# The Cold War in South Asia

The Cold War in South Asia provides the first comprehensive and transnational history of Anglo-American relations with South Asia during a seminal period in the history of the Indian subcontinent, between independence in the late 1940s, and the height of the Cold War in the late 1960s. Drawing upon significant new evidence from British, American, Indian and Eastern bloc archives, the book re-examines how and why the Cold War in South Asia evolved in the way that it did, at a time when the national leaderships, geopolitical outlooks and regional aspirations of India, Pakistan and their superpower suitors were in a state of considerable flux. The book probes the factors that encouraged the governments of Britain and the United States to work so closely together in South Asia during the two decades after independence, and suggests what benefits, if any, Anglo-American intervention in South Asia's affairs delivered, and to whom.

PAUL M. MCGARR is Lecturer in US Foreign Policy in the Department of American and Canadian Studies at the University of Nottingham. He has published widely on aspects of transnational politics, economics, defence, intelligence and security, and post-colonial culture.

# The Cold War in South Asia

*Britain, the United States and the Indian Subcontinent 1945–1965*

Paul M. McGarr

**CAMBRIDGE**
UNIVERSITY PRESS

# CAMBRIDGE
## UNIVERSITY PRESS

University Printing House, Cambridge CB2 8BS, United Kingdom

Cambridge University Press is part of the University of Cambridge.

It furthers the University's mission by disseminating knowledge in the pursuit of education, learning and research at the highest international levels of excellence.

www.cambridge.org
Information on this title: www.cambridge.org/9781107595507

© Paul M. McGarr 2013

First published 2013
First paperback edition 2015

*A catalogue record for this publication is available from the British Library*

*Library of Congress Cataloguing in Publication data*
McGarr, Paul M., 1969–
The Cold War in South Asia : Britain, the United States and the Indian subcontinent, 1945–1965 / Paul M. McGarr.
    pages   cm
Includes bibliographical references and index.
ISBN 978-1-107-00815-1 (hardback)
1. South Asia–Foreign relations–20th century.   2. South Asia–Foreign relations–
Great Britain.   3. South Asia–Foreign relations–United
States.   4. Great Britain–Foreign relations–South Asia.   5. United States–
Foreign relations–South Asia.   6. Cold War.   7. India–Foreign relations–20th
century.   8. Pakistan–Foreign relations–20th century.   I. Title.
DS341.M43   2013
327.54009′045–dc23
2013013496

ISBN 978-1-107-00815-1 Hardback
ISBN 978-1-107-59550-7 Paperback

# Contents

# Acknowledgements

This book is the product of a long-held fascination with contemporary South Asia and its interaction with the wider global community. Over the past decade, I have accumulated many debts in striving to better understand and explain the evolution of India and Pakistan's role in the Cold War. Much of this work is based on primary research in archives on three different continents, and would have proved impossible to complete without the support of a host of individuals and institutions. Financial support has come from the British Arts and Humanities Research Council; the Mellon Fund; the History Department at Royal Holloway, University of London; the Department of American and Canadian Studies at the University of Nottingham; and the Rothermere American Institute at the University of Oxford. Numerous librarians and archivists in the United Kingdom, the United States and India have extended invaluable help with the identification of research materials.

Without the generous support, wise counsel and unstinting encouragement of Professor Matthew Jones of the University of Nottingham, this project would not have seen the light of day. It was my extreme good fortune that as a doctoral candidate Matthew agreed to take me under his academic wing. A number of additional scholars have played an important part in bringing this book to fruition. At Royal Holloway, University of London, Tony Stockwell and Sarah Ansari acted as astute and incisive sounding boards on matters South Asian. Colleagues at the University of Hertfordshire, where I held a visiting research fellowship, offered sound advice and innumerable moments of good cheer. Likewise, at the University of Warwick, Richard Aldrich, Chris Moran and Simon Willmetts, with whom I had the privilege to work on the AHRC-sponsored research project *Landscapes of Secrecy: The Central Intelligence Agency and the Contested Record of US Foreign Policy, 1947–2001*, helped to make this a better book. The Department of American and Canadian Studies at the University of Nottingham is a wonderfully convivial place in which to work on the history of the United States' foreign policymaking. At Nottingham, I have been privileged to receive the support and encouragement of Graham Thompson, Celeste-Marie Bernier, Sharon Monteith and Judie Newman. Eric Pullin, at Carthage College, proved an invaluable intellectual collaborator.

Another significant debt is owed to the faculty and participants of the 2010 National History Centre International Seminar on Decolonization in Washington, DC. Under the guiding hand of Wm. Roger Louis, and his able assistants, Miriam Cunningham, Dane Kennedy, Philippa Levine, Pillarisetti Sudhir and the incomparable Jason Parker, I was able to develop and refine my understanding of the Cold War in the context of post-war decolonisation. Fellow seminarians, and most especially Rob Fletcher, Andrew Cohen, Gerard McCann, Greg Harper, Rachel Leow and Mathilde Von Bulow, helped to make the seminar a truly memorable experience. In 2007, an earlier excursion to Washington, on this occasion to take part in the George Washington University/University of Santa Barbara/London School of Economics International Graduate Student Seminar on the Cold War, proved equally important in the evolution of this study. In the United Kingdom, I benefited enormously from a research fellowship at the University of Oxford Rothermere American Institute (RAI) in the Michaelmas term of 2011. Under the guidance of the Institute's Director, Nigel Bowles, the RAI provided an ideal forum in which to hone my research conclusions.

My greatest debt of gratitude remains to my family, who have endured the frequent bouts of distraction and prolonged absences associated with the completion of this study with exceptional good grace. My three young sons, Robert, William and Oliver, cheerfully came to accept, if not understand, their father's preoccupation with South Asia, while my wife, Louise, helped to sustain the project with her unstinting support and encouragement. It is to Louise, with much love, that this book is dedicated.

# A note on the political geography of Pakistan

Between August 1947, when Pakistan came into existence as an independent sovereign state, and 1958, the country's national capital was the city of Karachi. Situated in the southern province of Sind, on the coast of the Arabian Sea, Karachi was then, and remains today, Pakistan's largest city, principal port and major financial centre. In 1958, under the direction of Pakistan's president, General (later Field Marshal) Mohammad Ayub Khan, the national capital was shifted from Karachi to the northern city of Rawalpindi, the headquarters of Pakistan's armed forces. At the same time, Ayub Khan announced plans to construct a new and purpose-built seat of government at Islamabad, adjacent to Rawalpindi. Several factors lay behind Ayub Khan's decision to relocate Pakistan's capital. Chief amongst them was the desire to devolve some of the bureaucratic power and influence concentrated in Karachi. A more northerly capital was also considered to be easier to defend, more accessible from all corners of the country and to have the advantage of being closer to the military hierarchy in Rawalpindi, who exerted considerable sway over Pakistani politics. The official transition of Pakistan's capital from Rawalpindi to Islamabad was completed on 14 August 1967, the twentieth anniversary of the country's independence from British rule. In the narrative that follows, Karachi, Rawalpindi and Islamabad are all deployed as synonyms for the government of Pakistan during the periods in which they served as the nation's capital.

# Abbreviations

| | |
|---|---|
| AID | Agency for International Development |
| CAB | Cabinet Papers |
| CCP | Chinese Communist Party |
| CDS | Chief of Defence Staff |
| CENTO | Central Treaty Organization |
| Chicom | Chinese Communist(s) |
| CIA | Central Intelligence Agency |
| CPI | Communist Party of India |
| CRO | Commonwealth Relations Office |
| DLF | Development Loan Fund |
| EEC | European Economic Community |
| FO | Foreign Office |
| *FRUS* | Foreign Relations of the United States |
| GNP | Gross national product |
| GOP | Government of Pakistan |
| HMG | Her Majesty's Government |
| IAF | Indian Air Force |
| IB | Delhi Intelligence Bureau |
| IBRD | International Bank for Reconstruction and Development |
| ICA | International Cooperation Administration |
| JCS | Joint Chiefs of Staff |
| JFKL | John F. Kennedy Library |
| JIC | British Joint Intelligence Committee |
| LBJL | Lyndon Baines Johnson Library |
| LOC | Library of Congress |
| MAAG | Military Assistance Advisory Group |
| MAP | Military assistance programme |
| MEA | Ministry of External Affairs |
| MI5 | British Security Service |
| MiG | Mikoyan i Gurevich (Soviet fighter aircraft) |
| MoD | Ministry of Defence |

| NARA | National Archives and Records Administration |
| NATO | North Atlantic Treaty Organization |
| NEA | Bureau of Near Eastern, South Asian and African Affairs, Department of State |
| NEFA | North-East Frontier Agency |
| NMML | Nehru Memorial Museum and Library |
| NSAM | National Security Action Memoranda |
| NSC | National Security Council |
| PLA | People's Liberation Army |
| PLP | Parliamentary Labour Party |
| PRC | People's Republic of China |
| PREM | Prime Minister's Office files |
| RAF | Royal Air Force |
| RCAF | Royal Canadian Air Force |
| SAM | Surface-to-air missile |
| SEATO | South East Asia Treaty Organization |
| SLO | Security Liaison Officer |
| SOA | Office of South Asian Affairs, Department of State |
| UK | United Kingdom of Great Britain and Northern Ireland |
| TNA | United Kingdom National Archives |
| UN | United Nations |
| UNSC | United Nations Security Council |
| US | United States of America |
| USAF | United States Air Force |
| USIA | United States Information Agency |
| USIS | United States Information Service |
| USSR | Union of Soviet Socialist Republics |

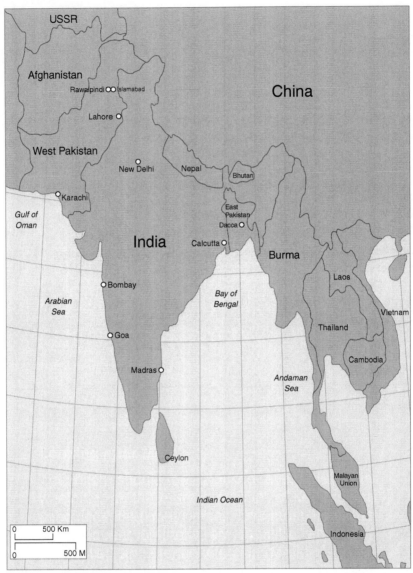

Map 1 South Asia post-1947

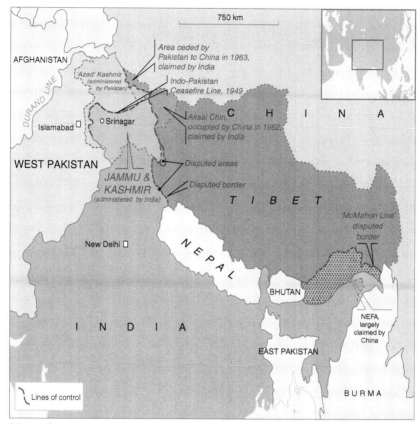

Map 2 South Asian territorial disputes, 1947–65

# Introduction

The British Raj is over, the American demi-Raj is ending, and both have left interesting legacies.

Daniel Patrick Moynihan, US ambassador to India, 1 September 1973[1]

On 8 January 1958, Britain's prime minister, Harold Macmillan, touched down in a specially chartered Britannia aeroplane at New Delhi's Palam airport to begin the first leg of a whirlwind five-week Commonwealth tour. The first serving British premier to visit South Asia since the end of the British Raj, in August 1947, Macmillan was apprehensive about the reception that awaited him in India. Over the previous two years, Anglo-Indian relations had sunk to a post-independence nadir. In 1956, Britain and India had fallen out during the Suez and Hungarian crises. In the case of the former, the Bombay daily, *The Indian Express*, had excoriated Macmillan's predecessor, Anthony Eden, for providing 'Britain with her most inglorious hour'. By ordering British troops into Egypt to seize the Suez Canal, the *Express* opined, Eden had been guilty of launching a, 'wanton and senseless ... [and] barbaric onslaught ... on a small West Asian country'.[2] The following year, the Indian government reacted with cold fury when Britain backed a resolution in the United Nations Security Council that reiterated calls for a plebiscite in the contested, and largely Indian-controlled, territory of Kashmir.

To Macmillan's great relief, he met with a warm and effusive greeting in India. In a welcoming speech delivered on Palam's aircraft apron, India's prime minister, Jawaharlal Nehru, downplayed Anglo-Indian tensions and instead emphasised India's 'unique' shared heritage with Britain.[3] As if to underscore Nehru's point, after responding to the Indian premier's address, Macmillan chatted casually with two Indian

[1] Moynihan to Alistair Cooke, 1 September 1973, I-353, Folder India Correspondence C 4 1973–5, Daniel P. Moynihan Papers, Manuscript Division, Library of Congress, Washington, DC.

[2] 'Eden Has Provided Britain With Her Most Inglorious Hour', 8 November 1956, *The Indian Express*.

[3] *The Times*, 9 January 1958.

soldiers sporting British campaign medals from the Second World War, and greeted General K. S. Thimayya, India's Chief of Army Staff, with a familiar, 'How are things going? We last met at my house.' In subsequent talks with Indian ministers and officials, Macmillan was delighted to discover that 'Indian leaders from Mr. Nehru downwards showed no disposition to rake over recent disagreements'. Indeed, when the British leader departed from India five days later, he did so, 'impressed by the respect in which the British people were now held and the balanced view which was taken by leaders of opinion on the value of their connection, past and present, with Britain'.[4]

In fact, by the time Macmillan had entered 10 Downing Street almost exactly a year earlier, the arrival of the Cold War in South Asia had already set in train a series of events that, over the next decade, would precipitate a steep decline in British power and authority in the Indian subcontinent. In the early 1960s, Britain continued to exercise a preponderant external influence over the political, economic and cultural affairs of India and Pakistan, and in India's case, its armed forces as well. By the early 1970s, following almost two centuries of regional hegemony, the onset of superpower intervention in the region had reduced the United Kingdom to the role of bit player in South Asia. Speaking in London, in October 1971, at the Chatham House headquarters of the Royal Institute of International Affairs, India's then prime minister, Indira Gandhi, observed that 'in Britain, which has such close historical ties with us, there is a wide gap in the understanding of the forces which have shaped our great history and which are influencing us today'. India's interaction with Britain, Gandhi intoned, had ceased to be determined by the 'old myth' of imperial and Commonwealth solidarity. Moving forward the value that India attached to its relationship with the United Kingdom, India's leader noted pointedly, would be based not on sentiment but rather a 'rational' assessment of Britain's standing in the post-war world.[5]

In 1947, when India and Pakistan first emerged as independent nation states, the administration of President Harry S. Truman in the United States paid little heed to the momentous events taking place in South Asia. At the time, Truman and his Secretary of State, George C. Marshall, were far more concerned with contemporaneous developments in Western Europe. Chronic post-war economic, political

---

[4] 'Prime Minister's Commonwealth Tour', 4 June 1958, CAB 129/93, C (58), 120, The United Kingdom National Archives, Kew, London.
[5] Indira Gandhi address to the Royal Institute of International Affairs, Chatham House, London, 29 October 1971. Indira Gandhi, *India: The Speeches and Reminiscences of Indira Gandhi, Prime Minister of India* (London: Hodder & Stoughton, 1975), p. 185.

and social tensions appeared poised to rebound to the Soviet Union's advantage, and sweep communist regimes to power in Italy, France and across the Mediterranean littoral. Chester Bowles, America's ambassador to India at the time, bemoaned the lack of interest that senior US government officials displayed toward the subcontinent. Washington, Bowles subsequently complained, was inclined to interpret the region through a 'Kiplingesque' prism, imagining India to be 'an ancient land of cobras, maharajahs, monkeys, famines, polo players, over-crowded with cows and babies'.[6] In the mid-1950s, as American policymakers identified a growing need to compete with the Soviet Union for 'hearts and minds' in the developing world, the United States began to reconsider the value of nascent post-colonial nations as Cold War allies, and none more so than India and Pakistan. From a strategic standpoint, South Asia acquired new significance in official American thinking, initially as a bulwark against Soviet expansion into the Middle East, and latterly as a buffer to restrict the spread of Chinese Communist influence in South East Asia. In 1954, the government of Dwight D. Eisenhower entered into a military alliance with Pakistan, and toward the end of the decade scaled up American economic and political support for India. At the beginning of the 1960s, the Kennedy administration expanded the United States' commitments in South Asia, frequently intervening in the affairs of the subcontinent alongside an, often reluctant, British partner.

Indeed, between the mid-1950s and mid-1960s, American governments sponsored a host of diplomatic initiatives in South Asia, and lavished $12 billion in economic and military aid on India and Pakistan with little, if any, substantive returns to show for their investments. To Washington's frustration, rather than confront a purported communist 'threat' to the subcontinent, Indian and Pakistani leaders channelled their nations' energy and resources into a sterile and enervating internecine feud. Following the Indo-Pakistani War of 1965, Kennedy's successor, Lyndon Johnson, turned his back on the subcontinent and redirected American power into holding the line against communism in South East Asia. In December 1965, US Under Secretary of State George Ball jibed that the Soviets were now free to 'break their lance' in South Asia.[7] By the time that Indira Gandhi delivered her Chatham House speech, late in 1971, the US Embassy in New Delhi lamented that Washington had come to see India as 'an oversized political entity lacking cohesion with massive economic and social problems which

---

[6] Chester Bowles, 'America and Russia', *Foreign Affairs*, 49 (July 1971), 636–51.
[7] Brief for Ayub Khan Visit, 14 December 1965, President's Office Files, Jack Valenti meeting notes, Lyndon Baines Johnson Library, Austin, Texas.

threaten its viability and preclude its ability to wield power effectively and entail the provision of endless external existence'. 'Evidently,' one American diplomat recorded, 'White House strategists view India much more as a drainpipe than a fountain head.'[8]

This book offers a re-examination of how and why the Cold War in South Asia evolved in the way that it did, at a time when the national leaderships, geopolitical outlooks and regional aspirations of India, Pakistan and their superpower suitors, were in a state of considerable flux. In August 1947, as the last British flag was hauled down in South Asia, a new 'Great Game' began to take shape in the subcontinent. In common with its nineteenth-century antecedent, immortalised in the pages of Rudyard Kipling's novel *Kim*, over the next two decades Britain, the United States, the Soviet Union and the People's Republic of China (PRC) vied for influence in a region that, in the early 1960s, represented a major theatre in the global Cold War.[9] More particularly, this study critically re-evaluates the remarkable collaborative efforts undertaken by governments in Great Britain and the United States after 1947, to engineer an Indo-Pakistani rapprochement; recast the nature of India's relationship with the West; and minimise Soviet and Chinese sway in the subcontinent. Moreover, in placing the ongoing political, economic, territorial and military rivalry between India and Pakistan (and India and China) in a broad historical context, this monograph calls into question the efficacy of post-war Anglo-American interventions in South Asia, and elsewhere on the global stage.

This book was not conceived as a conventional history of post-war Anglo-American diplomatic relations. Others have ably and extensively covered that particular historical canvass.[10] Nor is its intention to rake over the well-worn, and now clichéd ground, of post-war British

---

[8] Lee T. Stull (US Embassy Delhi) to Anthony C. E. Quainton (State Department), 28 December 1971, RG 59, Bureau of Near Eastern and South Asian Affairs Records Relating to India 1966–75, Lot, 76D30, Box 20, Folder Mrs Gandhi 1971, National Archives and Records Administration, College Park, Maryland.

[9] Rudyard Kipling, *Kim* (London: Macmillan, 1901). For an historical context on the Victorian 'Great Game', see Peter Hopkirk, *The Great Game: On Secret Service in High Asia* (London: John Murray, 1990); and Robert Johnson, *Spying for Empire: The Great Game in Central and South-East Asia, 1757–1947* (London: Greenhill Books, 2006).

[10] Notably, Nigel J. Ashton, *Kennedy, Macmillan and the Cold War: The Irony of Interdependence* (Basingstoke: Palgrave Macmillan, 2002); C. J. Bartlett, *'The Special Relationship': A Political History of Anglo-American Relations since 1945* (London: Longman, 1992); John Dickie, *'Special' No More: Anglo-American Relations: Rhetoric and Reality* (London: Weidenfeld and Nicolson, 1994); David Dimbleby and David Reynolds, *An Ocean Apart: The Relationship between Britain and America in the Twentieth Century* (London: Hodder & Stoughton, 1988); Alan Dobson, *The Politics of the Anglo-American Economic Special Relationship, 1940–87* (Brighton: Wheatsheaf, 1988); John Dumbrell, *A Special Relationship: Anglo-American Relations in the Cold*

'decline' and American 'hubris'. There already exists a voluminous body of work, of variable merit, addressing such themes.[11] Rather, it sets out to trace how and why the extension of the Cold War into the Indian subcontinent, precipitated by the United States' military alliance with Pakistan in 1954, and the inevitable Soviet riposte that followed, transformed South Asia from an international backwater into an important locus of superpower rivalry. In the first half of the 1960s, an unprecedented period of regional instability shattered the political status quo in India and Pakistan, and placed both countries' relationships with the international community, and each other, on a new and very different footing. In the space of five years, South Asia was buffeted by the backwash from a collapse in India's relations with the PRC; Moscow's estrangement from Beijing; the Sino-Indian border war of 1962; the end of the Nehru era; and a fresh bout of Indo-Pakistani hostilities. Simultaneously, Britain's traditional position of authority in the subcontinent was severely proscribed by broader global trends. Tellingly, when Harold Wilson tried to intercede in the affairs of India and Pakistan toward the end of the 1960s, one member of the British cabinet recorded that New Delhi and Islamabad 'just ignored him'.[12]

The conclusion that this study draws, explicated in the chapters that follow, is that collaborative Anglo-American interventions in the Indian subcontinent in the early Cold War period invariably proved to be misguided, ineffectual and counterproductive. In contrast to the more carefully calibrated actions of the Soviet Union and PRC, British and American policymakers plunged together into the morass of South Asian politics on the basis of a series of highly questionable and often contradictory assumptions: that India and Pakistan could be cajoled into settling their differences; that the spectre of Communist Chinese power would persuade India to abandon its policy of non-alignment;

*War and After* (Basingstoke: Palgrave Macmillan, 2000); Matthew Jones, *Conflict and Confrontation in South East Asia, 1961–1965: Britain, the United States, and the Creation of Malaysia* (Cambridge University Press, 2002); Wm. Roger Louis and Hedley Bull (eds.), *The Special Relationship: Anglo-American Relations Since 1945* (Oxford: Clarendon Press, 1986); and David Reynolds, 'A "Special Relationship"? America, Britain and the International Order Since the Second World War', *International Affairs*, 62, 1 (1985–6), 1–20.

[11] See, for example, Corelli Barnett, *The Verdict of Peace: Britain between Her Yesterday and the Future* (London: Macmillan, 2001); Saki Dockrill, *Britain's Retreat from East of Suez: The Choice between Empire and the World?* (London: Palgrave Macmillan, 2002); David Halberstam, *The Best and the Brightest* (London: Barrie and Jenkins, 1972); Chalmers Johnson, *Blowback: The Costs and Consequences of American Empire* (London: Little Brown, 2000); and John W. Young, *The Labour Governments 1964–1970*, vol. 2: *International Policy* (Manchester University Press, 2003).

[12] Denis Healey, *The Time of My Life* (London: Michael Joseph, 1989), p. 280.

and that the dependence of India and Pakistan on Western economic and military aid would deter those countries from turning to the Soviet Union and PRC for support. In the process, having started from a position of considerable strength in 1947, by the end of 1965, British and American relations with India and Pakistan were in tatters. Moscow and Beijing, meanwhile, stood poised in the wings to assume the roles of New Delhi's and Islamabad's best friends.

This study is not the first to focus attention upon the ebb and flow of superpower rivalry in the developing world in the latter half of the twentieth century. Over the past decade, military, diplomatic, social, economic and cultural historians have diligently probed the complex factors that helped to define the exchange between the 'centre' and the 'periphery' during the Cold War.[13] An extensive and growing body of literature has documented American, British, Soviet and Chinese interventions in greater Asia after 1945. Notable recent accounts, the focus of which has centred primarily on East and South East Asia, have shed new light on the causes, contours and consequences of the Cold War outside Europe.[14] In a South Asian context, Chen Jian's *Mao's China and the Cold War* and articles by Mikhail Y. Prozumenshchikov and Vojtech Mastny, have offered up valuable insights into previously obscure aspects of Eastern bloc policy in the subcontinent.[15] Earlier works, chiefly by American scholars, have directly addressed the United States' interaction with post-independent South Asia. As early as 1972, William J. Barnds, in *India, Pakistan and the Great Powers*, highlighted the difficulties that successive US administrations, from Truman to Johnson, had encountered in attempting to navigate the turbulent waters of South

---

[13] An outstanding example of which is the Bancroft prize-winning study by Odd Arne Westad, *The Global Cold War: Third World Interventions and the Making of Our Times* (Cambridge University Press, 2007).

[14] For example, Tuong Vu and Wasana Wongsurawat (eds.), *Dynamics of the Cold War in Asia: Ideology, Identity, and Culture* (New York: Palgrave Macmillan, 2009); Christopher E. Goscha and Christian F. Ostermann (eds.), *Connecting Histories: Decolonization and the Cold War in Southeast Asia, 1945–1962* (Palo Alto: Stanford University Press, 2009); Zheng Yangwen, Hong Liu and Michael Szonyi (eds.), *The Cold War in Asia: The Battle for Hearts and Minds* (Leiden: Brill, 2010); Anthony Day and Maya H. T. Liem (eds.), *Cultures at War: The Cold War and Cultural Expression in Southeast Asia* (Ithaca, NY: Cornell University Press, 2010).

[15] Chen Jian, *Mao's China and the Cold War* (Chapel Hill: University of North Carolina Press, 2001); Mikhail Y. Prozumenshchikov, 'The Sino-Indian Conflict, the Cuban Missile Crisis, and the Sino-Soviet Split, October 1962: New Evidence from the Russian Archives', *Cold War International History Project Bulletin*, no. 8–9 (1996–7), 251–7; and Vojtech Mastny, 'The Soviet Union's Partnership with India', *Journal of Cold War Studies*, 12, 3 (2010), 50–90.

Asian politics. In the 1990s, Robert J. McMahon's thought-provoking survey of the United States' relationship with India and Pakistan, *The Cold War on the Periphery: The United States, India and Pakistan*, Andrew J. Rotter's *Comrades at Odds: The United States and India, 1947–1964* and Dennis Merrill's *Bread and the Ballot: The United States and India's Economic Development, 1947–1963*, amongst others, broke new ground by exploring the diplomatic, cultural and economic aspects of America's relationship with the Indian subcontinent.[16] Remarkably given the importance that British policymakers continued to attach to South Asia after 1947, Anita Inder Singh's 1993 monograph, *The Limits of British Influence: South Asia and the Anglo-American Relationship 1947–56*, remains one of the only studies to have given sustained attention to post-war British policy in the subcontinent.[17]

Nonetheless, despite the important contributions made by these authors, it has only recently become possible to interrogate the broad history of Cold War in South Asia from a transnational perspective. Existing studies of superpower intervention in India and Pakistan were written at a time when the pertinent official records on South Asia were only just becoming available on both sides of the Atlantic, and when no comparable Eastern European, Chinese, Indian or Pakistani documentation had yet seen the light of day. Since the mid-1990s, significant new archival material has become available to researchers. In the United Kingdom, William Waldegrave, Minister for Open Government in John Major's administration, oversaw the declassification and release of previously embargoed files from the Cabinet Office, the Home Office, the Foreign Office, Ministry of Defence and the Intelligence Services. Likewise, in archives across Eastern Europe, the PRC and India, although it has hardly been a case of open sesame, a substantial amount of new government documentation has begun to emerge. This, in turn, has helped to transform scholarly understanding of previously opaque

---

[16] William J. Barnds, *India, Pakistan and the Great Powers* (London: Pall Mall, 1972); Robert J. McMahon, *The Cold War on the Periphery: The United States, India and Pakistan* (New York: Columbia University Press, 1994); Dennis Merrill, *Bread and the Ballot: The United States and India's Economic Development, 1947–1963* (Chapel Hill: The University of North Carolina Press, 1990); Andrew Rotter, *Comrades at Odds: The United States and India, 1947–1964* (London: Cornell University Press, 2000). See also Dennis Kux, *India and the United States: Estranged Democracies, 1941–1991* (Washington, DC: National Defense University Press, 1993), and *The United States and Pakistan, 1947–2000: Disenchanted Allies* (Baltimore: The Johns Hopkins University Press, 2001).

[17] Anita Inder Singh, *The Limits of British Influence: South Asia and the Anglo-American Relationship, 1947–56* (London: Pinter, 1993).

aspects of the Sino-Indian conflict, and challenged conventional interpretations of how and why the Sino-Soviet split influenced Moscow's
and Beijing's relations with South Asia.[18]

This study is based on recently released documents in the British
National Archives; the India Office collections of the British Library;
the Bodleian Library at the University of Oxford; Churchill College
Archives at the University of Cambridge; the US National Archives; the
US Library of Congress; the Dwight D. Eisenhower, John F. Kennedy,
Lyndon B. Johnson and Richard M. Nixon Presidential Libraries; the
Butler Library at Columbia University; the Indian National Archives;
and the Nehru Memorial Museum and Library, as well as other archival sources and published primary and secondary material. One of the
key contributions this study makes is to bring to the fore new docu-
mentary evidence that gives lie to the fallacy that the Cold War, in
a South Asian context at least, was conducted in a Free World ver-
sus Communist binary. In doing so, it emphasises the power of local
agency and the extent to which foreign interventions in the region were
beholden to potent political, ethnic, communal, religious and cultural
forces. Moreover, it questions prevailing conceptions, not only of the
nature and impact of superpower initiatives in South Asia, but also of
how and why the Cold War played out across the developing world as
it did. In recent years, India's emergence as a global economic force, a
revival in rhetoric surrounding Sino-Indian rivalry and the advent of
the so-called 'War on Terror' have brought South Asia to the forefront
of global attention once again. This book is intended, above all, to stimulate debate on the evolution of modern South Asia and to act as a spur
to further research in the field. Engaging meaningfully with the history
of India's and Pakistan's relations with the broader international community, I would contend, is more relevant and important today than
ever, as we head into what many commentators have characterised as
the 'Asian century'.

[18] For example, Vladislav Zubok, 'The Khrushchev–Mao Conversations, 31 July–3
August 1958 and 2 October 1959', *Cold War International History Project*, Bulletin
12–13 (Fall/Winter 2001); and Surjit Mansingh, 'Indo-Soviet Relations in the Nehru
Years: The View from New Delhi', Parallel History Project on Cooperative Security
(February 2009).

# 1    India, Pakistan and the early Cold War, 1947–1956

On 15 August 1947, having dominated the political and economic land-scape of South Asia for two centuries, Britain quit the Indian subcontinent and transferred power to the newly constituted sovereign states of India and Pakistan. The decision taken by Clement Attlee's Labour government to relinquish Britain's Indian Empire, the jewel in the imperial crown and the most potent symbol of the nation's global status, had an immediate and lasting impact on the United Kingdom's international standing. Two years earlier, as Attlee's administration set about the task of rebuilding an imperial superpower exhausted and impoverished by six years of enervating global conflict, Britain's grip on India had begun to fracture. In New Delhi, the Viceroy of India, Archibald Wavell, confided to his diary that an erosion in British authority in the subcontinent had left him, 'still legally and morally responsible for what happens in India ... [but without] nearly all power to control events; we are simply running on the momentum of our previous prestige'.[1]

Although publicly committed to a policy of early independence for India, the Attlee administration's failure to advance a schedule for self-government produced rumblings of discontent in South Asia. The Labour Party had a long tradition of anti-imperialism. Nonetheless, Attlee, whose personal association with India dated from his service on the Simon Commission in 1927, along with other senior members of the British cabinet, retained a sentimental attachment to the allure of empire. Wavell considered both Ernest Bevin, Britain's Foreign Secretary, and Albert Alexander, Labour's minister of defence, to be 'in reality imperialists ... [who] dislike any idea of leaving India'.[2] The

[1] Entry for 31 December 1946, in Pendrel Moon (ed.), *Wavell: The Viceroy's Journal* (London: Oxford University Press, 1973), p. 402. See also R. J. Moore, *Escape from Empire: The Attlee Government and the Indian Problem* (Oxford: Clarendon Press, 1983), p. 338.

[2] Entry 24 December 1946, Moon (ed.), *Viceroy's Journal*, p. 399; *The Times*, 12 January 1946. See also Kenneth O. Morgan, *Labour in Power, 1945–1951* (Oxford: Clarendon Press, 1984), pp. 193–4.

9

Labour Party's manifesto for the 1945 general election, *Let's Face the Future*, made no reference to colonial issues. The British electorate, Labour's leadership judged, were more concerned with the advent of a new welfare state, a return to full employment and social equality, than imperial reform.[3] In a national opinion poll conducted in Britain in early 1947, three-quarters of respondents were unable to differentiate between a dominion and a colony, and over half of those interviewed failed to name a single British imperial territory.[4] In addition, as World War turned to Cold War after 1945, British civil and military leaders became anxious that without access to India's strategic, economic and martial resources, Britain's future as a global power would be compromised.[5] Moreover, the Attlee government's India policy faced intense scrutiny from a Conservative opposition, led by Winston Churchill, which insisted that relinquishing the Indian Empire was as unnecessary, as it was undesirable.[6]

A lack of political impetus in London on the India question allowed nationalist forces in the subcontinent to drive the pace of change in South Asia. In February 1946, the Royal Indian Navy mutinied in Bombay. The following month, as nationalist agitation in India threatened to spiral out of control, Attlee dispatched a Cabinet Mission to New Delhi to negotiate terms for a British withdrawal.[7] By September, a transitional Indian government was in place, and the talismanic Congress Party leader, Jawaharlal Nehru, was installed as its de facto premier and foreign minister. With the genie of political devolution out of the bottle in the subcontinent, in February 1947, Attlee produced a timetable for the end of British rule in India. Before a sombre House of Commons, the Labour premier confirmed that the Raj would be brought to an end by 31 March 1948, if not before.[8] Somewhat belatedly, Attlee's government recognised that by accelerating India's independence Britain stood a much better chance of retaining close economic and security links with the subcontinent. This, in turn, would go a long way to sustain British influence elsewhere in Asia. As it turned out, grandiose British plans for

[3] Partha Sarathi Gupta, *Imperialism and the British Labour Movement, 1914–1964* (London: The Macmillan Press, 1975), pp. 282–4.

[4] David Goldsworthy, *Colonial Issues in British Politics, 1945–1961: From 'Colonial Development' to 'Winds of Change'* (Oxford: Clarendon Press, 1971), p. 399.

[5] 'Strategic Position of the British Commonwealth', 2 April 1946, CAB 131/2, DO (46) 47, The United Kingdom National Archives, Kew, London (hereafter TNA).

[6] Entry for 31 August 1945, Moon (ed.), *Viceroy's Journal*, p. 168; Lord Butler, *The Art of the Possible: The Memoirs of Lord Butler* (London: Hamish Hamilton, 1971), p. 141.

[7] Sarvepalli Gopal, *Jawaharlal Nehru: A Biography*, vol. 1: *1889–1947* (London: Jonathan Cape, 1975), p. 311.

[8] Kenneth Harris, *Attlee* (London: Weidenfeld and Nicolson, 1982), p. 380.

a new and collaborative international partnership with India were misplaced. Nehru's administration had no intention of being seen to play second fiddle to the British on the world stage. Instead, India looked to carve out its own niche in global affairs as a leading force in the non-aligned movement. In a more limited sense, however, the goodwill that the Attlee government garnered in India from ending the Raj did help to preserve a surprising degree of British influence within South Asia after 1947.[9]

As Attlee sounded the death knell of Britain's Indian Empire, outside Westminster the United Kingdom was gripped by a 'great freeze', as the coldest winter weather for seventy years enveloped the country in a blanket of snow and ice. Britain's shivering inhabitants digested the news that India was to be granted independence in the midst of a fuel crisis, chronic industrial manpower shortages and, later that summer, a disastrous and short-lived flotation of sterling, all of which threatened economic disaster. With a prolonged period of national austerity on the horizon, Hugh Dalton, Attlee's Chancellor of the Exchequer, lamented the 'many different and unwelcome' foreign and domestic crises that had conspired to upset his party's ambitious plans to revive British post-war fortunes. Although 'not the end of the world', Dalton reflected soberly, Britain's straitened domestic circumstances and enforced imperial retrenchment had deflated the mood of national euphoria and optimism that had followed Labour's sweeping electoral victory, in July 1945. 'Never', the Chancellor lamented, 'glad confident morning again.'[10]

In fact, Britain went on to retain strong links with India and Pakistan well into the 1960s. Politically, economically, militarily and culturally, as well as in less obvious areas, such as security and intelligence liaison, the British remained a powerful force in South Asia after 1947. At the same time, the onset of imperial retrenchment led successive post-war British governments to view close collaborative relations with the United States as the new fulcrum of the United Kingdom's foreign policy. The notion of an Anglo-American 'special relationship' was embraced by Whitehall as a mechanism through which, in part, Britain could continue to play a leading global role.[11] In turn, in the

[9] John Darwin, *Britain and Decolonisation: The Retreat from Empire in the Post-War World* (London: Macmillan, 1988), pp. 152–3.

[10] Hugh Dalton, *High Tide and After: Memoirs 1945–1960* (London: Frederick Mueller, 1962), p. 205.

[11] See, for example, David Reynolds, 'A "Special Relationship"? America, Britain and the International Order Since the Second World War', *International Affairs*, 62, 1 (1985–6), 1–20; Nigel J. Ashton, *Kennedy, Macmillan and the Cold War: The Irony of Interdependence* (Basingstoke: Palgrave Macmillan, 2002); John Dumbrell, *A Special Relationship: Anglo-American Relations in the Cold War and After* (Basingstoke: Palgrave

early 1950s, as the Cold War in Asia turned hot, American policymakers came to see Britain's residual influence in the Indian subcontinent as an asset that, if harnessed correctly, could help to keep India and Pakistan out of the Communist bloc.

### The transfer of power in India: winning friends and influencing people

To the surprise of many foreign observers, the transfer of constitutional power from London to New Delhi and Karachi in the late summer of 1947 passed off in an atmosphere of general goodwill. The US ambassador to India in the early 1950s, Chester Bowles, attributed this phenomenon to the Attlee government's decision to withdraw from India, 'suddenly, peacefully and with dignity'. No such post-colonial amity had survived in Indonesia, Bowles observed, where the Dutch 'attempted to destroy the new republic by force and ... Left in shreds and tatters because they did not understand that colonialism was doomed in Asia'. Having passed through the Indonesian capital, Jakarta, en route to take up his post in India, Bowles witnessed workmen hauling down statues of former Dutch governor generals. In New Delhi, the American ambassador found that streets retained the names of former English viceroys and colonial administrators. 'Even a statue of [Sir John] Nicholson, who led the British against Indians during the "Mutiny"', Bowles was astonished to discover, had been left untouched.[12] Little appeared to have changed toward the end of the decade when Britain's prime minister, Harold Macmillan, visited India. After dining one evening with India's president, in what had formerly been the Viceroy's residence, the British premier reflected wryly that the plate and china retained heraldic emblems from the Raj, and that his wife, Dorothy, had been seated opposite a portrait of her grandfather, Lord Lansdowne, who had governed India half a century before.[13] Macmillan was not the only Western leader to reflect on the extent to which India seemed to be at ease with its colonial past. 'When I noted an impressive statue of King George V standing in a prominent place near the [president's] Palace,' America's president, Dwight D. Eisenhower, recorded on a visit to India's capital the following year, 'I could not help wondering whether

Macmillan, 2000); and Alan Dobson, *The Politics of the Anglo-American Economic Special Relationship, 1940–87* (Brighton: Wheatsheaf, 1988).

[12] Chester Bowles, *Ambassador's Report* (New York: Harper & Brothers, 1954), pp. 55–6.

[13] Harold Macmillan, *Riding the Storm, 1956–1959* (London: Macmillan, 1971), p. 385.

we in our early days of independence would have tolerated among us a statue of King George III.'[14]

Accounts from contemporary witnesses in the subcontinent celebrated the relative benevolence in which Indians and British alike had marked the passing of the Raj. One British businessman in India recalled that on 15 August, 'everybody [was] patting you on the back and shaking you by the hand. We were the British heroes, the British who had given them independence.'[15] On the same day in Madras, in southern India, the British governor, Sir Archibald Nye, was showered with flowers by cheering crowds as he travelled through the city.[16] In the east, in Calcutta, the influential daily newspaper *The Statesman* was inundated with correspondence from its Indian readership praising the British for 'the peaceful manner in which they decided to leave India – unheard of in the history of any empire ... [and which] enhanced British prestige and character'. Writing at the time to his brother Tom, Clement Attlee expressed his relief that the transfer of power had enabled Britain to 'come out with honour instead, as at one time seemed likely, of being pushed out ignominiously'.[17] Broadly speaking, a majority of India's new ruling elite shared Attlee's assessment. India's Foreign Secretary, K. P. S. Menon, spoke for many of his government colleagues when he reflected subsequently that the British had, albeit tardily, managed to exit the subcontinent with good grace. 'Nothing, it may be said,' Menon remarked in 1950, 'became the British in India more than their leaving of it.'[18] Not all Indians were as generous to their former colonial rulers. Another of *The Statesman*'s readers complained bitterly in September 1947 that 'Unlike the emperor who found Rome a city of bricks and left one of marble, the British found India flowing with milk and honey. They are leaving her divided, poverty-stricken, backward.'[19]

Notwithstanding the existence of a strong, if comparatively marginal strain of residual anti-British sentiment in South Asia, credit for the largely positive relationship that developed between India and Britain after 1947 can be attributed, to a substantial degree, to two men,

---

[14] Dwight D. Eisenhower, *The White House Years: Waging Peace, 1956–1961* (New York: Doubleday & Co., 1965), pp. 501–2.

[15] Charles Allen, *Plain Tales from the Raj: Images of India in the Twentieth Century* (London: Andre Deutsch, 1975), p. 256.

[16] Bowles, *Ambassador's Report*, p. 56.

[17] Clement Attlee to Thomas Attlee, 18 August 1947, MS. Attlee dep. 142, Clement Attlee Papers, Bodleian Library, University of Oxford.

[18] K. P. S. Menon, 'India's Foreign Policy', 1950, Speeches & Writings File No. 35, K. P. S. Menon Papers, Nehru Memorial Museum and Library (hereafter NMML).

[19] *The Statesman (Calcutta)*, 5 and 12 September 1947.

Jawaharlal Nehru, and India's spiritual leader, Mohandas Karamchand Gandhi. India's last Viceroy, Lord Louis Mountbatten, recorded that both Nehru and Gandhi 'bore no malice' toward the British, and that 'the remarkably friendly relations between Britain and India are mainly due to them'.[20] For his part, Nehru credited the 'unique example' of post-colonial Anglo-Indian goodwill to the importance that Gandhi had placed on non-violence and reconciliation throughout India's struggle for independence. 'Always he was telling us,' Nehru recounted in December 1956, ' "You are fighting for a principle, for independence. You are fighting against, let us say, British Imperialism; you are not fighting the British people; you are not fighting anyone British; be friendly with them." '[21]

Having been born and raised in one of the most anglicised families in early twentieth-century India, many of Nehru's political contemporaries believed that the Indian premier had been inculcated with an essentially 'pro-British' outlook. America's ambassador to India in the late 1940s, Loy Henderson, concluded that Nehru, 'although he had resented British colonialism … nevertheless had a great respect for British institutions and manners in general'. To one of Henderson's successors, John Kenneth Galbraith, Nehru joked that he would be remembered as the 'last Englishman to rule in India'.[22] To the chagrin of American policymakers, with the passing of British rule in the subcontinent, India's political elite redirected much of its anti-colonial zeal into attacks on 'US imperialism', be it cultural, political or economic. In the early 1950s, Larry Wilson, the cultural affairs officer at the US Consulate in Bombay, noted that it was, 'a funny thing, we try and try and have been trying, and yet we're not liked out here. The British are far better liked than the Americans!"[23] In 1952, having visited India as a United Nations envoy, former First Lady Eleanor Roosevelt reflected that

---

[20] Mountbatten's obituary for Nehru, May 1964, MB1/J304, Lord Mountbatten Papers, Hartley Library, University of Southampton (hereafter MBP).

[21] Nehru speech to UN General Assembly, New York, 20 December 1956, in Mushirul Hasan (ed.), *Selected Works of Jawaharlal Nehru*, Second Series, vol. 36, 1 December 1956–21 February 1957 (New Delhi: Oxford University Press, 2005), pp. 507–8.

[22] B. R. Nanda, 'Nehru and the British', *Modern Asian Studies*, 30, 2 (1996), 469–79; Henderson to Field, 7 June 1978, Box 8, Folder India Misc., Loy W. Henderson Papers, Manuscripts Division, Library of Congress (hereafter LWHP); John Kenneth Galbraith, *A Life in Our Times* (London: Andre Deutsch, 1981), p. 408.

[23] Wilson, cited in Saunders Redding, *An American in India: A Personal Report on the Indian Dilemma and the Nature of Her Conflicts* (New York: The Bobbs-Merrill Company, 1954), p. 41.

In India, after the departure of the British, the resentment previously felt towards them was in a large measure transferred to us. Never convinced that the British really intended to keep their promise to leave, the Indians were deeply impressed when they actually did, and the disappearance of their hostility was almost an overnight phenomenon ... They tend to remember the good things that the British did and to ignore the bad; and it is a fact that today the British are remarkably popular there.[24]

The *New York Times*' correspondent in New Delhi at the time, A. M. Rosenthal, agreed that an 'unhappy tendency' existed in India, 'to believe the worst of the US and to say little good about it'. Moreover, in Rosenthal's estimation, India's negative attitude toward the United States was, if not encouraged by Nehru, then certainly condoned by the Indian leader.[25] Like many Indians of his generation, Nehru had a wide circle of American friends, and yet appeared ill at ease in the company of Americans in general. The Indian premier extolled American vigour and technological achievement, yet admonished Washington for misusing its power and brandishing the United States' wealth in the face of Asia's poor.[26] Fear of 'American economic imperialism' and the 'Almighty American dollar', fuelled in part by the work performed by US non-governmental organisations in South Asia, such as the Ford and Rockefeller Foundations and the Fulbright programme, loomed large in the minds of Indian ministers.[27] In 1950, one senior official in the US Embassy in New Delhi assured the State Department that Nehru 'not only does not want but ... will subtly oppose the exertion of political leadership by the United States in this area of Asia'.[28] Nehru did try to dispel the impression amongst US policymakers that his administration had an anti-American bent. In conversation with John Sherman Cooper, US ambassador in India between February 1955 and April 1956, Nehru insisted that 'there was no truth in what some people said that we were hostile to America'. His government was 'not at all hostile' and 'wanted to be friends' with the United States, the Indian premier assured Cooper, 'but ... [India] certainly felt that American policies had

---

[24] Eleanor Roosevelt, *India and the Awakening East* (London: Hutchinson, 1954), p. 90.

[25] *The New York Times*, 1 July 1956.

[26] Surjit Mansingh, 'India and the United States', in B. R. Nanda (ed.), *Indian Foreign Policy: The Nehru Years* (New Delhi: Sangam Books, 1990), p. 52.

[27] Roosevelt, *Awakening East*, p. 91.

[28] Graham Parson to Sparks, 3 February 1950, RG 59, Office of South Asian Affairs, Lot file 57D373, Box 2, Folder Official informal Jan–May 1950, National Archives and Records Administration, College Park, Maryland (hereafter NARA).

been wrong and encouraged the very [aggressive and anti-democratic] tendencies which they had sought to put an end to'.[29]

## A changing of the guard: Britain, the United States and Pakistan

Although not overtly antagonistic, in many respects Pakistan's post-colonial relationship with Britain proved to be a good deal more difficult and fractious than that with India. In January 1933, Choudhary Rahmat Ali, a Cambridge-educated Muslim nationalist from the town of Balachaur, now part of the Indian province of Punjab, had first articulated the concept of Pakistan. In a pamphlet entitled *Now or Never; Are We to Live or Perish Forever?*, commonly known as the 'Pakistan Declaration', Rahmat Ali called for the establishment of a Muslim state in the north-west corner of British India, encompassing the provinces of Punjab, North-West Frontier Province, Kashmir, Sind and Balochistan.[30] Taking its name from the initials of its constituent parts, Pakistan also became known as 'The Land of the Pure', the term 'Pak' meaning 'pure' in Urdu, the lingua franca of north India's Muslim community.[31] By 1946, as Clement Attlee began to lose confidence in Wavell's ability to steer British India to independence without plunging the subcontinent into civil war, the once fanciful notion of Pakistan assumed an irresistible political momentum under the direction of Mohammed Ali Jinnah and his Muslim League.[32] The following year, Wavell was sacked, and the formidable task of winding up the Raj on terms acceptable to London, Nehru's Congress Party and Jinnah's Muslim League fell to Mountbatten.

The subsequent partition of British India along religious lines, and the horrific communal violence that it wrought, embittered London's relations with Pakistan. Specifically, Pakistan's government, under the leadership of Jinnah, believed that a close personal bond between

---

[29] Meeting between Nehru and John Sherman Cooper, 5 May 1955, in Ravinder Kumar and H. Y. Sharada Prasad (eds.), *Selected Works of Jawaharlal Nehru*, vol. 28, 1 February–31 May 1955 (New Delhi: Oxford University Press, 2001), p. 284.

[30] Pamphlet reproduced in G. Allana, 'Pakistan Movement Historical Documents' (Karachi: Department of International Relations, University of Karachi, nd [1969]), pp. 103–10; available at http://www.columbia.edu/itc/mealac/pritchett/00islamlinks/txt_rahmatali_1933.html.

[31] Anatol Lieven, *Pakistan: A Hard Country* (London: Penguin, 2012), p. 10.

[32] The collapse in Attlee's relationship with Wavell is examined in Glynn Irial, ' "An Untouchable in the Presence of Brahmins": Lord Wavell's Disastrous Relationship with Whitehall During His Time as Viceroy, 1943–47', *Modern Asian Studies*, 41, 3 (2007), 639–63.

Mountbatten and Nehru had resulted in the last Viceroy being less than impartial when it came to dividing up the Raj's physical inheritance between India and Pakistan.[33] Above all, a conviction took root amongst Pakistan's political class and wider public that Mountbatten had rigged the territorial division of the subcontinent in New Delhi's favour. Most seriously, Mountbatten was held culpable in Karachi for ensuring that the predominately Muslim state of Kashmir acceded to India, and not Pakistan. As a state breaking away from a far larger, more powerful and less than friendly neighbour, Pakistan's physical and psychological sense of insecurity was highly sensitised to British slights, real and imagined. Writing in the early 1960s, one British official turned journalist, with extensive experience in the subcontinent, both before and after partition, argued that Pakistanis, 'do not consider that fairness has ever been obtained [from Britain]. Always, at critical moments, in their view, the balance has been tilted to India's advantage.'[34] Revealingly, after stepping down as Viceroy, Mountbatten was invited by Nehru to remain in India as the country's first Governor General, an office that he held until June 1948. To Mountbatten's disappointment, the government of Pakistan elected not to follow India's lead. Although not quite a political car crash, Britain's strained relations with Pakistan echoed the fate of the official diplomatic vehicle assigned by London to its first High Commissioner in Karachi, Sir Laurence Grafftey-Smith. Two days after arriving at Karachi's docks, a falling tree flattened Grafftey-Smith's gleaming Rolls Royce limousine. Much like Anglo-Pakistani relations, one British official noted wryly, it was some time before the car was repaired and able to operate 'in proper shape'.[35]

Viewed in a global context, Pakistan was by no means a small country. Its eastern and western wings, separated by a thousand miles of Indian controlled territory, comprised a landmass four times the size of the United Kingdom and equivalent to that of Texas and Arizona combined. Alongside India, however, where a majority of the ruling Congress government resented its very existence, Pakistan appeared

---

[33] The mutual distrust and rancour that developed between Mountbatten and Jinnah is discussed in Ayesha Jalal, *The Sole Spokesman: Jinnah, the Muslim League and the Demand for Pakistan* (Cambridge University Press, 1985); Mohammed Ali Jinnah, *Speeches and Statements, 1947–1948* (Karachi: Oxford University Press, 1999); and most recently, Jaswant Singh, *Jinnah: India, Partition, Independence* (Oxford University Press, 2010).

[34] Ian Stephens, *Pakistan: Old Country/New Nation* (London: Penguin Books, 1964), p. 262.

[35] John M. Fasal to Cyril Pickard, 23 February 1984, RCMS 68/5 Pakistan papers, Cyril Pickard Papers, Royal Commonwealth Society Library, University of Cambridge.

something of a minnow. Burdened it seemed with 'every conceivable handicap', Pakistan was riven with deep-seated ethnic, racial, linguistic and economic divisions. Less than a quarter of India's size, and with a population only a fifth as large, Pakistan's economy was predominately agrarian and lacked India's industrial infrastructure. At the time of partition, Pakistan inherited less than 10 per cent of the subcontinent's steel output and manufacturing capability. The vast bulk of South Asia's commercial and military resources were retained by India.[36] The relative disparity in power and prestige between the two states was reflected in the correspondence sent by some British companies to the subcontinent, which, as late as the early 1960s, continued to be addressed 'Pakistan, India'.[37]

The absence of strong and effective political leadership further complicated the challenge that Pakistan faced in weaving its disparate social, territorial and parochial loyalties into a cohesive nation state. Jinnah, the *Quaid-i-Azam*, or 'Great Leader', who more than any other individual had been responsible for bringing Pakistan into being, was already a sick man at the time of independence and passed away in September 1948. In October 1951, an Afghan national, Syed Akbar, assassinated Pakistan's first prime minister, Liaquat Ali Khan, at a political rally in Rawalpindi. In assessing the impact of Ali Khan's untimely death, Gilbert Laithwaite, Britain's High Commissioner in Karachi, reported that it had

deprived Pakistan of a leader of great distinction, whose place it will be impossible to fill. His strong common sense, sound political judgment and impressive personality, coupled with an eminent record of service in the national cause, gave him a position of particular significance in Pakistan.[38]

In the absence of Ali Khan, the ruling Muslim League Party went into rapid decline. A succession of inept and corrupt national leaders proved unable, or unwilling, to tackle the formidable issues confronting Pakistan. Disputes over the role of Islam in the new state, and conflicts of interest between the country's western and eastern halves, meant that Pakistan had to wait until March 1956 before a national constitution was passed into law, the nation being governed in the interim under the

---

[36] Ian Talbot, *Pakistan: A Modern History* (London: Hurst & Company, 2009), pp. 95–9.

[37] Briefing paper on 'Pakistan' February 1961, Alexander Symon Papers, Mss Eur E367/14, 'Queen's Visit to Pakistan and Bangladesh – Symon's Dispatches as UK High Commissioner', India Office Select Materials, British Library.

[38] Gilbert Laithwaite to Secretary of State for Commonwealth Relations, 'Assassination of Mr. Liaquat Ali Khan', 29 October 1951, DO 201/2 Correspondence respecting Commonwealth Relations, volume II 1951, TNA.

1935 Government of India Act. One future president of Pakistan subsequently reflected that the country's politicians, 'did not make even ordinary efforts to resolve the problems in front of them'.[39] Pakistan's increasingly chaotic political landscape stood in stark contrast to that in neighbouring India. In New Delhi, Nehru and his Congress Party exercised an iron grip on power that transformed democratic India into a de facto one-party state, and spawned a political dynasty that has dominated Indian politics through to the present.[40]

The fragmented political history of the territories that came to form Pakistan made it unlikely that, even had Jinnah or Ali Khan lived on into the late 1950s, Pakistan could have emulated the same level of central control and national cohesion achieved in India. Prior to independence, although claiming to speak for all South Asia's Muslims, the Muslim League's intellectual capital and popular support had been drawn largely from the northern heart of the subcontinent, deep inside what was to become Indian territory. In the west, the Muslim majority regions of Sind, Balochistan, the North-West Frontier Province and Punjab had traditionally been dominated by a clutch of small and parochial political parties, with little or no links to the Muslim League. Early efforts by Pakistan's ruling elite to foster a sense of national unity and legitimise state authority were further complicated by its predominately Indian heritage. A significant proportion of senior Muslim League politicians, including Jinnah and Ali Khan, as well as leading Pakistani bureaucrats, businessmen and military officers were Mohajirs, or migrants, who had relocated from India to Pakistan at the time of partition. The decision to adopt Urdu as Pakistan's official state language added to the sense of dislocation much of the nation's citizenry felt from its leadership. The court language of the former Mughal rulers of central India, Urdu was spoken only by a minority of West Pakistan's population, and not at all by the Bengali inhabitants of the country's eastern wing.[41]

Indeed, by far the greatest conundrum facing Pakistan was how to keep its two constituent parts from fracturing under the weight of powerful fissiparous pressures. The physical distance between East and West Pakistan was mirrored by an equally wide chasm in the ethnic, social, economic and linguistic composition of the two wings. In the 1930s, Choudhary Rahmat Ali, and his fellow Muslim nationalists, had omitted East Bengal from their vision of Pakistan. At the time, it

[39] Mohammad Ayub Khan, 'Pakistan Perspective', *Foreign Affairs* (July 1960), 549.
[40] Talbot, *Pakistan*, p. 126.
[41] Lieven, *Pakistan: A Hard Country*, pp. 61–2.

appeared whimsical to contemplate the fusion of two such geograph-
ically distant and culturally diverse regions into a single nation state.
Speaking in a constituent assembly debate on 19 March 1956, Ataur
Rahman Khan, chief minister of East Pakistan, underlined the sense of
alienation that Bengalis felt in relation to West Pakistan. 'I feel a pecu-
liar sensation when I come from Dacca to Karachi', Khan observed.
'I feel physically, apart from mental feeling, that I am living here in
a foreign country. I did not feel as much when I went to Zurich, to
Geneva or Switzerland, or London as much as I feel here in my own
country that I am in a foreign land.'[42] For many of West Pakistan's
citizens, the existence of a common religious bond proved insufficient to overcome deep-rooted feelings of animosity and contempt for
their fellow countrymen in the East. A former Viceroy of British India,
Lord Curzon, had referred scathingly to the flood-prone Bengal as 'a
low-lying country, inhabited by low, lying people'. To British officials
stationed in West Pakistan in the 1950s, their hosts appeared to share
Curzon's prejudice.[43] Seen as an economically backward, socially radical and politically volatile trouble spot by West Pakistan's leaders, the
more populous eastern wing of Pakistan was frustrated by the imposition of constitutional checks and balances designed to keep power out
of Bengali hands. Festering resentment in Bengal over the imposition of
Urdu as Pakistan's sole official language eventually fuelled demands for
increased political autonomy in East Pakistan, and ultimately ignited
a campaign for secession from the Pakistani state that was to end in a
bloody denouement in December 1971.

Serious structural weaknesses in the nascent Pakistani state, and
looming external threats, predominately in the guise of India and
Afghanistan, fostered a national security culture in Pakistan, within
which political leaders distrusted their own constituencies, and the
armed services assumed a central role in the maintenance of national
cohesion. Having witnessed at first hand the communal slaughter and
military conflict with India in Kashmir that accompanied Pakistan's
birth, one of its future leaders later recorded that the experience had
proved instrumental in convincing him that 'Pakistan's survival was
vitally linked with the establishment of a well-trained, well-equipped
and well-led army'.[44] In a national radio broadcast on 8 October 1948,

---

[42] Constituent Assembly of Pakistan, *Debates*, 19 March 1956, vol. I, no. 4 (Government
of Pakistan), p. 216.
[43] Ivor Lucas, *A Road To Damascus: Mainly Diplomatic Memoirs from the Middle East*
(London: The Radcliffe Press, 1997), p. 54.
[44] Mohammad Ayub Khan, *Friends Not Masters: A Political Autobiography* (London:
Oxford University Press, 1967), p. 2.

Liaquat Ali Khan made clear that for Pakistan, 'The defence of the State is our foremost consideration. It dominates all other government activities. We will not grudge any amount on the defence of our country.' Five years later, one of Ali Khan's successors announced melodramatically that he would starve before allowing the country's defences to be weakened.[45] In the first few years after 1947, defence expenditure absorbed upward of 70 per cent of Pakistan's national budget, and continued to account for 60 per cent of total state spending into the mid-1950s. Pakistan's policymakers evidenced far less interest, and expended much less capital, in growing the country's economy or developing its representative institutions.[46]

Pakistan's leaders were painfully aware, however, that whatever proportion of national output was directed into the armed forces, it would never be sufficient to offset India's preponderant economic and military power. As early as October 1947, Pakistan sought to address this dilemma by approaching the United States for a $2 billion loan. By the middle of the following decade, to the alarm of New Delhi, Karachi resolved to underwrite Pakistan's long-term security by becoming a fully paid-up member of the Western alliance.[47] In early 1954, resurgent Arab nationalism undercut British plans for a Middle Eastern defence organisation encompassing Pakistan. In May that year, American dissatisfaction with British leadership in a region that Washington had previously recognised as London's preserve prompted the United States to sign a bilateral defence agreement with Pakistan. Pakistan went on to became a founder member of the Southeast Asia Treaty Organization (SEATO), an American-sponsored collective security body, the ostensible purpose of which was to contain Chinese Communist influence in Asia. In 1955, Pakistan deepened its security and defence relationships with the West by joining the Middle East Treaty Organization, or Baghdad Pact. Under Washington's aegis, this bound Britain, Iran, Iraq, Turkey and Pakistan together in a mutual security agreement designed to deter Soviet expansion into the oil rich Persian Gulf.

In a political context, Pakistan's strategic alignment with the United States provided the country's bureaucratic and military elite with a rationale for retaining a stranglehold on domestic power at the expense of democratic institutions and elected representatives. Removing

[45] *News Chronicle*, 9 October 1948; *Dawn (Karachi)*, 17 August 1953.
[46] Gilbert Laithwaite to Secretary of State for Commonwealth Relations, 'Budget 1954–55', 30 March 1954, DO 201/5 Correspondence respecting Commonwealth Relations, volume V 1954, TNA; Talbot, *Pakistan*, p. 96.
[47] Meeting between Nehru and Mikoyan, 26 March 1956, New Delhi, Subject File No. 19, 1956, Subimal Dutt Papers, NMML.

internal political interference from Pakistan's foreign policymaking was presented as a necessary sacrifice in order to safeguard the flow of US military and economic assistance that accompanied the nation's new status as 'America's most allied ally in Asia'.[48] In April 1953, Pakistan's Governor General, Malik Ghulam Muhammad, had laid the groundwork for a US-Pakistani alliance by installing a cipher, Muhammed Ali Bogra, as prime minister. Bogra's appointment was inspired less by his decidedly mediocre political record, and more by his reputation for malleability and pro-American attitude.[49] Addressing a public meeting in Karachi, on 12 August 1954, Bogra defended Pakistan's tilt toward the United States, stating defiantly that

From a policy of drift in international affairs, our approach is now firm and positive ... [Pakistan's alliance with the US] will enable us to strengthen our defences. The prospect of a strong Pakistan is unwelcome in certain unfriendly quarters, and in India we have witnessed a most strenuous and in some respects most amazing vehement opposition to the idea that we should strengthen our defence forces by receiving military aid from the USA. We shall not frame our policies to suit India. We are here to do what is in our own interests. We are therefore determined to go forward with the building up of our defence forces as fast and as rapidly as we possibly can ... Our decision to receive military aid from America is ... a most significant move forward in the consolidation and progress of our country.[50]

The decisions taken in Washington and London to welcome Pakistan formally into the Western bloc and, as he saw it, extend the Cold War to South Asia, prompted a bitter Nehru to confide to one associate:

I do not think that there are many examples in history of a succession of wrong policies being followed by a country as by the United States in the Far East during the past five or six years. They have taken one wrong step after another ... They think that they can solve any problem with money and arms. They forget the human element. They forget the nationalistic urges of people. They forget the strong resentment of people in Asia against impositions.[51]

In public, the Indian premier was equally scathing in his criticism of America's willingness to fund the modernisation and expansion of Pakistan's armed forces. Addressing a Congress Party meeting at Kalyani in West Bengal, in January 1954, Nehru openly called upon Pakistan to reject American arms. 'For India this is a serious matter ... ', Congress Party delegates were informed. 'The mere fact that war is

[48] Ayub Khan, *Friends Not Masters*, p. 130.
[49] Talbot, *Pakistan*, pp. 119–20.
[50] 'Prime Minister on Importance of Agreements with Turkey and USA', *Pakistan News*, vol. 7, no. 22, 21 August 1954.
[51] Nehru to Birla, 21 May 1954, G. D. Birla Papers, NMML.

likely to come to our frontiers is grave enough. The other fact that this military aid [to Pakistan] might possibly be utilized against India cannot be ignored. I earnestly trust that even at this stage this unfortunate development will not take place, and I say so not in hostility but in all friendship for the people of Pakistan.'[52] Having visited the subcontinent the previous year, Eisenhower's vice-president, Richard Nixon, dismissed Nehru's objections to a US-Pakistani alliance as 'primarily based upon the fact that he [Nehru] wants India to be the dominant nation in Asia and that he wants no competition from Pakistan or any other country'. The vice-president assured a gathering of Washington officials that Pakistan had struck him as a country with the requisite 'foundations for more stability than exists [elsewhere in Asia] ... Everyone [in Pakistan] looked to the United States with favour ... the people of Pakistan definitely want the military aid program ... the program should go through'.[53]

Nehru's unfavourable assessment of American 'pactomania' may not have impressed Nixon, but it did resonate with his fellow Indians. An Indian Institute of Public Opinion survey conducted between January and March 1956 in West Bengal, New Delhi and the southern state of Travancore-Cochin, found that a majority of Indians believed that military alliances in general made for war, were inherently aggressive and did not promote freedom. Furthermore, the poll revealed that Soviet collective security arrangements 'were consistently and rather highly regarded as being defensive in nature and as affecting the security of India and the freedom of the Asian people *favourably*, whereas American military alliances were considered to *unfavourably* affect the security of India and Asian freedom'.[54] Pakistan's transformation into the West's foremost Asian ally also brought Indian opprobrium down on the heads of the British. In June 1956, Malcolm MacDonald, who had taken up the post of High Commissioner in New Delhi the previous year, warned the Commonwealth Relations Office (CRO) in London that Britain's central role in the SEATO and Baghdad pacts had attracted 'growing criticism' in India, and threatened, 'to undermine quite seriously good relations between the two countries'.[55]

---

[52] 'Nehru to Pakistan: "Reject US Aid" ', *Commonwealth Observer*, 24 January 1954.

[53] 'Debriefing Meeting of Nixon's Trip with Officials from State Department, CIA, and Defense', 8 January 1954, Declassified Documents Reference System (DDRS), DDRS-269392-i1-9.

[54] 'Indian Attitudes Towards US and USSR', 25 May 1956, RG306, Records of the US Information Agency, Box 11, Folder S-25 56, NARA.

[55] MacDonald to Earl of Home, 19 June 1956, Despatches and official correspondence 1955–60, 42/3/5–6, 29 February–12 November 1956, 42/3/7–11, Malcolm MacDonald Papers, GB 033 MAC, Palace Green Library, University of Durham.

Elsewhere, the United Kingdom's association with SEATO and the Baghdad Pact did little to quell a lingering bitterness in Pakistan over the British government's purportedly pro-Indian bias. Back in 1950, Anglo-Pakistani tensions had risen after India was allowed to remain in the Commonwealth on becoming a republic. Although upset at what it interpreted as further evidence of the absence of even-handedness in Britain's South Asian policy, Pakistan stayed in the Commonwealth, partly to constrain India's international influence, and partly to ensure continued access to British economic aid and London's expertise in intelligence and foreign policy matters. Occasional fits of pique on the part of Pakistan, however, reminded London that all was not entirely well with Anglo-Pakistani relations. In March 1956, the government of Pakistan refused to allow an aircraft carrying Mountbatten, then Britain's First Sea Lord, to fly through its airspace en route to New Delhi.[56] Applauding this decision, one Pakistani citizen fulminated in a letter published by the semi-official Karachi newspaper, *Dawn*, that the '"Serpent" Lord Mountbatten ... [whose] hand is stained with the blood of thousands of innocent Muslims is nothing but the enemy of Pakistan. He is the declared enemy of Islam ... and Pakistan.'[57] For its part, Whitehall continued to set great store by its politico-military association with Pakistan. Lord Home reminded his cabinet colleagues that it was very much in Britain's interest to ensure that Pakistan did not become so disenchanted with the West that it turned to embrace neutralism, or worse still, the Eastern bloc. It would 'be exceedingly dangerous', Home contended in 1955, 'for us to lose our one reliable military ally in the Sub-Continent and in the East'.[58]

The existence of a strong mutual self-interest ensured that London and Karachi kept Anglo-Pakistani relations on a reasonably even keel during the early 1950s. However, as Pakistan's first minister for education, Ishtiaq Hussain Qureshi, underlined at the time, Pakistan's relationship with the United Kingdom was best characterised as, 'correct, but seldom warm'.[59] Moreover, as the British readily acknowledged, the extension of American power and influence into the Mediterranean and the Middle East in the years after 1945 weakened London's position in Pakistan. In a cable sent to the CRO in March 1954, Gilbert Laithwaite, Britain's High Commissioner in Karachi, confirmed that Pakistan's government, 'clearly sees that it is not we but the Americans

---

[56] Mountbatten note, 14 March 1956, MB1/I508, MBP.

[57] *Dawn*, 17 March 1956.

[58] Douglas-Home, 'Impressions of My Commonwealth Tour', 15 November 1955, CAB/129/78, TNA.

[59] Ishtiaq Hussain Qureshi, *The Pakistani Way of Life* (London: Heinemann, 1956).

who now have something to give, and who are ready and anxious to take political, diplomatic and military initiatives which for good reasons are not open to us'. Laithwaite reported that a recent conversation with Sir Khizar Hayat Tiwana, a former premier of the Punjab, had reinforced his impression that America was inheriting the grudging regard from sections of Pakistan society that had once been the preserve of the British. Many Pakistanis had come to the conclusion, Tiwana volunteered, that 'If I cannot have the brother and he can no longer help me, I may as well have the cousin.'[60]

### Britain and India after 1947: plus ça change, plus c'est la même chose?

In the immediate aftermath of India's independence, Britain clashed with the Nehru government over how best to resolve its dispute with Pakistan over Kashmir and, in 1948, in relation to Hyderabad's enforced integration into the Indian Union. On the whole, however, London and New Delhi worked diligently to preserve Indo-British amity. In 1951, Archibald Nye, by now Britain's High Commissioner to India, informed Loy Henderson, 'that relations between the United Kingdom and India were better now than they ever have been'. Indo-British relations, Nye crowed, were rooted in feelings of 'mutual confidence and cooperation'. 'Nehru was firmly attached to the Commonwealth', Henderson was assured, 'and could be depended upon to be a loyal [British] partner.'[61]

India's willingness to remain in the Commonwealth after becoming an independent republic and renouncing its status as a Dominion of the British crown, may, in small degree, have been influenced by Nehru's feelings of affinity toward Britain.[62] However, compelling practical considerations undoubtedly played a more important part in the decision. Participation in Commonwealth meetings provided Nehru and his ministers with an international political platform on which to promote India and reinforce the country's status as a leading nation within the developing world. From a macro-economic perspective, a significant proportion of India's trade was with Commonwealth countries. In 1949–50, a quarter of India's total imports came from the

---

[60] Gilbert Laithwaite to Sir Percivale Liesching, 'American Military Aid to Pakistan', 15 March 1954, DO 201/5 Correspondence respecting Commonwealth Relations, volume V 1954, TNA.

[61] Henderson to Eliot Weil, 19 February 1951, RG 59, Office of South Asian Affairs, Lot 59 D 75, Folder SOA General 1956, NARA.

[62] 'India's Relations with the Commonwealth', 10 November 1948, CAB 129/30, TNA.

United Kingdom, while the British market absorbed a similar level of India's exports. Six years later, on the eve of the Suez crisis, Indian trade with Britain had increased slightly in percentage terms, while that with both the United States and the Soviet Union, which taken together accounted for less than a fifth of India's total commercial activity, was in decline.[63] Moreover, New Delhi's foreign exchange reserves, totalling some £750 million, were locked into the British-controlled sterling area. India drew upon its sterling balances, which were held in London, to purchase foodstuffs from abroad, fund consumer imports and underwrite its development plans.[64]

Lower down the economic chain, *box-wallahs*, or British businessmen and industrialists based in the subcontinent, continued to fulfil an important financial and technical role in India after 1947. Up until the late 1960s, India's tea, mining and oil refining industries remained largely British-controlled concerns. In Calcutta, much of the city's infrastructure, including its electricity supply and public transport system, was owned and operated by private companies based in London. The Calcutta Tramways Company remained in British hands until July 1967 when, to the dismay of its shareholders, it was expropriated by the Communist state government of West Bengal.[65] Having visited the subcontinent in 1955, Alec Douglas-Home, Britain's Secretary of State for Commonwealth Relations, lauded the 'vigorous' British business community in India. The vibrant British commercial presence in the subcontinent, Home advised his cabinet colleagues, was doubly significant given that 'America, with all her money and strength, makes no headway in winning their [Indians] confidence'. 'In so far as any country from the West can exercise influence', the Commonwealth Secretary added, 'the task of holding them [India] lies upon us.'[66]

In military terms, India also remained heavily reliant on Britain to supply its armed services with the bulk of their training and equipment. Under the Raj, India's army, navy and air force had been imbued with the structures, practices and traditions of the British military. In the post-independence period, British officers continued to nurture

---

[63] Blaker to Banks, 'Monthly Statistics of Foreign Trade of India and Annual Statement of Foreign Trade of India', 29 September 1961, DO 133/145, TNA.

[64] 'India's Future Relations with the Commonwealth: Implications for Commonwealth Countries', February 1949, SWIN III 3/1, Earl of Swinton Papers, Churchill Archives Centre, Churchill College Cambridge (hereafter SWP).

[65] Sir Percival Griffiths to John Tilney, 14 November 1967, HC-1-118-2-11, John Tilney Papers, Houses of Parliament Archives, London.

[66] Douglas-Home, 'Impressions of My Commonwealth Tour', 15 November 1955, CAB/129/78, TNA.

a network of connections, both formal and informal, which had been built up between the armed services of the two countries during the previous two hundred years.[67] At the invitation of Nehru's government, senior British military personnel retained important posts in India's armed forces for a considerable time after independence. General Sir Roy Bucher served as head of the Indian Army until 1949. Air Marshal Sir Thomas Elmhirst continued to run the Indian Air Force until 1950. The Indian Navy remained under the leadership of senior officers seconded from the Royal Navy until as late as April 1958.

Less obvious, but equally important, was the close liaison and training relationships that the British Security Service (MI5) established with India's intelligence service, the Delhi Intelligence Bureau (IB). With the approval of India's first director of intelligence, T. G. Sanjevi, and his successor B. N. Mullik, who assumed control of the IB in July 1950, MI5 stationed a declared, or overt, Security Liaison Officer (SLO) in New Delhi. SLOs provided advice and support to the IB. This encompassed guidance on counter-espionage operations directed against the Communist Party of India, and included the exchange of security-related information between London and New Delhi. MI5 was careful not to engage in acts of subterfuge or espionage on Indian soil.[68] The introduction of a British SLO in India proved so successful that it was replicated in Pakistan and, as the Cold War escalated in the early 1950s, across the wider British Empire and Commonwealth.[69] Mullik subsequently acknowledged that the intimacy of the intelligence relationship established between India and Britain led Nehru to suspect that the IB was guilty of simply 'dishing out intelligence which the British continued to supply to it'.[70] In 1955, one MI5 SLO in New Delhi, John Allen, confirmed that Mullik preferred to keep the Security Service's presence in India as quiet as possible. Were Nehru or officials from the Indian Ministry of External Affairs to get wind of the extent of the IB's collaboration with MI5, Mullik had explained to Allen, it was likely that much of their current security liaison activity would have to be curtailed.[71]

---

[67] S. R. Mehrotra, 'Nehru and the Commonwealth', in Nanda, *Nehru Years*, pp. 38–9.
[68] 'Visit of Captain Liddell (Security Service) to the Middle East', 9 June 1947, Confidential Annex to JIC (47) 33rd Meeting (0), CAB 159/1, TNA. See also Christopher Andrew, *The Defence of the Realm: The Authorized History of MI5* (London: Allen Lane, 2009), pp. 137 and 481.
[69] 'Security Service Representative in Pakistan', 5 November 1947, JIC (47) 75th Meeting (O), CAB 159/2, TNA.
[70] B. N. Mullik, *My Years with Nehru, 1948–1964* (New Delhi: Allied Publishers, 1972), p. 57.
[71] Andrew, *Defence of the Realm*, pp. 445–6.

The last MI5 officer left New Delhi in the late 1960s not at India's behest, but as consequence of swingeing cuts forced on the Security Service by a Whitehall bureaucracy in search of overseas economies.[72] By 1965, MI5 was under pressure from the Treasury to implement annual cost savings of £100,000. The Security Service recalled SLOs from Tanzania, Ghana, Ceylon and Gibraltar, and started the process of shutting down stations in Australia and Malta. In an effort to save its Indian SLO from a similar fate, the then director general of MI5, Roger Hollis, enlisted the support of John Freeman, Britain's High Commissioner to India. Freeman's insistence that removing MI5's presence in India would 'risk destroying a liaison which it might be very difficult if ever to re-establish' failed to move the British Cabinet Secretary, Sir Burke Trend. On being informed by Hollis's successor, Martin Furnivall Jones, of MI5's decision to withdraw its SLO from New Delhi, S. P. Varma, then head of the IB, expressed deep misgivings at Britain's decision to terminate an intelligence connection with India that stretched back over twenty years. It was regrettable, Varma wrote to Furnivall Jones, that London had seen fit to end 'the longstanding contact at a personal level which has proved invaluable to us'.[73]

In another sense, the legacy of British imperialism in the subcontinent, although in so many respects deleterious and divisive, left behind a deep and enduring cultural imprint that many Indians embraced and, where possible, turned to their advantage. The Indian polymath and poet Rabindranath Tagore was not alone in linking the intellectual foundations of Indian nationalism to the liberal idealism espoused by the British philosophers John Locke, John Stuart Mill and John Bright. One observer of post-independence Indian politics noted that the British had found it impossible not to advance the principle, if not the practice, of free speech and self-government, which, in turn, laid the basis for India's independence movement.[74] Speaking in January 1961, India's president, Dr Rajendra Prasad, an ardent Indian nationalist and implacable opponent of imperialism, reflected that the British impact upon India had, 'been in many ways an abiding one'. On the principle that 'nationalism should never acquire an exclusive character', Prasad welcomed the extent to which India had assimilated, adapted and exploited some of the 'finer aspects' of Anglo-Indian exchange. 'English language and literature play a prominent part in our lives, and the whole English tradition colours and conditions some of our ways of thought', India's president observed. 'The influence of British jurisprudence can still be

---

[72] Hollis to Burke Trend, 13 November 1965, CO 1035/171, TNA.
[73] Andrew, *Defence of the Realm*, p. 481.
[74] Bowles, *Ambassador's Report*, p. 56.

traced in our law. Above all, we have sought to develop the British methods of policies and government, adapting them to our own context.'[75]

The British were well aware that their broad institutional, cultural and economic influence in the subcontinent, while 'permeating the fabric of Indian life', did not readily translate into direct authority over the Indian government's political outlook or policymaking. Moreover, the British recognised that in the age of the superpowers their standing in South Asia constituted a wasting asset. In the long term, Britain did not have the strategic resources to contest the expansion of American and Soviet influence in South Asia. Besides which, British officials recognised that a new and younger generation of Indians would be, 'less likely to be as receptive to the "legacy" of British influence as the older generation who lead Press and public affairs in India today'.[76] In the early 1960s, Whitehall sought to identify exactly when 'the old British influence' in India had begun to ebb. With the benefit of hindsight, it seemed probable that by the early 1950s the British High Commission in New Delhi had started to play a 'rather anomalous and much less effective role' than hitherto. From 1956, in the wake of the Suez crisis, a diminution in British political authority in India appeared to be more discernible.[77] Yet, throughout the 1950s, British officials continued to enjoy easy and privileged access to the higher echelons of the Indian government. Malcolm MacDonald, who served as Britain's High Commissioner in New Delhi in the later half of the decade, would invariably begin his working day with a visit to India's Ministry of External Affairs (MEA). Over an off-the-record chat with the MEA Secretary General, Sir Raghavan Pillai, a stalwart of the pre-independence Indian Civil Service, MacDonald would discuss issues raised in the overnight cable traffic he had received from Whitehall.[78] The retention of such informal connections encouraged some British officials to persist in the belief that a deep-rooted 'general sympathy' between India and the United Kingdom would continue to act as an emollient when differences arose between London and New Delhi.[79] More significantly still,

[75] Rajendra Prasad, New Delhi, 21 January 1961, in Valmiki Choudhary (ed.), *Dr. Rajendra Prasad: Correspondence and Select Documents*, vol. 21, January 1960 to February 1963 (New Delhi: Allied Publishers Limited, 1995), p. 306.
[76] 'India's Future Relations with the Commonwealth: Implications for Commonwealth Countries', February 1949, SWIN III 3/1, SWP; Dunelm Brown to Simmons, 8 September 1961, DO 133/145, TNA.
[77] J. S. P. Mackenzie, 'UK Influence in India', 19 September 1961, DO 133/145, TNA.
[78] David Malcolm McBain, Private Secretary to Malcolm MacDonald, DOHP 50, interviewed 27 April 2000, British Diplomatic Oral History Programme, Churchill College Cambridge.
[79] Blaker to Simmons, 19 September 1961, DO 133/145, TNA.

policymakers in the United States retained the impression, well into the following decade, that the British were capable of influencing Nehru's government in ways that Washington could not.[80]

## The Soviet Union and South Asia

Until Joseph Stalin's death in 1953, the USSR's relationship with South Asia was inhibited by the Soviet dictator's conviction that nascent post-colonial states were little more than imperialist puppets. In 1950, one Indian official recorded that the state-controlled Soviet press seemed determined to portray India as 'a stronghold of reaction, a persecutor of democratic forces, a hanger-on of the Anglo-American bloc, and the harbinger of a new Imperialism in the East'.[81] The Indian government, and much of the country's media, exercised 'great restraint in its attitudes towards the Soviet Union', and invariably ignored Moscow's brickbats. In large part, Indian equanimity reflected a consensus amongst the country's policymakers that an open Indo-Soviet breach would compromise the nation's policy of Cold War non-alignment.[82] To the Nehru administration's relief, toward the end of the Stalin era signals had started to emerge from Moscow of a softening in the Soviet attitude toward India. Having previously shunned contact with Indian diplomats, during the course of 1953 the Soviet leadership began to meet with Sarvepalli Radhakrishnan, India's ambassador to the USSR. Andrey Vishinsky, the Soviet foreign minister, started to attend receptions at the Indian Embassy in Moscow, and in New Delhi, the Soviet ambassador displayed a new and 'sudden affability' toward his Indian hosts. The 'tendentious propaganda' that the Soviet Union had directed against India also ceased.[83] More substantively, the Soviets began to take India's side in its dispute with Pakistan over Kashmir.[84]

[80] Victor Martin to Gore-Booth, 29 August 1961, DO 133/145, TNA.
[81] K. P. S. Menon, 'India's Foreign Policy', 1950, Speeches & Writings File No. 35, K. P. S. Menon Collection, NMML.
[82] *Ibid.* The evolution of India's relations with the Soviet Union have been analysed in works such as Robert C. Horn, *Soviet-Indian Relations: Issues and Influence* (New York: Praeger, 1982); Peter J. S. Duncan, *The Soviet Union and India* (London: Routledge, 1989); Ramesh Thakur and Carlyle A. Thayer, *Soviet Relations with India and Vietnam, 1945–1992* (New York: St. Martin's Press, 1992); and, most recently, Vojtech Mastny, 'The Soviet Union's Partnership with India', *Journal of Cold War Studies*, 12, 3 (2010), 50–90.
[83] P. N. Kaul, 'The Scope for Developing Trade Relations with USSR', 1954, Ministry of External Affairs, D/3042/Europe, National Archives of India (hereafter NAI).
[84] Graham Parson to Sparks, 3 February 1950, RG 59, Office of South Asian Affairs, Lot file 57D373, Box 2, Folder Official informal Jan–May 1950, NARA; P. N. Kaul, 'The Scope for Developing Trade Relations with USSR', 1954, Ministry of External Affairs, D/3042/Europe, NAI.

Nehru's government welcomed signals that a more constructive phase in India's relationship with Moscow could be on the horizon. Aside from the strategic advantage that the Indian government identified in maintaining friendly relations with both Cold War blocs, many Indians, Nehru included, did not share the visceral antipathy for communism prevalent in the United States and much of Western Europe. As an avowed socialist, the Indian premier acknowledged and admired Soviet accomplishments in fields as diverse as economic planning, education and healthcare.[85] Moreover, as one Indian official noted, Soviet calls for 'the end of colonialism and racial discrimination and for redistribution of world wealth, are by no means disagreeable to India'.[86] Nehru had first visited the Soviet Union in 1927. The future Indian leader's impressions of the USSR, which he committed to print the following year in a work entitled *Soviet Russia: Some Random Sketches and Impressions*, were uniformly upbeat. The seemingly egalitarian structure of Soviet society, its programme of crash industrialisation and central planning, and its policy of agricultural collectivisation, were presented by Nehru as models of sound social and economic progress.[87] In common with many left-wing intellectuals at that time, Nehru came to be associated with transnational anti-imperialist movements sponsored by communist front organisations. In the 1930s, when the less-edifying aspects of the tyrannical regimes of Lenin and Stalin were exposed, Nehru qualified his earlier, utopian vision of the Soviet Union. In a character sketch of the Indian leader produced by the US State Department in the mid-1950s, Nehru was portrayed as an individual who 'as a young man … sympathised with and was fascinated by the Soviet attempt to create a new society'. 'The intellectual appreciation of Marxist ideology', was not, however, considered by American officials to have 'significantly affected his [Nehru's] basic liberal humanism … he has found Communist official dogmatism, heresy hunts, and violence repugnant to his convictions.'[88] Having observed Nehru at close quarters, Loy Henderson deduced that the Indian prime minister was convinced that communism offered a 'grim and bleak' prescription for the future, and placed insufficient emphasis on the importance of individual and

---

[85] Nanda, *Nehru Years*, p. 5.

[86] K. P. S. Menon, 'India's Foreign Policy', 1950, Speeches & Writings File No. 35, K. P. S. Menon Collection, NMML.

[87] Jawaharlal Nehru, *Soviet Russia: Some Random Sketches and Impressions* (Allahabad: Law Journal Press, 1928).

[88] 'Nehru's Political Personality', 18 June 1956, RG 59, Office of South Asian Affairs, Lot 59 D 75, Folder 1956, NARA.

cultural freedom. Nehru, the American ambassador concluded, was 'a non-communist rather than an anti-communist'.[89]

The contention voiced by some American friends of India that Nehru had become 'disillusioned' with the USSR, and saw it as 'a dangerous aggressor', overstated the Indian leader's disenchantment with the Soviet Union.[90] Nonetheless, Moscow's ruthless subjugation of satellite states in Eastern Europe troubled Indian policymakers. The process of Stalinisation that occurred behind the Iron Curtain, one Indian senior official observed, suggested 'that the condition of Soviet friendship is political subservience'. Inside India, the Nehru government took a firm line with the Communist Party of India, arresting communist activists suspected of inciting civil disorder or engaging in political subversion. Prominent Russian diplomats, such as Alexandra Kollontai, took their Indian counterparts to task for the manner in which 'the true democrats [communists] in India were being ruthlessly persecuted by the Indian Government'.[91] Soviet protests had little effect on Nehru's aversion to indigenous Indian communism. On the campaign trail during India's first general election, which took place between October 1951 and February 1952, the Indian premier urged a crowd of communists waving red banners etched with the Soviet hammer and sickle motif, to 'go and live in the country whose flag you are carrying'.[92]

In a broader sense, international developments provided the impetus for New Delhi and Moscow to put their differences to one side, and continue to strengthen bilateral relations. Notably, Nehru's emergence as an influential figure in the international non-aligned movement, the first large-scale gathering of which occurred in Bandung in April 1955, coincided with a decision taken by the post-Stalin Soviet leadership to inaugurate an Afro-Asian front in the Cold War, the ideological battle lines of which had solidified in Europe. Indian officials embraced the 'new atmosphere created since Stalin's death', which saw the Soviet Union adopt a less ideological and 'far more practical and business-like' approach to Indo-Soviet affairs. Moscow, it seemed, had resolved to strengthen its political, commercial and cultural links with India 'on the basis, of mutual advantage' and, where possible, 'seek ...

[89] 'Jawaharlal Nehru', undated, Box 8, India Misc. folder, LWHP.
[90] Chester Bowles to John Foster Dulles, 20 March 1953, RG 59, Office of South Asian Affairs, Lot file 57D373, Box 3, Folder 'Ambassador Chester Bowles', NARA.
[91] K. P. S. Menon, 'India's Foreign Policy', 1950, Speeches & Writings File No. 35, K. P. S. Menon Collection, NMML.
[92] Frank Moraes, *Jawaharlal Nehru: A Biography* (New York: Macmillan, 1956), p. 143.

co-operation in international affairs'.[93] In June 1955, Nehru accepted an invitation to visit the Soviet Union and, later that autumn, Nikita Khrushchev, First Secretary of the Communist Party of the Soviet Union, and Nikolai Bulganin, the Soviet premier, travelled to India. When Nehru landed at Moscow airport, the entire Soviet presidium turned out to greet him. Over a two-week period, the Indian premier toured Leningrad, Georgia, the Ukraine and Soviet central Asia. Large and enthusiastic crowds were mobilised to greet Nehru wherever he went. The Indian leader's books were reprinted and published in Russian, Indian films were shown in Soviet cinemas, and Indian popular music broadcast over state radio. 'The unprecedented welcome given to a non-Communist statesman', one Indian diplomat gushed, 'is the most spectacular affirmation, yet made by the Soviet Government, of their belief in co-existence.'[94]

Discussions between Indian and Soviet officials during Nehru's visit to the USSR were largely confined to areas in which New Delhi and Moscow were in full agreement, such as the Chinese Communist claim on Taiwan, the implementation of the Geneva accords on Indo-China and the desirability of additional Indo-Soviet cultural and economic exchange. Working with Nehru and his government promised to advance Soviet interests in the developing world, Khrushchev noted later, and had little bearing on the underlying perception in Moscow that the Indian leader was essentially a Western flunky.[95] Back in Washington, State Department officials took comfort from the fact that, in terms of India's foreign policy, 'little or nothing new' appeared to have materialised from Nehru's Russian adventure.[96] In November, Khrushchev and Bulganin spent three weeks in India addressing rallies and inspecting farms, dams and steel mills across the subcontinent. In Kashmir, to New Delhi's delight and Pakistan's fury, Khrushchev publicly declared that the Soviet Union regarded the troubled state as an integral part of India.[97] Nothing occurred during the course of the Soviet leaders' visit,

[93] P. N. Kaul, 'The Scope for Developing Trade Relations with USSR', 1954, Ministry of External Affairs, D/3042/Europe, NAI.

[94] N. R. Pillai, 'A Visit to the Soviet Union: Some Impressions and Reflections', 29 July 1955, Subject File 16, June–July 1955, Subimal Dutt Papers. NMML; 'The Prime Minister's Visit to the Soviet Union', 6 July 1955, Subject File 16, June–July 1955, Subimal Dutt Papers, NMML.

[95] Nikita S. Khrushchev, *Memoirs: Time, People, Power*, vol. 3 (Moscow: Moskovskie Novosti, 1999), p. 317.

[96] Jones to Jernegan, 'Nehru–Bulganin Declaration', 23 June 1955, RG 59, Office of South Asian Affairs, Lot 59 D 75, Folder India Economic 1955, NARA.

[97] N. A. Bulganin and N. S. Khrushchev, *Visit of Friendship to India, Burma and Afghanistan: Speeches and Official Documents, November–December 1955* (Moscow: Foreign Languages Publishing House, 1955).

however, to suggest that India's foreign or domestic policy had shifted to the left.

Khrushchev's 'rugged personality ... good humour and plain speaking made him the people's favourite as well as the pressman's joy', one Indian diplomat noted.[98] Yet, the Soviet delegation's talks with Indian ministers proved to be stilted and uneventful.[99] Writing later to an American friend, Nehru's daughter, Indira Gandhi, emphasised that 'at no time [during their Indian visit] did anyone think that we were growing nearer to the communists, neither did Bulganin and Khrushchev think so'.[100] Indeed, while Nehru robustly defended India's right to cultivate ties with Eastern bloc nations that were 'very friendly to us', and rejected calls to outlaw the Communist Party of India on the grounds that such a move would 'approximate to dictatorship', the Indian premier continued to attack communist doctrine as fundamentally inimical to India and its people. In January 1960, speaking at a Congress Party rally at Ernakulam, in Kerala, Nehru declared that he opposed the CPI because

the policies they pursue and which they have in mind are not right. The basic approach of the party is not right and will not be conducive to the growth of India and the advancement of the Indian people. They will lead, as sometimes in the past, to conflict and trouble.[101]

In the economic sphere, India's relations with the Soviet Union did receive a boost from the exchange of visits between Nehru and Khrushchev in 1955. The Second Secretary in India's Moscow Embassy, P. N. Kaul, had long urged New Delhi to increase trade with the Soviet Union as a means of accelerating India's domestic development programme. Building stronger economic links with the USSR, Kaul argued, would also have the ancillary effect of placing, 'a healthy diplomatic pressure on the Western powers [to] ... pay more heed to our [India's] needs and requirements'.[102] Moreover, Indian officials

---

[98] K. P. S. Menon. 'The Annual Political Report of the USSR for 1955', 15 February 1956, Ministry of External Affairs, Research & Intelligence, Progs. Nos. 3 (30)-RI, 1956, NAI.

[99] 'Summary Record of a Talk between the Prime Minister of India and Mr. Bulganin and Mr. Khrushchev on 21 November 1955', 21 November 1955, Subject File 17, Nov–Dec 1955, Subimal Dutt Papers, NMML.

[100] Gandhi to Norman, Prime Minister's House, New Delhi, 23 February 1956, Dorothy Norman, *Indira Gandhi: Letters to an American Friend, 1950–1984* (New York: Harcourt Brace Jovanovich, 1985), p. 30.

[101] 'Reds Hinder Nation's Advance, Says Nehru' and 'Foreign Reds Irrelevant To Kerala Poll', *The Hindustan Times*, 13 January 1960.

[102] P. N. Kaul, 'The Scope for Developing Trade Relations with USSR', 1954, Ministry of External Affairs, D/3042/Europe, NAI.

calculated that the Soviets retained a strong self-interest in assisting India's industrial and agricultural development. In a note sent to the Ministry of External Affairs back in New Delhi, India's ambassador in Moscow, K. P. S. Menon, underlined that

The Soviet Government will not of course help us, any more than any other Government, in a spirit of altruism. They will help us because it will pay them to do so. They feel that generous assistance to India now will fetch dividends not only in Rupees and Roubles, but in India's goodwill, which is worth much to them, especially at a time when the USA is picking off one weak or compliant Asian state after another and hitching it to its waggon [sic].[103]

It was 'entirely consistent' with India's foreign policy, Menon added, to encourage 'a little competition' between the Soviets and the West when it came to furnishing India with technical assistance and economic aid. Doing so would also go some way to dispelling 'the impression, prevalent not merely in the Soviet Union, but in certain quarters in India itself, that while India is resolutely independent in political matters, her economy is getting increasingly enmeshed in Anglo-American schemes'.[104]

In the two years between 1955 and 1957, India's imports from the USSR increased seven-fold. Over the same period, India's exports to the Soviet Union grew at a similar rate.[105] India's economic 'flirtation with Russia' alarmed the British. 'The [Indian] papers are full of what Russian capital and technical skill can do to promote Indian expansion and development', Douglas-Home noted toward the end of 1955, 'and the Russians are responding with some good work.'[106] In April 1950, Frank Roberts, Britain's Deputy High Commissioner in New Delhi, had assured American colleagues that Soviet influence in India was likely to remain marginal for some considerable time to come. 'When anything really important happened here,' Roberts observed at the time, '[Sir Girija] Bajpai [India's minister for external affairs] invariably called in the United Kingdom High Commissioner and the American Ambassador, and he did not call in the Soviet Ambassador.'[107] Yet,

---

[103] K. P. S. Menon to R. K. Nehru, No. 5(1) EAFT/54, 30 April 1954, Ministry of External Affairs, D/3042/Europe, NAI.

[104] K. P. S. Menon to R. K. Nehru, No. 5(1) EAFT/54, 30 April 1954, Ministry of External Affairs, D/3042/Europe, NAI.

[105] Blaker to Banks, 29 September 1961, 'Monthly Statistics of Foreign Trade of India and Annual Statement of Foreign Trade of India', DO 133/145, TNA.

[106] Douglas-Home, 'Impressions of My Commonwealth Tour', 15 November 1955, CAB129/78, TNA.

[107] Memorandum of Conversation between Graham Parsons and Roberts, 19 April 1950, RG 59, Office of South Asian Affairs, Lot file 54D341, Box 18, Folder India–US Relations, NARA.

by the middle of the decade, the impact of the Soviet charm offensive in South Asia had become a matter of marked concern to Western officials. In May 1956, a survey conducted by the Indian Institute of Public Opinion found that respondents in the subcontinent typically viewed the Soviet Union as 'friendly to Asian countries', and home to an economic system that delivered 'a rise in the standard of all living in the country'. The Western capitalist model, meanwhile, was generally perceived by Indians to result in economic 'exploitation'.[108] 'Until yesterday,' K. P. S. Menon noted drily, 'Britannia ruled the waves of the Indian Ocean; now a new [Soviet] frigate, manned by pirates is entering the region!'[109]

### Hindee Chinee bhai-bhai

The Indian government's post-war relationship with Communist China proved to be every bit as tortuous and involved as that between New Delhi and Moscow.[110] On an individual level, Nehru admired, and felt indebted to, the exiled Chinese Nationalist leader Jiang Jieshi, otherwise known as Chiang Kai-Shek. During the Second World War, Jiang and his Kuomintang government had lobbied its American ally to press the British on the question of India's independence. For several months during the war Jiang's family cared for the children of one of Nehru's sisters, adding a personal dimension to the political bond between the two Asian leaders. In October 1949, when the Chinese Communist Party (CCP) overthrew the Kuomintang regime and ended China's long and enervating civil war, Nehru put sentiment to one side, and quickly recognised the new People's Republic of China (PRC). Nehru explained to Loy Henderson that while India would 'firmly oppose' Chinese attempts to 'infiltrate India with Communist ideology or with Communist agents', his government 'hoped [that] by maintaining friendly relations with Chinese nationalism to be of service to China and to assist in extricating that nationalism from the control of Communism'.[111] If the United States failed to do likewise, the Indian leader cautioned US officials, and attempted 'to prop up a man [Jiang]

---

108 'Indian Attitudes Towards US and USSR', 25 May 1956, RG 306, Records of the US Information Agency, Box 11, Folder S-25 56, NARA.

109 K. P. S. Menon, 'The Annual Political Report of the USSR for 1955', 15 February 1956, Ministry of External Affairs, Research & Intelligence, Progs. Nos. 3 (30)-RI, 1956, NAI.

110 Chester Bowles to John Foster Dulles, 20 March 1953, RG 59, Office of South Asian Affairs, Lot file 57D373, Box 3, Folder 'Ambassador Chester Bowles', NARA.

111 'Discussion with Prime Minister on Indian Foreign Policy', February 1950, Box 8, India Misc. folder, LWHP.

who ... has been so discredited', America would 'weaken' its influence in Asia.[112]

Above all, Nehru respected the manner in which the CCP, under Mao Zedong's leadership, had managed to unify and strengthen a nation that for so long had been enfeebled, divided and exploited. The CCP's success in reasserting China's national sovereignty, and defending its interests on the international stage, drew plaudits from New Delhi. India's leaders, a senior State Department official reflected, appeared to harbour a, 'complex, sympathetic ... feeling of kinship for China as an Asian power which has thrown off "white Western exploitation"'.[113] In the context of the Korean War, American diplomats suspected that Nehru, in common with a majority of Indians, were 'thrill[ed] to see a formerly weak oriental power suddenly become strong and able to sit across the table from us ... not acting in a cowed, humble fashion but even in an arrogant manner, looking us straight in the eye'.[114] India expressed support for the PRC in a more tangible form by calling for its admission to the United Nations; refusing to declare China an aggressor in Korea; declining to sign a Western-sponsored peace agreement with Japan, from which China was excluded; and by pressing for PRC representation at the Bandung Conference. Even more significant, was Nehru's decision to sign the Sino-Indian Treaty on Trade and Intercourse with Tibet in 1954, which incorporated the Panch Sheel, or Five Principles of Peaceful Co-existence. This committed India and China to uphold policies of mutual non-aggression; to respect each other's sovereignty and territorial integrity; to eschew interference in each other's domestic affairs; and to pursue policies of peaceful coexistence. The treaty was also notable as the instrument under which India formally relinquished its ancient claim to special rights and privileges in Tibet.[115]

A spirit of *Hindee Chinee bhai-bhai*, or Indian-Chinese brotherhood, took root in India following the signing of the Sino-Indian treaty. India and China had a history of political, cultural and economic exchange stretching back centuries. Both had endured long periods of foreign

[112] Chester Bowles to John Foster Dulles, 20 March 1953, RG 59, Office of South Asian Affairs, Lot file 57D373, Box 3, Folder 'Ambassador Chester Bowles', NARA.
[113] George V. Allen to Alex Jones, 6 August 1955, RG 59, Office of South Asian Affairs, Lot 59 D 75, Folder India 1955, NARA.
[114] Ambassador George V. Allen, 12 May 1954, Committee on Foreign Relations, United States Senate, Eighty-Third Congress, Second Session (Washington, DC: USGPO, 1954).
[115] The text of the Sino-Indian Treaty on Trade and Intercourse with Tibet is reproduced in A. Appadorai (ed.), *Select Documents on India's Foreign Policy and Relations, 1947–1972*, vol. 1 (New Delhi: Oxford University Press, 1982), pp. 459–66.

domination, and fought protracted struggles to reassert their independence. Both were confronted with formidable economic and social problems, exacerbated by runaway population growth, and faced an urgent need to refocus national energy and resources on delivering economic development. Given the domestic challenges confronting India, courting China's friendship was seen by the Nehru government as an eminently sensible policy. The contemporaneous decision taken by the United States to furnish Pakistan with military aid provided an additional strategic rationale for India to remain on good terms with its powerful Asian neighbour. In October 1954, Nehru visited China in a move designed to buttress India's relationship with the PRC. The Indian leader was impressed by the rapid strides that China had made in mobilising its enormous, and previously largely untapped, economic potential.[116] China's leaders, and in particular the nation's premier, Zhou Enlai, struck their Indian counterparts as essentially pragmatic individuals, with whom they could do business. Following his first encounter with Zhou, the distinguished Indian statesman Chakravarti Rajagopalachari recorded that 'frankly my impression was very favourable ... the Chinese Premier is I believe a good type of man and trustworthy'.[117]

Behind the expressions of goodwill toward China emanating from New Delhi, the Indian government remained wary of the regional implications of China's growing economic and political power. In 1955, Nehru confided to George Allen, US Assistant Secretary of State for Near Eastern and South Asian Affairs, that 'The thought of 500 million Chinese working hard and in a reasonably unified way constantly frightens me.' Ideologically, economically and strategically, Asia's two predominant powers were natural competitors. The Nehru government, Washington observed, was 'keenly aware that Asia is now being offered through China another kind of economic system to which the Indian people may turn if democracy should fail'. Nonetheless, Nehru and his closest political advisers discounted the possibility that China would seek to dominate India through force of arms. Mao Zedong's regime appeared too preoccupied with tackling China's own formidable social and economic problems, and consolidating the CCP's grip on power, to contemplate external military adventures in the absence of a direct threat to Chinese interests. Furthermore, the Himalayan

---

[116] Allen to Alex Jones, 16 November 1955, 'Indo-US Relations', RG 59, Office of South Asian Affairs, Lot file 57D373, Box 6, Folder Memo File 1955, NARA.
[117] Rajagopalachari to R, 8 December 1956, File 46, Fourth Instalment, C. Rajagopalachari Papers, NMML.

barrier separating the two countries was generally perceived to rule out a large-scale Chinese incursion into India.[118]

In October 1950, Beijing's military annexation of Tibet had unsettled Indian policymakers. Nehru's public reaction to the Chinese decision to 'liberate' Tibet was muted. Privately, however, the Indian premier condemned China's action as 'rather foolish'. In a letter written to his sister, Nehru reflected that Beijing's use of force had evoked a 'strong feeling' in many Indians 'of being let down by them [China]'.[119] China's absorption of Tibet, and subsequent construction of a new network of roads and military airfields within the country, led some Indian politicians to question whether Beijing's next move might be to challenge Indian influence in Nepal, Sikkim and even Assam.[120] In 1954, Indian officials began to express concern at the movement of Chinese patrols through territory astride the Sino-Indian border that was claimed by New Delhi. In view of the political and economic cost of qualifying India's entente with China, not least in terms of increased military spending, Nehru opted not to take a robust line with Beijing on the border issue. India's parliament, press and people remained largely in the dark as simmering tension on the Sino-Indian border intensified throughout the latter half of the 1950s.[121]

### Britain, the United States and the early Cold War in South Asia: empire, race and ideology

In 1947, South Asia barely registered on the political radar of President Harry S. Truman's administration in Washington. Truman, his Secretary of State, George C. Marshall, and senior American foreign policymakers were focused instead on events taking place in Western Europe. Political turmoil, economic volatility and rising social tension appeared poised to undermine Europe's post-war recovery and, in the process, threaten the United States' long-term security and prosperity. Fears that the Soviet Union might exploit turbulence on the

[118] Allen to Alex Jones, 6 August 1955, RG 59, Office of South Asian Affairs, Lot 59 D 75, folder India 1955, NARA.
[119] Nehru to Vijaya Lakshmi Pandit, 1 November 1953, Vijaya Lakshmi Pandit Papers, NMML.
[120] Ambassador George V. Allen, 12 May 1954, Committee on Foreign Relations, United States Senate, Eighty-Third Congress, Second Session (Washington, DC: USGPO, 1954).
[121] Sarvepalli Gopal, *Jawaharlal Nehru: A Biography*, vol. 3: *1956–1964* (London: Jonathan Cape, 1984), pp. 33–4; Sumit Ganguly, 'The Prime Minister and Foreign and Defence Policies', in James Manor (ed.), *Nehru to the Nineties: The Changing Office of the Prime Minister in India* (London: Hurst & Company, 1994), p. 143.

borders of its Eastern bloc satellites, and attempt to extend communist influence into the Aegean and across the wider European continent, prompted the US government to promulgate the Truman Doctrine and the Marshall Plan. In this context, the emergence of India and Pakistan as sovereign nations appeared, from Washington's perspective at least, as a matter of peripheral concern.[122] Indeed, with little industrial or technical infrastructure, a largely unskilled workforce and a dearth of commodities or raw materials, the subcontinent's size, spiralling population and endemic poverty made it appear more of a troublesome burden, than a strategic Cold War asset. Illuminatingly, in September 1947, in a report prepared for Truman by the newly established Central Intelligence Agency, South Asia was ranked at the bottom of the United States' list of regional priorities, below Western Europe, the Middle East and South East Asia.[123]

The Truman administration's ambivalent attitude toward India and Pakistan was reflected in its willingness to defer to the British in matters South Asian. Pakistan first approached the United States for military and economic assistance as early as the autumn of 1947.[124] In response, Washington curtly informed Pakistani government officials that such requests should be redirected to London. Marshall's successor at the State Department, Dean Acheson, later reflected that the Pakistanis 'were always asking for arms and I was always putting them off'.[125] In May 1950, the British and American governments formally agreed 'that the United Kingdom should "take the lead" in South Asian affairs'. Having rationalised that the regional objectives of Britain and the United States, 'if not identical, were certainly similar in most respects', the State Department reached an understanding with Whitehall that American diplomats acknowledged 'amounted in a very real sense to the delegation to the British of the conduct of an important segment of our relations with India and Pakistan'.[126] Above all, the British were expected to use their residual influence in India and Pakistan to bolster

---

[122] The strategic rationale that underpinned the Truman administration's Cold War foreign policy is addressed in detail in Melvyn P. Leffler, *A Preponderance of Power: National Security, the Truman Administration and the Cold War* (Stanford University Press, 1992); and David G. McCullough, *Truman* (New York: Simon & Schuster, 1992).

[123] 'Review of the World Situation as it Relates to the Security of the United States', 12 September 1947, CIA reports File, Harry S. Truman Papers, Harry S. Truman Library, Independence, Missouri (hereafter HSTL).

[124] Talbot, *Pakistan*, p. 119.

[125] Acheson cited in Selig Harrison, 'Pakistan and the United States', *New Republic*, 10 August 1959, p. 14.

[126] 'The Present Situation', February 1951, RG 59, Office of South Asian Affairs, Lot file 57D373, Box 3, Folder London Talks February 1951, NARA.

South Asia's association with the West, and keep communist influence out of the subcontinent.[127] In New Delhi, Loy Henderson accepted, somewhat reluctantly, that the multitude of global burdens assumed by the United States after 1945 had made it necessary to 'trust our [British] partners to take the lead in some areas'.[128]

In his subsequent dealings with British government officials and his Indian hosts, Henderson discerned a distinct absence of mutual trust and understanding. In 1948, before arriving in India to take up his ambassadorial posting, Henderson had been disconcerted by an encounter in London with the British Foreign Secretary, Ernest Bevin. During an interview with the American ambassador, Bevin informed Henderson that Nehru had become increasingly critical of US foreign policy in his discussions with British ministers. The Indian premier, Henderson was advised, had even hinted that India might consider withdrawing from the Commonwealth were London to continue pri-oritising its relationship with Washington over that with New Delhi. To Henderson's consternation, Bevin suggested that, in order to mol-lify Nehru, it might be prudent for Archibald Nye to forgo displays of particular friendliness toward American officials in India and, from time to time, publicly criticise the United States and its foreign policy. After Henderson refused point blank to countenance such a duplicitous arrangement, Bevin quickly backed away from the idea.[129] Almost a year later, however, Henderson was to be found complaining to Dean Acheson about British conduct in India. British officials in the sub-continent, the ambassador observed, appeared uniformly convinced 'that the development of closer relations between India and the United States will in some way or other result in a deterioration of the relations between Great Britain and India'. 'There is no doubt', Acheson was notified, 'that such a belief exists [in British circles] and that it affects the actions of those who share it.'[130]

More particularly, Henderson suspected that his British counterpart, Archibald Nye, whom he discerned to be 'no admirer of the United States', had 'not always been as frank with us as we have with him'. In January 1951, Henderson informed Washington that evidence had come

---

[127] 'United States Objectives with Respect to South Asia', February 1951, RG 59, Office of South Asian Affairs, Lot file 57D373, Box 3, Folder London Talks February 1951, NARA.

[128] Henderson to McGhee, 8 January 1951, RG 59, Office of South Asian Affairs, Lot file 57D373, Box 3, Folder Official Informal Letters Jan–June 1951, NARA.

[129] Loy Henderson Oral History, Washington, DC, 14 June and 15 July 1973, pp. 170–3, HSTL.

[130] Henderson to Acheson, 18 June 1949, Box 8, India Misc. folder, LWHP.

to his attention, which suggested that the British High Commission in New Delhi had not merely been ignoring Indian censure of the United States, but had 'been inclined to take the initiative in criticizing us'. Furthermore, Henderson believed that secret conversations had occurred between British and Indian officials on developments in the Far East, 'which both were carefully hiding from us [the United States]'. The British even appeared, the American ambassador noted, to have encouraged the Indians to deny Washington access to strategic information on Beijing's attitude to Asian security issues gleaned from Chinese sources. All of which, Henderson underlined to his superiors back at the State Department, pointed to the conclusion that 'we cannot trust the British to represent our partnership in South Asia. We must work with them but we cannot put ourselves in their hands.'[131]

During the first half of 1951, figures inside the State Department began to echo Henderson's assessment of Britain's limited utility as an American partner in the Indian subcontinent. In February 1951, ahead of talks with the British in London, officials from the State Department's Office of South Asian Affairs suggested that

Regardless of the fact that the British may reluctantly realize that their survival as a nation depends in large measure on US assistance, it is perfectly possible that many Britishers derive a certain satisfaction from the fact that the US is suspect in an area from which the British have been forced to withdraw, and the importance of British commercial relations with India in particular is such that many British officials and businessmen may hope that 'anti-American' feeling will react to their advantage. It is therefore doubtful that any useful purpose would be served by requesting British assistance in eliminating 'anti-American' feeling in South Asia. This would appear to be a task, which we must tackle ourselves.[132]

Besides which, Washington had become increasingly exasperated by what it saw as an unwillingness on the part of the British government 'to say or do anything which will offend' India. American officials were irritated by the refusal of their British colleagues to challenge the Indian 'aberration' of non-alignment, or take a robust position on the Kashmir dispute in the United Nations Security Council. By following Britain's lead in South Asia, and finding itself 'perennially on the fence', the United States found itself 'damned' by both India and Pakistan, 'and accused by each of favouring the other'. The time had come it seemed,

---

[131] Henderson to McGhee, 8 January 1951, RG 59, Office of South Asian Affairs, Lot file 57D373, Box 3, Folder Official Informal Letters Jan–June 1951, NARA.
[132] 'International Position of South Asian Countries', February 1951, RG 59, Office of South Asian Affairs, Lot file 57D373, Box 3, Folder London Talks February 1951, NARA.

for the US government to 'critically examine … an agreement [with Britain] which limits our freedom to conduct relations with India and Pakistan'.[133]

From Britain's viewpoint, a consensus inside Westminster on working to contain communism in Asia through a process of political rather than military containment helped pave the way for a series of joint Anglo-Indian diplomatic initiatives in the early 1950s. Notably, in late 1952, at the United Nations in New York, the coordinated efforts of British and Indian diplomats proved instrumental in removing a Sino-American impasse over the non-forcible repatriation of prisoners of war in Korea which, in turn, made possible the signing of an armistice the following year. Similarly, in 1954, at the Geneva conference on Indochina, Anthony Eden, Britain's Foreign Secretary, received valuable behind-the-scenes assistance from Krishna Menon, Nehru's international troubleshooter, which helped to seal an agreement ending French colonial rule in South East Asia.[134] At the same time, the US government found itself bogged down in disagreements with India over whether Communist China should be admitted to the UN; the desirability of New Delhi's involvement in talks to end the Korean and Indochina conflicts; American H-bomb tests in the Pacific; and a host of other minor foreign policy issues. As the decade wore on, the Eisenhower administration did work successfully with the Indian government to reduce international tension, in particular during the Suez crisis in 1956, and in the Lebanon in 1958. Relations between India and the United Kingdom, and more especially between India and the United States, were, however, often disturbed by festering differences over Cold War ideology, racialism and colonialism, and by the existence of deep-seated personal antagonisms between senior policymakers on all three sides.

Above all else, the Nehru government's strident advocacy of Cold War non-alignment proved to be an enduring source of irritation and frustration between British, American and Indian leaders. On 7 September 1946, in his first broadcast on All India Radio as India's interim prime minister, Jawaharlal Nehru made abundantly clear the value that he placed on upholding India's independence in the foreign policy field.

---

[133] 'The Present Situation', February 1951, RG 59, Office of South Asian Affairs, Lot file 57D373, Box 3, London Talks February 1951, NARA.

[134] Nehru to Chief Ministers, 22 June 1954, in G. Parthasarathi (ed.), *Jawaharlal Nehru: Letters to Chief Ministers, 1947–1964*, vol. 3: *1952–1954* (New Delhi: Oxford University Press, 1989), p. 576. See also Anita Inder Singh, *The Limits of British Influence: South Asia and the Anglo-American Relationship, 1947–56* (London: Pinter, 1993), pp. 98–105, pp. 174–6.

'We propose as far as possible', Nehru advised his fellow countrymen, 'to keep away from the power politics of groups, aligned against one another, which have led in the past to world wars and which may again lead to disaster on an even vaster scale.'[135] India's development as a secular, democratic, socially progressive and economically vibrant state, Nehru reasoned, hinged on securing technical and financial support from both the East and the West, and avoiding entanglement in debilitating external conflicts. At the same time, the Indian premier added, if his government could occasionally assume the role of an honest broker, and help to defuse East–West tension, so much the better, and all the more so if, in consequence, India's global image and prestige received a boost.[136]

The evangelical zeal with which Nehru promoted the merits of non-alignment, both at home and abroad, rankled with Western policymakers. In June 1948, shortly before returning to the United States, America's first ambassador to India, Henry Grady, confided to K. P. S. Menon that 'he was leaving India with a sense of frustration'. India's insistence on equating the United States with the Soviet Union, Grady observed, 'was annoying to his countrymen', and had compromised his ability to garner support for India on Capitol Hill. 'Was it necessary', Menon was asked pointedly, 'to put the USA and the Soviet Union on exactly the same footing? Was it necessary to tar them with the same brush? Was not the USA a truer friend of democracy than the Soviet Union?'[137] John Foster Dulles certainly felt such a comparison to be unjustified and unconscionable. In June 1956, the US Secretary of State informed a public gathering at Iowa State University that 'except under very exceptional circumstances' non-alignment was 'an immoral and short-sighted conception'.[138] Nehru continued to think otherwise. Addressing the Lok Sabha (lower house of India's parliament) a year earlier on the eve of the Bandung Conference of Afro-Asian countries, the exasperated Indian leader complained:

It has almost become impossible to consider any matter logically, reasonably or by itself. Everything is to be considered, we are told, from the communist or anti-communist point of view because the world is divided into communist and anti-communist parts. There is no other way of dealing with the situation

---

[135] Text of Nehru's broadcast cited in Nanda, *Nehru Years*, p. 3.
[136] Nehru to Chief Ministers, 3 June 1954, in *Letters to Chief Ministers*, vol. 3: *1952–1954*, p. 553; 'Nehru's Political Personality', 18 June 1956, RG 59, Office of South Asian Affairs, Lot 59 D 75, Folder 1956, NARA.
[137] K. P. S. Menon, 'India's Foreign Policy', 1950, Speeches & Writings File No. 35, K. P. S. Menon Collection, NMML.
[138] *The New York Times*, 10 June 1956.

according to some powers and authority. Now this has made difficult to understand any question much less to solve it. This is a simple, rather naïve view of the world, that you must belong to this bloc or that bloc and if you do not, either you are foolish or there is some mischief behind your attitude ... It is a dangerously simple way of looking at things and because of this simple thinking, the world might suddenly find itself on the brink of disaster.[139]

In public, Nehru insisted that India's non-alignment and commitment to world peace precluded the nation's taking sides in any future global conflagration. 'We have absolutely no intention of throwing ourselves into war even if the rest of the world goes to war', the Indian leader declared categorically in April 1955. 'Let there be no doubt about it. We will not go to war [even] if there is war all over the world.'[140] In private discussions with British and American officials, however, Nehru adopted a more flexible position. On several occasions, Nehru went out of his way to reassure Archibald Nye and Loy Henderson that, in the final analysis, India would support the West in a general war with the Soviet Union. In February 1950, the Indian premier confided to Henderson, 'that in spite of the efforts of India to remain neutral, in the event of a World War ... eventually India would be drawn into it, and ... it [India] would not side with the Communists'.[141] Journalists with close links to the Indian government, such as Frank Moraes, reinforced Nehru's message in confidential exchanges with British and American diplomats. In June 1953, during an off-the-record discussion with Jack Yeaman Bryan, a United States Information Service Officer stationed in Bombay, Moraes explained that the 'pressures of geography, history, and internal economy' required India to avoid an open commitment in the Cold War struggle between East and West. Nonetheless, should India be compelled to commit to one side or the other, Moraes added, 'we know that the decision will be in favour of the West'.[142]

Indian blandishments, however well intentioned, had little impact on a seemingly ubiquitous American distaste for non-alignment. Prominent dissenters, such as Chester Bowles, struggled in vain to persuade their countrymen that it was against US interests for Nehru's government to formally align itself with the Western bloc, make enemies of India's Soviet and Chinese neighbours, and leave America to pick up the tab

---

[139] 'Bandung Conference of Historic Importance', *The Hindustan Times*, 1 April 1955.

[140] *Ibid.*

[141] 'Discussion with Prime Minister on Indian Foreign Policy', February 1950, Box 8, India Misc. folder, LWHP; Henderson to Eliot Weil, 19 February 1951, RG 59, Office of South Asian Affairs, Lot 59 D 75, Folder SOA General 1956, NARA.

[142] Bryan to Bartlett, 26 June 1953, RG 59, Office of South Asian Affairs, Lot file 57D373, Box 3, Folder Press and Publication in India, NARA.

for an escalation in Indian defence spending.[143] The British Chiefs of Staff had noted back in February 1949 that, even had New Delhi welcomed Western military aid, it remained improbable 'that the Allies will, even by 1957, be able to make any significant contribution to help India in her defence'. 'This fact is certain profoundly to affect India's defence policy', Britain's military commanders emphasised, 'and may well – until such time as she herself raises adequate forces to meet the external threat – cause her to adopt an attitude in war which she appreciates is unlikely to provoke Russia into attacking her.'[144] The strategic logic underpinning India's policy of non-alignment made little impression on a majority of Anglo-American political and popular opinion which, as K. P. S. Menon noted bitterly, persisted in viewing India as, 'neutral, passive and weak-kneed'. 'Our determination to follow an independent foreign policy', Menon grumbled, 'is a constant irritant to the Great Powers.'[145]

The importance that the Indian government placed upon the abolition of colonialism, ending racial discrimination and instituting an equitable redistribution of global wealth and resources injected additional friction into New Delhi's intercourse with the West. Musing upon the fixation that Anglo-American leaders evidenced with the struggle between communist 'oppression' and 'enlightened' liberal-capitalism, in the course of an Indian parliamentary debate in the spring of 1955, Nehru asked bluntly:

But what about some little things happening in the continent of Africa? What about the things happening in the colonial territories? What about the tragedy that is taking place in the Dominion of South Africa where hundreds and thousands of people are being lifted up bodily from there, taken away somewhere else? Why do we not hear the champions of freedom talk about this? Why are they so silent? They simply pass it over. They should realise that people in Asia and Africa may not shout very much about it, but they feel it more than communism and anti-communism. It is a human problem for us, this racialism, and it will become more dangerous than any other of [the] world's problems today ... [it penetrates] deep down into our minds and hearts and we feel it strongly.[146]

For its part, Whitehall felt aggrieved at stinging and, in its view, unwarranted brickbats from Nehru and his ministers over the languid pace at

---

[143] Chester Bowles interview cited in Redding, *An American in India*, pp. 22–3.
[144] 'Military Implications of India's Possible Future Status', Chiefs of Staff Committee, February 1949, SWIN III 3/1, SWP.
[145] K. P. S. Menon, 'India's Foreign Policy', 1950, Speeches & Writings File No. 35, K. P. S. Menon Collection, NMML.
[146] 'Bandung Conference of Historic Importance', *The Hindustan Times*, 1 April 1955.

which Britain was moving to relinquish control of its colonial empire in Africa and Asia. Washington harboured a similar sense of pique over the Indian premier's criticisms of the United States' willingness to prop up repressive French, Belgian and Portuguese imperialism in Indochina, the Maghreb and sub-Saharan Africa. In siding with European Cold War allies and choosing to ignore indigenous nationalist movements across the developing world, Nehru trumpeted, post-war American administrations had shown themselves to be 'not sincerely opposed to colonialism'.[147] In March 1953, in a valedictory message sent to John Foster Dulles from New Delhi, the outgoing US ambassador, Chester Bowles, impressed upon the incoming Secretary of State that Nehru believed the United States to be guilty of, 'compromising ... [its] principles to win the approval of Western Europe'. Washington would be 'on much firmer ground', the Indian premier counselled Bowles, if it stopped supporting morally bankrupt colonial regimes and associated America with 'the rising tide of colored peoples throughout the world'.[148]

Indian censure of America's 'regressive' approach to colonialism was infused with an added piquancy by the existence of *de jure* racial discrimination in the southern United States under the Jim Crow system. From the late 1870s, the passage of laws in state legislatures throughout the former Confederacy, the southern states that had seceded from the United States between 1861 and 1865, mandated the racial segregation of public services between black and white citizens under the principle of 'separate but equal'. In practice, this imposed a stultifying burden of economic and social disadvantage on the majority of America's African-American population. In February 1951, Loy Henderson asserted before a gathering of American foreign service officers that India 'cannot fully trust the democratic professions and the sincerity of the motives of any country which permits its people to practice racial discrimination or which fails to give its unqualified support to the struggle for the elimination of racial discrimination everywhere'.[149] In 1957, at the time of the Little Rock Central High School integration crisis in Arkansas, an opinion poll commissioned in India by the United States Information Agency found that press coverage of the crisis had left nearly half of all respondents surveyed with a 'bad' or 'very bad' opinion of the

---

[147] Henderson address to US Foreign Service Officers, February 1951, Box 8, India Misc. folder, LWHP.

[148] Chester Bowles to John Foster Dulles, 20 March 1953, RG 59, Office of South Asian Affairs, Lot file 57D373, Box 3, Folder 'Ambassador Chester Bowles', NARA.

[149] Henderson address to US Foreign Service Officers, February 1951, Box 8, India Misc. folder, LWHP.

United States.[150] Unsavoury incidents involving American and British nationals within the subcontinent reinforced Indian convictions that the West did not take the issue of racialism sufficiently seriously. In 1955, the State Department sent the *Minneapolis Tribune*'s African-American journalist, Carl Rowan, on a goodwill tour of India. After hearing Rowan speak at public meetings, many Indians headed off to their local USIS library in search of his prize-wining book, *South From Freedom*. They failed to locate it on the library's bookshelves. Rowan's work on race had been labelled as 'controversial' back in Washington, and stamped as unsuitable for export.[151] Three years earlier, in the summer of 1952, the African-American academic Saunders Redding had undertaken a similar mission in India on behalf of the US government. 'No matter where I went', Redding subsequently recorded, 'or with whom I talked or what the original subject of conversation, Indians were always coming back at me with America's race prejudice. It was a shadow in which I moved. It evoked scorn, or patronage, or pity.'[152]

The experience in India of a third American emissary, Major Sammy Lee, an Olympic diving champion of Korean ancestry, demonstrated that the British could be just as bigoted and inept when it came to racial matters. In the mid-1950s, a British-run Club retained control of Calcutta's only Olympic-standard swimming pool. The Club's management turned down a request from the local American consulate for Lee to stage an exhibition performance in the pool for Calcutta's citizenry. Indians, the British management explained tartly, were not permitted on Club grounds. It might be possible, American officials were told, for Lee to perform for a white audience. The Club's managers added, however, that even this concession 'was stretching things a bit as Lee himself shouldn't really be allowed to put on an exhibition on their premises, he being of Korean extraction'.[153] To the exasperation of Whitehall diplomats, elements of the British expatriate community in Pakistan displayed an equally hidebound and unenlightened approach toward the local population. Once the preserve of senior British administrators and military officers, membership of the prestigious Punjab Club in Lahore went into steady decline after 1947. In the mid-1950s, Club membership was opened up to the local Western business

---

[150] USIA Report, R-169-62 (R), 29 November 1962, RG 306, Records of the US Information Agency, Box 12, Folder R169-62, NARA.

[151] George V. Allen to Alex Jones, 6 August 1955, RG 59, Office of South Asian Affairs, Lot 59 D 75, Folder India 1955, NARA.

[152] Redding, *An American in India*, p. 48.

[153] George V. Allen to Alex Jones, 6 August 1955, RG 59, Office of South Asian Affairs, Lot 59 D 75, Folder India 1955, NARA.

community by its British board, 'but unfortunately *not*', incredulous Whitehall mandarins noted at the time, 'to Pakistanis'.[154]

Ideological and cultural tensions between India, Britain and the United States were magnified during much of the 1950s by clashes of personality and perspective between senior foreign policymakers in London, Washington and New Delhi. Most conspicuously, the abrasive character and purportedly pro-communist sympathies of Krishna Menon, one of Nehru's oldest friends and closest confidants, ruffled Western feathers. From his position as India's representative to the UN and, from April 1957, his nation's minister of defence, American officials, in particular, resented Menon's propensity to meddle in issues ranging from the Korean War to the Hungarian and Suez incidents of 1956. State Department officers who dealt with Menon on a regular basis disparaged the Indian interlocutor as 'venomous', 'violently anti-American' and 'a tough, poisonous bastard'.[155] To many in the United States, Menon represented the embodiment of Indian naivety and Cold War hypocrisy. Nehru's government loudly extolled the virtues of non-alignment and the importance of self-determination, yet inexplicably it seemed, courted the Soviets and ignored UN calls to implement Security Council resolutions on Kashmir. Krishna Menon, above all other Indians, one US ambassador to New Delhi observed retrospectively, 'epitomized non-alignment and anti-Americanism, at least in the eyes of a lot of Western officials and the American public'.[156]

The Truman administration evidenced some concern at Krishna Menon's socialist background, but it was under the Eisenhower government that American antipathy for Menon reached its peak.[157] Fed details of Menon's links to British communists by MI5, and bitterly critical of his unsolicited forays in Cold War diplomacy, Eisenhower's administration formed a deeply negative view of Menon.[158] The US president looked upon Nehru's chief foreign policy adviser as 'a master at twisting words and meaning of others', and an unscrupulous intriguer driven 'by an ambition to prove himself the master international manipulator

---

[154] Briefing paper on 'The Punjab Club, Lahore', February 1961, Alexander Symon Papers, Mss Eur E367/14, 'Queen's Visit to Pakistan and Bangladesh – Symon's Dispatches as UK High Commissioner', India Office Select Materials, British Library.

[155] Arthur W. Hummel, Jr, Oral History Interview, 13 July 1989, Foreign Affairs Oral History Project, Library of Congress, Washington, DC (hereafter FAOHP).

[156] Christopher Van Hollen, Oral History Interview, 23 January 1990, FAOHP.

[157] US Embassy to Curry, 5 August 1947, KV/2/2511-2; MI5 to US Embassy, 15 August 1947, KV/2/2511-2, TNA.

[158] SLO Washington to DG MI5, 7 December 1954, KV/2/2514-2; and, DG to SLO Washington, 9 December 1954, KV/2/2514-2, TNA.

and politician of the age'.[159] Back in January 1947, while serving as a
Republican Party adviser to America's UN delegation, John Foster
Dulles had publicly denounced Menon as a 'confirmed Marxian' and a
disciple of the Soviet foreign minister, Vyacheslav Molotov.[160] After he
became Secretary of State, Dulles' opinion of Menon remained sharply
critical. In May 1954, Dulles warned colleagues on the National
Security Council that Nehru's roving international emissary was, 'a
pretty bad fellow' and a 'troublemaker'.[161]

Nehru resented Dulles' treatment of Menon, which, given his intimate association with the maverick Indian diplomat, the prime minister interpreted as a thinly disguised attack on himself. Dulles, the
Indian premier concluded, was 'narrow-minded', 'bigoted' and a 'great
menace'. 'He [Dulles] thinks every one must agree with him', Nehru
informed the Chinese leader Mao Zedong, in October 1954, 'and a man
like him might take any move.'[162] In turn, Menon excoriated Dulles
for his denunciation of non-alignment, orchestration of the United
States' military alliance with Pakistan and tolerance of European colonialism.[163] With a 'formidable incompatibility of temperament' adding
spice to their political differences, Dulles and Menon clashed repeatedly, in public and in private.[164] In July 1955, in the aftermath of the
first Taiwan Straits crisis, one typically prickly exchange between the
two saw Dulles accuse Menon of being a Communist Chinese lackey.
In response, Menon made it widely known in diplomatic circles that
the Indian government regarded Dulles as the principal threat to peace
and stability in Asia. Rather than engage meaningfully with the substantive international issues of the day, contemporary observers noted
that 'a great part' of the interplay between Dulles and Menon during

---

[159] Eisenhower Diary Entry, 14 July 1955, DDE Diary Series, Box 9 Ann Whitman
File, Dwight D. Eisenhower Library, Abilene, Kansas (hereafter DDEL). See also
Eisenhower, *Waging Peace*, p. 107.

[160] Kurt Stiegler, 'Communism and "Colonial Evolution": John Foster Dulles' Vision
of India and Pakistan', *Journal of South Asian and Middle Eastern Studies*, 12 (Winter
1991), 74–5.

[161] 198th Meeting of the National Security Council, Thursday 20 May 1954, *Foreign
Relations of the United States* (hereafter *FRUS*), *1952–54*, vol. XII (Washington, DC:
Government Printing Office, 1984), p. 497; Allen to State Department, 31 March
1954, *FRUS, 1952–1954*, vol. XIII (Washington, DC: Government Printing Office,
1982), pp. 1193–4.

[162] Nehru meeting with Mao Zedong, Beijing, 2 October 1954, in Ravinder Kumar and
H. Y. Sharada Prasad (eds.), *Selected Works of Jawaharlal Nehru*, Second Series, vol.
27, 1 October 1954–31 January 1955 (New Delhi: Oxford University Press, 2000),
p. 34.

[163] Gopal, *Nehru: 1956–1964*, p. 46.

[164] Nehru is reported to have commented that 'Krishna Menon is my Answer to Dulles'.
M. O. Mathai, *Reminiscences of the Nehru Age* (New Delhi: Vikas, 1978), p. 55.

the 1950s was invariably, 'taken up with the process of getting under each other's skins'.[165]

Toward the end 1956, two international incidents brought underlying tensions between India, Pakistan, the United States and Great Britain to a head. In July, the Egyptian government of Gamal Abdel Nasser took the West by surprise and nationalised the Suez Canal, wrenching control of the waterway from its Anglo-French owners. Known as the 'Highway to India', from its opening in November 1869 the canal had served as a prime economic and strategic artery between Europe and Asia. The British government's subsequent decision toward the end of 1956 to collude with France and Israel in a ham-fisted bid to seize back control of the Suez Canal by force was condemned by India and Pakistan as an ill-judged and unwarranted reversion to gunboat diplomacy. Angry crowds gathered outside the gates of the British High Commission in New Delhi, and burnt an effigy of Britain's premier, Anthony Eden. In Pakistan, the Anglo-French-Israeli assault on a fellow Muslim country provoked outrage. Violent anti-British demonstrations broke out in Karachi, Lahore and Dhaka. One young Swedish tourist, newly arrived in Karachi, caused wry amusement amongst the city's expatriate British community by donning a large hand-printed sign that proclaimed, 'I AM *NOT* BRITISH'.[166] In Lahore, British diplomatic buildings were surrounded by baying mobs. To the relief of the resident British First Secretary, Frank Miles, the senior Pakistani police officer charged with protecting British property in Lahore, Fazal Mahmud, happened to be one of the finest seam bowlers in world cricket at that time, and a teammate of Miles' at the local Gymkhana Club. In consequence, demonstrations in the city met with an unusually robust response from the local police force, and British consular buildings emerged unscathed.[167]

In the United States, the Eisenhower administration was left seething at the British decision to launch an assault on Egyptian sovereignty without first taking Washington fully into its confidence. The Eden government's reckless and inept military adventurism, State Department officials bemoaned, had dealt a severe blow to British prestige within the developing world.[168] India's High Commissioner in London, Vijaya

[165] 'Dulles–Menon Talks', 13 July 1955, CIA-RDP79R00904A000200030007-9, CREST, NARA; *The Economist*, 5 July 1955.
[166] Morrice James, *Pakistan Chronicle* (London: Hurst, 1992), pp. 43–6.
[167] Frank Miles, DOHP 58, Interview September 2002, British Diplomatic Oral History Programme, Churchill College Cambridge.
[168] Memorandum of conversation between Richard Casey and Walter Robertson, Washington, DC, 8 November 1956, RG 59, Pakistan–Afghanistan Affairs 1950–6, Lot file 57D421, Box 11, Folder UK and Commonwealth Relations, NARA.

Lakshmi Pandit, recorded that Britain's relations with New Delhi had begun the year with a 'fund of goodwill … which was brimming over'. Following the Suez debacle, Pandit lamented, '1956 … turned out to be the most difficult year for Indo-British relations since independence'.[169] India's ambassador in Egypt, Ali Yavar Jung, loudly condemned the Anglo-French intervention in Egypt, asserting that it was motivated primarily by 'malice and revenge, [and] the desire to restore and resume abandoned colonial positions'. The British and French, Jung fulminated, had deceived friends and allies, betrayed those whose security they had guaranteed, and displayed 'utter disregard and violation of international ethics and law'.[170] At one stage it seemed possible that India and Pakistan might withdraw from the Commonwealth over the Suez crisis. From Karachi, Britain's High Commissioner in Pakistan, Sir Alexander Symon, who had begun his diplomatic career as a lowly assistant clerk in the India Office shortly after the end of the First World War, informed London that Britain's intervention in Egypt had created a groundswell of indignation and anger in Pakistan, where the episode had been generally interpreted as an 'out-dated act of colonialism' and 'a stab in the back of the Arabs'. The lesson that many Pakistanis had drawn from the crisis, Symon underscored, was that Britain could no longer 'maintain its position and succour its allies in the Middle East'. Following Suez, it had become 'widely held' in Pakistan, Symon cautioned, 'that it is to America that Pakistan must in future look for many of the things (including physical protection and even moral leadership) that she formerly expected to obtain from the United Kingdom'.[171]

Having united in denouncing Britain's conduct in the Middle East, India and the United States differed sharply in their responses to a second, contemporaneous crisis unfolding in Eastern Europe. In October, a popular uprising erupted in Hungary against the country's Soviet-backed Marxist government. The Soviets' use of the Red Army to crush 'counter-revolutionary' forces in Hungary, in an operation that claimed the lives of thousands of Hungarian citizens and hundreds of Soviet soldiers, was widely reviled by the global international community. The Indian government's reaction to events in Eastern Europe was more equivocal. In a speech in Calcutta on 9 November, Nehru

---

[169] Vijaya Lakshmi Pandit to MEA, No. 3(48)-R&I/57, NAI.
[170] Ali Yavar Jung, 'Political Reports for the Months of October and November 1956', 4 February 1957, No. 23 – Research and Intelligence 56, Ministry of External Affairs, NAI.
[171] 'Effects of the Middle East Crisis' and 'Review of the Effects of the Middle East Crisis', A. C. B. Symon to Lord Home, 6 and 27 December 1956, DO 201/7, Correspondence respecting Commonwealth Relations, volume VII 1956, TNA.

categorised the Hungarian revolt as 'a civil conflict' marked by 'mutual killings'. On the same day in New York, Krishna Menon voted against a resolution in the UN General Assembly that called on the Soviet Union to withdraw its troops from Hungary. The 'markedly different' tone adopted by the Indian government in response to acts of Anglo-French aggression in Suez and the Soviet aggression in Hungary exasperated the Eisenhower administration. In private, Nehru condemned the Soviet intervention in Hungary as a moral outrage that had left India's citizens 'deeply shocked'.[172] However, in common with much international opinion, Eisenhower was dismayed at Nehru's hesitancy in publicly condemning the Soviets' military intervention in Eastern Europe.[173] Inside the subcontinent, the influential social activist and former political associate of Nehru's, Jayaprakash Narayan, added his voice to a growing number of Indians uneasy at their prime minister's apparent willingness to employ 'double standards ... unworthy of this country [India]'. Speaking at a public meeting in Bombay, on 11 November, Narayan declared:

The world has witnessed in recent days two examples of the most cynical assault on human freedom; one in Egypt and the other in Hungary. To Egypt Mr. Nehru's reaction was immediate and firm and righteous. It was a reaction of which every Indian and every freedom-loving citizen of the world could be proud. But for many days there was not even a whisper heard from New Delhi about Hungary. Then one fine morning the papers reported Mr. Nehru's chief adviser on foreign policy, Mr. Krishna Menon, as having stated that the Hungarian question was a domestic affair of the Hungarian people. It was an astonishing statement that left me aghast.[174]

On 19 November, in the face of increasing pressure at home and abroad to take a firmer line with Moscow, Nehru did, albeit belatedly, issue a statement in the Indian parliament that indicated his disapproval at the USSR's actions in Hungary.[175] By that time, however, the events of the autumn of 1956 had placed India's relationships with Britain and the United States under considerable strain. On 10 January 1957, Britain's Chancellor of the Exchequer, Harold Macmillan, replaced a discredited Anthony Eden as prime minister. Ten days later, Dwight

---

[172] Nehru to K. P. S. Menon, 28 June 1958, No. 462-PMO/58, Subject File No. 20 June 1958, Subimal Dutt Papers, NMML.

[173] Eisenhower, *Waging Peace*, p. 108; Clyde Sanger, *Malcolm MacDonald: Bringing an End to Empire* (Liverpool University Press, 1995), p. 368.

[174] '"Double Standard" In Foreign Policy: J.P.'s Scathing Criticism of India's Stand On Hungary', *The Indian Express*, 12 November 1956.

[175] Sarvepalli Gopal, *Jawaharlal Nehru: A Biography*, vol. 2: *1947–1956* (London: Jonathan Cape, 1979), pp. 291–9.

Eisenhower was sworn in for a second term as president of the United States. For the remainder of the decade, as the Cold War cast an ever longer shadow over the Indian subcontinent, the Macmillan and Eisenhower governments would work closely together in a bid to rejuvenate and strengthen flagging Western influence in South Asia.

Eisenhower, Macmillan and the 'New Look'
      at South Asia, 1957–1960

On 20 January 1957, in a low-key ceremony in the East Room of the White House, witnessed by eighty or so relatives, aides, maids, ushers and cooks, Dwight D. Eisenhower was sworn in for a second four-year term as president of the United States by Chief Justice Earl Warren. The following day, as the sun struggled to break through a dull and overcast Washington sky, Eisenhower re-enacted the inaugural ceremony before a 20,000-strong crowd in front of the Capitol building. Looking remarkably fit for a man who during his first term in office had suffered a severe heart attack and undergone an emergency abdominal operation, the sixty-six-year-old Eisenhower delivered a short thirteen-and-a-half-minute address entitled, 'The Price of Peace'. Flanked by members of the House of Representatives and the Senate, many of whom had opposed long-term foreign aid programmes, the president warned his fellow Americans that moving forward they would be called upon to make sacrifices in the pursuit of peace and prosperity. 'We must use our skills and knowledge and, at times, our substance, to help others rise from misery, however far the scene of suffering may be from our shores', Eisenhower intoned. 'For wherever in the world a people knows desperate want, there must appear at least the spark of hope, the hope of progress or there will surely rise at last the flames of conflict.'[1]

The prominence that Eisenhower gave to the developing world in his inaugural address, and the strong case that it made for the Western powers to materially assist nations less fortunate than themselves, reflected the president's concern that the locus of the Cold War had shifted away from Europe to the more volatile battlefields of Asia, Africa and the Middle East. New sovereign nations spawned by the acceleration of European decolonisation occupied important strategic positions, and controlled access to many of the raw materials that fuelled

---

[1] Dwight D. Eisenhower, 'Second Inaugural Address', 21 January 1957, *The American Presidency Project*, www.presidency.ucsb.edu/ws/?pid=10856; *The New York Times*, 22 January 1957.

the West's industrial economy. Moreover, the embryonic constitutional structures, inexperienced political leaderships and endemic poverty of many post-colonial states suggested that they were vulnerable to external subversion. The 'divisive' and 'dark' force of international communism, Eisenhower cautioned his fellow Americans, 'strives to capture, to exploit for its own greater power, all forces of change in the world, especially the needs of the hungry and the hopes of the oppressed'.[2]

In India, where the Nehru government's ambitious second five-year plan had been launched the previous April, Eisenhower's call for the transfer of technical and economic resources from the First to the Third World received an unsurprisingly warm welcome.[3] Toward the end of his first presidential term, the Soviet Union's growing interest in South Asia encouraged Eisenhower to adopt an increasingly benign attitude toward Indian non-alignment. In July 1955, Nehru discerned that some 'hopeful' signs had begun to emerge from the United States, 'such as the recent eclipse of McArthies [sic] and Knowlands, [and] the differences between Dulles and Eisenhower and the slightly more conciliatory outlook of the latter'.[4] Furthermore, the provision of greater US economic aid to India, and the negotiation of bilateral trade agreements, appeared set to reinvigorate the United States' relationship with New Delhi. Likewise, during the second half of 1956, the Nehru government's desperate need for foreign capital to finance its expansive development plans led Indian officials to begin 'soft-pedalling' their criticisms of American foreign policy.[5]

Having been forced to postpone a visit to the United States the previous July after Eisenhower had been taken ill, in December 1956 Nehru flew to Washington for talks with the American president. Although he had never set foot in South Asia, Eisenhower had long been fascinated by the region's history and politics. The two leaders had met before, in 1949, at Columbia University, when Eisenhower had served briefly as its president. On that occasion the two men had got along well, and Eisenhower's renowned affability helped to ensure that seven years later, during talks held on 17 and 18 December at the White House and on the president's Gettysburg farm, the national leaders cemented a personal

---

[2] Dwight D. Eisenhower, 'Second Inaugural Address', 21 January 1957, *The American Presidency Project*, www.presidency.ucsb.edu/ws/?pid=10856.

[3] *The Indian Express*, 22 January 1957.

[4] K. P. S. Menon, 'The Prime Minister's Talks with Soviet Leaders', 12 July 1955, Subject File 16, June–July 1955, Subimal Dutt Papers, Nehru Memorial Museum and Library (hereafter NMML).

[5] Clark to Lord Home, 27 February 1958, FO 371/135947, The United Kingdom National Archives, Kew, London (hereafter TNA).

rapport. 'I liked Prime Minister Nehru', Eisenhower later reflected. 'He sincerely wanted to help his people and lead them to higher levels of living and opportunity; I think it only fair to conclude that he was essential to his nation.'[6] Back in the subcontinent, an exuberant Indian press extolled the 'highly successful and cordial series of talks between the two statesmen'. British officials in India noted that Nehru's encounter with Eisenhower had left the Indian premier 'in a friendly state of mind and, despite his dislike of many aspects of American culture and policy, with a new regard for President Eisenhower and for the average American citizen'.[7]

Shortly after Nehru's departure from the United States, Eisenhower approved a recommendation to increase US economic assistance for India, contained in National Security Council (NSC) report 5701. The NSC study asserted that the USSR and PRC had embarked upon, 'an intensive campaign to roll back the free world position in South Asia'. The Soviets, in particular, were presented as aggressively pursuing the expansion of communist influence in the subcontinent by 'capitalizing on [Indian] aspirations for economic improvement through substantial offers of aid, trade, and credits on easy terms and ostensibly with no political strings attached'. The Nehru government's foreign policy, and especially its advocacy of non-alignment, the report's American authors conceded, would 'on occasion bring India into opposition with US programs and activities'. Nonetheless, Eisenhower was urged to sanction an increase in technical and material support for India's second five-year plan on the basis that 'a weak India might well lead to the loss of South and South East Asia to Communism [whereas] a strong India would be an example of an alternative to Communism in an Asian context'.[8]

At the same time, the arrival of Ellsworth Bunker as America's ambassador in New Delhi, in March 1957, acted as an additional stimulus to the Eisenhower administration's efforts to build bridges with India. A successful businessman turned diplomat, Bunker had served briefly as US ambassador to Argentina and Italy, and worked for three years as president of the American Red Cross. Convinced that a strong, stable and democratic India was vital to the future political and economic

[6] Dwight D. Eisenhower, *The White House Years: Waging Peace, 1956–1961* (New York: Doubleday & Company, 1965), pp. 106–8; p. 113.

[7] Clark to Lord Home, 27 February 1958, FO 371/135947, TNA.

[8] National Security Council Report, NSC 5701, 'Statement of Policy on US Policy Toward South Asia', 10 January 1957, RG 59, S/S-NSC Files, Lot 63 D 351, NSC 5701-Memoranda, National Archives and Records Administration, College Park, Maryland (hereafter NARA).

security of Asia, Bunker enthusiastically championed the recommendations contained in NSC 5701. Over the course of his service in India, the US ambassador would earn Nehru's respect and admiration for the dedication and professionalism with which he strove to improve Indo-US relations.[9] By the time Bunker departed from the subcontinent in March 1961, Washington's relationship with New Delhi, although still plagued by periodic bouts of friction, had improved immeasurably. Lauding Bunker as a true friend of India, *The Indian Express* observed that 'It is no exaggeration to say that his work has prepared the ground for the closer relationship to which both countries are looking forward.'[10]

### Eisenhower, Macmillan and the Anglo-American relationship in South Asia

Having slumped to a post-war nadir during the Suez crisis in 1956, the following year proved to be a turning point in Britain's relations with the United States, India and Pakistan. On 10 January, Harold Macmillan replaced a sick and politically crippled Anthony Eden as Britain's prime minister. Macmillan's immediate priority was to repair the breach in Anglo-American relations caused by events in the Middle East, and to begin the process of restoring Britain's tattered international reputation. Within days of entering 10 Downing Street, Macmillan mounted a robust defence of Britain's great power status in a national televised broadcast. Adopting a tone of Churchillian defiance, the new British premier observed that:

Every now and again since the war I have heard people say: 'Isn't Britain only a second- or third-class power now? Isn't she on the way out?' What nonsense! This is a great country, and do not let us be ashamed to say so … Twice in my lifetime I have heard the same old tale about us being a second-class power, and I have lived to see the answer … So do not let us have any more defeatist talk of second-class powers and of dreadful things to come. Britain had been great, is great, and will stay great, provided we close our ranks and get on with the job.[11]

---

[9]  Bunker later reflected that 'my relations with him [Nehru] couldn't have been more satisfactory or more congenial, as far as I was concerned'. Ellsworth Bunker, Oral History, 1979, Butler Library, Columbia University, New York.

[10]  *The Indian Express*, 21 March 1961. A comprehensive account of Bunker's time as US ambassador in India is provided in Howard B. Schaffer, *Ellsworth Bunker: Global Troubleshooter, Vietnam Hawk* (Chapel Hill: The University of South Carolina Press, 2003).

[11]  Harold Macmillan broadcast from 10 Downing Street, 21 January 1957, British Pathé, www.britishpathe.com/record.php?id=32594.

For all his public bluster, Macmillan was too shrewd a politician not to have absorbed the principal lesson of the Suez debacle, namely that Britain was no longer capable of taking significant action on the world stage without American support. In October, the new British premier travelled to Washington for three days of talks with Eisenhower and senior members of the president's cabinet. During his stay in the United States Macmillan was assiduous in playing up his Anglo-American credentials. Macmillan's formidable mother, Nellie Belles, had been born and raised in Spencer, Indiana. In addition, the prime minister had worked harmoniously alongside Eisenhower and other senior American military and political figures during the Second World War, while acting as Britain's resident minister in North Africa and the Mediterranean. John Foster Dulles welcomed the fact that moving forward Macmillan and Eisenhower could be expected to 'build on a close personal friendship' and 'discuss ... common problems in an atmosphere of mutual confidence'. Indeed, by the end of his American visit, Macmillan had persuaded his hosts to confine the events of Suez to the past, and work with his government in 'formulating common policies and plans for resisting Soviet encroachment ... throughout the world'.[12] Accordingly, on 25 October, the White House released a joint Anglo-American communiqué entitled, 'Declaration of Common Purpose by the President and the Prime Minister of the United Kingdom', in which Eisenhower made plain his intention to recast and reinvigorate the United States' Cold War relationship with Britain.[13]

Earlier that year, Britain's High Commissioner in New Delhi, Malcolm MacDonald, travelled in the opposite direction from South Asia to the United Kingdom, in an attempt to smooth over strained Indo-British relations. During a series of meetings with Macmillan, officials from the Commonwealth Relations Office, Members of Parliament and newspapers editors, MacDonald worked tirelessly to stifle an upsurge in anti-Indian sentiment occasioned by the Suez crisis, and fuelled by New Delhi's censure of Britain's conduct in the latest round of United Nations Security Council debates on Kashmir. Writing to Nehru in early March, Lord Mountbatten expressed optimism that MacDonald's efforts in London would prove to be a 'turning point to the good after so many terrible misunderstandings and friction'.[14] In

---

[12] 'Anglo-American Discussions, Washington, DC', 23/24 October 1957, PREM 11/2329, TNA.

[13] Dwight D. Eisenhower, 'Declaration of Common Purpose by the President and the Prime Minister of the United Kingdom', 25 October 1957, *The American Presidency Project*, www.presidency.ucsb.edu/ws/?pid=10941.

[14] Mountbatten to Nehru, 15 March 1957, Subject File S. No. 62, Vijaya Lakshmi Pandit Papers, NMML.

seeking to patch up their relationship with India, the British were less anxious than the Eisenhower administration that a Soviet economic and political offensive in South Asia could marginalise Western influence in the subcontinent. 'India's permanent interest', Lord Home observed, 'lies in keeping a foot firmly in the Western camp. Russia and China are too dangerous for her to do otherwise.'[15] Moving forward, policy-makers in Whitehall were, however, conscious that the American and Soviet focus on India meant that the 'affairs of the sub-continent are going to be of increasing concern to the United Kingdom in the political and economic fields'. Indeed, although broadly welcoming 'the new Indian regard' for Eisenhower and his administration, British officials expressed regret that the deployment of American economic power in South Asia was likely to result in a diminution of 'Indian respect for our [British] material power and influence in international and particularly in Asian affairs'.[16] In this context, the hollowness of Macmillan's 'great power' rhetoric was evident when, on 15 March, the British premier informed MacDonald not to expect any additional financial assistance in his campaign to win back Indian goodwill. 'I would not wish to mislead Mr. Nehru into thinking that we can see any large untapped financial resources here which he might call upon to step up development in India', Macmillan informed the High Commissioner. 'Of course, India's development needs are enormous, but as you yourself know, we are in no position to do much more than we are doing at the moment.'[17]

The rancour that lingered on in Indo-British relations in the twelve months following the Suez crisis caused Harold Macmillan to approach his first visit to the subcontinent as prime minister, in January 1958, with some anxiety. In the event, Macmillan received an effusive reception when he stopped off briefly in New Delhi during a whirlwind tour of the Commonwealth. The British premier was both surprised and delighted to find that Nehru was willing to forgive and forget recent Anglo-Indian differences.[18] The previous year, Malcolm MacDonald's missionary work in London had succeeded in convincing a sceptical British establishment to invest 'time and patience' in mending its broken relationship with India. In return, Whitehall hoped to stimulate 'a

[15] Lord Home, 'Anglo-Indian Relations', 28 June 1957, C (57), 149, CAB 129/87, TNA.
[16] Clark to Lord Home, 27 February 1958, FO 371/135947, TNA.
[17] Macmillan to MacDonald, 15 March 1957, 42/12/22, Malcolm MacDonald Papers, Palace Green Library, University of Durham (hereafter MMP).
[18] 'Prime Minister's Commonwealth Tour', 4 June 1958, C (58), 120, CAB 129/93, TNA.

change of emphasis in India's foreign policy and through that in her attitude towards the West'.[19] Nearly two years later, in October 1959, MacDonald assured Macmillan that Britain's 'enlightened attitude to the new India' had paid dividends. The British High Commissioner noted with gratification that following Macmillan's goodwill visit to the subcontinent, a 'great change for the better' had taken place in relations between India and Britain. In response, Macmillan assured MacDonald that he had 'always felt that India is the key to the East. If we can keep that friendship, the other problems will be capable of solution.'[20] The following summer, officials at the CRO were to be found crowing with satisfaction over the astonishing transformation that had occurred in Britain's standing in India. From its post-Suez nadir, London's relationship with New Delhi had bounced back to a 'remarkably good' extent.[21] In the eyes of India's prominent astro-logical community, even the stars appeared to be realigning in Britain's favour. Writing in Lucknow's *Sunday Standard*, its resident astrologer, Gangadhar Iyer, disparaged talk of Britain's waning global influence. The United Kingdom's 'progressional chart', Iyer assured his reader-ship, provided irrefutable evidence 'that there will be a resurgence of Britain as a mighty world power before long'.[22]

The British suspected that a more prosaic factor had helped to accel-erate the normalisation of Anglo-Indian affairs. Communist China's 'aggressive occupation' of territory claimed by India, Whitehall rea-soned, had provided Nehru's government with a strong incentive to improve relations with the West. Toward the end of the 1950s, rising tension along the Sino-Indian border prompted India to begin 'looking around instinctively for powerful friends in case of serious trouble'.[23] In late 1960, India signed a landmark agreement to purchase twenty-nine US military transport aircraft, effectively terminating the IAF's estab-lished buy-British policy. Having sealed the transport aircraft deal with India, Malcolm MacDonald looked on with a mixture of admiration and envy as Washington arranged for planes to be 'removed from U.S.A.F.

[19] Lord Home, 'Anglo-Indian Relations', 28 June 1957, C (57), 149, CAB 129/87, TNA.
[20] MacDonald to Macmillan, 19 October 1959, 42/7/66–67; and Macmillan to MacDonald, 23 October 1959, 2/12/28, MMP.
[21] 'India: Shifts in Indian Foreign Policy', MacDonald to Home, 13 July 1960, DO 196/125, TNA.
[22] 'Saturn's Transit in Britain's Horoscope', 18 August 1957, *The Sunday Standard*, Lucknow.
[23] 'India: Shifts in Indian Foreign Policy', MacDonald to Home, 13 July 1960, DO 196/125, TNA.

service, repainted and flown over at a week's notice for use in the Indian Air Force'.[24] Macmillan's government reacted with a sense of unease to a development that threatened their virtual monopoly over the provision of India's military hardware. The British took comfort, however, in the Eisenhower administration's evident willingness to honour the spirit of the 'Declaration of Common Purpose', and work in collaboration with the United Kingdom in South Asia. The State Department welcomed some 'friendly commercial rivalry' between Britain and the United States in India. Nonetheless, American officials saw little merit in seeking to usurp British influence in the subcontinent and, in so doing, risk weakening the, 'the basic position [of dominance] which the free world has enjoyed economically and psychologically in India up to the present'.[25]

Indeed, in striving to bolster British and American relationships with India, the Macmillan and Eisenhower governments found themselves competing less with each other, and more with the Soviet Union. As Sino-Indian border tensions continued to fester around the turn of the decade, Nehru's government placed increasing importance on the value of India's association with Moscow. Indian officials, the British rationalised, 'realise that if Russia threw her weight behind China on this [border] issue, the future prospect for India would be very black indeed; they appreciate that if Russia on the other hand were to use her influence in Peking to restrain Chinese policy toward India, silver linings would appear on otherwise dark clouds'.[26] Indian pragmatism, Whitehall suspected, was increasingly likely to manifest itself in the 'pretty cold-blooded calculation that the price of keeping Soviet approval is somewhat higher in presentational matters than the price of obtaining American and British support'.[27]

### Moscow calling: the Soviet economic and political offensive in India

The upturn in economic activity between India and the Soviet Union in the aftermath of Nikita Khrushchev's visit to the subcontinent in 1955, and Nehru's reciprocal journey to the USSR later the same

[24] 'India: Effects of American and Soviet Economic Assistance', MacDonald to Sandys, 21 October 1960, DO 196/125, TNA.
[25] Bartlett to Lewis Jones, 9 July 1959, RG 59, Office of South Asian Affairs 1957–9, Lot 62D43, Box 24, Folder India Economic 1959 2 of 2, NARA.
[26] 'India: Shifts in Indian Foreign Policy', MacDonald to Home, 13 July 1960, DO 196/125, TNA.
[27] 'India: A General Review', Gore-Booth to Sandys, 26 May 1961, DO 196/74, TNA.

year, continued to gather pace throughout the later half of the 1950s. Soviet financial assistance to India, although eventually dwarfed by that of the United States, quickly came to represent an important element in the Indian government's economic planning at this time. Moreover, the expansion in India's commercial relationship with the USSR served as a catalyst for the development of closer political, cultural and military ties between Moscow and New Delhi. Significantly, when it came to meting out economic and technical aid, the Soviets were careful to channel their support for India into highly visible projects, such as the Suratgarh State Farm, the Bhilai steel mill, which Khrushchev lauded as 'the Indian equivalent of our Magnitogorsk', and the thermal power station at Singrauli, in Uttar Pradesh. British officials in India noted wistfully that the Soviets were adept at extracting 'maximum propaganda out of their aid, and also established themselves at a series of key points in India's plans from which they will gain substantial commercial, and perhaps political, advantage in future years'. In trading terms, the value of goods and services passing between India and the USSR more than tripled in the three years between 1956 and 1959, rising from £20 million to £67 million per annum.[28] In 1958, following the signing of a bilateral trade agreement, Indian tea, coffee, spices, tobacco and hessian was imported in ever-larger quantities by Moscow. In return, Soviet industrial equipment, and the petrol, oil and lubricants needed to operate and maintain it, flooded into India. By the end of the decade, the Soviets' willingness to supply India with significant volumes of heavily discounted crude oil had enabled New Delhi to reduce its purchases of more expensive Anglo-American petroleum by almost 12 per cent.[29]

As Indo-Soviet economic relations proceeded from strength to strength, a steady flow of Indian ministers and delegations were welcomed to the USSR. Rajendra Prasad, India's president, Morarji Desai, the country's finance minister, K. D. Malviya, minister for oil and natural resources, Panjab Rao Deshmukh, Nehru's agriculture minister, and Dr Homi Bhabha, chairman of India's atomic energy commission, amongst others, all beat a path to Moscow's door. 'This was very different from the state of affairs in my first year [in the Soviet Union

---

[28] The US provided over £750 million of aid toward India's first and second five-year plans (1951–61), in comparison with the Soviets' £109 million. 'India: Effects of American and Soviet Economic Assistance', MacDonald to Sandys, 21 October 1960, DO 196/125, TNA.

[29] K. P. S. Menon, 'Annual Political Report for the Year 1960', 5 January 1961, K. P. S. Menon Collection, Subject File No. 5, 1960–1, NMML.

in 1952]', India's ambassador K. P. S. Menon observed wryly, 'when an Indian in Moscow was as rare a sight as an Eskimo.'[30] At the same time, the Soviets moved to broaden and deepen their political ties with Nehru's government by sending their head of state, Kliment Voroshilov, first deputy prime minister, Frol Kozlov, and minister of culture, Yekatarina Furtseva, on goodwill missions to India. In February 1960, Khrushchev spent a week in India on his way to Indonesia, and used the opportunity to sign a cultural agreement with Nehru that expanded Indo-Soviet exchange in education, the arts, science and technology. Later that year, India accepted a Soviet offer to supply the Indian Air Force with AN-12 military transport aircraft on easy financial terms, establish a training programme for IAF pilots in the USSR and provide specialised military engineering equipment suitable for use on the mountainous Sino-Indian border.[31]

Nehru attributed much of the improvement in Indo-Soviet relations to Khrushchev's influence. The Soviet leader 'particularly likes India', Nehru informed the British, and had been impressed by the warmth extended to him by the Indian people and, on a more practical level, the first-hand evidence he had witnessed of India's 'progress in the economic and social fields'.[32] Khrushchev painted a similarly rosy picture of the USSR's relationship with India. 'So far as Indo-Soviet friendship was concerned,' the Soviet leader assured an Indian diplomat in 1960, 'there was not a single cloud on the sky.'[33] Equally, a concomitant deterioration in China's relationship with the Soviet Union played an important part in drawing New Delhi and Moscow closer together. Khrushchev's determination to reduce international Cold War tensions, and willingness to reach a pragmatic accommodation with the United States, widened an ideological breach between Moscow and Beijing that had been growing since the passing of Stalin. Specifically, China's leaders derided Khrushchev for retreating from the global struggle to advance communism, and pursuing a policy of 'peaceful co-existence' with the Eisenhower administration, exemplified by the Soviet leader's twelve-day tour of North America in September 1959. The previous year, the People's Republic of China had angered the Soviets

---

[30] *Ibid.*    [31] *Ibid.*

[32] 'A Talk with Mr. Nehru', 19 October 1959, 42/7/63, MMP.

[33] K. P. S. Menon, 'Annual Political Report for the Year 1960', 5 January 1961, K. P. S. Menon Collection, Subject File No. 5, 1960–1, NMML; Indian Embassy Moscow to Ministry of External Affairs, 6 November 1960, Ministry of External Affairs, Europe East, Progs. Nos. 8(14), 1960, National Archives of India, New Delhi (hereafter NAI).

by peremptorily dismissing Moscow's proposal to integrate submarine operations in the Pacific.[34] In turn, the Soviet Union reacted by withdrawing technical support for China's fledgling nuclear programme. Moreover, although Moscow maintained a neutral stance in public on Sino-Indian matters, Soviet leaders came to believe that China was largely responsible for worsening relations between Beijing and New Delhi. In August 1959, following a clash between Indian and Chinese border patrols, the Soviets left the PRC in no doubt that it considered China to be at fault for provoking the incident.[35] With the Soviet Union increasingly uneasy 'at the prospect of China growing mightier and mightier', and New Delhi anxious to avoid Moscow 'supporting China on her frontier disputes with India', Nehru and Khrushchev found common cause in seeking to frustrate any expansionist ambitions harboured by Beijing.[36]

Back in Washington, the State Department looked on with increasing concern as India's relationship with the Soviet Union bloomed in the latter half of the 1950s. Ominously for American policymakers, analysis conducted by US officials suggested that the Communist bloc was extremely well positioned to exploit economic weakness in the developing world to its political advantage. In March 1959, an economic report produced by the State Department emphasised that ten years previously Soviet gross national product (GNP) had been roughly one third that of the United States. With the Soviet economy's annual growth rate running at between 6 and 7 per cent, compared with America's 2 to 3 per cent, Soviet GNP was projected to have grown to half that of the United States by 1970. 'It is possible', the report underlined, 'that they [the USSR] may overtake us by the end of the century.' Such a prospect appeared all the more unpalatable in Washington, given the fact that the Soviets were estimated to be spending 20 per cent of their GNP on foreign economic and military aid, or approximately twice that spent in percentage terms by the United States. 'In other words,' one

---

[34] Memorandum of conversation between Mao Zedong and Nikita Khrushchev, Beijing, 31 July 1958, Archive of the President of the Russian Federation, Woodrow Wilson Center, The Cold War International History Project Digital Archive, www.wilsoncenter.org/digital-archive (hereafter CWIHP).

[35] Memorandum of conversation between Mao Zedong and Nikita Khrushchev, 3 October 1959, Archive of the President of the Russian Federation, CWIHP; 'Record of Prime Minister's Talk with Dalai Lama', 24 April 1959, File 9, Subimal Dutt Papers, NMML. See also Vojtech Mastny, 'The Soviet Union's Partnership with India', *Journal of Cold War Studies*, 12, 3 (2010), 56–7.

[36] 'A Talk with Mr. Nehru', 19 October 1959, 42/7/63; 'Note on a Talk with the American Ambassador', 21 July 1960, 42/11-104-5, MMP.

State Department official emphasised, 'with half the product, Russia's [foreign aid] effort is already equal to that of the US in absolute dollar terms.'[37]

Although, on the face of things, they had more to lose commercially from an influx of Soviet trade and aid into the subcontinent, the British government generally evidenced less concern than Washington over New Delhi's burgeoning economic and political links with Moscow. The British, one American diplomat complained, looked upon the Soviet economic offensive in India 'with more equanimity than we do'. The British saw a moderate amount of Soviet financial investment in India as a positive development. Soviet capital, Whitehall reasoned, could help to boost Indian economic growth, and in turn, underwrite political stability in the subcontinent by strengthening the popularity of Nehru's Congress Party. Furthermore, both the Soviet Union and the United States had encountered difficulties in translating the financial assistance that they provided to developing world nations into political capital. 'On the whole', Malcolm MacDonald reassured London, 'recent history does seem to show that a determined country (as, for instance, Egypt during the last decade) can, perhaps at some risk, swallow the jam of aid and spit out the pill of influence.'[38] The Eisenhower administration differed with the relatively benign British view of the Soviet Union's foreign aid policy. It appeared fanciful to American officials to expect that the Soviet Union would willingly contribute to the successful economic development of a non-communist society. Ultimately, it seemed more likely in American eyes that Moscow would aggressively seek to exploit any economic leverage it acquired in South Asia to foster a political and social climate conducive to a communist takeover.[39] Moreover, as Ellsworth Bunker made clear to MacDonald, momentum generated in the United States in favour of assisting India economically would rapidly dissipate should the 'Indians appear too sympathetic to Russia and too critical of America'.[40]

In this context, the financial crisis that engulfed India in 1957 generated considerable anxiety in Washington. Food shortages, rising defence spending driven by Pakistan's accumulation of American arms, and the

---

[37] R. H. Slover, 'Sino-Soviet Economic Offensive and its Effect on US Foreign Policy', 24 March 1959, RG 59, Lot 62D172, Box 1, Military Aid and Programs and the Draper Committee, 1957–62, Folder India, NARA.

[38] 'India: Effects of American and Soviet Economic Assistance', MacDonald to Sandys, 21 October 1960, DO 196/125, TNA.

[39] Bartlett to Lewis Jones, 9 July 1959, RG 59, Office of South Asian Affairs 1957–9, Lot 62D43, Box 24, Folder India Economic 1959, NARA.

[40] 'Note on a Talk with the American Ambassador', 21 July 1960, 42/11-104-5, MMP.

spiralling costs of raw materials and capital goods created a gaping hole in the Indian government's finances. Simply put, Nehru's administration lacked the foreign exchange reserves to fund the ambitious plans set out in its second five-year plan. With India's economy teetering on the edge of disaster, Ellsworth Bunker painted a grim picture of the likely political consequences of an Indian financial collapse. Were such a scenario allowed to unfold, Bunker informed the State Department on 4 June 1957, 'there was a strong possibility of the accession to power of some kind of extremist government'.[41] It was highly probable, if not certain, Bunker advised John Foster Dulles, that the communists would gain the most benefit from political uncertainty in India. The cost of losing India to communism, Bunker added dramatically, was certain to be 'even higher than the loss of China to the Free World'.[42]

Bunker's dire warnings of India's vulnerability to a communist take-over were amplified by the results of nationwide elections held in India between February and March 1957. On a national level, some 60 per cent of India's one hundred and ninety-two million eligible voters handed the ruling Congress Party an overwhelming victory. In the central parliament, Congress captured 371 of the 492 available seats. At a regional level, Congress fared almost as well, winning overall majorities in eleven of India's thirteen state assemblies. However, media coverage of the election results, inside and outside the subcontinent, largely ignored the Congress Party's successes. Instead, newspaper headlines focused on events in the southern state of Kerala, where the Communist Party of India (CPI), which maintained close links to Moscow, defeated the incumbent Congress administration. 'This must be the first time in history', Malcolm MacDonald informed Whitehall, 'that a Communist administration with anything approaching the jurisdiction and powers of the Kerala Government has been put into office by wholly democratic means.' In 1952, in India's first general election, the CPI had enjoyed some limited success in the southern states of Madras, Travancore-Cochin and Hyderabad. Five years later the Communists gained significant political ground, not only in Kerala, but also in the northern Congress heartland of Uttar Pradesh, Bihar and the Punjab. By exploiting the economic grievances of many Indians in areas such as land ownership, poverty and unemployment, Communist candidates

---

[41] Memorandum of conversation, 4 June 1957, 'Indian Financial Problems', RG59, State Department Central Files, 891.00/6-457, NARA.
[42] Bunker to John Foster Dulles, 19 November 1957, RG 59, State Department Central Files, 791.5 MSP/11-1957, NARA.

managed to double the share of the votes that they had received in 1952, and secured a presence in every one of India's state legislatures.[43]

Having travelled through Kerala shortly after the CPI government assumed power, Henry Ramsey, America's consul-general in Madras, reported back to the State Department that the 'Communists are moving skilfully and non-dramatically within constitutional limitations to consolidate [their] position'. Ramsey failed to share the optimism expressed by some Congress Party leaders that the Communist 'beachhead' in Kerala would flounder, once it became apparent that the state's economic problems could not be resolved overnight. The 'lack of realism' evident amongst local Congress Party activists in the state, whose inefficiency, corruption and shambolic political organisation had paved the way for the CPI's victory, disconcerted Ramsey. '[N]either [the] Kerala Congress nor central [Congress Party] has evolved a clear strategic line either to displace or replace [the] Communists', the American consul-general cautioned Washington, 'and in EMS [Namboodiripad, the CPI state leader] and his Cabinet, Congress is confronted with a shrewd, young, zealous, closely-knit team.'[44]

In a bid to prevent the election result in Kerala being repeated elsewhere in India, the White House instructed the State Department to increase the amount of publicity given to American assistance programmes in the subcontinent. In addition, plans were made for US economic aid and development projects to be redirected, wherever possible, to 'bear more directly on the situation in South India'.[45] More controversially, President Eisenhower authorised the Central Intelligence Agency to mount a covert operation to subvert the CPI administration in Kerala. Between 1957 and 1959, by secretly channelling funds to local Congress Party officials and labour leaders, the CIA promoted industrial unrest and political turmoil in the state. In July 1959, amidst scenes of mounting violence and disorder in Kerala, the CPI government was dismissed from office under an executive order issued by India's president.[46] In combination, the Kerala episode, the

[43] MacDonald to Home, 'India: General Elections, 1957', 30 April 1957, DO 35/3167, TNA.
[44] Ramsey to Secretary of State, No. 347, 1 May 1957, RG 59, Office of South Asian Affairs India Affairs 1944–57, Lot 57D373, Box 8, Folder Kerala Aug–Dec 1957, NARA.
[45] Simons to Adams, 21 November 1957, RG 59, Office of South Asian Affairs India Affairs 1944–57, Lot file 57D373, Box 8, Folder Kerala Aug–Dec 1957, NARA.
[46] In 1979, Ellsworth Bunker confirmed that in the late 1950s the CIA had funnelled money to the Congress Party through S. K. Patil, a Congress leader in Maharashtra, to foment a campaign of opposition to the Communist administration in Kerala. See Ellsworth Bunker, Oral History, 18 June and 17 July 1979, Butler Library, Columbia University, New York, pp. 67–8. Junior US officials, such as David S. Burgess,

Soviet Union's growing interest in the affairs of the subcontinent, and the formidable economic challenges confronting India prompted the Eisenhower administration to radically rethink its South Asian policy. Encouraged by a bipartisan cross-section of influential American foreign policy practitioners and commentators, who perceived India to be dangerously vulnerable to the forces of communism, internally and externally, the US government embarked upon an unprecedented political and economic intervention in the Indian subcontinent. Over the course of the next decade, Washington's attempt to 'save' India for the free world was, however, destined to yield decidedly mixed and often unforeseen results.

### The Eisenhower administration and the 'New Look' at South Asia

The injection of significantly higher levels of US economic aid into India's ailing economy formed a central plank in the Eisenhower administration's strategy to curtail, and ultimately reverse, the inroads made by communism in South Asia. In February 1957, in the wake of NSC 5701, William Rountree, Assistant Secretary of State for Near Eastern, and South Asian and African Affairs, began to urge senior administration officials to impart substance into the United States' rhetoric on developing world aid. In memoranda sent to John Foster Dulles on 4 and 8 February, Rountree echoed Ellsworth Bunker's concern at the seriousness of the economic problems facing India. Without prompt US financial intervention, Rountree advised Dulles, an Indian financial disaster was probable, which, in turn, threatened India's long-term future as a functioning democracy.[47] In response, Dulles established an interagency committee where representatives drawn from the State Department, Treasury and International Cooperation Administration (ICA) explored how the United States could best assist in propping up India's ailing economy. Having met first in March, when the committee reported back to Dulles in May, it identified a gap of between $700 and $900 million in the cost of the commitments set out in India's second

---

Labour attaché at the US Embassy in New Delhi between 1955 and 1960, have since corroborated Bunker's revelation. See David. S. Burgess, Oral History, 7 April 1991, The Foreign Affairs Oral History Project (hereafter FAOHP) http://memory.loc.gov/ammem/collections/diplomacy/. Daniel Patrick Moynihan, US ambassador to India in the early 1970s, also confirmed that the CIA was used to fund Congress Party campaigns against the CPI in Kerala and West Bengal. See Daniel Patrick Moynihan, *A Dangerous Place* (Boston: Little Brown, 1978), p. 41.

[47] Rountree to John Foster Dulles, 4 and 8 February 1957, RG 59, State Department Central Files, 4 and 8 February, 791.5-MSP2-457; 791.5-MSP/2-857, NARA.

five-year plan and the foreign exchange reserves available to Nehru's government to service them. Dulles was encouraged to help New Delhi bridge the yawning chasm in India's finances by increasing access to commodity assistance, and offering the Indian government access to cheap capital through the newly established Development Loan Fund (DLF), Export–Import Bank and, if necessary, the World Bank. State Department officials went even further and, over opposition from their more fiscally conservative colleagues in the Treasury and ICA, suggested that the administration consider approaching Congress for authorisation to offer India an emergency long-term loan.[48]

With America in the midst of an economic downturn of its own, many of Eisenhower's cabinet, Dulles included, were reluctant to ask Congress to appropriate exceptional funds for overseas aid. The caution exhibited by senior administration officials over the issue of Indian economic assistance was augmented by the knowledge that Nehru's government had few friends on Capitol Hill, where India's non-alignment and willingness to court the Communist bloc rankled with America's legislators. Having returned to Washington in the middle of the year to rally political support for an emergency package of economic aid for India, Ellsworth Bunker encountered opposition and disappointment at every turn. After meeting with a group of prominent Republican and Democratic Senators, including Lyndon Johnson, William Knowland, George Aitken and Mike Mansfield, and the House of Representatives majority leader, John McCormick, a downbeat Bunker reluctantly concluded that 'it would be extremely difficult, if not impossible, to get special legislation [for India] in this session [of Congress]'.[49]

Throughout the late summer of 1957, the spectre of an Indian economic implosion continued to occupy the attention of the State Department. In August, one background report received by the US Information Agency (USIA) from the State Department evaluated India's 'prospects for attaining some reasonable measure of economic growth and political maturity by means of essentially democratic processes ... [as] "poor" to only "moderately good"'.[50] The previous month, a significant impediment to the State Department's efforts to secure

---

[48] Report of the Interdepartmental Working Group on India, 'The Economic Problem of India', 2 May 1957, Subject subseries, Records of the Chairman of the Council on Foreign Economic Policy (CFEP), Dwight D. Eisenhower Library, Abilene, Kansas (hereafter DDEL).

[49] Bunker to Bartlett, 27 June 1957, RG 59, NEA/SOA Files, Lot 62 D 43, India – June–December 1957, NARA.

[50] 'A Preliminary Fact Book on India', 19 August 1957, RG 306, Office of Research Special 'S' Reports 1953–83, Box 12 Folder S-36 57, NARA.

additional American financial support for India had, however, been removed. In July, Robert Anderson, an economic liberal and champion of foreign aid, succeeded George Humphrey, a fiscal conservative and influential opponent of welfare spending at home and developmental assistance abroad, as Eisenhower's Treasury Secretary. Later that autumn, India's finance minister, T. T. Krishnamachari, and G. D. Birla, an eminent Indian industrialist, visited the United States in a bid to remove concerns harboured by American policymakers over the Nehru government's 'socialist' economic agenda. Back in India, British officials observed that Krishnamachari had gone

daringly far in his attempts to allay American suspicion about Indian economic policies. His observations or insinuations that India had no serious intention of nationalising anything important, that the United States was more socialistic (in terms of publicly owned industrial capacity) than India and that Indian socialism relied on private enterprise, apart from startling many Americans, excited violent criticism of him from Leftish factions in India.[51]

During the latter half of that year, as financial conditions worsened in the subcontinent, Indian government leaders continued to throw conspicuous gestures of goodwill in the United States' direction. In November, in a highly unusual move, Nehru addressed a conference of the American Technical Co-operative Mission in India, and expressed deep gratitude for the contribution that American aid had made to the subcontinent's economic development. The Indian premier's speech was significant less for its content, observers noted at the time, than for the mere fact that Nehru 'should have addressed the [American] conference at all'.[52] Rather than accentuate areas of Indo-American discord in public statements on issues such as Kashmir, nuclear weapons and collective security pacts, Indian government officials began to conspicuously play up similarities in the democratic outlook of the two countries. At the same time, India's newspapers and magazines started to publish more articles and editorials favourable to the United States.[53]

In October, with Krishnamachari back in India, a cabal of senior State Department officials led by Rountree, and including the Deputy Under Secretaries of State for Economic and Political Affairs, C. Douglas Dillon and Robert Murphy, pressed John Foster Dulles to support an approach to Congress for increased economic aid to India, 'on a scale which would enable that country to complete the core of the Second

---

[51] Clark to Lord Home, 27 February 1958, FO 371/135947, TNA.
[52] *Ibid.*     [53] *Ibid.*

five-year plan'.[54] After digesting Rountree's plea, Dulles endorsed
the provision of $250 million of annual US aid to New Delhi over a
three-year period. In arguing that the time had come for the administration to take a more assertive stand on the question of Indian aid,
Dulles drew heavily upon events in Kerala. In a note sent to Eisenhower
on 4 November, the Secretary of State reminded the president that

the Communists [had recently come] ... to power in the economically depressed
Indian state of Kerala. It is feared that if the second Five Year Plan fails they
may extend their power to the more populous and strategically situated province of Bengal. This could trigger off a chain reaction, which would lead to
growing extremism and separatism in other parts of the country. The chances
of chaos and a Communist advent to power in the sub-continent would be
vastly increased. Loss of this area to Communist control would undermine the
West's position throughout free Asia.[55]

Within days of aligning himself with the State Department's pro-India
lobby, Dulles began to have second thoughts about the wisdom of
forging ahead with an aid package for India that would necessitate
Congressional approval. Changing tack, and adopting a more circumspect attitude, Dulles suggested to Eisenhower that it might be
more prudent to provide India with financial support through a series
of short-term loans provided by the Export–Import Bank, the DLF
and third parties, such as West Germany. 'The danger of a spectacular defeat in Congress is very great', Dulles cautioned Eisenhower
on 12 November, '... better to pick up bits and pieces ... and get the
Ex[port]–Im[port] Bank to put up additional funds.'[56]

In the first quarter of 1958, Dulles' piecemeal approach to Indian
aid began to deliver economic succour to Nehru's hard-pressed government. The Eisenhower administration confirmed its intention to
underwrite a $225 million loan to India, and make increased quan-
tities of heavily subsidised wheat and other foodstuffs available to New
Delhi under Public Law 480, or the Food for Peace programme. Later
that year, State Department officials, working in conjunction with the
World Bank, cajoled Britain, West Germany, Canada and Japan to join
the United States in forming an international aid consortium. In short
order, the consortium members pledged $350 million in emergency aid
to India. Although representing somewhat less financial assistance than

---

[54] Murphy, Dillon and Rountree to Dulles, 'Financial Assistance to India', 16 October
   1957, RG 59, Central Files, 791.5-MS/10-1657, NARA.
[55] Dulles to Eisenhower, 'Aid to India', 4 November 1957, Whitman Files, Dulles–Herter
   Series, DDEL.
[56] Memorandum of Eisenhower meeting with Dulles, Nixon, Dillon, Herter, 12
   November 1957, RG 59, Central Files, 711.11-El/11-1657, NARA.

the Indian government had hoped to receive from Washington, the first tentative steps taken by Eisenhower's administration's to alleviate India's economic problems were, nonetheless, 'received with relief and genuine gratitude' in the subcontinent. Significantly, the magnitude of American economic aid to India did prove sufficient for Nehru to feel obliged to reaffirm his government's ongoing commitment to the principle of non-alignment. In a letter sent to his chief ministers in July, the Indian premier emphasised that he was alert to the danger that 'even after a country has become independent, it may continue to be economically dependent on other countries. This kind of thing is euphemistically called having close cultural and economic ties.'[57]

In a broader sense, the Eisenhower government's desire to go further and faster in accelerating India's economic development toward the end of the 1950s was assisted by a gradual softening of the political consensus in the United States in relation to the provision of development aid in general, and the provision of development aid to India in particular. In the Senate, rising political stars such as John F. Kennedy and Hubert Humphrey came to public prominence by arguing that it was in America's wider interest to help stimulate the economic development of democratic India. A failure to do so, it was suggested, risked seeing Communist China emerge as Asia's dominant economic force. In June 1958, Kennedy joined forces with Ellsworth Bunker's predecessor in New Delhi, the Republican congressman from Kentucky, John Sherman Cooper, to table a bipartisan motion in the Senate calling for a substantial increase in US economic assistance to India. Away from Capitol Hill, prominent economists such as Walt W. Rostow and Max Millikan, working within the Massachusetts Institute of Technology's Center for International Studies, made a powerful intellectual case for investing American taxpayer dollars in the Indian subcontinent. Were India's economic growth allowed to stall for want of foreign capital, Millikan pronounced in February 1959,

the chances of a repetition of the recent history of China would be great. A strictly authoritarian regime would almost certainly come ultimately to power [in India] and the prospects are high that it would be a Communist-dominated regime, subservient at least in part to the foreign-policy interests of Moscow ... [losing 400 million people to the Communist bloc would be] a blow to American

[57] Nehru to Chief Ministers, 13 July 1958, New Delhi, in G. Parthasarathi (ed.), *Jawaharlal Nehru: Letters to Chief Ministers, 1947–1964*, vol. 5: *1958–1964* (New Delhi: Oxford University Press, 1989), pp. 87–8; Clark to Lord Home, 27 February 1958, FO 371/135947, TNA.

interests of the most serious sort ... [and necessitate defence spending] ... much larger than any proposed economic aid allocations.[58]

Around the turn of the decade, influential media commentators, including such luminaries as Walter Lippmann, had joined the Indian developmental bandwagon. In November 1958, writing in his nationally syndicated column 'Today and Tomorrow', Lippmann submitted that communism was gaining ground rapidly in Asia by virtue of its association with efforts to increase 'the power and the standard of living of a backward people'. It was in India, Lippmann asserted, with its endemic poverty, teeming multitudes, fledgling democracy and highly developed bureaucratic structures, that the West should make a stand against a red tide sweeping across Asia. 'There is little doubt in my mind', Lippmann assured his readership, 'that if we and our Western partners could underwrite and assure the success of India's development it would make a world of difference ... It would put an end to the enervating feeling of fatality and of inevitability, to the sense that communism is the only way of the future.'[59] On meeting Lord Louis Mountbatten at an American Embassy reception in London, the US vice-president, Richard Nixon, warmly endorsed Lippmann's central thesis. Nixon, Mountbatten reported back to the British Foreign Secretary, Selwyn Lloyd, 'told me that he intended to do everything in his power to get the US Government to support the policy outlined by Walter Lippmann'.[60] Early the following year, Nixon made clear his conversion to the cause of Indian economic development when, on welcoming delegates to a Washington conference on Indo-US relations, the vice-president declared, 'what happens in India, insofar as its economic progress is concerned in the next few years, could be as important, or could even be more important in the long run, than what happens ... with regard to Berlin'.[61]

In New Delhi, Ellsworth Bunker expressed a mixture of relief and satisfaction that 'Washington has somehow come to believe that as a matter of cold fact it is not in the United States' interest to see India's

---

[58]  Max F. Millikan, 'India', 20 February 1959, RG 59, Lot 62D172, Box 1, Military Aid and Programs and the Draper Committee, 1957–62, Folder India, NARA; see also Walt W. Rostow, *Eisenhower, Kennedy and Foreign Aid* (Austin: University of Texas Press, 1985).

[59]  Walter Lippmann, 'Meeting Soviet Challenge in Asia and Africa: India, the Test for US Policy', *The Guardian*, 13 November 1958.

[60]  Mountbatten to Selwyn Lloyd, 4 December 1958, DL10345/5, FO 371/135947, TNA.

[61]  Selig Harrison (ed.), *India and the United States* (New York: Macmillan, 1961), p. 144.

economy collapse'.[62] The State Department proved unable to extract the full measure of economic assistance for India from a parsimonious Congress which, in its view, Nehru's government warranted. Nevertheless, over the course of Eisenhower's second term of office, which ended in January 1961, the provision of annual American developmental aid to India more than tripled. Moreover, by the middle of the following decade, the Public Law 480 programme initiated by Eisenhower's administration had helped to stave off famine in the subcontinent by supplying India with $1.5 billion of discounted American wheat, rice and other food grains. At the same time, the Eisenhower government's strategy of deploying American economic power in support of Nehru's government saw Washington's Cold War alliance with Pakistan come under severe strain.

### The United States and Pakistan: an alliance under strain

In seeking to roll back what it perceived to be a dangerous and rising tide of communist influence in India, the Eisenhower administration faced a conundrum. The more economic and political support that the United States provided to non-aligned India, the more Washington's relationship with Pakistan, one of its staunchest partners in the developing world, faltered. How far could the United States go to promote India's economic development and muffle the siren call of communism in India, American policymakers pondered, without forfeiting the US-Pakistani alliance? The Department of Defense and the CIA, in particular, attached considerable importance to the strategic and intelligence dimension of the United States' association with Pakistan. As a member of both SEATO and the Baghdad Pact, Pakistan helped to confer a degree of political legitimacy on Western collective security structures within the developing world. In addition, Pakistan's position between the Middle East and Asia placed it within striking distance of the Soviet Union, PRC and the oilfields of the Persian Gulf. Accordingly, the Pentagon valued American access to the country's military facilities and airfields. Under secret protocols negotiated with Pakistan's government in 1957, the CIA also maintained a significant and highly prized intelligence presence in Pakistan. The Agency operated listening posts and ran U-2 aerial reconnaissance flights from bases in northern Pakistan, at Badaber, Peshawar and Lahore, which

---

[62] Bunker to Bartlett, 9 December 1958, RG 59, Lot 62D43, Box 2, South Asian Affairs, 1957–9, Folder Indian 1958, NARA.

gathered intelligence on missile development and nuclear tests behind the Iron and Bamboo Curtains.[63]

As the Eisenhower administration's efforts to furnish India with greater economic assistance gained political traction in the United States, officials in the State Department debated how best to mitigate Pakistan's growing unease at Washington's 'tilt' toward India. Only by removing the principal sources of Indo-Pakistani enmity and friction, it seemed, would the United States be free to fully develop economic, political and, in Pakistan's case, military relations with South Asia. As a first step, in April 1958, William Rountree invited Morrice James, Assistant Under Secretary of State at the Commonwealth Relations Office, to Washington for two days of talks on the subcontinent. James agreed with his American colleagues that three core areas of contention lay at the heart of the ongoing antagonism between India and Pakistan. These encompassed disputes over control of the contested state of Kashmir; access to the waters of the Indus River and its principal tributaries; and regional defence spending. British officials were a good deal more sceptical than their American colleagues that third-party intervention could help to resolve differences between India and Pakistan, particularly when it came to such an emotive issue as Kashmir. Nevertheless, the CRO agreed to support a US-led mediation initiative in the subcontinent, or 'package plan'. By bundling together relatively straightforward technical issues, such as the Indus Waters dispute, where agreement between India and Pakistan appeared possible, with more intractable problems, such as Kashmir, the State Department hoped to broker a comprehensive and durable Indo-Pakistani settlement.[64]

In the event, to Eisenhower's chagrin, when the 'package plan' was presented to the Indian and Pakistani governments on 16 May 1958, it met with a mixed response. As British and American officials had anticipated, Pakistan, who had the most to gain from a change in the regional status quo, welcomed the Western initiative. In New Delhi, Nehru failed to see why his government should risk compromising India's grip on Kashmir by participating in an American-led mediation exercise. In consequence, the Indian government effectively vetoed Eisenhower's

---

[63] NSC 5909/1, 'Statement of US Policy Toward South Asia', 21 August 1959, RG 59, S/S-NSC Files, Lot 63 D 351, NSC 5909 Series; and Adams to Rountree, 'Review of Our Military Aid Program to Pakistan', 5 May 1959, RG 59, Central Files, 790D.5-MSP/5-559, NARA. See also Stephen Cohen, 'US Weapons and South Asia: A Policy Analysis', *Pacific Affairs*, 49 (1976), 49–69.
[64] US–UK Talks, 16–18 April 1958, 'Proposals for Reduction of Tension between India and Pakistan', 25 April 1958, RG 59, Lot 62D43, Package Folder 2, NARA.

proposal.[65] Ellsworth Bunker had forewarned Washington that just such an Indian reaction was likely. The previous year, within weeks of arriving in the subcontinent, Bunker had left the State Department in no doubt that Nehru, in common with the overwhelming majority of India's political establishment, viewed the retention of Kashmir as a 'vital [Indian] national interest'. The Indian premier, Bunker underlined, was adamant that when it came to Kashmir, 'this fact constitutes a reality which foreign governments have to face'.[66]

A separate State Department initiative taken forward by the World Bank president, Eugene Black, did eventually deliver a resolution to the Indus Waters dispute. The Indus River, and its five main tributaries, irrigated thirty million acres of agricultural land in the north-west of the subcontinent, the crops from which fed forty million Pakistanis and ten million Indians. At the time of partition, the headwaters of the Indus passed under Indian control, affording New Delhi a stranglehold over much of West Pakistan's food production. In September 1960, India and Pakistan signed an agreement, brokered by Black, which assigned Pakistan rights to the waters of the Indus, Jhelum and Chenab rivers, and awarded India control of the Ravi, Sutlej and Beas waterways. Crucially, the treaty, under which the World Bank agreed to fund the construction of a series of new canals and dams in the subcontinent, guaranteed water security for Pakistan's principal agricultural provinces of Sind and Punjab, the breadbasket of South Asia.[67]

When Nehru flew to Pakistan on an IAF Viscount aircraft to sign the Indus Waters Treaty on 19 September 1960, a crowd of one hundred thousand people turned out at Karachi airport to welcome the Indian premier. Pakistan's president, Field Marshall Mohammad Ayub Khan, set the tone for what many hoped would prove to be a watershed in Indo-Pakistani relations by greeting Nehru with a warm handshake as he descended from the steps of his aeroplane. On the ten-mile drive from the airport to the centre of Karachi, crowds lined the route and shouted 'Welcome Nehru' and 'Nehru Zindabad', or 'Long Live Nehru', as the official motorcade swept by. Later that day, at a signing ceremony held on the spacious green lawns of the Presidential House, a thousand specially invited guests heard Nehru echo the prevailing mood of optimism. Lauding the achievement of India and Pakistan in overcoming a 'very difficult and complex problem' that had 'troubled'

[65] Nehru to Eisenhower, 7 June 1958, RG 59, Presidential Correspondence, Lot 66 D 204, Folder Nehru, NARA.
[66] Bunker to State Department, 3 April 1957, RG 59, State Department Central Files, 690D.91/4-357, NARA.
[67] Ian Talbot, *Pakistan: A Modern History* (London: Hurst & Company, 2009), p. 112.

both nations for 'many years', the Indian prime minister reflected that the Indus Waters agreement was

certainly memorable ... because in spite of the problem and harassing delays, success has come at last. We are going to have many benefits out of this arrangement, but greater than the material advantages are the psychological and emotional benefits. It is a symbol of unity and co-operation between the two neighbouring countries.[68]

Many Pakistani government officials harboured an expectation that the prevailing spirit of Indo-Pakistani goodwill that had helped to solve the 'economic' problem posed by the Indus Waters issue would translate into greater Indian flexibility on common 'political' questions, and, above all, the Kashmir dispute. In Ayub Khan's view, the Indus Waters agreement merely reinforced the imperative of reaching 'an amicable and just' settlement with India over Kashmir. 'The very fact that Pakistan had to be content with the waters of three western [Indus] rivers', the Pakistani president subsequently recorded, 'underline[d] the importance for us of having physical control over the upper reaches of these rivers to secure their maximum utilization for the growing needs of West Pakistan. In my mind, therefore, the solution of the Kashmir issue acquired a new sense of urgency on the conclusion of this Treaty.'[69] Yet, try as it might, when it came to the stickier questions of cajoling India and Pakistan to agree a compact on Kashmir, or consider a regional defence arrangement, the United States proved unable to replicate the success of the Indus Waters intervention.

Indeed, the emergence in October 1958 of a new, and more cohesive national government in Pakistan, led by Ayub Khan, ensured that for the balance of Eisenhower's presidency, Indo-Pakistani relations, and in consequence, Pakistan's alliance with Washington, experienced considerable strain. Ayub Khan came to power in Pakistan amidst a background of escalating social and economic tension, smouldering friction between the country's eastern and western wings, and political inertia on the part of a moribund national Constituent Assembly. One British diplomat serving in Karachi at the time observed that Pakistan's politicians evidenced 'little trace of real concern for the country, and so much – and so scantily concealed – concern for their own unrestricted access to the pork-barrel of patronage and power'.[70] For a brief period,

---

[68] 'Over A Lakh of People Greet Nehru On Arrival in Karachi' and 'Nehru and Ayub Sign Indus Waters Treaty', *National Herald*, Lucknow, 20 September 1960.
[69] Mohammad Ayub Khan, *Friends Not Masters: A Political Autobiography* (London: Oxford University Press, 1967), p. 107 and p. 113.
[70] Morrice James to Gilbert Laithwaite, Easter Monday 1955, MSS EUR F 138/149, Sir John Gilbert Laithwaite Papers, India Office Select Materials, British Library.

between September and December 1954, Pakistan's eastern wing came back under the control of the British Chief Justice of East Bengal, Sir Thomas Ellis. In a throwback to the days of the Raj, following the dismissal of East Bengal's parliament and the imposition of direct rule, Ellis found himself constitutionally responsible for running the more populous half of Pakistan. When parliamentary authority was eventually restored in Bengal, conflict between the Krishak Sramik Party (KSP) and the dominant Awami (or People's) League led Awami members to bodily remove an incumbent KSP assembly speaker from his chair in the midst of one session, declare him insane and have him locked up in a secure hospital. Two days later, when an Awami League representative occupied the vacant speaker's post, a violent mêlée ensued, in which KSP rivals pelted the speaker's chair with pieces of furniture, killing its new occupant.[71]

During the three-year period between August 1955 and October 1958, no less than five prime ministers came and went in Pakistan. The prevailing atmosphere of political chaos and governmental apathy inside the country was captured in a letter that Huseyn Shaheed Suhrawardy wrote to Richard Nixon in October 1957, shortly after he had stepped down as Pakistan's premier. Before signing off his letter to Nixon, Suhrawardy remarked casually, 'I forgot to tell you that I am no more the Prime Minister of Pakistan. In fact, it does not seem to have made any difference to me. I forgot when I was Prime Minister that I was Prime Minister, and I forget when I am not Prime Minister that I am not Prime Minister. Does this make sense?'[72] On 7 October 1958, under pressure from Pakistan's army to take decisive action and end the political malaise afflicting the country, the nation's president, Iskander Mirza, declared a state of martial law and dismissed the incumbent prime minister, Sir Feroz Khan Noon, and his ministry. Mirza went on to abrogate Pakistan's constitution, dissolve the National Assembly and its provincial legislatures, and outlaw all political parties. In a 1,400-word statement that accompanied the imposition of martial law, Mirza excoriated the country's political class for waging a 'ruthless' struggle for personal power and privilege that had culminated in the 'prostitution of Islam for political ends'.[73]

General Mohammad Ayub Khan, then Commander-in-Chief of the army, was quickly installed as Chief Martial Law Administrator and

[71] Ian Stephens, *Pakistan: Old Country/New Nation* (London: Penguin Books, 1964), pp. 298–9.
[72] H. S. Suhrawardy to Nixon, 19 October 1957, Box 13 Folder Pakistan 1957–61, Vice Presidential Papers, Cushman Files PPS 320, Richard Nixon Presidential Library and Museum, Yorba Linda, California.
[73] *Dawn (Karachi)*, 8 October 1958.

the new prime minister of Pakistan. Once in office, Ayub Khan wasted little time wresting the presidency from Mirza's grip, and sending his predecessor off into political exile in London. The new president's priority was to tackle the widespread abuse of political power, corruption and endemic factionalism, which he believed had brought Pakistan to 'the brink of a civil war'.[74] On 28 August 1958, shortly before the declaration of martial law, Ayub Khan recorded in his personal diary that he had received

very depressing reports about economic distress, maladministration through political interference, frustration and complete loss of faith by the people in the political leadership inclusive of the President. The general belief is that none of these men have any honesty of purpose, integrity or patriotism ... The general belief is emerging that even I and the army are failing to do our duty by not saving the people from these tyrants.[75]

In his first public address after assuming power, Pakistan's new leader reiterated his determination to put an end to the 'ceaseless and bitter' internecine war that the country's politicians had waged against each other, 'regardless of the ill effects on the country'.[76]

Having become increasingly exasperated by the political turmoil engulfing Pakistan, British and American policymakers broadly welcomed the advent of Ayub Khan's military administration. A large and robust Pathan from Pakistan's rugged North-West Frontier Province, at well over six feet tall, Ayub Khan was physically imposing, and appeared outwardly self-assured. Educated for a short period at the Aligarh Muslim University, where he absorbed the modernising and Western-orientated principles espoused by its founder, Sir Syed Ahmed Khan, Pakistan's president had left the subcontinent in the 1920s to study at the British Army's Royal Military Academy at Sandhurst. The first foreign cadet at Sandhurst to reach the rank of corporal, Ayub Khan went on to serve with distinction as an officer in the British Indian Army in Burma during the Second World War. An enthusiastic tennis player, golfer and participant in field sports, Ayub Khan also claimed a keen interest in the study of literature and art, to

---

[74] Ayub Khan interview with Altaf Gauhar, Rawalpindi, 23 June 1964, in Nadia Ghani (ed.), *Field Marshal Mohammad Ayub Khan: A Selection of Talks and Interviews, 1964–1967* (Karachi: Oxford University Press, 2010), p. 103.

[75] Ayub Khan, *Friends Not Masters*, p. 68.

[76] Mohammad Ayub Khan, 8 October 1958, *Speeches and Statements by Field Marshal Mohammad Ayub Khan*, vol. 1, October 1958–June 1959 (Karachi: Pakistan Government Publications, 1959), p. 2. See also *Dawn*, 8 October 1958; and, Ayesha Jalal, *The State of Martial Rule: The Origins of Pakistan's Political Economy of Defence* (Cambridge University Press, 1990).

the amusement of British officials. While blessed with many admirable traits, the country's president was not considered by British diplomats in Pakistan to be a man of culture. Ayub Khan, one senior British official later opined, was 'notably antipathetic to intellectuals, and an out-and-out philistine'.[77]

One colourful literary episode that the Pakistani president proved eager to play down occurred in the summer of 1963, when the British tabloid newspaper, the *News of the World*, serialised the memoir of Christine Keeler, the femme fatale at the heart of the Profumo scandal. To the dismay of the Pakistan government, Keeler claimed that Ayub Khan had frolicked with her in the swimming pool at Lord Astor's Cliveden mansion in the Buckinghamshire countryside where, three years earlier, she had embarked on relationships with the British Secretary of State for War, John Profumo, and a Soviet naval attaché, Yvegeny Ivanov. Having denied the veracity of Keeler's story, and lodged a strong protest with the British government, Pakistani officials moved quickly to suppress news of Ayub Khan's supposed association with the Profumo affair in the country's newspapers.[78] In Karachi, Britain's High Commissioner, Morrice James, observed:

Though the newspapers here have reported with gusto the details of the Ward–Keeler–Profumo case, there have been surprisingly few references to the Ayub–Keeler aspect; indeed the Press here were evidently told to keep off the subject ... this shows what an effective degree of control the Pakistan Government can exert over the Pakistan newspapers when it wants to.[79]

In an aside to James that perhaps revealed more about his own political ambition than Ayub Khan's character, Zulfikar Ali Bhutto, Pakistan's foreign minister, observed caustically that it seemed 'incongruous for an interesting thing like that to happen to such a very dull man'.[80]

More prosaically, having followed his rise through the ranks of Pakistan's armed forces, British and American officials deemed Ayub Khan to be just the type of strong-willed, upright and efficient administrator that Pakistan needed.[81] Although previously content to steer

---

[77] Morrice James, *Pakistan Chronicle* (London: Hurst, 1992), p. 108.
[78] CRO to Karachi, No. 1225, 17 June 1963, DO 196/5; Iftikhar Ali (Pakistan Deputy High Commissioner) to Cyril Pickard (Assistant Under Secretary of State, CRO), 19 June 1963, DO 196/5, TNA.
[79] Morrice James to Saville Garner, 5 July 1963, DO 196/5, TNA.
[80] James, *Pakistan Chronicle*, p. 110.
[81] 'Pakistan: The President', 16 February 1960, PREM11/3902, TNA; Langley to Secretary of State, 5 October 1958, No. 775, RG 59, State Department Central Files, 790D.00/10-558, NARA.

clear of domestic politics, between October 1954 and August 1955, Ayub Khan had served briefly as minister of defence in the emergency government of Ghulam Muhammad.[82] Significantly, Pakistan's future president did take particular care to cultivate good relations with political leaders in the United States, impressing Richard Nixon as a man for the future when the two had first met, in 1953.[83] Once in power, the American press warmed to Ayub Khan, lauding him as 'the Asian "de Gaulle"' and a leader 'who gets things done'.[84] Having duly promised to reintroduce a form of democracy that 'the people could understand', Ayub Khan moved quickly to stamp his authority on Pakistan. Political parties remained banned, 'troublemakers' were imprisoned, a crackdown was initiated on the nation's black economy, and fixed prices introduced in shops for staples such as milk and vegetables.[85]

Although unmistakably authoritarian, Ayub Khan's administration won plaudits in the West for its willingness to champion a radical agenda of socio-political reform. Taking his cue from earlier political innovators close to home, such as Mohammed Ali Jinnah and Sir Syed Ahmed Khan, and in a broader context, the Turkish social-revolutionary, Mustafa Kemal Ataturk, Ayub Khan implemented a crash programme of modernisation that was intended to safeguard Pakistan's survival and prosperity in the face of growing internal and external pressures. In part, this involved recasting a constitutional system in Pakistan modelled on British parliamentary democracy that took 'for granted too many prerequisites which do not really exist in a country like Pakistan'.[86] Low rates of literacy, poor communication networks and a predominantly rural population whose allegiance to powerful feudal barons was underpinned by strong bonds of kinship and patronage undoubtedly qualified Pakistan's democratic credentials. An alternative 'Basic Democracy' system would, Ayub Khan proclaimed, enable Pakistan to reap benefits from a brand of democracy that was, 'simple to understand, easy to work and cheap to sustain ... [and likely to deliver] reasonably strong and stable governments'.[87] Under the scheme, Pakistan's two wings were divided into 40,000 constituencies, each with an average population of 1,000. Each constituency returned one representative,

---

[82] 'Note by Sir Gilbert Laithwaite on General Ayub', 28 October 1958, PREM 11/3902, TNA.
[83] Nixon to Ayub Khan, 19 April 1960, Box 409 Folder M. Ayub Khan, Pre-Presidential Papers of Richard Nixon, General Correspondence Series 320, Richard Nixon Presidential Library and Museum, Yorba Linda, California.
[84] 'Pakistan's Ayub Khan: The Asian "de Gaulle"', *Newsweek*, 19 April 1960.
[85] Talbot, *Pakistan*, pp. 154–6.
[86] Mohammad Ayub Khan, 'Pakistan Perspective', *Foreign Affairs* (July 1960), 550.
[87] *Ibid.*, p. 551.

or Basic Democrat, by universal franchise. Ever-larger administrative groups then combined to elect representatives at local, district and provincial levels. The 'Basic Democracy' experiment garnered praise in the United States, where it was widely represented as a bold attempt to break an enervating cycle in which post-colonial nations experienced 'pseudo-parliamentary democracy, chaos, then strong-man rule'. In the pages of *Newsweek*, Ayub Khan was congratulated for confronting the 'disconcerting fact ... [that] not every young nation is ready for fully fledged democracy'.[88] In Pakistan, the propensity of the state to manipulate the 'Basic Democrat' system to favour approved representatives drew widespread condemnation and weakened the legitimacy of Ayub Khan's government. In villages and cities across Pakistan, Basic Democrats 'came to be ridiculed as *Bekas*, or helpless, Democrats'.[89]

In social terms, Ayub Khan's administration turned Pakistan into a testing ground for a raft of 'modernisation' initiatives in the fields of education, public health, land reform and civil administration.[90] Ambitious programmes were launched to kick-start economic growth and overcome problems associated with runaway population expansion, agricultural underproduction and industrial stagnation. Showpiece projects such as the new model town constructed at Korangi, seven miles north-east of Karachi, were referenced as symbols of a new and forward-looking Pakistan. Women's rights were advanced through laws making divorce less arbitrary and the implementation of measures to discourage the practice of polygamy and promote the use of birth control. The secular thrust of Ayub Khan's vision of modernity saw the 'Islamic' designation removed from the official nomenclature of the Republic of Pakistan. By departing so fundamentally from the interpretation of Islamic orthodoxy promoted by Pakistan's influential *ulama*, or arbiters of Muslim laws and customs, the Pakistan government made a powerful political enemy.[91] Toward the end of his period in office, Ayub Khan berated the 'idiots or rascals' amongst Pakistan's *ulama*

[88] 'Pakistan's Ayub Khan: The Asian "de Gaulle"', *Newsweek*, 19 April 1960.
[89] Anatol Lieven, *Pakistan: A Hard Country* (London: Penguin, 2012), p. 156.
[90] The most influential treatise on 'modernisation theory' at the time was Walt W. Rostow's *The Stages of Economic Growth: A Non-Communist Manifesto* (Cambridge University Press, 1960). Rostow went on to serve in the Kennedy administration in the early 1960s, and had a significant impact on US international economic policy. See Chapter 3.
[91] Lord Saint Brides to Major General S. Shahid Hamid (Pakistan minister for information and broadcasting), 'The Projection of Pakistan in Western Countries in 1979', 17 August 1979, RCMS 68/6 Morrice James Papers, Royal Commonwealth Society Library, University of Cambridge.

who 'in the name of Islam … are dead against progress and society having the right to think for itself'. Through repeated efforts to discredit his government's attempts 'to bring enlightenment and salvation' to the Muslim *millat*, or nation, Pakistan's president complained, conservative elements within the *ulama* had shown themselves to be 'the deadliest enemy of the educated Muslim'.[92]

Economically, the Pakistani state ploughed capital investment into its industrial and agricultural sectors in a bid to pump-prime growth. Over the course of Pakistan's second five-year plan (1960–5), agricultural production surged, annual manufacturing output rose by 11.5 per cent, and per capita income increased by 14 per cent. The benefits associated with economic growth, however, were not evenly distributed across Pakistani society, and served to inflame rather than to ameliorate smouldering class tensions and regional animosities. In 1960, the annual growth rate in East Pakistan of 5.2 per cent lagged well behind that in West Pakistan at 7.2 per cent. The poorest sections of Pakistani society were hit hardest by rises in the costs of consumer goods and foodstuffs brought on by an inflationary spiral, a decline in average real wages, and inadequacies in the provision of housing, transport and sanitation in the country's burgeoning urban centres. Ultimately, the maldistribution of wealth that accompanied Pakistan's economic boom was to prove politically toxic, as the absolute numbers of the country's citizenry living in poverty soared.[93]

Further afield, Pakistan's government displayed a similar degree of energy and enterprise in seeking a modus vivendi with its India neighbour. In May 1959, Ayub Khan proposed putting in place a loose Indo-Pakistani arrangement for the joint defence of the subcontinent. Nehru brusquely dismissed the Pakistani initiative as incompatible with his government's aversion to mutual security pacts. 'We do not propose to have a military alliance with any country, come what may', the Indian leader announced in the Rajya Sabha (upper house of the Indian parliament) on 4 May, 'and I want to be clear about it.'[94] The following September, when the two South Asian leaders met at Muree, a hill station in northern Pakistan, Ayub Khan was equally unsuccessful in his efforts to persuade Nehru to revisit the Kashmir question. 'I did not get the impression that Nehru was interested in any long-term and lasting

---

[92] Diary entry for Tuesday 6 September 1966, in Craig Baxter (ed.) *Diaries of Field Marshal Mohammad Ayub Khan, 1966–1972* (Karachi: Oxford University Press, 2007), p. 5.

[93] Record of meeting between James and Freeman in Karachi, 1 and 2 February 1966, FO 371/186952/F1041/30, TNA; Talbot, *Pakistan*, pp. 169–71.

[94] 'India: The Lone Fireman', *Time*, 18 May 1959.

[Indo-Pakistan] solution', Ayub Khan noted later. 'He was, perhaps, not averse to the dialogue going on for the time being, but he was not visualizing a future of understanding between the two countries.'[95]

In a broader international context, America's burgeoning relationship with India, and Washington's apparent inability to soften Nehru's uncompromising attitude on matters of mutual Indo-Pakistani interest, encouraged Ayub Khan's government to underwrite Pakistan's national security by cultivating closer ties with its Russian and Chinese neighbours. In May 1960, the Pakistan government's unease over the continued utility of its alliance with the United States multiplied following the downing of an American U-2 spy plane over the Soviet Union. The American aircraft had entered Soviet airspace after taking off from a US facility at Peshawar, in northern Pakistan. In the wake of the U-2 incident, Nikita Khrushchev chided Pakistan's ambassador in Moscow, pointedly asking the diplomat, 'Where is this place Peshawar? We have circled it in red on our maps.' Khrushchev need only have consulted the pages of *Newsweek* or *The New York Times* for the answer to his question. To the consternation of Pakistani officials, both American publications had printed large maps identifying the location of US military bases inside Pakistan.[96] One month after the U-2 debacle, Pakistan reached an agreement with Moscow to mount a joint search for oil deposits in the vicinity of Attock, close to the Soviet–Pakistan border. Shortly afterwards, to India's fury, Rawalpindi confirmed its intention to enter into negotiations with the PRC to demarcate the border between China and Azad, or Free, Pakistani-occupied Kashmir. Pakistan's message to Washington was clear. In the absence of a comprehensive Indo-Pakistani accord, the United States' rapprochement with India would be treated by Pakistan as a direct threat to the country's national interests. Over the following decade, Eisenhower's successors in the White House would confront the inconvenient fact that, in seeking to hedge American bets in the Indian subcontinent, the United States risked squandering the loyalties of both old allies and new friends.

### 'India loves Ike'

In December 1959, as his second term in office came to a close, President Eisenhower set off on a nineteen-day valedictory trip around the globe,

[95] Ayub Khan, *Friends Not Masters*, pp. 125–8; Bunker to Bartlett, 24 December 1959, RG 59, Office of South Asian Affairs, 1957–9, Lot file 62D43, Box 24, Folder India Economic 1959 2 of 2, NARA.
[96] 'Call by Pakistan Foreign Minister Qadir on Secretary: The U-2 Incident and Soviet Pressures on Pakistan', 2 June 1960, RG 59, State Department Central Files, 033.90D11/6-260, NARA.

or 'Flight to Peace' tour. Eisenhower had long harboured an ambition
to visit the Indian subcontinent, and on 7 December he became the first
American president to step foot in South Asia when his Boeing 707 jet
touched down at Karachi's Mauripur airport. After spending just forty
hours in Pakistan, a good portion of which was spent taking in a cricket
test match between Pakistan and Australia, another presidential first,
Eisenhower moved on to India, passing briefly through Afghanistan en
route. In a reflection of the direction in which his foreign policy priorities had shifted over the previous four years, Eisenhower remained
in India for five days, between 9 and 14 December. As Air Force One
appeared in the skies over New Delhi, escorted by eighteen Hunter jet
fighters from the Indian Air Force, Eisenhower's Indian counterpart,
Rajendra Prasad, Jawaharlal Nehru, the entire Indian cabinet, two
thousand assorted dignitaries and many more well-wishers, assembled
to greet the US leader. As Eisenhower emerged onto the airport tarmac,
he was met with 'thunderous applause and loud cheers'. Throughout
the twelve-mile road journey into the centre of India's capital, crowds
thirty-to-forty deep lined the route, eager to catch a glimpse of 'India's
American friend'.[97] Nehru was taken aback by the response of ordinary Indians to Eisenhower's arrival, informing his American guest that
New Delhi had not witnessed such an outpouring of popular enthusiasm since the country's Independence Day celebrations, back in August
1947. 'The whole teeming boisterous, confused, happy crowd outdid
in size anything I had ever seen,' Eisenhower later recorded, 'including those of the victory celebrations in the great cities of America and
Europe.'[98]

Indian and American officials had anticipated that Eisenhower
would receive a warm welcome in New Delhi. The importance that
the president had come to place on assisting the economic and social
progress of countries within the developing world, and in India above
all, had earned him many friends in the subcontinent. Even so, as
Indira Gandhi confided to an American acquaintance, the interest
and genuine affection that Eisenhower generated amongst her com-
patriots 'exceeded our expectations'.[99] In an uncharacteristic display
of ebullience, Ellsworth Bunker reported that the president's visit to

---

[97] 'India News', Newspaper issued by the Information Service of India, Indian Embassy,
Washington, DC, 15 December 1959, Box 43, Folder 1959, Dorothy Norman Papers,
Butler Library, Columbia University, New York.

[98] Eisenhower, *Waging Peace*, p. 499.

[99] Indira Gandhi to Dorothy Norman, New Delhi, 22 December 1959, in Dorothy
Norman, *Indira Gandhi: Letters to an American Friend, 1950–1984* (New York:
Harcourt Brace Jovanovich, 1985), p. 46.

India had been 'an unprecedented success'. 'Nothing remotely comparable to it has even happened here before', Bunker informed the State Department. 'The President's ability to project his personality, his integrity of character and purpose, his simplicity and friendliness to the average Indian was extraordinary.' In the American ambassador's view, Eisenhower's five days in India had a transformative impact on Indo-US relations. The president, Bunker cabled back to Washington, 'succeeded in breaking down the last psychological barriers which had grown up between our two countries after World War II; these barriers had been gradually diminishing from the time of Suez and the President completed the job'.[100]

On a personal level, Nehru and Eisenhower proved to be just as relaxed and comfortable in each other's company as they had back in 1956. In a speech delivered in the American leader's presence on 11 December, the Indian premier reflected upon the 'exhibitions of popular love and enthusiasm' that Indians at all levels had extended to the president. Eisenhower, Nehru added, was 'a great person', who had 'found an echo in the hearts of our millions'.[101] Significantly, India's prime minister took a more sober view of the wider implications for India's relations with the United States of Eisenhower's visit to the subcontinent. It was 'all to the good', Nehru informed his chief ministers once Eisenhower had left India, 'that there is a greater mutual understanding between these two countries now'. 'That does not mean, as some people imagine', the Indian prime minister continued, 'that we have moved away from our basic policies.'[102]

Indeed, as the Eisenhower government discovered, and, in turn, subsequent administrations in the United States would reluctantly come to concede, American economic and military intervention in the Indian subcontinent invariably yielded disappointing political returns. By the time Eisenhower left the Oval Office in January 1961, feelings of Indo-US amity had reached new and unprecedented heights. Yet, in taking a 'New Look' at South Asia, Eisenhower was unable to substantively affect India's foreign policy, dampen Indo-Pakistani enmity or check Soviet influence in the subcontinent. Washington's shift in regional policy, however, did succeed in placing the United States'

---

[100] Bunker to Bartlett, 24 December 1959, RG 59, Office of South Asian Affairs, 1957–9, Lot 62D43, Box 24, Folder India Economic 1959 2 of 2, NARA.

[101] Nehru's Speech at Opening of World Agricultural Fair, 11 December 1959, RG 59, Office of South Asian Affairs, 1957–9, Lot 62D43, Box 24, Folder India Economic 1959 2 of 2, NARA.

[102] Nehru to Chief Ministers, New Delhi, 15 December 1959, in *Letters to Chief Ministers*, vol. 5: *1958–1964*, p. 343.

alliance with Pakistan under unparalleled strain. The notion that complex and interconnected regional problems could prove resistant to the application of American power sat uncomfortably with Eisenhower's youthful and activist successor. Over the following three years, John F. Kennedy, and the best and brightest members of his New Frontier, would deepen America's involvement in the subcontinent, confident that they could succeed where previous US policymakers had failed, and establish close and constructive relations with both India *and* Pakistan.

# 3    The best of friends: Kennedy, Macmillan and Jawaharlal Nehru

In November 1959, while campaigning in California to secure the Democratic Party's nomination for the following year's presidential election, the United States Senator for Massachusetts, John F. Kennedy, declared that

no struggle in the world deserves more time and attention from this [Eisenhower's] Administration – and the next – than that which now grips the attention of all of Asia … that is the struggle between India and China for the economic and political leadership of the East … We want India to win that race with Red China. We want India to be a free and thriving leader of a free and thriving Asia.[1]

Elected to the Senate back in 1953, Kennedy's early political career had been plagued by serious bouts of ill health and prolonged absences from Washington. By the late 1950s, however, Kennedy had completed a remarkable physical and political transformation. Repositioning himself as a contender to succeed Eisenhower as America's 35th president, Kennedy championed the notion that the Cold War's locus had shifted away from the entrenched battle lines of Western Europe, and toward the fluid political landscape of the developing world. It was in the developing world, Kennedy believed, that America should abandon its traditional emphasis on formal alliances and military pacts, and instead adopt a flexible approach toward non-alignment and the provision of developmental aid. Failure to do so, the Senator suggested, would risk key non-aligned states such as India, Indonesia and Egypt falling under communist sway, tilting the balance of Cold War forces decisively against the West.[2]

[1] Kennedy Speech delivered at Riverside, California, 1 November 1959, *The Strategy of Peace* (New York: Popular Library Publishers, 1961), pp. 177–8.
[2] See, for example, Kennedy's speech to the United States Senate delivered on 25 March 1958, 'The Choice in Asia – Democratic Development in India'. John F. Kennedy, *A Compilation of Statements and Speeches Made During His Service in the United States Senate and the House of Representatives* (Washington, DC: Government Printing Office, 1964), pp. 591–608.

No country figured more prominently in Kennedy's thinking than India. A committed internationalist and keen student of foreign affairs, Kennedy looked upon the preservation of a strong and democratic India as a prerequisite for the containment of communism in Asia. In his estimation, the contest between India and the PRC to become Asia's dominant power represented nothing less than '*the* decisive struggle in the Cold War'.[3] With the PRC outpacing India in steel production, industrial capacity, literacy rates and domestic consumption, Kennedy worried that a failure to contain Communist China would leave subsequent generations of Americans facing an apocalyptic future. Looking forward into the 1970s, he speculated that, left unchecked, the PRC, with 700 million citizens, nuclear weapons, a Stalinist internal regime and an expansionist outlook, would pose the greatest threat to global peace and security since the end of the Second World War.[4]

Calls for a programme of expanded American financial assistance to India, and greater tolerance on the part of his countrymen toward Nehruvian non-alignment, became key foreign policy planks in Kennedy's bid for the White House.[5] In March 1958, in conjunction with John Sherman Cooper, Republican Senator for Kentucky and one-time US ambassador to India, Kennedy placed the Kennedy–Cooper Resolution before the US Senate. The Resolution, through which India eventually received $150 million in exchange credits from the Export–Import Bank, and a further $75 million from a newly established overseas loan fund, cemented Kennedy's image as a leading advocate of Third World development. Two years later, in April 1960, as the race to succeed Eisenhower gathered pace, another former US ambassador to India, and one of Kennedy's principal foreign policy advisers at the time, Chester Bowles, underscored the strategic rationale for accelerating India's development, in an influential article published by the journal *Foreign Affairs*. Amongst the newly independent nations of Asia, Bowles contested, India alone had the requisite economic and military potential to prevent Communist China with its 'inadequate resource base, spiralling population, ruthless Communist leadership and intense

---

[3] Kennedy, *Strategy*, p. 264.
[4] 'President Kennedy News Conference 59', Washington, DC, 1 August 1963, *Public Papers of the Presidents of the United States* (hereafter *PPP-US*), *John F. Kennedy, 1963*, The American Presidency Project, www.presidency.ucsb.edu/ws/.
[5] Kennedy had declared in 1959, 'if neutrality is the result of a concentration on internal problems, raising the standard of living of the people and so on ... I would accept that'. Kennedy's interview with *Harper's Magazine*, 9 December 1959, reproduced in Kennedy, *Strategy*, pp. 260–8.

nationalist spirit ... [from] develop[ing] fiercely expansionist tendencies directed toward the weaker neighbouring states to the south'.[6]

Having narrowly defeated Richard Nixon in November's presidential election, Kennedy and his fledgling administration moved swiftly to offer India economic and political support. Indeed, Kennedy's inauguration on the steps of the Capitol building, on a bitterly cold January morning in 1961, heralded the beginning of a new and controversial phase in the United States' relationship with South Asia. Strengthening America's existing relationship with India, Kennedy's government recognised, threatened an open schism in the US alliance with Pakistan. When accepting the Democratic Party's presidential nomination back in July 1960, the future president had proclaimed that his country stood 'on the edge of a New Frontier ... of unknown opportunities and perils'.[7] However, the hubris of Kennedy's 'New Frontier' administration, as it subsequently came to be known, coupled with the president's personal conviction that India had a pivotal role to play in the Cold War in Asia, encouraged the White House to run significant risks with US-Pakistani relations.[8] Although striving, like Eisenhower before him, to foster close ties with India and Pakistan, once in office, Kennedy leaned toward India. Setting to one side formal US security commitments to Rawalpindi, and the presence of valued American intelligence assets on Pakistani soil, Kennedy's administration resolved that, 'if we must choose amongst these countries, there is little question that India ... is where we must put our chief reliance'.[9]

## America's new best friend

In seeking to build upon the rapprochement in Indo-US relations begun under Eisenhower, the Kennedy administration faced an uphill battle in overcoming a propensity amongst Americans and Indians alike to view the other through a distorted cultural prism. As previously noted, during the 1950s popular American perceptions of India and its

[6] Chester Bowles, 'The "China Problem" Reconsidered', *Foreign Affairs*, 38 (April 1960), 477.

[7] Presidential Candidate John F. Kennedy, Acceptance Speech, Democratic National Convention, Los Angeles, 15 July 1960, TNC-191-E5, John F. Kennedy Library, Boston, Massachusetts (hereafter JFKL).

[8] Komer to McGeorge Bundy, 6 January 1962, *Foreign Relations of the United States* (hereafter *FRUS*), *1961–1963*, vol. XIX (Washington, DC: Government Printing Office, 1996), p. 180.

[9] Stephen Cohen, 'US Weapons and South Asia: A Policy Analysis', *Pacific Affairs*, 49 (1976), 49–69; Komer to Bundy, 6 January 1962, *FRUS, 1961–1963*, vol. XIX, p. 180.

inhabitants were largely negative. In the foreign policy field, Americans generally looked upon India's government as unashamedly hypocritical and woefully naive. The US media delighted in lambasting Jawaharlal Nehru's supposed duplicity in endorsing Cold War non-alignment and Gandhian principles of non-violence while at the same time resorting to military force whenever India's interests appeared threatened, most evidently in Kashmir in 1947, Hyderabad in 1948 and Goa in 1961.[10]

Within the upper echelons of Kennedy's government, an aversion toward Indians in general, and senior Indian policymakers in particular, was endemic. Having replaced Ellsworth Bunker as US ambassador in New Delhi with a prominent economist and close political associate, the Harvard academic John Kenneth Galbraith, Kennedy subsequently characterised the appointment as Galbraith's 'period of penance'.[11] Likewise, although some Kennedy acolytes would later assert that 'the President liked Nehru',[12] his brother Robert provided a typically more candid appraisal of their relationship. Far from warming to India's premier, Robert Kennedy revealed that his elder sibling found Nehru to be arrogant and condescending.[13] Moreover, the White House felt deep irritation at the anti-American sentiment expressed by some Indian government officials and, in particular, Nehru's defence minister, Krishna Menon.[14] In choosing to ignore Indian invective and forge closer ties with Nehru's government, Kennedy placed political expediency above personal sentiment. Robert Komer, Kennedy's charismatic National Security Council (NSC) adviser on South Asia, underlined that, from the administration's perspective, when it came to dealing with India, strategic necessity trumped cultural prejudice. 'No Westerner who goes [to South Asia],' Komer asserted, 'unless he's a terrible romantic or a mystic ... ends up liking Indians better than Pak[istani]s. The

[10] Revealingly, having interviewed a cross-section of influential Americans in the mid-1950s, Harold Issacs' pioneering study of Indo-US relations found that only 28 per cent of those polled held a favourable impression of India. The majority of respondents with a negative attitude typically attributed this to India's 'defensive arrogance', which in turn induced feelings of 'annoyance, antipathy, and even outrage'. Harold Issacs, *Scratches on Our Minds: American Views of China and India* (New York: John Day, 1958), pp. 328–9 and 381–2. On this subject, see also Andrew Rotter, *Comrades at Odds: The United States and India, 1947–1964* (London: Cornell University Press, 2000), p. 20.

[11] Theodore Sorensen, *Kennedy* (New York: Harper & Row, 1965), p. 395.

[12] *Ibid.*, p. 578.

[13] Gerald Strober and Deborah Strober (eds.), *'Let us Begin Anew': An Oral History of the Kennedy Presidency* (New York: Harper Collins, 1993), Robert Kennedy interviews with John Stewart, 20 July and 1 August 1967, p. 437. See also Robert J. McMahon, *The Cold War on the Periphery: The United States, India and Pakistan* (New York: Columbia University Press, 1994), p. 281.

[14] Phillips Talbot, Oral History (hereafter OH), 27 July 1965, pp. 17–18, JFKL.

Pak[istani]s are just much more engaging ... it was almost despite our prejudices that we were going in that [India's] direction.'[15]

Within the subcontinent, a reciprocal antipathy toward American culture and values flourished among influential sections of Indian society. On a visit to the subcontinent in 1958, Harold Macmillan noted with wry amusement that Nehru had 'deplored the Americanisation of India' and had introduced strict limits on the domestic broadcast of American popular music.[16] Equally, the distaste that Kennedy felt toward Nehru was returned in full measure by the Indian leader. Nehru, who had enjoyed a notably convivial relationship with President Eisenhower, privately dismissed Kennedy as 'brash, aggressive and inexperienced'.[17] However, from the late 1950s, as economic aid from the United States began to flood into the subcontinent in ever-larger quantity, many Indians, from Nehru downward, began to moderate the tone of their anti-American rhetoric. In July 1960, Britain's High Commissioner in India, Malcolm MacDonald, observed with surprise that Indians, at all levels, had started to 'revise their earlier critical, and even hostile, attitude to America'.[18] The roots of this transformation, the British suspected, lay in Nehru's recognition that the success or failure of India's economic development plans hinged, to a substantial degree, on the continued flow of capital investment from the United States.[19] Accordingly, whatever mutual distaste lay beneath the veneer of goodwill established between India and the United States in the late 1950s, Kennedy and Nehru were far too pragmatic and politically savvy to allow it to intrude into the conduct of Indo-US relations.

In fact, having closely followed Kennedy's evolution into a prominent advocate of Indian economic development, Nehru welcomed his election victory over Richard Nixon. Responding in kind, speaking before a joint session of Congress, Kennedy went out of his way to praise the Indian leader's 'soaring idealism'.[20] So eager was Kennedy to inject substance into his administration's pro-Indian rhetoric that, while

[15] Robert Komer, OH, 30 January 1970, pp. 32–3, JFKL.
[16] 'Prime Minister's Commonwealth Tour', 4 June 1958, CAB 129/93, C (58), 120, The United Kingdom National Archives, Kew, London (hereafter TNA).
[17] According to Gopal, of the post-war US presidents, Truman's 'cocky vulgarity' offended Nehru, as did the ostentatious 'affluence and glitter' surrounding Kennedy's Camelot. It was Eisenhower's embodiment of 'sincerity and goodwill' that the Indian leader found most appealing. Sarvepalli Gopal, *Jawaharlal Nehru: A Biography*, vol. 3: *1956–1964* (London: Jonathan Cape, 1984), pp. 189–90.
[18] 'India: Shifts in Indian Foreign Policy', Malcolm MacDonald to Lord Home, 13 July 1960, DO 196/125, TNA.
[19] 'India: November 1960 to May 1962', Gore-Booth to Sandys, 7 June 1962, DO 196/75, TNA.
[20] Gopal, *Nehru: 1956–1964*, p. 187.

still president-elect, he convened a special taskforce to examine ways of further stimulating India's economic development. Walt W. Rostow, MIT's guru of Third World development and proponent of modernisation theory, led the taskforce. Rostow had come to public prominence in 1960 with the publication of his assault on Marxist economic theory, *The Stages of Economic Growth: A Non-Communist Manifesto*. Outlining five stages of growth through which all economies passed, Rostow's book argued that it was incumbent upon the United States and other Western nations experiencing an 'age of mass consumption' to assist less developed countries, such as India, to achieve economic 'take-off'.[21] An economic adviser to Kennedy since 1957, Rostow had provided the then Senator for Massachusetts with the intellectual ammunition to attack the Eisenhower administration for leaving underdeveloped economies to stagnate, and failing to stem the appeal of Marxism–Leninism in the Third World.[22]

When Rostow's taskforce concluded that India should be offered massive US financial support, Kennedy endorsed its principal finding.[23] In the Kennedy administration's first foreign aid budget for the fiscal year 1962, India was subsequently allocated an unprecedented $500 million in economic assistance. The remainder of the developing world was left to make do with less than half this figure.[24] Eager for other Western countries to follow his administration's example, Kennedy applied political pressure on America's allies to supply India with similarly generous amounts of developmental aid. In April 1961, at an international aid meeting in Washington, sponsored by the International Bank for Reconstruction and Development (IBRD), US officials cajoled a consortium of countries, including Britain, West Germany and Japan, to match an American commitment to pump $1 billion dollars into the first two years of India's third five-year plan (1961–6).[25] Unsurprisingly, Kennedy's success in securing greater international economic assistance for India was well received in New Delhi. Writing to Kennedy in the aftermath of the aid consortium meeting, Nehru expressed

---

[21] Walt W. Rostow, *The Stages of Economic Growth: A Non-Communist Manifesto* (Cambridge University Press, 1960), p. 134. See also Walt W. Rostow, *Diffusion of Power: An Essay in Recent History* (New York: Macmillan, 1972).

[22] An insightful analysis of Rostow's relationship with Kennedy can be found in David Milne, *America's Rasputin: Walt Rostow and the Vietnam War* (New York: Hill and Wang, 2008). See also Kimber Charles Pearce, *Rostow, Kennedy and the Rhetoric of Foreign Aid* (East Lansing: Michigan State University Press, 2001).

[23] McMahon, *Cold War on the Periphery*, p. 273.

[24] Dennis Merrill, *Bread and the Ballot: The United States and India's Economic Development, 1947–1963* (Chapel Hill: The University of North Carolina Press, 1990), p. 175.

[25] Ball to Kennedy, 19 April 1961, *FRUS, 1961–1963*, vol. XIX, p. 33.

his deep gratitude for 'the goodwill and generous assistance of the United States'.[26] Visiting the subcontinent at the time, John Sherman Cooper noted with satisfaction that following Kennedy's election, the United States' standing in India had reached new and unprecedented heights.[27]

The perception that India represented 'big business' in the Kennedy White House was reinforced by the appointment of high profile friends of India, such as Chester Bowles, Phillips Talbot and John Kenneth Galbraith, to senior positions in the new administration. In New Delhi, the Indian government looked on with approval as having first appointed Bowles as his Under Secretary of State, Kennedy broke with convention by naming a South Asian expert, Phillips Talbot, rather than a Middle Eastern specialist, as Assistant Secretary of State for Near Eastern and South Asia Affairs. Kennedy's decision to install John Kenneth Galbraith as his ambassador to India had an even greater impact in the subcontinent. A well-connected and vocal Democratic Party activist, the Harvard professor cut an imposing figure. Sir Paul Gore-Booth, Malcolm MacDonald's successor as Britain's High Commissioner in India, later reflected that he 'had to run all the time to keep up intellectually and physically with the six foot eight and half inches of Galbraith'.[28] On intimate political terms with Kennedy, Galbraith's presence in New Delhi ensured that Indian issues were never far from the top of the presidential in-tray.[29] Equally, as the author of such left-of-centre polemics as *The Affluent Society* and *The Liberal Hour*, Kennedy's emissary quickly established a rapport with India's socialist leader.[30] Galbraith reflected subsequently that 'Friendship with Nehru came easily ... our relations remained informal and infinitely agreeable.'[31]

With Kennedy's Secretary of State, Dean Rusk, preoccupied by the Soviet threat to Europe, Kennedy enjoyed ample latitude for indulging his interest in the Third World. Moreover, when it came to the Indian subcontinent, as one administration official with responsibility for South

---

[26] Nehru to Kennedy, 24 May 1961, cited in Gopal, *Nehru: 1956–1964*, pp. 187–8.
[27] 'Notes on My Talks in India', undated, circa January 1961, India, John Sherman Cooper, President's Office Files, JFKL.
[28] Paul Gore-Booth, *With Great Truth and Respect* (London: Constable, 1974), p. 74.
[29] Robert Komer, OH, 3 September 1964, p. 13, JFKL. The Pakistani government felt aggrieved that, as Ayub informed one Western diplomat, America's ambassador to Pakistan 'cut much [less] ice with Mr. Kennedy than Galbraith evidently did, who could "see Mr. Kennedy in his bathroom" if he wished to'. 'United States Diplomatic Affairs', Morrice James to Joe Garner, 10 February 1962, DO 19/132, f. 64, TNA.
[30] John Kenneth Galbraith, *The Affluent Society* (London: Penguin Books, 1958); *The Liberal Hour* (London: Hamish Hamilton, 1960).
[31] John Kenneth Galbraith, *A Life in Our Times: Memoirs* (London: Andre Deutsch, 1981), p. 407.

Asia confirmed, 'there really wasn't the same high degree of interest on the part of senior officials of the government than there was on the part of the President himself'.[32] Kennedy frequently ignored bureaucratic protocol and bypassed Rusk to deal directly with the State Department's South Asian desk officers. Administration officials responsible for South Asian affairs, such as Robert Komer, duly exploited every opportunity to encourage Kennedy's interest in the region. Like Kennedy, a Harvard graduate and Second World War combat veteran, Komer epitomised the aura of intellectual activism prized within New Frontier circles.[33] In Komer's view, the Eisenhower administration's policy of favouring 100 million Pakistanis over 500 million Indians made little sense. Arguably Kennedy's 'most effective advocate of a pro-Indian policy', Komer's formidable energy and uncompromising style ensured that the Washington bureaucracy came under sustained pressure to deliver Kennedy's agenda for change in the subcontinent.[34]

This was just as well, as Kennedy's decision to forge closer ties with Nehru's government encountered stiff resistance from the Pentagon and the State Department. The US defence establishment, in particular, having invested heavily in its relationship with Pakistan since 1954, was set against alienating a valued ally by developing closer American links to non-aligned India. Significantly, however, Robert McNamara, Kennedy's Secretary of Defense, was less averse to running risks with the United States' military relationship with Pakistan. Drafted in by Kennedy from the Ford Motor Company to run the Pentagon, McNamara arrived in Washington with the reputation as an intellectually formidable and politically inexperienced technocrat, wedded to the analytical principles of scientific management.[35] Prepared to challenge conventional military wisdom, McNamara calculated that the Pentagon's substantial investment in Pakistan had failed to deliver appropriate strategic returns. Rather than focus on the expansionist threat posed by its northern Soviet neighbour, Kennedy's Secretary of Defense highlighted the uncomfortable reality that instead, Pakistan had directed the vast majority of its US military assistance into preparing

[32] Robert Komer, OH, 18 June 1964, pp. 1–2, JFKL.
[33] Noam Kochavi, *A Conflict Perpetuated: China Policy during the Kennedy Years* (London: Praeger, 2002), pp. 74–5.
[34] See McMahon, *Cold War on the Periphery*, p. 275; John Prados, *Keepers of the Keys: A History of the National Security Council from Truman to Bush* (New York: Morrow, 1991), p. 232.
[35] The magazine *Business Week* characterised McNamara as a 'prize specimen of a remarkable breed in US industry – the trained specialist in the science of business management who is also a generalist moving easily from one technical area to another'. *Business Week*, 11 February 1961.

to fight a fratricidal conflict with India.[36] Frustratingly for Kennedy, at the State Department, Dean Rusk proved less willing than McNamara to countenance an adjustment in the United States' relationship with Pakistan. Naturally cautious, and with more than a hint of Dulles-era antipathy toward Indian non-alignment in his make-up, Rusk queried the necessity of revising America's established regional policy and tilting further toward India. Moreover, in the CIA, which attached great importance to its network of intelligence-gathering facilities inside Pakistan, Rusk found a powerful ally. 'There was a natural cleavage between the old [South Asian] policy and the new,' one administration figure later observed, 'and the institutional guardians of the old policy died fairly hard.'[37]

A goodwill visit that the US vice-president, Lyndon Johnson, made to India in May 1961 provided the Kennedy administration with an early opportunity to gauge whether the hand of friendship that it had extended to Nehru's government was likely to reap a political dividend. Characteristically, Johnson garnered headlines in India for his unorthodox and intensely personal diplomatic style. On his way to visit Old Delhi's historic Lal Qila, or Red Fort, the vice-president startled his police escort, press entourage and Indian onlookers by ordering his driver to a sudden halt and plunging into a sea of bodies jamming a narrow lane. Declaring loudly to a crowd of puzzled bystanders that 'India and America are friends and will ever so remain', Johnson proceeded to deliver a stump speech extolling the virtues of Indo-American amity, which a breathless State Department interpreter translated into halting Hindi.[38] Johnson's official reception in New Delhi, although warm, merely reaffirmed Nehru's commitment to an Indian foreign policy based on strict non-alignment. Notably, the vice-president's suggestion that Nehru work with the United States in containing communism in Asia fell flat.[39] Charging communist forces with sowing 'widespread discontent, and in some cases violent insurrection' across South East Asia, Johnson urged Nehru 'to speak out "in stirring and ringing tones" against Communist-led insurgencies in Laos and South Vietnam'.[40] Instead, India's premier stuck to vague platitudes emphasising his government's determination to promote regional stability.[41] Ignoring

[36] Robert Komer, OH, 30 January 1970, pp. 26–7, JFKL.
[37] *Ibid.*
[38] 'Roadside Speech', *National Herald*, Lucknow, 19 May 1961.
[39] Galbraith to Rusk, No. 2751, 19 May 1961, National Security File (NSF), Box 242A, 5/61, JFKL.
[40] Berger to Bowles, No. 1951, 21 May 1961, NSF, Box 242A, 5/61, JFKL.
[41] Johnson–Nehru talks, New Delhi, 18 May 1961, *FRUS, 1961–1963*, vol. XIX, pp. 41–2.

Nehru's rebuff, Johnson placed a positive spin on his encounter with the Indian leader. Having been met with 'friendliness beyond expectation', the vice-president reported back to Washington, he had left New Delhi with 'real hope that India can be induced to provide [regional] leadership'.[42]

Galbraith's reports from New Delhi provided Kennedy with an equally upbeat assessment of his administration's impact in the subcontinent.[43] Although conceding that American economic benevolence had yet to deliver tangible political results in India, it had, Galbraith suggested, enhanced the general Indian impression of Kennedy and his government as 'liberal and compassionate and much interested in Indian problems'.[44] Following a further round of official Indo-US talks, in New Delhi, in the summer, Chester Bowles proved similarly sanguine, noting with approval that the Indian premier appeared 'very favourably inclined toward the United States'.[45] Yet, as Johnson's experience in India had suggested, the Kennedy administration's ability to translate abundant Indian goodwill into political leverage with Nehru's government was to prove frustratingly elusive over the course of the subsequent three years.

## Clinging on: the Macmillan government and India

The Macmillan government had worked hard to place Anglo-Indian relations back on an even keel following the Suez crisis in 1956. Toward the end of 1961, however, Britain's relations with India once again took a turn for the worse. The previous October, when Sir Paul Gore-Booth replaced Malcolm MacDonald as Britain's High Commissioner in New Delhi, Indo-British relations remained good. The disintegration of MacDonald's marriage had led to the disgruntled High Commissioner being peremptorily recalled to London prior to an official visit to India and Pakistan by Queen Elizabeth II. Under the restrictive British social mores of the time, Whitehall deemed it inappropriate for a High Commissioner with divorce proceedings hanging in the air to receive the Queen. Having spent just one day with MacDonald in London, and rushing through the CRO's list of recommended Indian reading, which encompassed Rudyard Kipling's *Kim*, E. M. Forster's *A Passage to India*

---

[42] Berger to Bowles, No. 1951, 21 May 1961, NSF, Box 242A, 5/61, JFKL.
[43] Entry for 21 May 1961, New Delhi, John Kenneth Galbraith, *Ambassador's Journal: A Personal Account of the Kennedy Years* (Boston: Houghton Mifflin, 1969), p. 121.
[44] Galbraith to Rusk, No. 2767, 20 May 1961, NSF, Box 242A, 5/61, JFKL.
[45] Memorandum of conversation between Bowles and Nehru, New Delhi, 8–9 August 1961, *FRUS, 1961–1963*, vol. XIX, pp. 82–6.

and, perhaps more usefully, Nehru's *Discovery of India*, Gore-Booth arrived in the subcontinent in the late summer of 1960 full of optimism.[46] Writing to a fellow old Indian hand, Morrice James, Deputy UK High Commissioner in New Delhi, enthused that Gore-Booth 'has great drive and charm and will be a huge success here ... I think this will be a stimulating and constructive time'.[47] The upbeat attitude evidenced by British officials was reinforced by the reception that Queen Elizabeth received across India, in early 1961.[48] The first British monarch to visit the subcontinent since independence, in a speech broadcast over All India Radio on 1 March, the Queen thanked her hosts for the warmth of their welcome and suggested that the royal tour had 'set the seal on a new relationship between Britain and India'.[49]

Within a matter of months, any semblance of Indo-British goodwill had evaporated in the wake of a succession of disputes between London and New Delhi over colonial policy, the Congo, Britain's application to join the European Economic Community (EEC) and Commonwealth immigration. In September, having met with Krishna Menon, whom he had befriended back in the 1930s, Lord Mountbatten cautioned the CRO that he had 'never known him [Menon] in such a depressed state about relations between India and the UK.'[50] More seriously, the British noted that the Indian premier himself appeared 'aggressively and meanly out of sorts with the UK'[51] The 'sad and serious' deterioration that had taken place in Britain's relations with India, the CRO concluded, was due in large measure to Nehru's distaste for the United Kingdom's colonial policy. 'Mr. Nehru', British officials bemoaned, 'is the principal and most damaging mouthpiece of Indian anti-colonialism. It seems plain that his attitude derives more from innate personal prejudice than from factual knowledge of what happens in the Colonies.'[52]

---

[46] United Kingdom High Commission Notes for Officers appointed to New Delhi, undated, c. 1960, DO 35/2644, TNA; Gore-Booth, *Truth and Respect*, p. 264.
[47] Morrice James to Gilbert Laithwaite, 14 December 1960, MSS EUR F 138/149, Sir John Gilbert Laithwaite Papers, India Office Select Materials, British Library.
[48] See, for example, 'A Million People Cheer the Queen: Delhi's Affectionate Welcome', *National Herald*, Lucknow, 22 January 1961; '1,500,000 Hail Queen, Consort in Delhi', *The Hindustan Times*, New Delhi, 22 January 1961.
[49] 'Tour Has Set the Seal on New Indo-British Ties, Says Queen', *The Hindustan Times*, New Delhi, 2 March 1961.
[50] Mountbatten to Sandys, 19 September 1961, MB1/J284, Lord Mountbatten Papers, Hartley Library, University of Southampton.
[51] Belcher to Hampshire, 21 December 1961, DO 196/1, TNA.
[52] 'Policy of the Government of India on Colonial Affairs', IRD 113/05, undated, Secret paper prepared for Cabinet (C 54), FO 371/112214, TNA.

More accurately, Nehru's mounting irritation with the British stemmed from what the Indian leader considered to be a glaring inconsistency in the Macmillan government's approach to African nationalism. This, the CRO conceded, had begun 'colouring all Mr. Nehru's thoughts and utterances (and silences) about Britain'. On the one hand, Nehru welcomed the fact that London had moved progressively to grant self-government to the former British colonial territories of Ghana, Nigeria, Tanzania and Uganda. On the other hand, the Indian leader was 'baffled' by the Macmillan government's reluctance to exert pressure on fellow European colonial powers, and most notably Portugal, to follow its lead. To frustrated British officials in Whitehall, Britain's relationship with India appeared the victim of an unwelcome imperial hangover. While Nehru enthusiastically courted superpower sponsorship, the CRO grumbled, he appeared unable to dispel 'a residue of suspicion in his mind that the British leopard cannot wholly change its colonial spots'.[53]

Events in the Congo, where a bloody civil war had broken out following Belgium's precipitate decision to grant its former colony independence in June 1960, placed Britain's relationship with India under further strain. In Gore-Booth's judgement, fissures between Britain and India over the secession of the mineral-rich Congolese province of Katanga, and the UN's role in the conflict, where Indian soldiers made up part of a multinational peacekeeping force, threatened 'near disaster'.[54] Nehru faced strong domestic pressure to denounce foreign and, more particularly, Anglo-American interference in Congo's internal affairs. The Indian Socialist leader, Dr Ram Manohar Lohia, openly charged that the Congress Party's foreign policy 'had become power-orientated' and 'had betrayed the cause of colonial people'. The General Secretary of the Communist Party of India, Ajoy Ghosh, added to the chorus of criticism, singling out the Congo as a 'glaring instance' of Nehru's 'failure to take a firm stand on several anti-colonial issues'.[55]

Additional disquiet surfaced in New Delhi over the economic impact on India of British plans to join the EEC. In July 1961, after Macmillan's cabinet agreed to push ahead with an application for EEC membership, a disgruntled Nehru complained to his chief ministers that 'Just when

---

[53] Belcher to Hampshire, 21 December 1961, DO 196/1, TNA.

[54] Gore-Booth to CRO, No. 2154, 23 December 1960, PREM 11/3391, TNA; Gore-Booth, *Truth and Respect*, p. 278.

[55] 'Lohia Says India Has Betrayed Colonial People', 1 March 1961, 'CPI Report Attacks Govt. "Vacillation" On Anti-Colonial Issues', 17 April 1961, *National Herald*, Lucknow.

we are struggling with this export question comes a new blow from the European Common Market and the probability of the United Kingdom joining it ... the outlook is not a very happy one.'[56] Amendments to Britain's immigration policy at this time proved equally unpopular in the subcontinent. In 1948, the British Nationality Act had granted all Commonwealth subjects the right to British citizenship. During the 1950s, the British economy's demand for unskilled and low-paid workers attracted significant numbers of immigrants into the United Kingdom from the Caribbean, Africa and Asia.[57] As Britain's economy slumped around the beginning of the 1960s, political pressure grew within the United Kingdom to impose tighter controls on immigration. Proposals to give preference to skilled over unskilled migrants provoked resentment in India, where it was felt that this would disproportionately favour immigrants from the 'old', or 'white', Commonwealth countries.[58] During the course of 1961 alone, the scramble to beat the introduction of a new Commonwealth Immigrants Act saw 61,000 people leave South Asia for a new life in Britain.[59] 'The Commonwealth Citizens Immigration Bill', one Indian newspaper noted, 'has been widely resented in both official and unofficial circles as a piece of colour-bar politics, least expected of Britain at this late hour when imperialism is on its last legs.'[60]

On another level, Britain's increasingly fraught relations with India brought to the fore personal animosities and resentments that, in happier times, had lain dormant. In common with President Kennedy, Harold Macmillan, who had first met Nehru in New Delhi, in February 1947, was attracted by the Indian leader's political guile, intelligence and social sophistication.[61] Like Kennedy, Macmillan also regarded Nehru as smug and prone to acts of political hypocrisy. The British premier

---

[56] Nehru to Chief Ministers, New Delhi, 3 September 1962, in G. Parthasarathi (ed.), *Jawaharlal Nehru: Letters to Chief Ministers, 1947–1964*, vol. 5: *1958–1964* (New Delhi: Oxford University Press, 1989), pp. 524–5.

[57] At the beginning of the 1950s, the Black and Asian population of the UK numbered around 70,000 people. A decade later, it stood at 337,000. See Shamit Saggar, *Race and Politics in Britain* (London: Philip Allan, 1991), p. 49.

[58] Gore-Booth, *Truth and Respect*, p. 275.

[59] Dominic Sandbrook, *Never Had it So Good: A History of Britain from Suez to the Beatles* (London: Little Brown 2005), pp. 313–14.

[60] 'Delhi Diary: Indo-British Relations', *Amrita Bazar Patrika*, 18 December 1961.

[61] Following their first encounter in 1947, Macmillan had dismissed Nehru as 'charming but nervy ... [someone who] would not stand the racket of great events'. The Indian leader, Macmillan concluded, was 'not a man for storms; only a stormy petrel'. Entry for 4 February 1947, in Pendrel Moon (ed.), *Wavell: The Viceroy's Journal* (London: Oxford University Press, 1973), p. 417; Alistair Horne, *Macmillan, 1894–1956* (London: Macmillan, 1988), p. 311.

found that his Indian counterpart's pacifist rhetoric and preachy sermons in support of African nationalism grated, when set against India's sense of primacy within the developing world, and strident military posture toward Pakistan.[62] As Nehru confided to the Soviet premier, Nikita Khrushchev, although cordial, his relationship with Macmillan was 'not terribly intimate'.[63] Macmillan's frustration with Nehru surfaced most obviously following the outbreak of Sino-Indian hostilities in 1962. Mocking Nehru's bellicose public statements at that time, Macmillan observed that they appeared of a markedly 'different tone from that [previously] adopted by the protagonist of non-resistance and "non-alignment"'. India's leader, the British premier added caustically, appeared to have undergone a transformation from 'an imitation of George Lansbury into a parody of Churchill'.[64] With an evident distaste, the British premier reflected that Communist China had compelled his government to assist 'people [Indians] who for 12 years or more have attacked us ... like a camel looking down his nose at you'.[65]

The vexation Nehru's government engendered in Macmillan was replicated across Whitehall. In August 1963, after being recalled to London for talks, Ronald Belcher, Britain's Deputy High Commissioner in India, returned to the subcontinent with 'the impression ... of everyone's disliking and distrusting India – to such a degree that it seemed there was a danger of emotion being allowed more hand than reason in swaying our policies'. So disconcerted was Belcher by the strength of the anti-Indian feeling that he encountered in official British circles that he urged the CRO not to let

the present Government of India's undoubtedly irritating characteristics of stubbornness and ungratefulness ... divert attention from the basic fact that we are doing what we are for India, in the economic and defence fields, because it is in our own interest to do it.[66]

Belcher need not have worried. The CRO, as its officials readily conceded, did frequently experience 'moments of exasperation with India'. Rarely, if at all, however, was Whitehall's frustration 'allowed unduly to sway considered policy'.[67] Macmillan's government was aware that

[62] Alistair Horne, *Macmillan, 1957–1986* (London: Macmillan, 1989), pp. 415–16.
[63] 'Record of Talks between Prime Minister [Nehru] and Mr. Khrushchev in Calcutta, 1 March 1960', P. N. Kaul, Subject File No. 24 1960, Subimal Dutt Papers, Nehru Memorial Museum and Library (hereafter NMML).
[64] Harold Macmillan, *At the End of the Day, 1961–1963* (London: Macmillan, 1973), pp. 228–9.
[65] Kennedy/Macmillan talks, Nassau, 20 December 1962, *FRUS, 1961–1963*, vol. XIX, p. 451.
[66] Belcher to Pickard, 26 August 1963, DO 196/2, TNA.
[67] Pickard to Belcher, 19 September 1963, DO 196/2, TNA.

pursuing a foreign policy based upon anything other than shoring up Britain's precarious domestic position in the early 1960s invited political suicide, economic ruin and a collapse in the country's international prestige. Given India's financial, diplomatic and strategic importance to the United Kingdom, New Delhi was an ally that Macmillan's government could ill afford to do without.

### An alliance under strain

Pakistan's president, Mohammad Ayub Khan, had looked on with 'perplexity and dismay' as the United States bankrolled India's economic development in the late 1950s.[68] Viewed from Rawalpindi's perspective, by alleviating pressure on India's hard-pressed exchequer and freeing Nehru's government to divert a greater proportion of its own financial resources into India's armed forces, America's regional policy directly threatened Pakistan's sovereignty. In light of John F. Kennedy's vocal advocacy of increased Western developmental support for India, Pakistan's government had hoped that Richard Nixon would triumph in the 1960 US presidential election. William Rountree, America's ambassador in Karachi, observed that Kennedy's pro-Indian reputation had left Pakistan's policymakers with the 'impression ... that [Kennedy] ... looked with greater favour upon neutralists than upon allies'. In contrast, Nixon's reputation as a virulent anti-communist, it seemed, offered the hope that he would look less favourably than Kennedy upon non-aligned India.[69]

Kennedy's subsequent victory over Nixon unnerved Pakistani policymakers. From inside Pakistan, the American Embassy pressed the State Department to issue 'a statement at the earliest practicable date, which will reassure our Pakistani allies regarding our attitudes'.[70] Ayub Khan wasted little time in privately cautioning Kennedy not to take Pakistan's friendship for granted. 'It [the US-Pakistani alliance] cannot ... be sustained', Pakistan's leader wrote to the new American president in February 1961, 'if the attitude and policies of the West itself are calculated to undermine it or even create a sense of doubt in the minds of firm friends.'[71] In public, Ayub Khan vented his frustration that while the United States had actively lobbied Western industrialised

---

[68] Mohammad Ayub Khan, *Friends Not Masters: A Political Autobiography* (London: Oxford University Press, 1967), p. 132.
[69] Rountree to State Department, Karachi, 16 February 1961, *FRUS, 1961–1963*, vol. XIX, p. 9.
[70] Jones to Rusk, Washington, 31 January 1961, *FRUS, 1961–1963*, vol. XIX, pp. 2–3.
[71] Ayub Khan to Kennedy, Karachi, 16 February 1961, *ibid.*, vol. XIX, p. 11.

countries to supply India with record amounts of economic assistance, Pakistan's flow of developmental aid from Washington and its allies had been 'slashed'. In an interview broadcast on British television on 9 July 1961, Pakistan's president griped that

in respect of India, the United States made a special effort with the other contributing countries to persuade them to match the United States' effort. The United States went out of her way to bequeath a billion dollars as their contribution at a time when the Indian plan was not even worked out. In our case, all sorts of objections were raised. Some were genuine while some were, to my mind spurious – the sort of things which are designed to put off a caller ... I don't think the United States made any special effort [for Pakistan].[72]

To Pakistan's government, it appeared that a clique of pro-Indian 'Harvard intellectuals' had seized control of American foreign policy. In contrast to the close bond that had existed between US and Pakistani policymakers during Eisenhower's presidency, Kennedy appointees, such as Bowles and Galbraith, were lambasted in Pakistan's press as 'pro-Indian, pro-neutralist, lukewarm towards America's existing alliances, starry eyed, naïve, and largely out of touch with reality'. Ayub Khan's ministers refrained from openly endorsing the vilification of Kennedy's government in Pakistan's media. The British High Commission in Karachi confirmed to London, however, that 'neither we nor our American colleagues have any doubt that the [Pakistani] press campaign had Government sanction'.[73]

Back in March, Kennedy had despatched the veteran American diplomat and troubleshooter Averell Harriman to the subcontinent, in part to reassure Pakistan that the United States continued to value its alliance with Rawalpindi. Given the widely divergent perspectives held by Kennedy and Ayub Khan over the wisdom of transforming India into a de facto Western ally, Harriman faced an unenviable task. In typically forthright style, Kennedy's emissary confirmed to his hosts that Washington had no intention of downgrading its relationship with Pakistan. Harriman also made clear that the Kennedy administration's commitment to foster closer economic and political links to non-aligned states, India included, remained integral to its policy of containing communist influence in the developing world.[74] In turn, Ayub Khan confirmed that by blurring the distinction between formal allies and

---

[72] Mohammad Ayub Khan, *Speeches and Statements by Field Marshal Mohammad Ayub Khan*, vol. 4, July 1961–June 1962 (Karachi: Pakistan Government Publications, 1962), p. 6.
[73] 'US–Pakistan Relations', Golds to Martin, 13 June 1961, DO 196/132; 'Pakistan Foreign Policy', Martin to Walsh Atkins, 14 April 1961, DO 196/128, TNA.
[74] McMahon, *Cold War on the Periphery*, p. 278.

'friends', Kennedy's government would encourage Afro-Asian nations to question whether the benefits of alignment with the West continued to outweigh its associated risks. By way of illustration, Harriman was informed that Pakistan intended to take out its own regional insurance policy, and 'normalise' relations with its Soviet and Chinese neighbours. The message from Pakistan was clear: while its alliance with the United States remained a central component of its foreign policy, as long as Kennedy's South Asian loyalties remained suspect, Rawalpindi would seek to hedge its Cold War bets.[75]

Lyndon Johnson's presence in South Asia the following May provided the Kennedy administration with a further opportunity to build bridges with Pakistan. In the wake of his talks with Harriman, Ayub Khan had been disconcerted to discover that Washington had excluded his government from contingency planning for a SEATO-led intervention in Laos. Concluding that the disgruntled Pakistani leader needed a 'pat on the back', the State Department asked Johnson to brief Ayub Khan on his recent trips to Vietnam and Thailand, which it was hoped, would help 'strengthen the impression that we are definitely interested in Pakistan as an ally'.[76] At Ayub Khan's insistence, however, Pakistan's dispute with India over Kashmir dominated his exchanges with Johnson. Having prepared for an exercise in diplomatic glad-handing, an uneasy Johnson was instead forced to defend America's policy, in the face of strident demands from Ayub Khan that the United States use its economic leverage over India to cajole Nehru into reopening the question of Kashmir's sovereignty. Johnson was left in no doubt that Rawalpindi would interpret the Kennedy administration's attitude toward the Kashmir question as a litmus test of the United States' good faith toward Pakistan.[77] British officials in the subcontinent found their American colleagues 'justifiably depressed' in the aftermath of Johnson's visit. Rather than reassure Ayub Khan's government, the vice-president's evasiveness on the Kashmir question served only to heighten Pakistan's fears of an imminent American tilt toward India.[78] Questioning the timing, purpose and execution of Johnson's mission to Pakistan, on balance the British concluded that it had acted more as an irritant than a balm. 'Our American colleagues are far from happy about the impression made by their Vice-President in Pakistan',

[75] Rountree to Rusk, No. 1622, 22 March 1961, Box 526, Folder 12, Pakistan 1, Averell Harriman Papers, United States Library of Congress, Washington, DC (hereafter HP).
[76] 'Background Material, India', NSF, Box 242A, 5/61, JFKL.
[77] Rountree to Rusk, No. 2019, 21 May 1961, NSF, Box 242A, 5/61, JFKL.
[78] 'US–Pakistan Relations', Golds to Martin, 13 June 1961, DO 196/132, TNA.

the British High Commission cabled London; '[it appears to have] done the Americans little immediate good and perhaps some harm.'[79]

The disappointing outcome of Johnson's visit to Pakistan prompted the White House to bring forward an outstanding invitation for Ayub Khan to visit Washington.[80] In preparing for Ayub Khan's arrival in July, American officials considered how best to puncture the Pakistani leader's inflated expectation of the support that his government could expect to receive from the United States on contentious issues, such as Kashmir. In a minute to Walt Rostow, whom Kennedy had installed as his Deputy National Security Advisor, Robert Komer stressed the importance of the Kennedy–Ayub Khan talks. 'What happens in these three days', Komer prophesied, 'will determine US–Pakistan relations for the next three years.'[81] Rostow agreed that Kennedy's meeting with Ayub Khan was likely to 'cast a long shadow, for good or ill'. However, Rostow encouraged Kennedy not to pull any punches in confronting the Pakistani president's anticipated complaints on issues such as military aid, economic assistance and Kashmir. Noting that Ayub Khan prided himself on his directness, Rostow advised the US president that the Pakistani leader would 'measure you by the clarity, bluntness, and toughness of your responses, even if some of the toughness gives him less than he wants'.[82]

In the event, following a series of frank but amicable exchanges, Ayub Khan came away from Washington satisfied that he had extracted a number of important concessions from Kennedy, which, temporarily at least, served to stabilise US-Pakistani relations. Crucially, Kennedy gave the Pakistani leader a commitment to undertake 'a major effort' to persuade Nehru to open talks with Pakistan on Kashmir, when the Indian leader visited the United States in November. Furthermore, Ayub Khan was reassured by the State Department that were Nehru to spurn Kennedy's approach on Kashmir, the United States would support Pakistan should it to refer the matter back to the UN Security Council. Of almost equal importance to Pakistan's government was a pledge that Kennedy made to consult with Rawalpindi, should rising Sino-Indian tensions produce an Indian request for US military

[79] 'Pakistan: The Visit of the Vice-President of the United States', 16 June 1961, DO 196/132, TNA.
[80] 'President Ayub's State Visit to the United States', Viscount Hood to Lord Home, 27 July 1961, DO 196/132, TNA.
[81] 'Subject: Ayub Visit', Komer to Walt Rostow, 30 June 1961, NSF, Box 441, Pakistan, JFKL.
[82] 'The Ayub Visit: Two Key Questions', Walt Rostow to President Kennedy, 7 July 1961, NSF, Box 147A, Pakistan, JFKL.

assistance.[83] In a final gesture of goodwill, the White House delighted Ayub Khan by confirming its intention to honour an agreement struck by the Eisenhower administration to supply Pakistan with a squadron of advanced US F-104 supersonic fighter aircraft.[84]

Kennedy was far less content with the outcome of his encounter with Ayub Khan. Above all, the inability of senior Pakistani government officials to accept the pragmatic rationale underpinning his administration's strategy of developing India as an Asian counterweight to Communist China exasperated the American president. Inside the State Department, the Pakistani president's visit to Washington engendered a similar sense of frustration and foreboding. Discussions with the Pakistani delegation, American diplomats bemoaned, had 'gone around in familiar old circles without issues being resolved'.[85] The British were surprised at the extent of Ayub Khan's 'considerable personal success' in the United States. The Commonwealth Relations Office, however, doubted that it would have much, if any, significant impact on US regional policy. From a strategic perspective Pakistan's leader had merely papered over the widening cracks in his country's relationship with Washington. He had, nonetheless, at least cleared the air with Kennedy and won a measure of the president's personal regard.[86] This alone, London optimistically hoped, would provide Washington with a timely reminder that Pakistan remained an ally worth keeping.[87]

## Britain and Pakistan: a relationship in decline

In January 1958, Harold Macmillan had taken heart from the effusive reception that greeted him in India, on the South Asian leg of a Commonwealth tour. In Pakistan, the British premier received a noticeably less enthusiastic welcome that year. British officials in Pakistan attributed the lukewarm reaction generated by Macmillan's visit not to

---

[83] Memorandum of Conversation, Kennedy–Ayub Khan Talks, 3–5 p.m., Tuesday 11 July 1961, NSF, Box 147A, Pakistan, 7/61, JFKL.

[84] McMahon, *Cold War on the Periphery*, pp. 279–80.

[85] Phillips Talbot, OH, 27 July 1965, pp. 19–20, JFKL.

[86] Ayub Khan, who one British diplomat contended was 'notably antipathetic to intellectuals, and an out-and-out philistine', appeared less comfortable with the urbane Kennedy than he had been with Eisenhower, a fellow soldier-cum-politician. Kennedy, the Pakistani leader later reflected, 'struck me as a preoccupied and lonely man ... He seemed unsure of his grasp of things and I could see that he was surrounded by too many theoreticians, who are useful people to have but can sometimes divert one from the right and practical course of action.' Morrice James, *Pakistan Chronicle* (London: Hurst, 1992), p. 108; Ayub Khan, *Friends Not Masters*, p. 139.

[87] 'President Ayub's State Visit to the United States', Viscount Hood to Lord Home, 27 July 1961, DO 196/132, TNA.

'any absence of friendly feeling' between the two countries, but rather to the 'apparent indifference' that had come to characterise Pakistan's relationship with the United Kingdom.[88] Having looked to the United States for economic and military security since 1954, Pakistan's attitude toward Britain had developed along increasingly ambivalent lines. In September 1961, the British High Commission in Karachi observed that a majority of informed Pakistani opinion viewed its former colonial ruler as

a rather nice old thing, getting a bit past it ... a shade old-fashioned and odd at times and keeps some disreputable friends: but experienced, and wise ... and tries to be helpful ... and the help, when it is forthcoming, is worth having.[89]

In general, Pakistan's government continued to treat its British counterpart with 'a measure of friendly respect'. Nonetheless, Whitehall recognised that within Pakistan there existed 'a tendency to regard Britain as a spent force'. Taken as a whole, Pakistan's perception of the United Kingdom as a rapidly waning global power was seen by London as overblown and premature, yet understandable. 'It is perhaps naturally difficult for any people which recalls the sun of the British Empire at its zenith', one British diplomat reflected soberly, 'to measure accurately the angle of its decline.'[90]

Morrice James, who had arrived in Pakistan in 1961 to take up the post of British High Commissioner, quickly concluded that Anglo-Pakistani relations were in the midst of a transitional phase. Since 1947, James' predecessors had laboured assiduously to promote a 'special' relationship between Britain and Pakistan, based largely on the maintenance of residual colonial connections. This strategy, James reasoned, had now run its course. In the coming decade, James cautioned Whitehall, 'British influence [in Pakistan] would have to be earned in the present, and not founded on sentiment or goodwill'.[91] Placed in the context of the Macmillan government's inability to compete with the Soviet and American superpowers' growing economic investments in South Asia, James' assessment did not augur well for Britain's future position in the subcontinent. The British conceded that, viewed from Pakistan's perspective:

Our military strength ... does not remotely compare with that of the superpowers. Our economic strength yields an enviable and magnetic prosperity

---

[88] 'Prime Minister's Commonwealth Tour', 4 June 1958, CAB 129/93, C (58), 120, TNA.
[89] 'Pakistan: Foreign Policy', Walsh Atkins to Sandys, 27 September 1961, DO 196/132, TNA.
[90] *Ibid.*    [91] James, *Pakistan Chronicle*, p. 72.

at home: it seems paradoxical then that we are unable or unwilling to display as much generosity in our aid to Pakistan as is thought to be due to us. And the shadows of rockets and sputniks obscure the pioneers of radar and the jet engine.[92]

In searching for the means to preserve residual British influence in Pakistan, officials at the CRO latched onto the hope that President Ayub Khan might develop into a valuable ally. Standing well over six feet tall, and 'broad and robust in proportion', the Sandhurst-trained Ayub Khan exuded an aura of calm authority. In contrast to the enigmatic Nehru, British officials saw Pakistan's leader as a refreshingly uncomplicated character, possessing much 'common sense, sincerity, directness and balance'. Moreover, the firm grip that Ayub Khan held over his cabinet colleagues suggested to the British that 'a very great deal clearly depends on his attitude toward us and our relations with him'. The product of a British military system in which he had served with distinction, Ayub Khan was thought to be an Anglophile at heart. 'I believe', Alexander Symon, Britain's then High Commissioner in Pakistan, informed London in 1960, 'he likes our ways and is basically friendly toward us.'[93]

On occasions, Ayub Khan's words and deeds appeared to support Symon's analysis. In August 1961, in a keynote foreign policy speech delivered before Pakistan's Institute of International Affairs, the Pakistani president made a succession of 'friendly and helpful remarks' on the value of the Commonwealth and the importance of the SEATO and CENTO collective security organisations. The latter, with Britain as its nominal head, had helped to shore up Western interests in the Middle East since 1955. The content and tone of Ayub Khan's observations, British officials in Pakistan gloated subsequently, 'could scarcely have been improved if we had written them ourselves'.[94] Yet, Ayub Khan was equally willing to adopt a strong anti-British posture when it suited his political interests. Notably, in July 1960, when British economic assistance to Pakistan failed to meet his government's expectations, the president publicly excoriated Macmillan's government. The British, Ayub Khan contended, retained an obligation to Pakistan to make up the leeway of '200 years of slavery'. After all, Pakistan's president suggested:

[92] 'Pakistan: Foreign Policy', Walsh Atkins to Sandys, 27 September 1961, DO 196/132, TNA.
[93] 'Pakistan: The President', Symon to Home, 16 February 1960, PREM 11/3902, TNA.
[94] 'Pakistan: Foreign Policy', Walsh Atkins to Sandys, 27 September 1961, DO 196/132, TNA.

It was during the period of imperial rule that the British industrial development started and gained momentum with resources which to a large extent were taken from the colonial areas ... So far as the area now forming Pakistan is concerned, its manpower was generally employed to man the British Armies to maintain and protect the Empire. For this reason, this part of the Indian sub-continent was purposely kept industrially backward so that the populace would not be diverted into other channels of employment ... the English-speaking world ought to feel a special responsibility to assist Pakistan in attaining a reasonable posture of advancement. It is not just a claim. It is in fact a dictate of history.[95]

Such rhetoric, as Morrice James submitted, gave lie to the fallacy that historic ties or personal affinities, rather than raw political and economic power, could substantively influence Britain's standing within Pakistan. Indeed, to Whitehall's chagrin, Britain's former colonial association with the subcontinent appeared to confer substantial residual responsibilities, yet offer little compensatory authority in South Asia. Notably, the United Kingdom's decision to pursue British entry into the EEC, its imposition of stricter controls on Commonwealth immigration, and concern over the treatment of Pakistani communities in Britain's northern industrial cities, all placed a strain on London's relations with Rawalpindi.[96] The British did maintain a significant military association with Pakistan's government through the SEATO and CENTO pacts. Financially, British companies continued to hold a sizeable stake in Pakistan's economy. Politically, the Commonwealth served as a common bond. Nonetheless, around the beginning of the 1960s, such connections represented wasting assets. The preponderant levels of economic and military support provided to Pakistan by the United States ensured that it was to Washington that Ayub Khan listened, and not London. Whitehall readily acknowledged that with America having supplied $1,166 million of the $1,497 million in foreign aid received by Pakistan between 1947 and 1960, 'The Pakistanis are realistic in their attitude to the USA whose material support is now perhaps the most important factor (other than India) in Pakistan's international relationships.'[97] Revealingly, up until 1958, Whitehall continued to place emphasis upon the 'value, which the Pakistan armed forces attach to the traditional links that bind them to their British counterparts'.[98] Just

[95] Mohammad Ayub Khan, 'Pakistan Perspective', *Foreign Affairs* (July 1960), 547–56.
[96] 'Pakistan: Some Reflections', James to Sandys, 6 June 1962, DO 196/3; 'Pakistan: Visit of the Secretary of State for Commonwealth Relations', James to Sandys, 7 July 1962, DO 196/213, TNA.
[97] Sandys brief for Pakistan visit, 16 December 1960, DO 196/100, TNA.
[98] 'Prime Minister's Commonwealth Tour', 4 June 1958, CAB 129/93, C (58), 120, TNA.

two years later, the CRO lamented that Pakistan's army and air force had become 'almost entirely dependent on the United States'.[99]

## Kennedy, Macmillan and South Asia

When viewed from a broad geostrategic perspective, Pakistan's decision to turn away from Britain and toward the United States was unsurprising. In the post-war period, Britain's retention of Empire and Commonwealth, permanent membership of the United Nations Security Council (UNSC) and possession of a nuclear deterrent masked a systemic decline in its economic and military power. On several occasions, financial crises sparked by Britain's wide-ranging and costly overseas commitments had threatened to cripple its fragile economy. In the 1950s, with the defence budget consuming 10 per cent of the gross national product (GNP), and one in seven of the populace tied up in the armed services, the international competitiveness of British industry slumped.[100] Swingeing defence cuts, when they arrived courtesy of the Sandys' White Paper in 1957, provided a clear insight into the shallowness of Britain's great power pretension. By placing emphasis on its relatively cheap nuclear deterrent and phasing out conscription, the Macmillan government averted economic implosion. The price for doing so, however, was a significant erosion of Britain's conventional military capability, with the British Army halving in size between 1956 and 1962.[101]

In contrast, following a period of peace and prosperity during the Eisenhower era, John F. Kennedy inherited an American economy seven times the size, and a defence budget ten times as large, as that of Great Britain.[102] Glaring disparities in Anglo-American resources failed to dent Harold Macmillan's optimism that the 'Declaration of Common Purpose', which he had agreed with Eisenhower in October

---

[99] Sandys brief for Pakistan visit, 16 December 1960, DO 196/100, TNA.

[100] David Reynolds, *Britannia Overruled: British Policy and World Power in the 20th Century* (London: Longman, 1991), p. 211.

[101] Paul Kennedy, *The Realities Behind Diplomacy: Background Influences on British External Policy, 1865–1980* (London: Allen & Unwin 1981), p. 374.

[102] By 1963, US GNP stood at $560 billion, compared with Britain's $81 billion; America's share of world manufacturing output at 35.1 per cent, compared to Britain's 6.4 per cent; and, US defence expenditure at $52.2 billion, compared with Britain's $5.2 billion. See Paul Kennedy, *The Rise and Fall of the Great Powers: Economic Change and Military Confrontation 1500 to 2000* (London: Unwin Hyman, 1988), p. 495, and *Realities*, p. 341. See also Nigel Ashton, 'Managing Transition: Macmillan and the Utility of Anglo-American Relations', in Richard Aldous and Sabine Lee (eds.), *Harold Macmillan: Aspects of a Political Life* (Basingstoke: Macmillan, 1988), pp. 242–3.

1957, would allow Britain to retain a significant, if necessarily subsidiary global role, alongside the United States.[103] The British Foreign Office shared Macmillan's sanguine assessment of the Anglo-American 'partnership'. As the 1960s dawned, FO officials lauded Britain's success in 'consolidating and extending our position as the first ally of the United States'. The 'co-ordination of policy' between London and Washington, Whitehall crowed in January 1960, had 'never been so far-reaching and satisfactory'.[104] Others took a less charitable view of the Anglo-American relationship. Memorably, the *Beyond the Fringe* review struck a chord with the British public when satirising Macmillan's transparent effort to mask the nation's post-war decline. Addressing theatre audiences in the guise of Britain's ageing premier, the comedian Peter Cook proclaimed:

Good evening. I have recently been travelling around the world on your behalf and at your expense, visiting some chaps with whom I hope to be shaping your future ... I went to America, and there I had talks with the young, vigorous President of that great country, and danced with his very lovely lady wife. We talked of many things, including Great Britain's role in the world as an honest broker. I agreed with him, when he said that no nation could be more honest; and he agreed with me, when I chaffed him, and said that no nation could be broker.[105]

The existence of strong personal ties between senior figures in the Macmillan and Kennedy governments ensured that Britain maintained intimate working relations with the United States after Eisenhower's departure from the White House, in January 1961. Having assiduously cultivated Eisenhower's goodwill, Macmillan fretted over the improbability of replicating such a close bond with his youthful successor.[106] The apprehension that Macmillan harboured in relation to Kennedy emerged clearly in a valedictory note that he sent to Eisenhower, as the latter prepared to leave office. 'I cannot of course', the fawning British prime minister wrote, 'ever hope to have anything to replace the sort of relations that we have had.'[107] In particular, Macmillan harboured

[103] Nigel Ashton, 'Harold Macmillan and the "Golden Days" of Anglo-American Relations Revisited, 1957–63', *Diplomatic History*, 29 (September 2005), 722.

[104] 'The Future of Anglo-American Relations', 5 January 1960, PREM 11/2986, TNA.

[105] Both Kennedy, on New York's Broadway, and Macmillan, in London's West End, attended performances of the review. Ronald Bergan, *Beyond the Fringe ... and Beyond: A Critical Biography of Alan Bennett, Peter Cook, Jonathan Miller, Dudley Moore* (London: Virgin, 1989), pp. 33–4; Humphrey Carpenter, *That Was Satire That Was: The Satire Boom of the 1960s* (London: Phoenix, 2002), p. 104.

[106] Alistair Horne, 'The Macmillan Years and Afterwards', in Wm. Roger Louis and Hedley Bull (eds.), *The Special Relationship: Anglo-American Relations Since 1945* (Oxford: Clarendon, 1986), p. 90.

[107] Harold Macmillan, *Pointing the Way, 1959–1961* (London: Macmillan, 1972), p. 284.

reservations that the generation gap between himself and Kennedy would undermine their working relationship. Two years previously, *The Economist* had lampooned Macmillan for his Edwardian affectation, noting sardonically that the Conservative Party confronted the unenviable challenge of 'trying to project in 1958 a Prime Minister obstinately determined to reflect 1908'.[108] Moreover, toward the end of 1960, Harold Evans, Macmillan's Press Secretary, had noted that his sixty-six-year-old boss had begun 'feeling his age'.[109]

Macmillan's concern at how the transition from the Eisenhower to the Kennedy administrations would affect British fortunes was understandable. The Suez debacle in 1956 had provided a salutary lesson in the folly of Britain acting on the post-war international stage without at least tacit American support. Moreover, for Macmillan, in particular, it had demonstrated the pivotal role personal relationships could assume at the highest level of Anglo-American diplomacy. With Anthony Eden's handling of the Middle Eastern crisis having alienated Eisenhower, it was only following Eden's resignation in January 1957, and Macmillan's subsequent assumption of power, that transatlantic relations returned to something approaching cordiality.[110] In fact, Macmillan need not have worried. Of his Western contemporaries, as one of Kennedy's intimates confirmed, it was Macmillan whom the president 'saw first, liked best and saw most often'.[111] Both shared a dry biting wit, and retained a strong affinity for British history and literature. Outside the glare of the political arena, the complicated and often duplicitous personal lives of both leaders appeared to provide them with a further common bond. In 1920, shortly after his marriage to Lady Dorothy Cavendish, Macmillan's wife had embarked upon what was to prove a lifelong liaison with the Conservative MP Robert Boothby. Although the marriage survived Macmillan's discovery of the affair in 1929, it came to represent little more than a sham. Kennedy's troubled marriage to Jacqueline Bouvier was equally notable for its extramarital dimension, in this instance on the part of the president, who indulged in a succession of casual sexual encounters.[112] Reflecting on the surprise expressed by outsiders that he had established so close a rapport

[108] *The Economist*, 15 February 1958.
[109] Harold Evans, *Downing Street Diary: The Macmillan Years, 1957–1963* (London: Hodder & Stoughton, 1981), pp. 127–8.
[110] Alan Dobson, *The Politics of the Anglo-American Economic Special Relationship, 1940–87* (Brighton: Wheatsheaf, 1988), p. 161.
[111] Sorensen, *Kennedy*, p. 558.
[112] Kennedy's marital transgressions have been documented in lurid detail, in such works as Seymour Hersh, *The Dark Side of Camelot* (New York: Back Bay Books, 1998).

with the British leader, Kennedy once explained, 'I feel at home with Macmillan because I can share my loneliness with him.'[113]

The potency of Anglo-American relations also drew considerably on the presence in Washington, from October 1961, of Sir David Ormsby Gore as Britain's ambassador. In Macmillan's estimation, Ormsby Gore developed a degree of influence at the centre of the American policymaking process, 'unique in the annals of the British Embassy in Washington'.[114] A Kennedy family friend since the 1940s, Ormsby Gore's relationship with the president was sufficiently close, officially and socially, to facilitate his inclusion in Kennedy's inner circle. Having stated that 'I trust David as I would my own Cabinet', Kennedy regularly employed the British ambassador as a confidential sounding board.[115] Macmillan observed that the young American president's world revolved around three interconnecting circles, fashionable people, intellectuals and politicians, and that Ormsby Gore enjoyed the unique distinction of being a party to all three.[116]

Tellingly, however, given the chasm in economic and military power between the United Kingdom and the United States, the Macmillan government's ability to connect on a personal level with Kennedy invariably failed to translate into meaningful British influence over US policy. Macmillan was not informed in advance of the disastrous Bay of Pigs operation that Kennedy authorised against Cuba in April 1961, nor did the American president extend to Britain a role at that year's superpower summit in Vienna.[117] Similarly, Macmillan's subsequent attempts to embellish the significance of his role during the Cuban Missile Crisis in the autumn of 1962 rang hollow, when set against Ormsby Gore's reflection that 'I can't honestly think of anything said from London that changed ... US action – it was chiefly reassurance to JFK.'[118] Toward the end of his premiership, so low had Macmillan's stock fallen in Washington, that following a final meeting with Kennedy, in June 1963 at Birch Grove, Macmillan's Sussex home,

---

[113] Nigel J. Ashton, *Kennedy, Macmillan and the Cold War: The Irony of Interdependence* (Basingstoke: Palgrave Macmillan, 2002), p. 194. See also John D. Fair, 'The Intellectual JFK: Lessons in Statesmanship from British History', *Diplomatic History*, 30 (January 2006), 119–42; and Robert Dallek, *John F. Kennedy: An Unfinished Life, 1917–1963* (London: Allen Lane, 2003), pp. 52–4.

[114] Macmillan to Ormsby Gore, 29 April 1962, Macmillan letters, c.333, April 1962, Harold Macmillan Papers, Bodleian Library, University of Oxford.

[115] Sorensen, *Kennedy*, p. 559.

[116] Horne, *Macmillan, 1957–1986*, p. 307.

[117] John Turner, *Macmillan* (London: Longman, 1994), p. 159.

[118] Horne, *Macmillan, 1957–1986*, p. 382.

the British press reported that Kennedy had been dismayed at his host's 'bumbling and old-fashioned' performance.[119]

From the very beginning of Kennedy's presidency, the British government acknowledged that the preservation of 'satisfactory' bilateral relations with the United States presented significant challenges. Anglo-American tension existed in areas as diverse as European integration, Middle Eastern policy and nuclear strategy, all of which threatened the continuation of harmonious ties. The British aimed to minimise Anglo-American friction with Washington by emphasising the 'positive factors' that they brought to the transatlantic table, principally sterling's role alongside the US dollar as an instrument for international financial stability, and their dependability as a staunch ally in the United States' crusade against communism. However, it was through leadership of the Commonwealth, with its expanding membership of Afro-Asian nations, that the British hoped to maximise their political capital within the White House. In January 1960, the Foreign Office had reflected that given the United States' focus on the Third World as a crucial Cold War battleground, 'it is our [Britain's] influence and knowledge of the world outside Europe, especially in the Commonwealth, which has most value today in the eyes of Americans'.[120]

It was in this sense, that the British identified an opportunity to 'preserve the Anglo-American partnership' by being seen to 'do all in our power to support India as the counter-attraction to China in Asia'.[121] The British did not share Kennedy's almost pathological belief that China harboured expansionist and hegemonic regional ambitions. In Macmillan's view, a policy based on accommodation with the Chinese, rather than an inherently antagonistic American approach, predicated on an inevitable clash of interests, offered greater prospects for bringing peace and stability to Asia.[122] The British were also a good deal less sanguine than Washington that India could act as an effective counterweight to the PRC. In the opinion of the Foreign Office, having absorbed 'incomparably more external aid' than China with little impact on its economic performance, India appeared illustrative of the fact that external assistance alone failed to provide a panacea for redressing 'backwardness'. Economic progress was driven by the will and energy of the general populace, British officials contended,

[119] Richard Lamb, *The Macmillan Years: The Emerging Truth* (London: John Murray, 1995), pp. 367–8.
[120] 'The Future of Anglo-American Relations', 5 January 1960, PREM 11/2986, TNA.
[121] *Ibid.*
[122] Horne, *Macmillan, 1957–1986*, pp. 416–17.

and although 'that upsurge of will and energy is certainly manifest in China: it does not yet seem to be very evident in India'.[123]

Whitehall's priority in India was not centred on containing a communist threat to South Asia that London regarded as overstated, but on protecting Britain's valuable commercial and political assets in the subcontinent. In the early 1960s, the British accepted that they had come to rank as only 'one of many' influential external powers in India, and 'in strict terms of power and cash, not among the first'.[124] Significantly, Macmillan's government harboured a concern that left unchecked, India's developing ties with the United States might have 'prejudicial effects on our own position in India'. Writing to the CRO from New Delhi, in August 1961, Sir Paul Gore-Booth emphasised that the British government 'must and do exercise a moderating influence in an Indian direction on the Americans ... yet not to the extent that the Americans get fed up'.[125] Conveniently for the British, the largely illusory nature of their residual power in South Asia appeared to retain currency within Kennedy's government. Politically, as head of a Commonwealth, incorporating India and Pakistan; militarily, as India's principal supplier of arms; and financially, as New Delhi's major trading partner, the British were seen by Washington as an influential regional player. 'The Americans', CRO officials noted with surprise, '... seem to have a respect for the amount of influence which they imagine we carry with the Indians.'[126]

From its standpoint, the Kennedy administration saw a number of advantages in working closely with the British in the Indian subcontinent. Forging an Anglo-American partnership in South Asia offered Washington some prospect that Britain would take on a portion of the financial burden involved in accelerating India's economic development. In addition, a prominent British role in joint political and economic initiatives in the subcontinent, the Kennedy administration anticipated, would help to deflect some of the criticism that its regional policy could expect to draw from Pakistan, and a US Congress largely antipathetic toward Nehru's government. In rationalising the value of coordinating

[123] 'UK Brief for NATO Far Eastern Experts Meeting', Paris, 14 March 1962, FO 371/164871, TNA.

[124] Gore-Booth to CRO, 10 December 1960, DO 196/1, TNA. Malcolm MacDonald, Gore-Booth's predecessor in New Delhi, reached much the same conclusion, informing Whitehall earlier that year that British authority in India represented a 'wasting asset', based on 'acquired prestige' and 'established connexions'. 'India: Effects of American and Soviet Economic Assistance', MacDonald to Sandys, 21 October 1960, DO 196/125, TNA.

[125] Gore-Booth to Victor Martin, 4 August 1961, DO 133/145, TNA.

[126] Victor Martin to Gore-Booth, 29 August 1961, DO 133/145, TNA.

action with the British in South Asia, Dean Rusk observed, in May 1963, that:

It's important ... for our own people here to see some other flags flying when we go charging off to the assistance of other people that are in trouble. We are carrying about as much of a load as we can carry with the notion that we are the gendarmes of the universe and here's the greatest member of the British Commonwealth in terms of size ... I think we'd be hard pressed to tell our own people why we are doing this with India when even the British won't do it, the Australians won't do it, the Canadians won't do it. We need to have those other flags flying on these joint enterprises.[127]

From a broader strategic standpoint, Anglo-American collaboration in the Indian subcontinent made considerable sense. The British and American governments both wished to foster stability and economic development in the region. Both were eager to minimise the extension of Soviet and Chinese influence across Asia. Both favoured a rapprochement between India and Pakistan, and the eventual coordination of those countries' defences against external communist threats. Moreover, although keen to cultivate political and military ties with India, neither party in the Anglo-American camp advocated that India should formally abandon non-alignment. British and American officials doubted that Nehru's government could be persuaded to relinquish the benefits that it derived from its relationship with the USSR, principally Soviet economic aid and Moscow's support in the UNSC on the Kashmir question.[128] Furthermore, both the Macmillan and Kennedy administrations considered that the political and financial price of entering into a formal alliance with India was likely to prove prohibitively expensive.[129]

In a memoir published in the late 1970s, one prominent former Permanent Under Secretary at the Commonwealth Relations Office reflected that for much of the early Cold War period the 'ultimate aims' of British and American policy in South Asia remained in 'complete harmony'. Such unanimity of purpose, the British official added, was often compromised in practice by 'strong differences' between London and Washington 'as to how these [common aims] could be best achieved'.[130]

---

[127] NSC Meeting on India, 9 May 1963, Meetings Recordings, Tape No. 86 (1), JFKL.
[128] Kaysen to Kennedy, 3 November 1962, *FRUS, 1961–1963*, vol. XIX, p. 367.
[129] See 'Military Aid to India', Sir Algernon Rumbold (CRO) to Peck (FO), 16 November 1962, FO 371/164929/FC1063/10 (E), TNA; Saville Garner to Sandys, 15 November 1962, FO 371/164929/FC1063/13, TNA; and Galbraith, *Ambassador's Journal*, 16 November 1962, p. 479.
[130] Joe Garner, *The Commonwealth Office, 1925–1968* (London: Heinemann, 1978), p. 403.

During its brief term in office, the Kennedy administration was to press Harold Macmillan's government to play an ever-greater part in the delivery of its ambitious South Asian strategy. In turn, a yawning disparity in Anglo-American resources, and sharp tactical differences between Kennedy and Macmillan over the optimum means of achieving common strategic objectives, invariably placed the British in a position where they were unwilling, or felt unable, to meet the expectations placed upon them by Washington. Between 1961 and 1963, a series of politico-military shocks, from India's 'liberation' of Goa to the outbreak of Sino-Indian hostilities, shattered the Indian subcontinent's established equilibrium. In the process, the New Frontier's partnership with the British in South Asia, and the foundations on which the United States had based its relationships with India and Pakistan since 1947, gradually unravelled.

# 4    Upsetting the apple cart: India's 'liberation' of Goa

At the stroke of midnight on 17 December 1961, thirty thousand Indian Army troops under the command of Lieutenant General J. N. Chaudhury launched 'Operation Vijay'. Moving simultaneously against the Portuguese enclaves of Goa, Daman and Diu, on India's western coastline, Chaudhury's men quickly brushed aside token opposition from local Portuguese garrisons. In New Delhi, on being informed that Indo-Portuguese hostilities had broken out, America's ambassador to India, John Kenneth Galbraith, predicted that India would seize control of Goa in 'one day and [with] no casualties to speak of'.[1] Galbraith's assessment proved prescient. By the morning of 19 December, with units of the Sikh Light Infantry in control of Goa's capital, Panjim, Portugal's 460-year presence on the Indian subcontinent had been brought to an ignominious end.[2]

The Portuguese presence in India dated back to the early sixteenth century. Then, following a short conflict against the local Bijaper sultanate, Portugal had annexed a swathe of territory surrounding the port of Goa and claimed sovereignty over the smaller trading posts of Daman, Diu, Dadra and Nagar Haveli. In 1961, Portugal's South Asian Empire, which covered 1,500 square miles of the Indian subcontinent, was home to a predominantly ethnically Indian population of some half a million people. The British colonial presence in South Asia had ended back in August 1947 with the creation of India and Pakistan. In October 1954,

---

[1] John Kenneth Galbraith, *Ambassador's Journal: A Personal Account of the Kennedy Years* (Boston: Houghton Mifflin, 1969), Entry for 20 December 1961, New Delhi, p. 285. Galbraith subsequently informed US Under Secretary of State George Ball that 'The Indians in Goa encountered about the same resistance as the Governor visiting the Iowa State fair but the casualties were less.' Operation Vijay claimed forty-five Portuguese and twenty-two Indian lives. Galbraith to Ball, 19 December 1961, Record Group (RG) 59, Records of Under Secretary of State George Ball, Box 21, National Archives and Records Administration, College Park, Maryland (hereafter NARA).

[2] D. K. Palit, *War in High Himalaya: The Indian Army in Crisis, 1962* (London: Hurst, 1991), pp. 153–4.

following somewhat tardily in British footsteps, the French had placed their territorial possessions in the subcontinent under de facto Indian governance.[3] To the Indian government's chagrin, however, Portugal displayed no inclination to follow suit.[4] Between 1947 and 1961, India's prime minister, Jawaharlal Nehru, made a series of unsuccessful attempts to engage the Portuguese government in bilateral discussions on Goa's future.[5] Under the leadership of Prime Minister António de Oliveira Salazar, whose authoritarian Estado Novo, or 'New State' government, had come to power in Portugal in 1932, the nation's colonies in Asia and Africa were categorised as 'Overseas Provinces', and came to be regarded as an integral part of the Portuguese state.[6]

More practically, the Salazar government's refusal to discuss the legitimacy of Portuguese rule in Goa was linked to the fate of the country's southern African possessions, Angola and Mozambique. Of itself, Goa was of little economic or strategic importance to Portugal. In contrast, its African colonies provided the Portuguese exchequer with valuable foreign exchange revenues from the export of cotton, maize, sugar, palm oil, groundnuts, sisal, coffee and diamonds. In 1953, Angola and Mozambique accounted for 16 per cent of Portugal's imports and provided a market for 27 per cent of its exports.[7] Conceding the principle of self-determination in Goa, Lisbon reasoned, would increase international pressure on Portugal to do likewise in its African Empire. To the Indian government's irritation, Portuguese colonialism was tacitly endorsed by the Eisenhower administration in the United States, which looked upon Salazar's government as an important Cold War ally. From 1951, the Portuguese had provided fellow NATO members with access to prized military staging facilities in the Azores and Cape Verde Islands. Five years later, in July 1956, Salazar signed a further agreement permitting NATO aircraft to operate out of Espinho, in northern Portugal, and Montijo, to the south of Lisbon. Moreover, as political

---

[3] Arthur Rubinoff, *India's Use of Force in Goa* (Bombay: Popular Prakashan, 1971), p. 31. The French presence in India dated from 1723 and was centred on the five trading ports of Pondichéry, Karikal, Yanaon, Mahé and Channdanagar.

[4] Weil to Talbot, Washington, 6 December 1961, *Foreign Relations of the United States* (hereafter *FRUS*), *1961–1963*, vol. XIX (Washington, DC: Government Printing Office, 1996), p. 146.

[5] Henceforth, Goa will be employed as a general term for all Portugal's South Asian possessions, inclusive of Daman and Diu.

[6] Salazar was influenced by the work of Brazilian scholar Gilberto Freyre, whose theory of Lusotropicalism emphasised the multicultural, multiracial and pluricontinental aspects of Portugal's national identify. See Franco Nogueira, *Salazar*, 6 vols. (Coimbra: Atlântida, 1977–85), and Filipe Ribeiro de Meneses, *Salazar: A Political Biography* (London: Enigma, 2010).

[7] *The Economist*, 17 April 1954.

developments elsewhere in the mid-1950s threatened American access to military facilities in Iceland and Morocco, Washington attached increasing value to NATO's bases on Portuguese soil.[8]

The Eisenhower government's relationship with Portugal acted as a festering source of Indo-US friction. In December 1955, the US Secretary of State, John Foster Dulles, infuriated Indians by issuing a joint communiqué with Paulo Cunha, Portugal's foreign minister, which made reference to Lisbon's Asian 'provinces'. Compounding his diplomatic gaffe, when journalists queried the communiqué's use of the term 'province', Dulles blithely responded, 'As far as I know, all the world regards it [Goa] as a Portuguese province.'[9] Speaking before a rally of Goan expatriates in Bombay, Jawaharlal Nehru stated that he had been 'astonished' at the 'extraordinary statement ... made by the responsible head of the Foreign office of this great country, America'.[10] The Soviet premier, Nikita Khrushchev, seized on Dulles' remark, and took delight in publicly contrasting the Soviet Union's endorsement of nationalist movements in Africa and Asia with the United States' support for anachronistic colonial regimes.[11] Tacitly acknowledging the currency that Khrushchev's rhetoric carried in the developing world, Britain's premier, Harold Macmillan, used his 'Winds of Change' address before South Africa's parliament, in February 1960, to call for a more enlightened European response to the upsurge in national consciousness sweeping across Afro-Asia.[12] Salazar shunned Macmillan's counsel. As other European nations planned for a wave of decolonisation in the early 1960s, Portugal bucked the trend. Denying the inevitability of imperial retreat, Salazar's government instead fell back on an increasingly brutal programme of colonial repression.

In this context, the Portuguese presence in Goa met with growing opposition inside India. In July 1954, Indian inhabitants of the small and

---

[8] 'The Anglo-Portuguese Alliance', 12 April 1962, CAB 129/109, C (62) 60, The United Kingdom National Archives, Kew, London (hereafter TNA).

[9] Rubinoff, *Goa*, pp. 67–8. America's ambassador to India, John Sherman Cooper, subsequently faced the uncomfortable task of attempting to 'explain' Dulles' statement to an incredulous Nehru. 'Developments Relating to Goa and Afghanistan', 8 December 1955, RG59, Office of South Asian Affairs Regional Conf. and Country Files, Box 3 Goa, NARA.

[10] Nehru address in Bombay, 4 June 1956, in Mushirul Hasan, H. Y. Sharad Prasad and A. K. Damodaran (eds.), *Selected Works of Jawaharlal Nehru*, Second Series, vol. 33, 1 May 1956–20 June 1956 (New Delhi: Oxford University Press, 2004), p. 412.

[11] B. M. Jain, 'The Kennedy Administration's Policy towards Colonialism: A Case Study of Goa, 1961, in the Indian Context', *The Indian Journal of American Studies* 14 (July 1984), 146.

[12] Harold Macmillan, *Pointing the Way, 1959–1961* (London: Macmillan, 1972), pp. 473–82.

isolated inland enclaves of Dadra and Nagar Haveli rose up and, with the help of volunteer organisations, such as the United Front of Goans, evicted Portuguese administrators. The following year, the Indian government imposed a trade embargo on Goa, and, in July 1955, suspended diplomatic relations with the Portuguese.[13] That August, a *satyagraha*, or campaign of non-violent resistance, was launched in Goa, but failed to dislodge the Portuguese. It did succeed, however, in inflaming anti-Portuguese sentiment across India after several Indian protesters were killed by Portuguese troops. While Jawaharlal Nehru never explicitly ruled out India's use of force to 'liberate' Goa, on numerous occasions after 1947, both in public and private, his rhetoric left the strong impression that his government would not sanction military action against the Portuguese.[14] In April 1955, in the lead-up to the conference of Afro-Asian nations in Bandung, Indonesia, Nehru declared that in India

we think ahead and we see the world situation as it is and we do not wish to do something even in a small way, indulging in violence etc., which may have bigger repercussions ... We are prepared to wait a little because inevitably the end must be the one we aim at, our objectives must be realized. It is inconceivable, it is impossible – and I do not care what other Powers in the world support Portugal – for Portugal to imagine that they can remain in India.[15]

However, as nationalist sentiment in the developing world gathered pace in the early 1960s, Nehru encountered ever-stronger pressure to change tack and adopt a more forceful response to the Goa problem. At the beginning of 1961, the Indian prime minister came under fire from opponents in the Lok Sabha, or lower house of India's parliament, for his government's weakness in failing to counter a spate of Chinese incursions into northern India, and adopting a 'do-nothing' policy against the Portuguese in the south. In March that year, public interest in the Goa question was reignited when the speaker of the Lok Sabha, M. A. Ayyangar, opened a 'National Convention on Goa' in New Delhi. The advent of a high-profile campaign in India's press calling for the territory's immediate 'liberation', which was financed by Goan expatriates, added to Nehru's discomfort.[16] With a general

---

[13]  Habibur Rahman, 'India's Liberation of Goa and the Anglo-American Stand', *Journal of South Asian Studies*, 19, 1 (1996), 38.

[14]  Nehru to Chief Ministers, 23–4 January 1958, in G. Parthasarathi (ed.), *Jawaharlal Nehru: Letters to Chief Ministers, 1947–1964*, vol. 5: *1958–1964* (New Delhi: Oxford University Press, 1989); Delhi to CRO, No. 244, 18 August 1961. FO 371/159705, TNA; Sarvepalli Gopal, *Jawaharlal Nehru: A Biography*, vol. 3: *1956–1964* (London: Jonathan Cape, 1984), pp. 190–1.

[15]  'Bandung Conference of Historic Importance', *The Hindustan Times*, 1 April 1955.

[16]  Weil to Talbot, Washington, 6 December 1961, *FRUS, 1961–1963*, vol. XIX, p. 147.

election due in India early in 1962, the domestic clamour for action in Goa threatened to turn the electoral process into a referendum on Nehru's anti-colonial credentials.[17]

At a conference of non-aligned nations held in Belgrade in September 1961, Indian passivity in the face of Portugal's refusal to discuss Goa's sovereignty led African nationalists to openly question Nehru's commitment to the anti-imperial cause. India lacked the military capability to tackle Chinese provocations in the north, and American policymakers began to ponder whether Nehru's government might be 'tempted to answer its foreign policy critics by making at least a demonstration of force against Goa'.[18] Frank Moraes of *The Indian Express* felt likewise, noting that Nehru might favour 'stamping on a [Portuguese] mouse in the kitchen when there was a [Chinese] tiger at the door'.[19] Stung by the criticism that he had received in Belgrade, once back in New Delhi, Nehru convened an international seminar on the 'Problems of the Portuguese Colonies'. The seminar's delegates, who included the Labour MP and future British minister Anthony Wedgwood Benn, arrived in India in a belligerent mood. African representatives, in particular, implored Nehru to erase Portugal's colonial presence from South Asia, if necessary through the use of force. Reflecting subsequently on the symposium's impact on his thinking, the Indian premier confessed that it had left his administration 'keyed up ... we were in a receptive mood, searching for something to do'.[20]

A pretext for action in Goa arrived the following month, when news reached New Delhi of a series of clashes between Portuguese troops and Indian citizens on the territory's borders. The most serious of these, which occurred on 24 November near the island of Anjadev, claimed the life of an Indian fisherman. Demanding swift retaliation, India's press embarked upon a vociferous anti-Portuguese propaganda campaign. Much of the Indian media's reporting in relation to Goa took on a sensationalist and highly emotive tone. The left-wing magazine *Link* alleged implausibly that 'some foreigners with experience in methods of torture gained in Hitler's concentration camps have been hired [by Portugal] to work as guards and use their knowledge on Goan nationalists'.[21] To the US State Department, reports in sections of the Indian press alleging that Goa stood on the verge of rebellion appeared fanciful.

[17] Delhi to CRO, No. 2126, 30 November 1961, FO 371/159705/D1024/19, TNA.
[18] Weil to Talbot, Washington, 6 December 1961, *FRUS, 1961–1963*, vol. XIX, p. 147.
[19] Arthur M. Schlesinger Jr, *A Thousand Days: John F. Kennedy in the White House* (Boston: Houghton Mifflin, 1965), p. 529.
[20] *The Times*, 29 December 1961. See also *The Daily Telegraph*, 21 October 1961.
[21] Rubinoff, *Goa*, pp. 85–6.

Aside from a small number of poorly trained and ill-equipped activists working for the Azad Gomantak Dal, or Free Goa Army, American officials noted that 'the majority of Goans are relatively passive in [the] present situation'.[22]

In New Delhi, John Kenneth Galbraith marvelled at the flimsy pretexts used by Indian newspapers to inflame public opinion. An uninformed reader, the US ambassador observed wryly, 'could conclude from the [Indian] papers that Portugal is about to take over the entire India Union. Aggression is charged although it amounts to little more than the firing of a rifle in the air – and it is not clear by whom.'[23] Britain's High Commissioner in India, Sir Paul Gore-Booth, concurred with Galbraith. 'The Indian Press campaign', he observed subsequently, 'recalled a Nazi propaganda build up ... selective, slanted and emotional.'[24] By the beginning of December 1961, both the British and American governments had become increasingly concerned that Indian jingoism was approaching the point at which Nehru might feel compelled to send the Indian Army into Goa. In a speech delivered in Allahabad, on 2 December, Nehru stated that his government could 'no longer tolerate the reign of Portuguese terror' in Goa, and would 'take suitable action at the right time'.[25] Discounting Nehru's private assurances that his government continued to favour a negotiated settlement of Indo-Portuguese differences, British and American officials began to consider how they might avert an outbreak of hostilities in the Indian subcontinent.[26]

### The limits of Anglo-American diplomacy

In Whitehall, the Commonwealth Relations Office was acutely aware that conflict between India and Portugal would place Harold Macmillan's government in an extremely awkward position. The British financial, military and political stake in India necessitated the preservation of strong Anglo-Indian ties. Equally, Anglo-Portuguese treaties signed in 1661 and 1899 committed Britain to defend Portugal's overseas

---

[22] Talbot to Ball, Washington, 12 December 1961, *FRUS, 1961–1963*, vol. XIX, pp. 153–5.
[23] Galbraith, *Ambassador's Journal*, New Delhi, 8 December 1961, pp. 274–5, and New Delhi, 11 December 1961, p. 276.
[24] 'India: The Invasion of Goa', Gore-Booth to Sandys, 29 December 1961, PREM 11/3837, TNA.
[25] *The Sunday Express*, 3 December 1961.
[26] *The Times*, 4 December 1961.

territories.[27] In Washington, the Kennedy administration was equally disturbed by the prospect of an armed clash between Portugal, a valued NATO ally, and India, a country central to its strategic vision for Asia. In particular, American officials were concerned that an Indian military assault on Goa would adversely affect the international community's willingness to bankroll India's development, and imperil the country's chances of outpacing the People's Republic of China as Asia's dominant economic power. Moreover, by utilising force to resolve a territorial dispute, India appeared likely to set a dangerous global precedent, most especially in 'promot[ing] further chaos in Africa, where India has done so much to try to restore order, as in the Congo'.[28]

In New Delhi, uncertainty reigned during early December, as Nehru vacillated between launching a military strike on Goa and continuing to pursue a negotiated settlement with the Portuguese.[29] By way of illustration, *The Times* noted that after Nehru had publicly rejected further Indo-Portuguese talks, members of the ruling Congress Party had tabled a Lok Sabha motion calling for Lisbon to be issued with a final ultimatum to quit Goa or face the consequences. To the consternation of puzzled colleagues, however, Nehru promptly backtracked and opposed the parliamentary motion, explaining that he still hoped to resolve the Goa crisis peacefully.[30] A series of contradictory statements from Indian government ministers added to the atmosphere of confusion. One cabinet clique, led by India's finance minister, Morarji Desai, stressed the 'precautionary' nature of the government's decision to mobilise India's armed forces.[31] Another, led by India's defence minister, Krishna Menon, asserted that 'the die is cast, India's patience is at last exhausted ... Portuguese colonialism is now to be driven out'.[32]

Despite mounting pressure to act against the Portuguese, Gore-Booth informed the CRO on 8 December that Nehru seemed not to have

---

[27] 'The Anglo-Portuguese Treaty', 13 December 1961, FO 371/159707/D1024/52, TNA.

[28] Weil to Talbot, Washington, 6 December 1961, *FRUS, 1961–1963*, vol. XIX, p. 147.

[29] 'India: The Invasion of Goa', Gore-Booth to Sandys, 29 December 1961, PREM 11/3837, TNA.

[30] *The Times*, 9 December 1961.

[31] Desai subsequently criticised Nehru's handling of the Goa crisis, lamenting that it had squandered 'the moral respect which India commanded in the international field'. Morarji Desai, *The Story of My Life*, vol. 2 (Oxford: Pergamon Press, 1979), p. 190.

[32] *The Times*, 5 December 1961. In the first week of December, the British noted that Indian Army units had begun converging on Goa in brigade strength, and that the crew of the Indian aircraft carrier *Vikrant* had been recalled from leave to Bombay. Delhi to CRO, No. 2154, 4 December 1961, FO 371/159705, TNA.

reached an irrevocable decision to send the Indian Army into Goa.[33] Galbraith shared the British assessment. Confirming Nehru's irresolution, the American ambassador nevertheless cautioned Washington that in the prevailing climate of heightened Indo-Portuguese tension, a single incendiary incident could trigger an Indian military response.[34] Faced with an apparently narrowing window of opportunity, in London, Macmillan's government debated how best to tackle the 'urgent and acutely embarrassing situation' developing in India. Arguing that Britain was already overburdened with Asian problems, the South East Asia desk at the Foreign Office urged caution. 'Getting into this squabble', its officials insisted, would 'do ourselves nothing but harm with the Indians ... [inviting their] utmost bitterness to any interference on our part.'[35] Nehru, it was suggested, might well ascribe a colonial motivation to British calls for Indian restraint, leaving a bad taste in New Delhi's mouth. In this sense, the FO suggested, American diplomatic intervention was more likely to yield positive results.[36] From India, Gore-Booth voiced his agreement. Preponderant Western influence on the subcontinent, he rationalised, now lay with the Americans, who stood 'a much better chance than we do of being able to mediate in this dispute'. The FO's Central Department also favoured an American-led approach to the Goa problem but, in addition, pushed for a British show of support for the Portuguese. In the Central Department's assessment, should NATO, 'and above all her ancient [British] ally', fail to uphold Portuguese interests in South Asia, Salazar might retaliate by withdrawing from the Western alliance or denying RAF aircraft access to Portuguese airspace and strategically valuable staging facilities.[37]

In taking into account their treaty commitments to the Portuguese, the British pondered whether it might be possible to circumvent their obligation to defend Portugal's colonies by providing Salazar's government with less direct forms of military assistance. Previous British governments had ruled out military action against India, or any other member of the Commonwealth, as 'unthinkable'. Yet, as the Foreign Office emphasised, such a convenient escape clause would prove worthless should

---

[33] Gore-Booth to CRO, No. 338, 8 December 1961, FO 371/159707/D1024/60, TNA.

[34] Galbraith to State Department, 10 December 1961, *FRUS, 1961–1963*, vol. XIX, p. 152.

[35] 'Warner Note on Goa', 8 December 1961, FO 371/159706/D1024/30, TNA. Elsewhere in Asia, at this very moment the British were disengaging from support for the Dutch claim on West Irian. See Matthew Jones, *Conflict and Confrontation in South East Asia, 1961–1965: Britain, the United States, and the Creation of Malaysia* (Cambridge University Press, 2002).

[36] FO to Ormsby Gore, No. 9164, 8 December 1961, FO 371/159706/D1024/24, TNA.

[37] 'Warner Note on Goa', 8 December 1961, FO 371/159706/D1024/30, TNA.

the Chinese move against Portuguese Macao, or Indonesia attack East Timor. 'I should hate to think that we were obliged to engage the might of Communist China', one British official reflected, 'on behalf of the 400 year-old, six square-miles, territory of Macao.'[38] Disconcertingly for Macmillan's government, before it could act, Salazar followed up calls for British diplomatic support with a request to use RAF bases in Aden and Mauritius for the staging of Portuguese troops and military equipment bound for Goa.[39] While not ruling out Portuguese access to RAF facilities, the British played for time. Lisbon was informed that its use of Aden and Mauritius was 'technically impractical' and, that while diplomatic channels remained open, Britain preferred not to compromise its ability to act as an honest broker by appearing to take sides in the Goa dispute.[40] However, in the final analysis, although reconfirming that Britain could not engage in hostilities against India, Macmillan's cabinet agreed that if pressed, it would consider granting the Portuguese access to alternative RAF facilities.[41] Notifying Nehru only of the former decision, Macmillan somewhat disingenuously underlined his government's determination to avoid military entanglement in the Indo-Portuguese dispute. Tellingly, in his reply to the British premier, Nehru offered no such guarantee.[42]

As the British struggled to sidestep Portugal's unwelcome call for support, incongruously, American officials suggested that Macmillan's government should cajole Salazar into offering India concessions with respect to Goa's sovereignty. Acknowledging that the Kennedy administration held more sway in New Delhi than the British, somewhat implausibly, Galbraith claimed the opposite to be true in Lisbon. As 'the only people who have any influence on the Portuguese', the American ambassador proposed that Britain should prod Salazar to grant India a greater economic and cultural say in Goa's affairs.

---

[38] 'The Anglo-Portuguese Treaty', 13 December 1961, FO 371/159707/D1024/52, TNA.
[39] Britain's ambassador in Lisbon, Sir Archibald Ross, had been asked by the Portuguese Foreign Ministry on 5 December to arrange for London to issue a warning to Nehru against the use of force in Goa. The British demurred, informing the Portuguese disingenuously that the Goa question was a bilateral matter between India and Portugal. Ross to FO, No. 619, 5 December 1961, and FO to Lisbon, No. 1004, 6 December 1961, FO 371/159706, TNA.
[40] 71st Cabinet Conclusions, Goa, 12 December 1961, CAB 128/35, CC (61); 74th Cabinet Conclusions, Goa, 14 December 1961, CAB 128/35, CC (61), TNA.
[41] FO to Lisbon, No. 1035, 12 December 1961, PREM 11/3837, TNA; 'Portuguese Request for Facilities at British Airfields for Reinforcements for Goa', 12 December 1961, FO 371/159707/D1024/56; 74th Cabinet Conclusions, Goa, 14 December 1961, CAB 128/35, CC (61), TNA.
[42] Gopal, *Nehru: 1956–1964*, p. 197.

Gore-Booth dismissed Galbraith's proposal as misguided. At best, the British High Commissioner reasoned, such a transparent attempt to sustain a Portuguese presence in the Indian subcontinent would buy a day or two of negotiations with Nehru's government before the fundamental sticking point of Goa's long-term sovereignty reared its head.[43] The CRO endorsed Gore-Booth's analysis. Given Salazar's track record, it seemed that 'they [the Portuguese] may well prefer to be thrown out of Goa after a brief resistance rather than climb down in the face of an Indian threat'. Although not ruling out British mediation should Indo-Portuguese tempers cool, in the interim, the CRO counselled that approaching Salazar was 'likely to achieve nothing and merely make the Portuguese less inclined to listen to us later'.[44] The British Embassy in Lisbon agreed. In a warning to Whitehall, embassy officials counselled that Salazar would deeply resent Britain 'responding to an ally's appeal for help by advising surrender'. Earlier American efforts to encourage the Portuguese government to cede greater autonomy to its overseas territories, it was noted, had been badly received. Following Washington's lead appeared likely only to 'add insult to injury'.[45]

Inside the Kennedy administration, an analogous debate raged over the merits of balancing a warning to India against taking military action in Goa, with a statement condemning colonialism. Throughout early December, Galbraith badgered Washington to adopt a 'bolder and more dramatic' approach to the Goa question. Supporting India's claim on Goa and strengthening Indo-US ties, he argued, would better serve Asia's future and America's wider interests than condoning Portuguese imperialism.[46] Kennedy's Secretary of State, Dean Rusk, disagreed. Mindful of Portugal's importance to NATO, Rusk acceded to a request from Salazar that American officials refrain from any public comment on the colonial dimension of the Goa dispute.[47] Siding with Galbraith, the State Department's South Asia desk challenged Rusk's edict. Asking Nehru's government to reject a military resolution to the Goa quarrel, its officials insisted, while refusing to denounce Portugal's colonial policy, risked provoking an anti-American backlash in India. The time had come, Rusk was urged, 'to deal with the issue [Goa] as a whole'.[48]

---

[43] Gore-Booth to CRO, No. 2248, 14 December 1961, PREM 11/3837, TNA.
[44] CRO to Delhi, No. 3926, 14 December 1961, PREM 11/3837, TNA.
[45] Lisbon to FO, No. 651, 15 December 1961, PREM 11/3837, TNA.
[46] Weil to Talbot, Washington, 6 December 1961, *FRUS, 1961–1963*, vol. XIX, p. 146.
[47] Schlesinger, *Thousand Days*, pp. 527–8.
[48] Weil to Talbot, Washington, 6 December 1961, *FRUS, 1961–1963*, vol. XIX, p. 148.

The appeal from the State Department's South Asian specialists left Rusk unmoved. On 8 December, following a request for American support from Portugal's foreign minister, Franco Nogueira, Rusk instructed Phillips Talbot, US Assistant Secretary of State for Near Eastern and South Asian Affairs, to issue the Indian government with a firm warning against launching a military assault on Goa.[49] In New Delhi, Galbraith criticised the timing and tenor of Talbot's missive. To Indians, the ambassador lamented, it had implied that Washington was both susceptible to Portuguese pressure and willing to condone an anti-quated brand of imperialism. Moreover, by offering the Indian government nothing more in compensation than vague platitudes reaffirming America's commitment to self-determination in the developing world, the State Department had provided Nehru with little hope that diplomacy alone could end Portugal's presence in the subcontinent.[50] In Rusk's defence, his deputy, Under Secretary of State George Ball, informed Galbraith that the 'Portuguese will not give an inch [on Goa] and an approach from us would only bring recriminations and bitter comparisons to our consistent stand on [not] negotiating in [the] face of [the] threat of force in Berlin and elsewhere'.[51] Dispirited, Galbraith reflected later that he had 'hardly imagined that I would be undercut in such a flaccid and incompetent manner by our own management'.[52] So inexplicable had Dean Rusk's timidity seemed in the face of 'incredible' Portuguese proposals, which included a suggestion that Pakistani divisions be deployed along India's border to intimidate Nehru, that a member of Galbraith's embassy staff 'conclude[d] that the [US] policy was to support the Portuguese fully and that I was out of step'.[53]

When news reached the US Embassy in New Delhi during the second week of December that Indian Army units were massing on Goa's borders, Galbraith's suspicion that Washington's refusal to exert pressure on Salazar would force Nehru's hand appeared well founded.[54] M. J. Desai, Nehru's foreign minister, confirmed the sense of growing Indian frustration over the Goa impasse. A staunch advocate of non-violence,

---

[49] State Department to New Delhi, Washington, 8 December 1961, *FRUS, 1961–1963*, vol. XIX, pp. 149–50; Ormsby Gore to FO, No. 3333, 8 December 1961, FO 371/159706/D1024/24, TNA.

[50] Galbraith to State Department, New Delhi, 10 December 1961, *FRUS, 1961–1963*, vol. XIX, p. 152.

[51] Ball to New Delhi, Washington, 14 December 1961, *FRUS, 1961–1963*, vol. XIX, pp. 157–8.

[52] Galbraith, *Ambassador's Journal*, New Delhi, 18 December 1961, pp. 281–5.

[53] Galbraith to Rusk, 19 December 1961, RG 59, Lot 72 D 192, Box 41, Folder G, NARA.

[54] Galbraith to State Department, New Delhi, 10 December 1961, *FRUS, 1961–1963*, vol. XIX, p. 152.

Desai confided in Galbraith that events were now 'passing rapidly beyond his hands'. Only immediate and substantial Portuguese concessions on Goa's future sovereignty, Desai suggested, could now avert Indian military action. In response, a despondent Galbraith cabled Washington on 15 December that an Indian invasion of Goa, 'probably tomorrow', appeared inevitable.[55] The State Department, he recorded in his diary that evening, would 'have to give me something fairly good to stop it'.[56]

In fact, late on 15 December, as India's army prepared to move into Goa, the American ambassador's desperate pleas to Indian ministers to be given more time to frame a diplomatic solution to the crisis caused Nehru to step back from the military precipice. Suspending 'Operation Vijay' for forty-eight hours, the Indian premier expressed the hope that a last-minute agreement with the Portuguese might still be possible.[57] A 'disturbed' Krishna Menon was far less sure that Salazar could be made to see reason, and pressed Nehru to reverse his decision. Cautioning that 'there will be trouble' if Indian troops were left kicking their heels on Goa's border, Menon prodded Nehru to set a new D-Day for a military assault.[58] Back in Washington, at Galbraith's prompting, Kennedy instructed the State Department to exploit the brief window of opportunity afforded by Nehru to redouble diplomatic efforts to avert an Indo-Portuguese clash. With Dean Rusk travelling in Europe, the job of keeping the peace in Goa fell to George Ball. Having first reiterated to India's ambassador in Washington, B. K. Nehru, the dim personal view that Kennedy would take were New Delhi to initiate hostilities against the Portuguese,[59] Ball offered the Indian government a carrot to offset the diplomatic stick that the United States had brandished in Nehru's face throughout the Goa crisis. Were India to agree to a six-month standstill on military action, Ball confirmed, the Kennedy administration would 'undertake a serious effort' to broker a settlement between Lisbon and New Delhi.[60]

[55] *Ibid.*, p. 160.
[56] Galbraith, *Ambassador's Journal*, New Delhi, 15 December 1961, p. 279.
[57] Gopal, *Nehru: 1956–1964*, p. 197.
[58] Michael Brecher, *India and World Politics: Krishna Menon's View of the World* (London: Oxford University Press, 1968), pp. 130–1.
[59] Memorandum of conversation between Ball and B. K. Nehru, 15 December 1961, George Ball Papers, Box 5 of 9, India, 1961–3, John F. Kennedy Library, Boston, Massachusetts (hereafter JFKL).
[60] George Ball meeting with Ambassador Nehru, 16 December 1961, RG 59, Lot 65 D 330, NARA.

For Galbraith, Ball's offer represented too little, too late. The State Department proposal, he carped, was 'unspecific and badly hedged'.[61] Nehru shared Galbraith's reservations, and the American ambassador's subsequent bid to sell the six-month formula to the Indian government failed. Given the depth of Salazar's feeling on the colonial question, and Washington's reluctance to press Lisbon on the issue, Nehru saw no advantage in continuing to postpone the day of reckoning in Goa. Indeed, by demanding an immediate resolution to the crisis, the prime minister conceded, Indian public opinion had driven his cabinet 'beyond [the] point of no return'. Reporting back to Washington, Galbraith noted that Nehru had 'virtually told me' that Indian military action was now inevitable.[62] The American ambassador's frustration at his failure to prevent the outbreak of Indo-Portuguese hostilities was vented not at the Indian government, but the State Department. In a stinging cable to Rusk, an angry Galbraith insisted that 'this episode was avoidable'. The Indian cabinet, he observed, had been 'deeply divided' on the merit of sending troops into Goa and, with Nehru wavering, effective American intervention could have tilted the scales back in favour of a negotiated settlement. To nullify the voices calling for the 'liberation' of Goa within his government, the Congress Party and the Indian press, Galbraith maintained, Nehru had required nothing more than a prompt and firm American commitment that the Portuguese would not be allowed to 'sit on their asses with the classic stolidity of the last fourteen years'. The State Department's refusal to address such a basic requirement 'until it got to the highest levels', he added, 'was deplorable'.[63]

Last ditch efforts made by the British to halt India's march toward war proved similarly ineffective. Citing the pressures of cabinet business, Nehru granted Gore-Booth only the briefest audience in which to restate the British case against Indian military action. Ignoring the High Commissioner's invitation to rule out an assault on Goa, a tired

---

[61] Galbraith, *Ambassador's Journal*, New Delhi, 18 December 1961, p. 284. Nehru later referred to the American initiative as well intentioned but 'rather vague'. A. Appadorai (ed.), *Select Documents on India's Foreign Policy and Relations, 1947–1972*, vol. 2 (New Delhi: Oxford University Press, 1985), pp. 435–40.

[62] Galbraith to State Department, New Delhi, 17 December 1961, *FRUS, 1961–1963*, vol. XIX, pp. 161–2.

[63] Galbraith to Rusk, 19 December 1961, RG 59, Lot 72 D 192, Box 41, Folder G, NARA. Galbraith reiterated his claim to Kennedy's National Security Advisor, McGeorge Bundy, stating that had Ball acted earlier, 'I could then have thrown a block in with Nehru and had some hope of success'. Galbraith to McGeorge Bundy, 26 December 1961, National Security File (NSF), Box 106, India, General, 12/1/61–12/3/61, JFKL.

and exasperated Nehru snapped back that, 'If nothing happened about Goa he would have to resign – not immediately but within a short period.'[64] Harold Macmillan retained little sympathy for Salazar's outmoded imperial pretensions, noting privately that 'it was absurd of the Portuguese to try to hold onto it [Goa]'.[65] Mindful, however, of the wider international implications of India's use of force, the British premier wrote to Nehru on 13 December in a bid to stay his hand. Lauding India's global standing as a beacon of morality and restraint, Macmillan cautioned Nehru that the annexation of Goa would squander this reputation and risk igniting a series of regional conflagrations. Were India to forsake the rule of international law, Macmillan opined, 'I feel sure that President Sukarno would then consider himself justified in making a military attack on New Guinea, and I fear that many of the new African states would have recourse to the same methods in order to solve their feuds and jealousies.' Nehru's reply landed on Macmillan's desk late on 17 December, as four thousand miles away the Indian Army marched into Goa.[66]

## The United Nations debate on Goa

In the wake of India's annexation of Goa, Nehru justified his government's action by pointing to resolutions denouncing Portuguese colonialism that the United Nations General Assembly had passed in 1960 and 1961. Asserting that the UN had legitimised India's claim on Goa, Nehru insisted that given Salazar's refusal to negotiate a peaceful transition of power, India's 'police action' constituted an act of national liberation rather than international aggression.[67] From the Indian government's perspective, the oppressive character of the colonial administration in Goa provided an additional and compelling rationale for terminating Portuguese rule in the subcontinent. Citing acts of intolerable Portuguese provocation, Nehru argued that a combination of increased repression and escalating social disorder inside Goa had forced his hand. 'It appeared to us', the Indian prime minister informed the world's media on 28 December, 'that if we had really called off the whole thing we would probably have had to shoot down our people in

---

[64] Delhi to CRO, No. 2238, 13 December 1961, FO 371/159707/D1024/54, TNA.

[65] Macmillan to Menzies, 19 December 1961, MSS Macmillan, dep. c. 332, f. 293, Harold Macmillan Papers, Bodleian Library, University of Oxford (hereafter HMP).

[66] Macmillan to Nehru, 13 December 1961, PREM 11/3837, TNA.

[67] Gopal, *Nehru: 1956–1964*, p. 194.

considerable numbers or stand by and witness the Portuguese shooting them.'[68]

In an exchange of correspondence with Macmillan, Nehru maintained that the responsibility for failing to resolve the Goa crisis peacefully lay with Salazar. Unnecessary and ill-judged acts of Portuguese aggression, the Indian leader informed Macmillan, had whipped popular Indian sentiment into an indignant frenzy. 'As a democratic leader', Nehru intoned, 'you will appreciate that there are limits to what one can do against a widespread and resentful public opinion.' For Nehru, the decision to send Indian troops into Goa, though regrettable, constituted 'the lesser of two evils'. Had India not acted decisively, he assured his British counterpart, the despotic Portuguese administration would have responded to spiralling civil disorder inside Goa with lethal force.[69] However, despite robustly defending his government's handling of the Goa emergency, Nehru did express reservations at the wider implications of resolving international disputes at the point of a gun. Speaking at a press conference in New Delhi, in late December, the prime minister confessed 'that one of the considerations that had made him hold his hand [in relation to Goa] for 14 years was the misgivings he felt about the consequences in the world at large of India's use of force'.[70] For his part, Gore-Booth concluded that the decision to send the Indian Army into Goa had 'produced a tremendous moral revulsion in Nehru who later undoubtedly realised that he had been wrong'.[71]

The Portuguese government responded to India's assault on Goa by asking the UN Security Council to convene in emergency session. Meeting in New York on 18 December, Adlai Stevenson, America's ambassador to the United Nations, placed a draft resolution before Security Council members that called for an immediate ceasefire in Goa, the withdrawal of Indian forces and the resumption of Indo-Portuguese talks. The British UN delegation, headed by Sir Patrick Dean, hesitated to associate itself with a resolution that was certain to antagonise the Indian government. Having counted on Britain's backing within the Security Council, Dean's equivocation angered the Kennedy administration.[72] Summoned to the State Department, the British ambassador in Washington, David Ormsby Gore, was curtly informed by Dean

---

[68] Nehru Press Conference, 28 December 1961, Appadorai (ed.), *Relations*, vol. 2, p. 434.
[69] Nehru to Macmillan, 17 December 1962, PREM 11/3837, TNA.
[70] *The Times*, 29 December 1961.
[71] Conversation between Lord Home and Gore-Booth, 22 June 1962, DO 196/127, TNA.
[72] Ball call with Ambassador Elbrick, Lisbon, 16 December 1961, George Ball Papers, Box 5 of 9, India, 1961–3, JFKL.

Rusk that the White House was 'very unhappy' with the stance Britain had taken in New York. In the circumstances, Rusk emphasised, though regrettable, it was clearly appropriate for the Western members of the Security Council to censure India for what amounted to an act of aggression. Were the British government not to endorse Stevenson's Security Council resolution, Rusk added pointedly, bar the French, the Kennedy administration would be 'left almost alone in taking an initiative with which he assumed we [Britain] fully agreed'. The US government would take a dim view, Ormsby Gore made plain to London, were it forced to confront India's ire without British support.[73]

On leaving Rusk's office, Ormsby Gore immediately contacted Dean in New York and urged his colleague to reverse course and co-sponsor Stevenson's resolution.[74] Capitulating, Dean despatched an apologetic note to the Foreign Office late on 18 December justifying his decision. 'I agreed to co-sponsor the United States draft Resolution', he advised the British Foreign Secretary, Lord Home, 'only after holding out against doing so for as long as possible, since the Americans would otherwise have been in a very isolated position. The president personally appealed to Her Majesty's Ambassador in Washington to secure our co-sponsorship, and in the circumstances I thought it right to avail myself of the discretion which you had given me.'[75] Dean's initiative in using his 'discretion' to change tack and back Stevenson in the Security Council proved timely. Back at the Foreign Office, Home had come out firmly in favour of Britain taking a robust stand against India's decision to occupy Goa. In Home's view, New Delhi's use of force represented a clear breach of 'the rule of law', threatened 'very grave' international repercussions and therefore necessitated a firm British riposte. Calling India's acting High Commissioner in London, T. N. Kaul, to the Foreign Office, Home informed the Indian diplomat that his government's behaviour had undermined its international reputation and the wider work of the United Nations.[76] 'If India's action were not condemned in the United Nations,' Home insisted to cabinet colleagues the next day, 'Indonesia would be encouraged to launch a similar attack on West Irian.' Anticipating that the Soviet Union would use their Security Council veto to block a resolution denouncing India, Home suggested placing a motion deploring Indian aggression before the UN

[73] Ormsby Gore to FO, No. 3451, 19 December 1961, PREM 11/3837, TNA.
[74] Ibid.
[75] Dean to FO, No. 2616, 18 December 1961, FO 371/159708/D1024/77(B), TNA.
[76] The Foreign Secretary's interview with Kaul, 18 December 1961, FO 371/159710/D1024/105, TNA.

General Assembly, in order to uphold the organisation's credentials as the guardian of international law.[77]

Home remained exercised by events in Goa when Kennedy, Macmillan, and leading British and American officials met on the island of Bermuda, later in December. Revisiting the Security Council's shortcomings in responding to acts of international aggression, Home pressed the Americans to participate in a concerted Western effort to resist 'a tendency to ignore the [UN] Charter when colonial matters came up'. What would the United Nations response be, the British Foreign Secretary asked, 'if China attacked Hong Kong or Spain Gibraltar? Could we afford to let this issue drop?' Unimpressed, Dean Rusk dismissed what he considered to be an exaggerated show of British imperial sensitivity. His government, the US Secretary of State observed cuttingly to Home, 'did not think that the anti-colonialism of the Afro-Asians was aimed at the British'.[78] Rusk's impatience with Home belied the wider sense of indignation that he felt at India's decision to use force against the Portuguese. Anxious, however, not to derail the Kennedy administration's plan to transform Nehru's government into a tacit Western ally, Rusk confined his criticism of India to a terse private exchange with B. K. Nehru. Placing a call to the Indian ambassador on 17 December, Rusk left him in no doubt that he 'deplore[d] the Indian action after all our efforts to prevent violence', and regretted the fact that this would 'undoubtedly put a strain on public attitudes [toward India] in this country'.[79] In the same vein, the following day Rusk instructed Adlai Stevenson 'to make our views known very sharply to the Indians privately [at the UN]'. 'The [Indian] double standard', the Secretary of State added caustically, 'is becoming a triple standard.' Moving forward, however, Rusk ordered American diplomats to mute public criticism of India's action in Goa. If questioned by the press, State Department officials were advised to voice expressions of sorrow, rather than anger, at the regrettable turn of events in South Asia.[80]

The stinging rebuke that Stevenson subsequently aimed at Nehru's government during the Security Council's debate on Goa paid little heed to Rusk's directive. As expected, Stevenson's resolution calling for a return to the status quo ante in Goa was defeated by a Soviet veto. In response, the American ambassador engaged in a remarkable display

---

[77] 75th Conclusions, Goa, 19 December 1961, CAB 128/35, CC (61), TNA.
[78] Home conversation with Rusk, 21 December 1961, PREM 11/3782, TNA.
[79] Rusk telephone conversation with Ambassador Nehru, 17 December 1962, RG 59, Lot File 79 D 192, Box 45, NARA.
[80] Rusk telephone conversation with Ambassador Stevenson, 18 December 1962, RG 59, Lot File 79 D 192, Box 45, NARA.

of hyperbole, asserting that the Security Council's failure to condemn India's act of aggression 'could end with its death'. 'The failure ... to call for a cease-fire tonight in these simple circumstances', Stevenson continued, 'is a failure of the United Nations ... This approach can only lead to chaos and to the disintegration of the United Nations.' Seizing on Stevenson's remarks, the British and American press added to the prevailing sense of crisis. In London, *The Times* reported that the Soviet use of its Security Council veto had 'left the United Nations headquarters in a state of shock and almost super-charged emotionalism'.[81] Of more immediate concern to senior British and American officials, however, was the positive impact that Soviet support for India had had on Moscow's standing in Asia and Africa. The Soviet president, Leonid Brezhnev, who happened to be visiting Bombay on the evening of 20 December, revelled in the propaganda opportunity presented by the Goa crisis. Speaking at a banquet hosted in his honour by the State Governor of Maharashtra, Brezhnev emphasised his delight at being on hand to witness 'a great event in the life of your motherland, the liberation of the land of India from the last remnants of colonialism'.[82] While the Soviets' anti-imperialist credentials received a welcome boost during the Goa saga, in contrast, by appearing to side with the Portuguese, London and Washington won few friends in the developing world.[83]

Back in New Delhi, Galbraith was stunned by Stevenson's 'unfortunately emotional' performance at the UN. The invective and lack of balance in Stevenson's rhetoric appeared especially injudicious given the importance that the Kennedy administration placed on the United States' relationship with India. While excoriating India at some length for the errors of its ways, Galbraith observed, Stevenson had made no comment whatsoever on the pernicious nature of Portuguese colonialism.[84] Nehru was incensed by the tone of Stevenson's verbal assault on India. While his government had expected a mild show of American disapproval in the aftermath of Goa, they were taken aback by the ferocity of Stevenson's 'emotional outbursts'. Protesting formally to Phillips Talbot, B. K. Nehru noted that by allowing Stevenson to publicly vent his spleen, Washington had 'handled [Goa] in the "wrong way"' and

[81] 'Failure of Goa Cease-Fire Call Could be End of UN', *The Times*, 20 December 1961, p. 8.
[82] 'Liberation of Goa a Great Event – Brezhnev', 21 December 1961, *National Herald*, Lucknow.
[83] *The Times*, 20 December 1961.
[84] Galbraith, *Ambassador's Journal*, New Delhi, 20 December 1961, p. 286.

needlessly alienated Indian opinion.[85] In common with Galbraith, Nehru suspected that Stevenson's Security Council outburst stemmed, in large part, from his desire to repay Krishna Menon in kind for the vitriolic anti-American tirades that the Indian defence minister had delivered over a number of years from the floor of the UN.[86] Somewhat ironically, given his own reputation for histrionics in the Security Council chamber, Menon added his own voice to the chorus of Indian criticism heaped upon Kennedy's UN ambassador. 'Stevenson could have made a token protest,' Menon noted, 'but instead of that he took it [Goa] as though it was like the *Anschluss*.'[87]

### Kennedy, Macmillan and the impact of Goa on India's relations with the West

On a personal level, the timing of India's 'police action' in Goa, coming five weeks after Nehru had visited the United States, offended President Kennedy. Reasoning that Indian contingency plans for an assault on Goa must had been formulated prior to his talks with Nehru in Washington, Kennedy took the Indian prime minister's silence on the subject to be an act of bad faith. Moreover, for the exasperated American president, Nehru's subsequent exercise in self-justification betrayed a troubling inability to confront the negative consequences of a poorly conceived Indian decision.[88] Aside from its adverse impact on New Delhi's relations with Pakistan and India's standing on Capitol Hill, American intelligence sources indicated that Nehru's show of strength in Goa might prove to be a serious strategic blunder. It seemed possible that the wave of popular euphoria in India generated by Nehru's decision to give the Portuguese a bloody nose, would translate into domestic pressure on his government to produce an encore against the far more formidable Chinese.[89] In such circumstances, analysts at the Central Intelligence Agency concluded, 'the Goa affair could prove to have been a real boomerang'.[90]

---

[85] Talbot meeting with B. K. Nehru, 29 January 1962, RG 59, NEA INC Lot 65 D 415, Entry 5252, Box 1, Kashmir, NARA.

[86] Dennis Kux, *India and the United States: Estranged Democracies, 1941–1991* (Washington, DC: National Defense University Press, 1993), p. 197.

[87] Brecher, *World Politics*, p. 134.

[88] Talbot meeting with B. K. Nehru, 29 January 1962, RG 59, NEA INC Lot 65 D 415, Entry 5252, Box 1, Kashmir, NARA.

[89] Indian opinion polls indicated that 97 per cent of the population supported the forceful annexation of Goa. See Rubinoff, *Goa*, p. 100.

[90] 'Afterthoughts', CIA report, 16 January 1962, NSF, Box 106A, India, General, 1/1/62–1/31/62, JFKL.

Galbraith conceded that the Goa episode had turned American opinion against India. Even so, he cautioned Washington against taking matters too far and provoking a schism in the United States' relations with New Delhi. 'India is the strongest of the non-Communist countries in this part of the world,' Galbraith reminded the State Department, 'and we cannot avoid doing business with her.'[91] In contrast, the State Department's Europeanists were reluctant to let India off the hook too lightly. Brushing aside India's attack on a NATO ally, some in the State Department argued, risked undermining the organisation's unity. In the White House, Kennedy came down firmly on the side of Galbraith. With characteristic pragmatism, the president observed that given the decisiveness with which India had evicted the Portuguese, his administration 'really didn't have any alternative to doing a bit of grumbling but going along'.[92] Making any further diplomatic protest, such as recalling American diplomats from New Delhi, seemed a futile exercise that would serve only to embitter already strained Indo-US ties. Kennedy had previously downplayed the notion that India's annexation of Goa would set a dangerous precedent for the resolution of other territorial disputes. Prior to the outbreak of hostilities on the Indian subcontinent, the American president had confided to Macmillan, 'let's face it, if at the end of the day Goa becomes Indian and West Irian becomes Indonesian, neither you in Britain or we in America are going to suffer any irrevocable damage. We must keep a sense of perspective about this.'[93] Kennedy was much more concerned with the negative consequences that the Goa dispute would have on American perceptions of India. While insisting that US economic assistance to India carried no strings, Kennedy urged Nehru to recognise that Congressional control over the executive purse dictated that 'we must both weigh the effects of action by one country on public opinion and political action in the other'.[94] Adopting a 'rather philosophical attitude', Kennedy contented himself with privately chastising Nehru for damaging India's 'general international reputation', and more pertinently, '[its] position in Washington'.[95]

[91]  Galbraith, *Ambassador's Journal*, New Delhi, 26 December 1961, p. 293.
[92]  Phillips Talbot, 13 August 1970, Oral History (OH) interview, JFKL, p. 67.
[93]  Lord Harlech, OH interview, JFKL.
[94]  Kennedy to Nehru, Washington, 18 January 1962, *FRUS, 1961–1963*, vol. XIX, pp. 197–9.
[95]  Robert Komer, OH, 3 September 1964, p. 14, JFKL; Phillips Talbot, OH, 13 August 1970, p. 67, JFKL; Desai, *My Life*, vol. 2, p. 192.

In the final analysis, neither India nor the United States wished to see differences over Goa dislocate their bilateral relations.[96] The significant political capital that Kennedy had invested in forging closer ties with India precluded an American schism with New Delhi. He would, Kennedy assured Nehru on 18 January, work to 'ensure that damage to our common interests is temporary. Good and fruitful relations with India have been a matter of great concern to me for many years.'[97] Underlining the Kennedy administration's position, Dean Rusk confirmed in a US television broadcast aired the same month that, 'We [America] have a basic interest in the economic and social development of India, and we have not abandoned that policy or interest.'[98] Accordingly, 'without undue publicity', Washington was soon arranging for the release of economic aid payments to India, which it had suspended following the outbreak of Indo-Portuguese hostilities. Moreover, having embargoed the shipment of arms to New Delhi once fighting had broken out in Goa, following an enquiry from the Indian government in early January concerning the purchase of US aircraft, missiles and communications equipment, Kennedy's National Security Council advisers recommended 'that in the near future we resume consideration of such sales'.[99]

The clash between India and Portugal, the British Secretary of State for Commonwealth Relations, Duncan Sandys, informed the House of Commons on 18 December, had placed Macmillan's government 'in a most painful position'.[100] For Galbraith, by 'taking no positions' at all during the crisis in an attempt to avoid alienating Lisbon or New Delhi, the British succeeded merely in 'getting the worst of it from both sides'.[101] Macmillan's government took a different view. The fact that Britain had emerged from a potentially disastrous diplomatic predicament with its relations with India and Portugal intact, if battered, was considered to be cause for considerable satisfaction. Lord Home lamented that the Anglo-Portuguese alliance had 'suffered heavily

---

[96] Robert J. McMahon, *The Cold War on the Periphery: The United States, India and Pakistan* (New York: Columbia University Press, 1994), p. 282.

[97] Kennedy to Nehru, Washington, 18 January 1962, *FRUS, 1961–1963*, vol. XIX, pp. 197–9.

[98] Jain, 'Goa', 151.

[99] NEA paper on South Asian Affairs, Washington, undated, *FRUS, 1961–1963*, vol. XIX, pp. 185–8; Komer to McGeorge Bundy, Washington, 12 January 1962, *FRUS, 1961–1963*, vol. XIX, p. 190.

[100] Sandys' Commons statement on Goa, 18 December 1961, DSDN 8/10, Duncan Sandys Papers, Churchill Archives Centre, Churchill College Cambridge (hereafter DSP).

[101] Galbraith, *Ambassador's Journal*, New Delhi, 15 December 1961, p. 279.

because they [Portugal] felt that, in not giving them assistance against India, we were being untrue to the alliance'.[102] Although sharply critical of 'Britain's ineffectual intervention in the Goa Affair', Salazar nevertheless confirmed to the French daily *Le Figaro* that 'the English, whom we very much like ... remain our allies'.[103] Remaining on the periphery of events appeared to have served British interests well. 'We have', CRO officials reflected, 'reasonably successfully resisted efforts by Portugal and India to involve us in mopping up operations after Goa, which could only have been an embarrassment to us in our relations with both countries.'[104]

In private, Duncan Sandys took additional solace from his assessment that while Goa had 'been a very real shock here', in the long term, 'it may not be such a bad thing that Nehru should have fallen off his undeserved pedestal'.[105] British friends of India adopted a less judgemental position. Musing upon Nehru's conduct during the Goa crisis, Britain's Chief of Defence Staff, Lord Mountbatten, informed Gore-Booth that while he remained 'personally very sorry' that Nehru had authorised military action, 'I will never believe he [Nehru] cooked [it] up.' In Nehru's defence, Mountbatten noted that in any case, 'after our own incredible behaviour at Suez, we are not in a very strong position to criticise'.[106] For his part, a saddened Gore-Booth took consolation from his conviction that the British had done everything possible to avert India's use of force. On colonial issues, London simply carried little influence in New Delhi. 'Even the Americans', he observed, 'with all the professional friends of India in the [Kennedy] Administration and with all that India needs from them, were unable to influence things.'[107] The Foreign Office agreed, and while the Macmillan government's reluctance to intervene in the Goa affair was undoubtedly motivated by a strong element of self-interest, more than a grain of truth existed in the British contention that while the 'United States might be able to promote a negotiated solution [between India and Portugal] ... there is little we can do to help'.[108]

In reviewing the events of December 1961, Gore-Booth later concluded that an irrepressible combination of factors had prompted Nehru

[102] 'The Anglo-Portuguese Alliance', 12 April 1962, CAB 129/109, C (62) 60, TNA.
[103] *The Times*, 29 December 1961.
[104] Mills to de Zulueta, 5 January 1962, PREM 11/3837, TNA.
[105] Sandys to Gore-Booth, 20 December 1961, MS.Gorebooth 85, Paul Gore-Booth Papers, Bodleian Library, University of Oxford (hereafter GBP).
[106] Mountbatten to Gore-Booth, 20 December 1961, MS.Gorebooth 85, GBP.
[107] Gore-Booth to Sandys, 18 December 1961, DSDN 8/10, DSP.
[108] 'FO Brief for Bermuda Dec. 1961', 20 December 1961, FO 371/159709/D1024/99, TNA.

to lance the Goan boil. An upsurge of jingoistic sentiment inside India had fostered a belligerent attitude within Nehru's cabinet. Concerted pressure from African nationalists for India to confront Portuguese colonialism had played on New Delhi's mind. In addition, the Nehru government's seeming impotence in the face of Chinese violations of India's Himalayan border, and the contrasting political advantage an act of toughness in the south offered, had played its part in the decision to unleash the Indian Army.[109] The influence that Krishna Menon wielded over Nehru during the Goa crisis also attracted British attention. As India's defence minister, Menon had borne the brunt of the criticism that had been levelled at Nehru's government for its failure to secure the country's northern border. Moreover, a large Goan community resided in Menon's North Bombay parliamentary constituency. As Menon's political opponents were quick to point out, the embattled Indian minister had much to gain politically from orchestrating a victorious military campaign against the Portuguese. With this in mind, Gore-Booth observed that 'it is said frequently in Delhi that Mr. Menon hustled Mr. Nehru into the Goan action for his own electoral and general political purposes ... Many people [are] describing Goa as "Krishna Menon's War".'[110]

Nehru angrily dismissed rumours that Menon had been behind the decision to use force in Goa as completely baseless and 'utterly irresponsible'. Speaking to journalists on 28 December, the Indian premier stated defiantly, 'We [the Congress Party] are certainly responsible [for Goa]. But it was something which was demanded by every party in the country ... I was surprised and amazed that some ... had said that this was brought about to gain a few votes in the elections.'[111] Nehru had a point. In the wave of euphoria that engulfed India following Goa's 'liberation', even the prime minister's bitterest domestic critics publicly supported his decision to evict the Portuguese. The prominent Sarvodaya, or Ghandian, social activist, Jayaprakash Narayan, while deploring the use of violence in general terms as 'immoral and an offence against humanity', defended its application in the case of Goa. 'No Government in the world has accepted Gandhian non-violence, and disarmed and forsworn never to use force', Narayan informed the Indian press on 21 December. 'According to the accepted political

[109] 'India: The Invasion of Goa', Gore-Booth to Sandys, 29 December 1961, PREM 11/3837, TNA.

[110] *Ibid.*

[111] 'No Vote-catching Device', 29 December 1961, *National Herald*, Lucknow.

ethics of nations, force was never more justified than the force employed by India in Goa.'[112]

Of more concern to London was the prospect that Menon might exploit a surge in his personal popularity in India to sabotage the Nehru government's efforts 'to minimise the damage to their relations with ourselves and the Americans which that [Goan] operation inflicted'.[113] Reports reaching Washington indicated that Menon had been busy manipulating the Goa episode to fuel anti-Americanism inside India. One CIA source inside the Indian government quoted the defence minister as claiming that American indignation 'over Goa is only because a black nation has thrown out a white nation. We now know who our friends are. I would kick their [American] aid in the face unless they brought it to my doorstep.'[114] Such sentiment appeared to resonate with Nehru. At a press conference held by the Indian premier in New Delhi, on 28 December, Nehru bemoaned the schism that the Goa operation had provoked, 'to put it crudely, between black and white [global opinion]'.[115]

The equally troubling possibility that a politically ascendant Menon might exploit the 'very marked mood of popular [Indian] chauvinism that has been unleashed by Goa' to push Nehru into a confrontation with Pakistan, alarmed Whitehall. Calming London's nerves, Gore-Booth reassured the CRO that while such a Machiavellian scheme might well appeal to Menon as a means of distracting public attention from the more intractable challenge to India's security posed by the Chinese, an Indo-Pakistani conflict remained unlikely, at least in the short term. Menon's proclivity to engage in bellicose anti-Pakistani rhetoric was disconcerting, the British High Commissioner conceded, but his capacity to cajole Nehru into a second round of hostilities against the much tougher military proposition posed by Pakistan was doubtful.[116]

A final twist in the saga of Krishna Menon and Goa surfaced at the beginning of February 1962. In discussion with Vijaya Lakshmi Pandit, Nehru's sister and India's former High Commissioner to the UK, Sir David Eccles, Macmillan's minister of education, was informed that 'Krishna

---

[112] 'J.P. Happy Over Victory in Goa: Regrets India Had To Use Violence', 21 December 1961, *National Herald*, Lucknow.

[113] Gore-Booth to Hampshire, 14 January 1962, DO 196/126, TNA.

[114] 'Comments by Krishna Menon on Indian Foreign Policy', CIA report, 9 January 1962, NSF, Box 106A, India, General, JFKL.

[115] 'Action in Goa Only After Lisbon Rejected US Moves: P.M. Distressed Over Western Criticism', 29 December 1961, *National Herald*, Lucknow.

[116] Gore-Booth to Hampshire, 14 January 1962, DO 196/126, TNA.

Menon had threatened the Prime Minister with a military coup if Mr. Nehru refused to give the order to invade [Goa].' Her brother, Pandit implied, had proved reluctant to challenge Menon at the time, having concluded that Menon's growing power over the Indian defence establishment made him 'capable, in all senses of the word' of staging a *coup d'état*. Gore-Booth disparaged Pandit's allegation. Although agreeing that little would inhibit Menon in his pursuit of power, the High Commissioner reasoned that the defence minister 'must be aware of his own unpopularity ... with a considerable proportion of the Army, and in political circles, which must make him doubt whether a coup would be successful'. In short, Gore-Booth advised the CRO that, with the outcome of a coup so uncertain, 'Mr. Menon is too clever to run this kind of risk.'[117] American intelligence sources lent credence to Gore-Booth's suspicion that Pandit's accusation against Menon had been motivated in large part by her desire to deflect responsibility for the use of force in Goa away from her brother. In the CIA's estimation, Nehru had pulled the strings in relation to Goa, with Menon serving very much as the 'whipping boy'.[118]

In early 1962, reflecting back on a tumultuous few months in South Asia, Gore-Booth noted that India appeared to have 'drifted ... a little away from Britain'. By way of illustration the High Commissioner cited Nehru's 'extraordinary performance in writing a letter to President Kennedy about Goa saying that he is far more disturbed at the British attitudes as shown in the Congo than he is by American criticisms'. Kennedy's New Frontier, it seemed, had usurped the once pre-eminent influence that Britain had enjoyed in post-independence India. '[T]he pity', Gore-Booth ruminated, 'is that sourness towards us coincides with a greater warmth toward the Americans induced by the coming to power in Washington of the professional friends of India; but perhaps ... it is better for one of the principal Western powers to be in the doghouse rather than both.'[119] The dominant American position on the subcontinent did, however, offer some compensating advantage for the British. With Washington's economic aid 'no longer expressed mainly by promise, but ... showing itself in performance', it appeared that 'our [British] association with the Americans now sometimes takes the edge off Indian criticism of ourselves'.[120] Moreover, although the Goa crisis

[117] 'Krishna Menon', and 'Appendix II: A Military Coup by Krishna Menon', Gore-Booth to Saville Garner, 3 February 1962, DO 196/209, TNA.
[118] 'Afterthoughts', CIA report, 16 January 1962, NSF, Box 106A, India, General, JFKL.
[119] 'Mr. Nehru', Gore-Booth to Saville Garner, 19 February 1962, DO 196/210, TNA.
[120] 'India: November 1960 to May 1962', Gore-Booth to Sandys, 7 June 1962, DO 196/75, TNA.

had exposed tactical differences between the Kennedy and Macmillan governments, their strategic visions for South Asia remained consistent. As Gore-Booth elucidated:

... we [Britain] have to think beyond this [Goa] episode in terms of living together with India in the Commonwealth and the world. Even if feelings are not quite the same as they were, our stake and the stake of the free world in India, are such ... that living with the Indians is going to continue to be terribly important both from the point of view of the £300 million we have invested here and from the strategic point of view of the relation between India on the one hand and China and communists in S.E. Asia on the other.[121]

### Pakistan's response to Goa

In Pakistan, news of India's 'police action' in Goa was received with alarm and considerable foreboding. Writing to Macmillan on 22 December, Pakistan's president, Mohammad Ayub Khan, complained that by resorting to force to settle their dispute with the Portuguese, Nehru's government had undermined the United Nations and demonstrated its belief in the principle that 'might is still right'.[122] Moreover, as the British Foreign Office noted, events in Goa had 'confirm[ed] their [Pakistan's] view that it is India's military capability and capacity which can be dangerous to peace and not merely India's intentions'. In this sense, Ayub Khan's government feared that 'the opening of a new aggressive phase in Indian policy' would jeopardise its hold over East Pakistan, and the portion of Azad, or 'free' Kashmir, under its control.[123] Such insecurity was reflected in Pakistan's press, which in the aftermath of Goa called for an increase in defence spending, the country's withdrawal from SEATO and the establishment of closer military links between Pakistan and China. Such measures, influential newspapers such as *Dawn* claimed, represented a necessary form of insurance against 'an unscrupulous and bellicose [Indian] neighbour'.[124] Espousing his own crude South Asian domino theory, on 23 December, Pakistan's president informed the British that a combination of Indian aggression, greater Soviet economic and military support for New Delhi, and Western deference to Nehru's government,

---

[121] Gore-Booth to Clutterbuck, 22 December 1962, DO 196/1, TNA.
[122] Ayub Khan to Macmillan, No. 1726, 22 December 1961, MSS Macmillan, dep. c.344, f. 430, HMP.
[123] Brief for Sir David Eccles's Visit to India and Pakistan, January 1962, FO 371/166357/ D1041/22, TNA.
[124] Karachi to CRO, No. 243, 23 December 1961, DO 196/66, TNA.

threatened the security not only of his own country but also that of Nepal, Sri Lanka, Burma and Malaya. The Anglo-American refusal to intervene militarily on the Indian subcontinent in support of their Portuguese ally had, Ayub Khan charged, 'already started rumblings in Asia' as to the extent to which Western collective security guarantees remained credible.[125]

British officials were quick to dismiss what they perceived to be an excessive Pakistani concern that the Goa affair signalled the beginning of a shift to an expansionist Indian foreign policy. In a joint letter to London, Britain's High Commissioners in India and Pakistan maintained that, 'while we can foresee a deterioration in Indo-Pakistan relations, extending into the long period, we do not think that India is more likely to attack Pakistan than she was before "Goa"'.[126] Hedging their bets, however, the British upheld their policy of avoiding entering into a commitment to defend Pakistan in the event of Indian aggression.[127] Washington was less equivocal. Attempting to ease Pakistan's sense of insecurity, Dean Rusk informed Aziz Ahmed, Pakistan's ambassador to the United States, that unlike the 'muddled' colonial issue surrounding Goa, the Kennedy administration was committed to preserving Pakistan's national sovereignty. The Portuguese and Pakistani situations, Rusk insisted, 'were as different as night and day'.[128] Kennedy personally reinforced Rusk's message during a separate meeting with Ahmed. Pronouncing Pakistan a 'different proposition' than Goa, the American president characterised the inflammatory post-Goa rhetoric of Indian politicians, such as Krishna Menon, as little more than hot air. Endorsing the British line, Kennedy assured a sceptical Ahmed that the likelihood of an Indian attack on Pakistan remained just as improbable after Goa as it had been before.[129]

Unconvinced by the benign Anglo-American reading of India's regional intentions, the Pakistan government issued a series of warnings to London and Washington that its status as an ally of Britain and the United States ought not to be taken for granted. Toward the end of 1961, disparaging comments made by Pakistani officials on the future of CENTO led the British to conclude that 'we may be in for an acute attack

---

[125] Ayub Khan to Macmillan, 23 December 1961, PREM 11/3837, TNA.
[126] James to Hampshire, 27 December 1961, DO 196/66, TNA.
[127] Macmillan to Ayub Khan, T.3/62, 4 January 1962, PREM 11/3837, TNA.
[128] Rusk meeting with Aziz Ahmed, Washington, 3 January 1962, *FRUS, 1961–1963*, vol. XIX, p. 173.
[129] Ball to Karachi, Washington, 26 January 1962, *FRUS, 1961–1963*, vol. XIX, pp. 205–6.

of malaise in Pakistan's feelings towards the Organization generally'. During a CENTO council meeting in Turkey, in March 1962, Pakistan's representatives refused to endorse the alliance's strategic plans on the grounds that they failed to adequately address the military threat posed by India. Pushing for a revision of CENTO treaty obligations to encompass collective defence against non-communist aggression and subversion, the Pakistanis made it clear that they now considered non-aligned India a greater menace to South Asia's security than either the Soviet Union or the People's Republic of China. In its present form, a senior Pakistani official reasoned, his countrymen 'might feel that CENTO was not much use generally ... since the United States ... would, in any case, always come to the help of regional countries against Communist attack ... and membership of the Organization had the disadvantage of attracting criticism from Russia and neutrals'.[130]

Pakistan's growing disenchantment with what it regarded as inadequate Anglo-American security guarantees perturbed Harold Macmillan. 'This is a serious matter', the British premier scrawled in a note to his advisers. 'What is the ... likelihood of Pakistan leaving CENTO?'[131] A British straw poll conducted in early April, based on input from the High Commissions in New Delhi and Karachi, the Foreign Office and the CRO, provided some reassurance for Macmillan. 'In the present circumstances', it concluded, 'there is little likelihood of Pakistan leaving CENTO.' More likely was a prolonged bout of Pakistani griping, incorporating attacks on the inadequacies of both Anglo-American political and economic support in general, and the Western military alliance structure in particular. Calculating that there was little immediate action they could take to mitigate Pakistan's ill temper, the British resigned themselves to an uncomfortable, and hopefully transitory, period of Anglo-Pakistani friction.[132] On a bilateral basis, Ayub Khan's government fared equally badly in attempting to extract economic and political concessions from Washington in the wake of Goa. In an aide-mémoire presented to the State Department, Pakistan requested that the United States halt the sale of military equipment to India, increase its own share of American military aid, place a cap on US economic assistance to New Delhi and publicly commit to defend Pakistan against external aggression.[133] In

[130] Burrows (Ankara) to FO, No. 355, 17 March 1962, PREM 11/4922, TNA.
[131] Burrows (Ankara) to FO, No. 356, 17 March 1962, PREM 11/4922, TNA.
[132] Samuel to de Zulueta, 5 April 1962, PREM 11/4922, TNA.
[133] NEA paper on South Asian Affairs, Washington, undated, *FRUS, 1961–1963*, vol. XIX, pp. 185–8.

response, Kennedy offered a disappointed Ayub Khan nothing more than a private 'reaffirmation' of his administration's commitment to underwrite Pakistani autonomy.[134]

Indeed, far from securing additional Western support, the hectoring and 'offensive' tone adopted by Pakistani government officials led some of their American counterparts to conclude that 'we ought to consider a new tack in our relations with Pakistan'. As the National Security Council specialist on South Asia affairs Robert Komer emphasised, Ayub Khan's government, by continuing to utilise the US-Pakistani alliance primarily as a mechanism to deter Indian, rather than communist aggression, expected the Kennedy administration to take 'a position which runs contrary to our larger strategic interests in the area'.[135] Refining such sentiments in a note to Kennedy, Komer suggested that Ayub Khan ought to be left in no doubt that America's commitment to Pakistan did not imply that the United States would unquestioningly side with his government in its disputes with India. Encouraging Kennedy to look ahead, Komer cautioned that in a climate of deteriorating Sino-Indian relations, unless Pakistan was made to understand that the United States was set on building India up as an Asian counterweight to Communist China, a future US-Pakistani schism was inevitable. 'If [the] Sino-Indian dispute gets worse,' Komer advised Kennedy, 'we'll face major military sales to India, probably at a discount. Ayub will [then] raise hob unless … he already knows we are determined on this course.'[136] The risks in taking a tough line with Pakistan were presented to Kennedy as negligible. Aside from America's intelligence facilities in northern Pakistan, and 'a paper commitment to SEATO and CENTO', Komer argued that the Pakistani alliance provided the United States with little of value. Moreover, Ayub Khan's government remained heavily dependent upon American financial and military aid. 'Pakistan', Kennedy was assured, 'needs the US connection more than we need it.'[137]

---

[134] Kennedy to Ayub Khan, Washington, 26 January 1962, *FRUS, 1961–1963*, vol. XIX, p. 208.

[135] Komer to McGeorge Bundy, Washington, 6 January 1962, *FRUS, 1961–1963*, vol. XIX, pp. 179–81.

[136] 'State Briefing Paper on South Asia Issues', Komer to President Kennedy, 11 January 1962, NSF, Box 230, Regional Security, South Asia, General, 1961–3, JFKL.

[137] Komer to McGeorge Bundy, Washington, 6 January 1962, *FRUS, 1961–1963*, vol. XIX, pp. 179–81.

Komer's assessment proved overly optimistic. For the remainder of the decade, the dichotomy between Pakistani and American interpretations of their mutual alliance roles and responsibilities, was to consistently impede the United States' efforts to reshape the political landscape of South Asia.

# 5    Allies of a kind: Britain, the United States and the 1962 Sino-Indian War

As dawn broke in the eastern Himalayas on 20 October 1962, two flares arced high into the sky over the Thag La Ridge, a precipitous and densely forested escarpment dominating the border between India's North-East Frontier Agency (NEFA) and the Tibet region of China. Moments later, Indian Army positions in the valley below came under ferocious assault by Chinese forces. Outnumbered and taken by surprise, the Indians fell back in disarray. Within a matter of hours, one Rajput battalion facing the Chinese had 90 per cent of its men killed, wounded or taken prisoner.[1] Two days later, having routed the 7th Indian Infantry Brigade in the NEFA, advanced units of the Chinese People's Liberation Army (PLA) were deep inside north-eastern India. At the opposite end of the Himalayas, a coordinated Chinese thrust on India's north-western border met with similar success.[2] In New Delhi, asked by journalists to confirm when and where the Chinese invasion of India would be checked, the country's shell-shocked defence minister, Krishna Menon, replied despondently, 'The way they [the Chinese] are going there is not any limit to where they will go.'[3]

The origins of the Sino-Indian border conflict are long, complex and contentious.[4] On departing from South Asia in August 1947, the British

---

[1] D. K. Palit, *War in High Himalaya: The Indian Army in Crisis, 1962* (London: Hurst, 1991), p. 240; Neville Maxwell, *India's China War* (London: Cape, 1970), pp. 388–9. Official Indian casualty figures for the war listed 1,383 killed, 1,696 missing and 3,968 captured. Comparable Chinese numbers, although unpublished, were undoubtedly smaller. No Chinese prisoners were captured by Indian forces.

[2] Robert J. McMahon, *The Cold War on the Periphery: The United States, India and Pakistan* (New York: Columbia University Press, 1994), pp. 286–7.

[3] *The Times*, 22 October 1962.

[4] The best account of the border war remains Maxwell's *India's China War*. See also Yaccov Vertzberger, 'India's Border Conflict with China: A Perceptual Analysis', *Journal of Contemporary History*, 17, 4 (1982), 607–31; Michael Brecher, 'Non-Alignment Under Stress: The West and the India–China Border War', *Pacific Affairs*, 52, 4 (1979–80), 612–30; John Garver, *Protracted Contest: Sino-Indian Rivalry in the Twentieth Century* (Seattle: University of Washington Press, 2001), pp. 58–62. A 507-page official history of the border conflict, written in 1992 by the History Division of the Ministry of Defence of India, remains classified. However, leaked versions of the report are widely

149

left India with a contested northern border. In the eastern Himalayas, India and China both claimed sovereignty over 90,000 square kilometres (35,000 square miles) of territory, roughly approximating to the present Indian state of Arunchal Pradesh. In the north-west, a second Sino-Indian territorial dispute centred on ownership of the Aksai Chin plateau, 38,000 square kilometres (14,700 square miles) of arid desert, wedged between the Indian region of Ladakh, Tibet and the Chinese province of Xinjiang.

Quiescent until the late 1950s, the significance of the border dispute between India and China grew as relations between the two countries, which had blossomed earlier in the decade after the signing of the Panch Sheel accord in 1954, and an ensuing spirit of *Hindee Chinee bhai-bhai*, turned rancorous.[5] In 1957, discord between New Delhi and Beijing surfaced after China announced that it had constructed a highway between Xinjiang and Tibet, part of which bisected the Aksai Chin plateau.[6] The road provided a valuable strategic link between China and the previously inaccessible region of Western Tibet, which had long been a hotbed of Tibetan resistance to Chinese rule. To the Indian government's chagrin, China dismissed protests that the highway violated India's sovereignty.[7] In 1959, Sino-Indian relations deteriorated further following Nehru's decision to grant political asylum to Tibet's spiritual leader, the Dalai Lama, and thousands of his supporters, in the aftermath of an abortive Tibetan revolt against Chinese rule. Incensed that Nehru had provided Tibetan exiles with a safe haven and suspicious that the Indian government was colluding with the CIA to foment unrest inside Tibet, Beijing took an increasingly dim view of what it saw as a provocative and unwarranted intrusion by New Delhi into China's internal affairs.[8]

---

available on the World Wide Web. See, for example, S. N. Prasad (ed.), *History of the Conflict With China, 1962* (New Delhi: History Division, Ministry of Defence, 1992), available at Parallel History Project on Cooperative Security, Zurich, www.php.isn.ethz.ch/collections/coll_india/SecretHistory.cfm?navinfo=96318.

[5] The 'Panch Sheel' or 'Five Principles of Peaceful Co-existence' were incorporated into the 1954 Sino-Indian Treaty on Trade and Intercourse with Tibet. These encompassed commitments to mutual non-aggression and respect for national sovereignty. The slogan and policy of *Hindee Chinee bhai-bhai*, or Indian-Chinese brotherhood, was popularised in India following the treaty, the text of which is reproduced in A. Appadorai (ed.), *Select Documents on India's Foreign Policy and Relations, 1947–1972*, vol. 1 (New Delhi: Oxford University Press, 1982), pp. 459–66.

[6] William J. Barnds, *India, Pakistan and the Great Powers* (London: Pall Mall Press, 1972), p. 143; Dennis Kux, *India and the United States: Estranged Democracies, 1941–1991* (Washington, DC: National Defense University Press, 1993), pp. 161–2.

[7] Maxwell, *India's China War*, pp. 254–5.

[8] 'Chinese Intentions against India', Joint Intelligence Committee (JIC) report, 22 November 1962, CAB 158/47, The United Kingdom National Archives, Kew,

Later in 1959, clashes between Indian and Chinese border guards in the NEFA and Aksai Chin led to a series of vituperative exchanges on the border question between Nehru and Chinese premier, Zhou Enlai. After returning from a visit to Beijing in November, the eminent Indian lawyer, Danial Latifi, cautioned Nehru that public opinion in China appeared 'to have worked itself up to a considerable pitch' on the border question. 'As you know, probably too well,' Latifi informed the Indian premier, 'it is difficult *in any country* to make concessions once the public has been told it [contested territory] forms part of the national homeland.'[9] Within the subcontinent, the appearance of inflammatory literature produced by obscure organisations, such as the Chinese People's Anti-Expansionists Committee, which lambasted 'Indian imperialism' as a 'threat to Asian unity', had an equally incendiary impact on popular sentiment, and increased pressure on the Indian government not to 'appease' China.[10] Opening a debate on Sino-Indian relations in the Rajya Sabha on 8 December, Nehru attacked the Chinese government for adopting an 'expansive and aggressive attitude'. 'We believe peace is better than war, that war is unutterably bad', the Indian premier declared. 'Nevertheless, if a country's freedom or integrity or honour is attacked we have to defend that with war, if necessary.'[11]

In April 1960, the prospect of a negotiated settlement to the border imbroglio receded further into the distance, when Nehru rejected Zhou's offer to renounce China's claim on the NEFA if India did likewise with respect to Aksai Chin. Condemning Zhou's 'efforts to conceal the [border] crisis behind a barrage of pleasantries and platitudes', *The Indian Express* observed that the Chinese premier's 'attempts to make a hundred flowers bloom in the garden of Sino-Indian "eternal friendship" have withered at the roots'.[12] With both sides jostling to stake out their respective territorial claims over the following two years, in print and on the ground, confrontations between Indian and Chinese frontier

London (hereafter TNA). See also Sarvepalli Gopal, *Jawaharlal Nehru: A Biography*, vol. 3: *1956–1964* (London: Jonathan Cape, 1984), pp. 81 and 89, and Robert J. McMahon, 'US Policy toward South Asia and Tibet during the Early Cold War', *Journal of Cold War Studies*, 8, 3 (2006), 141. For a Chinese perspective on Sino-Indian relations see Chen Jian, *Mao's China and the Cold War* (Chapel Hill: University of North Carolina Press, 2001), pp. 78–9.

[9] Latifi to Nehru, 27 November 1959, Subject File 423, Third Instalment, P. N. Haksar Papers, Nehru Memorial Museum and Library, New Delhi (hereafter NMML).

[10] 'Ban on Booklets Disputing India's Border', *National Herald*, Lucknow, 10 December 1959.

[11] 'Non-alignment and Co-existence Big Fact Of Today – Nehru', *National Herald*, Lucknow, 9 December 1959.

[12] 'Chou Faces Chinese Wall: A Hundred Flowers Wither Away', *The Indian Express*, 22 April 1960.

forces grew in regularity and intensity.[13] By the autumn of 1962, with meaningful bilateral dialogue on the border dispute at an end, and substantial Indian and Chinese military forces standing toe to toe at either end of the Himalayas, the countdown to India's 'cartographic war' was underway.[14]

When the Chinese assault on India unfolded in October 1962, Nehru envisaged that his nation would face a long and arduous struggle for survival. In a broadcast over All India Radio, on the evening of 22 October, the Indian premier portrayed China's assault as the greatest menace that had confronted India since independence. In bitter tones, Nehru declared:

There are not many instances in history where one country, that is India, had gone out of her way to be friendly and cooperative with the Chinese Government and people, and to plead their cause in the councils of the world, and then for the Chinese Government to return evil for good and even go to the extent of committing aggression and invade our sacred land. No self-respecting country and certainly not India, with her love of freedom, can submit to this, whatever the consequences may be.[15]

War fever soon took a grip in India. A national State of Emergency was declared, parliament recalled, slit trenches dug in public gardens and army recruiting stations inundated with eager applicants. In Rajasthan, the village of Bardhana Khurd announced that it would send one son from each of its families to join the army. In the streets of New Delhi, students burned effigies of Mao Zedong, and signed pledges in their own blood to defend India. Industrial workers across the country declared a moratorium on strikes, and manufacturers pledged to raise their productivity. The Communist Party of India (CPI) abandoned class solidarity, and lambasted Beijing's 'act of invasion' in the pages of its weekly newsletter, *New Age*. More prosaically, in a move promptly dubbed 'ornaments for armaments', India's finance minister, Morarji

---

[13] Gopal, *Nehru: 1956–1964*, p. 100; Maxwell, *India's China War*, pp. 231–2.

[14] JIC Weekly Review, 18 September 1962, CAB 179/9, TNA; Stanley Wolpert, *Nehru: A Tryst with Destiny* (Oxford University Press, 1996), p. 473; Nehru to Chief Ministers, 3 September 1962, in G. Parthasarathi (ed.), *Jawaharlal Nehru: Letters to Chief Ministers, 1947–1964*, vol. 5: *1958–1964* (New Delhi: Oxford University Press, 1989), p. 523; Exchanges between New Delhi and Beijing prior to the border war are available in Appadorai, *Relations*, vol. 1, pp. 450–650.

[15] 'Menace to Freedom', 22 October 1962, in S. N. Prasad (ed.), *Prime Minister on Chinese Aggression* (New Delhi: Publications Division, Ministry of External Affairs, 1963), pp. 1–2.

Desai, called for public donations of money, gold and valuables, to help pay for the nation's defence.[16]

Nehru was initially reluctant to concede that China's attack on India might compel his government to abandon its policy of non-alignment. In the lead-up to the border war, the Indian premier characterised the acceptance of foreign military aid as akin to 'becoming somebody else's dependent', which was a state of affairs India would never accept, 'even if disaster occurs on the frontier'.[17] On 23 October, as Chinese forces surged into northern India, Nehru reiterated his position. 'We are not going to give up our basic principles because of the present difficulty', he asserted publicly. 'Even this difficulty will be more effectively met by continuing that policy.'[18] The scale of India's military collapse on the northern border, however, forced Nehru to qualify his 'basic principles'. On 25 October, before an audience of state officials, India's humbled leader conceded that his nation had been guilty of, 'getting out of touch with the modern world [and] ... living in an artificial atmosphere of our own creation'.[19]

In Britain and the United States, the Macmillan and Kennedy governments approached the outbreak of Sino-Indian hostilities as an opportunity to establish a 'closer understanding, within their general policy of non-alignment, between India and the West'. This in turn, it was envisaged, would provide a platform from which Nehru's government could be encouraged to adopt a less benign view of communism in general, and the threat to world peace posed by the Soviet Union and PRC in particular.[20] For the remainder of 1962, the determination of British and American policymakers to exploit the Sino-Indian War as a mechanism for tilting Jawaharlal Nehru's government toward the West, acted as the catalyst for unprecedented Anglo-American intervention in South Asia. Moreover, by actively supporting India in its conflict with China, the Kennedy and Macmillan administrations came to question

---

[16] Prasad (ed.), *Conflict With China*, p. 386; Gore-Booth to Garner, 26 October 1962, DO 196/75, TNA; Maxwell, *India's China War*, p. 414; *The Times*, 27 October 1962; CIA Daily Intelligence Bulletin, 28 October 1962, National Archives and Records Administration, College Park, Maryland (hereafter NARA).

[17] Maxwell, *India's China War*, pp. 392 and 411.

[18] Delhi to CRO, No. 1645, 23 October 1962, DO 196/165, TNA.

[19] Gopal, *Nehru: 1956–1964*, p. 223. The official Indian history of the border conflict noted that, confronted by a determined and skilful Chinese offensive, 'The Indian Army ... fought like the British Army, unimaginative, elephantine, rule-bound and road-bound.' Prasad, *Conflict With China*, p. xxii.

[20] CRO to Delhi and Karachi, 15 November 1962, FO 371/164929/FC 1063/13 (B), TNA; Roger Hilsman, *To Move a Nation: The Politics of Foreign Policy in the Administration of John F. Kennedy* (New York: Delta, 1967), pp. 331–2; Chester Bowles, *Promises to Keep: My Years in Public Life, 1941–1969* (New York: Harper, 1971), p. 437.

the utility of their associations with India, Pakistan and, in a South Asian context, each other.

### International reaction to the border war

The British government's concern at India's deteriorating relationship with China had been muted before the autumn of 1962. In part, this reflected Whitehall's belief that China's territorial designs in South Asia were limited, and a suspicion that the Nehru government's bellicose rhetoric had undermined diplomatic efforts to settle the Sino-Indian border dispute.[21] Equally, while perturbed at London's detachment from events unfolding on the Indian subcontinent, Sir Paul Gore-Booth rationalised that 'over the last year the Indians in their attitude and policy towards Britain have done little to prepare sympathy for themselves'.[22] During mid-October, with Chinese and Indian forces heavily engaged, the Foreign Office vacillated over whether to issue an unsolicited expression of British solidarity for India. Nehru, the FO judged, could interpret the intercession of an 'imperialist power' as an affront to Indian non-alignment, while China might respond to British meddling by escalating hostilities.[23] It was only as India's embattled army confronted, in Harold Macmillan's words, 'a bit of a Dunkirk', and after Washington had publicly condemned Chinese aggression, that the British voiced support for India.[24] Prodded by the CRO, on 23 October, Macmillan sent Nehru an open letter expressing Britain's sympathy for India's plight, and reconfirming his government's endorsement of New Delhi's claim on the NEFA.[25]

In the United States, the Kennedy administration was distracted for much of October 1962 by a concurrently unfolding crisis in the Caribbean, where American U-2 reconnaissance aircraft had identified

---

[21] Bruce to Rusk, No. 1664, 22 October 1962, National Security File (NSF), Box 107A, John F. Kennedy Library, Boston, Massachusetts (hereafter JFKL). Notably, India adopted the 'forward policy' in 1961, which saw its army aggressively patrol disputed territory along the north-eastern border.

[22] Delhi to CRO, No. 1623, 20 October 1962, DO 196/165, TNA. Anglo-Indian relations had been strained by disputes over the UK's EEC application, British colonial policy, Goa's 'liberation', Kashmir and the Indo-Soviet MiG deal. See Paul Gore-Booth, *With Great Truth and Respect* (London: Constable, 1974), p. 294.

[23] 'Expression of Sympathy for India', 21 October 1962, FO 371/164914/FC 1061/86, TNA; Peck memorandum, 22 October 1962, FO 371/164914/FC 1061/92, TNA.

[24] Entry for 23 October 1962, d.47, Harold Macmillan Diaries, Bodleian Library, University of Oxford (hereafter HMD); Brubeck to Bundy, 15 October 1962, *FRUS, 1961–1963*, vol. XIX, pp. 341–2.

[25] Macmillan to Home, 22 October 1962, FO 371/164914/FC 1061/94, TNA; FO to British Embassies, No. 416 Guidance, 23 October 1962, DO 196/165, TNA.

Soviet ballistic missile sites under construction in Cuba.[26] Nonetheless, on 22 October, before addressing the American people on the Cuban emergency, Kennedy found time to speculate with Congressional leaders on the likelihood that events in the Caribbean and South Asia formed part of a coordinated Sino-Soviet assault on Western interests. Four days later, with the United States Navy having placed Cuba under quarantine, Kennedy discussed the Sino-Indian clash with B. K. Nehru, India's ambassador to the United States. Puzzled by the timing, motivation and implications of the Chinese attack on India, Kennedy pondered, 'Does anybody know the mystery of the Communist system? What is their reason for doing this? This is the question. What is it they're getting out of this? They take you [India] on. Why don't they take us on in Vietnam or something? Why are they taking you on?'[27] Moreover, having ventured that the Sino-Indian border clash would force Moscow to side with either India or China, enhance the prospect of an Indo-Pakistani rapprochement, and foster closer military ties between Nehru's government and the West, Kennedy privately mused that the conflict in South Asia could prove just as fateful for American global interests as the Cuban Missile Crisis.[28]

As Kennedy suspected, China's assault on India did place the Soviet Union in a quandary. Despite the emergence of serious strains in its relationship with the PRC during the late 1950s, exacerbated in part by Moscow's unease at Beijing's bellicose approach to the Sino-Indian border dispute, the Soviet leadership was reluctant to effect an open breach with fellow Communists by publicly censuring Mao Zedong's government.[29] Equally, India's status as a leading member of the non-aligned movement had encouraged the Soviets to invest substantial economic and political capital in courting Nehru's government.

---

[26] Galbraith grumbled that 'Washington continues [to be] totally occupied with Cuba', and with 'a considerable war' on his hands he had received little guidance. John Kenneth Galbraith, *Ambassador's Journal: A Personal Account of the Kennedy Years* (Boston: Houghton Mifflin, 1969), New Delhi, 26 October 1962, pp. 435–6.

[27] President Kennedy meeting with B. K. Nehru, 26 October 1962, Meetings Recordings, Tape No. 40, JFKL.

[28] Noam Kochavi, *A Conflict Perpetuated: China Policy during the Kennedy Years* (London: Praeger, 2002), pp. 148–50.

[29] Dong Wang, 'The Quarrelling Brothers: New Chinese Archives and a Reappraisal of the Sino-Soviet Split, 1959–1962', Working Paper No. 49, The Cold War International History Project, Woodrow Wilson International Center for Scholars, Washington, DC (hereafter CWIHP), p. 17. See also Mikhail Y. Prozumenshchikov, 'The Sino-Indian Conflict, the Cuban Missile Crisis, and the Sino-Soviet Split, October 1962: New Evidence from the Russian Archives', *Cold War International History Project Bulletin*, no. 8–9 (1996–7), pp. 251–7; and Vojtech Mastny, 'The Soviet Union's Partnership with India', *Journal of Cold War Studies*, 12, 3 (2010), 50–90.

In February 1960, an attempt by Nehru to garner Soviet support for India's position on the border question had come to nothing. Having broached the subject during talks with Khrushchev in New Delhi, the Soviet leader conceded to Nehru that the Sino-Indian territorial dispute represented a 'most embarrassing question ... The difficulty is that we think that you and China are friendly and peace-loving countries ... We would not like our relations with either of our two friends to cool off.' Ruling out Soviet mediation on the grounds that it would 'only make matters worse', Khrushchev stressed that India and China would have to reach a mutually satisfactory settlement under their own aegis.[30] As Anastas Mikoyan, the Soviet politburo veteran, later reinforced to India's president, Sarvepalli Radhakrishnan, a negotiated solution to the Sino-Indian conflict would make the Indians happier, the Chinese happier, but as a titular friend of both countries, the Soviet Union happiest of all.[31]

Mikoyan was only partially correct. In August 1962, at a secretive party conference at Beidaihe, the summer retreat of China's Communist leadership, Mao Zedong won backing from the CCP hierarchy to implement a revolutionary foreign policy directly at odds with the Soviet strategy of peaceful coexistence. By the first week of October, Mao had determined to utilise Sino-Indian tension as a test bed for a new and more aggressive Chinese approach to international affairs, by responding to the next border skirmish with India with an overwhelming show of military force. On 8 October, Moscow received notification from the Chinese of their intention to escalate the border dispute.[32] Once the Sino-Indian dispute had erupted into open hostilities, the concurrent Cuban Missile Crisis shaped the Soviets' initial response to the border conflict. Any thoughts Moscow might have harboured of acting as an honest broker between Beijing and New Delhi were quickly overtaken by the Soviet Union's need to secure Chinese support, as toward the end of October, the Cuban stand-off threatened to escalate into a global conflagration.

Having previously taken a detached line in its coverage of the Sino-Indian dispute, as fighting between India and China intensified,

---

[30] 'Record of the Talk between Prime Minister of USSR Mr. N. S. Khrushchev and Prime Minister of India at the Latter's Residence, 12 February 1960', P. N. Kaul, 13 February 1960, Subject File No. 24 1960, Subimal Dutt Papers, NMML.

[31] Galbraith to Rusk, No. 709, 2 September 1962, RG 59, Box 2135, NARA.

[32] Niu Jun, '1962: The Eve of the Left Turn in China's Foreign Policy', CWIHP Working Paper No. 48, CWIHP; John W. Garver, 'China's Decision for War with India in 1962', in Alastair Iain Johnson and Robert S. Ross (eds.), *New Directions in the Study of China's Foreign Policy* (Stanford University Press, 2008), pp. 116–20.

the Soviet daily *Pravda* swung firmly behind Mao's government. At the UN, the Soviet representative, Valerian Zorin, called for India to enter into peace talks with China, a message that Nikita Khrushchev reaffirmed privately in written exchanges with Nehru.[33] Conscious that the Cuban crisis lay behind Moscow's tilt toward Beijing, and confident that India would continue to receive the support of Britain and the United States, Nehru reacted magnanimously to the application of Soviet pressure. Moreover, preserving cordial Indo-Soviet relations helped Nehru to preserve the outward appearance of Indian non-alignment, and reduced the possibility that the border war would act as a catalyst for a lasting Sino-Soviet rapprochement.[34] Speaking in the Lok Sabha, Nehru emphasised that Moscow had been a good friend to India and, as an ally of the Chinese, could not be expected to openly compromise its relations with Beijing. 'We have and have had their [Soviet] goodwill and good wishes all along', Nehru assured his fellow parliamentarians, 'and that is a consolation to us and we certainly hope to have that in future.'[35] Such an accommodating attitude exasperated Washington. Khrushchev, Kennedy tartly observed to B. K. Nehru, 'ought to either give you some equipment, or he ought to be of some political help, or he ought to be discredited'.[36]

On 26 October, as barely a week into the border fighting Indian forces stood on the verge of an ignominious defeat, Jawaharlal Nehru issued an unprecedented call to the international community for 'sympathy and support'. The impact of this very public qualification of Indian non-alignment, Gore-Booth noted, 'lay in the fact that it had to be delivered, of all people, by Jawaharlal Nehru'.[37] Within India, Nehru's decision was welcomed in the press and by the opposition Swantantra

---

[33] *The Times*, 28 October 1962; M. Y. Prozumenshchikov, 'The Sino-Indian Conflict, the Cuban Missile Crisis, and the Sino-Soviet Split, October 1962'; Gopal, *Nehru: 1956–1964*, pp. 221–3; Allen Whiting, *The Chinese Calculus of Deterrence* (Ann Arbor: University of Michigan Press, 1975), p. 131.

[34] 'Far Eastern Dept. Note', 12 November 1962, TNA, FO 371/164919/FC 1061/189, TNA; New Delhi to Sandys, 14 November 1962, DO 196/172, TNA.

[35] Nehru speech to Lok Sabha, 14 November 1962, in S. N. Prasad (ed.), *We Accept China's Challenge: Speeches in the Lok Sabha on India's Resolve to Drive out the Aggressor* (New Delhi: Government of India, Ministry of Information and Broadcasting Publications Division, 1962), p. 15.

[36] B. K. Nehru Meeting, 26 October 1962, Meetings Recordings, Tape No. 40, JFKL. Nehru's pragmatism bore fruit early in November when, with the Cuban crisis over, the Soviets reasserted their neutrality in relation to the Sino-Indian dispute.

[37] Gore-Booth to Saville Garner, 26 October 1962, DO 196/75, TNA.

Party.[38] In private, the Indian leader brooded over the wider implications of internationalising the Sino-Indian conflict. Writing to the British philosopher and peace campaigner Bertrand Russell, Nehru emphasised that 'we do not want this frontier war with China to continue and even more certainly we do not want it to spread and involve the nuclear powers'. Given India's plight, however, Nehru lamented that he had been left with 'no choice' but to 'somewhat affect' India's independence, and appeal for military assistance from abroad.[39] In conversation with Galbraith, on 29 October, the Indian premier put things more bluntly, expressing his hope to the American ambassador 'that this would not mean a military alliance between the United States and India'.[40] Lacking the financial resources to purchase desperately needed military equipment from abroad on commercial terms, Nehru's government nonetheless worked to retain a veneer of Indian non-alignment. Indian missions in 'friendly countries' were duly instructed to make discreet enquiries with a view to obtaining military supplies on easy credit terms, and in return for the payment of non-convertible Indian rupees.[41]

The immediate military priority for Nehru's government was tackling the Indian Army's deficiency in automatic rifles. Practical considerations, chiefly compatibility with existing equipment, led Indian officials to favour the acquisition of British small arms. Meeting India's needs in this area, the British reasoned, would amass valuable political credit with Nehru, while taking the opposite course 'could do much harm' to Indo-British relations. Furthermore, with the Americans indicating their willingness to supply India with modern rifles, broader economic considerations came into play. 'We should', Gore-Booth suggested to Whitehall, 'presumably not wish to miss ... bringing about continued use by [the] Indian Army of standard British equipment.'[42] This point was not lost on the Indians, who made it abundantly clear to the British that 'most things could be obtained from the United States if this was easier'.[43] Taking Gore-Booth's cue, Duncan Sandys expedited

---

[38] 'Preliminary World Reactions to the Sino-Indian Conflict', 8 November 1962, NSF, Box 108, JFKL; Nehru to Chief Ministers, 1 January 1963, in *Letters to Chief Ministers*, vol. 5: *1958–1964*, p. 564.

[39] Nehru to Bertrand Russell, 4 December 1962, in Sarvepalli Gopal (ed.), *The Essential Writings of Jawaharlal Nehru*, vol. 2 (Oxford University Press, 2003), pp. 313–14.

[40] Galbraith, *Ambassador's Journal*, New Delhi, 29 October 1962, p. 445.

[41] Chiefs of Staff (COS) (62) 69th Meeting, 1 November 1962, FO 371/164916/FC 1061/137, TNA.

[42] Delhi to CRO, No. 1629, 21 October 1962, FO 371/164914/FC 1061/82, TNA; Ormsby Gore to FO, No. 2723, 29 October 1962, FO 371/164880/F1195/11/G, TNA.

[43] Delhi to CRO, No. 1748, 1 November 1962, DO 194/24, TNA.

the delivery of automatic weapons to the subcontinent as a gift from the British people to India. In offering India support, Sandys reassured Nehru that the Macmillan government would be 'most careful in any public statements ... to avoid saying anything which might embarrass you ... or prejudice in any way your policy of non-alignment'.[44]

When the full scale of India's appetite for Western military aid became apparent in early November, it stunned British and American officials. Initial Indian government estimates placed the cost of the country's long-term military requirements as high as $1 billion, and were quickly dismissed by the British as 'unrealistic'.[45] A subsequent Indian request for $60–70 million dollars of emergency Anglo-American military aid 'shocked' Galbraith.[46] Yet, while rejecting India's military planning as impractical, the British welcomed it in principle as symbolising a 'dramatic change' in Nehru's foreign policy. Duncan Sandys had given Nehru the impression that, in coming to his government's assistance, Britain would do its best to maintain the appearance of Indian non-alignment. However, in conversation with David Bruce, America's ambassador in London, Sandys welcomed India's new and unexpected dependence on the West as a 'great opportunity ... [for] making a real break in India's policy of neutralism'.[47] Consequently, proposals from the CRO that Britain offer India a £5 million loan to purchase military equipment, and establish an Anglo-Indian 'lend-lease' agreement under which the UK retained ultimate title over the weaponry that it despatched to the subcontinent, were vetoed by Sandys. The purpose of providing India with British military assistance, Macmillan's Secretary of State for Commonwealth Relations scolded his officials, was not to uphold a facade of Indian Cold War neutrality, but rather to 'tie the Government of India down quickly to the acceptance of [Western] military aid before their tempers against the Chinese have time to cool'.[48]

American policymakers failed to share Sandys' enthusiasm for abrogating Indian non-alignment. Galbraith, in particular, thought it inappropriate and counterproductive to exploit India's desperate need for arms.[49] Greater long-term dividends, the US ambassador argued, could

---

[44] Sandys to Nehru, 26 October 1962, CRO to Delhi, No. 2250, DSDN 8/1, Duncan Sandys Papers, Churchill Archives Centre, Churchill College Cambridge (hereafter DSP).

[45] Saville Garner to Sandys, 1 November 1962, DO 194/24, TNA; 'Military Aid for India', 2 November 1962, DO 194/24, TNA.

[46] Galbraith, *Ambassador's Journal*, New Delhi, 1 November 1962, p. 453.

[47] Sandys meeting with Bruce, 2 November 1962, DO 196/175, TNA.

[48] *The New York Times*, 1 November 1962; 'Military Aid for India', 2 November 1962, and Rumbold to Picket, 5 November 1962, DO 194/24, TNA.

[49] Galbraith to Kennedy, No. 1647, 21 October 1962, NSF, Box 107A, JFKL.

be derived from being seen to have helped an Indian friend, rather than acquired a reluctant ally. If nothing else, expecting Nehru to align India with the West appeared unrealistic, given the benefits that his government derived from Soviet economic aid and Moscow's political support in the United Nations.[50] Kennedy endorsed Galbraith's approach, readily accepting a request from B. K. Nehru that American expressions of support for India avoid any reference to military aid.[51] Writing to Jawaharlal Nehru on 28 October, Kennedy affirmed his commitment to 'translate our support into terms that are practically most useful to you'.[52]

It was not only Indian political considerations that influenced London and Washington's thinking on the provision of military aid to Nehru's government. Pakistan's alarm at the shipment of Western arms to India posed an added challenge for British and American officials. In Pakistan's National Assembly, during an emotive debate laden with expressions of anger and indignation, the arrival of 'large-scale' British and American military assistance to India was unanimously condemned. In Karachi, mobs of protesters invaded the USIS library compound, while in Rawalpindi, an angry crowd besieged Flashman's Hotel, which catered to a predominately Western clientele. Widespread anger on Pakistan's streets against British and American support for India led to the imposition of Section 144 orders in Karachi, Lahore, Peshawar and Rawalpindi, which banned public gatherings of five or more people.[53] At the same time, on the principle that 'my enemy's enemy is my friend', Ayub Khan's administration reaffirmed that its response to the establishment of a more intimate military relationship between India and the West would be to cultivate closer Sino-Pakistani ties.[54] As had become clear in the aftermath of the Goa episode, however, the Kennedy administration was prepared to run considerable risks with US-Pakistani relations. In Washington, senior officials made light of Pakistan's reaction to events unfolding in the subcontinent, and disparaged Ayub Khan's threat to foster a new strategic alliance with Beijing as 'temper tantrums'.[55] With far less leverage over Pakistan

---

[50] Kaysen to Kennedy, 3 November 1962, *FRUS, 1961–1963*, vol. XIX, p. 367.
[51] B. K. Nehru Meeting, 26 October 1962, Meetings Recordings, Tape No. 40, JFKL; Rusk to Galbraith, 27 October 1962, *FRUS, 1961–1963*, vol. XIX, pp. 352–3.
[52] Galbraith, *Ambassador's Journal*, New Delhi, 26 October 1962, p. 439, and 28 October 1962, p. 442.
[53] Ian Talbot, *Pakistan: A Modern History* (London: Hurst & Company, 2009), p. 173.
[54] Rusk to McConaughy, 16 October 1962, *FRUS, 1961–1963*, vol. XIX, p. 345.
[55] Komer to Kaysen, 2 November 1962, NSF, Box 146, JFKL. Pakistani ire had been stoked by Ayub Khan's personal sense of betrayal after Kennedy reneged on a pledge to consult him before arming India. Mohammad Ayub Khan, *Friends Not Masters: A Political Autobiography* (London: Oxford University Press, 1967), p. 145; McConaughy

than the United States, but with a substantial commercial and political stake in the country, the British were less dismissive of Pakistan's growing sense of disillusionment with the West. Optimistically, the CRO hoped that Pakistan would tolerate Britain's support for India 'as an emergency and an exceptional measure'.[56] In Karachi, Britain's High Commissioner, Morrice James, was less sanguine. Following the despatch of Western arms to India, James noted, Pakistan's foreign minister, Muhammed Ali Bogra, and finance minister, Abdul Qadir, had called for Pakistan to withdraw from SEATO and CENTO, and adopt a non-aligned foreign policy.[57] In the absence of an Indo-Pakistani rapprochement, by offering Nehru's government military aid, James cautioned London presciently, 'We could well find that we had forfeited Pakistan friendship and Western alignment once and for all without gaining any lasting advantage in India.'[58]

### The coordination of Anglo-American military aid to India

In November, a significant constraint on United States' intervention in the Sino-Indian border war disappeared, when Krishna Menon resigned from Nehru's cabinet. Labelled by the Western press as 'India's Rasputin' and the 'Hindu Vishinsky', Menon had gained an invidious reputation in the 1950s for his vitriolic criticism of US foreign policy and contrasting empathy for the Soviet Union.[59] State Department officials, in particular, regarded Menon as 'venomous' and an 'unpleasant mischief-maker'.[60] Having first met Nehru in pre-war London, Menon went on to form an intimate personal and political bond with the Indian leader. Nehru found Menon's socialism, intelligence and acerbic wit attractive.[61] In return, Menon enthusiastically championed issues close to Nehru's heart, from the merits of non-alignment to the righteousness of India's claim on Kashmir. 'Menon', Gore-Booth emphasised to

meeting with Ayub Khan, 5 November 1962, pp. 370–3, and State Department to McConaughy, 5 November 1962, *FRUS, 1961–1963*, vol. XIX, pp. 391–2.

[56] Saville Garner to Sandys, 1 November 1962, DO 194/24, TNA; 'Military Aid for India', 2 November 1962, DO 194/24, TNA.

[57] 'Pakistani Plans for Military Action in Kashmir', 14 November 1962, NSF, Box 108, JFKL; 'The Five-Fold Dilemma: The Implications of the Sino-Indian Conflict', Hilsman to Rusk, 17 November 1962, NSF, Box 108A, JFKL.

[58] James to CRO, No. 1502, 7 November 1962, DO 189/245, TNA.

[59] Wolpert, *Nehru*, p. 487.

[60] Arthur W. Hummel, Jr, Oral History Interview, 13 July 1989, Foreign Affairs Oral History Project, http://memory.loc.gov/ammem/collections/diplomacy/ (hereafter FAOHP).

[61] Gopal, *Nehru: 1956–1964*, p. 129.

the CRO, 'is felt to be one of the Nehru family (in a way that no other Minister is or has been) ... indeed Nehru behaved towards Menon in a manner so paternal as to suggest that he saw in Menon the son that he had always so much wanted to have.'[62] British officials shared many of their American colleagues' reservations when it came to Menon. The CRO categorised him as a 'fierce anti-American', 'unscrupulous, egotistical and unreliable'.[63] When informing London, in September 1957, that Menon had left India en route to the United States, Malcolm MacDonald observed acidly, 'Of course he ought to be going to New York to see a psycho-analyst, not to attend the Assembly of the United Nations.'[64]

From the outset of the border war, while keen to utilise the conflict as a means of strengthening Indo-US relations, American officials were inclined 'to have decently in mind the pounding we have been taking from Krishna Menon'.[65] Given the antipathy that Menon engendered within the United States, the Kennedy administration worried that his position as India's defence minister would compromise Congress' willingness to fund an Indian military aid programme.[66] On 23 October, Galbraith candidly informed India's Foreign Secretary, M. J. Desai, that Menon represented one of the 'more serious problems' obstructing the flow of US arms to India.[67] Three days later, in Washington, Kennedy pointedly emphasised to B. K. Nehru that in aiding India, 'We [the United States] don't want to, in any way ... have Krishna enter into this ... he is a disaster and makes all the thing [sic] much more complicated. Your judgment is that he will continue, however, as defense minister?'[68] In an effort to resolve the Menon 'problem', Carl Kaysen, Kennedy's Deputy National Security Advisor, approached the British with a plan to discredit the Indian defence minister. Specifically, Kaysen suggested that the British government might plant stories in European newspapers highlighting Menon's culpability for India's humiliation at the hands of the Chinese. Although agreeing that Menon was 'somewhat ill in mind', and worried by the Indian minister's Machiavellian influence over Nehru,[69] the British rejected Kaysen's plan. Attacking Menon in the Western press, Britain's ambassador in Washington, David Ormsby

---

[62] Gore-Booth to Saville Garner, 15 December 1962, DO 196/209, TNA.
[63] Saville Garner to Crombie, 9 February 1954, DO 35/9014; Clutterbuck to Garner, 21 October 1954, KV 2/2514/3, TNA.
[64] MacDonald to Lord Home, 18 September 1957, PREM 11/2361, TNA.
[65] Galbraith, *Ambassador's Journal*, New Delhi, 23 October 1962, pp. 428–31.
[66] Galbraith to Kennedy, No. 1647, 21 October 1962, NSF, Box 107A, JFKL.
[67] Galbraith, *Ambassador's Journal*, New Delhi, 23 October 1962, p. 431.
[68] B. K. Nehru Meeting, 26 October 1962, Meetings Recordings, Tape No. 40, JFKL.
[69] New Delhi to Sandys, 14 November 1962, DO 196/172, TNA.

Gore, advised Kaysen, was 'more likely to save Menon than send him under'.[70]

In the event, Krishna Menon's Waterloo came soon enough. Psychologically shattered by China's attack on India, the depth of Menon's defeatism shocked Chester Ronning, Canada's High Commissioner in New Delhi. In conversation with the defence minister, Ronning was taken aback by Menon's talk of a ten-year Sino-Indian War, in which Chinese forces might occupy territory as far south as Madras.[71] As October ended, the scale of India's military humiliation had made Menon's position in government untenable. Faced with accusations that his mismanagement of the defence portfolio had left India powerless in the face of Chinese aggression, a clamour mounted inside India for Menon's head.[72] In order to silence Menon, Gore-Booth informed London, opponents had taken to sabotaging his microphone at public meetings.[73] Nehru, however, kept faith with his defence minister, calculating that to abandon a close political confidant and fellow champion of non-alignment would be widely interpreted as evidence of a shift in India's foreign policy.[74] Only reluctantly, and following an ill-judged bid to save Menon by demoting him from defence minister to minister for defence production, did Nehru accept his friend's 'resignation' on 7 November.[75]

Unlike the Kennedy administration, Macmillan's government saw Menon's departure from the Indian cabinet as a mixed blessing. Although welcoming the advent of a new and more accommodating attitude toward Britain and the United States on the part of India's defence ministry, a suspicion lingered within Whitehall that the Americans would prove to be the prime beneficiaries of Menon's political demise. Gore-Booth reflected that while Menon had 'tolerated on sufferance' Britain's leading role in training and equipping India's armed forces, American defence contractors had remained an 'anathema' to the former defence minister. This satisfactory state of affairs appeared unlikely to continue under Menon's successor.[76] Paradoxically, while rejoicing in the removal of a 'symbol of anti-Americanism', Galbraith

[70] Ormsby Gore to FO, No. 2717, 29 October 1962, DO 196/166, TNA.
[71] Gopal, *Nehru: 1956–1964*, p. 131; Galbraith, *Ambassador's Journal*, New Delhi, 25 October 1962, p. 435.
[72] *The New York Times*, 1 November 1962.
[73] Gore-Booth to Saville Garner, 7 November 1962, DO 196/75, TNA.
[74] CIA Daily Intelligence Bulletin, 1 November 1962, NARA.
[75] Gore-Booth, *Truth and Respect*, p. 295; Gopal, *Nehru: 1956–1964*, p. 13; Steven Hoffmann, *India and the China Crisis* (Berkeley: University of California Press, 1990), pp. 203–6.
[76] New Delhi to Sandys, 14 November 1962, DO 196/172, TNA.

warned Washington against attaching too much significance to Menon's demise. References to non-alignment retained 'great evocative power' in India, the American ambassador noted, while 'phrases like military blocs, military alliances, even Pentagon still have a bad sound'.[77] In echoing Galbraith's caution, Averell Harriman, the veteran American diplomat serving as Kennedy's Assistant Secretary of State for Far Eastern Affairs, took a different tack. China's attack on India offered a valuable opportunity to co-opt the Nehru government into support-ing the global struggle against communism, Harriman conceded, but in so doing, care was needed to avoid committing US resources 'in a bad place at a bad time ... [and] in such a way that our prestige is in his [Nehru's] hands'.[78]

Ironically, while American diplomats urged Washington to tread warily in coming to India's assistance, an uneasiness took root in Whitehall that the conflict between India and China would prompt the Kennedy administration to offer Nehru's government massive mil-itary aid. For the cash-strapped British, such a development posed a direct threat to their lucrative and politically valuable position as India's principal quartermaster. In an effort to influence the American position on military aid, the British invited US government officials to the United Kingdom for talks on the Sino-Indian War.[79] Arriving in London in early November, a team of Americans led by William Bundy, Deputy Assistant Secretary of Defense, quickly concurred with the British that China's incursion into India was likely to prove limited. More significantly, Bundy secured British agreement that the primary Anglo-American objective in supporting India was to bring about a 'closer understanding' with Nehru's government within the context of Indian non-alignment.[80] On this point, British officials pushed Duncan Sandys' radical agenda for bringing India tacitly into the Western alli-ance to one side. Crucially, the British did reach an understanding with their American colleagues that, in the short term, India need only be supplied with the weaponry necessary to stave off a military col-lapse. As a medium-term measure, the British and Americans proposed

---

[77] Galbraith, *Ambassador's Journal*, New Delhi, 1 November 1962, p. 454; Galbraith to State Department, 1 November 1962, *FRUS, 1961–1963*, vol. XIX, pp. 361–2.

[78] 'United States Policy in the Sino-Indian Conflict', 3 November 1962, Box 536, Folder 1, Averell Harriman Papers, United States Library of Congress, Washington, DC (hereafter HP).

[79] Sandys meeting with Bruce, 2 November 1962, DO 196/175, TNA.

[80] 'Opening Meeting on Sino-Indian Conflict', 12 November 1962, FO 371/164929/ FC 1063/10, TNA; '2nd Meeting on Sino-Indian Conflict', 12 November 1962, FO 371/164929/FC 1063/10 (C), TNA; CRO to Delhi and Karachi, 15 November 1962, FO 371/164929/FC 1063/13 (B), TNA.

equipping five Indian Army divisions. This operation was also, however, to be 'strictly limited' to 'reasonable quantities' of defensive equipment, such as automatic rifles, communication sets and winter clothing.[81] To the relief of British officials, Bundy and his team readily accepted the premise that by closely regulating the scale of assistance provided to India, Britain and the United States could mitigate Pakistani anxieties and limit the risk of China escalating hostilities. The provision of minimal Anglo-American martial support to Nehru's government also appeared to be a prudent means of constraining Indian jingoism, while still providing some sway over New Delhi's military strategy.[82] To the CRO, the American government's aversion to making an open-ended commitment to defend India was especially reassuring. In fact, to Whitehall's surprise, Bundy had appeared 'particularly anxious to listen to our views and, indeed, to accept our leadership in handling matters in Delhi'.[83]

In India, Galbraith's take on the 'London talks' was less effusive. Inadequate recommendations from 'minor bureaucrats', the ambassador fumed, had failed to give appropriate weight to public sentiment in India, which demanded swift retribution against Chinese perfidy. 'After lecturing the Indians for years on the aggressive tendencies of the Chinese Communists,' Galbraith observed, 'we cannot now turn around and explain that these chaps are really lambs.'[84] Gore-Booth shared Galbraith's apprehension at the unexpectedly parsimonious level of Anglo-American military assistance to India that had been agreed in London. The Nehru government's appreciation of Western support following China's attack on India, the High Commissioner reflected, had shown early signs of delivering political dividends. India had voted for an Anglo-American resolution at the UN on nuclear testing in early November, when a majority of the Afro-Asian non-aligned bloc chose to abstain. In future, such an accommodating Indian attitude promised to benefit Western interests on issues as diverse as Berlin, Cuba, the Congo and, in particular, colonial Africa.[85] Indeed, in the weeks following the outbreak of the border war, an unprecedented upsurge was recorded in British and American standing in India. In surveys conducted by the Indian Institute of Public Opinion, the percentage

---

[81] CRO to New Delhi, 15 November 1962, FO 371/164929/FC 1063/13 (D), TNA.

[82] CRO to New Delhi, 15 November 1962, FO 371/164929/FC 1063/13 (C), TNA; 'Meeting on Sino-Indian Conflict', 13 November 1962, FO 371/164929/FC 1063/10 (D), TNA.

[83] Saville Garner to Sandys, 15 November 1962, FO 371/164929/FC 1063/13, TNA.

[84] Galbraith, *Ambassador's Journal*, New Delhi, 16–17 November 1962, pp. 478–80.

[85] Gore-Booth to Sandys, 14 November 1962, DO 196/172, TNA.

of Indians with a 'favourable' opinion of the United States soared from 34 per cent at the beginning of October, to a record 89 per cent in early November. Corresponding figures for the British leapt from 22 to 79 per cent, while the Soviet Union's 'favourable' rating fell from 47 to 33 per cent.[86] Appearing to deny India an effective defence against Chinese aggression, Gore-Booth cautioned Whitehall, risked Britain and the United States precipitating 'such a let down from our newly and dramatically improved relations that we should lose any chance of achieving the major aims set out'.[87] Unsurprisingly, in Pakistan, Morrice James took a different view. The Anglo-American proposals fleshed out in London, he cabled to the CRO, underestimated the 'violent and irrational' reaction that would follow were Britain and the United States to continue arming India. 'The London papers', James warned, 'make the future [in South Asia] out to be a good bit tidier and more manageable than it will in fact prove.'[88]

## The Commonwealth role in India's defence

A lull in Sino-Indian fighting during late October, had sparked optimism in New Delhi that after pausing to regroup, its forces would throw the Chinese back across India's northern border. India's media, fed misleading accounts of preparations for an assault on Chinese positions in the NEFA by government officials, raised public expectations that a large-scale offensive was imminent. On 12 November, Nehru's home minister, Lal Bahadur Shastri, declared confidently to journalists that 'India was now strong enough to repulse the Chinese attacks and was building its military might to drive the invaders from Indian soil'.[89] Indian sabre-rattling, Nehru's dismissal of peace overtures from Beijing, and ominous reports of Chinese troop movements in the north, alarmed Galbraith. What had seemed 'essentially a border conflict', he mused on 13 November, now seemed poised to develop into 'something more serious', burdening the United States with a hazardous and expensive commitment to defend India. Nehru's anxiety over the demise of

---

[86] 'Impact of Chinese Border Attack upon Delhi Opinions of the United States, Britain and the Soviet Union', R-54–63 (R), 29 March 1963, RG 306, Records of the US Information Agency Office of Research, 'R' Reports 1960–3, Box 14, Folder R54–63, NARA.

[87] Delhi to CRO, 19 November 1962, FO 371/164929/FC 1063/13 (F), TNA.

[88] Karachi to CRO, No. 1463, 18 November 1962, FO 371/164929/FC 1063/13 (E), TNA.

[89] Maxwell, *India's China War*, p. 422.

non-alignment was misplaced, the American ambassador mused wryly, 'it is we that should be doing the worrying'.[90]

Back in Washington, Robert Komer disagreed. Komer welcomed the possibility of an escalation in Sino-Indian fighting as a heaven-sent opportunity for transforming Indo-US relations.[91] On 15 November, Komer's wish was granted when, in the most significant show of force since the PLA had moved across the Yalu River into Korea, in October 1950, Beijing ordered a second major Chinese assault on Indian positions in the NEFA and Ladakh. In a repeat of the October debacle, India's army disintegrated under the weight of a renewed Chinese onslaught. In Ladakh, more than forty Indian guard posts were overrun, and the strategically vital Chushul airfield subjected to Chinese artillery fire. In the NEFA, PLA troops occupied the towns of Walong and Bomdila, and in the process eliminated the only significant military force standing between them and the densely populated plains of northern India. As news of fresh reverses in the north filtered through to New Delhi, panic gripped the Indian capital for the second time in a month. Morarji Desai assured an incredulous Galbraith that the Soviets were supplying China with petroleum via a trans-Tibetan pipeline, and that Chinese plans to seize Calcutta's harbour had been discovered aboard a Polish ship anchored in the Indian port.[92] Over 200 members of the CPI were rounded up by the Indian government and thrown into gaol, amongst them leaders of the official opposition in the states of West Bengal, Kerala and Andhra Pradesh. Orders were issued for the internment of all Chinese nationals and people of Chinese origin living in Assam and the border districts of West Bengal. Throughout the NEFA, civil administration collapsed as the Chinese advanced. In Tezpur, a city of 50,000 inhabitants, local officials deserted their posts, the district treasury burnt its currency reserves, gaols were flung open, hospital doctors abandoned their patients, and a frightened and bewildered population was left alone to ponder an uncertain fate. The once-bustling Tezpur, India's official history of the border war subsequently confirmed, was transformed into 'a ghost city. The collapse of law and order was complete.'[93]

On 19 November, Nehru responded by publicly announcing that the Indian government had approached Britain and the United States for 'massive' military aid. 'We are not going to tolerate this kind of

[90] Galbraith, *Ambassador's Journal*, New Delhi, 13 November 1962, pp. 474–5.
[91] McMahon, *Cold War on the Periphery*, p. 287.
[92] Galbraith to Rusk, No. 1898, 20 November 1962, NSF, Box 108, JFKL.
[93] Prasad (ed.), *Conflict With China*, p. 372. See also *The Times*, 22 November 1962 and 26 November 1962.

invasion of India', Nehru proclaimed. 'India is not going to lose this war, however long it lasts and whatever harm it may do us.'[94] The Indian premier's decision to abrogate non-alignment sprang from his conviction that in the absence of foreign military assistance, large swathes of the subcontinent would come under Chinese control. Lal Bahadur Shastri had warned Nehru that with India's defensive line in the NEFA shattered, the Chinese were free to walk unopposed into Assam and Bengal. Underlining his point, Shastri had contingency plans prepared to destroy Assam's oilfields before they fell into Chinese hands.[95] In Calcutta, the writer V. S. Naipaul noted wild tales circulating within the city's bazaars. 'The Indian Marwari merchants', Naipaul recorded, were said to be '... making enquiries about business prospects under Chinese rule; the same rumour had it that in the South the Madrasis, despite their objection to Hindi, were already learning Chinese.'[96] With India's plight seemingly 'desperate', Nehru sent an urgent and top-secret request to President Kennedy for immediate American military intervention in the Sino-Indian conflict. Only direct US military action, Nehru insisted, could avert 'nothing short of a catastrophe for our country'. Concern that retaliatory Chinese air-raids against Indian cities, such as Calcutta, 'might result in panic', caused Nehru to baulk at using the Indian Air Force against the advancing PLA forces.[97] Instead, the Indian leader called on Kennedy to underwrite a Western air war against the Chinese. It was imperative, Nehru advised the stunned US president, that twelve squadrons of American supersonic fighters, two squadrons of bombers and a mobile radar network be despatched to India with the utmost haste.[98]

Concluding that Nehru was 'clearly in a state of panic', Kennedy questioned whether the ageing Indian leader's judgement had completely deserted him.[99] Galbraith reacted with similar dismay. Having repeatedly denied accusations that the Kennedy administration was plotting to cajole India into becoming a member of the Western alliance,

---

[94] *The New York Times*, 20 November 1962.
[95] Gopal, *Nehru: 1956–1964*, p. 228. Political considerations aside, the British noted that Assam's loss would have 'serious economic effects on India'. Its tea crop earned £100 million per year in foreign exchange (30 per cent of India's export revenue), while its wells provided 12 per cent of India's annual oil consumption. COS (62) 73, 20 November 1962, DO 196/168, TNA; 'Chinese Intentions against India', JIC Report, 22 November 1962, CAB 158/47, TNA.
[96] V. S. Naipaul, *An Area of Darkness: A Discovery of India* (New York: Vintage Books, 2002), pp. 264–5.
[97] Prasad (ed.), *Conflict With China*, p. xiii.
[98] Ormsby Gore to FO, No. 2901, Nehru to Kennedy, 20 November 1962, FO 371/164880/F1195/44/G (A), TNA.
[99] Ormsby Gore to Macmillan, No. 2899, 20 November 1962, DO 196/168, TNA.

the US ambassador was disconcerted to find the Indian government 'pleading for military association'.[100] Sceptical that the latest Chinese attack would develop into a full-scale invasion of India, Dean Rusk instructed Galbraith to make Nehru aware that he would need to meet some stiff preconditions before America considered direct intervention in the Sino-Indian War. These encompassed maximum Indian mobilisation of its own political and military resources; moves by New Delhi toward an Indo-Pakistani rapprochement; and the marshalling of support from the British Commonwealth and those nations within South East Asia, such as Thailand, Burma and Malaya, with a mutual interest in containing China. Moreover, if, having made every effort to help itself, Nehru's government still sought American military support, as a quid pro quo, Washington expected India to relinquish its Cold War neutrality.[101]

Given the United States' extensive global commitments, and the unpalatable prospect of reprising a Sino-American clash akin to the Korean War, Rusk was particularly anxious that the British Commonwealth take the lead in supporting India, while Washington 'trailed somewhat behind'.[102] Kennedy concurred. Aware that Britain's limited resources could not sustain such a position for long, the US president nevertheless calculated that working through Macmillan's government offered short-term advantages. Specifically, it promised to make American intervention in South Asia more palatable to Pakistan and the wider international community; offset Congressional opposition to unilateral American action overseas; and bind London to burden-sharing arrangements in the subcontinent. After debating how to respond to India's predicament with senior members of his cabinet, Kennedy rationalised, 'I would think you would, you must, figure India a British mission ... I think the British ought to take the lead here.'[103] The president wasted little time in communicating this feeling to the British. When it came to defending India from communism, Kennedy informed Ormsby Gore,

[100] Galbraith, *Ambassador's Journal*, New Delhi, 19 November 1962, p. 486; Galbraith to Rusk, No. 1898, 20 November 1962, NSF, Box 108, JFKL.

[101] Rusk to Delhi, 20 November 1962, *FRUS, 1961–1963*, vol. XIX, p. 400; Ormsby Gore to FO, No. 2900, 20 November 1962, DO 196/168, TNA; Ormsby Gore to Macmillan, No. 2899, 20 November 1962, DO 196/168, TNA.

[102] 'Presidential Meeting on Sino-Indian Conflict', 19 November 1962, *FRUS, 1961–1963*, vol. XIX, pp. 395–6.

[103] Sceptical the British would commit the necessary resources to guarantee India's security, US Secretary of Defense Robert McNamara nevertheless conceded, 'Now if we want to operate behind the façade of the British ... I suspect from a political point of view that is a very wise thing to do.' 'Sino-Indian War', 19 November 1962, Meetings Recordings, Tape No. 62, JFKL.

on 19 November, with their 'exceptional knowledge of India and as ... leader of the Commonwealth ... the United Kingdom, had an exceptionally important role to play'.[104] Reinforcing Kennedy's message, Rusk pressed Macmillan's government to organise a coalition of the 'old' Commonwealth countries (Canada, Australia and New Zealand) to assist India. Such a Commonwealth bloc, Rusk recommended to the British, could suspend grain sales to China; call a Commonwealth summit to procure wider international support for India; persuade Pakistan to propose conciliatory talks with New Delhi; and even loan retired British military personnel to India's armed forces.[105] Equally, Galbraith was instructed by the State Department to ensure that Nehru's government 'insist on maximum Commonwealth support ... Specifically, any requests for assistance made of us should also be addressed to the British.'[106]

In Downing Street, Harold Macmillan vacillated over the wisdom of waging war at India's side. During talks with the Labour Party leader Hugh Gaitskell, Macmillan indicated that while Britain would offer India help, 'We could not become involved in a war with China.'[107] Duncan Sandys was less sure. Having queried the status of Anglo-American contingency plans for intervention in India with the British Chiefs of Staff, Sandys reminded Macmillan that if the Chinese advance into India continued, 'the United States and Britain may be obliged to threaten armed intervention'.[108] On 20 November, with an absent Sandys receiving hospital treatment for a back ailment, Macmillan steered his cabinet away from talk of British military action in the subcontinent. Noting that the Chinese had not yet advanced beyond their territorial claim

---

[104] 'Presidential Meeting on Sino-Indian Conflict', 19 November 1962, *FRUS, 1961–1963*, vol. XIX, pp. 395–6; Ormsby Gore to FO, No. 2899, 19 November 1962, FO 371/164929/FC 1063/14, TNA.

[105] No doubt in a throwback to his Second World War service in the China–India–Burma theatre, Rusk informed the British that while 'He supposed that Field Marshal Slim was now too old there were undoubtedly other capable officers who had served under him available.' Ormsby Gore to FO, No. 2899, 19 November 1962, FO 371/164929/FC 1063/14/G, TNA; Grant to Talbot, 7 December 1962, RG59, Lot70D265, Box 13, NARA.

[106] State Department to New Delhi, 20 November 1962, *FRUS, 1961–1963*, vol. XIX, p. 401; S. Mahmud Ali, *Cold War in the High Himalayas: The USA, China and South Asia in the 1950s* (New York: St. Martin's Press, 1999), pp. 153–4.

[107] Macmillan meeting with Gaitskell, 20 November 1962, PREM 11/3859, TNA. At Nehru's request, Macmillan had sent some mountain artillery to India and approved £10 million in military aid for New Delhi. Nehru to Macmillan, 20 November 1962, DO 196/168, TNA; 'Co-ordination of Indian Arms Requirements', 20 November 1962, DO 196/168, TNA.

[108] Ministry of Defence (MoD) Minute, 19 November 1962, DO 196/168; Sandys to Macmillan, 20 November 1962, FO 371/164921, TNA.

line in northern India, the British premier suggested that Beijing's objective might remain limited to administering Nehru with a punitive lesson in realpolitik.[109] Viewed in this light, diplomatic initiatives, such as encouraging India to trade land for peace with Pakistan, or appeal to the United Nations for support against Chinese aggression, appeared more appropriate options.[110] The next day, as news reached London that the Chinese drive into India had gathered momentum, Macmillan was forced to reconsider his position and plan for the worst. 'Should all other efforts to stop the Chinese fail,' the prime minister cabled to Commonwealth leaders, 'we and the Americans and perhaps our other Western Allies may need to intervene militarily.'[111] Given the British government's preoccupation with a domestic economy already overburdened with foreign commitments, and its concern at Pakistan's reaction to British support for India, the wider ramifications of Macmillan's dilemma were not lost on US policymakers.[112] At the State Department, American officials reasoned that

Macmillan probably regards the Chinese attack on India as an acid test of the value of the Commonwealth and of Britain's ability to act as a world power. Consequently, he will probably stretch far to provide British leadership and material assistance both in fact and appearance. Macmillan will also seek to stimulate a comparable response from the Commonwealth ... This may alter fundamentally the relations of India to Britain (and the Commonwealth) on the one hand and to the US on the other. Such a metamorphosis in turn is likely to affect Britain's attitude toward the United States.[113]

As Washington had anticipated, Macmillan responded to American calls for action by conceiving a high-profile gesture of Commonwealth support for India. Specifically, this envisaged redeploying the Commonwealth Brigade (a mixed force of British, Australian and New Zealand troops based in Malaya) to the Indian subcontinent. It was intended that the Brigade's mission would be restricted to policing a

---

[109] Ormsby Gore to FO, No. 2900, 20 November 1962, DO 196/168, TNA; 'Sino-Indian Conflict', 20 November 1962, CAB 130/189, GEN.779, TNA.

[110] The Foreign Office received one bizarre diplomatic overture from Field Marshal Montgomery. Citing friendships with Mao Zedong, Zhou Enlai, Chen Yi (foreign minister of the PRC) and Nehru, Monty, as possibly 'the only person in the Western world who knows these four persons intimately', offered his services as a mediator in the Sino-Indian dispute. Whitehall declined the offer. Montgomery to FO, 19 November 1962, FO 371/164921/FC 1061/228, TNA.

[111] Macmillan to Diefenbaker, Menzies, Holyoake and Tunku Abdul Rahman, 21 November 1962, DO 196/169, TNA.

[112] Peck paper, 2 November 1962, FO 371/164929/FC 1063/1, TNA; 'Meeting on Sino-Indian Conflict', 20 November 1962, CAB 130/189, GEN.779, TNA.

[113] 'Current Political Scene in the United Kingdom', 13 December 1962, NSF, Box 238, Folder 2, JFKL.

buffer zone between Indian and Pakistani-occupied Kashmir, which in turn, would free up Indian forces for use against the Chinese. Although confident that Pakistan would support his proposal, Macmillan recognised that securing Indian agreement would prove to be more problematic. Nehru's Foreign Secretary, M. J. Desai, confirmed as much when he informed Galbraith that the ruling Congress Party hierarchy would never countenance the return of British troops to the subcontinent. In such a scenario, Desai explained, his fellow Indians would 'never believe that the British aren't somehow coming back [for good]'.[114] Equally, the British Chiefs of Staff pointed out that a decision to send the Brigade to India would require approval from Australia, New Zealand and Malaya. Such approval appeared unlikely to be forthcoming, not least because in releasing troops from service in Malaya those countries would find themselves unable to meet SEATO treaty commitments elsewhere.[115] So it proved. Having floated the Commonwealth Brigade proposal, a chastened Macmillan received a series of 'discouraging noises' from Canberra and Wellington, and was left with little choice but to abandon the scheme.[116]

### The Harriman and Sandys missions

Having been disconcerted by the confused and panic-stricken messages emanating from Nehru's government, toward the end of November the Kennedy administration went in search of accurate information on the situation in India, before deciding whether to commit additional American resources to the Sino-Indian War. 'We as a government are without any foundations for decision making', Robert McNamara observed on 19 November. 'We don't know enough about the situation [in India]. We need a sort of a Taylor mission to do for India what they did for South Vietnam.' Brushing aside Dean Rusk's contention that this should be left to the British, Kennedy approved the despatch of a high-level fact-finding mission to the subcontinent.[117] Having discovered through Ormsby Gore that British thinking had developed along similar lines, agreement was reached between London and Washington to coordinate the activities of a British mission bound for India,

---

[114] Galbraith to Rusk, No. 2298, 9 December 1962, NSF, Box 109, JFKL.
[115] COS (62) 73, 20 November 1962, DO 196/168, TNA.
[116] Macmillan to Menzies and Holyoake, 21 November 1962, DO 196/170, TNA; 'Sino-Indian Conflict', 20 November 1962, CAB 130/189, GEN.779, TNA; Menzies to Macmillan, 30 November 1962, DO 196/170, TNA; Norton Minute, 4 December 1962, FO 371/164921/FC 1061/233/G (A), TNA.
[117] 'Sino-Indian War', 19 November 1962, Meetings Recordings, Tape No. 62, JFKL.

headed by Duncan Sandys, and its American equivalent, under Averell Harriman.[118]

Shortly before midnight on 20 November, with the Harriman and Sandys missions en route to New Delhi, the Chinese government surprised the world by announcing that its forces inside India would halt all offensive operations and observe a unilateral ceasefire within the following twenty-four hours. Nine days later, the PLA began withdrawing to positions 20 kilometres behind the line of Sino-Indian control that had existed prior to November 1959. By effectively trading its claim on the NEFA for control over Aksai Chin, China had imposed on Nehru's government the border settlement that Beijing had tried, and failed, to secure diplomatically. British officials judged that the Chinese decision most likely reflected Mao Zedong's calculation that with Western intervention in the border war looming, the Sino-Indian fighting threatened to escalate from a successfully managed local conflict into a major war, fraught with political and military uncertainty. Moreover, the Chinese were well placed to play the role of peacemaker, having humbled India in the eyes of the Afro-Asian world, undermined Nehru's commitment to non-alignment and secured their immediate territorial objectives.[119] Back in Washington, the United States Information Agency reasoned that the Chinese had 'won a decided propaganda victory with the ceasefire initiative'. In sum, the USIA suggested:

Peking's net gain thus far in the dispute exceeds any net loss. If Peking wanted to inflate its power image in Asia and recoup ground lost to the 'great leap forward' failures, it has succeeded. If Peking wanted to challenge the mettle of the pro-Western bloc or the unity of the neutralist nations, it has likewise succeeded. If Peking designed to tarnish the image of its most formidable opponent in the area, India, it succeeded.[120]

Inside the Oval Office, Kennedy responded to the ceasefire announcement with a mixture of grudging admiration and relief. 'There is no doubt who is in control over there [China]', Kennedy commented to advisers. 'Can you imagine the difficulty we would have with the Pentagon in pulling back and giving up territory that had cost that

---

[118] Ormsby Gore to FO, No. 2899, 19 November 1962, FO 371/164929/FC 1063/14/G, and Ormsby Gore to FO, 20 November 1962, FC1063/16 (C), TNA; Sandys to Macmillan, 13 November 1962, DSDN 8/12, DSP.

[119] 'Chinese Intentions against India', JIC Report, 22 November 1962, CAB 158/47, TNA; Ledward to McKenzie-Johnston, 24 November 1962, FO 371/164930/FC 1063/35G, TNA.

[120] 'World Reaction to the Sino-Indian Conflict', 31 January 1963, R-8-63 (A), RG 306 Records of the US Information Agency Office of Research, 'R' Reports 1960–3, Box 13, Folder R8–63, NARA.

many casualties, no matter how great the political end it served?'[121] As the British noted, however, the timing of Beijing's action had, nonetheless, left India 'somewhat more committed to the West than would have been the case had the Chinese acted two days earlier'.[122]

The Sandys and Harriman missions arrived in India with cautious briefs. Harriman's instructions from Kennedy were to listen to Indian officials, assess the political and military situation on the ground, and effect a show of American solidarity with Nehru's government.[123] Likewise, Macmillan impressed upon Sandys that his remit was primarily consultative. Hasty or open-ended commitments to India were to be avoided, given the broader economic and political constraints that London confronted. In this sense, an ancillary objective of the British and American missions was to prod the Indian government into accepting that the most immediate and effective means of improving its national security would be to settle outstanding Indo-Pakistani differences.[124] The British found it incongruous that while India pressed for Western military aid to fight the Chinese, a substantial proportion of its own armed forces continued to be deployed along the frontier with Pakistan.[125] Americans shared the sense of frustration at India's reluctance to confront new subcontinental realities. Ormsby Gore reported 'strong criticism' in the US press over Nehru's inexplicable failure to concentrate more Indian firepower against the Chinese.[126] Inflammatory statements by Indian officials fuelled Anglo-American exasperation. Even defeat by the Chinese, Morarji Desai stated publicly, was preferable to India making concessions to Pakistan. Similarly, American officials observed that while Nehru acknowledged the logic of pooling Indian and Pakistani resources to meet a Chinese threat to South Asia, the Indian leader had moved only 'very slowly, dangerously slowly' toward reconciliation with Pakistan.[127]

The principal sticking point in Indo-Pakistani relations remained Kashmir. With India more dependent than ever on Anglo-American military and economic aid as a consequence of the border war, Ayub Khan urged Kennedy and Macmillan to use Western leverage to force

[121] Hilsman, *To Move a Nation*, pp. 338–9.
[122] 'Sino-Indian Conflict: Policy Situation', 22 November 1962, DO 196/172, TNA.
[123] Kennedy to Harriman and Galbraith, 23 November 1962, *FRUS, 1961–1963*, vol. XIX, p. 405, and Galbraith to Washington, No. 2032, 24 November 1962, *FRUS, 1961–1963*, vol. XIX, p. 405.
[124] Macmillan to Ayub Khan, 20 November 1962, FO 371/164921/FC 1061/223, TNA; Kennedy to Harriman, 25 November 1962, *FRUS, 1961–1963*, vol. XIX, p. 406.
[125] Macmillan to Sandys, 22 November 1962, DO 196/169, TNA.
[126] Ormsby Gore to FO, No. 586, 20 November 1962, FO 371/164921, TNA.
[127] 'Report of the Harriman Mission', undated, Box 536, Folder 1, HP.

Nehru to settle the Kashmir dispute.[128] The notion of engineering a quid pro quo, under which India's receipt of Western military aid would be traded for a Kashmir accord, alarmed Galbraith. Indians would recoil from the implication that America and Pakistan were colluding to enforce the surrender of their territory, the ambassador cautioned the State Department, while at the same the Chinese were grabbing land in the north. 'For God's sake,' Galbraith implored Washington, '...keep Kashmir out of it.'[129] The CRO agreed. 'In no circumstances', its officials argued, 'should we get ourselves into the position of undertaking to put pressure on Mr. Nehru as regards Kashmir.' Doing so risked causing severe damage to Anglo-Indian relations and exacerbating existing Indo-Pakistani tension, and offered little hope of success.[130] Macmillan took a different view. For the British premier, India's reliance on Anglo-American support represented a 'most propitious moment' to nudge Nehru toward a Kashmir accord. Accordingly, Macmillan advised Sandys, 'in so far as Western military assistance with India will make her dependent upon us ... [to] use all our influence in favour of a [Kashmir] settlement'.[131] Wary of alienating Indian opinion and derailing his strategic vision of transforming India into a bulwark against Chinese Communism, Kennedy adopted a position midway between that of Galbraith and Macmillan. Rather than establishing a direct link between the delivery of Western military aid and progress toward a Kashmir settlement, Harriman was authorised by Kennedy to impress upon Nehru that American support came with an *expectation* that New Delhi would take concrete steps to end enervating Indo-Pakistani enmity.[132]

Once on the ground in New Delhi, Harriman quickly concluded that the conditions necessary to engineer a Kashmir settlement were not in place. Nehru's cabinet and the Indian public, Harriman judged, appeared psychologically unprepared to make significant territorial concessions to Pakistan.[133] Sandys felt less inhibited in pressing Indian government officials to extend Ayub Khan an olive branch. Wasting little time, the British Secretary of State for Commonwealth Relations

[128] Ayub Khan to Macmillan, 5 November 1962, FO 371/164919/FC 1061/198, TNA; McConaughy to Talbot, 27 October 1962, *FRUS, 1961–1963*, vol. XIX, p. 355.

[129] Galbraith, *Ambassador's Journal*, New Delhi, 28 October 1962, pp. 441–2.

[130] 'Pickard Situation Summary', 19 November 1962, FO 371/164921/FC 1061/227, TNA.

[131] Macmillan to Sandys, 22 November 1962, DO 196/169, TNA; Entry for 17 November 1962, d.47, HMD.

[132] Kennedy to Harriman, 24 November 1962, NSF, Box 146, JFKL.

[133] Harriman, Sandys, Ayub Khan talks, 28 November 1962, *FRUS, 1961–1963*, vol. XIX, p. 410.

immediately began to lobby Indian cabinet ministers to give ground on Kashmir. During one interview with Nehru, the 'highly emotional' Indian premier slammed his fist against a table and insisted to Sandys that defeat by China must not be followed by 'surrender to Pakistani blackmail'.[134] Such bluster, Sandys predicted, would temper once Indians accepted that political opposition at home would make it impossible for Kennedy and Macmillan to build up India's armed forces in the face of continued Indo-Pakistani hostility.[135] From their perspective, the Americans were content for Sandys to draw the Indian government's political fire and browbeat Nehru into opening up a dialogue with Pakistan on Kashmir,[136] which, in late November, the notably reluctant Indian leader agreed to do.

In the immediate aftermath of Beijing's ceasefire declaration, given the scale of India's defeat at China's hands, Harriman and Sandys found the Nehru government's requests for military assistance to be relatively modest. In the short term, the Indian Chiefs of Staff ruled out offensive operations against the Chinese. In consequence, New Delhi looked to the West to re-equip three Indian Army divisions that had been badly mauled by the Chinese, and arm three additional divisions that were to be raised from scratch. This effectively represented a single division increment on the military aid levels that British and American officials had agreed during October's 'London Talks'. India's medium-term ambitions were more expansive. On the assumption that Indian forces would resume offensive operations against the Chinese in 1964 or 1965, Indian Army commanders proposed raising fifteen new divisions. Such talk appeared dangerously irresponsible to British and American military experts. Even with substantial external support, increasing the Indian Army's manpower from 400,000 to 2,000,000 men within two years threatened to impose an intolerable burden on the nation's brittle economy. Indian plans for the IAF were equally extravagant, and encompassed the modernisation of existing aircraft and a doubling of the number then in active service.[137] Such wholesale

[134] Sandys to CRO, No. 62 Secret, 27 November 1962, FO 371/164930/FC 1063/24 (G), TNA.
[135] Gore-Booth to Sandys, 'India: Visit by the Secretary of State, the Parliamentary Under-Secretary of State and the Chief of the Imperial General Staff', 24 December 1962, DO 196/171, TNA; Sandys to CRO, No. 71 Secret, 29 November 1962, DSDN 8/1, DSP.
[136] Kaysen to Kennedy, 3 December 1962, NSF, Box 109, JFKL.
[137] Gore-Booth to Sandys, 'India: Visit by the Secretary of State, the Parliamentary Under-Secretary of State and the Chief of the Imperial General Staff', 24 December 1962, DO 196/171, TNA; Sandys to CRO, No. 58, 26 November 1962, DSDN 8/1, DSP; Macmillan had noted, 'Her [India's] economy is pretty sticky now. How will it stand the new strains of the China war?' Entry for 5 November 1962, d.47, HMD.

reforms, the British High Commission in New Delhi reported back to London, 'in terms of Pakistan, finance, and of future affiliation of the Indian Air Force ... make our hair stand on end'.[138] After some haggling, Harriman and Sandys secured an agreement with Indian government officials to confine the Indian Army's growth, at least initially, to the original six-division plan. No consensus emerged, however, from repeated Anglo-American attempts to convince senior IAF officers that their grandiose plans to update and expand the Indian airforce were unworkable.[139]

While Harriman and Sandys agreed on the need to check India's military aspirations, less unity of purpose was apparent in their attitudes to Indian non-alignment. Specifically, despite American misgivings, once in the subcontinent, Sandys chose to revisit his agenda for aligning India with the West. Buoyed by platitudes from Indian ministers that hinted at the country's growing disillusionment with non-alignment, Sandys mistakenly concluded that Nehru's government was willing to fundamentally revise its approach to foreign affairs.[140] Harriman and his staff were more sceptical that Indian ministers, and the nation's wider public, were ready to become formal Western allies.[141] On meeting Nehru, the State Department staffer Roger Hilsman was struck by the Indian leader's marked reluctance to discuss the broader political ramifications of China's attack on India. 'His letters to Kennedy asking for help had painted a desperate picture,' Hilsman recalled, 'but face to face Nehru seemed to want to avoid talking about it all.'[142] Nehru's rhetoric reinforced American thinking. 'Some critics of our policy want us to give up non-alignment', the Indian premier wrote to his chief ministers in December, 'and definitely want us to join

---

[138] Belcher to Pickard, 14 November 1962, DO 164/70, TNA.

[139] Gore-Booth to Sandys, 'India: Visit by the Secretary of State, the Parliamentary Under-Secretary of State and the Chief of the Imperial General Staff', 24 December 1962, DO 196/171, TNA. The British had their own economic rationale for limiting Anglo-American military assistance to India. Alarmed that Harriman's mission had 'turned itself into a fully fledged MAAG group', the cash-strapped British feared the Pentagon flexing its military muscle and usurping their traditional position as India's quartermaster. Meeting between the US and UK missions, 27 November 1962, DO 196/170, TNA; MoD minute, 28 November 1962, DO 196/170, TNA.

[140] Delhi to CRO, No. 2071, 25 November 1962, DO 196/169, TNA; Sandys to CRO, No. 58, 26 November 1962, DSDN 8/1, DSP; Gore-Booth to Sandys, 'India: Visit by the Secretary of State, the Parliamentary Under-Secretary of State and the Chief of the Imperial General Staff', 24 December 1962, DO 196/171, TNA.

[141] 'Report of the Harriman Mission', undated, Box 536, Folder 1, HP.

[142] Hilsman, *To Move a Nation*, p. 331; Kaysen to Kennedy, 3 December 1962, NSF, Box 109, JFKL.

the Western military bloc ... This would be completely wrong and harmful ...'[143]

Disconcerted by Sandys' determination 'to achieve a new relationship with India which he defined rather loosely as "alignment"', Harriman took solace from the private reassurances provided by British officials that the Commonwealth Secretary's position did not reflect HMG policy. Sandys' own civil servants at the CRO reminded their minister that Anglo-American agreement had been reached during the 'London Talks' to preserve Indian non-alignment. Moreover, with domestic opinion in the United States opposed to a formal alliance with India, Sandys was cautioned that retrospectively challenging this policy was 'likely to lead to strong counter-argument by ... President [Kennedy]'.[144] Equally, confident that the erosion of Nehru's political authority occasioned by the border war would eventually see India move closer to the West, American policymakers continued to regard calls to rush into a 'formal' association with New Delhi as unnecessary and counterproductive. Forcing Nehru's government into the Western alliance risked alienating Pakistan, diminishing India's own effort to meet the Chinese threat, and provoking an Indo-Soviet schism, with its attendant risk of a Sino-Soviet rapprochement.[145] In Macmillan, however, Sandys found a kindred spirit. Only by bringing India fully into the West's collective security system, the British leader suggested to Kennedy, would Beijing be made to think twice about launching further incursions into South Asia, 'for they would never be sure that they would not draw upon themselves the nuclear reply'.[146] American policymakers demurred. 'Macmillan seems ... to have adopted Duncan Sandys' view that India should be drawn into CENTO or SEATO', the National Security Council (NSC) subcommittee on South Asia noted. 'This strikes us as nonsense. The pacts are weak, they still have bad connotations in India and we can achieve the same ends more easily through direct bilateral arrangements.'[147]

Perhaps the most significant outcome of the Harriman mission was the impetus that it provided to those in Washington, such as Dean Rusk, who argued that the British should assume a prominent role in India's

---

[143] Nehru to Chief Ministers, 22 December 1962, in *Letters to Chief Ministers*, vol. 5: *1958–1964*, pp. 547–57.

[144] Pickard Memorandum, 12 December 1962, DO 196/175, TNA.

[145] 'Report of the Harriman Mission', undated, Box 536, Folder 1, HP; Galbraith, *Ambassador's Journal*, New Delhi, 27 November 1962, p. 498.

[146] Macmillan to Kennedy, 13 December 1962, *FRUS, 1961–1963*, vol. XIX, pp. 430–2.

[147] 'Recommendations of NSC Subcommittee on South Asia for Nassau Talks', 16 December 1962, NSF, Box 109, JFKL.

defence. 'The successful pattern of close cooperation with the British on the political and military problems arising out of the Sino-Indian conflict should be continued,' Harriman urged the State Department, 'with the British being encouraged to appear to be a half step ahead whenever possible.'[148] From President Kennedy's perspective, keeping the British out in front in India continued to appear a prudent means of reducing pressure on his administration's relationship with Pakistan, limiting US military overextension and guarding against a direct Sino-American clash. Equally, from a domestic perspective, soundings taken amongst members of the Senate Foreign Relations Committee revealed an ongoing resistance to unilateral American intervention in South Asia.[149] Likewise, with the cost of the 'emergency' military aid package to India endorsed by Harriman and Sandys estimated at $120 million, the White House was eager to split this expense with Britain and the Commonwealth, as much as possible, on a fifty-fifty basis.[150]

Accordingly, Macmillan confronted American pressure throughout late 1962 to deliver some form of Commonwealth support for India. Kennedy's appeals for the British to 'give drive and unity' to the Commonwealth, however, merely laid bare that organisation's short-comings as a proxy for the United States in South Asia.[151] Financially, anxiety over Britain's balance of payments account led Macmillan's Treasury to oppose granting India additional military aid over and above the £10 million that the British cabinet had approved back in October.[152] Logistically, the Ministry of Defence declared that it was simply beyond Britain's means to source and deliver $60 million of military supplies to India.[153] Renewed British efforts to solicit contributions for India's defence from Australia, Canada and New Zealand, 'in order to reduce the financial burden falling upon us', met familiar resistance.[154] Noting Canberra's miserly response to India's calls for international assistance,

---

[148] 'Report of the Harriman Mission', undated, Box 536, Folder 1, HP.
[149] Harriman conversation with Fulbright, 4 December 1962, Box 537, Folder 1 and Harriman to Rusk, 18 December 1962, Box 536, Folder 2, HP; Harriman to McGeorge Bundy, 10 December 1962, NSF, Box 109, JFKL.
[150] 'Recommendations of NSC Subcommittee on South Asia for Nassau Talks', 16 December 1962, NSF, Box 109, JFKL; Meeting of the Executive Committee of the NSC, 3 December 1962, *FRUS, 1961–1963*, vol. XIX, p. 418, and NSAM No. 209, 10 December 1962, *FRUS, 1961–1963*, vol. XIX, p. 429.
[151] Ormsby Gore to Lord Home, No. 202, 11 December 1962, FO 371/164925/FC 1061/313, TNA.
[152] Boyd Carpenter to Macmillan, 12 December 1962, T 317/138, TNA.
[153] MoD minute to Macmillan, 11 December 1962, DO 196/175, TNA.
[154] Macmillan to Kennedy, 13 December 1962, *FRUS, 1961–1963*, vol. XIX, p. 430; Ormsby Gore to FO, No. 3094, 8 December 1962, DO 196/175; 'Military Aid for India', 21 December 1962, DO 196/171, TNA.

American officials rued that 'The Australian contribution [to India's defence] ... ought to be measured in terms of millions of dollars rather than in thousands of dollars.'[155] Likewise, when challenged by Dean Rusk to arrange for Australia and Canada to suspend sales of wheat to China, the half-hearted and ineffectual British response exasperated the Secretary of State.[156] Disinclined to imperil their own commercial relationship with Beijing by organising a Commonwealth trade embargo, the British, in any case, lacked the authority to influence Canberra or Ottawa's economic policy.[157] As the Kennedy administration belatedly came to acknowledge, the Sino-Indian War had landed Macmillan's government, as the Commonwealth's principal power, with 'embarrassing' financial and military obligations that it was ill equipped to meet.[158]

### The Nassau Summit

In mid-December, as Kennedy prepared to travel to Nassau in the Bahamas for his second Anglo-American summit meeting with Macmillan, the British premier's disappointing performance in mobilising Commonwealth support for India led American officials to reassess the value of working in South Asia with a partner lacking in 'urgency'.[159] British lethargy, the State Department speculated, ought perhaps to have been expected from a government in London 'which calls itself conservative ... and which is directed by a leader whose birthdate is Victorian and whose manners are Edwardian'.[160] In an effort to retain Washington's confidence, Macmillan provided Kennedy with a crumb of comfort on the eve of their Nassau meeting. Certain that once it had been scrutinised more fully by Anglo-American experts, the $120 million estimate that Harriman and Sandys had placed on India's military needs would be revised downward, Macmillan agreed in principle to 'share' the bill for India's defence with the Kennedy administration.[161]

---

[155] Grant to Talbot, 7 December 1962, RG 59, Lot 70D265, Box 13, NARA.
[156] Ormsby Gore to Lord Home, No. 202, 11 December 1962, FO 371/164925/FC 1061/313, TNA.
[157] The CRO observed, 'It would be contrary to our political aims and economic interests to refuse to trade with China.' Emery to Belcher, 8 October 1963, DO 196/4, TNA.
[158] 'Current Political Scene in the United Kingdom', 13 December 1962, NSF, Box 238, Folder 2, JFKL.
[159] Komer to Kennedy, 16 December 1962, *FRUS, 1961–1963*, vol. XIX, pp. 434–7.
[160] 'Current Political Scene in the United Kingdom', 13 December 1962, NSF, Box 238, Folder 2, JFKL.
[161] Macmillan to Kennedy, 13 December 1962, *FRUS, 1961–1963*, vol. XIX, p. 430.

British munificence did little to dispel nagging American doubts over the efficacy of the Anglo-American partnership in the Indian subcontinent. On balance, the NSC Subcommittee on South Asia continued to endorse a multilateral response to the Sino-Indian War. 'The British', it concluded, 'should remain a half-step ahead of us so long as they have the will and capability to do so.' American patience, however, was wearing thin. 'Should they flag,' the subcommittee added tellingly, 'we should take whichever steps are necessary to keep this opportunity [of drawing India closer to the West] from slipping through our fingers.'[162]

The outcome of the Anglo-American discussions at Nassau failed to assuage American concern over the Macmillan government's approach to South Asian affairs. Two issues dominated exchanges on the Sino-Indian War between British and American leaders: Indian air defence and Indo-Pakistani relations. On the air defence question, as elsewhere, Kennedy looked to the Commonwealth to provide a lead.[163] For Macmillan, this opened up the disturbing possibility of the RAF becoming engaged in an air war with China without direct American support. Averse to offering India a security guarantee on a par with that extended to formal allies, such as Pakistan, but with none of the attendant responsibilities, the British judged India's formal association with the West as an appropriate price for the provision of air defence. Kennedy felt otherwise, and again disputed the benefit that Britain and the United States would derive from compelling India to compromise its non-alignment.[164] The Anglo-American impasse spawned a suitably equivocal compromise. Deferring an immediate decision on the air defence issue, Kennedy and Macmillan instead agreed to send a joint mission to the subcontinent to re-evaluate India's air defence requirements. The solution had the advantage of meeting Kennedy's objective of providing Nehru with a show of Western support, and satisfied Macmillan by avoiding any unilateral British commitment to defend India.[165] To some frustrated American officials, however, such as Galbraith, British timidity had spurned a valuable opportunity to enhance Western influence with India, by offering Nehru's government firmer military support

---

[162] 'Recommendations of NSC Subcommittee on South Asia for Nassau Talks', 16 December 1962, NSF, Box 109, JFKL.

[163] New Delhi to State Department, 30 November 1962, *FRUS, 1961–1963*, vol. XIX, pp. 415–17.

[164] Sandys to Macmillan, 10 December 1962, DO 196/175; 'Air Support for India: Political Assessment', 12 December 1962, FO 371/164925/FC 1061/314; Macmillan/Kennedy Talks, Nassau, 20 December 1962, PREM 11/4229, TNA.

[165] Macmillan/Kennedy Talks, Nassau, 20 December 1962, PREM 11/4229, TNA.

without any associated political strings.[166] Nehru was less disappointed with the air defence compromise. With the border ceasefire holding and domestic opposition to a Western 'air umbrella' becoming increasingly vocal, the Indian premier was happy for the Chinese to receive a clear signal of Anglo-American military intent, while at the same time, nominally at least, India's non-alignment remained intact.[167]

Further disagreement bedevilled British and American discussions at Nassau on Indo-Pakistani relations and, more specifically, the issue of Kashmir. On the British side, Macmillan and Sandys reiterated the case for rationing the supply of military aid to India in a bid to squeeze Nehru's government into a political settlement with Pakistan. It was noted that Nehru faced a growing domestic clamour not to barter away Indian interests in Kashmir, while Ayub Khan's decision to court Beijing had turned popular Indian sentiment against Pakistan. With the Chinese threat to India abating, the British worried that, in the absence of external pressure, Nehru would continue to stonewall on Kashmir, provoking a schism between Pakistan and the West. Equally exercised by India's increasingly hard-nosed stance on Kashmir, Kennedy nevertheless favoured a more cautious line. Linking Anglo-American military aid to a Kashmir settlement was 'pushing things too far', the American president argued, and risked squandering the considerable Indian goodwill that Britain and the United States had accumulated over the previous two months. More precisely, Kennedy feared that by hitting Nehru too hard on Kashmir, his government might precipitate a Sino-Indian reconciliation. 'In three months from now,' Kennedy mused, 'the Indians might say they were unable to get arms from the West without giving up Kashmir and therefore they had no alternative to making a deal with the Chinese.' Procrastinating, Kennedy and Macmillan deferred a second important decision, this time on long-term military aid for India, until the spring of 1963, when the results of ongoing Indo-Pakistan talks would be clearer.[168] Nonetheless, with the British eager to force the pace with Nehru's government on Kashmir, and London more inclined than the Americans to make military aid contingent upon an Indo-Pakistani settlement, the stage had been set for what would prove to be a frustrating, discordant and ultimately unsuccessful Anglo-American foray into the Kashmir quagmire.

---

[166] Galbraith to Rusk, No. 5061, 24 June 1963, NSF, Box 110, JFKL

[167] Gopal, *Nehru: 1956–1964*, p. 253; Vijaya Lakshmi Pandit, *The Scope of Happiness: A Personal Memoir* (London: Weidenfeld & Nicolson, 1979), p. 274.

[168] Macmillan/Kennedy Talks, Nassau, 20 December 1962, PREM 11/4229, TNA; Gore-Booth to CRO, No. 242, 21 December 1962, DO 196/171, TNA.

# 6  Quagmire: the Anglo-American search for a Kashmir settlement

For the United Kingdom's High Commissioner to India, Sir Paul Gore-Booth, it ranked as the 'most unusual episode in the history of relations between India and Britain and India and the West generally'.[1] The event in question occurred in New Delhi, in May 1963, when senior British, American and Indian policymakers met to discuss the dispute between India and Pakistan over control of the state of Jammu and Kashmir. Following a week of frenetic diplomatic activity, which Gore-Booth confessed had left him 'not only physically but mentally somewhat breathless', by the end of May, Anglo-American bonds were strained, and India's patience with what it saw as unwarranted foreign interference in its internal affairs, all but exhausted.[2] More significantly, however, by the end of the trilateral talks, India's premier, Jawaharlal Nehru, had agreed in principle to third-party mediation of what he had hitherto insisted was a strictly bilateral issue between India and Pakistan. In the spring of 1963, it seemed, Anglo-American diplomacy had brought India and Pakistan tantalisingly close to resolving the Kashmir dispute, one of the most deleterious and vexing legacies of the Indian subcontinent's partition in August 1947.

The Anglo-American decision to push for a mediated settlement to the Kashmir dispute came after months of fruitless talks between India and Pakistan, which the British and American governments had sponsored in the wake of the Sino-Indian border war. The rationale for Anglo-American intercession in the Kashmir dispute lay in its propensity to prolong enervating Indo-Pakistani enmity, which in turn threatened to undermine the political, economic and military stability of South Asia. Moreover, following its military humiliation at the hands of Communist China in late 1962, by continuing to divert its scarce resources into an internecine squabble with Pakistan, Nehru's

---

[1] Gore-Booth to Sandys, 10 June 1963, DO 196/122, The United Kingdom National Archives, Kew, London (hereafter TNA).

[2] *Ibid.*

government threatened the Kennedy administration's plan to develop democratic India into an Asian counterweight to the PRC. British and American hopes that a significant step had been taken in May 1963 on the road to a Kashmir settlement, however, ultimately proved misplaced. The attempt to mediate a Kashmir settlement, as with other Kashmir proposals London and Washington had co-sponsored during the previous two years, succumbed to the corrosive effect of Indian equivocation, inflated Pakistani expectation and Anglo-American discord. In this sense, the Kennedy and Macmillan governments' intervention in the Kashmir dispute was rendered ineffectual by the same forces, both internal and external to the subcontinent, which combined to frustrate wider British and, more especially, American policy initiatives in South Asia, in the early 1960s.

Situated in the far north-west corner of the Indian subcontinent, the 85,000-square-mile (220,000 square kilometres) state of Jammu and Kashmir occupies a strategic location between India, Pakistan, the Tibet and Xinjiang regions of China, and, beyond the narrow Wakhan corridor controlled by Afghanistan, the Soviet Union. The state's political and economic life centres on its capital Srinagar, nestled within the Vale of Kashmir (Kashmir Valley), a fertile plain eighty-five miles (137 kilometres) long by twenty-five miles (forty kilometres) wide and enclosed by a mountainous hinterland. In the early 1960s, over three-quarters of the state's four million inhabitants were Muslims, with Hindu and Buddhist minorities concentrated in Jammu, in the south, and Ladakh, in the north-east.[3] The origins of the Kashmir dispute lay in the partition agreement that Britain brokered between Nehru's Congress Party and Mohammed Ali Jinnah's Muslim League before departing from the Indian subcontinent, in August 1947. In part, this required each of British India's 350 semi-autonomous princely states to accede to either India or Pakistan. However, as South Asia celebrated its independence, Hari Singh, the Hindu Maharaja of Jammu and Kashmir, determined to preserve his kingdom's autonomy and prevaricated over signing an instrument of accession with New Delhi or Karachi.

Toward the end of 1947, the horrific communal violence between Hindu, Muslim and Sikh that accompanied partition, spilled over into Kashmir from the neighbouring Punjab, wrecking Hari Singh's plans. In October, on the pretext of defending fellow Muslims, and with the collusion of Pakistan's government, heavily armed Pathan tribesmen from the North-West Frontier Province swept into the Kashmir Valley

---

[3] India–Pakistan Summary, 17 April 1959, RG 59, Lot 62D172, National Archives and Records Administration, College Park, Maryland (hereafter NARA).

and advanced on Srinagar. With his own private army in full retreat, a desperate Hari Singh appealed to the Indian government for urgent military assistance. Nehru authorised an operation to airlift Indian troops into Srinagar only after Hari Singh had agreed to Kashmir's integration into the Indian Union. Subsequent fighting between the Indian Army and irregular Pakistani forces in Kashmir dragged on into 1949. Under UN auspices, a ceasefire agreement was eventually brokered, which left India in control of two-thirds of the state, including the Vale, while Pakistan retained a foothold in the mountainous north, which it subsequently referred to as Azad, or 'free', Kashmir.[4]

Nehru and his Congress Party had gone to considerable lengths following India's independence to forge a unitary and secular nation from the subcontinent's diverse religious, ethnic, linguistic and caste groupings. For the Indian leader, the notion that Kashmir should adhere to Pakistan simply because its inhabitants were predominately Muslim, threatened to undermine communal harmony and the very principles on which the Indian republic had been founded. In July 1953, writing to India's last Governor General, and then Chief Minister of Madras, Chakravarti Rajagopalachari, Nehru stressed that 'anything that happens there [Kashmir] has larger and wider consequences'. 'The "problem of Kashmir"', Rajagopalachari was assured, '[is] symbolic of … our secular policy in India.'[5]

Equally, to Pakistan's government, the existence within the Indian union of a state with an overwhelming Muslim majority challenged the *raison d'être* for Pakistan's existence, and undermined the nation's commitment to Muslim solidarity.[6] As many Congress leaders, such as Rajagopalachari, privately conceded, when it came to Kashmir, Pakistan's leaders invariably found themselves 'in a worse situation than Nehru in regard to public pressures and emotional bondage'.[7] In late 1947, in an effort to resolve this conundrum, Britain's last Viceroy and the Indian republic's first Governor General, Lord Louis Mountbatten, persuaded Nehru that once law and order had been re-established within Kashmir, the state's population should decide by means of a plebiscite

[4] Sumit Ganguly, *Conflict Unending: India-Pakistan Tensions since 1947* (New York: Columbia University Press, 2001), pp. 16–17; William J. Barnds, *India, Pakistan and the Great Powers* (London: Pall Mall Press, 1972), pp. 38–43.

[5] Nehru to Rajagopalachari, 31 July 1953, Subject File 123 C, Fifth Instalment, C. Rajagopalachari Papers, Nehru Memorial Museum and Library, New Delhi (hereafter NMML).

[6] Robert J. McMahon, *The Cold War on the Periphery: The United States, India and Pakistan* (New York: Columbia University Press, 1994), pp. 20–1.

[7] Rajagopalachari to Shiva Rao, 12 May 1964, Subject File 92, Fourth Instalment, C. Rajagopalachari Papers, NMML.

whether its future lay with India or Pakistan. International support for a Kashmiri plebiscite was subsequently enshrined in resolutions passed by the United Nations Security Council in August 1948 and January 1949. Agreement between India and Pakistan on the preconditions necessary for a state-wide ballot, however, which hinged on mutual troop withdrawals and the composition of a transitional Kashmiri administration, proved elusive.

With the passage of time, and with India firmly in control of Kashmir's prime real estate, the attitude of Nehru's government hardened against any substantive changes to the territorial status quo. Consequently, sporadic exchanges between India and Pakistan on Kashmir's future floundered. Specifically, talks held between Nehru and Pakistani leaders, such as Muhammed Ali Bogra, in 1953, and Mohammad Ayub Khan, in 1959, and attempts to advance the Kashmir issue at the United Nations in 1957 and 1958, came to nothing. Anglo-American intervention in the dispute at the end of the 1950s proved to be equally ineffectual.[8] Undaunted by the seemingly intractable nature of the Kashmir conundrum, on taking office in January 1961, the Kennedy administration embarked upon an audacious and politically hazardous attempt to remove the primary source of friction between India and Pakistan. Indeed, under President Kennedy's aegis, between 1961 and 1963, American and British involvement in South Asia's most obstinate problem entered a new and unparalleled phase.

## Kennedy, Kashmir and the United Nations

The Kennedy administration was well aware that American intercession in the Kashmir dispute risked the United States' estrangement from India, or Pakistan, or possibly both countries.[9] In early 1961, however, reports from the US Embassy in Karachi suggested that from a Pakistani perspective, at least, such intervention could prove timely. Ayub Khan's government, it seemed, had concluded that Nehru would never risk forfeiting India's preponderant territorial stake in Kashmir by agreeing to hold a state plebiscite. In conversations with American Embassy officers, Pakistani officials began to hint that Rawalpindi would be willing to renounce its claim on the whole of Kashmir, if an agreement could be reached to partition the state between India and Pakistan on a more

---

[8] US–UK talks, 16–18 April 1958 and 'Proposals for Reduction of Tension between India and Pakistan', 25 April 1958, RG 59, Lot 62D43, Package folder 2, NARA.

[9] McMahon, *Cold War on the Periphery*, p. 282.

equitable basis.[10] As expected, the signals on Kashmir emanating from New Delhi were far less encouraging. On meeting with Nehru, in March 1961, Kennedy's ambassador at large, Averell Harriman, found the Indian premier to be in uncompromising mood. India would reject any Kashmir accord with Pakistan, Nehru confirmed, which required New Delhi to sanction anything other than minor adjustments to the existing line of control.[11] Troublingly for Washington, Pakistan associated Nehru's intransigence on Kashmir with the Kennedy administration's reluctance to attach political strings to its 'vast' economic aid programme in India. Moreover, in the first half of 1961 popular pressure to 'liberate' Kashmir mounted in Pakistan. In May, US Vice-President Lyndon Johnson was left in no doubt when he visited the subcontinent that Ayub Khan's government expected its American allies to take a firm line with Nehru on Kashmir. The extent of Kennedy's willingness to support Rawalpindi's claim on the contested state, Johnson was informed, would be taken as *the* barometer of his administration's goodwill toward Pakistan.[12]

In a bid to temper Pakistan's expectations in relation to Kashmir, a visit to the United States that Ayub Khan was scheduled to make in November was brought forward to July by the White House.[13] In advance of his arrival in Washington, Pakistan's president irritated the Kennedy administration by encouraging his country's semi-official press to portray the upcoming meeting with his American counterpart as one of 'epochal' importance to the future of South Asia.[14] Once in the United States, Ayub Khan exploited an appearance on the nationally televised 'Meet the Press' to pile further pressure on his host. Asked by American journalists how far Kennedy could go in influencing Nehru on Kashmir, Ayub Khan replied, 'We will see how far he can go. He should be able to go a long way.'[15] Pakistan's faith in the utility of American power to resolve the Kashmir dispute perturbed Kennedy's foreign policy advisers. Within the NSC, Robert Komer lamented the

---

[10] Rountree to Weill, Karachi, 8 February 1961, *FRUS, 1961–1963*, vol. XIX, pp. 6–7.

[11] Harriman/Nehru meeting, New Delhi, 23 March 1961, Box 526, Averell Harriman Papers, United States Library of Congress, Washington, DC (hereafter HP).

[12] Rountree to Rusk, No. 2019, 21 May 1961, and No. 2023, 22 May 1961, National Security File (NSF), Box 242A, John F. Kennedy Library, Boston, Massachusetts (hereafter JFKL). The British concurred that Johnson's visit had prompted an officially sanctioned Pakistani 'psychological campaign of pressure on the Americans' for action on Kashmir. 'Pakistan: The Visit of the Vice-President of the United States', 16 June 1961, DO 196/132, TNA.

[13] Viscount Hood to Lord Home, 27 July 1961, DO 196/132, TNA.

[14] Komer to Walt Rostow, 30 June 1961, NSF, Box 441, JFKL.

[15] Mohammad Ayub Khan, *Friends Not Masters: A Political Autobiography* (London: Oxford University Press, 1967), p. 137.

fact that Ayub Khan's government stubbornly refused to accept that by pressing Nehru too hard, the United States would 'throw India back into the hands of Peiping and Moscow'.[16] Given their divergent perspectives on Kashmir, Kennedy's exchanges with Ayub Khan on the issue proved tense. Repeated exhortations from the Pakistani president to link American aid to India with movement toward a Kashmir settlement were dismissed by Kennedy as inimical to their common objective of containing communism. 'It [was] in the interest of all of us', Kennedy reminded his Pakistani guest, 'that India should not collapse.'[17] Despite their differences on Kashmir, however, Kennedy had no wish to exacerbate rising anti-American sentiment in Pakistan by sending Ayub Khan home empty-handed. To the State Department's dismay, in his final exchange with the Pakistani delegation, the president went further than he had planned, and agreed to 'make a major effort' with Nehru on Kashmir when the Indian leader visited Washington in November. Should the initiative with Nehru fail to yield results, Kennedy added, the American government would back Pakistan's calls for a fresh debate on Kashmir at the UN Security Council.[18]

Back in the subcontinent, British and American officials in India expressed deep misgivings at the commitments that Kennedy had provided to Ayub Khan. Simmering animosity between India and Pakistan, an upsurge in communal tension, and a forthcoming Indian general election, all appeared to militate against any moderation in Nehru's outlook on Kashmir.[19] In mid-August, Gore-Booth impressed upon the CRO that India's government remained convinced that by relinquishing its hold on Kashmir, the sectarian violence that it had worked so hard to suppress after the horror of partition would flare up once again. Moreover, with China contesting India's sovereignty in parts of Ladakh, which abutted Kashmir, senior Indian Army commanders advised Nehru that the Kashmir Valley was of 'vital strategic importance' to the defence of the country's northern border. Equally, as a descendant of Kashmiri Brahmins, Nehru's personal stake in the dispute also factored heavily in Anglo-American thinking. Although 'rational about

---

[16] Komer to Walt Rostow, 30 June 1961, Box 147A, and Rostow to Kennedy, 7 July 1961, NSF, Box 441, JFKL.

[17] Kennedy–Ayub Khan talks, Tuesday 11 July 1961, NSF, Box 147 A, JFKL. Phillips Talbot reflected that Kennedy saw American economic power as a paper tiger in the South Asian context. 'He [Kennedy] felt the quarrels [between India and Pakistan] to be so bone-deep that threats to change the levels of US aid would be unlikely to help erase them.' Phillips Talbot, OH, 27 July 1965, p. 22, JFKL.

[18] Kennedy–Ayub Khan talks, 11 July 1961, NSF, Box 147 A, JFKL.

[19] Galbraith to State Department, New Delhi, 28 June 1961, *FRUS, 1961–1963*, vol. XIX, p. 59.

practically everything', Gore-Booth observed, Nehru was 'so emotionally involved over the integration of his family's homeland into India,
that on Kashmir at least he is completely irrational'. Nehru's psychological baggage was such, the British High Commissioner suggested, that
'we shall have to wait for Mr. Nehru's successor before we can have an
Indian Government willing to consider a compromise'.[20]

The conditional assurance that Kennedy had given Ayub Khan to
support a UN Security Council resolution on Kashmir was of particular concern to British and American officials. The British failed to
conceive how it would be possible to avoid alienating either India or
Pakistan during a Security Council debate. Bilateral talks appeared
a more productive way forward, and only then in an atmosphere of
improved Indo-Pakistani relations.[21] The State Department was largely
in tune with British thinking. Taking Kashmir before the United
Nations would, its officials concluded, merely increase Indo-Pakistani
tension, harden negotiating positions on both sides and 'set back rather
than promote the kind of quiet discussions which are essential to bringing about a solution'.[22] The prospect of a UN debate increased, nonetheless, after Kennedy met with Nehru in Washington, in November
1961. On Kashmir, Nehru remained implacable. The Indian people
and parliament, Kennedy was chided by his visitor, would tolerate only
minor territorial adjustments in the state. To do otherwise would open
the Pandora's box of communalism, undermining the fabric of Indian
national unity and threatening the security of India's forty-five million Muslims.[23] 'The danger to India ... is not communism', Nehru
was fond of reminding his civil servants. 'It is Hindu right-wing communalism.'[24] The Indian leader's robust defence of his government's
Kashmir policy convinced Washington that any breakthrough on the
issue would have to wait until the following spring. By then, it was
hoped, with India's general election out of the way and the political dust
having settled in New Delhi, Nehru might adopt a more conciliatory
position.[25]

[20]  Gore-Booth to Sandys, 14 August 1961, FO 371/164873/F 1041/8, TNA.
[21]  *Ibid.*
[22]  'President Ayub's Visit', 11–18 July 1961, RG 59, NEA INC LOT 65 D 415, Box 1,
      NARA.
[23]  Kennedy–Nehru talks, Washington, 7 November 1961, *FRUS, 1961–1963*, vol. XIX,
      pp. 131–4.
[24]  Y. D. Gundevia, *Outside the Archives* (New Delhi: Sangam Books, 1984), pp. 208–9.
[25]  Rountree to State Department, Karachi, 13 December 1961, *FRUS, 1961–1963*, vol.
      XIX, pp. 158–9.

Determined that Kashmir remain at the top of the subcontinent's political agenda, a disappointed Ayub Khan responded to the Kennedy–Nehru talks by publicly confirming Pakistan's intention to place the dispute back before the UN Security Council.[26] In a bid to avoid such an eventuality, the White House pressed Nehru to open an Indo-Pakistani dialogue on Kashmir following India's general election.[27] The American initiative was overtaken, however, by India's 'liberation' of Goa, in December 1961. India's 'act of aggression', Ayub Khan subsequently informed Kennedy, had underscored the urgency of mobilising international pressure on Nehru to implement the UN Security Council resolutions calling for a plebiscite in Kashmir.[28] In response, on the condition that Pakistan withdraw its demand for a UN debate, Kennedy offered the services of the World Bank president, Eugene Black, who had been instrumental in resolving the Indus Waters dispute, to mediate a Kashmir settlement.[29]

To Kennedy's irritation, Ayub Khan accepted his offer of American mediation but also prevaricated over turning away from the UN.[30] Worse still, Nehru's government rejected the 'Black proposal' out of hand. In making the case for mediation, American officials had urged India to recognise the strategic value of working with Pakistan to counter the looming threat of 'the political use of the A-bomb by the Communist Chinese to threaten Asia'. Moreover, from a tactical standpoint, the immediate aftermath of India's general election, in February 1962, was represented as offering the ruling Congress Party a five-year cushion within which to absorb domestic political fallout from a Kashmir settlement. Likewise, Ayub Khan would be able to seize a similar window of opportunity in which to make unpopular concessions on Kashmir, before Pakistan's impending reversion to parliamentary government later that year.[31] Such arguments left Nehru unmoved. For the Indian leader, accepting Kennedy's mediation proposal was certain to bring further unwelcome pressure on his government to endorse the partition of Kashmir along religious lines. 'The two-nation theory in regard to Kashmir will have the most disastrous consequences in the whole of India', Nehru rationalised.

[26] *The Times*, 27 November 1961.
[27] Komer to McGeorge Bundy, Washington, 28 December 1961, *FRUS, 1961–1963*, vol. XIX, p. 164.
[28] Ayub Khan to Kennedy, Rawalpindi, 2 January 1962, *FRUS, 1961–1963*, vol. XIX, pp. 170–1.
[29] Komer to McGeorge Bundy, 12 January 1962, NSF, Box 230, JFKL.
[30] *The Times*, 13 January 1962; Ayub Khan to Kennedy, Karachi, 18 January 1962, *FRUS, 1961–1963*, vol. XIX, pp. 202–3.
[31] Talbot–B. K. Nehru meeting, 29 January 1962, RG 59, NEA INC Lot 65 D 415, Box 1, NARA.

'Not only will our secularism end, but India will tend to break up.'[32] Having personally sanctioned the 'Black proposal', Kennedy made the Indian government aware that he was 'real mad' at Nehru's summary rebuff.[33] From Washington, it appeared that Nehru's unreasonable fear of what India might have to concede to settle its differences with Pakistan had led the Indian premier to spurn mediation and instead play a waiting game, in the implausible hope that Ayub Khan and his successors would eventually come to accept the status quo in Kashmir.[34]

As Washington had expected, Pakistan's government reacted to Nehru's intransigence by accelerating its efforts to bring the Kashmir dispute before the Security Council. Irked at having been dragged into a public spat between India and Pakistan, when the Security Council convened in New York to discuss Kashmir, on 22 June 1962, the Kennedy administration focused its energies on limiting the divisive impact of the debate. The British resolved 'to remain in the background as far as possible and to leave the running to the Americans'.[35] In a bid to extract some diplomatic sting from the Security Council's deliberations, American officials drafted a moderate Kashmir resolution, which they hoped would prove objectionable to neither India nor Pakistan, and persuaded five 'impartial' non-permanent members of the Council (Ireland, Chile, Venezuela, Ghana and the United Arab Republic) to act as its sponsors. By associating a broad cross-section of international opinion with an innocuous Kashmir resolution, the State Department concluded optimistically, the debate on Kashmir could be concluded quickly and quietly.

The Indian government had other ideas. A series of objections raised during the debate by Indian diplomats, prompted the British UN delegation to complain bitterly that their Indian colleagues were 'unwilling to accept any resolution put forward by the Five-Power group that had any content in it whatsoever'.[36] During the 'sorry affair' that ensued, a coordinated effort by Britain and the United States to appease Pakistan, by pushing an anodyne Kashmir resolution through the Security Council, was vetoed by the Soviet Union at India's behest. Britain's ambassador

[32] Nehru to M. C. Chagla, Indian High Commissioner to UK, 2 August 1962, cited in Sarvepalli Gopal, *Jawaharlal Nehru: A Biography*, vol. 3: *1956–1964* (London: Jonathan Cape, 1984), p. 216.

[33] Ormsby Gore to FO, No. 286, 31 January 1962, FO 371/166358/D 1041/51, TNA; *The Times*, 1 February 1962.

[34] Bowles to State Department, Karachi, 3 March 1962, *FRUS, 1961–1963*, vol. XIX, p. 219.

[35] Sir Patrick Dean to Lord Home, 9 July 1962, DO 196/141, TNA.

[36] *Ibid.*; Cleveland and Talbot to Ball, Washington, 22 June 1962, *FRUS, 1961–1963*, vol. XIX, p. 290.

to the United Nations, Sir Patrick Dean, complained to London that Indian officials had 'sneered at my arguments and, particularly at my appeal for understanding between Commonwealth members'.[37] In the Lok Sabha, Nehru voiced his 'deep regret and sorrow' that Britain and the United States had chosen to pursue a course in New York that had 'hurt and injured' India, and fostered 'doubt in our minds about [Western] … goodwill'.[38] Believing itself, and not the Indian government, to be the injured party, Kennedy's administration bridled at Nehru's barbs. India's attitude during and immediately following the UNSC debate, Dean Rusk cabled Galbraith in New Delhi, had induced feelings of 'intense irritation in Congressional and government circles here'.[39]

The Security Council saga proved entirely counterproductive from the Kennedy administration's perspective, fuelling Indo-Pakistani friction and straining its relationships with Nehru and Ayub Khan. 'We got nothing practical for Pakistan', Galbraith rued. 'We got a bad press in India.'[40] In the circumstances, Washington resolved to 'stand back for a while and try to gain perspective' on the Kashmir issue. Pakistan's government felt much the same, having all but abandoned hope of reaching a Kashmir settlement while Nehru remained at India's helm. Given the Indian leader's age and declining health, Ayub Khan resigned himself to waiting for a 'successor government [in India] … more tractable and more inclined [to] work reciprocally toward better Indo-Pak[istan] relations'.[41] Within a matter of months, however, with hostilities having broken out between India and China, the Kashmir question was once again pushed to the top of the subcontinent's political agenda.

### The Sino-Indian War and the Indo-Pakistan talks on Kashmir

While the British government had largely looked on from the sidelines as the Kennedy administration had attempted to broker a Kashmir settlement, the onset of the Sino-Indian War prompted the British and American governments to exchange roles. From late 1962,

---

[37] Sir Patrick Dean to Lord Home, 9 July 1962, DO 196/141, TNA.
[38] New Delhi to State Department, No. 4165, 24 June 1962, RG 59, 690D.91/6-2462, NARA; *The New York Times*, 24 June 1962.
[39] Rusk to Galbraith, Washington, 2 July 1962, *FRUS, 1961–1963*, vol. XIX, pp. 296–7; McGeorge Bundy to Galbraith, 3 July 1962, NSF, Box 107, JFKL.
[40] Galbraith to Kennedy, New Delhi, 25 June 1962, *FRUS, 1961–1963*, vol. XIX, pp. 292–4.
[41] McConaughy to State Department, Karachi, 13 July 1962, *FRUS, 1961–1963*, vol. XIX, pp. 303–5.

it was the British and, in particular, Macmillan's Secretary of State for Commonwealth Relations Duncan Sandys, who pushed hardest for an Indo-Pakistani rapprochement, inclusive of a Kashmir settlement. China's incursion into northern India, US officials concluded, had hardened Indian opinion against relinquishing control of any territory in Kashmir. In marked contrast, after visiting the subcontinent in November, Sandys came away convinced that the shock of China's incursion into India had convinced powerful elements within Nehru's cabinet that a new and more flexible Kashmir policy was called for.

In Sandys' estimation, India's Home Minister Lal Bahadur Shastri, Minister for Economic and Defence Co-ordination T. T. Krishnamachari and Defence Minister Yashwantrao Chavan were all willing to endorse a compromise settlement with Pakistan in some form.[42] A 'dramatic and almost incredible change in everyone's attitude and thinking' had occurred in India, the Commonwealth Secretary judged, since his previous visit to South Asia in July. In a cable he sent from New Delhi, on 26 November, Sandys informed Macmillan that 'India's leaders have suddenly woken from a long day dream and are for the first time facing up to the harsh realities of power politics.'[43] As Sandys' more sceptical colleagues in the Foreign Office were quick to point out, however, Nehru's cabinet retained a powerful incentive to court Western goodwill by playing up the prospects for a Kashmir settlement, while India continued to lock horns with the Chinese. Were India's security situation to improve, FO officials suggested, the country's enthusiasm for burying the hatchet with Pakistan was likely to wane.[44]

In this respect, an encounter between Sandys and India's Foreign Secretary, M. J. Desai, proved illuminating. Prior to China's announcement of a unilateral ceasefire, Desai had indicated that India would 'probably have to move further if there is in fact to be a [Kashmir] settlement'.[45] Once the ceasefire was in place, the Indian minister's position shifted markedly. 'While Kashmir must be settled in due course (perhaps in a year or two),' Desai informed Sandys on 23 November, 'Pakistan had made a habit of producing loud and hostile and highly irresponsible noises for a number of years without fatal results.'[46] Desai's U-turn failed to dent Sandys' optimism that real progress was possible

---

[42] Sandys–Lal Bahadur Shastri meeting, 25 November 1962, and China Committee minutes, 26 November 1962, DO 196/170, TNA.
[43] Sandys to CRO, No. 58, 26 November 1962, DSDN 8/1, Duncan Sandys Papers, Churchill Archives Centre, Churchill College Cambridge (hereafter DSP).
[44] Norton Minute, 28 November 1962, FO 371/164924/FC 1061285, TNA.
[45] Delhi to CRO, No. 2009, 21 November 1962, FO 371/164924, TNA.
[46] Delhi to CRO, 23 November 1962, FO 371/164930/FC 1063/24 (A), TNA.

on Kashmir. In keeping London apprised of his discussions with Indian ministers and officials, Sandys presented a uniformly upbeat analysis of the prospects of a Kashmir accord. India's Commonwealth Secretary, Y. D. Gundevia, Whitehall was advised, had called for an 'urgent settlement' of the Kashmir dispute, and momentum was building within the Congress Party for a rapprochement with Pakistan. Moreover, although Nehru had initially been 'most reticent' when it came to Kashmir, even the Indian premier, Sandys added implausibly, now 'seemed a changed man'.[47]

In late November, Sandys' determination to pursue a Kashmir agreement led him to embark upon a round of shuttle diplomacy between India and Pakistan. Having first secured Nehru's grudging commitment that his government would sit down with Pakistan to discuss Kashmir's future, British attention focused on persuading Ayub Khan to do likewise.[48] From Ayub Khan's standpoint, his government's position inside Pakistan risked being undermined were fresh Indo-Pakistan talks to follow the well-worn pattern of heightened expectation, followed by disillusionment and mutual recrimination when nothing of substance emerged. Accordingly, Sandys' meeting with Ayub Khan in Rawalpindi, on 28 November, was intended to reassure the Pakistani president that India's dependence on Anglo-American military assistance 'had now put Britain and America in a position to exert some pressure on her [India] to settle the Kashmir problem'. Emphasising that London and Washington would closely monitor the progress of bilateral talks between India and Pakistan once they were underway, Sandys informed Ayub Khan that between them, Britain and the United States 'should be able to use our influence to help bring them [the talks] to a successful conclusion'.[49] Buoyed by subsequent signs from American officials that the Kennedy administration would throw its weight behind Sandys' initiative, Ayub Khan gave the green light to the resumption of Indo-Pakistan discussions on Kashmir.[50]

---

[47] Sandys to CRO, No. 58, 26 November 1962, DSDN 8/1, DSP; China Committee minutes, 26 November 1962, DO 196/170, TNA.
[48] Sandys to CRO, No. 62 Secret, 27 November 1962, FO 371/164930/FC 1063/24 (G), TNA.
[49] Sandys to CRO, No. 71 Secret, 29 November 1962, DSDN 8/1, DSP.
[50] Gore-Booth to Sandys, 'India: Visit by the Secretary of State, the Parliamentary Under-Secretary of State and the Chief of the Imperial General Staff', 24 December 1962, DO 196/171, TNA; Harriman–Sandys–Ayub Khan meeting, 28 November 1962, *FRUS, 1961–1963*, vol. XIX, p. 409. Sandys' success in cajoling Nehru and Ayub Khan to revisit the Kashmir question took Macmillan back to his Mediterranean service during the Second World War, with 'the famous conference in Casablanca and the reluctant handshake between Giraud and de Gaulle'. Kennedy was similarly appreciative, applauding the British minister for pulling off a 'fine stroke'. Harold

Two days later, on 30 November, in the words of Sir Paul Gore-Booth, 'all hell broke loose'.[51] Goaded by inflammatory Indian press reports that claimed a Kashmir settlement with Pakistan would result in the state's formal partition, and pressed in the Lok Sabha to issue a rebuttal, Nehru appeared to rule out any substantive changes to the existing situation in Kashmir. 'Anything which involved upsetting the present arrangement in Kashmir', the Indian premier assured fellow parliamentarians, 'would be very harmful to the people of Kashmir as well as to future relations between India and Pakistan.' Nehru's statement provoked uproar in Pakistan, and prompted Ayub Khan to denounce 'the imposition on the talks of a pre-condition totally unacceptable to Pakistan'.[52] Aghast, Duncan Sandys took the first flight back to New Delhi, where he proceeded to browbeat a 'none too pleased' Nehru into 'clarifying' that his Lok Sabha statement did not imply any 'intention to limit the scope of the [Kashmir] discussions or ... the consideration of any solutions'.[53]

Anxious to avoid charges of having cajoled a reluctant Nehru into giving ground on Kashmir, Sandys subsequently downplayed his role in getting India and Pakistan back around the negotiating table. While newspapers on both sides of the Atlantic lauded the Commonwealth Secretary's diplomatic success, Sandys later informed the House of Commons that his role in bringing India and Pakistan together had been a 'limited one'.[54] Gore-Booth felt otherwise. Sandys' forthright approach had 'inevitably ... left scars' on Nehru, the British High Commissioner acknowledged, but his 'energetic intervention' had proved instrumental in capitalising upon the opportunity afforded by the Sino-Indian border war to promote an Indo-Pakistani rapprochement.[55] Although similarly impressed by Sandys' dynamism, Macmillan nevertheless harboured reservations that his minister's accomplishment would ultimately be subsumed in a resurgence of subcontinental rancour. 'Whether any child will ever be conceived and born after

Macmillan, *At the End of the Day, 1961–1963* (London: Macmillan, 1973), pp. 231–2; Ormsby Gore to Home, No. 202, 11 December 1962, FO 371/164925/FC 1061/313, TNA.

[51] Paul Gore-Booth, *With Great Truth and Respect* (London: Constable, 1974), p. 302.

[52] SEA 56/5/1 M, 11 January 1963, DO 196/171, TNA.

[53] Despatch No. 29, Annex 'C', Sandys statement in New Delhi, 1 December 1962, DO 196/171 and Annex 'D', Nehru statement in New Delhi, 1 December 1962, DO 196/171, TNA; 'Report of the Harriman Mission', undated, Box 536, Folder 1, HP; Gore-Booth, *Truth and Respect*, p. 302.

[54] Sandys statement to House of Commons, 3 December 1962, DO 196/170, TNA.

[55] Gore-Booth, *Truth and Respect*, p. 302.; Gore-Booth to Sandys, 'India: Visit by the Secretary of State, the Parliamentary Under-Secretary of State and the Chief of the Imperial General Staff', 24 December 1962, DO 196/171, TNA.

this shotgun wedding,' the British premier confided to his diary on 3 December, 'I rather doubt.'[56]

Macmillan's pessimism was mirrored in Washington, where US policymakers continued to doubt that Anglo-American influence alone would ever prove sufficient to persuade India to make the concessions necessary for a Kashmir settlement. '[O]nly *Chinese* pressure will compel Nehru to settle Kashmir', Robert Komer argued in early December. 'Undue US/UK or Pakistani pressure will only get Nehru's back up.'[57] Mindful of India's centrality to America's wider Asian policy, US officials were reluctant to push too hard for a Kashmir accord and risk alienating Nehru's government in the process. In this sense, as Indian officials undoubtedly suspected, the Kennedy administration placed greater emphasis on its relationship with India than it did on resolving the Kashmir dispute. In the final analysis, as the NSC Subcommittee on South Asia rationalised, 'While a Kashmir settlement is important, [the] defense of the sub-continent is even more important. For this reason, [US] military assistance to India and Pakistan probably would continue to be in our national interest even if the two countries failed to solve this problem.'[58]

### Internationalisation and partition

Characteristically, the Kennedy administration expected the British to undertake a leading role in overseeing the first round of Indo-Pakistan talks on Kashmir, which were scheduled to begin in late December 1962. By taking a back seat, Washington hoped to allay New Delhi's suspicion that the United States was colluding with Harold Macmillan's government against India's interests, and at the same time, protect US prestige from undue damage should the bilateral talks collapse.[59] Moreover, securing London's agreement to spearhead a renewed Anglo-American effort on Kashmir appeared to be a relatively straightforward matter. 'Macmillan must recognize the usefulness of the Commonwealth concept as a framework for continued pressure [on Kashmir],' the State Department reasoned, 'and hence should be receptive to our suggestion that HMG stay a half step ahead of us, at least as far as the public is

---

[56] Entry for 3 December 1962, d.47, Harold Macmillan Diaries, Bodleian Library, University of Oxford.
[57] Komer to McGeorge Bundy, 7 December1962, NSF, Box 420, JFKL.
[58] 'Recommendations of NSC Subcommittee on South Asia for Nassau Talks', 16 December 1962, NSF, Box 109, JFKL.
[59] Talbot to Ball, 12 December 1962, RG 59, NEA INC Lot 65D 415, NARA.

concerned.'[60] The American plan to work through the British, however, was hampered by Macmillan's reservations that a Kashmir agreement was achievable, and the persistence of Anglo-American differences over linking the provision of Western military assistance to India with progress toward a Kashmir settlement.[61]

Moreover, by the eve of the first meeting between Indian and Pakistani officials in Rawalpindi, Indian public opinion had swung decisively back against an accommodation with Pakistan. Nehru, Gore-Booth noted, had reverted to stating that he was 'not at present thinking in terms of more than the frontier adjustment in Pakistan's favour'.[62] For its part, Pakistan's actions added to the air of fatalism surrounding the Kashmir talks. Shortly before the talks were due to commence, Ayub Khan's government took the provocative step of signing an agreement with Beijing, which in part delineated China's border with Azad Kashmir, territory that India claimed as its own. Conducted in a glacial atmosphere of suspicion and mistrust, the Rawalpindi meeting accomplished little, and ended with India and Pakistan rehashing well-established arguments for and against a plebiscite in Kashmir.[63] When a second round of talks, held in New Delhi in mid-January, failed to move beyond a vague consideration of the criteria for demarcating an international boundary within Kashmir, Ayub Khan appealed for American help. Writing to Kennedy on 26 January, Pakistan's president complained that while India appeared ready to make minor territorial concessions elsewhere in the state, when it came to the Vale of Kashmir, Nehru appeared 'unwilling to part with it under any circumstances'. Given this impasse, Kennedy was advised that a Kashmir settlement would now 'largely turn on the extent of the contribution you can make and the degree of influence you can bring to bear on India to see reason'.[64] With India having warned Washington against interfering directly in the Kashmir talks, Kennedy responded by insisting that his influence would continue to be 'more helpful behind the scenes'.[65] The British agreed. Given the likelihood that any proposals put forward by a third

---

[60] Kennedy–Macmillan Nassau Meeting, 13 December 1962, RG 59, NEA INC Lot 65D 415, Kashmir, Box 1, NARA.

[61] Macmillan–Kennedy Talks, Nassau, 20 December 1962, PREM 11/4229, TNA; Macmillan–Kennedy Talks, Nassau, 20 December 1962, *FRUS, 1961–1963*, vol. XIX, pp. 450–3.

[62] Gore-Booth to CRO, No. 242, 21 December 1962, DO 196/171, TNA.

[63] CRO to Sandys, No. 207, 29 December 1962, DSDN 8/1, DSP; James to Snelling, 4 January 1963, DO 196/147, TNA.

[64] Ayub Khan to Kennedy, 26 January 1963, DO 196/149, TNA.

[65] Delhi to CRO, No. 1 Secret, 1 January 1963, FO 371/170637/F 1041/2; Kennedy to Ayub Khan, 6 February 1963, DO 196/149, TNA.

party would alienate one, or potentially both sides in the dispute, any temptation to intercede and push along the stuttering Indo-Pakistan discussions was viewed by the CRO as very much a last resort.[66]

Nonetheless, while continuing to emphasise their detachment from the ongoing Kashmir negotiations, as a contingency, British and American officials began to formulate proposals that could be introduced into the talks, 'if and when the time is ripe'. The CRO favoured putting forward a scheme to internationalise the Vale of Kashmir, initially for a period of ten years, during which time India and Pakistan would enjoy unfettered access to the valley and its environs. Once the ten-year period had elapsed, steps would then be taken to allow the Vale's inhabitants, 'in one way or another to decide their own future'. Discreet soundings taken by the British indicated that Ayub Khan would prove receptive to internationalisation, the proviso being that responsibility for the administration of the Vale would be placed in the hands of a consortium of Commonwealth countries, rather than the UN, thus precluding any Soviet involvement.[67]

Ayub Khan's qualification prompted Macmillan's government to fret over the investment in British blood and treasure that would be required to police an internationalisation scheme, particularly if a liberation movement sponsored by either India or Pakistan sprung up in the Vale. Such a scenario, the Ministry of Defence cautioned, 'might pose as big a problem ... as did the Enosis movement to the British Government in Cyprus'.[68] In New Delhi, Indian ministers reacted with open hostility to what many interpreted as a piecemeal ploy to wrest Kashmir from India. Internationalisation, Y. D. Gundevia bluntly informed Gore-Booth, 'simply would not work'.[69] Undaunted, the British considered tempering Indian opposition to an internationalisation plan with economic inducements, guarantees to uphold the Vale's independence

---

[66] Delhi to CRO, No. 2 Secret, 1 January 1963, FO 371/170637/F 1041/2, TNA.
[67] Karachi to CRO, No. 132 Confidential, 24 January 1963, FO 371/170637/F 1041/6 (G), TNA. The Foreign Office objected to American involvement in policing an internationalised Vale on the grounds that it would be difficult to 'expect the Chinese to believe, that if the Americans got into the area ... they would avoid the temptation to use it as a base for anti-Chinese activities ... [making] it hard to blame the Chinese if they took pretty vigorous measures to keep the Americans out of Kashmir'. The Americans were equally wary that the participation of 'old' Commonwealth countries might give the impression of 'the resumption of "white" administration in the sub-continent'. De la Mare (FO) to Emery (CRO), 24 January 1963, and Gore-Booth meeting with Galbraith, McConaughy and Talbot, 6 February 1963, DO 196/148, TNA.
[68] Karachi Military Attaché to MoD, 10 March 1963, DO 196/150, TNA.
[69] Delhi to CRO, No. 244 Confidential, 22 January 1963, DO 196/148, TNA.

during a transition phase, and an Anglo-American commitment to defend India against a Chinese attack in Ladakh.[70]

The alternatives to internationalisation appeared less than satisfactory to the CRO. Kashmiri independence was dismissed as unacceptable to both India and Pakistan, and in any case likely to leave 'a weak state in ... a key geographical position [which] could be a dangerous source of future international friction'. Likewise, condominium status was deemed unworkable given the rancorous state of Indo-Pakistani relations. Equally, the Indian government had repeatedly and forcefully ruled out a state-wide plebiscite.[71] Partition was regarded as similarly problematic.[72] Britain's High Commissioner to Pakistan, Morrice James, warned London that Ayub Khan's government would not survive 'accept[ing] a solution which would be so deeply unpopular as partitioning the Vale. Indeed he would be accused of consenting to a Kashmiri Munich or worse.'[73] Likewise, Indian officials indicated to the British that while they were prepared to show some flexibility in discussing the redistribution of territory to the north or west of the Kashmir Valley, 'their readiness for concession stopped there, and there could be no question of offering to give up the Vale or Srinagar'.[74]

The Kennedy administration favoured partition over internationalisation. State Department plans for a Kashmir settlement envisaged Pakistan assuming control of the northern third of the Vale, with India retaining control over the remainder, including Srinagar. As compensation for its minority stake in the Kashmir Valley, it was expected that Pakistan would receive 'substantial' additional territory elsewhere in Kashmir.[75] Although conceding that its partition scheme was 'quite pro-Indian' and had only a 'slender' chance of success, American officials considered the disadvantages of internationalisation to be greater. Convinced India would reject internationalisation 'in any form', the

---

[70] Snelling to Sandys, 18 January 1963, DO 196/147, TNA. Subsequent Anglo-American discussion touched on the possibility of bringing Ladakh formally under the SEATO umbrella, 'since SEATO was ... directly orientated against China'. Anglo-American meeting on Kashmir, 4 February 1963, DO 196/149, TNA.

[71] Snelling to Sandys, 18 January 1963, DO 196/147, TNA.

[72] CRO to New Delhi (No. 235) and Karachi (No. 17), 20 January 1963, DO 196/148, TNA.

[73] Karachi to CRO, No. 152, 30 January 1963, DO 196/148, TNA.

[74] Delhi to CRO, No. 244 Confidential, 22 January 1963, DO 196/148, TNA.

[75] Ormsby Gore to FO, No. 172, 16 January 1963, DO 196/147, TNA. The Americans envisioned Pakistan's 'additional sweeteners' encompassing most of Kashmir's Riasi district, facilities for the storage of Chenab waters, access rights to the entire Vale, and improved US trade agreements and development cooperation. Ormsby Gore to FO, No. 318, 29 January 1963, DO 196/148, TNA.

State Department was also concerned that such a scheme would facilitate Chinese encroachment into South Asia. Nehru's government 'would have no incentive to defend Ladakh', American officials reasoned, 'if there was nothing [Indian] behind it'.[76]

The divergence in Anglo-American thinking on Kashmir led Britain's ambassador in Washington, David Ormsby Gore, to suggest that London clear the air with Kennedy's administration, 'before we get too far apart'.[77] Thinking along similar lines, the US Assistant Secretary of State for South Asia, Phillips Talbot, urged the British to guard against the impression developing on the subcontinent 'that Britain favoured internationalisation (and thus Pakistan) while United States favoured partition (and thus India)'.[78] A subsequent meeting between Talbot and Sandys in London, on 4 February, duly established an Anglo-American modus operandi for the third round of Indo-Pakistan talks, which were due to take place in Karachi, later that month.[79] In essence, Britain and the United States agreed to hold off introducing their own formulae for a Kashmir settlement, and to stick to encouraging both sides in the dispute to start 'drawing lines on maps'.[80]

The outcome of the third round of Kashmir talks merely confirmed the gaping chasm that existed between the governments of India and Pakistan over where an international boundary should be drawn within the state. While India envisaged only minor territorial adjustments along the existing line of control, Pakistan laid claim to the whole of the Kashmir, bar a small sliver of land in the south-west of Jammu. Both parties, the British observed, had been 'shocked' by the extreme positions adopted by the other. After three rounds of bilateral talks, and with no settlement in sight, British and American officials speculated that with public patience in Pakistan wearing thin, Ayub Khan might be tempted to condemn Indian intransigence and withdraw from

[76] Komer to Kennedy, 26 January 1963, NSF, Box 109, JFKL; Ormsby Gore to FO, No. 318, 29 January 1963, and Delhi to CRO, No. 343 Confidential, 30 January 1963, DO 196/148, TNA.

[77] Ormsby Gore to FO, No. 318, 29 January 1963, DO 196/148, TNA.

[78] Karachi to CRO, No. 161 Secret, 3 February 1963, DO 196/148, TNA. Nehru frequently chastised the British for being 'always so pro-Pakistani', asking Macmillan pointedly on one occasion 'why the British Government always seemed to be psychologically wrong about the handling of this question [Kashmir]'. Nehru to Macmillan, 30 August 1963, MSS Macmillan c. 346, Harold Macmillan Papers, Bodleian Library, University of Oxford (hereafter HMP).

[79] Talbot meeting with CRO, 5 February 1963, DO 196/148, TNA, and CRO to Delhi and Karachi, No. 409 and No. 282 Confidential, 5 February 1963, DO 196/148, TNA.

[80] Gore-Booth meeting with Galbraith and McConaughy, 6 February 1963, DO 196/148, TNA; Kennedy to Ayub Khan, Washington, 7 February 1963, *FRUS, 1961–1963*, vol. XIX, pp. 492–3.

further discussions.[81] In the event, Anglo-American pressure persuaded Pakistan's president to agree to hold another meeting with the Indians in Calcutta, in March. However, Ayub Khan made clear that unless significant progress toward a settlement was forthcoming, Pakistan would reject a fifth round of talks.[82] Judging, somewhat implausibly, that in the wake of the Karachi round 'a fair chance' still existed of pulling off a Kashmir deal, Dean Rusk pressed for a more active US role in the Kashmir negotiations.[83] The State Department, Rusk confirmed to Kennedy, 'were asking permission to get in from up to our ankles to up to our knees'.[84]

## Galbraith's bazaar bargain and the 'elements' initiative

Dean Rusk's plans to deepen American involvement in the Kashmir dispute were almost overtaken on the eve of the Calcutta round, when Pakistan's foreign minister, Zulfikar Ali Bhutto, threw 'a spanner into the works' by travelling to Beijing to sign the border agreement with China that Ayub Khan's government had negotiated back in December.[85] Pakistan's 'obtrusive flirtation with the Chinese', Gore-Booth observed, threatened to derail further dialogue on Kashmir.[86] As it was, the Calcutta discussions went ahead, but with Bhutto's Chinese stunt having brought smouldering Indo-Pakistani hostility out into the open, negotiators on both sides responded by blithely reiterating the tired and irreconcilable positions they had staked out previously, in Karachi. The Calcutta talks, Galbraith lamented, had accomplished nothing, and 'just barely avoided being ridiculous'.[87] Having concocted his own plan to break the deadlock on Kashmir, Galbraith approached Rusk for permission to offer Nehru 'a crude bazaar-level' bargain. At its heart, this proposed asking the Indian government to cede a 'substantial' portion of the Kashmir Valley to Pakistan, in return for a 'sizable' programme of long-term American military aid, encompassing the provision of transport aircraft,

[81] James to Snelling, 15 February 1963, and 'Pakistan Fortnightly Summary, Part 1', 15 February 1963, DO 196/149, TNA.
[82] Morrice James, *Pakistan Chronicle* (London: Hurst, 1992), pp. 94–5.
[83] Rusk to Kennedy, 20 February 1963, RG 59, NEA INC Lot 65 D 415, Box 1, NARA.
[84] Presidential discussion on Kashmir, Washington, 21 February 1963, *FRUS, 1961–1963*, vol. XIX, pp. 508–10.
[85] Sandys to CRO, No. 33, Sandys to Garner, 24 February 1963, DSDN 8/2, DSP; Galbraith to Harriman, 26 February 1963, Box 463, HP.
[86] Gore-Booth to Sandys, 6 March 1963, DO 196/127, TNA.
[87] Galbraith, *Ambassador's Journal: A Personal Account of the Kennedy Years* (Boston: Houghton Mifflin, 1969), Calcutta, 15 March 1963, p. 556.

supersonic fighters and pilot training.[88] In Washington, Galbraith's proposal was dismissed as risky and premature. Suspecting that, in part, it reflected the ambassador's desire to settle the Kashmir issue before his term of service in India came to an end in May, Robert Komer argued that 'we neither can nor should move fast enough to meet the timetable of his [Galbraith's] own personal convenience'.[89] Deriding the 'bazaar bargain', Dean Rusk observed to Kennedy that it was

designed to purchase not a settlement, but an immediate breakthrough from the Indian side. The price is an open-ended military commitment to India. Since this is just the thing, which the Pakistanis fear most, we would expect them to react violently. This would reduce the likelihood of a Kashmir settlement and increase Indo-Pak[istan] tensions. We would, therefore, suffer a severe setback in our efforts to strengthen subcontinental defense against Communist China.[90]

Ignoring State Department instructions not to approach the Indians with his bazaar bargain, Galbraith presented it to Nehru during a ninety-minute interview, on 15 April.[91] The Indian premier reacted by angrily denouncing Galbraith's implication that a Kashmir settlement would necessitate India relinquishing control over a significant chunk of the Vale.[92] Nehru, a chastened Galbraith reported back to Washington, was now telling everyone who would listen 'that we were real bastards as compared with Ike who ... [had] offered India an even more generous supply of shooting irons with no mention of Kashmir at all'.[93] Conceding that Galbraith had pushed Nehru 'harder and more precisely than was wise', Robert Komer understood, but did not excuse, the ambassador's insubordination. Having become 'disgusted with what he regarded as US/UK shilly-shallying' on Kashmir, Komer counselled Kennedy, Galbraith had taken 'a chance in order to move the ball forward, and it backfired'.[94]

The State Department's own response to the 'badly lagging tempo' of the Calcutta round was to work with the British to formulate a set of 'elements', or general limits of a 'feasible' Kashmir settlement.[95] British

[88] Galbraith to State Department, New Delhi, 25 March 1963, *FRUS, 1961–1963*, vol. XIX, pp. 526–9.

[89] Komer to McGeorge Bundy, 27 March 1963, NSF, Box 109A, JFKL.

[90] Rusk to Kennedy, 31 March 1963, RG 59, NEA INC Lot 65 D 415, Box 1, NARA.

[91] Kennedy to Galbraith, 28 March 1963, NSF, Box 109A, JFKL; Presidential meeting on Kashmir, Washington, 1 April 1963, *FRUS, 1961–1963*, vol. XIX, pp. 535–7.

[92] Galbraith to Rusk, New Delhi, 15 April 1963, *FRUS, 1961–1963*, vol. XIX, pp. 546–8; Galbraith, *Ambassador's Journal*, New Delhi, 22 April 1963, p. 564.

[93] Galbraith to Rusk, No. 4068, 19 April 1963, NSF, Box 126A, JFKL.

[94] Komer to Kennedy, 24 April 1963, NSF, Box 110, JFKL.

[95] Rusk to Kennedy, Washington, 31 March 1963, *FRUS, 1961–1963*, vol. XIX, pp. 529–34; Ormsby Gore to London, No. 135, 1 April 1963, FO 371/170641 and

and American officials agreed that the 'elements' should reflect both India's and Pakistan's determination to hold some form of territorial stake in the Kashmir Valley, and the need for each party to have unrestricted access to and from the Vale. In addition, safeguards were required to protect India's special interest in Ladakh, and Pakistan's reliance on the waters of the Chenab River. Furthermore, a set of clearly defined arrangements were necessary to guarantee political freedom, population movement, and economic and tourist development, within the Vale. After being presented with an outline of the 'elements' on 11 April, the Pakistan government's reaction was muted. Although continuing to rule out the partition of the Kashmir Valley, Zulfikar Ali Bhutto conceded that the 'elements' provided a useful framework for addressing the mutual economic and security interests of India and Pakistan in Kashmir.[96] India's response was less equivocal. Writing to Macmillan on 22 April, Nehru complained:

> We have been rather concerned by the way in which US and UK representatives have been running about from place to place, while Indo-Pakistan talks are being held, but this latest development of the presentation of a vague and imprecise Plan, without any reference to the Government of India is, to say the least, an ill-considered and injudicious step.[97]

Characterising the 'elements' as 'totally unacceptable to us', Nehru attacked the idea of partitioning the Vale as a recipe for 'chaos and confusion' that would make it impossible for India to defend Ladakh against a future Chinese attack.[98] In part, the strength of the Indian premier's hostility to the 'elements' can be attributed to a bureaucratic faux pas on the part of British and American officials. Inexplicably, Ayub Khan's government was shown a written copy of the 'elements' proposal a week earlier than India, fuelling Nehru's suspicion that the plan had been conceived following Western collusion with Pakistan.[99] More significantly, however, Nehru's reaction underlined his discomfort at being forced to confront some hard choices.[100] Having 'suddenly found we were serious [on Kashmir], when previously he had thought we were merely going through the motions', the State Department concluded,

CRO to Delhi and Karachi, Nos. 1059 and 658 Secret, 6 April 1963, FO 371/170638/F 1042/44 (C), TNA.
[96] James, *Pakistan Chronicle*, pp. 97–8.
[97] CRO to Delhi and Karachi, Nos. 754 and 1312, 23 April 1963, DO 196/151, TNA.
[98] *Ibid.*
[99] Komer to Kennedy, 24 April 1963, NSF, Box 110, JFKL.
[100] 'Indo-Pakistan Relations', FO No. 233 Guidance, 30 April 1963, DO 196/151, TNA; Komer to Kennedy, 24 April 1963, NSF, Box 110, JFKL.

Nehru had consciously played up India's late receipt of the elements so as to avoid entering into serious debate on their substance.[101]

Following hard on the heels of Galbraith's 'bazaar bargain', the elements fiasco antagonised Nehru, and further frustrated Pakistan's expectation that American intervention could force a breakthrough on Kashmir. Moreover, the State Department worried that by summarily rejecting the elements proposal, Nehru had provided his enemies on Capitol Hill with ammunition to cut US aid appropriations to India. With Congress due to review a foreign aid bill later in 1963, Kennedy's administration had hoped to offset American distaste for Nehru's foreign policy, if not by settling the Kashmir dispute, then at least by evidencing some progress toward that goal. 'At the minimum,' Robert Komer had warned Kennedy back in March, 'we must get the Indians to be sufficiently forthcoming that the failure [of Kashmir talks] can be attributed to Pakistan.'[102] With Indo-US discord over Kashmir threatening the Congressional funding that it believed was necessary to transform India into a credible economic and military rival to Communist China, the Kennedy administration resolved to get Nehru 'back in tune with us'.[103]

## Kashmir and Anglo-American military aid to India

As its efforts to engineer a Kashmir settlement floundered, pressure on the Kennedy administration to scale back American support for Nehru's government extended beyond Capitol Hill. Frustrated by Nehru's dogmatism, the British had made it clear to Washington toward the end of March, 'that unless real progress is made towards a Kashmir settlement, a fairly serious difference may develop between the US and the UK on the question of further aid to India'.[104] Still convinced that Nehru would never agree to the concessions necessary for a Kashmir accord unless doing so was made a precondition for delivery of Western military assistance to his government, British officials bemoaned that their American colleagues 'did not seem to be as tough-minded as

---

[101] Wriggins to Cameron, 23 April 1963, RG 59, NEA INC Lot 65 D 415, Box 1, NARA.

[102] Komer to Kennedy, 2 March 1963, NSF, Box 126A, JFKL. Kennedy subsequently suggested that were the Kashmir talks broken off, much could be made of Pakistan's ties to the PRC in order to deflect Congressional criticism away from India. NSC Meeting on India, 9 May 1963, Meetings Recordings, Tape No. 86 (1), JFKL.

[103] Rusk to Kennedy, 25 April 1963, NSF, Box 110, JFKL.

[104] Armstrong (London Embassy) to Grant, 29 March 1963, RG 59, NEA INC Lot 65 D 415, Box 1, NARA.

we were on the question of not giving aid to India'.[105] Washington, it seemed, risked giving Nehru the impression that whatever happened with regard to Kashmir, India was assured of US support. Toward the end of April, the British sought a guarantee from Dean Rusk that the United States would not discuss the provision of long-term military aid with Nehru's government while a Kashmir settlement still appeared possible. '[T]hough the Indians should not be told they would not get any further arms aid,' Duncan Sandys suggested to Rusk, 'they should be under no illusion that further aid was "in the bag".'[106] Britain's Foreign Secretary, Lord Home, went further, baldly stating to Rusk his conviction that the Kashmir problem would remain intractable until the United States threatened to withdraw military and economic aid from India.[107] Senior American officials, however, dismissed the British argument as counterproductive.[108] 'President Kennedy', Walt Rostow of the State Department's Policy Planning Council informed the British wryly, 'had observed that everyone believed that threats to withdraw American aid would be effective if used on someone else.'[109]

Indian sensitivity toward any correlation between the delivery of Anglo-American military aid and progress toward a Kashmir settlement came to the fore in May. With Dean Rusk, Phillips Talbot and Duncan Sandys having travelled to New Delhi to impress upon Nehru the need for his government to adopt a fresh and more conciliatory approach toward the Kashmir problem, Indian officials began openly speculating that Britain and the United States were delaying decisions on long-term military aid in order to coerce India into a Kashmir settlement. To British consternation, India's press enthusiastically took up the story after latching onto an article published in *The Economist* on 25 April, which suggested 'that the views and policy of the United States and Britain in the matter of arms aid were not wholly at one, and that it was Britain which most favoured turning the screw'.[110] Such media coverage was particularly unwelcome for Macmillan's government, given the domestic political capital that Harold Wilson's Labour Party had made of 'unaccountable delays' in the despatch of British aircraft spares to India which, Wilson claimed, had grounded a 'considerable part' of the IAF.[111] As the Americans observed, 'Harold

---

[105] 'The Indian War Machine', 29 March 1963, PREM 11/4301, TNA.
[106] Sandys–Rusk meeting, 29 April 1963, DO 196/152, TNA.
[107] Home–Rusk meeting, 30 April 1963, DO 196/151, TNA.
[108] Rusk to Kennedy, 31 March 1963, RG 59, NEA INC Lot 65 D 415, Box 1, NARA.
[109] 'Mr. Rostow's Visit to Karachi', 6 April 1963, DO 196/151, TNA.
[110] 'India Fortnightly Summary, Part 1', 10 May 1963, DO 196/152, TNA.
[111] Transcript of Prime Minister's Questions, 2 May 1963, PREM 11/4306, TNA.

Wilson's recent parliamentary interventions have brought anxiety that India-Pak[istan] disputes may enter domestic politics, with Labor [sic] supporting India's case while [Macmillan's] government appears increasingly pro-Pakistani.'[112] Moving swiftly to head off such charges, Duncan Sandys took Wilson to task on the dangers of turning Britain's relations with India and Pakistan into a partisan 'political football'.[113]

In a bid to quell further speculation over a connection between British and American military aid to India and the Kashmir dispute, Duncan Sandys injudiciously informed Nehru that while no such link existed, the favourable impact of a settlement on public opinion on both sides of the Atlantic would ease the flow of Western arms to India.[114] Rationalising this approach, Britain's Cabinet Secretary, Burke Trend, observed to Macmillan that 'It would clearly be wrong to attempt to blackmail India into a Kashmir settlement. But it would be equally wrong to ignore the effect of this running sore on India's ability to defend herself against China, on her relations with Pakistan, and on Pakistan's relations with us.'[115] However, by publicly airing the assurance that he had received from Sandys that Anglo-American military aid to India was not linked to Kashmir, without mentioning its associated qualification, Nehru caused eyebrows to be raised in the Western press. If true, *The Times*' New Delhi correspondent reported, Nehru had revealed

a major change in the British and American line ... Six months ago Mr. Sandys was going out of his way to explain to the Indians that there could be no question of large-scale military aid unless there was first a [Kashmir] settlement with Pakistan ... and Mr. Harriman ... was endorsing every word.[116]

In reality, Kennedy's inclination had always been to provide India with American military assistance come what may. Moreover, by May 1963 administration officials such as Robert Komer, and America's new ambassador designate to India, Chester Bowles, had begun to argue that the Western effort to facilitate a Kashmir settlement had run its course. The time had come, Komer suggested, for breaking with the British and arming New Delhi.[117] Bowles, in particular, asserted that

[112] Talbot to Rusk, No. 1047, 9 May 1963, NSF, Box 110, JFKL.
[113] Pickard to Gore-Booth, Karachi/London, 7 May 1963, MSS.Gorebooth 86, Paul Gore-Booth Papers, Bodleian Library, University of Oxford (hereafter GBP).
[114] Kennedy and Rusk on India and Pakistan, 6 May 1963, Meetings Recordings, Tape No. 85 (2), JFKL; 'India Fortnightly Summary, Part 1', 10 May 1963, DO 196/152, TNA.
[115] Trend to Macmillan, 14 May 1963, PREM 11/4306, TNA.
[116] *The Times*, 3 May 1963.
[117] Komer to Harriman, 16 May 1963, Box 481, HP.

Washington's close association with Macmillan's government had weakened American influence over India. Indians retained a strong mistrust of 'the old British Tory tactics of playing Muslims against Hindus', Bowles noted. 'As a consequence, while *our* friendly motives in pressing for a Kashmir settlement *are generally accepted*, British motives are looked on with deep suspicion.'[118] This was not to say that powerful elements within the US government, chiefly in the Pentagon and State Department, shared such sentiment. 'They still think, like the UK, that we should stall until the Indians move on Kashmir,' Komer observed, 'ignoring the hard lesson of the last six months that Kashmir won't come that easily.'[119]

Such logic informed the American approach to Kennedy's meeting with Macmillan in June at Birch Grove, the British premier's Sussex home. From the White House's perspective, the Birch Grove talks provided a timely opportunity to 'vigorously' dispel lingering British thoughts that a Kashmir settlement constituted a prerequisite for the provision of long-term Western military aid to India.[120] In fact, the portion of the Anglo-American communiqué addressing Kashmir and military aid for India that emerged from the Birch Grove meeting was sufficiently equivocal to satisfy both Kennedy and Macmillan. In publicly committing Britain and the United States to continue 'providing further military aid to [India to] strengthen her defences against the threat of renewed Chinese Communist attack',[121] the communiqué provided Kennedy with the means to reassure Nehru of American good faith. Equally, in neglecting to state how much military aid India might expect to receive, of what type, and when, Macmillan claimed that the West's leverage over New Delhi remained intact. Pakistan begged to differ. Whereas India welcomed the reaffirmation of Western support, in Pakistan the reaction to the Birch Grove talks was scathing. Karachi's *Morning News* charged Kennedy and Macmillan with delivering a 'cold and calculated insult to Pakistan'. The unconditional pledge that Britain and the United States had given to arm India, the semi-official daily *Dawn* added, had killed the last hope of a Kashmir settlement and presented Pakistan with 'a challenge which will not be taken lying down'.[122] While Washington's attitude toward Indian military aid was dominated by the fear of a Sino-Indian rapprochement,

---

[118] 'US Policy toward India', Bowles memorandum, 4 May 1963, NSF, Box 314, JFKL.
[119] Komer to Kennedy, 17 May 1963, NSF, Box 433, JFKL.
[120] Komer to Kennedy, 21 June 1963, NSF, Box 110, JFKL.
[121] Birch Grove Joint Communiqué, 30 June 1963, PREM 11/4586, TNA.
[122] Karachi to CRO, No. 978, 2 July 1963, DO 196/154, TNA.

the British were more concerned that growing anti-Western opinion in Pakistan would see Ayub Khan's government reach out to Beijing. By July 1963, the CRO had concluded that the time had come for London 'to start mending fences' with Pakistan.[123]

### Mountbatten, mediation and 'Delhi week'

Although forced to invest a good deal of time and effort in calming the Indian government's anxieties over links between Kashmir and Anglo-American military aid, the chief purpose of Duncan Sandys' and Dean Rusk's presence in the subcontinent that spring was to promote a mediated settlement to the Kashmir dispute. Having lost faith in the efficacy of bilateral Indo-Pakistan talks, Rusk convinced President Kennedy that by bundling Kashmir into a broad package of issues, encompassing other areas of dispute between India and Pakistan, and subjecting these to external mediation, 'everybody gets something out of it and can bounce that off against the pain'.[124] In a bid to smoke out Nehru's position on third-party mediation, the Macmillan government co-opted the assistance of Britain's Chief of Defence Staff, and India's last Viceroy, Lord Louis Mountbatten. Duncan Sandys asked Mountbatten to utilise 'his good will and his close personal relationship' with Nehru, to open up a window into the Indian leader's thinking. Mountbatten's role was especially significant, given Sandys' own fractious relationship with Nehru, who resented the Commonwealth Secretary's 'bullying and patronising manner'.[125]

After arriving in New Delhi, Mountbatten spent the afternoon of 30 April with Nehru, 'reminiscing about old days and about the family'. The following day, the last Viceroy and the first prime minister of India got down to the business of Kashmir. Remarkably, Mountbatten succeeded in convincing Nehru that it was in his government's broader interest to explore a mediated solution to the Kashmir problem. After 'much weary thought' on the Indian premier's part during the forty-eight hours following his encounter with Mountbatten, and after some judicious prodding from his British friend on how history might

[123] Pickard to Sandys, 25 July 1963, DO 196/129, TNA.
[124] A final, sixth round of talks took place in New Delhi over 15–16 May 1963, which saw each side reiterate their established and irreconcilable positions regarding the Kashmir dispute, Pakistan demanding a plebiscite and India formalisation of the status quo; Kennedy/Rusk on India and Pakistan, 6 May 1963, Meetings Recordings, Tape No. 85 (2), JFKL.
[125] Mountbatten/Nehru meetings, 30 April and 2 May 1963, MB1/J302, Lord Mountbatten Papers, Hartley Library, University of Southampton (hereafter MBP); Sandys to CRO, No. 21 Secret, 6 May 1963, DSDN 8/3, DSP.

judge him were he seen to have wilfully obstructed a settlement, Nehru approved the appointment of an external mediator to examine all areas of Indo-Pakistani discord, including Kashmir.[126] As Nehru had previously insisted that the Kashmir dispute was for India and Pakistan to resolve alone, free from outside interference, Mountbatten received credit, inside and outside the subcontinent, for the Indian premier's unexpected volte-face.[127] '[B]y the time he [Mountbatten] had talked for a couple of hours with N[ehru] about Kashmir,' Gore-Booth reflected, 'we were in a different India.'[128]

The British proved less able to agree to a process with their American partners for moving the mediation initiative forward. To avoid Pakistani suspicions that they 'were selling something cooked up in Delhi', Sandys agreed with Dean Rusk that the mediation idea should be presented to Ayub Khan as unobtrusively as possible, preferably through resident British and American officials in Karachi.[129] To American irritation, and against the advice of the CRO, Sandys subsequently had a change of heart and decided to take up the matter with Pakistan's president in person. Smarting over the British reversal, Rusk and Galbraith pressed a reluctant Sandys into postponing his departure for Pakistan by forty-eight hours, while Morrice James and Walter McConaughy, the American ambassador to Pakistan, assessed Ayub Khan's likely reaction. Sandys proceeded to use his extended stay in New Delhi to secure Indian approval of a draft text confirming that a mediator would be appointed to facilitate discussion between India and Pakistan on Kashmir and other related problems. At the request of Indian officials, Sandys struck out reference to Kashmir in the text and, overruling Gore-Booth's objection that Pakistan would find the revision unacceptable, wired the document to James in Karachi.[130]

On informing the Americans of his action, an exchange ensued between Sandys and Galbraith that, Gore-Booth estimated, 'Messrs. Metro, Goldwyn and Meyer with all their resources could not have bettered'. Storming into the British High Commission, Galbraith charged Sandys with crass judgement and bad faith in negotiating with the Indians behind the United States' back. Moreover, by securing the Indian government's prior endorsement of the mediation text, and omitting from it any mention of Kashmir, the British were deemed to have guaranteed its rejection by Pakistan. '[R]oaring with rage and

[126] Mountbatten/Nehru meetings, 30 April and 2 May 1963, MB1/J302, MBP.
[127] Gopal, *Nehru: 1956–1964*, pp. 260–1.
[128] Gore-Booth to Belcher, 8 May 1963, MSS.Gorebooth 86, GBP.
[129] Galbraith, *Ambassador's Journal*, New Delhi, 5 May 1963, p. 569.
[130] Gore-Booth to Pickard, 5 May 1963, MSS.Gorebooth 86, GBP.

practically bumping into all the walls of the room in turn', Galbraith assured a stunned Sandys, '…that he had been long enough in political life to know how to break someone and he was going to do just that from that moment on.'[131] In order to avert 'a major Anglo-American row', at Gore-Booth's urging, Sandys agreed to rip up the mediation document. In return, Galbraith qualified his accusation of British bad faith. Having brokered an uneasy truce, Gore-Booth was left pondering what impact the mediation shambles would have on future Anglo-American collaboration in the subcontinent.[132] 'I think I want a rise in salary,' the British High Commissioner subsequently cabled Whitehall, 'and then I shall be prepared to ask whether there are any other little jobs you want me to do as part of the CRO.'[133]

Back in Pakistan, Ayub Khan expressed scepticism that a mediation initiative would prove worth the effort unless further Anglo-American military aid to India was made dependent on Nehru's acceptance of a mediator's recommendations.[134] In the face of Pakistani doubts, Kennedy and Macmillan pushed Ayub Khan not to turn his back on mediation. Writing to the Pakistani president on 17 May, Macmillan claimed, 'If Pakistan were to reject the proposal she would incur a heavy responsibility and forfeit a great deal of sympathy and support in the eyes of the rest of the world. I beg you, therefore, to give it most serious thought.'[135] In response, Ayub Khan accepted the principle of mediation on the condition that safeguards were put in place to prevent unreasonable obstinacy or procrastination on India's part. These included placing a time limit of three months on the mediation process; suspending Western consideration of long-term military aid to India while mediation was ongoing; and ensuring that a mediator's terms of reference referred specifically to Kashmir.[136] Such preconditions, the British reasoned, reflected Pakistan's 'crisis of confidence' in the West. 'The Pakistanis', the CRO noted, 'distrust our judgement, do not accept that there is a Chinese threat to India and regard themselves as

[131] *Ibid.* Galbraith later reflected, 'Not for years have I had such a bruising clash and I enjoyed it.' Galbraith, *Ambassador's Journal*, New Delhi, 5 May 1963, p. 571.

[132] Gore-Booth to Belcher, 8 May 1963, MSS.Gorebooth 86, GBP. London reassured Gore-Booth that 'I don't think you need be too worried about the effect of all this on our relations with the Americans.' Phillips Talbot, it was noted, had reacted to Galbraith's report of his encounter with Sandys with 'fascinated interest and some amusement'. Pickard to Gore-Booth, 7 May 1963, MSS.Gorebooth 86, GBP.

[133] Gore-Booth to Pickard, 5 May 1963, MSS.Gorebooth 86, GBP.

[134] McConaughy to State Department, Karachi, 6 May 1963, *FRUS, 1961–1963*, vol. XIX, pp. 577–9.

[135] Macmillan to Ayub Khan, No. 1021 Secret, 17 May 1963, DO 196/152 TNA.

[136] McConaughy to State Department, Karachi, 17 May 1963, *FRUS, 1961–1963*, vol. XIX, pp. 596–9.

neglected and ignored.' Considerable effort was required on the part of Britain and the United States to repair relations with Ayub Khan's government, Whitehall concluded, if mediation was 'to have any chance of success'.[137]

An additional challenge for the Kennedy and Macmillan governments was finding a mediator acceptable to both India and Pakistan. The CRO favoured a British mediator. 'Britain has an historic mission in India', Sandys was advised. 'Although America, with greater material resources, must often be looked to in the affairs of the West to provide the bulk of the money, we often have the brains which, in the wider interest, ought to be brought to bear.'[138] From a shortlist of British candidates compiled by the CRO, the recently retired Cabinet Secretary, Lord Normanbrook, and Macmillan's Lord Chancellor until July 1962, Lord Kilmuir, were strongly favoured. To London's surprise, however, Gore-Booth poured cold water on the idea of a British mediator. The Indians, he stressed, felt that

both in general and in particular over Kashmir, the Americans are more favourably disposed to them than we. Indian reasoning is compounded from, among other things, a belief (now enshrined in the folklore of Independence) that the British always found the Muslims of the subcontinent more sympathetic than the Hindus and favoured them accordingly ... and a very practical awareness that the Americans have a great deal more to offer than we have.[139]

Heeding the warning from New Delhi, on 28 June, Sandys informed Dean Rusk that he considered a US mediator, and preferably Eugene Black, most appropriate. India and Pakistan, the Commonwealth Secretary added, 'were more dependent on American aid and therefore more likely to pay attention to what an American nominee would say'. With Black committed elsewhere, however, Washington pondered whether the former US ambassador to India, Ellsworth Bunker, or Roswell Gilpatric, US Deputy Secretary of Defense, might prove adequate alternatives.[140] Pakistan's proposal that the former US president, Dwight Eisenhower, be considered for the mediator role, received short shrift in Washington. Aside from concerns that Eisenhower might not be physically up to the task, American officials were concerned by the domestic political implications of such an appointment. Noting the tendency for liberal Democrats to laud India while the sympathies of conservative Republicans lay with Pakistan, the Kennedy administration

---

[137] Pickard to Sandys, 25 July 1963, DO 196/129, TNA.
[138] CRO Minute on Kashmir Mediator, undated, DO 196/153, TNA.
[139] Allen (New Delhi) to Emery (CRO), 6 June 1963, DO 196/153, TNA.
[140] Anglo-American meeting on Kashmir, 28 June 1963, DSDN 8/20, DSP.

reasoned that, 'If Ike came up with a pro-Pakistan proposal it would be easy and tempting for Republicans by giving [it their] all-out support to embarrass [the] administration and damage its India policy.'[141]

Debate over the merits of various potential mediators threatened to prove redundant in early July, when India suddenly developed cold feet over subjecting the Kashmir dispute to mediation. On 1 July, in discussion with Gore-Booth and Galbraith, Y. D. Gundevia observed that having just holidayed in Kashmir, Nehru had returned to New Delhi with 'the feeling that there could be a revolution in the Valley if there was any further talks of partition or internationalisation'. Citing deteriorating Indo-Pakistani relations as an impediment to a settlement, and ignoring Anglo-American protestations that by doing so India would make Pakistan the injured party, Gundevia suggested suspending the mediation proposal.[142] The Nehru government's waning support for mediation received added impetus later that month, when Chester Bowles arrived on the subcontinent to replace Galbraith as US ambassador to India. To the consternation of colleagues back in Washington, who suspected he had succumbed to 'an obvious Indian attempt to take him into camp', Bowles strongly supported the Indian line that in the prevailing climate of Indo-Pakistani hostility, mediation would prove 'futile' and counterproductive.[143]

By the summer of 1963, although increasingly doubtful that mediation could work, White House officials continued to press its merit as a means of containing anti-Indian sentiment in the United States during Congress' deliberations on Kennedy's foreign aid bill.[144] For its part, concern within Macmillan's government that a collapse in the Kashmir process would have a disastrous impact on Pakistan's relations with the West ensured that the British remained firm advocates of mediation.[145] Consequently, the British and American governments pressed ahead and, on 7 August, presented India and Pakistan with a communiqué that proposed the appointment of a mutually acceptable mediator with a remit to produce recommendations 'on Kashmir and other related matters' within six months.[146] Attacking the communiqué's timing,

[141] John Kenneth Galbraith, *Letters to Kennedy* (London: Harvard University Press, 1998), pp. 125–6; Galbraith to Rusk, No. 4967, 18 June 1963, NSF, Box 110, and Komer to Galbraith, 19 June 1963, NSF, Box 111, JFKL.
[142] Delhi to CRO, No. 1918 Confidential, 1 July 1963, and CRO to Delhi, No. 2423 Confidential, 3 July 1963, DO 196/154, TNA.
[143] Bowles to Rusk, New Delhi, 30 July 1963, *FRUS, 1961–1963*, vol. XIX, pp. 624–6; Komer to McGeorge Bundy, 31 July 1963, NSF, Box 110A, JFKL.
[144] Komer to Kennedy, 12 August 1963, President's Office Files, Box 123, JFKL.
[145] CRO to Delhi and Karachi, Nos. 2792 and 1533, 31 July 1963, DO 196/154, TNA.
[146] Ministerial Brief No. 6 for Bhutto Visit, 14 October 1963, DO 196/155, TNA.

M. J. Desai informed Gore-Booth and Bowles that, given the prevailing atmosphere of recrimination between India and Pakistan, were Nehru to endorse it, 'both Parliament and the Indian public would think he was quite mad'.[147] On 11 August, confirming as much in a letter sent to Kennedy, an indignant Nehru lambasted the 'rabidly anti-Indian' posture adopted by Ayub Khan's government. Mediation, the Indian premier insisted, was 'not only not practical politics in the context of Pakistan's current attitudes, but would only result in irritating the people in India and in dampening their ardour and keenness to face the Chinese threat'.[148] Two days later, during a debate in the Lok Sabha, Nehru openly questioned the value of mediation when India would only countenance minor territorial adjustments in Kashmir, 'which Pakistan has a thousand times ruled out'.[149]

In response, Kennedy impressed upon Nehru that 'such a negative statement on mediation' might undercut his administration's ability to deliver economic and military aid to India.[150] Ominously, on 9 August, the House of Representatives Foreign Affairs Committee had warned India and Pakistan that it would recommend drastic reductions in US assistance to both countries, unless more progress was made on settling the Kashmir dispute.[151] Having 'counted heavily' on the mediation initiative to outflank domestic critics attacking the size of India's financial allocation in his foreign aid bill, an exasperated Kennedy cautioned Nehru that 'we must know more clearly what you propose to do [on Kashmir] … you do not rule out mediation but suggest the necessary preparatory work be done by quiet diplomacy … but how is this to be done?'[152] With his Congress Party facing intense scrutiny over its handling of the Sino-Indian conflict, however, and having been subjected during August to the first parliamentary motion of no confidence in his premiership since independence, Nehru had little incentive to court further domestic disapprobation by loosening India's grip on Kashmir. Emphasising this point in a cable to London, on 19 August, Gore-Booth counselled that

[147] Delhi to CRO, No. 2344 Confidential, 8 August 1963, DO 196/154, TNA; Gore-Booth to Belcher, New Delhi, 9 August 1963, MSS.Gorebooth 86, GBP.
[148] Nehru to Kennedy, New Delhi, 11 August 1963, *FRUS, 1961–1963*, vol. XIX, pp. 632–5.
[149] *The Times*, 14 August 1963.
[150] Kennedy to Nehru, Washington, 15 August 1963, *FRUS, 1961–1963*, vol. XIX, pp. 639–40.
[151] *The New York Times*, 10 August 1963.
[152] Kennedy to Nehru, Washington, 15 August 1963, *FRUS, 1961–1963*, vol. XIX, pp. 639–40.

the present process of trying to get mediation launched is at any rate for the time being a process of papering over a crack. There is little evidence here ... of a present willingness by those in power to accept any solution which would come remotely within range of acceptability by the other party ... in our policies towards the sub-continent we should reckon with the Kashmir problem continuing to be intractable for some considerable time to come.[153]

Pakistan saw the Anglo-American mediation communiqué as fundamentally flawed, with Bhutto grumbling that it failed to take full account of the safeguards that he had specified back in May.[154] By making it plain before the conclusion of Indo-Pakistan negotiations on Kashmir that New Delhi could count on American support against China come what may, Bhutto asserted that Washington had 'wrecked the possibilities of an Indo-Pakistan settlement and so, by its own actions, furthered close relations between Pakistan and China'.[155] To a bitter Ayub Khan, it appeared that Kennedy had decided 'that India should have all sympathy and support and that Pakistan would be well advised not to raise any difficulties'.[156] Sceptical that mediation could work unless India was convinced that continued Anglo-American military aid was contingent upon reaching a settlement with Pakistan, Ayub Khan's government preferred not to expose itself to the domestic censure that would follow yet another setback on Kashmir.[157] Accordingly, when US Under Secretary of State George Ball travelled to South Asia in September 1963 with the intention of smoothing over the Kennedy administration's strained relations with Pakistan, Ayub Khan suggested that the mediation plan should be dropped. If the United States wished to continue pushing on Kashmir, Ball was informed, 'she should do so in Delhi'.[158]

Conceding defeat in the face of the conflicting demands that India and Pakistan had imposed on the Anglo-American search for a Kashmir settlement, by the late summer of 1963, Dean Rusk's focus switched to insulating the Kennedy administration from criticism for plunging into the Kashmir quagmire. America's embassies in South Asia were instructed to publicise the rationale behind US intervention in Kashmir, stress that the positions adopted by Nehru and Ayub Khan

---

[153] Delhi to CRO, No. 2419 Confidential, 19 August 1963, DO 196/154, TNA.
[154] Karachi to CRO, No. 1230 Confidential, 17 August 1963, DO 196/154, TNA.
[155] Zulfikar Ali Bhutto, *The Myth of Independence* (London: Oxford University Press, 1969), p. 63.
[156] Ayub Khan, *Friends Not Masters*, p. 146.
[157] McConaughy to State Department, Karachi, 23 August 1963, *FRUS, 1961–1963*, vol. XIX, pp. 649–53.
[158] Karachi to CRO, No. 1330 and Karachi to CRO, No. 1331, 6 September 1963, DO 196/154, TNA.

had prevented the United States from facilitating a settlement, and confirm that the task of taking Kashmir forward was now in the hands of India and Pakistan.[159] Acknowledging that Anglo-American pressure for a breakthrough on Kashmir had become 'an extreme irritant which the Indians (and possibly the Pakistanis too) wished to have no more of', the British took a similarly pragmatic view of their failed attempt to resolve the subcontinent's most pernicious problem. '[If] we are going to embark on these techniques again at a later date,' Whitehall reflected soberly, in December 1963, 'the time and circumstance will need to be chosen very carefully.'[160]

[159] Rusk to Karachi, Washington, 28 August 1963, *FRUS, 1961–1963*, vol. XIX, pp. 655–6.
[160] O'Brien (New Delhi) to Emery (CRO), 4 December 1963, DO 196/156, TNA.

# 7 Realigning India: Western military aid and the threat from the north

On 2 May 1962, a report in the London *Daily Mail* set alarm bells ringing in Whitehall. The Indian government, the *Mail* revealed, had been negotiating with the Soviet Union to purchase a squadron of its latest MiG-21 supersonic fighters, and secure a licence from Moscow to manufacture additional MiGs in Indian factories in the subcontinent. Having discounted the veracity of the *Mail*'s scoop, the Commonwealth Relations Office was taken aback when enquiries made by the British High Commission in New Delhi confirmed its authenticity. Nehru's government, British officials complained bitterly, had 'behaved abominably' by seeking to acquire advanced Soviet weaponry behind London's back.[1] It was not strictly the military implication of India's interest in a small number of Soviet fighters that most exercised Harold Macmillan's government. The British were more concerned that closer ties between India and the USSR in the security field would weaken Britain's political and economic influence in South Asia, and at the same time, damage India's own broader interests. Above all, Whitehall worried that a US Congress ill disposed to New Delhi's military flirtation with the Soviet Union would withdraw economic aid critical to India's development.[2] 'It will break my heart to see [the US] Congress turn this [economic aid] down if they feel you have gone over to the Russians for your Armament', Lord Mountbatten counselled Nehru, '... [I] do not see how you could get along without it.'[3]

After departing from South Asia in 1947, the United Kingdom retained close military links with the armed forces of India and Pakistan. In the United States, the Truman administration looked upon the subcontinent as primarily a British preserve, and rebuffed several

---

[1] Briefing paper for Sandys talks with Nehru, undated, *circa* June 1962, DO 196/124, The United Kingdom National Archives, Kew, London (hereafter TNA).
[2] Delhi to CRO, No. 629, 5 May 1962, and CRO to Delhi, No. 828, 3 May 1962, PREM 11/3836, TNA.
[3] Mountbatten to Nehru, London, 14 June 1962, MB1/J302, Lord Mountbatten Papers, Hartley Library, University of Southampton (hereafter MBP).

requests from Pakistan for US military assistance in the early 1950s. An upsurge in Arab nationalism and decline in British influence across the Middle East later in the decade, prompted the Eisenhower government to re-evaluate Pakistan's utility as a regional American ally. In May 1954, Washington concluded a Mutual Defence Assistance Agreement with Karachi, and Pakistan moved decisively into America's sphere of military influence.[4] Britain remained India's principal military quarter-master, however, and continued to furnish India's army, navy and air force with the bulk of its equipment and training well into the 1960s. In early 1962, when New Delhi's prospective purchase of Soviet fighters entered the public domain, the Indian Air Force operated predomi-nately British-supplied Vampire, Gnat, Hunter and Canberra combat aircraft, alongside a small additional complement of French, American and Soviet transport aeroplanes.[5]

Britain's financially lucrative and strategically significant position at the heart of India's defence establishment had come under pressure back in the 1950s. In 1955, Anthony Eden's government fought off a Soviet attempt to sell the IAF its newest bomber, the Ilyushin IL-28. From an Indian perspective, the Soviet bomber had a number of advantages over its British equivalent, the Canberra. In comparison with the Canberra, the IL-28 was significantly cheaper, easier to maintain and more readily available. Only after Eden had personally stepped in to authorise the sale of Canberras to India at a heavily discounted price, and Lord Mountbatten had applied considerable personal pressure on Nehru to maintain the IAF's buy-British policy, did the Indian government decline the Soviet offer.[6] At the same time, Nehru made plain to the British that his government's decision did not preclude future Indian purchases of military equipment from the Soviet bloc.[7] Moving forward, British officials remained wary of a looming Soviet threat to the United Kingdom's virtual monopoly over the provision of India's military hardware. In June 1957, when India expressed an interest in procuring Britain's Hunter fighter, Lord Home, then Secretary of State for Commonwealth Relations, observed wryly, 'I rather expect them

[4] Makins to Eden, 28 October 1954, FO 371/112307, TNA.
[5] K. Subrahmanyam, 'Nehru and the India–China Conflict of 1962', in B. R. Nanda (ed.), *Indian Foreign Policy: The Nehru Years* (New Delhi: Sangam Books, 1990), pp. 114–15.
[6] Eden to Eisenhower, 1 February 1956, PREM 11/1399, TNA.
[7] Nehru to Eden, 23 March 1956, PREM 11/3836, TNA. In February 1957, after hag-gling with the British for over a year, India signed a contract to purchase sixty-eight Canberras.

[India] to say that they cannot pay unless we lend them the money and to hold the threat of purchase from Russia over our heads.'[8]

At the beginning of 1960, a series of articles surfaced in the Western and Indian press that indicated Nehru's government was in favour of developing closer military relations with the Soviet Union. In March 1961, India signed a contract with the Soviets to purchase eight Antonov-12 military transports on favourable financial terms. Agreement was also reached between Moscow and New Delhi to send IAF pilots to the USSR for training.[9] Worryingly for British officials, in rationalising his government's decision to turn to the Soviets for big-ticket military items, Nehru publicly reiterated that London should no longer assume that it had first refusal on satisfying India's military requirements.[10] Indeed, as the Sino-Indian border dispute continued to fester, the British became increasingly aware of the growing strategic value that India placed on its relationship with the Soviet Union.[11] Nehru's government, Whitehall suspected, had calculated that it could bolster India's security by forging closer political, economic and, to a lesser extent, military ties to the USSR, without running an undue risk of forfeiting British and American support.[12]

In fact, during the first half of the 1960s, British and American policy-makers waged a determined and often fractious battle with their counterparts in India and Pakistan to preserve the West's dominant strategic position in South Asia. In the process, India's and Pakistan's relationship with Britain and the United States, and at times, the Anglo-American partnership itself, came under serious strain.[13] Debates and disagreements arose within, and between, the governments of India, Pakistan, Great Britain and the United States over the extension of Soviet military influence in South Asia; the provision of Anglo-American military assistance to India; and the most appropriate means of providing the subcontinent with an air defence network. Rather than draw India closer to the West, as intended, British and American leaders discovered

[8]  'Anglo-Indian Relations', 26 June 1957, CAB 129/87, C (57) 149, TNA.
[9]  Arthur Stein, *India and the Soviet Union: The Nehru Era* (University of Chicago Press, 1972), pp. 126 and 204.
[10]  'Record of Informal Conversations with Mr. Nehru, Prime Minister of India', 13–15 May 1960, MB1/J303, MBP.
[11]  'India: Shifts in Indian Foreign Policy', MacDonald to Home, 13 July 1960, DO 196/125, TNA.
[12]  'India: A General Review', Gore-Booth to Sandys, 26 May 1961, DO 196/74, TNA. See also 'Note on a Talk with the American Ambassador', 21 July 1960, GB 033 MAC, Malcolm MacDonald Papers, Palace Green Library, University of Durham (hereafter MMP).
[13]  Robert Komer, 18 June 1964, pp. 15–16, Oral History (OH), John F. Kennedy Library, Boston, Massachusetts (hereafter JFKL).

to their chagrin that by attaching political strings to the provision of military aid, India and Pakistan were encouraged to turn eastward for an alternative means of underwriting their national security.

## The Indo-Soviet MiG deal

In May 1962, when news of India's plans to purchase supersonic fighter aircraft from the Soviet Union became public, Nehru's government was forced onto the defensive. In response to shrill criticism from Britain and the United States, Indian ministers emphasised that, in part, their interest in purchasing Soviet fighters had been prompted by events in Washington. Indian policymakers acknowledged that the security threat posed by deteriorating Sino-Indian relations had influenced their decision to upgrade the IAF's ageing fleet of fighters. Officials in New Delhi added, however, that the Indian government had also felt compelled to respond to an agreement that President Kennedy had reached with Ayub Khan, in July 1961, to supply Pakistan with America's F-104 supersonic fighter. India's defence minister, V. K. Krishna Menon, pointedly informed the British that he had been 'bound to look at all possibilities [for enhancing India's defence], since once again thanks to American help Pakistan were getting technically ahead and there was a threat of unknown proportions from China'.[14] Reflecting upon India's clash with Britain and the United States over the 'MiG deal', *The Times of India* observed:

> The feeling in informed circles here [New Delhi] is that the Kennedy administration finding itself in a politically embarrassing situation as a result of the Indian move to acquire Soviet supersonic jets … has only herself to thank for it … it has actually contributed to the current military tension and political ill-feeling between the two countries [India and Pakistan] by … equip[ping] the Pakistan Air Force with the latest American supersonic jets.[15]

From a financial standpoint, the underlying weakness of India's economy, and the paucity of its foreign exchange reserves, made it all but impossible for Nehru's government to purchase expensive Western fighter aircraft. India could ill afford to pay the going market rate for supersonic fighters, and New Delhi's policy of non-alignment effectively ruled out the acceptance of military aid from abroad. Unlike commercial British and American defence manufacturers, however, the state-controlled Soviet economy obscured the MiG-21's true

---

[14] Delhi to CRO, No. 633, 7 May 1962, PREM 11/3836; Sandys to CRO, No. 26, 17 June 1962, T 317/362, TNA.
[15] *The Times of India*, 13 May 1962.

production cost. Consequently, Moscow was able to 'sell' India military equipment at artificially low prices, and in exchange for 'soft' non-convertible Indian rupees, while nominally preserving the appearance of Indian non-alignment.[16] Moreover, the MiG's comparatively simplistic design gave it an additional advantage over its more sophisticated Western counterparts. The Indian government's long-term goal was to achieve military self-sufficiency, with indigenous defence contractors servicing the nation's security needs. For the IAF, this translated into the requirement for an Indian company to manufacture a foreign-designed fighter, of comparable performance to Pakistan's F-104, under licence in the subcontinent.[17] Assembling the Soviet MiG in India was a far less daunting technical proposition than surmounting the considerable challenge of building more complex British or American aircraft.[18]

Back in London, news that India had been negotiating with the Soviets to acquire cutting-edge military technology, without first consulting Britain, its established military supplier, was received in Whitehall with a mixture of confusion and indignation. 'What is happening?', a bemused Mountbatten wrote to Nehru's sister, Vijaya Lakshmi Pandit. 'How dismal it all is.'[19] New Delhi's action was not universally popular within Indian political circles. India's High Commissioner in London, Mahommedali Currim (M. C.) Chagla, voiced misgivings to the British over the negative impact that an Indo-Soviet MiG deal would have on India's relations with the West. 'Indian well-wishers in responsible positions', Chagla assured Mountbatten, 'had done everything in their power to counteract it [the MiG deal].'[20] In June 1962, one such 'well-wisher', India's president, Sarvepalli Radhakrishnan, assured the British that he was pressing Nehru to postpone a decision on supersonic fighters. India's premier, Radhakrishnan observed, 'had not foreseen the strength of American and British opposition to the proposed fighter deal'. 'He [Nehru] might well be glad to find some way out of

---

[16] Galbraith to State Department, 13 May 1962, *Foreign Relations of the United States* (hereafter *FRUS*), *1961–1963*, vol. XIX (Washington, DC: Government Printing Office, 1996), p. 256; Delhi to CRO, No. 758, 28 May 1962, PREM 11/3836, TNA.

[17] Subrahmanyam, 'Nehru and the India–China Conflict of 1962', in Nanda (ed.), *The Nehru Years*, p. 116.

[18] Gore-Booth to Sandys, 8 June 1962, DO 196/127; Nehru to Macmillan, 30 June 1962, T 317/363, TNA.

[19] Mountbatten to Vijaya Lakshmi Pandit, London, 20 June 1962, MB1/J325, Folder 1, MBP.

[20] Mountbatten to Gore-Booth, 21 June 1962, MS.Gorebooth 85, Gore-Booth Papers, Bodleian Library, University of Oxford (hereafter GBP).

the deal,' India's president intimated, 'if this did not involve too much loss of face.'[21]

Britain's Secretary of State for Commonwealth Relations, Duncan Sandys, dismissed the significance of an anti-MiG lobby in India. '[The] more right-wing Ministers, including Mr. Morarji Desai [India's finance minister],' Sandys scoffed, 'have not got the guts to stand up to Mr. Nehru against Mr. Krishna Menon and the pro-Russian faction.'[22] Sandys 'deplored' the prospect that India might operate a 'half-Russian half-British Air Force'. Classified Anglo-American military technology provided to the IAF would, he insisted, inevitably fall into the hands of Eastern bloc technicians overseeing the delivery of MiGs to the sub-continent.[23] Privately, however, as Britain's High Commissioner in India, Sir Paul Gore-Booth, acknowledged, London accepted that in a purely military sense, India's acquisition of a small number of Soviet fighters 'would not, of course be the end of the world'. Politically, the picture was more complicated. In particular, the British worried that US legislators would punish Nehru for purchasing Soviet fighters by slashing American investment in India's third five-year plan. This, in turn, opened up the unpalatable prospect that India's leader would 'opt for defiance and desperation' in the face of American economic pressure, and appeal to Moscow for financial support, further weakening Britain's position in South Asia.[24]

At the US Embassy in New Delhi, John Kenneth Galbraith echoed the British concern that by turning to the Soviets for advanced military hardware, India would alienate Capitol Hill and forfeit the American taxpayer dollars that were driving forward its economic development.[25] Galbraith reasoned that a significant reduction in American financial assistance to India was likely to see the improvement in Indo-US relations that had taken place since the late 1950s 'arrested and possibly reversed'.[26] Such apprehension appeared justified when, on 11 May,

[21] Belcher to Sandys, 22 June 1962, DO 189/371, TNA. Nehru partially validated such thinking, expressing his surprise at the Western 'furore' over India's interest in MiGs. 'I did not expect this,' he wrote in early July 1962, 'as I thought that foreign governments cannot object to a commercial transaction which we consider favourable to us.' 10 July 1962, Pahalgam (Kashmir), in G. Parthasarathi (ed.), *Jawaharlal Nehru: Letters to Chief Ministers, 1947–1964,* vol. 5: *1958–1964* (New Delhi: Oxford University Press, 1989), p. 506.
[22] Snelling to Saville Garner, 25 June 1962, DO 189/371, TNA.
[23] CRO to Delhi, 12 May 1962, PREM 11/3836, TNA.
[24] Gore-Booth to Saville Garner, 12 June 1962, CAB 21/5685; FO brief for Lord Home, FO 371/164881, 4 June 1962, TNA.
[25] Galbraith to Rusk, No. 3537, 8 May 1962, National Security File (NSF), Box 106A, JFKL.
[26] Galbraith to Rusk, 18 May 1962, *FRUS, 1961–1963,* vol. XIX, pp. 248–50.

the Senate Foreign Relations Committee voted for a 25 per cent cut in US economic aid to India. Acting Committee Chairman, Senator John Sparkman of Alabama, made clear to Washington's press corps that the vote was intended to signal Congress' irritation at the direction that Nehru's foreign policy was taking.[27] Inside the White House, Robert Komer took a more relaxed view of events unfolding in New Delhi. A token show of Soviet military support for India, the National Security Council's resident expert on South Asia suggested, might in fact work to Washington's advantage, by encouraging Nehru to become more openly critical of the People's Republic of China.[28] Llewellyn Thompson, America's ambassador in Moscow, agreed. In Thompson's opinion, an Indo-Soviet MiG deal was unlikely to 'lead to Indian dependence upon [the] Soviet Union in other military fields ... [yet] would place serious further strain on their [Soviet] relations with [the] Chicoms'.[29]

Inside the State Department, Dean Rusk hatched a plan to outflank the Soviets. This hinged on persuading the British government to offer its Lightning supersonic fighter to India, as an alternative to the MiG.[30] American officials dismissed the possibility of selling their own F-104 aircraft to New Delhi. In the unlikely event that Nehru's government could be cajoled into accepting tacit American military assistance, in the form of a cut-price sale of F-104s, such an arrangement appeared certain to encounter opposition from a US Congress largely antipathetic to India.[31] Furthermore, as Pakistan's ambassador to the United States, Aziz Ahmed, made clear to Rusk, his government would look upon the Kennedy administration's sale of F-104s to India as, 'an unfriendly act'.[32] Relations between Washington and Rawalpindi had come under significant strain during the previous six months in the wake of the Goa affair and America's abortive intervention in the Kashmir dispute. Accordingly, the White House was reluctant to further provoke Ayub Khan's regime, and risk the closure of 'near vital' US intelligence-gathering facilities in northern Pakistan, or precipitate Rawalpindi's withdrawal from the CENTO and SEATO pacts.[33]

[27] *The New York Times*, 12 May 1962.
[28] Komer to McGeorge Bundy, 9 May 1962, *FRUS, 1961–1963*, vol. XIX, pp. 242–3; Komer to McGeorge Bundy, 22 May 1962, NSF, Box 420, JFKL.
[29] Thompson to Rusk, No. 3025, 22 May 1962, RG 59, 791.5622, 5-962, Box 2135, NARA.
[30] Ormsby Gore to FO, No. 1421, 20 May 1962, PREM 11/3836, TNA; Komer to McGeorge Bundy, 25 May 1962, NSF, Box 420, JFKL.
[31] Kennedy to Macmillan, No. 4023, 8 June 1962, CAB 21/5685, TNA.
[32] Rusk meeting with Aziz Ahmed, 21 June 1962, *FRUS, 1961–1963*, vol. XIX, pp. 285–7.
[33] Komer to McGeorge Bundy, 9 May 1962, *FRUS, 1961–1963*, vol. XIX, pp. 242–3.

Over the summer of 1962, senior American policymakers, including President Kennedy, pushed Harold Macmillan's government to offer India an alternative to the MiG deal.[34] The British response was unenthusiastic. In the Foreign Office's view, the chances of selling India the Lightning were 'not hopeful'. Overcoming India's interest in Soviet aircraft appeared primarily a 'political rather than military' problem. Anglo-American opposition to an Indo-Soviet MiG deal had received extensive international press coverage. Nehru, British officials felt, would consequently 'have to produce publicly the strongest reasons for ordering fighters elsewhere than from Russia'.[35] Equally, Whitehall was concerned that an 'appalling precedent' would be established, were the RAF to sell its latest fighter aircraft to another Commonwealth country. 'Everybody in Africa and elsewhere', the British suspected, 'would want them too.'[36] Nonetheless, the implications for Britain's wider international interests of allowing India's purchase of Soviet fighters to go unchallenged were not lost on Macmillan's government. The United Kingdom's trading and investment relationships with India generated significant revenues for the British exchequer. The likelihood that an Indo-Soviet MiG deal would weaken India's fragile economy, by acting as the catalyst for a reduction in American economic aid to the subcontinent, weighed heavily on British minds. Likewise, the British were reluctant to dismiss out of hand a proposal strongly endorsed by the White House. It would be as well, the British Foreign Secretary, Lord Home, was counselled by his officials, to consider 'the effect on Anglo-US relations of rejecting, at this stage, a scheme in which President Kennedy is personally so closely interested'.[37]

In early June, having debated the matter at some length, the British cabinet agreed to consider offering the Lightning to India, 'on specially favourable terms', if the transaction's financial and political costs were 'underwritten by the American Government'. Specifically, the British expected Kennedy's administration to make up 'the difference between the true cost of such an offer to us and the artificially favourable terms which alone would make the offer attractive to the Indian Government'.[38] In order to insulate their interests in the subcontinent

---

[34] Kennedy to Macmillan, 1 June 1962; Macmillan to Kennedy, 4 June 1962; and Kennedy to Macmillan, 4 June 1962, *FRUS, 1961–1963*, vol. XIX, pp. 261–2.

[35] Delhi to CRO, No. 760, 29 May 1962, PREM 11/3836; FO to Washington, No. 4053, 1 June 1962, CAB 21/5685, TNA.

[36] Gore-Booth to Belcher, 21 June 1962, MS.Gorebooth 85, GBP.

[37] Briefing paper for Home meeting with Rusk, 22 June 1962, FO 371/164881, TNA.

[38] Meeting Gen. 767/1, 4 June 1962, CAB 21/5685, TNA. At a cost of £450,000 per aircraft, the Lightning was considerably more expensive than the MiG-21, which

from the full impact of a Pakistani backlash, the British also expected Washington to openly support the sale of British supersonic fighters to India.[39] The strength of Pakistan's opposition to the sale of advanced Western fighters to India became abundantly clear to the British when Duncan Sandys visited the subcontinent, in July. Having got wind of a prospective sale of Lightnings to India, the semi-official Karachi daily *Dawn* rounded on Macmillan's government for hatching a 'sinister' plot to compromise the security of a loyal ally. 'Pakistani pilots', Ayub Khan informed Sandys bluntly, 'would dislike being shot down by British planes just as much as by Russian planes.'[40]

Earlier in the year, a balance of payments crisis, shortfalls in the provision of external funding for India's latest five–year plan, and a sharp deterioration in the country's trading performance, had forced the Indian government to introduce a domestic austerity programme.[41] This, as the London *Times* observed, left India's future economic welfare more dependent on Western beneficence than ever before.[42] In mid-June, Harold Macmillan and Duncan Sandys set about exploiting India's economic vulnerability in a bid to scupper the MiG deal. On 15 June, Sandys emphasised to Morarji Desai, that by turning toward Moscow and alienating the US Congress, Nehru's government would transform the 'cheap MIG ... [into] the most expensive aeroplane the Indians had ever bought'. In a subsequent interview with Nehru, Sandys went further and suggested that New Delhi's interest in the MiG was 'inconsistent' with the provision of British economic assistance to India, since a purchase of Soviet combat aircraft would 'needlessly ... jeopardise incomparably larger sums of aid from America'.[43]

Moscow was reportedly prepared to sell to India for the equivalent of £300,000. CRO to Delhi, No. 1168, 6 June 1962, PREM 11/3836, TNA.

[39] Britain's High Commissioner to Pakistan, Morrice James, cautioned London that if Britain or the United States supplied India with supersonic fighters, Pakistanis would react 'emotionally rather than rationally', increasing the likelihood that Ayub Khan's government would make 'some dramatic gesture of dissatisfaction with Western alignment'. Karachi to CRO, Nos. 643 and 648, 2 and 4 June 1962, PREM 11/3836, TNA.

[40] James to Sandys, 7 July 1962, DO 196/213, TNA.

[41] In June 1962, a concerned CRO recorded that having aimed to maintain sterling balances of £94 million, itself 'not a high target', Indian reserves had declined to just £73 million, and appeared likely to drop further. Rumbold to Milner-Barry, 12 June 1962, T 317/362, TNA.

[42] *The Times*, 16 June 1962.

[43] Sandys' interview with Morarji Desai, 15 June 1962, DO 121/239; Sandys to CRO, No. 26, 17 June 1962, T 317/362, TNA.

In the Commonwealth Secretary's view, the MiG affair offered a timely opportunity to admonish India for its 'double standards'. On 25 June, Sandys observed that

reducing our future support for India's economic development ... will inevitably hurt our own business interests. But there comes a point beyond which we really cannot allow India indefinitely to take our goodwill for granted, while all the time currying favour at our expense with the Russians.[44]

Sir Paul Gore-Booth, in common with senior officials at the CRO, including the Deputy Under Secretary Algernon Rumbold, considered Sandys' willingness to use Western economic aid as a blunt political weapon to be both dangerous and counterproductive. By appearing 'to link aid crudely with MiGs', Rumbold argued, Britain was certain to raise Indian hackles.[45] Moreover, reducing or suspending Anglo-American fiscal support for India appeared certain to hit Britain's interests in the subcontinent particularly hard, and risk pushing Nehru's government 'into the opposite [Soviet] camp once and for all'.[46] The British Treasury, Board of Trade, and Bank of England, echoed such sentiments. Britain held the world's biggest trading and investment stake in India, and Whitehall's financial mandarins agreed that were Britain to precipitate an economic crisis in the subcontinent, 'the consequences for our [UK] interests in India would be immediate, disastrous and permanent'.[47] Or, as the Treasury put it, 'merely risk cutting off our nose to spite our face'.[48]

Besides which, British officials doubted that, having worked so hard to steer its Foreign Aid Bill through the House of Representatives without significant cuts, the Kennedy administration could be persuaded to change tack and curb its economic aid programme in India.[49] Selwyn Lloyd, Macmillan's Chancellor of the Exchequer, maintained that merely suggesting to the Americans that economic aid to India should be linked to the cancellation of a MiG deal would invite trouble. It was a 'certainty' in Lloyd's view, that Nehru would get wind of such an approach, and portray Britain's action as 'a deplorable attempt ...

---

[44] Sandys to Gore-Booth, 25 June 1962, MS.Gorebooth 85, GBP.
[45] Rumbold to Milner-Barry, 12 June 1962, T 317/362, TNA.
[46] Gore-Booth to Belcher, 25 June 1962, MS.Gorebooth 85, GBP.
[47] Rumbold to Sandys, 27 June 1962, DO 196/1; Pliatzky to Milner-Barry, 27 June 1962, T 317/363, TNA.
[48] Milner-Barry to Hubback, 27 June 1962, T 317/363, TNA.
[49] The House of Representatives had passed the Kennedy administration's $817 million request for aid to India in full, leaving the White House optimistic that after some Congressional haggling, the cuts imposed by the Senate back in May would be largely restored. Ormsby Gore to FO, No. 441, 13 July 1962, CAB 21/5685, TNA; Rusk to Galbraith, 27 July 1962, *FRUS, 1961–1963*, vol. XIX, pp. 314–16.

to take the United States Administration into partnership with us in a form of blackmail'.[50] The Kennedy administration was equally sensitive to the political implications being seen to link the provision of Western economic aid to India with the Nehru government's proposed acquisition of Soviet fighters. In communicating to Nehru his anxiety at the strength of anti-Indian feeling that the Indo-Soviet MiG deal had generated within the US Congress, President Kennedy instructed Galbraith to deliver his message to the Indian premier verbally, 'in view of [its] possible repercussions'.[51]

Even so, Nehru's determination to assert India's independence of action when it came to the MiG affair, saw the Indian leader bridle at what he perceived to be the imposition of Anglo-American duress. On 23 June, Nehru informed India's parliament that 'no independent country and certainly not India, can agree to the proposition that our purchases of aircraft or anything can be vetoed by another country'. Although the West had publicly 'agreed we can buy where we like and what we like', Nehru fumed, 'behind it all, although it is not said as a threat, behind it all is the question of aid'.[52] In the Western media, the last week of June was categorised as 'a period of fuming, frustration and political rethinking in New Delhi'.[53] The 'almost overt' tactics of coercion adopted by Macmillan's government, and to a lesser degree the United States, one British broadsheet noted, 'had the predictable consequence of uniting all extremes of [Indian] opinion behind Mr. Nehru'.[54]

As it turned out, following a series of protracted and at times fractious exchanges, Kennedy and Macmillan failed to reach agreement on the terms under which the Lightning should be offered to India. Writing to Macmillan on 24 July, Kennedy confided that he had become 'increasingly concerned about the ... financial cost' of subsidising the sale of British fighters to New Delhi.[55] The British premier's insistence that Kennedy publicly associate the United States with such a transaction had an equally salutary effect inside the Oval Office, and led Robert Komer to fulminate against 'Macmillan's repeated effort to get us to share the rap publicly'.[56] The British premier's own reservations about the wisdom of contesting the Indo-Soviet MiG deal were laid bare in

[50]  Lloyd to Sandys, 28 June 1962, CAB 21/5685, TNA.
[51]  Kennedy to Nehru, 21 June 1962, *FRUS, 1961–1963*, vol. XIX, pp. 283–4.
[52]  Nehru speech to Rajya Sabha, 23 June 1962, T 317/363, TNA.
[53]  *The New York Times*, 1 July 1962.
[54]  *The Times*, 5 July 1962.
[55]  Kennedy to Macmillan, 24 July 1962, CAB 21/5685, TNA.
[56]  Komer to McGeorge Bundy, 24 July 1962, NSF, Box 420, JFKL.

his personal diary. 'We cannot afford to *give* the Indians ... our own fighters – with more to follow', Macmillan recorded, on 19 June. 'Nor can they [India] pay because they have no money ... we cannot really do it. Moreover, a gift to India of this kind will enrage the Pakistanis.'[57] By the end of July, Washington had effectively abandoned its attempt to prevent India's acquisition of Soviet fighters. 'At this point', Robert Komer rationalised, 'further frenetic efforts on our part [against the MiG deal] will merely depreciate our currency further [with the Indian government] and create bad blood. We should now begin thinking of how best to ... recover our footing in India.'[58]

Paradoxically, the outbreak of Sino-Indian hostilities in October, and India's subsequent acceptance of military assistance from the West, provided an added incentive for the Nehru government to press ahead with the MiG deal. In November, the British observed that in an effort to retain the appearance, if not the substance, of non-alignment, Nehru had been 'playing down his gratitude to the West ... and playing up any signs of Russian friendliness – and his evident anxiety to secure the Migs [sic]'.[59] In conversation with Ronald Belcher, Britain's Deputy High Commissioner in New Delhi, the Indian premier underlined that the delivery of a handful of Soviet fighters to the IAF was of negligible military value. The MiG deal's importance to India, Nehru stressed, was in its 'very great' potential to undermine Sino-Soviet relations. Likewise, by the close of 1962, as Sino-Indian hostilities petered out, and recriminations in the wake of the Cuban Missile Crisis further poisoned relations between Moscow and Beijing, the Soviets were happy to 'punish' China by supplying India with MiGs. In December, India's defence minister, Yashwantrao Chavan, confirmed that the Indo-Soviet MiG deal would go ahead.[60] A few months earlier, the British and American governments had been aghast at the prospect of India purchasing Soviet fighter aircraft. Since then, the transformative effect of the Sino-Indian border war had rendered such a concern largely redundant. The Macmillan and Kennedy governments now had more pressing issues to deal with in the subcontinent, foremost amongst which was how to respond to a request from Nehru's government to furnish India with a comprehensive system of air defence.[61]

[57] Entry for 19 June 1962, d.45, Harold Macmillan Diaries, Bodleian Library, University of Oxford (hereafter HMD).

[58] Komer to McGeorge Bundy, 26 July 1962, NSF, Box 107, General, India, JFKL.

[59] Gore-Booth to Sandys, 14 November 1962, DO 196/172, TNA.

[60] Belcher to CRO, No. 1923, 15 November 1962, DO 196/168; Belcher to CRO, No. 2214, 5 December 1962, PREM 11/4307, TNA.

[61] Second session on Sino-Indian dispute at Nassau, 20 December 1962, *FRUS, 1961–1963*, vol. XIX, pp. 456–7.

### Indian air defence

During the Sino-Indian border war, British and American officials went to considerable lengths to dissuade Nehru's government from escalating India's conflict with China by deploying the IAF to attack PLA forces. Engaging the PLA from the air as it moved through the thickly wooded terrain of northern India would, British and American officials agreed, prove militarily ineffective and risk drawing the West into an aerial war with China over the subcontinent.[62] India would be better advised, Galbraith assured Chavan, 'to keep quiet, win time and be suspicious of the possibilities of air power'.[63] At the height of the border war, a flustered Nehru had ignored Galbraith's counsel and appealed to President Kennedy for American combat aircraft to be sent to India. To Kennedy's relief, Beijing's decision to declare a unilateral ceasefire on 20 November had a sobering effect on the Indian premier. On 21 November, T. T. Krishnamachari, India's minister for economic and defence coordination, informed Sir Paul Gore-Booth that the Indian cabinet were 'extremely anxious to avoid having to invite foreign manpower to India to help defend the country "thus turning it into another Korea"'.[64] Nevertheless, as an uneasy peace descended over the subcontinent, Nehru's government concluded that until India could modernise and expand its own air force, some form of interim support from the USAF and RAF was needed to safeguard the nation's northern cities from the threat of Chinese bombing.

The scale of Indian plans to revamp the IAF shocked British and American officials. New Delhi envisioned doubling the number of fighter squadrons operated by the IAF and modernising the remainder of its existing fleet.[65] To the British, such wholesale reform, quite apart from raising alarming political issues, not least with Pakistan, appeared to be both technically and economically 'beyond India's

---

[62] Galbraith to Rusk, Nos. 1898 and 1899, 20 November 1962, NSF, Box 108, JFKL. The roots of Galbraith's regard for the military limitations of air power lay in his experience as a member of the US Strategic Bombing Survey in Europe and Japan during the Second World War. See Richard Parker, *John Kenneth Galbraith: His Life, His Politics, His Economics* (New York: Farrar, Straus and Giroux, 2005), pp. 177–90.

[63] John Kenneth Galbraith, *Ambassador's Journal: A Personal Account of the Kennedy Years* (Boston: Houghton Mifflin, 1969), New Delhi, 22 November 1962, pp. 492–3.

[64] Gore-Booth to CRO, No. 2004, 21 November 1962, DO 196/169, TNA.

[65] Gore-Booth to Sandys, 'India: Visit by the Secretary of State, the Parliamentary Under-Secretary of State and the Chief of the Imperial General Staff', 24 December 1962, DO 196/171, TNA.

capacity'.[66] The Indian economy had laboured prior to China's attack, in November 1962. In its aftermath, India's anticipated annual economic growth rate was revised downward from 5 per cent to 2.3 per cent. Emphasis on military spending over economic development seemed certain to exacerbate the Nehru administration's financial problems.[67] With India facing severe economic pressures at home, a formidable Chinese enemy and a deterioration in its relationship with Pakistan, anxiety mounted amongst US policymakers that 'if India tried to carry all three burdens she would break her back'.[68] The Soviet Union shared the Anglo-American worries over the wider economic impact of India's rearmament plans. 'Militarization always brings a heavy burden on the people', the Soviet premier, Nikita Khrushchev, cautioned India's ambassador to Moscow, T. N. Kaul, in late 1962, 'and this is particularly true for India, for which militarization would be a veritable scourge.'[69] Moreover, as the British noted, it seemed to many expert observers that India could, 'in fact, have a very useful air force by rationalising what they possess now'.[70]

Although the British considered it 'unlikely' that China would consider bombing New Delhi or Calcutta, Indian officials received an assurance from their British counterparts that 'formed squadrons from other countries' would be able to fly in at short notice and effectively neutralise such a threat, were it to materialise.[71] It would be even better, the Macmillan government noted privately, for India to enhance its air defences by purchasing British 'Bloodhound' or 'Thunderbird' surface-to-air missiles (SAMs). The latter would provide India with a tangible show of British support, generate orders for British defence contractors and, most importantly of all, avoid a scenario in which RAF fighters might have to shoot down Chinese aircraft over South Asia.[72] 'A British or American pilot could on some perhaps misunderstood instruction from an Indian Air Force officer', Duncan Sandys emphasised, 'land us in a war with China.'[73]

---

[66] Meeting between Lall and British Mission Air Officers, 27 November 1962, DO 196/170, TNA.
[67] 'Report of the Harriman Mission', undated, Box 536, Folder 1, Averell Harriman Papers, United States Library of Congress, Washington, DC (hereafter HP).
[68] 'Mr. Rostow's Visit to Karachi', 6 April 1963, DO 196/151, TNA.
[69] Memorandum of conversation between Kaul and Khrushchev, 24 November 1962, T. N. Kaul Papers, Nehru Memorial Museum and Library (hereafter NMML).
[70] Air Vice Marshall Wykeham on the Indian Air Force, Appendix 2 Annex to COS (62) 477, 22–30 November 1962, DO 196/71, TNA.
[71] Meeting between Lall and British Mission Air Officers, 27 November 1962, DO 196/170, TNA.
[72] China Committee minutes, 26 November 1962, DO 196/170, TNA.
[73] Sandys meeting with Chavan, 27 November 1962, DO 196/170, TNA.

Having previously voiced similar reservations to the British, a number of American officials, including Galbraith, later warmed to the idea of placing a Western 'air umbrella' over India. The onset of winter in the Himalayas, and the consequent implausibility of Sino-Indian hostilities resuming before the spring thaw of 1963, suggested that such a scheme could bind India closer to the West without Britain and the United States running an undue military risk. In early December, India's Foreign Secretary, M. J. Desai, broached the possibility of putting a 'tacit air defence pact' in place between New Delhi, London and Washington. Galbraith implored the State Department to seize the Indian offer 'by the ears'.[74] Back in Washington, Dean Rusk and Robert McNamara favoured the British Commonwealth assuming the lead role in India's air defence. With a host of pressing military commitments elsewhere, the Pentagon was content to play a subsidiary role to the British, and restrict American support to the IAF to the provision of radar, technical assistance and Sidewinder air-to-air missiles.[75] In a broader political context, the State Department considered that rotating squadrons of Commonwealth fighters through the subcontinent would prove less contentious on Capitol Hill, and in Rawalpindi, than the appearance of American combat aircraft in the skies over New Delhi. 'Indian air defence is a field', Rusk informed an incredulous Galbraith, 'in which we are going to insist on Commonwealth leadership.'[76]

In mid-December, the Kennedy administration's National Security Council Subcommittee on South Asia recommended that the United States seek a firm commitment from Macmillan's government that British fighters would be despatched to South Asia should China attack India from the air.[77] China's premier, Zhou Enlai, the subcommittee noted, had indicated that his government understood Britain's obligation to come to the assistance of a fellow Commonwealth member, such as India. American intervention in any future Sino-Indian dispute, Zhou had added, 'would not be similarly "understood"'. Furthermore, Moscow had signalled that a military compact between India and the United States might compel the Soviet Union to honour its own security commitments to China. Limited British military support for

[74] Galbraith, *Ambassador's Journal*, New Delhi, 1 December 1962, p. 504, and 2 December 1962, pp. 504–5.
[75] JCS Memorandum to McNamara, JCSM-996–62, 14 December 1962, NSF, Box 109, JFKL.
[76] Rusk to Galbraith, 5 December 1962, RG 59, Central Decimal File, 1960–3, Box 2136, 791.5622/10-2062, NARA.
[77] 'Recommendations of NSC Subcommittee on South Asia for Nassau Talks', 16 December 1962, NSF, Box 109, JFKL.

India was deemed likely to have little, if any, impact upon Sino-Soviet relations.[78]

The British were horrified at Washington's suggestion that the United Kingdom enter into a bilateral military arrangement with India. Duncan Sandys insisted that it was militarily impractical for the RAF to operate over India without the much more powerful USAF by its side. Furthermore, in the absence of an American pledge to defend Britain's interests elsewhere in Asia, and most especially in Hong Kong, the United Kingdom would be left vulnerable to Chinese reprisals outside the subcontinent were it to defend India's airspace. Equally, by issuing India with a formal security guarantee, the Commonwealth Secretary argued, Britain would enrage Pakistan and risk enticing China to dent Western prestige by further bloodying India's nose. Inviting 'a major trial of strength between China and the West', Sandys feared, might well end in 'nuclear war'.[79] The Foreign Office echoed Sandys' concern that sending British fighters to India was 'likely to bring about the very result which we want to avoid, which is an extension and a widening of the area of conflict'.[80] Rather than dismiss the Kennedy administration's approach on Indian air defence out of hand, Harold Macmillan opted to parry the American proposal. Sending Commonwealth *and* American air squadrons on periodic tours to India, Macmillan informed Kennedy on 13 December, might offer an attractive means of augmenting India's air defence. However, British participation in such a scheme would only be possible, Macmillan added, on the understanding that his government accepted no 'formal or moral obligation to participate in an Indian war with China'.[81]

During the Anglo-American summit held in Nassau, in December, Kennedy conceded that Commonwealth and American fighter squadrons could rotate through India on an alternate basis. In Kennedy's view, regular visits to India by a token force of British and American combat aircraft would act as a deterrent to the Chinese; be cheaper than modernising the IAF; draw Nehru's government closer to the West without openly compromising Indian non-alignment; and go some way toward muting Pakistan's anxiety at New Delhi's burgeoning military ambition. Nervous that such an initiative could eventually escalate into a 'very large commitment', the British pressed for a distinction to be maintained between the Western military assistance that had been

[78] 'Air Defense of India', 17 December 1962, Box 537, Folder 7, HP.
[79] Sandys to Macmillan, 10 December 1962, DO 196/175, TNA.
[80] 'Air Support for India: Political Assessment', 12 December 1962, FO 371/164925, TNA.
[81] Macmillan to Kennedy, 13 December 1962, *FRUS, 1961–1963*, vol. XIX, p. 432.

provided to India during the 'emergency phase' of the Sino-Indian War, and any air defence proposal put forward in its aftermath. Nehru's government, Sandys declared to his American colleagues, needed to clearly understand that Britain and the United States would not be 'providing planes to shoot [at the] Chinese'.[82]

At Averell Harriman's suggestion, as a first step, Kennedy and Macmillan agreed to approach Nehru's government with an offer to send a high-profile US–Commonwealth military mission to the subcontinent to evaluate India's air defence requirements.[83] Even so, British policy-makers continued to harbour doubts that, 'however much we may wrap ourselves round with provisos', the United Kingdom's participation in an Indian air defence scheme would embitter Anglo-Pakistani relations and threaten to involve Britain in a war with China.[84] British disquiet was exacerbated by the reluctance of the Australian and Canadian governments to support the air mission. It was only after the application of strong pressure by Macmillan, and a personal assurance from the British premier that participation would not obligate either country to defend India, that the Australian prime minister, Robert Menzies, and his Canadian counterpart, John Diefenbaker, were persuaded to sign up to the air mission proposal.[85]

At the end of December, Nehru 'categorically welcomed' a joint Anglo-American offer to send an air mission to India.[86] The following month, on the eve of its arrival in the subcontinent, the air mission became the focus of a political controversy. To the surprise of New Delhi's press corps, Galbraith 'volunteered the information' that the Indian government had been talking to Britain and the United States about the possibility of Western fighter squadrons defending India's cities from Chinese attack. The 'air umbrella' revelation drew a stream of questions from excited India press correspondents on the probable Soviet reaction to such a scheme; whether it heralded a formal Indo-US alliance; and how it would effect Indian non-alignment.[87] Galbraith's indiscretion drew an equally excited, and generally averse, reaction from Indian politicians, prompting Nehru to issue a series of less than candid denials that his government had ever entertained the notion of

[82] Macmillan/Kennedy Talks, Nassau, 20 December 1962, PREM 11/4229, TNA.
[83] *Ibid.*
[84] Home to Macmillan, 12 January 1963, FO 371/170644, TNA.
[85] See Ottawa to CRO, No. 53, 16 January 1963 and CRO to Ottawa, No. 61, 18 January 1963, DO 196/35; Canberra to CRO, No. 46, 18 January 1963 and Macmillan to Diefenbaker and Menzies, Nos. 67 and 78, 21 January 1963, DO 164/35, TNA.
[86] Delhi to CRO, No. 2447, 29 December 1962, DO 196/171, TNA.
[87] Galbraith, *Ambassador's Journal*, New Delhi, 24 January 1963, pp. 539–40.

placing a Western air umbrella over India. Writing to his chief ministers on 2 February, Nehru stated:

There has been some talk in the newspapers about a so-called 'air umbrella'. I do not know quite how this talk has begun because there has been no discussion of this subject between us and the Anglo-American teams that have come here ... That will [sic] not only be politically wrong, but also will produce a feeling in the country which comes in the way of active [defensive] preparation.[88]

India's premier, Galbraith mused, appeared confused by Anglo-American plans to augment India's air defence capabilities, 'even though he requested the arrangements'. 'One must defend India', the US ambassador reflected sardonically, 'in a properly neutral way.'[89]

After spending several weeks in India during January and February, the US–Commonwealth air mission delivered its interim report in early March. The report recommended that Britain and the United States enhance India's radar and ground control systems; supply the IAF with air-to-air missiles; establish contingency plans to deploy Western fighters to India in an emergency; and hold regular joint training and familiarisation exercises with the IAF in the subcontinent.[90] On 25 April, Kennedy met with senior members of his cabinet to review the air mission's proposals. After some cursory debate between McNamara and Rusk over the military necessity of supplementing India's air defences with Western combat aircraft, and the extent to which doing so would increase the risks of a Sino-American clash, Kennedy shut off further discussion by coming down firmly on the side of the air mission's findings. 'I think we ought to be considering this [air umbrella]', Kennedy decreed. 'It isn't going to cost us very much. It's something we would do anyway, it's something we would want the Chinese to know we were going to do in order to avoid having to do it, it would be much cheaper than getting into a major military [commitment in India] ... we ought to do it.'[91]

The British remained uneasy that Washington's estrangement from the PRC appeared to have encouraged 'the Americans ... to view with much greater equanimity than we ... the prospect of a shooting war developing between the West and China'.[92] With a valuable trading stake

---

[88] Nehru to Chief Ministers, 2 February 1963, in *Letters to Chief Ministers*, vol. 5: *1958–1964*, p. 571.

[89] Galbraith, *Ambassador's Journal*, New Delhi, 11 February 1963, p. 546.

[90] 'Synopsis of Joint Report by Commonwealth/United States Air Defence Mission to India, March 1963', 7 March 1963, FO 371/170644, TNA.

[91] President's Meeting on India, 25 April 1963, Meetings Recordings, Tape No. 83 (2), JFKL.

[92] 'The Indian War Machine', 29 March 1963, PREM 11/4301, TNA.

in China, and the security of Hong Kong to consider, Macmillan's government were eager to remain on good terms with Beijing. In January, the British invited Lu Hsu-Chang, China's vice-minister for foreign trade, to visit the United Kingdom. 'It is important for our trade with China that we do this', Lord Home informed Sandys, '... we are so badly in need of export outlets it would, I think, be difficult to justify to Parliament and public a more rigid attitude towards China, out of deference to India.'[93] During the first quarter of 1963, a belief hardened amongst Britain's principal foreign policymakers that the United Kingdom's wider Asian interests militated against the country's participation in India's air defence. Nehru's government would be better served, British ministers concurred, by following Pakistan's example and managing external threats to India's sovereignty by joining a Western-backed organisation for collective security, such as SEATO. Accordingly, in late April, after reviewing the air mission's report, Macmillan's cabinet decided to reject its recommendations.[94]

### Anglo-American military aid and the preservation of Indian non-alignment

At its heart, the Macmillan government's position on Indian air defence reflected a wider concern in Whitehall that were Britain to offer New Delhi long-term military assistance, it would be morally obligated to uphold India's sovereignty. Entering into a tacit military alliance with India, British officials suspected, was a 'comparatively simple' proposition for the Americans, given Washington's strategic focus on India as a 'key country' in Asia. Britain's position on the issue was deemed to be 'more complex'. Helping to fund the expansion and modernisation of India's armed forces, it was felt, would break the British precedent against granting fellow Commonwealth countries military assistance; invite calls from Pakistan for similar treatment; exhaust the UK's 'extremely limited' military stockpiles; and quite possibly embroil London in an open-ended commitment to defend India.[95] 'Long-term military assistance was a business in which the United States was already well established', Sir Cyril Pickard, Under Secretary of State at the CRO, reflected. 'Britain was not in it and did not wish to enter it.'[96]

---

[93] Home to Sandys, 11 January 1963, DO 196/4, TNA.
[94] Cabinet minutes, 25 April 1963, CAB 128/37, CC 26 (33), TNA.
[95] 'Defence and Economic Aid to India', 4 April 1963, DO 164/68, TNA.
[96] 'British/United States Talks on Military Aid for India', 25 June 1963, DO 164/4, TNA.

Unbeknownst to British officials, senior members of the Kennedy administration shared many of their reservations about seeking a de facto military partnership with India. The size of India's appetite for Western military assistance, over and above that in the air defence arena, astonished Washington. Plans drawn up by New Delhi called for the West to bankroll a sweeping overhaul of India's defence establishment by means of a $1.6 billion five-year military assistance programme (MAP). From a financial standpoint, Galbraith considered that a much more modest $500 million of external military assistance, over a similar timeframe, would be more than sufficient to meet India's security needs. Robert McNamara took an even more parsimonious approach, arguing that $300 million of military aid over three years could adequately shore up India's defences.[97] The Nehru government's talk of creating a twenty-five-division army by 1965 was, McNamara stated, 'completely unrealistic on the grounds of finance, manpower and the demands which their requirements would make of the Commonwealth and United States'.[98] America's legislators were equally inimical to spending US taxpayer dollars arming India while Indo-Pakistani tensions, particularly over Kashmir, continued to fester. In February 1963, Averell Harriman observed that 'the Congressional situation … is such that we will have difficulty saving what we are now doing for India economically – let alone undertaking a long-range military program – unless there is disengagement with Pakistan'.[99] Two months later, with no sign of an Indo-Pakistani rapprochement on the horizon, Turner Cameron, the State Department's Director of South Asian Affairs, suggested that the Kennedy administration would be unwise to seek Congressional backing for a significant Indian MAP for the remainder of 1963.[100]

Kennedy was inclined to defy Congress and press ahead with an offer of military assistance to India, albeit at a level closer to that envisaged by McNamara rather than New Delhi. In the president's opinion, a stable, democratic and Western-orientated India remained crucial to a non-nuclear balance of power in Asia. Kennedy also feared that a failure on the part of his administration to support India might see Nehru turn to the Soviets for military aid, or even seek to patch up his differences with China. Besides which, Kennedy reasoned that providing India with $100 million of annual military assistance over three

[97] Robert J. McMahon, *The Cold War on the Periphery: The United States, India and Pakistan* (New York: Columbia University Press, 1994), pp. 297–8.
[98] Harriman conversation with Senator William J. Fulbright, 4 December 1962, Box 537, Folder 1, HP.
[99] Harriman to Galbraith, 15 February 1963, Box 463, Folder 1, HP.
[100] Cameron to Talbot, 10 April 1963, RG 59, NEA INC Lot 65 D 415, Box 1, NARA.

years was 'not going to put much of a strain on us'.[101] It was in this context that the Kennedy administration reacted with a mixture of irritation and exasperation when Macmillan's government rejected the US–Commonwealth air mission's recommendations. In an NSC meeting on 9 May, McGeorge Bundy, Assistant to President Kennedy for National Security Affairs, suggested that the British 'really don't accept our basic view that there is a revolution in policy in the subcontinent. I think that's what it comes down to.' Reflecting upon the importance of the air defence scheme as a mechanism for deterring future Chinese aggression against India, Kennedy mused that

I don't think there's any doubt that this country is determined we couldn't permit the Chinese to defeat the Indians. Don't know what we're doing if we were. We might as well get out of South Korea and South Vietnam ... We would quite obviously use nuclear weapons if we were really going to be overrun in ... India ... [the question is] is a deterrent necessary to the Chinese and therefore do we want to express a guarantee at this time, and secondly in what way can we get the most political mileage out of it if we give the guarantee to the Indians, and the least political heat from the Pakistanis, and do we need the British to go with us on it.[102]

In answering the latter question, Dean Rusk assured his cabinet colleagues that the British Commonwealth's participation in India's defence retained value. Commonwealth support for India would ease domestic reservations over the administration's willingness to assume new obligations in India, and help to avoid US military overextension. It remained essential, Rusk argued, to 'have those other flags flying on these joint enterprises'. Sensitive to the political complications inherent in the United States offering India a unilateral military guarantee, Kennedy decided to press the British to reconsider their position on air defence.[103] At the same time, the president confirmed that he was prepared to break with Macmillan over the issue, if necessary. On 10 May, Kennedy issued NSAM 243, which instructed Rusk and McNamara to explore 'how we can best proceed unilaterally should the United Kingdom prove reluctant to commit itself to joint arrangements for the air defence of India'.[104] American reservations over the Macmillan government's willingness to work with the United States in South Asia multiplied in early May, after Phillips Talbot met with

---

[101] President's Meeting on India, 25 April 1963, Meetings Recordings, Tape No. 83 (2), JFKL.

[102] NSC Meeting on India, 9 May 1963, Meetings Recordings, Tape No. 86 (1), JFKL.

[103] *Ibid.*

[104] NSAM No. 243, 10 May 1963, NSF, Box 314, JFKL.

senior British officials in the subcontinent. Sandys, Gore-Booth and Pickard all intimated to Talbot that while Britain remained 'extremely anxious' to coordinate its regional policy with Washington, when it came to offering India military aid, 'the UK wants [the] US [to] go slow'. At best, Talbot concluded, it seemed that the British could be cajoled into a limited expansion of their existing military commitments to India, notably in air defence and defence production, particularly if much of this could be disguised as an extension to existing economic aid programmes. Obtaining London's commitment to anything beyond this appeared more problematic.[105] 'The British are pursuing their own different and limited goals [in India]', Galbraith confirmed to Washington, 'and are not … concerned with what could be costly and disastrous for us.'[106]

On 14 May, Kennedy called on Macmillan to reconsider his government's dismissal of the air mission's recommendation that Western fighter squadrons undertake joint training exercises alongside the IAF in the subcontinent. 'Indian support is so essential to a satisfactory non-nuclear balance of power in Asia', Kennedy stated in a letter to the British premier, 'that we don't want to risk unduly any Indian backsliding from their determination to counter the Chinese Communist threat.'[107] The following day, in an ill-judged reply, the ageing British premier attempted to educate America's youthful president in the lessons of history. Macmillan informed Kennedy that he had been struck by a parallel between the events of the summer of 1914, in which he had played a part, and the current situation in India. Having entered into a defensive military arrangement with the French on the eve of the First World War, Britain had subsequently felt morally compelled to participate in a wider conflict on the European continent. Taking on a commitment to defend Indian airspace, Macmillan suggested, would risk 'putting ourselves now in a [similar] position where we should ultimately no longer have a free choice'.[108] Kennedy responded by turning Macmillan's Great War analogy on its head. Quoting from volume one of Winston Churchill's *World Crisis*, he countered that had Britain's commitment to France been less equivocal, war might have been averted in 1914. 'Ever since Nassau we have regarded this [air defence] as a joint enterprise, and are anxious to keep it so', Kennedy cautioned

[105] Talbot to Rusk, No. 1047, 9 May 1963, NSF, Box 110, JFKL.
[106] Galbraith to Rusk and Kennedy, No. 44539, 16 May 1963, NSF, Box 110, JFKL.
[107] Kennedy to Macmillan, 14 May 1963, FO 371/170644, TNA.
[108] Macmillan to Kennedy, 15 May 1963 FO 371/170644; Macmillan to Kennedy, 15 May 1963, PREM 11/4593, TNA.

Macmillan. 'But if you do not feel that it is possible to go ahead on this basis, my inclination would be to make the proposal alone.'[109]

Kennedy's ultimatum troubled Macmillan. Britain's refusal to participate in an Indian air defence scheme, the British leader fretted, could sour transatlantic ties and risk 'serious damage to our relations with India'.[110] Home, Sandys, and Peter Thorneycroft, Britain's minister for defence, came to share Macmillan's concern. Given Kennedy's determination to offer India assistance in the field of air defence, some form of British involvement appeared preferable to being left out in the cold. On 28 May, on condition that Anglo-American military support for India would only be triggered by an unprovoked act of Chinese aggression of a magnitude requiring external assistance, 'and that we would be the judges of that necessity', the British cabinet swung behind the air umbrella proposal.[111]

While the British and Americans wrangled over whether, and on what terms, India should be offered help with air defence, opinion hardened in New Delhi against the air umbrella concept. Having previously asked the United States to defend India's airspace, India's policymakers underwent a collective change of heart in the first half of 1963. 'The main reason for this change', Sandys observed on 13 May, 'is that they realise that a defence arrangement of this kind [an Anglo-American air umbrella] would constitute an important military link with the West and would be generally regarded as a thinly veiled abandonment of India's traditional policy of non-alignment.'[112] After visiting India in the spring, Dean Rusk noted the Nehru government's growing unease at the prospect of Commonwealth and American aircraft operating alongside the IAF in India. 'I think they [Nehru's government] would prefer not to have this take place', Rusk advised Kennedy, 'we are not sure they are asking for it … they may decide not to have something that clearly pins them to an alignment.'[113]

The following month, as Kennedy prepared to visit Macmillan's Sussex home, Birch Grove, for a further round of Anglo-American talks, rumours surfaced of Soviet plans to sell India cut-price SAMs. American officials worried that Nehru might seize upon Moscow's offer as an alternative means of bolstering India's air defences more in

[109] Kennedy to Macmillan, 23 May 1963, FO 371/170644, TNA.
[110] Macmillan to Home, 24 May 1963, FO 371/170644, TNA.
[111] 'Military Aid for India', 13 May 1963, CAB 129/113, C (63) 82; Cabinet minutes, 28 May 1963, CAB 128/37 CC (63) 35, TNA.
[112] 'Military Aid for India',13 May 1963, CAB 129/113, C (63) 82, TNA.
[113] NSC Meeting on India, 9 May 1963, Meetings Recordings, Tape No. 86 (1), JFKL.

keeping with 'his cherished non-alignment policy'.[114] The British were just as anxious about American plans to loan India transport aircraft, provide New Delhi with road-making equipment, fund a plant for the production of small arms and ammunition in the subcontinent, and assist in training Indian Army officers. 'In the light of these United States offers,' Sandys advised his cabinet colleagues, 'it is clear that our response [on military aid] to the Indians cannot be wholly negative.'[115] Having virtually monopolised the supply of equipment and training to the Indian armed forces since 1947, the CRO was conscious 'that if we did not work rather rapidly on this subject [arms aid] ... we should find that the Americans, with all the advance work which they have done, would be in a fair way to transforming and annexing the Indian Armed Services'.[116] Ignoring objections from the Treasury, which maintained that Britain's parlous finances made it impractical to contest the 'unfortunate' expansion of American military influence in the subcontinent, Macmillan sided with Sandys and decided to increase British military aid to India over and above the $60 million that had been agreed at the Nassau meeting.[117] An extra $10 million to $20 million of British martial assistance was set aside for India. In addition, London pledged to raise its contribution to India's third five-year plan from $60 million to $84 million. Representing Macmillan's volte-face on Indian military aid as 'a major change in UK policy' that would never have occurred without the application of American pressure, Robert Komer noted that Washington was 'rather pleased' at Britain's unexpected change of heart.[118]

At the Birch Grove meeting, which took place on 29–30 June, the British gave Kennedy further cause for satisfaction by thrashing out a compromise agreement with American officials on Indian air defence. The British confirmed that RAF squadrons could participate in joint manoeuvres with the IAF in the subcontinent, on condition that London and Washington would undertake merely to *consult* with New Delhi were India subjected to further Chinese aggression.[119] On 9 July, British and American officials presented Nehru's government with a formal proposal to conduct joint US-Commonwealth-Indian air

---

[114] Komer to Kennedy, 21 June 1963, NSF, Box 110, JFKL; 'Talks with President Kennedy Indo-Pakistan Questions', 27 June 1963, FO 371/170644, TNA.
[115] 'Further Military Aid for India', 27 May 1963, CAB 129/113, C (63) 92, TNA.
[116] Gore-Booth to Saville Garner, 11 June 1963, MS.Gorebooth 86, GBP.
[117] Boyd-Carpenter to Sandys, 9 July 1963, T 317/360, TNA.
[118] Komer to McGeorge Bundy, 6 June 1963, NSF, Box 420, JFKL.
[119] Anglo-American meeting on India, 28 June 1963, DSDN 8/20, Duncan Sandys Papers, Churchill Archives Centre, Churchill College Cambridge (hereafter DSP).

defence exercises in India later that year. Nehru deliberated for a week before accepting the Anglo-American offer. Indian government spokesmen presented the agreement to a sceptical press as a 'training' arrangement, under which American and Commonwealth aircraft would assist the IAF in its preparations to meet an aerial threat from the north. 'The defense of India, including its air defense', India's media was assured, 'is wholly and solely the responsibility of the Government of India.'[120] Many Indians felt otherwise, and a chorus of domestic criticism was directed at Nehru's administration for compromising the nation's policy of non-alignment by agreeing to conduct joint military exercises with foreign forces on India soil.[121]

The US-Commonwealth-Indian air exercises, code-named Shiksha, or 'training', went ahead in November 1963. One squadron of RAF Javelin fighters, a second of USAF Super-sabres and two Australian Canberra bombers, the latter of which served as mock Chinese targets, flew sorties alongside squadrons of Indian Gnat and Hunter fighters in the environs of New Delhi and Calcutta.[122] By the 25 November, the 750 Western military personnel seconded to the operation had left India, leaving behind them two American-supplied mobile radar stations.[123] Western journalists grumbled that India's government had imposed a virtual news embargo on Shiksha. 'The apparent reason for the information blackout', the *New York Times*'s New Delhi correspondent trumpeted, 'is the political embarrassment caused to "nonaligned" India by the presence here of British and United States squadrons and ground personnel.'[124]

Indeed, the combination of a diminishing Chinese threat to Indian security, strident domestic opposition to the presence of foreign military forces on Indian soil, and signs that Soviet support for his government was returning, provided Nehru with sufficient impetus to kill off the air umbrella scheme. Having sidestepped an attempt by General Maxwell Taylor, Chairman of the US Joint Chiefs of Staff, to garner India's reaction to Shiksha, Nehru quietly vetoed a second round of joint air exercises in India, which had been scheduled to take place in April 1964.[125] In the final twist of what had been a dizzying series of

---

[120] *The New York Times*, 3 July 1963.
[121] *The New York Times*, 2 September 1963.
[122] 'Brief for Air Exercise Shiksha', 20 October 1963, NSF, Box 433, JFKL.
[123] A. Appadorai (ed.), *Select Documents on India's Foreign Policy and Relations, 1947–1972*, vol. 2 (New Delhi: Oxford University Press, 1985), pp. 182–3.
[124] *The New York Times*, 17 November 1963.
[125] 58th meeting of the US/Australian/British/Canadian co-ordinating group, 19 December 1963, DO 164/72, TNA.

British, American and Indian political gyrations on the air umbrella affair, Nehru assured the Rajya Sabha, in December 1963, that there was no question of foreign troops, ships or *aircraft* participating in India's defence.[126]

### All change: Lyndon Johnson, Alec Douglas-Home and South Asia

In July 1963, Chester Bowles had returned to India to begin his second stint as US ambassador. Within a few months of arriving back in the subcontinent, Bowles was suffering from 'genuinely low' morale. 'It was his [Bowles] hard luck', Robert Komer noted in November, 'to get back to Delhi just as the steam went out of our India enterprise.'[127] Having strongly endorsed Galbraith's proposal that the United States offer India a five-year $500 million programme of military aid, the new ambassador discovered that, on this issue, and much else besides, his was a lone voice in the Kennedy administration. Hampered by an indifferent relationship with Dean Rusk, and the generally low esteem in which he was held by Kennedy's closest coterie of advisers, Bowles' warnings that a penny-pinching approach to military aid risked squandering the Indian goodwill that America had accumulated since the late 1950s went unheeded. In October, Britain's ambassador in Washington, Sir David Ormsby Gore, informed London that the State Department and Pentagon had adopted an increasingly 'unenthusiastic' and 'non-committal' attitude in response to Indian enquiries on military aid. To their consternation, Indian officials were advised that difficulties with Pakistan and on Capitol Hill, where a Foreign Aid Bill was well behind schedule, made it impossible to confirm when additional American funding for military assistance might become available, and even then, 'any new [Indian] requests would have to compete with existing projects'.[128] Bowles' British counterpart, Sir Paul Gore-Booth, expressed similar frustration at the Macmillan government's reluctance to allocate financial resources to the Indian subcontinent. 'It is frankly too depressing to think about it for long at this end', Gore-Booth lamented to a colleague at the CRO. 'How the whole vast machinery of a former Empire gets itself tied into futile knots over [military aid] … it

[126] Sarvepalli Gopal, *Jawaharlal Nehru: A Biography*, vol. 3: *1956–1964* (London: Jonathan Cape, 1984), p. 253.
[127] Komer to McGeorge Bundy, 12 November 1963, NSF, Box 111, JFKL.
[128] Ormsby Gore to FO, No. 3219, 17 October 1963, PREM 11/4867, TNA.

is just utterly out of proportion and make us look stupid, irresolute and inefficient in the eyes of the ... Indians.'[129]

In early November, in an effort to resolve the impasse on military aid, Bowles persuaded the Indian government to scale down its request for American martial assistance to $375 million.[130] Having brokered a deal in New Delhi, Bowles returned to the United States to sell his proposal in Washington. On 13 November, the ambassador met briefly with Kennedy, and was encouraged by the president to whip up support for a new initiative on Indian military aid, ahead of an NSC meeting at the end of that month.[131] Less than a fortnight later, as Kennedy made his fateful visit to Dallas, Robert Komer informed McGeorge Bundy that 'JFK's sense [is] that *we should get on with our Indian enterprise. We've* been marking time too much because of Congress and the Pak[istani] s.' It appeared possible, Komer added optimistically, that a 'clear policy decision' on Indian military assistance would emerge from the meeting on India that Kennedy had scheduled on his return from Texas.[132]

Instead, abrupt changes at the top of both the United States and British governments drained what little momentum remained from the Anglo-American debate on Indian military aid. On 22 November, following Kennedy's assassination, Lyndon Johnson was sworn in as America's 36th president aboard Air Force One, at Love Field in Dallas. Johnson took charge of a traumatised nation, and inherited responsibility for a swathe of pressing domestic and foreign policy problems. Issues left over from his predecessor's foray into the politics of the Indian subcontinent, the new president quickly decided, would have to wait while more urgent priorities were addressed, at home and abroad. At the same time, a new Conservative administration led by the now Sir Alec Douglas-Home, who in order to succeed Macmillan as Britain's prime minister, in October 1963, had renounced his hereditary peerages, pondered the future of British policy in South Asia. Britain's High Commissioner in Pakistan, Morrice James, urged the new government in London to consider carefully the strain that British military support for India in the aftermath of the Sino-Indian War had imposed on the United Kingdom's traditional policy of even-handedness in the subcontinent. 'Pakistanis from the President downwards', James advised the CRO, 'believe Britain has chosen to back India rather than them', firstly, in order to stay onside with Americans, and secondly, to protect

---

[129] Gore-Booth to Belcher, 9 August 1963, MS.Gorebooth 86, GBP.
[130] Robert Komer, 3 September 1964, OH, JFKL.
[131] Komer to McGeorge Bundy, 22 November 1963, Box 481, HP.
[132] Komer to McGeorge Bundy, 22 November 1963, NSF, Box 433, JFKL.

business interests in India.[133] In New Delhi, Gore-Booth took a different view, and made the case for pressing ahead with a modest programme of British military aid for India. Doing so, he argued, would go a long way toward protecting Britain's political, military and economic influence in India; deterring Chinese aggression in South Asia; and strengthening Anglo-American relations. 'It is worth remembering the unhappy consequences, e.g. in Pakistan itself, of the monopolisation of Western defence aid by the United States which was such a disagreeable feature of the Dulles era', he reflected, 'neither the Americans nor the Indians want it here.'[134]

With some uncertainty surrounding Johnson's thinking on South Asian matters, the CRO issued Douglas-Home with a defensive regional brief in advance of his first substantive meeting with the American president, in Washington, in February 1964. Although satisfied that the White House appeared eager to continue Anglo-American collaboration in the subcontinent, British officials cautioned Douglas-Home that within the military sphere this constituted 'a difficult issue for us, requiring consideration in Cabinet'. Entering into a long-term military aid commitment with a fellow Commonwealth country, the CRO emphasised, 'would be a new departure of policy'. Moreover, it would place the British in an invidious position vis-à-vis Pakistan, given that in comparison with the United States, 'our economic aid is smaller and our military aid non-existent; but our private investment is far higher'.[135] In the event, British concern over the vigour with which Lyndon Johnson might seek to uphold his predecessor's regional legacy was misplaced. The advent of the Johnson administration, as Douglas-Home, and his Labour successor in 10 Downing Street, Harold Wilson, soon discovered, would herald the beginning of a new and markedly different chapter in the history of the United States' relations with India and Pakistan.

---

[133] James to Saville Garner, 18 January 1964, T 317/536, TNA.
[134] Gore-Booth to Saville Garner, 25 January 1964, T 317/536, TNA.
[135] CRO brief for Douglas-Home's visit to Washington, 31 January 1964, T 317/536, TNA.

# 8    The other transfer of power: Britain, the United States and the Nehru–Shastri transition

From his position as India's first prime minister, Jawaharlal Nehru accumulated a formidable amount of political power after 1947. On top of his prime ministerial responsibilities, Nehru managed India's external affairs portfolio, led its economic planning commission, ran the country's atomic energy programme and chaired the ruling Congress Party's Working Committee. Moreover, after the death, in December 1950, of India's home minister, and deputy prime minister, Vallabhbhai Patel, Nehru was left with few, if any, substantive political rivals. In 1958, Nehru's omnipotence prompted Britain's then High Commissioner to India, Malcolm MacDonald, to reflect that 'Mr. Nehru has hitherto exerted unchallenged and almost unqualified personal authority [in India]. In fact, Indian democracy already possesses some of the features of a typical Asian autocracy.'[1] By the following November, however, the arrival of Nehru's seventieth birthday had amplified long-standing debates, both inside and outside the Indian subcontinent, over when India's premier should step down from office and who should succeed him when he did.[2] Moreover, by the turn of the decade, with Nehru's health faltering, Sino-Indian relations deteriorating and Soviet interest in India growing, British and American policymakers evidenced anxiety about not only who, but perhaps more pertinently what forces, would shape the future of the world's largest democracy.[3]

Such concerns were brought into sharp focus following Nehru's visit to Washington, in November 1961. Kennedy had been assured before

[1] Malcolm MacDonald to Viscount Kilmuir, 6 October 1958, DO 35/8649, The United Kingdom National Archives, Kew, London (hereafter TNA). For further insights into Nehru's 'virtually unquestioned authority' within India, see Sumit Ganguly, 'The Prime Minister and Foreign and Defence Policies', in James Manor (ed.), *Nehru to the Nineties: The Changing Office of the Prime Minister in India* (London: Hurst & Company, 1994).

[2] Michael Brecher, *Succession in India: A Study in Decision-Making* (London: Oxford University Press, 1966), p. 6.

[3] *Time*, 24 August 1962; Welles Hangen, *After Nehru, Who?* (London: Rupert Hart-Davis, 1963).

Nehru's arrival in the United States that although approaching his seventy-second year, the Indian premier's 'power and presence remains basically undiminished'.[4] Instead, the American president found his guest tired and distracted, a shadow of what he had been led to expect.[5] Nehru's lacklustre performance in Washington was such that Kennedy's Secretary of State, Dean Rusk, concluded afterwards that the Indian government was 'in effect being run by others'.[6] In off-the-record briefings with American journalists, Rusk emphasised the Kennedy administration's disappointment that having touted Nehru as a dynamic totem for Asian democracy, instead, he had proved 'old and ill ... he is *in* office but he doesn't *fill* it'.[7] The British government felt similarly. On his way to meet with Kennedy in Washington, Nehru had stopped off in London. Having taken advantage of the Indian leader's presence in Britain to conduct informal talks on matters of common concern, Harold Macmillan recorded in his personal diary that Nehru appeared to be a spent force, 'much aged and very tired'.[8]

The following spring, Nehru was taken ill on the floor of the Lok Sabha, the lower house of India's parliament. Diagnosed as suffering from pyelonephritis, a viral infection of the urinary tract, the Indian prime minister spent much of the subsequent month in bed. On his doctor's advice, Nehru scaled back his workload, changed his diet and began taking more rest.[9] Nonetheless, Sir Paul Gore-Booth, who had replaced Malcolm MacDonald as Britain's High Commissioner in India in 1960, noticed a marked contrast in Nehru's behaviour before and after his illness. Nehru, Gore-Booth informed the Commonwealth Relations Office back in London, had emerged from his convalescence, 'noticeably slower in response. Less curious, more prejudiced, and, above all, more tired.'[10] MacDonald, who was passing through New Delhi at the time of Nehru's illness, confirmed that it had given India's leader 'an awful psychological shock'. Having 'hoped he [Nehru] was

---

[4] 'Nehru – 1961', undated, c. October 1961, National Security File (NSF), Box 106, John F. Kennedy Library, Boston, Massachusetts (hereafter JFKL).
[5] Kennedy lamented that his encounter with Nehru was 'a disaster ... the worst head-of-state visit I have had'. Arthur M. Schlesinger Jr, *A Thousand Days: John F. Kennedy in the White House* (Boston: Houghton Mifflin, 1965), pp. 523–6.
[6] Conversation between Home and Rusk, 10 December 1961, FO 371/159708/D 1024/61, TNA.
[7] C. L. Sulzberger, *Last of the Giants* (London: Weidenfeld & Nicolson, 1972), p. 906.
[8] Entry for 4 November 1961, d.44, 24 Oct 1961–24 Jan 1962, Harold Macmillan Diaries, Bodleian Library, University of Oxford (hereafter HMD).
[9] Sarvepalli Gopal, *Jawaharlal Nehru: A Biography*, vol. 3: *1956–1964* (London: Jonathan Cape, 1984), p. 266.
[10] Gore-Booth to Sandys, 7 June 1962, DO 196/75, TNA.

blessed with eternal youth', MacDonald observed, '... he had discovered with dismay that his body was that of an old man'.[11]

Nehru's physical and psychological deterioration was particularly unsettling for British and American policymakers given the formidable internal and external threats that India faced, and the absence of an obvious successor to its ailing premier. In June 1962, writing to his friend and Nehru's sister, Vijaya Lakshmi Pandit, Lord Louis Mountbatten spoke for many in Whitehall when lamenting that 'your wonderful brother is ill and losing his grip at a time when India needs his help and guidance more than ever'.[12] Nehru had always refused to be drawn on the subject of political succession. In February 1957, when asked by journalists to comment on how India would fare in his absence, Nehru gave a typically frosty rebuff. 'The question is foolish and meaningless', he retorted disingenuously, 'I am not running the country. India is shaping herself.'[13] Nehru maintained that by naming a preferred successor he would risk subverting India's democratic process, and perhaps more significantly, do the individual concerned more harm than good. Rationalising his position, Nehru argued that, 'If a certain person is named, you put that person at a disadvantage because there would be jealousies and the people would possibly react against something being imposed on them.'[14] By way of illustration, he cited the example of Sir Anthony Eden. After being groomed for power by Churchill, within months of taking office Eden had became embroiled in the Suez fiasco and had subsequently resigned under a cloud. The irony that a sick and politically ineffective Churchill had clung on to power far too long in the 1950s than was good either for himself, his country or, one might plausibly argue, the intensely frustrated Eden, appeared lost on the Indian premier.

## The erosion of authority

To Nehru's irritation, the world's media refused to let the succession question drop. In the summer of 1962, under the headline 'Who's Next', the American magazine *Time* ran a rule over Nehru's likely successors. On the basis that the Congress Party hierarchy would prefer a 'straw man' to follow Nehru, *Time* installed India's 'bland' home minister, Lal

---

[11] Malcolm MacDonald, *Titans and Others* (London: Collins, 1972), p. 233.
[12] Pandit to Mountbatten, 14 February 1962, and Mountbatten to Pandit, 20 June 1962, MB1/J325, Lord Mountbatten Papers, Hartley Library, University of Southampton (hereafter MBP).
[13] *The Times*, 12 February 1957.
[14] 'Mr. Nehru's Press Conference, Colombo', 15 November 1962, DO 133/51,TNA.

Bahadur Shastri, as the frontrunner.[15] A diminutive five feet and two inches tall, Shastri was physically inconspicuous and temperamentally unassuming. Christened 'The Sparrow' by his countrymen, Shastri had joined the pre-independence nationalist movement in northern India's United Provinces while still in his teens. Having served a seemingly obligatory political apprenticeship in British prisons in the 1940s, he rose steadily through the ranks of the Congress Party in the 1950s. Often underestimated by his contemporaries, Shastri's slight frame housed a steely inner core. 'Perhaps due to my being small in size and soft in tongue people are apt to believe that I am not able to be very firm with them', he informed fellow parliamentarians in November 1956. 'Though not physically strong I think I am internally not that weak.'[16] The CRO characterised Shastri as 'pleasant, intelligent, [and] highly public spirited'. Moreover, it noted that he had 'the rare reputation in Indian politics of complete freedom from corruption and political jobbery'. More significantly still, Shastri enjoyed Nehru's confidence, having performed admirably for many years as the Indian premier's 'faithful lieutenant'.[17] Nevertheless, serious question marks surrounded Shastri's health. A workaholic, like Nehru, in October 1959 Shastri suffered a serious heart attack. Although he subsequently appeared to have made a full recovery, many commentators dismissed his prime ministerial prospects on medical grounds. Equally, Shastri lacked a strong public profile outside northern India. In 1961, in a nationwide poll conducted by the Indian Institute of Public Opinion, he was ranked as only the fourth most likely person to succeed Nehru.[18]

The majority of political pundits saw Nehru's finance minister, Morarji Desai, as a better bet to become India's next prime minister. A former Chief Minister of Bombay, Desai had moved into central government in the mid-1950s and quickly established a reputation for austerity, both personally and politically. A devout Hindu, Desai practised yoga and spun khaddar, the homegrown cloth that under Mohandas Gandhi's aegis had become associated with India's independence

[15] *Time*, 24 August 1962.
[16] 'A Life Sketch of Mr. Lal Bahadur Shastri', 5 June 1964, *Indiagram*, No. 83.
[17] 'Mr. Lal Bahadur Shastri', June 1964, PREM 11/4864, TNA; 'Lal Bahadur Shastri', 15 January 1964, RG 59, Records Relating to Indian Political Affairs, 1964–6, Box 5, US National Archives and Records Administration, College Park, Maryland (hereafter NARA). For further insights into Shastri's life and politics, see C. P. Srivastava, *Lal Bahadur Shastri: A Life of Truth in Politics* (New Delhi: Oxford University Press, 1995).
[18] Hangen, *After Nehru*, p. 128. The three leading contenders were the Socialist Party leader Jayaprakash Narayan, and from the right and left wings of the Congress Party respectively, Morarji Desai, and India's defence minister Krishna Menon.

movement; championed prohibition; followed a spartan dietary regime; and adhered to a vow of celibacy. Born on 29 February, some thought it apt that Desai's birthday came around only once every four years.[19] Known for his fiscal conservatism, endorsement of free enterprise and pro-Western outlook, Desai was popular with the Congress Party's right wing and India's business community. By 1958, American officials had marked him out as a man to watch within the Indian cabinet, and 'one of the leading candidates for the prime ministership after Nehru'.[20] The British agreed, concluding that Desai was well placed in the succession stakes. 'If Mr. Nehru were to die tomorrow ...,' the CRO opined in July 1962, 'without having designated his successor it is reasonable to assume ... the appointment as Prime Minister of Mr. Morarji Desai.'[21] Welles Hangen, an NBC journalist based in New Delhi, felt likewise. In his influential book, *After Nehru, Who?*, which appeared in Indian bookstores that autumn, Hangen named Desai as the clear favourite to replace Nehru.[22]

While Desai's advocacy of free market economics, strident anti-communism, and pro-Western sympathies, won him plaudits in London and Washington, British and American officials considered that as a future leader of India he had serious drawbacks. Foremost amongst these was Desai's potential to act as a divisive influence within the Congress Party and India as a whole. 'Desai ...', the US State Department observed, 'is bitterly opposed by the [Congress] party's leftist faction and is disliked by the dominant party leaders of the south because of his inflexible attitudes.' Moreover, Desai was considered 'primarily a Hindu nationalist', whose elevation to the premiership would alarm India's Muslim community.[23] In a broader sense, Whitehall judged that when it came to the matter of Indo-Pakistani relations, 'the one issue that overrides all others and has consistently bedevilled India's relations with Britain', Desai's 'rigid and extreme anti-Pakistan convictions would make his appointment [as India's prime minister] little less than a disaster'.[24] Nehru appeared equally convinced that as India's

---

[19] Hangen, *After Nehru*, p. 33.

[20] 'Current Intelligence Weekly Summary', 22 May 1958, CIA-RDP79-00927A001700110001-2, CIA Records Search Tool (hereafter CREST), US National Archives and Records Administration, College Park, Maryland.

[21] 'Implications of Mr. Nehru's Death', 3 July 1962, DO 133/51, TNA.

[22] Hangen, *After Nehru*, pp. 29–32. Hangen identified seven other candidates for the premiership including Krishna Menon, Shastri and Nehru's daughter, Indira Gandhi.

[23] 'Morarji Desai', 15 January 1964, RG 59, Records Relating to Indian Political Affairs, 1964–6, Box 5, NARA.

[24] 'India after Nehru', 9 June 1964, PREM 11/4864, TNA.

leader, the combination of Desai's personality and politics would split rather than unite the nation.[25] Tellingly, in 1961, when Desai attempted to cement his credentials as prime minister in waiting by standing for the post of Deputy Leader of the Congress Party, Nehru stepped in to sabotage his candidacy.[26]

Disconcertingly for British and American policymakers, Desai's shortcomings opened up the alarming possibility that, either by default or design, Nehru would leave a door open for Krishna Menon to step into his shoes. By the summer of 1962, British and American officials had grown disturbed by the increasingly malevolent influence that Menon appeared to exercise over Nehru. In August, the British High Commission in New Delhi informed London that Nehru's 'decisions themselves are … less his own than they used to be … he is certainly more vulnerable to over-persuasion by men of determination, in particular Krishna Menon, who knows exactly what he wants and works with unscrupulous vigour to achieve it'.[27] Furthermore, unsettling reports began to surface in the international press that suggested that Nehru secretly favoured Menon as his successor.[28] 'If there's even a one in five chance [of Menon coming to power],' Robert Komer cautioned in July 1962, 'we ought to run plenty scared.'[29]

The Sino-Indian War, however, undid any plans that Menon may have harboured to succeed Nehru. As the principal architect of India's China policy, Nehru was left feeling betrayed, humiliated and depressed by the PRC's attack on India.[30] Moreover, Indians at all levels held Nehru partly culpable for the nation's defeat and, for the first time, began to seriously question their leader's judgement. 'Everywhere in Parliament and outside there is an ever increasing demand for the PM to go', Vijaya Lakshmi Pandit informed the American journalist and Nehru family friend, Dorothy Norman. 'God knows where all this will end. For my poor brother it [India's military humiliation] is a wound that cannot heal and the fact that he brought it on himself to a large

[25] Brecher, *Succession in India*, pp. 76–7.
[26] Hangen, *After Nehru*, pp. 45–6.
[27] Belcher to Sandys, 25 August 1962, DO 196/127, TNA.
[28] *Time*, 24 August 1962. Interestingly, as the doyen of the Congress Party's left wing, Menon was Moscow's choice to replace Nehru. In May 1962, Soviet leaders went as far as to instruct the KGB residency in New Delhi to initiate a covert pro-Menon propaganda campaign inside India. Disappointingly for the Kremlin, its results proved notably ineffective. Christopher Andrew and Vasili Mitrokhin, *The KGB and the World: The Mitrokhin Archive II* (London: Allen Lane, 2005), pp. 314–15.
[29] Komer to McGeorge Bundy, 16 July 1962, NSF, Box 441, JFKL.
[30] Vijaya Lakshmi Pandit, *The Scope of Happiness: A Personal Memoir* (London: Weidenfeld & Nicolson, 1979), p. 315; Ramachandra Guha, *India After Gandhi: The History of the World's Largest Democracy* (London: Macmillan, 2007), p. 338.

extent does not help.'[31] Above all, Nehru's critics rounded on the Indian premier for keeping faith with Menon.[32] Having at first resisted political pressure to sack his closest political confidant, the fact that Nehru was subsequently compelled to back down and accept Menon's 'resignation' was seen as significant by the British in two respects. Firstly, it confirmed 'that the Congress Party, which Mr. Nehru hardly ever seems to consult actively, has proved that, on occasion, it cannot be ignored'. Secondly, it effectively ended the political career of 'the person who seemed most likely to make the succession to Mr. Nehru difficult if not turbulent or violent'.[33]

The ebbing away of Nehru's authority in the aftermath of the Sino-Indian War intensified debates inside India over the need to identify a prime ministerial successor.[34] In December, British officials were informed by contacts inside the Congress Party that 'if it had not been that Nehru was the only politician with mass support, attempts would already have been made to oust him'.[35] Within a matter of months, Nehru's value as an electoral asset appeared less certain. Visiting New Delhi, in May 1963, Mountbatten was appalled by the levels of incompetence and corruption that he encountered. 'There is a complete lack of leadership', Mountbatten observed. 'Everybody is very pessimistic about the future. Several people have said to me "why don't you come back and run the country again?"'[36] With the economy under pressure, India's third five-year plan faltering, food shortages common, regional tensions festering and public outrage growing at endemic government graft, the Indian electorate turned against Nehru's government. In early 1962, Congress had won a resounding general election victory, securing 361 of the 494 seats in the Lok Sabha.[37] A year later, the Party suffered successive by-election defeats in Amroka, Farrukhabad and Rajkot, all seats that it had held in 1962.[38]

In July 1963, America's new ambassador in India, Chester Bowles, recorded his shock at the political developments that had taken place

---

[31] Pandit to Dorothy Norman, 22 November 1962, Box 140, Folder Pandit Mdm VJ, Dorothy Norman Papers, Butler Library, Columbia University, New York.

[32] 'An Ailing Nehru and the Indian Leadership', 24 January 1964, CIA-RDP79-00927A004300090002-6, CREST; Judith M. Brown, *Nehru: A Political Life* (New Haven: Yale University Press, 2003), p. 326.

[33] 'After Nehru, Who?', J. A. G. Banks, 26 November 1962, DO 131/151, TNA.

[34] Benjamin Zachariah, *Nehru* (London: Routledge, 2004), p. 251.

[35] Ormerod to Allen, 22 December 1962, DO 133/51, TNA.

[36] Philip Ziegler, *Mountbatten: The Official Biography* (London: Collins, 1985), p. 602.

[37] 'Indian Politics and the Succession Problem', 13 January 1964, CIA-RDP78-03061A000200050001-5, CREST.

[38] Zachariah, *Nehru*, pp. 252–3.

since he had last served in New Delhi, a decade previously. 'In my first twenty-four hours [in India]', Bowles confided to his diary, 'it is apparent that I will be a witness to the collapse of an era, or rather I should say to its petering out. Nehru was 80 per cent of Indian government authority; now he must be 30 per cent as the struggle for supremacy is on with a vengeance.'[39] Scenting political blood, the following month opposition MPs tabled a motion of no confidence in Nehru's government in the Lok Sabha. Nehru comfortably brushed off the challenge. In the process, however, he was subjected to the unedifying spectacle of his parliamentary opponents banging their seats and shouting 'Quit, Nehru quit!'[40] With his authority diminished, Congress leaders flexing their muscles, and critics sniping at him from the political sidelines, as the CIA noted, 'For the first time, Indian politicians, both within his party and outside it, seemed to be increasingly willing to contemplate a period when Nehru would not be around.'[41]

### Opportunities and threats

During the remainder of 1963, Nehru managed to keep his political opponents at bay with sporadic flashes of vigour and political acumen, most notably in turning the 'Kamaraj Plan' to his own advantage. Named after K. Kamaraj Nadar, Chief Minister of the state of Madras, and the dominant political figure in southern India, the plan was conceived by a coterie of senior Congress officials, known as 'The Syndicate', and was intended to reconnect the Party with Indian voters.[42] Under its terms, a number of prominent ministers, at both the state and national level, were marked out to quit government and go back to campaign for the Congress Party at a grass-roots level. Nehru seized upon the Kamaraj Plan as an opportunity to marginalise his opponents and stamp his authority on the succession question.[43] On 24 August 1963, he informed the Congress Party Working Committee

---

[39] Diary entry for 18 July 1963, Part IX, Series III, Diary 1, Box 392, Folder 158, Chester Bowles Papers, Sterling Memorial Library, Yale University, New Haven, Connecticut (hereafter CBP).

[40] Stanley Wolpert, *Nehru: A Tryst with Destiny* (Oxford University Press, 1996), p. 490.

[41] 'An Ailing Nehru and the Indian Leadership', 24 January 1964, CIA-RDP79-00927A004300090002-6, CREST.

[42] The 'Syndicate' included Kamaraj; the prominent Congress leaders from West Bengal and Maharashtra, Atulya Ghosh and S. K. Patil; Sanjiva Reddy, Chief Minister of Andhra Pradesh; and S. Nijalingappa, Chief Minister of Karnataka.

[43] 'An Ailing Nehru and the Indian Leadership', 24 January 1964, CIA-RDP79-00927A004300090002-6, CREST.

that six cabinet ministers and six chief ministers, including Morarji Desai and Lal Bahadur Shastri, would be the first to relinquish office under the plan. At a stroke, Nehru removed the two main contenders in the succession race from the locus of their political power, the Indian cabinet.[44]

Nehru's faltering health, however, ensured that his grip on power remained precarious. By the end of 1963, India's prime minister appeared physically and psychologically spent. In conversation with Gore-Booth, Vijaya Lakshmi Pandit confessed that she had become 'unable to guess with any accuracy how far he [Nehru] follows what goes on in meetings and conversations'.[45] Forced to observe the decline of a man he deeply admired, on 8 December, Chester Bowles noted mournfully in his diary, 'Why can't people leave rather that wilt and peter out?'[46] Judging that Nehru had entered a final and terminal decline, British and American officials focused increasingly upon the impact that the imminent succession struggle would have on India's internal stability and international relations. Many contemporary observers, not least the American author Harrison Salisbury, in his influential book *India: The Most Dangerous Decades*, had called into question India's ability to withstand fissiparous pressures in a post-Nehru era.[47] In London and Washington, policymakers were acutely aware that in a country notable for its cultural, linguistic and religious diversity, Nehru's power and prestige had acted as a great unifier. Even so, Nehru had worked tirelessly to preserve India's unity, security and communal harmony, and to keep the country economically solvent. Back in October 1958, Malcolm MacDonald had voiced 'scepticism as to the chances of this colossal multitude of people remaining a wholly compact nation'. For the majority of their history, MacDonald argued, Indians had been divided, and only forced together by exceptional internal figures or powerful external forces. 'In the near future much will depend on

---

[44] Nehru's action was widely interpreted, not least by Desai himself, as a move to wreck his finance minister's chances of becoming India's next premier. Lacking a strong regional base, and with opponents in control of the Congress Party in his home state of Gujarat, Desai's political strength rested to a substantial degree on his status as the second ranking member of the Indian cabinet after Nehru. Shastri, on the other hand, appeared to have far less to lose from a spell outside the government, and was expected to use it to consolidate his influence within the Congress Party. Gopal, *Nehru: 1956–1964*, p. 245; Morarji Desai, *The Story of My Life* (New Delhi: S. Chand, 1978), p. 204.

[45] Gore-Booth to Saville Garner, 3 January 1964, DO 196/311, TNA.

[46] Diary entry for 8 December 1963, Part IX, Series III, Diary 1, Box 392, Folder 158, CBP.

[47] Harrison Salisbury, *India: The Most Dangerous Decades* (Princeton University Press, 1960).

whether Mr. Nehru will be succeeded by a national leader', Britain's High Commissioner predicted, '... who can preserve a robust national unity.'[48] American officials were equally worried that in the absence of 'the old Gandhi–Nehru magic [that] had held everything together for the first 17 years of Indian independence', the country would fracture apart into a series of regional or ethnic blocs.[49]

Of the threats facing Nehru's successor, one of the most invidious was that of communal violence. Within India, the country's 360 million Hindus lived cheek by jowl with 50 million Muslims and 20 million followers of other minority religions, such as Sikhism, Jainism and Christianity. In January 1964, a spiral of religious and communal disturbances, that had begun in Kashmir the previous December, sparked anti-Hindu riots in East Pakistan that claimed twenty-seven lives. Seeking retribution, Calcutta's Hindus embarked on an anti-Muslim pogrom, which over the course of four days left hundreds dead.[50] The state government in West Bengal struggled to contain the communal violence in Calcutta and to prevent it from spilling over into the neighbouring state of Bihar. Exasperated by the lack of 'guts or grip' displayed by Bengal's Chief Minister, Britain's Deputy High Commissioner in Calcutta, Eric Norris, noted that at the height of the crisis while the police were 'complaining that they were desperately shorthanded ... [they] could still spare some 36 of their members to take part in gymkhana events at the Calcutta Horse show'.[51] Back in New Delhi, Indian officials admitted to Chester Bowles that it had taken some 'hard arm twisting' to keep inflammatory reports of the Calcutta violence out of the press, and the deployment of 5,000 troops to restore order in the city.[52] The depiction of the Calcutta riots that appeared in *Time* verged on the apocalyptic. 'The army clamped martial law on five of the city's 25 police districts,' *Time* reported, 'gunned down looters and arsonists in the streets, threw more than 10,000 demonstrators into jail. By the time order was restored, 200 were dead, 600 wounded, 73,000 homeless, and whole portions of the city razed.'[53]

---

[48] Malcolm MacDonald to Viscount Kilmuir, 6 October 1958, DO 35/8649, TNA.
[49] Ambassador Harmon E. Kirby, Oral History Interview, 31 August 1995, The Foreign Affairs Oral History Project, http://memory.loc.gov/ammem/collections/diplomacy/ (hereafter FAOHP).
[50] Benjamin Read to McGeorge Bundy, 16 January 1964, NSF Country File, India, Box 128, Folder, Lyndon Baines Johnson Library, Austin, Texas (hereafter LBJL).
[51] E. G. Norris to R. H. Belcher, POL 395/86/1, 14 January 1964, DO 196/342, TNA.
[52] Bowles to Rusk, 17 January 1964, NSF Country File, India, Box 128, Folder 1, LBJL.
[53] *Time*, 24 January 1964.

Some British officials serving in India at the time had witnessed at first hand the communal holocaust that engulfed the subcontinent in 1947. As a consequence, many had been left with an abiding sense of the fragility of the country's communal consensus. In early 1964, Britain's Acting High Commissioner in India, Ronald Belcher, reflected to his superiors in the CRO that

No one who saw as I did in the Punjab in 1947, the widespread and inhuman bestialities to which aroused communal passions can lead can have any doubt that Nehru was as right as he was sincere in his determination to make India a truly secular State. It is a major tragedy that he failed to see until too late how dangerously shallow the adherence of the Hindu majority was to this ideal.[54]

American officials echoed Belcher's anxiety. At the CIA, the Agency's South Asian analysts noted that the 'conservative and illiterate masses of India' were, on the whole, more susceptible to the emotionally charged sermons delivered by religious extremists, than they were to the measured rhetoric employed by proponents of secularism. In India's 1962 general election, the Bharatiya Jan Sangh, or Indian People's Party, the standard bearer of Hindu traditionalism, had polled only 6.1 per cent of the national vote. In its northern stronghold of Bihar and Madhya Pradesh, however, the Jan Sangh had given Congress a run for its money. For many of India's Muslims, Nehru embodied the nation's commitment to secularism, and as the CIA emphasised, was considered to be 'their best guarantee that the usual social and economic discrimination against Muslims by Hindus would at least not be officially countenanced'.[55] A new Indian premier, particularly one more associated with Hindu orthodoxy than Nehruvian agnosticism, faced an uphill battle to retain the confidence of his Muslim citizens. The CRO doubted that any future Indian government, whatever the strength of its opposition to communalism, 'can in all circumstances stand against it with the effectiveness of Nehru's instant and unquestioned resolution'.[56]

The looming spectre of civil disorder in India led British and American officials to question whether, moving forward, the country would remain a democracy. 'It is a mark of his [Nehru's] success', the British reflected, 'that so far India has remained a country where men can freely speak their minds. Will his successors be willing or able to

[54] 'India after Nehru', 9 June 1964, PREM 11/4864, TNA.
[55] 'An Ailing Nehru and the Indian Leadership', 24 January 1964, CIA-RDP79-00927A004300090002-6, CREST.
[56] 'India after Nehru', 9 June 1964, PREM 11/4864, TNA.

maintain this sort of vigilance to keep India on the democratic rails?'[57] Although Indians had readily assimilated the concepts of elections and of parliamentary debate, the idea of representative government was still a relatively recent phenomenon in the subcontinent. By the late 1950s, India's neighbour Pakistan, having initially embraced democracy, had drifted toward a more autocratic form of government dominated by the military. Having experienced at first hand the confusion and uncertainty that had followed the traumatic transition of presidential power from John F. Kennedy to Lyndon Johnson in November 1963, Robert Komer considered it possible that India might descend into 'disarray' on Nehru's death. 'A deep political crisis [in India]', Komer counselled senior Washington policymakers, 'is not inconceivable.'[58] In New Delhi, Gore-Booth echoed Komer's warning. 'Almost anything might emerge from all this [the succession] from the best to the worst', Britain's High Commissioner cabled London, on 3 January 1964. '[We are] trying to encourage them [Indians] to conduct affairs so as to give those who want to pursue a middle of the road political policy ... the greatest chance possible.'[59]

In another sense, British and American officials approached the end of the Nehru era as an opportunity to revitalise their governments' increasingly tense relationships with India. Having been feted by Indians for coming to their nation's aid during the Sino-Indian War, the British acknowledged that by the spring of 1964, Anglo-American relations with Nehru's government had come under 'serious strain'.[60] As has been stated previously, Britain and the United States had provoked Nehru's ire following the cessation of Sino-Indian hostilities by pressing India to reach an accommodation with Pakistan over Kashmir, and by proving unexpectedly parsimonious with their offers of military aid.[61] After Sir Patrick Dean, Britain's ambassador to the United Nations, criticised India's Kashmir policy in a Security Council speech, in early 1964, Indian diplomats boycotted British social functions. 'Anything favourable to India', a senior Indian official chastised Ronald Belcher, 'is always turned down by the CRO.'[62] Having written Nehru off as the principal impediment to progress on a range of regional issues from

---

[57] *Ibid.*
[58] Komer to McGeorge Bundy, 6 March 1964, NSF Country File, India, Box 128, Folder 3, LBJL.
[59] Gore-Booth to Saville Garner, 3 January 1964, DO 196/311, TNA.
[60] 'India: The Death of Mr. Nehru', 1 June 1964, PREM 11/4864, TNA.
[61] Surjit Mansingh, 'India and the United States', in B. R. Nanda (ed.) *Indian Foreign Policy: The Nehru Years* (New Delhi: Sangam, 1990), p. 167.
[62] Belcher to O'Brien, 4 May 1964, DO 133/151, TNA.

Indo-Pakistani rapprochement to economic liberalisation, policymakers in London and Washington looked forward to the arrival of a new, more progressive, and hopefully pro-Western regime, in New Delhi.[63]

## Endgame

On 6 January 1964, the hopes and fears that British and American officials voiced in relation to India's future acquired added piquancy when Nehru suffered a stroke during the Congress Party's annual conference in Bhubaneswar, in eastern India. Attempts by the Indian government to play down the seriousness of Nehru's illness contrasted with images of the listless Indian leader being carried in a wheelchair from the aeroplane that returned him to New Delhi, on 12 January.[64] Indian officials informed the British confidentially that Nehru had suffered a temporary occlusion, or failure of the blood supply to the brain, which had briefly paralysed his left side.[65] Back in Washington, the State Department immediately offered the Indian government American medical assistance. The State Department also asked leading American cardiologists to review Nehru's clinical background. The conclusions made for grim reading. 'Given Nehru's history,' the State Department was advised, 'a recurrence of thrombosis is likely. This might be in a day, week or decade. He [Nehru] is walking on eggs.'[66] Preparing for the worst, State Department officers began the macabre task of drafting condolence messages from Lyndon Johnson to India's president, Sarvepalli Radhakrishnan, Nehru's daughter, Indira Gandhi, and Vijaya Lakshmi Pandit.[67]

Although the Indian government maintained an upbeat picture of Nehru's condition, it quickly confirmed that the prime minister would take a break from official duties, with Gulzarilal Nanda, India's home minister, and T. T. Krishnamachari, the minister of finance, temporarily managing his day-to-day responsibilities.[68] By the end of January, Nehru had rallied sufficiently to make a brief public appearance at India's Republic Day parade, in New Delhi. Chester Bowles was far from alone, however, in expressing incredulity, when three days later

---

[63] 'India after Nehru', 9 June 1964, PREM 11/4864, TNA.
[64] *The Times*, 8 January 1964; 'Prime Minister's Health', 13 January 1964, PREM 11/4865, TNA.
[65] 'Mr. Nehru's Health', 5 February 1964, DO 196/311, TNA.
[66] 'Dr. Woodward on Nehru's Health', 10 January 1964, RG 59, Records Relating to Indian Political Affairs, 1964–6, Box 5, NARA.
[67] 'Scenario of Possible Actions Related to Prime Minister Nehru's Illness', 13 January 1964, RG 59, Records Relating to Indian Political Affairs, 1964–6, Box 5, NARA.
[68] 'Prime Minister's Health', 13 January 1964, PREM 11/4865, TNA.

the Prime Minister's press office announced that he had 'completely recovered'.[69] The British press chided Indian officials for 'glibly' asserting that Nehru had returned to full health, and thereby clouding the succession issue.[70] In fact, while Nehru continued to recuperate, senior members of his government shrank from taking important decisions, in part, because they had never before been expected to do so, and also because, with the succession question unresolved, they were inclined to keep their political powder dry. As long as Nehru's fate hung in the balance, American officials underlined, 'there will be a prolonged moratorium on decision-making within the Indian Government on a broad range of matters from fertilizers to fighters to factionalism'.[71]

On 22 January, a clearer picture emerged of Nehru's health, when it was announced that Lal Bahadur Shastri would return to the Indian cabinet as minister without portfolio. Shastri's responsibilities encompassed management of the Cabinet Secretariat and the departments of External Affairs and Atomic Energy, all of which Nehru had overseen before his stroke. The first of the 'Kamarajed' former ministers to rejoin the government, the British press feted Shastri as Nehru's heir.[72] Writing in *The Indian Express*, a popular New Delhi newspaper, Prem Bhatia observed with interest that the 'reactions in the West to Mr Shastri's recall to the Cabinet were prompt and so firmly favourable … which goes to show that the future leadership [of India], especially after the Prime Minister's illness, was a matter of genuine concern'.[73] Whitehall's response to the upturn in Shastri's fortunes was more guarded. Within the CRO, Shastri was still seen as something of an unknown quantity. His ministerial career to date had been limited and he lacked international experience, never having travelled outside South Asia. 'So far,' the British concluded in early February, 'he [Shastri] has merely revealed a potential to act as a good chairman with his powerful Ministerial colleagues.'[74]

While agreeing that Shastri's return to the Indian cabinet had made him 'the logical successor to Nehru as prime minister', American officials took an equally measured view of his qualifications for high

---

[69] Bowles to Rusk, 30 January 1964, NSF Country File, India, Box 128, Folder 1, LBJL.

[70] *The Daily Telegraph*, 27 January 1964.

[71] 'An Ailing Nehru and the Indian Leadership', 24 January 1964, CIA-RDP79-00927A004300090002-6, CREST.

[72] See, for example, *The Times*, 21 January 1964; *The Financial Times*, 23 January 1964; *The Guardian*, 23 January 1964; and *The Economist*, 25 January 1964.

[73] *The Indian Express*, 31 January 1964.

[74] 'Mr. Nehru's Health', 5 February 1964, DO 196/311, TNA.

office.[75] On one hand, Shastri had served as a loyal and able understudy to Nehru, appeared appropriately anti-communist and was a moderate when it came to economic and foreign policy. Moreover, after becoming a de facto member of the cabinet leadership committee alongside Nanda and Krishnamachari, he had quickly established himself as the dominant figure within that triumvirate.[76] However, Shastri lacked charisma and his health remained suspect. More seriously still was 'his unproven capacity for decision; in all of his life in politics, he has been someone's number-two man, never number one'. Nevertheless, Washington expected that the fifty-nine-year-old Shastri would prove a 'cautious, pragmatic and moderate' leader, whose views on domestic and international affairs chimed in with the broad consensus of the Congress Party.[77] Indeed, his popularity with Kamaraj and the Congress Party Syndicate was seen as one of Shastri's principal strengths.[78] From his position in the White House, Robert Komer concluded that Shastri was someone with whom the United States could do business. With 'Nehru on his last legs,' Komer counselled Lyndon Johnson, 'the emerging [Indian] leadership, especially Shastri – the heir apparent, looks good from our viewpoint. Now is the time to encourage them.'[79]

In March 1964, the Indian Institute of Public Opinion confirmed that Shastri was the popular choice to become India's next premier.[80] The chief rivals standing between Shastri and the leadership of India now appeared to be Morarji Desai, and Nehru's daughter, Indira Gandhi, who many commentators had begun to tout as a strong outside contender to succeed her father. Desai retained considerable support amongst the conservative wing of the Congress Party but, as the State Department noted, his political star had waned significantly in the subcontinent over the preceding twelve months. 'Should he fight hard and

[75] 'An Ailing Nehru and the Indian Leadership', 24 January 1964, CIA-RDP79-00927A004300090002-6, CREST.

[76] 'Central Intelligence Bulletin', 13 March 1964, CIA-RDP79-T0975A007500380001-7, CREST.

[77] 'An Ailing Nehru and the Indian Leadership', 24 January 1964, CIA-RDP79-00927A004300090002-6, CREST.

[78] Kamaraj's southern Indian origins and lack of fluency in either Hindi or English ruled him out of the succession race. Instead, he focused his formidable energy and considerable political talent on ensuring that Shastri was crowned as Nehru's successor. 'An Ailing Nehru and the Indian Leadership', 24 January 1964, CIA-RDP79-00927A004300090002-6, CREST.

[79] Komer to Johnson, 2 April 1964, NSF, Country File, India, Vol. II, Cables, 4/64–6/64, LBJL.

[80] The poll found that 26.9 per cent of respondents backed Shastri as India's next prime minister. Indira Gandhi and Morarji Desai were favoured by a comparatively paltry 5.9 per cent and 3.5 per cent, respectively. 'After Nehru, Who?', *Public Opinion Surveys of the Indian Institute of Public Opinion*, vol. IX, no. 5, February 1964.

imaginatively for the Prime Ministership he might obtain it,' American officials reasoned, 'but at some risk of splitting the party.' Moreover, with age and infirmity a central issue in the succession debate, although he remained in good health, at nearly sixty-eight years of age, Desai was considered to be 'probably past his peak'.[81]

In contrast, Indira Gandhi's political influence had blossomed as her father's grip on power had faded. A competent political performer in her own right, Gandhi had been an active president of the Congress Party between 1959 and 1960.[82] Although she disclaimed any interest in becoming India's next leader, in January 1964, Gandhi outperformed all other candidates in elections to the Congress Party Working Committee, and was rumoured to be in the running to take charge of India's Ministry of External Affairs.[83] Moreover, from her position as Nehru's nursemaid, appointments secretary and primary political sounding board, she seemed better placed than most inside the Indian government to affect the outcome of the succession process. In a cable sent to Washington on 28 January, Chester Bowles underlined that:

At present, Indira is in a key position. Having assumed a role similar to that of Mrs Woodrow Wilson, to whom she is being compared, she controls access to the PM and is [the] only person who regularly consults him. She is thus in [a] unique position to influence [the] PM on any issue, particularly on personalities. Indira is a person of strong likes and dislikes, is ambitious (regardless of her denials) and is reported to be opposed to attempts to put Shastri clearly in position of heir apparent.[84]

However, Gandhi held no elective office and had no experience inside government. A favourite of the Congress Party's left wing, she was seen by many to lack the broad-based appeal necessary to sustain a

---

[81] 'Morarji Desai', 15 January 1964, RG 59, Records Relating to Indian Political Affairs, 1964–6, Box 5, NARA.

[82] Notably, in 1959, Gandhi played an important role in persuading her father to take the controversial decision to dismiss the democratically elected Communist government in the southern state of Kerala. Robin Jeffrey, 'Jawaharlal Nehru and the Smoking Gun: Who Pulled the Trigger on Kerala's Communist Government in 1959?', *The Journal of Commonwealth and Comparative Politics*, 29 (1991), 72–85.

[83] O'Brien to CRO, 16 January 1964, DO 133/151, TNA.

[84] Bowles to Rusk, 28 January 1964, NSF Country File, India, Box 128, Folder 1, LBJL. To Gandhi's annoyance, she had been widely compared with Edith Bolling Wilson. Dubbed the 'first woman to run the American government', Mrs Wilson had been credited with acting as a de facto head of state for seventeen months after her husband, and 28th president of the United States, Woodrow Wilson, had suffered a debilitating stroke in October 1919. Inder Malhotra, *Indira Gandhi: A Personal Memoir and Political Biography* (London: Hodder & Stoughton, 1989), p. 77; Katherine Frank, *Indira: The Life of Indira Nehru Gandhi* (London: HarperCollins, 2002), p. 271.

challenge for the premiership.[85] Chester Bowles derided her long-term political future, asserting that although she might eventually end up in a future Indian cabinet, Gandhi 'would probably drift out of active politics in a year or two'.[86] Nonetheless, although it appeared unlikely, analysts at the State Department refused to discount an attempt by Congress apparatchiks to shoehorn Gandhi into the premiership, 'in an effort to retain her father's enormous prestige and mass popularity for the Congress Party'.[87] Likewise, the British rationalised that while Gandhi's inexperience would rule her out of contention in a 'normal' succession situation, in an emergency she 'would probably be willing to come forward'.[88]

By the spring of 1964, British and American officials had become exasperated with Nehru's refusal to step down from power and terminate his lame-duck administration. After calling briefly on Nehru in early March, a despondent Chester Bowles reported back to Washington that 'It was quite impossible to communicate with him [Nehru].' 'His mind was simply not in gear ... it is difficult for me to believe that he can last long as effective political force in India.'[89] A British account of a visit that Nehru paid to the All India Institute of Medical Sciences in New Delhi, the following month, made equally sombre reading. India's premier, a British official present recorded, 'looked terribly and pathetically old and absent'. When the Institute's principal expressed the hope that Nehru would continue to lead India for many years to come, the subsequent applause from the audience was 'quite invidiously small', and 'seemed to ... mean "Heaven forbid"'.[90] India's press evidenced similar dissatisfaction with the political lassitude afflicting New Delhi. Writing on 13 March in Calcutta's *Statesman*, Inder Malhotra observed that, at a time when the nation faced serious internal problems and a looming threat from China:

Most Congress MPs express themselves with varying degrees of anger, frustration and bitterness about the state of their party and Government. They acknowledge that they are virtually leaderless. And they lament that this pause

[85] Bowles to Rusk, 14 January 1964, NSF Country File, India, Box 128, Folder 1, LBJL.
[86] Bowles to Rusk, 20 March 1964, NSF Country File, India, Box 128, Folder 1, LBJL.
[87] 'Mrs. Indira Gandhi', 15 January 1964, RG 59, Records Relating to Indian Political Affairs, 1964–6, Box 5, NARA.
[88] 'After Nehru, Who?', J. A G. Banks, 26 November 1962, DO 131/151, TNA.
[89] Bowles to Rusk, 11 March 1964, NSF Country File, India, Box 128, Folder 2, LBJL.
[90] Ambler to Acting High Commissioner, New Delhi, 17 April 1964, DO 133/151, TNA.

in leadership should have occurred at a time when the situation cries out for dynamism and drive.[91]

Malhotra's broadside, the British noted, represented 'the most outspoken attack on the present "malaise" in Delhi yet to appear in an Indian newspaper'.[92] It was far from the last. Throughout the remainder of March and April, a steady clamour grew in the Indian press for Congress to evidence the smack of firm government, and replace Nehru with a new leader. Watching Nehru speak from the press gallery of a crowded Lok Sabha in early April, the influential editor of *The Indian Express*, Frank Moraes, noted in his diary that 'Nehru was pathetic to look at and hear, sitting like a stricken lion in his corner.'[93] In the pages of the following day's *Express*, Moraes implored parliament to act. 'The administrative machinery has begun to creak ominously', Moraes informed his readership. 'Drift is replacing direction.'[94]

Reasoning that Nehru could not go on for much longer, British and American officials turned to consider the impact that India's president, Sarvepalli Radhakrishnan, might have on the succession process. Chester Bowles was minded that, as the first president of India to preside over a change in prime minister, Radhakrishnan was well placed to establish a precedent for the future.[95] The seventy-four-year-old Radhakrishnan had acted as India's president since May 1962, having served as vice-president for the previous decade. A renowned scholar and former Oxford don, he came to the presidency determined to exercise more of the executive power vested in his office than had his predecessor, Rajendra Prasad. In constitutional terms, the Indian president's powers were impressive. He held supreme command of the country's armed forces, could declare a state of emergency, impose central rule in any state of the Indian union and, crucially, summoned and dismissed parliament and appointed prime ministers. Radhakrishnan took the last of these responsibilities extremely seriously and, as the CIA noted, was expected to 'seek to influence the choice of a successor to Nehru, either temporary or permanent, in any way he could'. Moreover, Radhakrishnan was politically conservative, and expected to favour a

---

[91] *The Statesman (Calcutta)*, 13 March 1964.

[92] Goldsmith to Molyneux, 13 March 1964, DO 131/151, TNA.

[93] Frank Moraes Diaries, Entry for 13 April 1964, PP MS 24 Box 2 Folder 12, 'Regent' Diary, Frank Moraes Papers, School of Oriental and African Studies, University of London (hereafter FMP).

[94] *The Indian Express*, 13 April 1964.

[95] Chester Bowles, *Promises to Keep: My Years in Public Life, 1941–1969* (New York: Harper, 1971), p. 578.

centre-right candidate to replace Nehru, or 'at least ... a moderate such as Shastri'.[96]

The British discovered that the vacillation at the heart of India's government had left Radhakrishnan 'deeply depressed'. Back at the end of January, Radhakrishnan had grumbled to Gore-Booth and Sir Olaf Caroe, the British diplomat turned scholar, that at a time when Asia was threatened on all sides by the forces of communism, India had lapsed into a national torpor. 'After we had left the President,' Gore-Booth reported back to Whitehall, 'Olaf Caroe said that what was quite clear to him was that we were watching the decision whether India would remain part of the free world. He added that he thought this was about the most important international issue at present. I agree with the first comment, and do not rush to disagree with the second.'[97] Radhakrishnan subsequently confirmed to Mountbatten that, as the CIA had suspected, he would not hesitate to make full and direct use of his constitutional powers in appointing India's next prime minister. Stating that India's next premier would need to be a moderate, conciliatory figure, acceptable to both the left and right wings of the Congress Party, Radhakrishnan made it clear to Mountbatten that he would 'intervene strongly and if necessary decisively against the candidature of Mrs. Gandhi if it were put forward'.[98] In fact, as the succession struggle approached its climax in the late spring of 1964, Indira Gandhi rejected entreaties from Congress Party officials to throw her hat into the leadership ring. Daunted by her lack of government experience, and emotionally drained by her father's long illness, Gandhi baulked at the prospect of succeeding her father.[99]

---

[96] 'An Ailing Nehru and the Indian Leadership', 24 January 1964, CIA-RDP79-00927A004300090002-6, CREST.

[97] Gore-Booth to Saville Garner, 18 January 1964, DO 133/151, TNA. *The Economist* concurred, arguing that the Congress Party's ability to manage the succession process in a timely and effective manner 'can legitimately be equated with the survival of India as a nation'. *The Economist*, 25 January 1964.

[98] Gore-Booth minute to Deputy High Commissioner, 30 January 1964, DO 133/151, TNA.

[99] One contemporary observer subsequently asserted that in an effort to clarify her leadership aspirations, on 30 May, Shastri approached Gandhi directly and suggested that she should succeed her father, using the words, 'ab app mulk ko sambhal leejiye' (you should now assume responsibility for the country). Gandhi declined, stating that she could not think of contesting the election while still mourning for her father. Srivastava, *Lal Bahadur Shastri*, p. 85. Frank Moraes recorded at the time that confidantes of Gandhi had suggested that she felt it would be 'vulgar' to step immediately into her father's shoes and 'was waiting till three chaps in a row proved their incompetence. Then as a symbol she'd step in.' Frank Moraes Diary Entry for 30 May 1964, PP MS 24 Box 2 Folder 12, 'Regent' Diary, FMP.

On 17 May, Jawaharlal Nehru suffered a second minor stroke while walking with Radhakrishnan in New Delhi's Mogul Gardens.[100] By 22 May, Nehru had recovered sufficiently to give what would be his last press conference. Badgered by journalists for a comment on the succession, Nehru chided his questioners, assuring them, 'My Life is not ending so very soon.'[101] The assembled press corps felt otherwise. An Indian journalist, and long-time admirer of the prime minister, noted privately that Nehru had made for 'A pathetic sight ... It was painful watching him.'[102] Later that day, Nehru left New Delhi to recuperate in the mountain air of Dehra Dun. On arrival, the prime minister found the weather to be cold and gloomy and, by 26 May, he was back at his desk in the capital. Early the following morning, Jawaharlal Nehru's abdominal aorta ruptured. Despite frantic efforts to save his life, at 1.44pm Indian Standard Time, on Wednesday, 27 May 1964, India's premier was declared dead.[103] When the news of Nehru's death was announced in India, the country came to a standstill. Government offices closed and shops pulled own their shutters. In New York, debate in the United Nations Security Council was suspended. Asked to comment on Nehru's passing, a spokesman for the Indian High Commission in London stated simply, 'For us it is like the shattering of the Himalayas.'[104]

In Downing Street, Britain's prime minister, Sir Alec Douglas-Home, decided at once to fly to New Delhi to attend Nehru's funeral. However, with Nehru's cremation scheduled to take place within twenty-four hours, Douglas-Home's decision threw Whitehall into a logistical flap. A BOAC aircraft capable of flying non-stop from London to New Delhi was hurriedly chartered, and Douglas-Home set off for India, accompanied by Lord Mountbatten, representing the Queen, George Brown, deputy leader of the Labour Party, Jivraj Mehta, India's High Commissioner in London, and Gore-Booth.[105] In Washington, Dean Rusk, whom Lyndon Johnson had asked to represent the United States at Nehru's funeral, faced a still greater challenge in reaching New Delhi. Made aware of Rusk's predicament, the Indian government took

---

[100] Brecher, *Succession in India*, p. 30.
[101] 'Mr. Nehru', Delhi to CRO, 22 May 1964, TNA.
[102] Entry 23 May 1964, PP MS 24 Box 2 Folder 12, 'Regent' Diary, FMP.
[103] Frank, *Indira*, p. 274.
[104] *The New York Times*, 28 May 1964.
[105] Gore-Booth had returned from India on leave, and had left London for a family holiday in the West of England. To the British ambassador's embarrassment an RAF helicopter was despatched to fetch him, while the British funeral party kicked their heels for two hours on the tarmac at Heathrow airport. 'Prime Minister's Visit to New Delhi, 27–29 May 1964', PREM 11/4864, TNA.

the unprecedented step of delaying Nehru's funeral ceremony by five hours.[106]

On 28 May, 3 million people stood in ranks up to ten deep as Nehru's funeral cortege wound its way slowly from his official residence in New Delhi, the Teen Murti Bhavan, through the narrow streets of the old city, to a cremation ghat beside the banks of the Jamuna River.[107] Having expected to bear witness to an outpouring of collective angst, many foreign observers were instead struck by the uncharacteristic display of Indian reserve that they encountered. Ronald Belcher informed the CRO that

there were virtually no signs of grief – even the cries that were raised from time to time were thought by many observers to have been led by small groups of individuals and were certainly not prolonged or universal. I am told by those who attended Gandhi's funeral that the contrast in emotional atmosphere was most striking ... Certainly the popular reactions we observed were more suggestive of the loss of an admired – even revered – leader than of one greatly beloved.[108]

The scramble to succeed Nehru continued quite literally over the dead premier's body, turning New Delhi, in the words of one Indian journalist, into a 'snake pit of intrigue'.[109] 'The moment he [Nehru] drew his last breath,' Krishna Menon subsequently recalled, 'the question of succession arose ... One or two people spoke to me about this in the house where he lay dead.'[110] It was not only Indian candidates for the premiership, however, whose thoughts turned to focus on the future rather than the past. Across New Delhi, the high-powered British and American delegations that had descended on the Indian capital for Nehru's funeral were busy attempting to influence the appointment of India's next prime minister.

Within hours of arriving in India on the morning of Nehru's funeral, Douglas-Home and Mountbatten held separate talks with Radhakrishnan at Rashtrapati Bhavan, the Indian president's official residence.[111] The mechanics of the succession process dominated their discussions. Mountbatten in particular, in a throwback to his vice-regal past, interfered shamelessly in India's internal affairs. During the hour that he spent with Radhakrishnan, Mountbatten lobbied for the

[106] Bowles, *Promises to Keep*, pp. 561–2.
[107] Brecher, *Succession in India*, p. 40.
[108] 'India: The Death of Mr. Nehru', 1 June 1964, PREM 11/4864, TNA.
[109] Entry for 1 June 1964, PP MS 24 Box 2 Folder 12, 'Regent' Diary, FMP.
[110] Michael Brecher, *India and World Politics: Krishna Menon's View of the World* (London: Oxford University Press, 1968), p. 215.
[111] 'Prime Minister's Visit to New Delhi, 27–29 May 1964', PREM 11/4864, TNA.

pro-Western Vijaya Lakshmi Pandit to be made minister for external affairs; questioned the Indian president's decision to appoint Gulzarilal Nanda as interim prime minister following Nehru's death; and exhorted Radhakrishnan to do everything in his power to see that Shastri was installed as India's next premier. Mountbatten was pushing against an open door. There was no doubt, Radhakrishnan reassured his guest, that Shastri would 'romp home by a big majority' once the Congress Parliamentary Party had gathered in New Delhi to select a new prime minister. Moreover, given Shastri's relative inexperience, particularly in the realm of foreign affairs, the Indian president felt confident that he would seek out his counsel on important matters, such as government appointments. He had high hopes, Radhakrishnan continued, 'of getting a sensible Government under Shastri and being able to influence him to be statesmanlike'. In the post-Nehru era, Mountbatten was informed, Britain could look forward to 'a new India, more forthcoming and friendly and less difficult'.[112]

Chester Bowles arrived at Rashtrapati Bhavan hot on Mountbatten's heels. Making a 'private call' on Radhakrishnan late on 28 May, Bowles expressed his concern that Shastri's elevation to the premiership remained in the balance.[113] Soothing ruffled American feathers, Radhakrishnan assured Bowles that Shastri enjoyed overwhelming support within the Congress Parliamentary Party. When Congress MPs met to select their next leader, which Radhakrishnan emphasised he had urged Party leaders to do 'very quickly', the Indian president predicted that Shastri would poll some three hundred votes. His nearest rival, Morarji Desai, was likely to receive less than one hundred, with Nanda some way behind that, in third place. A new Indian government under Shastri's leadership and 'more pro-West than ever', Bowles was advised, would be in place within days.[114] Nonetheless, to guard against any last minute surprises, Bowles took the precaution of inserting 'observers' into Shastri's and Desai's campaign teams. Nervous of being caught 'meddling in Indian affairs', the British instead opted to

[112] 'Mountbatten/Radhakrishnan Meeting', 28 May 1964, DO 196/311, TNA. Ronald Belcher warmly applauded Mountbatten's intervention in the succession process, informing the British Chief of Defence Staff that 'Your talk with the President was, as you know, of immense interest and help to us.' Belcher to Mountbatten, 12 June 1964, B1/J402 Lal Bahadur Shastri 1964, MBP.

[113] On 27 May, the State Department's South Asian analysts had advised senior policymakers that while Shastri was 'the obvious frontrunner', his selection as India's next prime minister was 'by no means certain'. Hughes to Acting Secretary, 27 May 1964, RG 59, Records Relating to Indian Political Affairs, 1964–6, Box 5, NARA.

[114] Rusk to Ball and Johnson, 29 May 1964, RG 59, Central Files 1964–6, POL 15-1 INDIA, NARA.

source information on the succession race through contacts inside the Congress Party. To the High Commission's satisfaction, these provided 'a running commentary on the state of play between the rival [leadership] factions'.[115]

On 1 June, as Radhakrishnan had predicted, soundings taken by Kamaraj amongst Congress MPs, cabinet ministers and the chief ministers of India's states, confirmed the strength of Shastri's support, and led Desai and Nanda to withdraw from the leadership contest.[116] The next day, in a display of party unity that had been conspicuously absent over the preceding eighteen months, Nanda proposed and Desai seconded Lal Bahadur Shastri as leader of the Congress Parliamentary Party. Shastri had, a relieved British High Commission reported back to London, been anointed as his nation's new leader, 'after a contest far less disruptive than many people here and abroad had apprehended'.[117] Or, as *The Guardian* observed drolly, 'with more dispatch, and much more dignity, than had the new Prime Minister of Britain'.[118]

### India's Harry Truman

Lal Bahadur Shastri had never met senior British or American government officials before he became India's prime minister. The man who had taken charge of the world's largest democracy was an enigma to all but a handful of middle-ranking British and American officials. Shastri had been bequeathed a host of potentially explosive political problems, from escalating food prices and disquiet over the adoption of Hindi as India's sole official language, to embittered Sino-Indian and Indo-Pakistani relations. Many Western observers drew comparisons between Nehru's passing and that of Franklin Delano Roosevelt, in the United States, almost twenty years earlier. On both occasions an iconic global figure had died in office during a period of national transition, and had been replaced by a relatively unknown figure, in Roosevelt's case, the former senator from Missouri, Harry S. Truman. 'Not many

---

[115] O'Brien to Emery, 2 June 1964, DO 196/311, TNA.
[116] The Soviet government had originally supported Nanda as Nehru's successor, but ordered the KGB residency in New Delhi to do all it could to support Shastri if Nanda's campaign flagged. Moscow's support for Shastri was almost certainly negative rather than positive, and aimed at keeping out Morarji Desai, who Moscow saw as an unconscionable right-wing Hindu extremist. Andrew and Mitrokhin, *KGB and the World*, p. 316.
[117] 'Nehru's Successor', Delhi to CRO, 2 June 1964, PREM 11/4864, TNA. Shastri was officially sworn in as India's prime minister on 9 June 1964.
[118] 'A New Prime Minister for India', *The Guardian*, 3 June 1964.

[people] knew Shastri', one American diplomat stationed in India at the time recalled. 'Who was he? What would he do?'[119]

Chester Bowles, who had had little contact with Shastri before he became prime minister, was immediately taken with India's new leader. 'His diminutive size has tended to underline the impression of a quiet, unassuming, weak, meek man', Bowles informed Dean Rusk. 'However ... I have been impressed with his intellectual qualities, his flexibility of mind and what appears to be an inner strength.'[120] The British High Commission in Delhi largely concurred with Bowles' assessment, noting in early June that Shastri's 'actions and speeches since he stepped forward from Nehru's overpowering shadow have shown an encouraging grasp and self-confidence'.[121] Likewise, having travelled to the subcontinent to interview Shastri that spring, the *Guardian*'s Commonwealth correspondent, Patrick Keatley, found India's new premier to be 'tough but just ... a man who is rock-sure of himself'. India 'needs a strong man', Keatley informed the British public, 'and she has got one'.[122] British and American policymakers did not expect Shastri to deviate significantly from the four pillars of Nehruvian policy: democracy; secularism; a mixed, socialist-orientated economy; and a non-aligned foreign policy. It was deemed likely, however, that he would evidence less of an 'attachment for the USSR and "socialism"' than Nehru and, in the long run, prove more flexible on a range of issues from Kashmir to the role played by private enterprise in the Indian economy.[123] Whereas Nehru had frustrated British and American officials with his 'emotional' and 'impressionistic' manner, Shastri was seen as pragmatic and reasonable.[124] 'I would assume', Bowles informed Washington on 1 June, 'that Shastri's policies would be inherently constructive, strongly anti-communist, internationally as well as domestically suspicious of [the] Soviet Union, desirous of better relations with Pakistan and friendly to us.'[125]

---

[119] Ambassador Brandon H. Grove, Oral History Interview, 14 November 1994, FAOHP.

[120] Bowles to Rusk, No. 3595, 1 June 1964, NSF Country File, India, Box 128, Folder 4, LBJL; Howard B. Schaffer, *Chester Bowles: New Dealer in the Cold War* (Cambridge, MA: Harvard University Press, 1993), pp. 288–90.

[121] 'India after Nehru', 9 June 1964, PREM 11/4864, TNA.

[122] 'A Sparrow's Strength', *The Guardian*, 6 June 1964.

[123] Hughes to Acting Secretary, 27 May 1964, RG 59, Records Relating to Indian Political Affairs, 1964–6, Box 5, NARA.

[124] 'India after Nehru', 9 June 1964, PREM 11/4864, TNA.

[125] Bowles to Rusk, 1 June 1964, NSF Country File, India, Box 128, Folder 4, LBJL.

Given Shastri's inexperience in the field of foreign affairs, Whitehall approached the Commonwealth Prime Ministers' Conference, which was scheduled to take place in London in July 1964, as an ideal opportunity to get to know the 'stranger' at the head of India's government and, more importantly, to influence his global outlook. 'What he [Shastri] learns – and how he learns it – at the Commonwealth Prime Ministers' Meeting', CRO officials suggested, 'will ... be of great importance.'[126] In particular, the British hoped to 'educate' Shastri on the Chinese threat to South East Asia and the principles underpinning London's security and colonial policies.[127] In a precursor of things to come, however, Shastri suffered a mild heart attack on 26 June, which forced him to cancel his trip to London.[128] To the British government's discomfort, when Shastri did make it to England, in December 1964, he proved to be a good deal less impressionable than had been expected. During four days of talks with British ministers, Gore-Booth noted that Shastri took unexpectedly strong positions in a number of key areas. On the colonial question, Shastri espoused 'independence for everyone'. When it came to economic aid, India's new leader admonished Britain for not doing more to help his country, stating baldly that 'our problems are bigger than yours'. Similarly, when discussion turned to Kashmir, Shastri disconcerted his hosts by adopting 'a rather surprisingly orthodox and rigid stand'.[129] For his part, Shastri was equally disappointed to find that the Labour Party's general election victory the previous October had made little impact on Britain's South Asian policy. On his return to New Delhi, the Indian premier confided to Frank Moraes that 'he had a good reception in Britain, but the Socialists had same attitude on Pakistan as the Tories'.[130] In the months ahead, Washington was to find

---

[126] 'India after Nehru', 9 June 1964, PREM 11/4864, TNA.

[127] 'Visit of the Prime Minister of India', 24 November 1964, DO 196/438, TNA.

[128] Given Shastri's clinical history, Western officials were disconcerted that he had been taken ill so soon after assuming power. Writing to Shastri in July, Malcolm MacDonald emphasised that 'The burden on the Indian Prime Minister in these times is appallingly heavy ... I do hope that you will take especially good care of yourself.' MacDonald to Shastri, 20 July 1964, Personal correspondence files from State House 1962–4, 49/4/44, Malcolm MacDonald Papers, Palace Green Library, University of Durham. The CIA noted that Shastri's latest coronary was less serious than his previous attacks, but that he had high blood pressure, was running a fever and had been told by his doctors to take several weeks rest. 'Details on Prime Minister Shastri's Heart Attack', CIA Intelligence Cable, 30 June 1964, Folder 4 India Cables Vol. II 4/64 to 6/64, NSF Country File, India, Box 128, Folder, LBJL.

[129] 'Retrospective Note on Mr. Shastri's Visit by the British High Commissioner in India', 3–6 December 1964, DO 196–438, TNA.

[130] Frank Moraes Diary Entry for 24 December 1964, PP MS 24 Box 2 Folder 12, 'Regent' Diary, FMP.

Shastri just as intractable as the British had found him. To the vexation of British and American policymakers, it would become all too apparent during the course of 1965, that while the characters and leadership styles of India's first and second prime ministers differed markedly, the substance of their politics did not.

# 9    A bumpy ride: Harold Wilson, Lyndon Johnson and South Asia

On a balmy mid-summer night, in June 1965, Britain's prime minister, Harold Wilson, rose to speak before a large audience packed inside London's Royal Festival Hall. Wilson had been invited to inaugurate an exhibition dedicated to the life of Jawaharlal Nehru. Amongst the long list of dignitaries that had gathered on London's South Bank to honour Nehru's memory were his daughter, Indira Gandhi, India's last viceroy, Lord Mountbatten, and the Labour leader who had presided over the transfer of power in India, in 1947, Clement Attlee. Wilson began his address by praising the vision and dynamism that Nehru had shown in transforming modern India into a unitary and secular democracy. To the surprise of many in the crowded auditorium, however, the British premier quickly turned to discuss contemporary political issues. India, and many of her Asian neighbours, Wilson asserted, occupied a position of immense strategic importance between the Western democracies and the totalitarian forces of communism. The British government, he announced, was fully committed to the preservation of the Indian subcontinent's geographical and political integrity. 'Britain's frontiers', Wilson observed memorably, 'are on the Himalayas.' The following morning, British newspapers derided the prime minister's rhetoric as overblown and 'Kiplingesque'. India's press was equally unimpressed by what they interpreted as an unwelcome and unsolicited attempt by Wilson to revive the *Pax Britannica*.[1] From across the political spectrum, the Festival Hall speech drew censure as ill conceived and out of touch with the economic and geopolitical realities governing Anglo-Indian affairs. Indeed, for the remainder of his premiership, Wilson's South Asia policy was to come under repeated fire from critics at home and abroad, as his Labour government struggled to redefine Britain post-imperial relationships with India and Pakistan.

Harold Wilson arrived in Downing Street on 16 October 1964, having narrowly defeated Alec Douglas-Home's incumbent Conservative

---

[1] 'Premier Pledges Support for India', *The Guardian*, 11 June 1965.

270

administration in that year's British general election. The Labour Party's election campaign portrayed the contest between the Labour and Conservative parties as a straight choice between a youthful, egalitarian and purportedly forward-thinking Wilson, and an aristocratic and anachronistic Conservative alternative, led by the former 14th Earl of Home. Wilson had launched his bid for power the previous January before an audience of Labour voters in Birmingham's Town Hall. The coming year, Wilson had announced, would bring 'A chance for change ... A chance to sweep away the grouse-moor conception of Tory leadership and refit Britain with a new image, a new confidence.'[2] In the event, after Douglas-Home fought a dogged and surprisingly adroit campaign, Wilson squeaked home with a parliamentary majority of five seats. At forty-eight years of age, Harold Wilson earned the distinction of becoming the youngest British prime minister to hold office since the Earl of Rosebery, back in the 1890s.

Wilson had been born into a lower-middle-class household in Huddersfield, West Yorkshire, during the First World War. Something of a child prodigy, Wilson's considerable academic talent was matched by a formidable work ethic. At the age of just twenty-one, the future prime minister became one of the twentieth century's youngest ever dons at Oxford University. Elected to parliament in the Labour landslide of 1945, Wilson went on to serve as President of the Board of Trade in the first Attlee government. One of only three Labour ministers in 1964 able to draw upon previous cabinet experience, Wilson had assumed leadership of his party the previous February, following the untimely death of Hugh Gaitskell. Respected rather than loved by the majority of the Parliamentary Labour Party (PLP), Wilson was admired for his formidable intelligence, extraordinary memory, quick wit and industry. Equally, once in power he quickly acquired a well-deserved reputation for deviousness, and was commonly regarded as a pragmatist, devoid of firm political convictions, and prone to crippling bouts of indecision.[3] The Labour politician and journalist John Freeman, who Wilson would

---

[2] Harold Wilson, *The New Britain: Labour's Plan: Selected Speeches 1964* (London: Harmondsworth, 1964), p. 10.

[3] For insights into Wilson's politics and personality, see in particular Ben Pimlott, *Wilson* (London: HarperCollins, 1992); Philip Ziegler, *Wilson: The Authorised Life* (London: Weidenfeld and Nicolson, 1993); Tony Benn, *Out of the Wilderness: Diaries 1963–67* (London: Hutchinson, 1987); Barbara Castle, *The Castle Diaries, 1964–1976* (London: Weidenfeld and Nicolson, 1980); Frank Pakenham Longford, *The Grain of Wheat: An Autobiography* (London: Collins, 1974) and *Eleven at Number Ten: A Personal View of Prime Ministers, 1931–1984* (London: Harrap, 1984); and Richard Crossman, *The Diaries of a Cabinet Minister*, vol. 1: *Minister of Housing 1964–66* (London: Jonathan Cape, 1975).

later appoint as Britain's High Commissioner to India, observed retro-spectively that 'If there were a word "aprincipled", as there is "amoral", it would describe Wilson perfectly.'[4] Predictably, some right-wing commentators offered more biting criticisms of Wilson's elastic polit-ical principles and apparently endless capacity for reinvention. In June 1964, shortly before his electoral triumph, the *Daily Mail* columnist Walter Terry observed acidly that he had identified at least 'ten faces of Harold': 'American Harold', 'Dynamic Harold', 'Basic Harold', 'Huddersfield Harold', 'Nationalize 'em Harold', 'Orthodox Harold', 'Intelligentsia Harold', 'Little Englander Harold', 'Capitalist Harold' and 'Russian Harold'.[5] Even this number, some wags in the Labour Party noted, was probably an underestimate.[6]

## 'We are a world power ... or we are nothing': Harold Wilson and South Asia

In the international sphere, Wilson arrived in office determined to arrest the seemingly inexorable post-war decline in Britain's global standing. In his first Guildhall speech, on 16 November 1964, Wilson declared grandiosely that 'if there is one nation that cannot afford to chalk on the walls: "World go home", it is Britain. We are a world power, and a world influence, or we are nothing.'[7] Above all else, Wilson resolved that his government would provide strong leadership to a reinvigorated Commonwealth and cement Britain's place as the United States' fore-most ally. These two central strands of Wilson's worldview, although increasingly difficult to harmonise as the decade wore on, remained the bedrocks of the Labour government's foreign policy throughout the 1960s. Moreover, it is significant that while seeking to deliver his ambi-tious international agenda, Wilson faced constant pressure from the Treasury to trim Britain's costly overseas commitments. From the day Wilson entered 10 Downing Street, until the devaluation of sterling, in November 1967, the Labour government was battered by a succession of monetary storms. The nation's economic fragility imposed increas-ing constraints upon Britain's ability to play a world role, and compli-cated the Wilson administration's relations with other nation states.[8] In

[4] Freeman interview with Philip Ziegler, cited in Ziegler, *Wilson*, p. 43.
[5] *The Daily Mail*, 19 June 1964.
[6] Dominic Sandbrook, *White Heat: A History of Britain in the Swinging Sixties* (London: Little Brown, 2006), p. 26.
[7] 'Mr. Wilson Denounces All Racial Prejudice', *The Times*, 17 November 1964.
[8] Interview with Sir Michael Palliser, 28 April 1999, Diplomatic Oral History Programme, Churchill College Cambridge.

particular, the correlation between Washington's willingness to prop up sterling and the substance of Wilson's foreign policy, although never as straightforward as some have suggested, would become increasingly apparent as Anglo-American tensions over the Vietnam War and Britain's military presence East of Suez, came to the fore later in the decade.[9]

On a personal level, Harold Wilson retained a sentimental attachment to the Commonwealth. Family connections in Australia provided the young Wilson with an early emotional connection to Britain's former Empire. It was the Commonwealth's capacity to place post-imperial Britain at the head of a global transnational network, however, which appealed to the politician in Wilson. Leadership of the Commonwealth, in his view, helped Britain to punch above its weight in the world. In May 1963, in an address to Labour Party activists in the north of England, Wilson called for greater investment in Commonwealth trade, cultural and scientific exchange, and social programmes. The 1964 Labour Party manifesto, *Let's Go with Labour for a New Britain*, underlined Wilson's determination to strengthen Commonwealth bonds.[10] The Labour leader's commitment to the Commonwealth continued after his arrival in Downing Street. In June 1966, when defending the need for a British military presence in the Indian Ocean, Wilson insisted to sceptics in the PLP that Britain and the Commonwealth remained important players on the international stage:

Is it really said that we have nothing to contribute except speeches that no one will listen to? I believe that Britain through history, through geography and Commonwealth connexion has a vital contribution to make – I believe a socialist Britain has even more. Perhaps there are some members who would like to contract out and leave it to the Americans and the Chinese, eyeball to eyeball,

[9] Much has been made of the Johnson administration's use of economic leverage over Britain to influence Wilson's foreign policy. Notably, Clive Ponting, *Breach of Promise: Labour in Power 1964–1970* (London: Hamish Hamilton, 1989) has contended that the Labour government compromised Britain's sovereignty in return for American guarantees of economic support. Others, including Pimlott, *Wilson*, John Dumbrell, *A Special Relationship: Anglo-American Relations in the Cold War and After* (Basingstoke: Palgrave Macmillan, 2000), and Diane Kunz, '"Somewhat Mixed up Together": Anglo-American Defence and Financial Policy during the 1960s', *Journal of Imperial and Commonwealth History*, 27, 2 (1999), 213–32, have, in the main, been more charitable to Wilson's government. The current balance of opinion maintains that in their financial negotiations with Washington, Wilson and his ministers played a weak hand with considerable skill, and invariably accepted American 'demands' only when they advanced London's own policy agenda.

[10] John W. Young, *The Labour Governments 1964–1970*, vol. 2: *International Policy* (Manchester University Press, 2003), p. 10.

to face this thing. The World is too small for that kind of attitude today. It is the surest prescription for a nuclear holocaust I could think of.[11]

In India, the Labour Party's return to power, in October 1964, was broadly welcomed by the ruling Congress Party. Labour's socialist outlook, and long association with India's fight for independence, sat more comfortably with many senior Congress figures than the Conservative Party's affinity for private enterprise, and 'regressive' attitude toward India prior to 1947. Writing to Wilson, on 17 October 1964, India's president, Sarvepalli Radhakrishnan, expressed satisfaction at Labour's election victory. 'We remember with gratitude that we got independence under the first Labour Government after the war', Radhakrishnan observed. 'I have no doubt that under your enlightened leadership our relations will get stronger.'[12] In response, Wilson assured India's president that his government would 'do all in its power to develop the closest possible relations with India and indeed to promote the whole Commonwealth concept as did our predecessors under Lord Attlee'.[13]

Other prominent Indians, including the prime minister, Lal Bahadur Shastri, were less convinced that a change in government in Britain offered much cause for celebration. The prospect that a Labour government would adopt a more enlightened approach to colonialism than its predecessor was offset in many Indian minds by a suspicion that Wilson would develop Britain's ties with the People's Republic of China (PRC). In opposition, the Labour Party's record on Communist China was mixed. Wilson had supported calls for the PRC's admission to the United Nations. He had also loudly condemned Beijing as the aggressor during the border war of late 1962.[14] Moreover, Labour appeared at one with the Conservative Party on the issue of Kashmir.[15] In Pakistan,

---

[11] 'Mr. Wilson Puts Case on Britain's Defence Role', *The Times*, 16 June 1966.
[12] Radhakrishnan to Wilson, 17 October 1964, PREM 13/973, The United Kingdom National Archives, Kew, London (hereafter TNA).
[13] Wilson to Radhakrishnan, 23 December 1964, PREM 13/973, TNA.
[14] Thomas L. Hughes to George Ball, 4 December 1964, NSF, Robert W. Komer Files, Box 53, Folder United Kingdom Jan 1964–Mar 1966 [2 of 2], Lyndon Baines Johnson Library, Austin, Texas (hereafter LBJL). Tony Benn, whose family had a long association with India, and who Wilson had appointed Post-Master General in October 1964, was taken aback by the strength of India's animus toward Communist China. Having met with India's minister for parliamentary affairs and communications in London in June 1965, Benn was disconcerted to find that when it came to China, his Indian guest appeared 'indistinguishable from John Foster Dulles speaking about Stalin at the height of the Cold War ... [and] was unwilling to contemplate any policy but international isolation for China'. Diary Entry for 21 June 1965, Benn, *Diaries 1963–67*, p. 277.
[15] Entry for 24 December 1964, PP MS 24 Box 2 Folder 12, 'Regent' Diary, Frank Moraes Papers, School of Oriental and African Studies, London (hereafter FMP).

Ayub Khan expressed reservations over the emphasis that Wilson had given to revitalising Britain's role in Asia. 'One does get the impression', Pakistan's president observed in February 1965, 'that the British want to re-establish ... imperialism, and are now having second thoughts on giving up on this part of the world, and want to come back rather heavy-footed.'[16]

Members of Wilson's own party acknowledged that India's and Pakistan's perceptions of Britain's international significance had shifted in parallel with the nation's post-war decline. In the subcontinent, Britain remained a significant player. British investments in India and Pakistan, which ranged from tea companies, such as James Finlay and McLeod Russell, to oil, chemical and manufacturing concerns, owned by Burmah Shell, ICI and Dunlop, were conservatively valued at £420 million. The United Kingdom remained the biggest single foreign investor in India, although Britain's traditional dominance of the Indian commercial market was under increasing challenge from countries such as West Germany, Japan and the United States.[17] Yet, Britain's healthy financial position in India and Pakistan could not disguise the reality that Wilson's administration governed under the shadow of an 'economic thundercloud'.[18] Saddled with a crippling balance of payments deficit, an embattled currency, and depressed growth and trade figures, Wilson's first Chancellor of the Exchequer, James Callaghan, cut government spending, raised taxes, and pressed for domestic and overseas economies. Having attended a reception at India House to celebrate Republic Day, the rising star of Labour's left wing Tony Benn recorded in his diary that 'The new [Indian] High Commissioner is Mr Mehta. He is a very old man and it rather suggests that the Indian government does not think that the London post matters very much.'[19]

In contrast, Wilson attached considerable importance to Anglo-Indian relations, a fact reflected in his decision to appoint a high-profile political ally, John Freeman, to replace a professional diplomat, Sir Paul

---

[16] Ayub Khan interview with British Correspondent, President's House, Rawalpindi, 6 February 1965, in Nadia Ghani (ed.), *Field Marshal Mohammad Ayub Khan; A Selection of Talks and Interviews, 1964–1967* (Karachi: Oxford University Press, 2010) p. 32.

[17] At the end of 1963, Britain accounted for 62.1 per cent of foreign investment in India, the United States 13.3 per cent, West Germany 2.5 per cent, Switzerland 1.6 per cent and Japan 0.7 per cent. Between 1962 and 1965, however, according to Indian government figures, British investment in India had grown by a paltry 7 per cent, while West Germany's had doubled, Japan's had increased by 80 per cent and the United States' by 30 per cent. *The Economist*, 11 September 1965.

[18] Michael Palliser, 'Foreign Policy', in Michael Parsons (ed.), *Looking Back: The Wilson Years* (The University of Pau Press, 1999), p. 23.

[19] Diary entry for 27 January 1964, Benn, *Diaries 1963–67*, p. 91.

Gore-Booth, as Britain's High Commissioner in New Delhi. A former Labour Member of Parliament, in 1951 Freeman had joined Wilson and Aneurin Bevan in resigning from the Attlee government, after minor charges were imposed on some National Health Service treatments to offset the financial demands of rearmament occasioned by the Korean War. In the mid-1950s, Freeman left parliament and carved out a successful career in political journalism, becoming editor of the left-of-centre weekly *New Statesman*. Wilson's offer of the High Commission in New Delhi took Freeman completely by surprise. Given just forty-eight hours to respond to the prime minister's invitation to become HMG's representative in India, Freeman accepted on the basis that, with Anglo-Indian relations in the midst of a transitional phase, the posting was likely to prove both interesting and challenging.[20] Indeed, Wilson left the new High Commissioner designate with the impression that he considered Britain's relations with India to be far too important to be left in the hands of officials from the Commonwealth Relations Office.[21] Members of the British establishment with close links to India, such as Lord Mountbatten, generally welcomed Freeman's appointment. Mountbatten regarded it as 'extremely fortunate' that a High Commissioner with such 'exceptional qualifications and connections' should represent Britain's interests in India.[22] For his part, America's ambassador in India, Chester Bowles, grumbled that unlike his own troubled relationship with the White House, the 'able new British Hi[gh] Com[missioner] John Freeman ... [enjoyed] significant personal influence' inside 10 Downing Street.[23]

### Harold Wilson, Lyndon Johnson and Anglo-American relations

The second pillar of Wilson's foreign policy centred upon the Anglo-American 'special' relationship, which toward the end of Harold Macmillan's embattled administration had come under considerable strain. Although no apologist for US foreign policy, Wilson was an Atlanticist at heart. He had first visited the United States in 1943,

---

[20] Peter Hall, DOHP 89, British Diplomatic Oral History Programme, Churchill College Cambridge.
[21] Ziegler, *Wilson*, p. 220.
[22] Mountbatten to Freeman, 7 May 1965, MB1/J507 Visit to India, May 1965, Lord Mountbatten Papers, Hartley Library, University of Southampton (hereafter MBP).
[23] Bowles to Rusk, No. 410, 28 August 1965, National Security File (NSF) Country File, India, Box 129 [2 of 2], Folder 2 India Cables [2 of 3], Vol. V, 6-65 to 9-65, LBJL.

as a wartime civil servant. The dynamism, technical innovation and military-industrial power that he encountered in the New World, left a deep impression on Wilson. In the 1950s, he watched with interest as the ascendancy of a conservative and increasingly moribund administration in the United States was eroded, and eventually eclipsed, by a young and charismatic leader espousing lofty promises of national renewal. Wilson's 1964 election campaign aped John F. Kennedy's 1960 presidential run in style and substance. In March 1964, in one interview, Wilson lauded Kennedy as a visionary who had brought much needed drive and intellectual rigour into the Oval Office. The Kennedy administration had taken the crucial step, Wilson argued, of shifting 'the whole [political] idea to a younger generation'.[24] With the encouragement of Tony Benn, whose earlier incarnation as a BBC producer saw him installed as Labour's chief media strategist, Wilson's 'New Britain' campaign drew brazenly upon Kennedy's 'New Frontier' rhetoric.[25]

Once in office, Wilson's political flexibility came to the fore, and the British premier promptly rebranded himself in Lyndon Johnson's image. During a press conference toward the end of 1964, Wilson announced shamelessly, 'I'm not a Kennedy. I'm a Johnson. I fly by the seat of my pants.'[26] In Wilson's case, although imitation represented perhaps the least sincere form of flattery, the British prime minister's ambitious international agenda demanded that he cultivate Kennedy's successor. The previous May, over dinner with journalists from *The Guardian*, at London's Connaught Hotel, Wilson had expressed breezy confidence that he would be able to 'establish a much more informal relationship with the American President ... [and] telephone and fly over as and when necessary, without the usual fuss of top-level meetings'.[27] Following talks with Johnson, in Washington in December 1965, Wilson provided his cabinet with an exuberant account of the close personal rapport that he had struck up with his Texan coucounterpart. Barbara Castle, Labour's minister for overseas development, noted how Wilson had come back from America 'full of beans'. 'Harold couldn't resist [informing the cabinet]', Castle recorded in her private journal, 'that he'd been asked to illuminate the [White House] Christmas tree: "the first time a PM has been asked to do this with the President since Churchill did it

[24] Pimlott, *Wilson*, pp. 283–4.
[25] Entry for 3 December 1963, Benn, *Diaries 1963–67*, pp. 80–1; Entry for 29 October 1964, Crossman, *Minister of Housing 1964–66*, p. 36.
[26] Christopher Brooker, *The Neophiliacs: The Revolution in English Life in the Fifties and Sixties* (London: Pimlico, 1992), p. 252.
[27] Entry for 5 May 1964, Benn, *Diaries 1963–67*, p. 108.

in 1943".'[28] Other Labour ministers reacted with a good deal of scepticism to Wilson's claims that a new and more constructive phase in Anglo-American relations was about to dawn. Toward the end of 1964, an incredulous Richard Crossman struggled not to laugh out loud as Wilson recounted to his cabinet how Johnson welcomed 'our new constructive ideas after an epoch of sterility' and had earnestly remarked upon 'the help which we had given him during the election and all that Harold Wilson's speeches had meant for him'. Wilson's performance, Crossman noted in his diary that evening, had been 'extremely funny, but I fear the humour was entirely unconscious'.[29]

The Johnson administration's reaction to Harold Wilson was less effusive. In advance of Wilson's arrival in Washington, in December 1964, a biographical sketch prepared by the State Department characterised the British premier as a 'loner' and a 'cold fish' with few close friends. Blessed with a 'brilliant mind, organizational ability ... and unusual political acumen', Wilson was also regarded, American officials noted, as 'a scheming opportunist and an egocentric'. 'He might best be summed up', one senior State Department figure suggested dryly, 'as a consummate politician.' Set alongside Lyndon Johnson's gregarious and outsized personality, Wilson appeared a colourless character.[30] On the face of things, the two leaders had little in common. Johnson's own view of Wilson may well have been influenced by the latter's reputation for duplicity. Moreover, the director of the Federal Bureau of Investigation, J. Edgar Hoover, warned the president that the British leader's alleged extra-marital affair with his political secretary, Marcia Williams, constituted a potential security risk. Although they enjoyed a healthy and workmanlike relationship, Wilson's mendacity and inveterate sponging undoubtedly irritated the American president.[31] 'I suppose', Johnson remarked on one occasion on being informed that Wilson had called a general election, 'I'll have that little creep camping on my doorstep again!'[32] George Ball, Johnson's Under Secretary of State, observed some years later that 'Harold Wilson ... was too ordinary, too much like other politicians with whom LBJ had dealt, and

[28] Entry for 21 December 1965, Castle, *Diaries, 1964–1976*, p. 37.
[29] Entry for 11 December 1964, Crossman, *Minister of Housing 1964–66*, p. 94.
[30] 'Visit of Prime Minister Wilson Dec. 1964 Briefing Book', December 1964, RG 59, Conference Files 1949–63, Lot file 60D110, CF 2461, Box 364, National Archives and Records Administration, College Park, Maryland (hereafter NARA); Hughes to Ball, 8 October 1964, NSF, Robert W. Komer Files, Box 53, Folder United Kingdom Jan 1964–Mar 1966 [2 of 2], LBJL.
[31] Young, *Labour Governments*, vol. 2, p. 21.
[32] Cited in Ziegler, *Wilson*, p. 324.

Johnson took an almost instant dislike to him.'[33] While Ball's verdict on Johnson's relationship with Wilson can be discounted as overly harsh, it is clear that the British premier's standing within the Oval Office was not nearly as high as he would have liked, or claimed to be the case.

In more general terms, the Johnson administration greeted Labour's return to power in the United Kingdom with relative indifference. Shortly before the October 1964 election, Thomas L. Hughes, the State Department's Director of Intelligence and Research, emphasised that although a Wilson government could be expected to place practical considerations ahead of party political dogma, and nurture 'the closest possible relations' with the United States, its views on a range of issues, from trade with Cuba to Communist China's admission to the UN, remained at odds with American policy.[34] Likewise, when it came to South Asia, Johnson did not share Wilson's view about the strategic importance of the Indian subcontinent. Having been propelled unexpectedly into the Oval Office following the assassination of John F. Kennedy, in November 1963, Johnson was confronted by a host of pressing domestic and foreign policy issues. Tying up the loose ends left over from Kennedy's interventions in South Asia was just one task on a long list of pressing problems that landed on Johnson's desk. Moreover, given the new president's resolve to carve out a political legacy at home rather than abroad, and the advent of more troublesome developments elsewhere in Asia, the affairs of the Indian subcontinent quickly slipped to the bottom of Johnson's to-do list.

### Lyndon Johnson and South Asia

To American officials who had spent the previous three years building up the United States' relationship with India in the face of bitter opposition from Pakistan and antipathy on Capitol Hill, it appeared possible that Lyndon Johnson would halt, or even reverse, the process of Indo-US rapprochement begun by President Eisenhower. Uncertain of Johnson's position in relation to India and Pakistan, Robert Komer, the NSC's resident South Asian expert, recalled that the then vice-president had warmed to Pakistan's president, Ayub Khan, during his visit to the subcontinent, in May 1961. The understanding between Pakistan's president and Johnson was much in evidence when the former travelled

---

[33] George Ball, *The Past Has Another Pattern: Memoirs* (New York: W.W. Norton & Company, 1982), p. 336.

[34] Hughes to Ball, 8 October 1964, NSF, Robert W. Komer Files, Box 53, Folder United Kingdom Jan 1964–Mar 1966 [2 of 2], LBJL.

to the United States later that year. Subjected to the full Johnsonian treatment, Ayub Khan was whisked off to Texas by the vice-president, conducted on a guided tour of Austin and San Antonio, and feted at a sumptuous barbecue held on Johnson's palatial ranch in the Lone Star State's rugged hill country. 'Why is it', Johnson remarked subsequently to one State Department official, 'that Jack Kennedy and you India lovers in the State Department are so Godammed ornery on my friend Ayub?'[35]

On 23 November 1963, Johnson's first full day in office, Komer voiced concern to his boss, McGeorge Bundy, that the US government might now shift back to become 'more pro-Pak[istan]'. Pakistan's leaders, Komer observed, had taken great heart from Johnson's elevation to the presidency. India's ambassador in Washington, B. K. Nehru, on the other hand, was reported to be 'exceedingly nervous'.[36] On a personal level, at least, Nehru's fears proved to be well founded. A frequent visitor to the Kennedy White House, the Indian ambassador's access to senior US policymakers dried up after November 1963. Sixteen months after Kennedy's death, Dean Rusk reminded Johnson that Nehru had 'not had a substantive talk with you since your assumption of the Presidency'.[37] The wider message that political observers drew from Nehru's spectacular fall from diplomatic grace troubled some of Johnson's advisers. 'More than most Ambassadors,' McGeorge Bundy wrote to the president, on 16 March 1965, 'Nehru is a man of vanity ... He feels you are not much interested in India or him, and hints of his feelings have gone back to India, where our Embassy has picked them up.' Revealingly, Bundy's memorandum was returned by Johnson with the terse rejoinder, 'No use ... my seeing him [Nehru] if he feels this way.'[38]

In a bid to head off a reversal in America's South Asian policy, Komer pressed Johnson to find space in his crowded schedule to meet with Chester Bowles. By helping to reiterate the central position that India had occupied in American strategic planning in Asia since the late

---

[35]  Robert W. Komer, Oral History, pp. 68–9, LBJL.
[36]  Komer to McGeorge Bundy, 23 November 1963, NSF, National Security Council History of South Asia, LBJL. Pakistan's High Commissioner to the United Kingdom, Aghampuakha Hilaly, confirmed to British officials that he expected Pakistan's relations with the United States to be much better under Johnson, 'who had already shown his understanding of Pakistan and there was much good will towards him'. Saville Garner to Cyril Pickard, 9 December 1963, DO 196/107, TNA.
[37]  Rusk to Johnson, 15 March 1965, NSF Country File, India, Box 129 [1 of 2], Folder 3 Memos & Misc. Vol. IV, 12-64 to 6-65, LBJL.
[38]  McGeorge Bundy to Johnson, 16 March 1965, NSF Country File, India, Box 129 [1 of 2], Folder 3 Memos & Misc. Vol. IV, 12-64 to 6-65, LBJL.

1950s, Komer hoped that Bowles, who had returned to Washington to negotiate the terms of a military aid package for New Delhi, would be able 'to get the new President ... firmly signed on to our Indian enterprise'.[39] Johnson's refusal to meet with Bowles left a gloomy Komer pondering whether much of the ground that the United States had gained in India since Eisenhower's second term might eventually be lost under its current leader. Indeed, unlike his predecessor in India, for the remainder of Johnson's presidency Bowles increasingly struggled to make his voice heard in the White House, or indeed, in New Delhi. Irritated by his ambassador's habitual and verbose sermons on the wisdom of supplying India with ever-greater amounts of US economic and military aid, Johnson ensured that their personal interaction was kept to a minimum.

In July 1965, when Bowles returned to Washington, Johnson made it clear to White House staff that 'he didn't want to see Bowles'. Concerned that Bowles risked becoming a lame duck in New Delhi, Robert Komer was reduced to pleading with McGeorge Bundy to arrange a face-saving meeting between the president and his ambassador. 'I know how much of a nuisance seeing Chet must seem to LBJ,' Komer argued, 'but the hard fact is that Chet's credibility would go way down if LBJ didn't see him.'[40] Within a year, however, even former allies such as Komer had begun to tire of Bowles' hectoring. 'Chet is back [in Washington] full of piss and vinegar,' Komer advised Johnson, in March 1966, 'and eager to tell you how to handle our Indian affairs.'[41] The anxiety felt by some senior US officials over Bowles' value as an advocate for closer Indo-US relations acquired added piquancy as question marks emerged over his health and political judgement. In November 1964, Bowles underwent an experimental brain procedure at a New York hospital to alleviate a growing paralysis occasioned by the onset of Parkinson's disease. Although seemingly successful, in the aftermath of Bowles' operation doubts increased in Washington over his effectiveness in New Delhi.[42] Many Indians felt likewise. During one lunchtime encounter with Bowles, Frank Moraes sat stunned as the US ambassador outlined a 'madcap' and 'crazy scheme' to accompany Indian newspaper editors

---

[39] Komer to McGeorge Bundy, 23 November 1963, NSF, Box 433, John F. Kennedy Library, Boston, Massachusetts (hereafter JFKL).
[40] Komer to McGeorge Bundy, 26 July 1965, NSF, Robert W. Komer Files, Box 13, Folder 1 Bowles 11-3-63-1965 [1 of 4], LBJL.
[41] Komer to LBJ, 23 March 1966, NSF Country File, India, Box 133, Folder 3 Prime Minister Gandhi Visit Papers [2 of 2] 3-27-30-66, LBJL.
[42] Komer to Johnson, 16 June 1965, NSF, Robert W. Komer Files, Box 13, Folder 1 Bowles 11-3-63-1965 [1 of 4], LBJL.

on a tour of South East Asia and illustrate first-hand the menace posed by communist subversion.[43] By the latter half of the 1960s, the State Department acknowledged that Indian government officials had simply 'stopped listening' to Bowles' well-worn and increasingly eccentric utterances.[44]

More encouragingly for disciples of Kennedy's South Asian policy, such as Robert Komer, Lyndon Johnson did offer some evidence early in his presidency that his ambivalence toward the subcontinent might cut both ways. Notably, Johnson seized the opportunity afforded by Zulfikar Ali Bhutto's presence at Kennedy's funeral, in November 1963, to excoriate Pakistan's foreign minister for his country's ongoing flirtation with Communist China.[45] Born into a wealthy and politically prominent family in the southern Pakistani province of Sind, Bhutto studied law at the universities of Oxford and California at Berkeley. A fiery orator with a penchant for expensive Western suits, in his youth the Pakistani minister spent a considerable amount of time in the United States. In 1950, Bhutto had cut his political teeth working on the campaign team of Helen Gahagan Douglas in her bitter contest against Richard Nixon for one of California's Senate seats. An admirer of Genghis Khan, Napoleon Bonaparte and Mao Zedong, Bhutto's critics chided that he was cut from much the same cloth as his ruthless and Machiavellian heroes.[46]

Bhutto had first come to international prominence in 1958, when he was appointed Pakistan's minister of commerce and became the youngest cabinet minister in the country's history. On the death of Muhammed Ali Bogra, in January 1963, Ayub Khan elevated Bhutto to the post of foreign minister. An ambitious and divisive figure, Bhutto was widely distrusted by policymakers, inside and outside Pakistan. In particular, Bhutto's promotion of closer Sino-Pakistani ties appeared to many British and American officials as a cynical and populist ploy designed to bolster his domestic political standing.[47] Australia's foreign minister, Paul Hasluck, who professed an 'intense' dislike for Bhutto,

[43] Entry for 13 July 1964, PP MS 24 Box 2 Folder 12, 'Regent' Diary, FMP.

[44] Howard Wriggins to Walt Rostow, 'Thoughts on India/Pakistan', 24 July 1967, NSF, Country File, Pakistan, Box 153, Folder 2, Pakistan Memos [1 of 2], Vol. VII, 10-66 to 7-67, LBJL.

[45] Note by Sir James Plimsoll (Australian High Commission, New Delhi) on talk with Chester Bowles, 6 December 1963, DO 196/156, TNA.

[46] 'Fact Sheet: Visit of Prime Minister Bhutto', 14 September 1973, Box 935 Folder 2, Pakistan Visit of Pres. Bhutto Sept 18 1973 [2 of 3], Richard Nixon Presidential Library and Museum, Yorba Linda, California.

[47] Morrice James, *Pakistan Chronicle* (London: Hurst, 1992), p. 110; Ball, *The Past Has Another Pattern*, pp. 282 and 315.

went as far as to label the Pakistani minister, 'pretty well a communist after the Chinese pattern'.[48]

Back in the autumn of 1963, having left Bhutto to kick his heels in Washington for four days before agreeing to meet with him, an exercised Johnson proceeded to leave the startled foreign minister in no doubt that he took an exceedingly dim view of Pakistan's ongoing flirtation with China. The US government, Bhutto was informed tartly, had been bitterly disappointed by the invitation to visit Pakistan extended by Ayub Khan to China's premier, Zhou Enlai. 'The strongest men in Congress in favour of Pakistan', Johnson pointedly reminded Bhutto, 'are also the strongest against the Chinese Communists.'[49] For all Johnson's bluster, however, he remained committed to preserving the US-Pakistani alliance. Rawalpindi's dissatisfaction with the United States, the new president rationalised privately, could in large part be attributed to American negligence in 'not giving him [Ayub Khan] a feeling of confidence in our motives', which, in turn, had encouraged 'the thought that we would abandon him in favor of India'. This misapprehension, Johnson instructed McGeorge Bundy, on 30 November 1963, 'he wished ... corrected in a most positive manner'.[50]

The following month, Johnson underlined his intention to adopt a new and more conciliatory approach to Pakistan. In early December, the foreign policy team that he had inherited from Kennedy urged Johnson to authorise a five-year military assistance programme for India, worth between $250 and $300 million. Failure to inject further substance into the support that the United States had offered to India following its clash with China, Johnson was advised, risked alienating New Delhi and encouraging the Indian government to expand its military relationship with the Soviets. Mindful of the outcry that would ensue in Pakistan were he to approve such a course of action, Johnson ignored his advisers, and instead deferred taking a decision on Indian military aid, pending the results of upcoming talks between General

[48] Diary entry for Monday, 14 June 1965, GBR/0014/HALY/15/3, 'Times' Diaries, Sir William John Haley Papers, Churchill Archives Centre, Churchill College Cambridge.

[49] Rusk to McConaughy, 2 December 1963, *Foreign Relations of the United States* (hereafter *FRUS*), *1961–1963*, vol. XIX (Washington, DC: Government Printing Office, 1996), pp. 694–6. George Ball recalled that as he left the Oval Office after meeting with Johnson, Bhutto 'turned on me furiously' to complain bitterly about the dressing down that he had received. Ball, *The Past Has Another Pattern*, p. 314.

[50] Johnson meeting with John McCone and McGeorge Bundy, Washington, 30 November 1963, *FRUS, 1961–1963*, vol. XIX, p. 693.

Maxwell Taylor, chairman of the Joint Chiefs of Staff, and Indian and Pakistani leaders.[51]

## Britain, the United States and the defence of South Asia

On succeeding Jawaharlal Nehru, India's second prime minister, Lal Bahadur Shastri, made plain that his two priorities would be national defence and agricultural productivity. Popularising the slogan *Jai Jawan Jai Kissan*, or praise to the soldier and to the cultivator, Shastri forged ahead with an ambitious programme of military expansion. On 21 September 1964, Y. B. Chavan, India's defence minister, outlined a five-year national defence plan in the Lok Sabha. This proposed a significant increase in the Indian Army's manpower and the transform-ation of the antiquated IAF into a large, up-to-date force, deploying some forty-five squadrons of modern aircraft.[52] Chavan's attempts to persuade the British to increase their contribution to India's rearma-ment programme met with a cool response from Harold Wilson's gov-ernment. Britain had provided India with £31 million in military aid following the outbreak of Sino-Indian hostilities. A further £4.7 mil-lion had been promised by London to fund New Delhi's purchase of British-built Leander-class frigates for the Indian Navy. During the same period, Pakistan received no military assistance from the United Kingdom. In November, Whitehall prevaricated when Chavan asked the British to finance India's acquisition of a submarine, a fleet of Daring-class naval escort vessels and forty refurbished Hunter fighter aircraft, at a cost of approximately £12 million. The following month, when Shastri visited London for talks with Harold Wilson, the Indian premier encountered similar difficulty in pinning his British counter-part down on the question of military aid.[53]

When considering India's request for military assistance, Wilson's government was mindful of the dangers to British interests in South Asia, and to wider Commonwealth unity, of being seen to take sides between India and Pakistan. Wilson's approach to the subcontinent, as one American official noted, hinged upon 'trying to perform the

---

[51] McGeorge Bundy and Komer to Johnson, Washington, 11 December 1963, *FRUS, 1961–1963*, vol. XIX, pp. 696–701.

[52] C. P. Srivastava, *Lal Bahadur Shastri: A Life of Truth in Politics* (New Delhi: Oxford University Press, 1995), pp. 115–16.

[53] Burke Trend to Wilson, 7 April 1965, 'Military Aid to India and Pakistan', PREM 13/390, TNA.

same balancing act that the Conservatives employed – not always successfully'.[54] In this respect, undertakings on military aid given to New Delhi by Macmillan's administration following China's incursion into northern India, placed its Labour successor in an awkward position. Macmillan had been careful not to commit Britain to a long-term military aid programme in India. The arms that London had provided to Nehru's government during the Sino-Indian War, and the subsequent pledges on military aid that emerged from the Anglo-American meetings at Nassau, in December 1962, and Birch Grove the following June, had, however, created an expectation in Indian political circles that Britain would continue contributing to India's rearmament effort.[55] While in opposition, Wilson's own rhetoric had left the impression that his party regarded the level of British military aid provided to India as derisory. In the House of Commons, the Labour leader had taken Macmillan to task for his 'unaccountable' failure to adequately support a fellow Commonwealth nation that had been subjected to Chinese aggression.[56] Wilson's political grandstanding, Sir Cyril Pickard, the Superintending Assistant Secretary at the CRO, informed American officials, had subsequently come back to haunt him. 'The new Labour government', Pickard observed in February 1965, '[now faced] the problem of its inability to deliver on the promises the Labour Party had made while it was in opposition.' Although the Indian government appeared 'willing to be patient where UK military aid is concerned', Pickard conceded that 'the possibility remains that the Indians harbour some sense of disillusionment on this score'.[57]

In purely financial terms, Britain's fragile economy limited the Labour government's ability to come to India's assistance. In its capacity as a member of the World Bank consortium providing economic aid to India, Britain had committed to supply New Delhi with £30 million of annual economic assistance, a figure that was expected to rise in future years. In March 1965, Wilson's Cabinet Secretary, Sir Burke Trend, who had spent much of his civil service career in the Treasury, cautioned the British premier that the overriding argument against

[54] Hughes to Ball, 4 December 1964, NSF, Robert W. Komer Files, Box 53, Folder United Kingdom Jan 1964–Mar 1966 [2 of 2], LBJL.
[55] Arthur Bottomley, 6 April 1965, 'Military Aid to India and Pakistan', CAB 129/121, TNA.
[56] Transcript of Prime Minister's Questions, 2 May 1963, PREM 11/4306, TNA.
[57] Anglo-American discussion on South Asia, 4 February 1965, RG 59, Records Relating to Indian Political Affairs 1964–6, Lot 69D52, Box 11 POL United Kingdom folder, NARA.

providing military aid to India 'is simply that we cannot afford to do so'.[58] Others, including Arthur Bottomley, Wilson's Secretary of State for Commonwealth Relations, took a more strategic view on the military aid question. The political impact of not providing India with any further military assistance, Bottomley assured his cabinet colleagues, 'would be very great, not least because India has such high expectations of support from a Labour Government'.[59] Making a 'judicious' financial investment in India, Bottomley argued, promised to deliver substantial long-term rewards by helping Britain to maintain its commercially lucrative and politically valuable position at the heart of India's military-industrial complex. Eighteen years after India's independence, residual British influence in the subcontinent was waning under pressure from the United States and the Soviet Union. 'Our expressions of support for India will need to be translated into practical assistance if they are to be made effective,' Bottomley insisted in April 1965, 'and military aid has a particular political significance.'[60]

Equally, the geostrategic value that Washington had attached to the Indian subcontinent over much of the previous decade, suggested to British officials that continuing to work in partnership with the Americans to strengthen India's defences against Communist China constituted 'an important element in our co-operation with the United States in Asia'.[61] Indeed, with the United States' commitment in South Vietnam deepening, the Johnson administration was wary of any sign that Britain's resolve to hold the ring against communism in Asia might be faltering, whether in Malaysia or India.[62] In another sense, after China's successful detonation of a uranium-235 device at its Lop Nor nuclear test site, on 16 October 1964, Wilson's government felt a greater need to reassure Indian policymakers, and a nervous Indian public, that they could continue to count on Western military support. Both Britain and the United States were particularly concerned that China's accession to the atomic club would prompt India to develop its own nuclear capability, diverting precious resources from the country's economic development and risking a dangerous regional arms race. On 11 December, Wilson warned his cabinet that 'the watershed of proliferation would be [broken] if India were compelled to make a nuclear weapon under threat from China'.[63]

[58] Burke Trend to Wilson, 30 March 1965, 'India: Military Aid and Nuclear Safeguards', PREM 13/390, TNA.
[59] Arthur Bottomley, 6 April 1965, 'Military Aid to India and Pakistan', CAB 129/121, TNA.
[60] *Ibid.*    [61] *Ibid.*
[62] Rostow to Johnson, 26 July 1966, NSF, Memos to the President, vol. IX, 43, LBJL.
[63] Entry for 11 December 1964, Crossman, *Minister of Housing 1964–66*, p. 94.

In the wake of the Chinese test, Zulfikar Ali Bhutto assured the British Defence Secretary, Denis Healey, that 'If India went ahead with the production of her own nuclear weapons, Pakistan would follow suit – whatever the economic sacrifice required.'[64] Although Shastri was known to be against developing an Indian bomb, Chavan and other senior Indian officials, such as the minister for defence production A. M. Thomas, made it known to the British that 'a growing tide of opinion' in the Congress Party opposed the Indian premier's 'negative' policy. Indians were acutely aware, Chavan noted, that they were 'faced by an enemy which believed in the inevitability of war, and of nuclear war at that'.[65] The previous March, Solly Zuckerman, the Ministry of Defence's Chief Scientific Adviser, had visited Trombay, the Indian equivalent of Britain's Harwell atomic research centre, as a guest of Dr Homi Bhabha, the director of India's Atomic Energy Programme. Zuckerman was struck by the 'hive of activity' that he encountered at Trombay. The 2,000 professional scientists India employed at the plant, he reported back to Wilson, were pressing ahead with preparations to construct an atomic device, 'in anticipation of a reversal of the present political decision'.[66]

Back in December 1964, Wilson had approached Shastri with a proposal that the three 'major' nuclear powers, Britain, the United States and the Soviet Union, provide a nuclear 'umbrella' to protect non-nuclear states from 'blackmail by third parties'. It soon became apparent, however, that with the Vietnam War souring East–West relations, the Soviets would refuse to join London and Washington in offering a nuclear guarantee to India that was so obviously directed at a fellow communist country.[67] From New Delhi's perspective, India's non-alignment made Soviet participation in any such a scheme a prerequisite. Having returned to London via Moscow for the Commonwealth Prime Ministers' Conference, in June 1965, Shastri confirmed to British officials 'that while they saw great advantage in a guarantee to the non-nuclear non-aligned Powers by the nuclear Powers, such a guarantee would only be acceptable if Russia joined in, and they realised that Russia would not join in any guarantee which would appear to be directed against China'.[68]

[64] Denis Healey to Michael Stewart and Bottomley, 3 May 1965, 'Nuclear "Umbrella"', PREM 13/373, TNA.
[65] Zuckerman to Wilson, 15 March 1965, 'India and the Bomb', PREM 13/973, TNA.
[66] *Ibid.*
[67] Note of Wilson meeting with Averell Harriman, 24 March 1965, PREM 13/973, TNA.
[68] 'Secret Background Note', 27 July 1965, PREM 13/973, TNA. Undeterred, Wilson pursued an extraordinary scheme to provide India with a 'nuclear umbrella' by

Prior to the collapse of the 'nuclear umbrella' proposal, Whitehall had assumed that organising a system of collective nuclear defence for India, were it to prove possible, would be, 'a long and complicated business'.[69] In the interim, the British worried that even if the development of an effective atomic delivery system remained beyond India's means for years to come, this would provide scant comfort to New Delhi's regional neighbours. 'You do not need a very sophisticated delivery system', Burke Trend reminded Wilson, 'to lob a nuclear bomb over the frontier into Pakistan.'[70] Senior officials, such as Trend, who on balance opposed British military aid to India, nevertheless conceded that perhaps the most effective means of persuading India not to develop atomic weapons lay in providing Shastri's government with 'some sort of assurance that the West is actively supporting them ... and that means, in the present context, [offering] a reasonable amount of conventional military aid'.[71]

Above all else, however, British policymakers were concerned by the effect a military aid programme for India would have on Anglo-Pakistani relations. The importance of retaining the impression, if not the substance, of impartiality in matters relating to India and Pakistan convinced British officials that the 'problem' of defending India from external threats had to be approached within a wider regional framework.[72] In early November 1964, Ayub Khan made it abundantly clear to Harold Wilson that Pakistan's government, and its people, would react in the most adverse terms were Britain to continue assisting India's 'massive rearmament programme'. Rehashing well-worn arguments, Pakistan's president insisted that in the face of an 'illusory' Chinese

redeploying Britain's Polaris submarines to the Indian Ocean. Having calculated that a future war with China was more likely than conflict with the Soviets, Wilson reasoned that sending the Polaris force East would appeal to left-wing Labour circles sympathetic to India, but opposed to his government's stance on Vietnam; garner support within the wider Labour Party for the retention of a British nuclear deterrent; and enable expensive conventional forces to be withdrawn from Asia. Remarkably, despite the opposition of cabinet colleagues, Wilson kept the option of Polaris redeployment open as late as mid-1968, when it was overtaken by the decision to withdraw British forces from East of Suez. See Matthew Jones and John Young, 'Polaris, East of Suez: British Plans for a Nuclear Force in the Indo-Pacific, 1964–1968', *Journal of Strategic Studies*, 33, 6 (2010), 1–24.

[69] Michael Stewart to Wilson, 3 March 1965, PREM 13/973; Burke Trend to Wilson, 7 April 1965, 'Military Aid to India and Pakistan', PREM 13/390, TNA.

[70] Burke Trend to Wilson, 30 March 1965, 'India: Military Aid and Nuclear Safeguards', PREM 13/390, TNA.

[71] Burke Trend to Wilson, 7 April 1965, 'Military Aid to India and Pakistan', PREM 13/390, TNA.

[72] Arthur Bottomley, 6 April 1965, 'Military Aid to India and Pakistan', CAB 129/121, TNA.

threat to the subcontinent, any expansion in India's armed forces 'cannot but be regarded by us as a serious threat to our [Pakistan's] security'. 'If India's military strength continues to grow through USA–UK help,' Wilson was cautioned, 'it would force Pakistan to seek additional arms from wherever she can obtain them and this would precipitate an arms race in this region.'[73]

Caught between its determination to preserve British influence in India, and at the same time avoid a breach in its relations with Pakistan, Wilson's cabinet eventually agreed to offer military aid to both countries. In rationalising this decision, Bottomley emphasised the 'vital' role that the subcontinent played in sustaining Britain's interests across Asia. 'If we lose India or Pakistan,' the Commonwealth Secretary argued, 'we should be suffering a political set-back which could not fail to affect our whole position East of Suez.' Providing India with a 'modest' amount of military assistance appeared a small price to pay for securing Britain's standing in New Delhi, keeping Indian armed forces 'basically British equipped', and helping to defend the subcontinent from communist aggression. If so doing necessitated compensating Pakistan with additional military aid, British ministers concluded, then so be it.[74] In April 1965, after some wrangling within the British Defence and Overseas Policy Committee over the appropriate size of a military aid programme for South Asia, Wilson's government offered to supply India with an Oberon-class submarine and thirty refurbished Hunter fighter aircraft, at an estimated cost to the British exchequer of £8 million. At the same time, Pakistan was offered its own Oberon submarine and British radar and communications equipment, worth a total of £5.5 million.[75]

In electing to embrace the 'the principle of parallelism' by arming India and Pakistan, the British fell into line with American policy in South Asia.[76] In December 1963, on returning from his fact-finding mission to the subcontinent, Maxwell Taylor advised Lyndon Johnson to provide long-term US military assistance to New Delhi and Rawalpindi. Growing Soviet and Communist Chinese influence in the region, Taylor recommended, ought to be challenged with a strong and tangible show of American support for India and Pakistan. More specifically, Taylor suggested that the United States offer India $50–60 million of annual

---

[73] Ayub Khan to Wilson, 13 November 1964, PREM 13/39, TNA.
[74] Arthur Bottomley, 6 April 1965, 'Military Aid to India and Pakistan', CAB 129/121, TNA.
[75] Burke Trend to Wilson, 7 April 1965, 'Military Aid to India and Pakistan', PREM 13/390, TNA.
[76] Komer to Johnson, 23 December 1963, NSC History of South Asia, NSF, LBJL.

military aid over a five-year period. In return for this aid, Shastri's government would be expected to limit the expansion of India's armed forces, maintain investment in the country's economic development, limit the procurement of Soviets arms, show restraint toward Pakistan and actively cooperate with the West in the containment of Communist China. As an interim gesture of American goodwill, Taylor proposed making $50 million of arms available to India immediately, to help re-equip its mountain divisions and bolster air defence.[77] In addition, Taylor advocated providing Pakistan with a similar five-year military assistance programme (MAP) of $50–60 million a year, the proviso being that Ayub Khan's government undertook 'a wholehearted change of attitude ... toward CENTO, SEATO, and the US'.[78]

The even-handed approach to India and Pakistan advocated by Taylor frustrated Robert Komer and Chester Bowles, who continued to make the case for an American tilt toward India. Bowles complained bitterly to Johnson that in recommending the provision of broadly comparable amounts of American military aid to India and Pakistan, Taylor had failed to adequately account for the vastly different threats faced by the two countries. India would need to be offered a minimum of $75–80 million in US military aid per year over a five-year period, Bowles grumbled, if he were to have 'a reasonable chance [of averting] ... the gradual strengthening of the pro-Soviet Menon forces in India, and the loss of a major opportunity to further United States interests in Asia'.[79] Although concerned that Bowles' 'wordy' cables from New Delhi were more likely to irritate Johnson than win him over, Komer felt that in pressing the case for additional military aid for India, the ambassador had a point. The Soviets had all but abandoned India during the Sino-Indian War, Komer reminded Johnson, but were 'now doing more than we to woo the India military establishment'. 'If India goes Communist, it will be a disaster comparable only to the loss of China', Komer added. 'Even if India reverts to pro-Soviet neutralism, our policy in Asia will be compromised. These risks are real, and the irony is that they are dangerous for Pakistan as well.'[80]

---

[77] Taylor to Johnson, 23 December 1963, NSF, General Taylor folder, International Meetings and Travel File, LBJL.

[78] Taylor Mission Report, 30 December 1963, NSF, Box 433, Taylor Mission, 12/63, Folder 2, JFKL.

[79] Bowles to Johnson, New Delhi, 27 December 1963, *FRUS, 1961–1963*, vol. XIX, pp. 727–30.

[80] Komer and Bundy to Johnson, 26 February 1964, NSF Country File, India, Box 128, Folder 3 India Memos & Misc. Vol. I, 12-63 to 3-64, LBJL.

Although mindful of the primacy that India had acquired over Pakistan in US strategic thinking, Lyndon Johnson was unwilling to sanction a major shift in America's South Asian policy by leaning toward New Delhi. Less comfortable in the realm of international affairs than in domestic politics, throughout his presidency Johnson was drawn toward the conservative, or seemingly 'safe' foreign policy option. More often than not, he reinforced, rather than challenged, received diplomatic wisdom. A naturally cautious, yet highly astute politician, Johnson reasoned that the advantages his administration might accrue from favouring India over Pakistan were outweighed by the considerable risks associated with adopting such a strategy, both at home and abroad. On 8 February 1964, Johnson approved the substance of Taylor's blueprint for a five-year MAP for India and Pakistan. In response, a downbeat Komer lamented Johnson's refusal to 'seize the nettle' and provide the Indian government with an unequivocal sign of American support, whatever Pakistan's protests. Johnson's decision to hedge his bets in South Asia, he reasoned, merely underlined the president's relative lack of interest in the region. 'I'm just not sanguine on the prospects of getting the subcontinent back on center stage', Komer informed McGeorge Bundy on 6 March. 'No matter how much more important it is in any long-term calculation than most other Afro-Asian problems.'[81]

### Losing friends and alienating people

During 1964, the Indian government became increasingly frustrated at Johnson's willingness to drag his heels over negotiations on the delivery of military aid. Having been sent to Washington in April on a goodwill mission by her father, Indira Gandhi ruffled American feathers by informing a correspondent from *The New York Times* that Indians were losing confidence in the US government. The 'favouritism' that America displayed toward Pakistan on issues such as Kashmir, Gandhi observed, had led many Indians to assume that 'the West is on Pakistan's side no matter what'.[82] Johnson challenged Gandhi's accusation of partiality during a meeting at the White House on 27 April. As a purportedly 'strong friend of India', Johnson assured his guest that the Pakistan government 'were much more unhappy about our policy toward India than India seemed to be about our policy toward

[81] Komer to McGeorge Bundy, 6 March 1964, NSF Country File, India, Box 128, Folder 3 India Memos & Misc. Vol. I, 12-63 to 3-64, LBJL.
[82] *The New York Times*, 22 April 1964.

Pakistan'. The White House was so full of 'pro-Indian' officials, such as Komer and McGeorge Bundy, the president joked, that he sometimes wondered whether the Indian government 'were subverting his staff'. Gandhi was unmoved by Johnson's bluff Texan diplomacy. Next to Kennedy, Gandhi, in common with many Indian government officials, concluded that Johnson was detached from South Asia affairs and either unwilling, or unable, to comprehend India's genuine sense of insecurity.[83]

In the aftermath of Gandhi's encounter with Johnson, Chester Bowles warned Washington that any further delay on the question of military aid was likely to see India drift inexorably toward the Soviet Union. Was it reasonable to expect an Indian government braced for an attack from China, Pakistan or possibly both, Bowles asked Dean Rusk, to 'wait on our [US] political conveniences'?[84] During the previous eighteen months, India had acquired Soviet MiG-21 fighters, AN-12 transport aircraft, MI-4 helicopters and advanced surface-to-air missiles. In short, Bowles complained, the 'Soviet Union is now extending more military assistance to India than is the United States'. Moreover, Moscow had stepped in to take up prestigious economic projects that the United States had initiated in India and subsequently abandoned. On 1 May, Bowles informed Washington that 'thunderous cheers' had echoed around the parliament building in New Delhi when it was announced that the Soviets would finance the construction of a steel plant at Bokaro, in eastern India, for which the Kennedy administration had failed to secure funding from Capitol Hill. A few days later, the subcontinent's media reported that Moscow had offered to supply India with a powerful radio transmitter, as an alternative to a broadcast mast that Washington had first proposed erecting, back in 1963.[85]

In part, Bowles' dire warnings of burgeoning Soviet influence in India were designed to pave the way for a long-term MAP agreement between the United States and India, when Chavan visited the United States at the end of May. On Chavan's arrival in Washington, it quickly became apparent that India's expectation of concluding an arms deal, in line with a five-year defence plan that New Delhi had prepared at

[83] Meeting of President with Mrs Indira Gandhi, 27 April 1964, NSF Country File, India, Box 128, Folder 5 Memos & Misc. Vol. II 4-64 to 6-64; CIA Intelligence Cable, 9 May 1964, B. K. Nehru to Y. D. Gundevia, NSF, Intelligence File, Box 7, Folder Codeword Material Vol. II [2 of 2], 3-64 to 10-64, LBJL.

[84] Bowles to Rusk, 12 March 1964, NSF Country File, India, Box 128, Folder 2 India Cables Vol. I [2 of 2], 12-63 to 3-64, LBJL.

[85] Bowles to Rusk, 16 and 17 May 1964, NSF Country File, India, Box 128, Folder 4 India Cables Vol. II, 4-64 to 6-64, LBJL.

America's request, was misplaced. Johnson's preference for keeping India on the end of a short tether led US Secretary of Defense, Robert McNamara, to offer Chavan just $50 million of military assistance for the fiscal year 1965, with no firm assurance of any further aid beyond that date. To compound India's displeasure, McNamara turned down a specific request from Chavan to supply the IAF with America's F-104 supersonic fighter.[86] As Bowles had predicted, having been disappointed by McNamara, the Indians turned back to the Soviets for help. In September, Chavan signed agreements in Moscow to purchase a further forty-five MiG-21 fighters and establish aircraft factories in India with the capacity to produce an additional 400 of the Soviet aircraft.

In Pakistan, news that the United States had offered India military assistance, albeit of a limited nature, provoked a furious response from the country's politicians. On 22 June, Zulfikar Ali Bhutto informed Pakistan's National Assembly that the Johnson administration's decision confirmed its 'utter disregard' for Pakistan's interests. 'The time has come', Bhutto stated, 'for Pakistan to undertake [a] reappraisal of its foreign policy and review her political and military commitments.' The American government, Pakistan's foreign minister added ominously, would have to choose between 'a system of alliances and betrayal of allies'.[87] The following day, Ayub Khan took a personal swipe at Johnson. In an interview published in the London *Daily Mail*, Pakistan's president declared, 'Today American policy is based on opportunism and is devoid of moral quality. Pakistan deeply regrets that although she has fulfilled all her commitments, she has been let down by politicians she regarded as friends.'[88] The outpouring of Pakistani vitriol directed at Johnson, and his administration's South Asian policy, infuriated the White House. Accusing the United States of betraying Pakistan, an enraged Robert Komer noted, was 'going a bit too far'.[89] If anything, American officials reflected coldly, Pakistan was the party guilty of gross disloyalty. Rawalpindi had, after all, courted Communist China and refused to support the United States in South Vietnam.[90]

Washington took particular exception to Ayub Khan's decision to roll out the red carpet for Zhou Enlai, in February 1964. As the Americans

---

[86] Rusk to Johnson, 15 June 1964, NSF Country File, India, Box 128, Folder 6 India Cables & Memos Vol. III, 7-64 to 11-64, LBJL.
[87] 'Anti-US Statements', 23 June 1964, NSF Country File, Pakistan, Box 151, Folder 1, Pakistan Cables Vol. II, 6-64 to 11-64, LBJL.
[88] Karachi to State Department, 24 June 1964, NSF, Pakistan, LBJL.
[89] Komer to Harriman and Talbot, 25 June 1964, NSF Country File, Pakistan, Box 151, Folder 1, Pakistan Cables Vol. II, 6-64 to 11-64, LBJL.
[90] State Department to Karachi, 29 July 1964, NSF, NSC Histories, South Asia, LBJL.

had feared, Zhou exploited the opportunity afforded by his eight-day visit to proclaim Chinese solidarity with Pakistan, and condemn the perfidious influence of Western neo-imperialism. Speaking, somewhat incongruously, from a Victorian bandstand in the quintessentially British setting of Karachi's Frere Hall Gardens, Zhou had played up China's historic trading and cultural links with the region that had gone on to become Pakistan. China and Pakistan, Zhou emphasised, had fought to secure their 'liberation' from foreign rule and reassert their independence and right to 'self-betterment'. While listening to Zhou's address, Britain's High Commissioner to Pakistan, Morrice James, found himself musing upon the irony of hearing China's premier deliver a strident anti-colonial polemic, in surroundings redolent of the English home counties circa 1890, while nearby, Pakistan's Navy band could be heard playing 'Dear Little Buttercup', from Gilbert and Sullivan's *HMS Pinafore*.[91] Johnson and his senior foreign policy advisers found it a good deal less humorous to read reports of banners proclaiming 'Chinese-Pakistani friendship' adorning buildings across Pakistan and pictures of the gold-starred red flag of Communist China fluttering in the streets surrounding the US Embassy in Karachi. During a press conference held at Rawalpindi airport, as Zhou sat surrounded by the Pakistan Air Force's new US supplied C-130 transport aircraft, Ayub Khan added to American discomfort. The one thing that had emerged clearly from his discussions with Zhou, Ayub Khan informed the world's press, was 'that the Chinese are prepared to be reasonable with anyone who is prepared to be reasonable with them'.[92]

Lyndon Johnson subsequently looked on with mounting exasperation as Pakistan settled a long-running border dispute with China, negotiated a trade deal with Beijing, reached agreement to institute a reciprocal commercial airline service between Chinese and Pakistani cities, and accepted a $60 million interest-free loan from America's communist adversary. By the summer of 1964, the American president's patience with Ayub Khan's 'China policy' had grown painfully thin. On 7 July, Johnson curtly informed Pakistan's new ambassador in Washington, Ghulam Ahmed, that his government's push to broaden and deepen its links with Communist China suggested that both the United States and Pakistan would 'have to re-evaluate the condition of our relationship'.[93] Despite the mounting tension in US-Pakistani relations

---

[91] James, *Pakistan Chronicle*, p. 112.
[92] 'How to be Friendly without Getting Seduced', *Time*, 28 February 1964.
[93] Memorandum of Conversation between Johnson and Ahmed, 7 July 1964, NSF, Pakistan, LBJL.

occasioned by Rawalpindi's entente with Beijing, however, both Johnson and Ayub Khan had good reason to avoid an open schism. Pakistan remained heavily dependent on receipts of American economic and military assistance that accounted for over half the country's external aid. Likewise, the CIA and Pentagon continued to place great value on US intelligence-gathering facilities situated in northern Pakistan.[94]

## Falling out

On 3 November 1964, Lyndon Johnson was elected president of the United States, winning 61 per cent of the popular vote in a landslide victory over his right-wing Republican opponent, Barry Goldwater. Almost exactly two months later, on 2 January 1965, Ayub Khan overcame an unexpectedly strong challenge from the Combined Opposition Parties, led by Fatima Jinnah, the Quaid-i-Azam's sister, to win Pakistan's first presidential election. Back in July 1962, Ayub Khan had reluctantly succumbed to pressure from opposition groups to regularise organised political activity, and passed the Political Parties Act. Having made political parties legal in Pakistan once more, Ayub Khan promptly formed the Convention Muslim League. The League was intended to counter rising popular opposition to the incumbent administration. Backed primarily by an alliance between independently minded regional dignitaries and traditional power brokers, the League had limited grass-roots appeal amongst ordinary Pakistanis disaffected with resurgent state-sponsored corruption and mismanagement. Despite utilising the full resources of the Pakistani state in a campaign widely criticised for flagrant electoral malpractice, Ayub Khan secured only 64 per cent of the votes cast by the country's 80,000 Basic Democrats. Standing under the banner of the Convention Muslim League Party, the Pakistani leader was defeated by Fatima Jinnah in Karachi, and came close to losing the vote in East Pakistan. Although able to claim a victory of sorts, the election confirmed the existence of widespread dissatisfaction in Pakistan with Ayub Khan's government. Lacking popular support, the president's authority came to hinge increasingly on his ability to retain control of Pakistan's army and state bureaucracy.[95]

---

[94] Executive Secretary United States Intelligence Board (USIB) to State, 17 March 1964, Report of conversation on 11 March between Talbot, McConaughy and Ayub Khan, Government House Lahore, NSF, Intelligence File, Box 7, Folder Codeword Material Vol. 2 [2 of 2], 3-64 to 10-64, LBJL. In 1965, Washington provided Pakistan with approximately $400 million in economic and military assistance.

[95] Anatol Lieven, *Pakistan: A Hard Country* (London: Penguin, 2012), pp. 66–7.

Shortly after Pakistan's election, Johnson extended a fig leaf to Rawalpindi, and invited Ayub Khan to Washington for talks. Perturbed by the steady deterioration in US-Pakistani relations, State Department officials convinced Johnson that with national elections in both countries now out of the way, a meeting with the Pakistani leader would offer a timely opportunity to begin building bridges.[96] Just days before Ayub Khan was due to arrive in Washington, the State Department's initiative to promote a rapprochement with Pakistan was thrown into disarray. During state visits to Beijing and Moscow in March and April, Ayub Khan had been openly critical of the United States' policy in post-war Asia, and more specifically, America's escalation of the war in Vietnam. When reports of the Pakistani president's public statements reached Washington, a furious Johnson abruptly rescinded Ayub Khan's invitation to visit the United States. Johnson was especially put out by the considerable international publicity that attended Ayub Khan's visit to China, between 2 and 9 March. In *The Indian Express*, an editorial by Frank Moraes entitled 'A Muslim De Gaulle' characterised the Pakistani president's tour of the PRC as 'triumphant'. The enthusiastic reception that Ayub Khan received throughout China, Moraes reflected, was 'very reminiscent of Nehru's visit in October 1954'.[97] On 6 March, at a banquet for China's leaders hosted by Ayub Khan at Pakistan's Beijing Embassy, the Pakistani president stated, 'It has been said that China fosters conflict and war. As a neighbour of China our experience has been to the contrary ... Pakistan is prepared to collaborate with China ... to strengthen the fabric of peace.'[98] Ayub Khan went on to aggravate a particularly sensitive political nerve of Johnson's by indirectly condemning America's military presence in South Vietnam. In a communiqué issued at the end of his Chinese visit, Pakistan's president joined his hosts in expressing support for 'national independence movements and struggles against all form of colonialism in Asia and Africa'.[99]

The newspaper headlines generated in the United States by Ayub Khan's trip to China persuaded Johnson that the Pakistani leader's presence in Washington would focus unwelcome Congressional attention on burgeoning Sino-Pakistani cooperation, and risk jeopardising support on Capitol Hill for his administration's foreign aid bill. Furthermore, Johnson strongly suspected that Ayub Khan would be drawn into

[96]  McConaughy to Rusk, No. 733, 12 January 1965, RG 59, Central Files 1964–6, POL 7 PAK, NARA.
[97]  Entry for 10 March 1965, PP MS 24 Box 2, Folder 14, 'Janta' Diary, FMP.
[98]  'Mao Seems Unmoved by Ayub's Peace Call', *The Washington Post*, 7 March 1965.
[99]  'China Silent As Ayub Asks Vietnam Talks', *The New York Times*, 8 March 1965.

commenting on the Vietnam War by America's media, adding to the White House's domestic political problems.[100] Senior American officials took solace in the hope that the cancellation of his meeting with Johnson would encourage Ayub Khan to re-evaluate his pro-China policy. In fact, although upset by Johnson's decision, Pakistan's president reacted defiantly to the White House's snub. On 20 April, in a confidential briefing delivered to government ministers in Rawalpindi, Ayub Khan defended his strategy of repositioning Pakistan between the Eastern and Western blocs. Asked by one official how any small country could survive as 'a lamb among lions', Ayub Khan insisted that Pakistan would prosper amongst American, Soviet and Chinese lions by the simple expedient of setting one against another. Pakistan's adroit diplomacy, Ayub Khan confidently asserted, would ensure that it continued to receive economic and military support commensurate with its position as one of the United States' foremost allies *and* remained on friendly terms with the Communist bloc.[101]

In seeking to arrest Ayub Khan's drift eastward, the Johnson administration wrestled with how best to utilise its economic leverage with Pakistan. Toward the end of April, Robert Komer advised Johnson that it was imperative to dispel Ayub Khan's illusion that he could 'have his cake and eat it too'. Were Rawalpindi to lean too much in the direction of Beijing, Komer underscored, the US Congress might well step in and cut off its economic and military assistance, instigating a rupture in US-Pakistani relations, and undermining the effort started under the Eisenhower administration to transform Pakistan into a modern, industrialised and pro-Western state. From the mid-1950s, American aid had played a crucial role in turning around Pakistan's economic fortunes. Roughly $3.2 billion in American grants and loans had helped to modernise Pakistan's industrial infrastructure. A further $1.5 billion of US aid had been directed into the Pakistan military. Pakistan's annual economic growth rate of between 4 and 6 per cent had led economists to cite the 'Pakistan example' as a model of what external investment could achieve in the developing world.[102] 'Our dilemma is that US economic aid is making Pakistan a real success story,' Robert Komer

---

[100] Ball to Rusk, 6 April 1965, NSF Country File, India, Box 129 [1 of 2], Folder 1 India Cables [1 of 2], Vol. IV, 12-64 to 6-65, LBJL.

[101] Komer to Bundy, 21 April 1965, NSF, NSC Histories, South Asia, LBJL; James, *Pakistan Chronicle*, p. 114.

[102] 'Should a Friend in Need, Be a Friend in Deed?', *Time*, 23 July 1965.

conceded, on 22 April, 'so we hate to cut back for political reasons (but the Pak[istanis] would hate it too).'[103]

Rather than cut aid to Pakistan, Johnson decided instead to apply diplomatic pressure on Rawalpindi by postponing a meeting of the World Bank's international aid consortium, which was scheduled to take place in Washington, on 27 July. On 3 July, American officials informed the Pakistani government that the consortium, which had been expected to make $500 million of additional economic aid available to Pakistan, would now meet on 27 September. In the interim, it was hoped that 'certain other problems' bedevilling US-Pakistani relations could be ironed out. The extent of Ayub Khan's 'repressed anger' at what he considered to be an 'unjustified' and 'punitive action' on the part of the US government, took American diplomats by surprise. Walter McConaughy, the US ambassador to Pakistan, informed the State Department that the Pakistani leader had taken news of the consortium's postponement 'quite hard – worse than I had anticipated'. Following a tense meeting with Ayub Khan, McConaughy warned Washington that the consortium's postponement looked certain to

precipitate a considerable stir and possibly an actual full-blown crisis in our relations with Pakistan. AYUB seems to feel that our postponement move challenges him, and strikes at [the] self-respect of [the] country by seeking to penalize Pakistan publicly for pursuing 'independent' foreign policy ... There is some danger of his reacting as if he has been 'driven to the wall.'[104]

In Rawalpindi, an enraged Zulfikar Ali Bhutto read out the US diplomatic note confirming the consortium's cancellation verbatim in Pakistan's National Assembly, provoking uproar in the parliamentary chamber. 'If we are not going to be ruled from No. 10 Downing Street,' one member of Pakistan's parliament exclaimed, 'then, by God, we are not going to be ruled by Wall Street.' The following day, Ayub Khan publicly denounced the Johnson administration's attempt to undermine Pakistan's autonomy. 'If friendship impinges on the sovereignty and independence of our country and is against our interests,' Pakistan's president declared defiantly, 'we no longer desire such friendship.' 'This is', one veteran US diplomat subsequently confided to an American journalist, 'the worst our relations [with Pakistan] have ever been.'[105]

---

[103] Komer to Johnson, 'Our Pakistan Affairs', 22 April 1965, NSF, NSC Histories, South Asia, LBJL.
[104] McConaughy to Rusk, 4 July 1965, RG 59, Central Files 1964–6, AID 9 PAK, NARA.
[105] 'Should a Friend in Need, Be a Friend in Deed?', Time, 23 July 1965.

At the same moment, America's relationship with India suffered a serious setback after Johnson determined, in an ill-judged display of regional 'even-handedness', to withdraw a long-standing invitation for Shastri to visit Washington.[106] In *The Times of India*, Johnson's 'unprovoked snub' was disparaged as an 'ill-deserved discourtesy'.[107] India's premier, government and media, Dean Rusk was advised by State Department officials, had 'reacted bitterly' to the cancellation of the state visit. Most Indians, indignant that Shastri had been treated on a par with Ayub Khan, who had 'been busy in Peking and elsewhere wooing Communist China', interpreted Johnson's action as a response to Shastri's criticism of America's Vietnam policy.[108] Shastri felt especially aggrieved at Johnson's rebuff, having been assured repeatedly by Chester Bowles that he could count on Washington's friendship. During their first meeting after Shastri had become India's leader, Bowles went out of his way to emphasise that 'as India's new Prime Minister he [Shastri] could count on President Johnson, Dean Rusk, me and everyone else in our gov[ernmen]t for understanding and support in good times or in bad'.[109] During 'a painful and difficult' interview with Bowles, on 20 April, Shastri informed the American ambassador that he was 'deeply hurt' that the US government had chosen to embarrass him 'before his country, his party and the world'. Advising Bowles that in his view a 'deep psychological gap' now existed between their two countries, Shastri confessed that he 'was at a loss to know how mutual confidence could be restored'. An angry and disconsolate Bowles informed the State Department that the crisis in Indo-US relations sparked by the cancellation of Shastri's state visit 'is the most serious I have encountered in many years in dealing with Indian people and government'.[110] Back in London, *The Economist* observed wryly that by rescinding the invitations that Ayub Khan and Shastri had received to visit the United

---

[106] Chester Bowles, *Promises to Keep: My Years in Public Life, 1941–1969* (New York: Harper, 1971), p. 581.
[107] Carl Rowan to Johnson, 19 April 1965, NSF, Robert W. Komer Files, Box 22 [1 of 2], Folder 6, LBJL.
[108] Bowles to Johnson and Rusk, 15 April 1965, Unnumbered, NSF Country File, India, Box 129 [1 of 2], Folder 2, India Cables [2 of 2], Vol. IV, 12-64 to 6-65, LBJL; and Thomas Hughes to Rusk, 16 May 1965, NSF, Robert W. Komer Files, Box 22 [1 of 2], Folder 6 Shastri Visit (Proposed) [2 of 3], LBJL.
[109] Bowles to State Department, 6 June 1964, RG 59, Central Files 1964–6, POL 1 INDIA–US, NARA; Bowles to Secretary of State, No. 3058, 27 April 1965, NSF Country File, India, Box 129 [1 of 2], Folder 2, India Cables [2 of 2], Vol. IV, 12-64 to 6-65, LBJL.
[110] Bowles to Rusk, No. 2970, 21 April 1965, NSF Country File, India, Box 129 [1 of 2], Folder 2, India Cables [2 of 2], Vol. IV, 12-64 to 6-65, LBJL.

States, Johnson had accomplished 'the unusual diplomatic feat of giving offence to both [India and Pakistan] simultaneously'.[111]

To the discomfort of American and British officials, the deterioration in the United States' relations with India and Pakistan coincided with a period of mounting tension in the Indian subcontinent. Back in February, a meeting of British and American officials at the Commonwealth Relations Office, in London, took a gloomy view of the outlook in South Asia. Having recently returned from the region, William J. Handley, the Deputy Assistant Secretary of State for South Asian Affairs, expressed concern that 'with India increasing its hold over the territory [of Kashmir], time is running out for Pakistan and there is a real danger that the Pak[istani]s might take some rash action'. The British agreed that following Shastri's decision to extend Articles 356 and 357 of the Indian Constitution to Kashmir, which empowered New Delhi to exercise direct rule in the state, Indo-Pakistani relations had entered a new and 'highly dangerous' phase. Cyril Pickard felt agreed that the rising frustration felt in Pakistan on the Kashmir question 'could explode at any time'. 'There exists', Pickard observed ominously, 'a real possibility of war over Kashmir.'[112] Within a matter of months, with America's standing in region at an all time low, the subcontinent was plunged once again into conflict. On this occasion, the second Indo-Pakistani War over the troubled state of Kashmir would have an unforeseen, dramatic and lasting impact on the British and American positions in South Asia.

---

[111] *The Economist*, 24 April 1965.
[112] Anglo-American talks on South Asia at CRO, 4 February 1965, RG 59, Records Relating to Indian Political Affairs 1964–6, Lot 69D52, Box 11 POL United Kingdom folder, NARA.

# 10   Triumph and tragedy: the Rann of Kutch and the 1965 Indo-Pakistani War

In the early hours of 24 April 1965, the 6th Brigade of Pakistan's army launched Operation Desert Hawk. Under the command of Brigadier Eftikhar Khan, Pakistani forces attacked and overwhelmed an isolated Indian military outpost at Sera Bet, in the Rann of Kutch, a desolate expanse of 'salt waste' wedged between the Arabian Sea to the west, the Pakistani province of Sind to the north and the Indian state of Gujarat to the south. By the end of April, Pakistan's army had over-run several more Indian positions in the Rann, and occupied a swathe of territory claimed by New Delhi.[1] In response, India rushed military reinforcements into the area and, for the first time since the conclusion of hostilities in Kashmir in January 1948, fighting broke out between brigade-sized forces from India and Pakistan.[2] Described by one visitor as 'a reeking reach of black tidal mudflats bounded with sand dunes and etched by dead streams of salt and scum', the Rann was uninhabited, bar a transient population of flamingos, wild asses and the occasional camel herdsmen, and of little economic value.[3] It seemed 'ridiculous' to the British High Commissioner in India, John Freeman, 'that two countries should quarrel so fiercely over a barren tract of land'. Yet, quarrel India and Pakistan did, and, as Freeman subsequently emphasised to the CRO, back in London, 'their quarrel very nearly led to war'.[4]

Title over the 7,000 square miles (18,000 square kilometres) of the Rann had been contested during the British Raj, and remained a matter of dispute at the time of India's independence, in August 1947. In 1938, the predominantly Muslim province of Sind formally challenged a

---

[1] B. C. Chakravorty, *History of the Indo-Pak War, 1965*, ed. S. N. Prasad (New Delhi: History Division, Ministry of Defence, Government of India, 1992), p. 31.

[2] Sykes to Bottomley, 'Pakistan: The Rann of Kutch Dispute', 16 July 1965, PREM 13/393, The United Kingdom National Archives, Kew, London (hereafter TNA).

[3] *Time*, 7 May 1965; Freeman to Bottomley, 'India: The Rann of Kutch Dispute', 16 July 1965, PREM 13/393, TNA.

[4] Freeman to Bottomley, 'India: The Rann of Kutch Dispute', 16 July 1965, PREM 13/393, TNA.

claim on the Rann lodged by the Hindu princely state of Kutch. Almost a decade later, at the time of the subcontinent's partition, Sind acceded to Pakistan, while Kutch became part of India. Pakistan's new national government wasted little time in asserting its claim on the Rann. On 14 July 1948, India was informed by Pakistan that the Sind–Kutch boundary remained 'in dispute' and 'must be settled'.[5] Pakistan argued that the Rann, which between June and October was transformed into a salt lake by seawater swept inland by the annual monsoon, was a dead sea and, under international law, should be divided equally between states situated on its boundaries. The Indian government rejected Pakistan's claim to the northern half of the Rann, and insisted that Survey of India maps published during the British occupation of the subcontinent confirmed that the entire area under dispute belonged to Kutch. Throughout the 1950s, a succession of small-scale skirmishes occurred between Indian and Pakistani patrols in the Rann. In January 1960, negotiations between Indian and Pakistani ministers ironed out a series of minor differences over the delineation of the India–West Pakistan border. However, both parties failed to reach an agreement on the Rann of Kutch question, and the matter was left unresolved pending further talks.[6]

Until early 1964, an uneasy peace was observed by India and Pakistan in the Rann. In February and May of that year, Pakistan attempted to advance its claim on Kashmir in the United Nations Security Council, without success. In the autumn, Lal Bahadur Shastri's government introduced legislation into the Lok Sabha to accelerate Kashmir's integration into the Indian Union. These twin setbacks to Pakistan's hope of wresting control of Kashmir away from India stirred Ayub Khan's administration into action. By aggressively prosecuting its interest in the Rann, Pakistan's government sought to refocus international attention upon outstanding areas of Indo-Pakistani rancour, and above all, the Kashmir dispute. Accordingly, at the beginning of 1965, Pakistan's elite Indus Rangers started to jostle with Indian forces for control of a ruined fort at Kanjarkot, on the north-west fringe of the Rann.[7]

At the same time, Shastri's authority in India was called into question as his government faced domestic criticism over its lacklustre response to food shortages, rising prices, a balance of payments crisis and concerns voiced in the south over plans to phase out English as an official

[5] Chakravorty, *Indo-Pak War*, p. 17.
[6] CRO Circular, No. 118, 'The Dispute between India and Pakistan over the Rann of Kutch', 28 April 1965, PREM 13/391, TNA.
[7] CRO to British High Commissions, 'The Dispute between India and Pakistan over the Rann of Kutch', 28 April 1965, PREM 13/391, TNA.

national language. Moreover, many Indians began to equate Pakistan's increasingly belligerent approach to the Rann dispute with that adopted by China prior to the Sino-Indian border war in 1962. In consequence, India's embattled premier found it politically expedient to take a tough line on the Rann issue.[8] In March, India staged a major military exercise in the Kutch region, code-named 'Arrow Head', in which powerful air, land and sea forces, including the nation's sole aircraft carrier INS *Vikrant*, were deployed in a considerable show of force.[9] Speaking at a public meeting in Hyderabad at the end of the month, Shastri urged Pakistan's leaders 'not to resort to the use of force to resolve minor disputes over demarcation ... [of] a few acres of land'. Should Pakistan seek to impose a military solution in Kutch, India's leader warned, 'then we [India] will have to act as the situation demands'.[10]

On 9 April, tension in the Rann increased after an exchange of fire occurred between large numbers of Indian and Pakistani soldiers on its northern edge. Over the following two weeks, both sides became embroiled in a cycle of attacks, counter-attacks and artillery duels, before, on 24 April, Pakistan's Army launched 'Desert Hawk', a powerful and decisive thrust toward the heart of the Rann. Two days later, India's defence minister, Yashwantrao Balwantrao (Y. B.) Chavan, informed the Lok Sabha that developments in Kutch 'necessitated certain [military] moves plus stoppage of leave and recall of [service] personnel on leave'.[11] India's armed forces were placed on high alert along the country's entire western border. In Pakistan, a general mobilisation was ordered, and Muhammad Musa, Commander-in-Chief of the army, instructed his soldiers to prepare to assume battle positions. For the first time since the late 1940s, the Indian subcontinent stood poised on the brink of general war.

### Averting war in the Rann: Britain, the United States and the Kutch dispute

Exactly how the crisis in Kutch had been allowed to assume such serious proportions, and precisely who was most to blame for it having done so, remained somewhat opaque to outside observers. At first, British

---

[8] Freeman to Bottomley, 'India: The Rann of Kutch Dispute', 16 July 1965, PREM 13/393, TNA.

[9] Chakravorty, *Indo-Pak War*, pp. 22–4; CRO to British High Commissions, 'The Dispute between India and Pakistan over the Rann of Kutch', 28 April 1965, PREM 13/391, TNA.

[10] *The Hindustan Times*, 22 March 1965.

[11] Chakravorty, *Indo-Pak War*, p. 34.

and American military and intelligence experts took a 'fairly relaxed' approach to the fighting in the Rann, characterising it as 'just another border incident' between India and Pakistan. In early April, American consular officials based in Bombay, directly to the south of Kutch, noted that their British colleagues were disposed 'towards putting blame on [the] Indians'. Pakistan patrols had been active in the Rann 'all along', the British reasoned, 'and the Indian[s] [were] just waking up to fact and reacting'.[12] As the fighting in Kutch intensified later that month, and 'confused and contradictory' accounts surfaced of events taking place to the north, the British qualified their earlier assessment of Indian culpability. Perplexed British officials in the subcontinent informed Whitehall that it was 'impossible to determine' whether India or Pakistan was most responsible for precipitating the crisis.[13] John Freeman eventually went further and concluded that 'the balance of right, although not the whole of it ... is on the Indian side in this tiresome affair'.[14] Chester Bowles took a more equivocal view than Freeman, advising Washington that 'no one can be sure' which party was primarily to blame for the Kutch episode. It seemed probable, Bowles suggested, 'that [the] fight [had] started by accident as in [the] case of two small boys pushing each other on [the] playground after school'.[15]

Besides which, Britain and the United States were less interested in apportioning responsibility for the Kutch imbroglio, and more concerned with ensuring that it did not escalate into a full-scale war between India and Pakistan. Specifically, British and American officials were disturbed to learn that following the Pakistani Army's strong showing in the Rann, where the terrain favoured forces attacking from the north, some members of Shastri's cabinet were calling for an Indian counter-attack outside Kutch, on more advantageous ground. In late April, Robert Komer informed McGeorge Bundy that the Kutch incident 'could build up into a real mess ... it might mean a major Pak/Indian war'. The State Department agreed, reasoning that the Indian public would not tolerate letting Pakistan 'get away with a Ladakh-type humiliation. So there's a strong chance of *Indian retaliation elsewhere,*

[12] Rewinkel to State Department, 10 April 1965, National Security File (NSF) Country File, India, Box 129 [1 of 2], Folder 2 India Cables [2 of 2], Vol. IV, 12-64 to 6-65, Lyndon Baines Johnson Library, Austin, Texas (hereafter LBJL).

[13] CRO Circular, No. 118, 'The Dispute between India and Pakistan over the Rann of Kutch', 28 April 1965, PREM 13/391, TNA.

[14] Freeman to Oliver Wright, 25 May 1965, PREM 13/392, TNA.

[15] Bowles to Rusk, No. 3210, 10 May 1965, NSF Country File, India, Box 129 [1 of 2], Folder 2 India Cables [2 of 2], Vol. IV, 12-64 to 6-65, LBJL.

where the odds favour them more.'[16] The British Commonwealth Relations Office feared that by widening its conflict with Pakistan beyond the Rann, India would risk precipitating widespread communal violence, a general conflagration on the subcontinent and possibly Chinese military intervention on the side of Pakistan.[17] The US Secretary of State, Dean Rusk, shared British anxieties. 'If hostilities came [between India and Pakistan]', Rusk informed Britain's ambassador in Washington, Sir Patrick Dean, 'they could not be confined to the military and … The resulting casualties would be comparable with those from a nuclear exchange.'[18]

On 26 April, British concern over the fighting taking place in the Rann prompted Harold Wilson to instruct John Freeman and Morrice James, Britain's High Commissioner in Karachi, to offer Shastri and Ayub Khan the British government's good offices in helping to bring about a cessation of hostilities.[19] When Freeman called on Shastri the following day to deliver Wilson's message, he found the Indian prime minister and his officials to be in a combative mood. On his way to meet with Shastri, Freeman dropped in on Chandra Shekhar (C. S.) Jha, India's Foreign Secretary. To Freeman's 'dismay', Jha confirmed that India was contemplating a military strike against a weak point in West Pakistan's defences, outside the Rann. 'You must understand', Jha informed the British High Commissioner, 'that there is now a danger of general war with Pakistan. India is most anxious to avoid this, but no government could face its public opinion if it took this lying down. The danger of war is unfortunately real.'[20] Freeman's interview with Shastri proved equally unsettling. The High Commissioner asked Shastri whether he had understood Jha correctly, when the Foreign Secretary had suggested that India was contemplating broadening its conflict with Pakistan. The Indian premier responded, Freeman reported back to Whitehall, 'with a silence which must have lasted 30 seconds and then said: "you are perfectly right"'. To senior policymakers in London and Washington, it appeared that the charges of weakness and vacillation levelled at Shastri by his domestic critics might have boxed the Indian prime minister into a political corner. 'Mr Shastri is a very worried man and as much about the political situation as the military', Freeman

---

[16] Komer to McGeorge Bundy, 26 April 1965, NSF Country File, Pakistan, Box 151, Folder 4, Pakistan Memos, Vol. III, 12-64 to 7-65, LBJL.

[17] CRO to Freeman, No. 1566, 27 April 1965, PREM 13/191, TNA.

[18] Sir Patrick Dean to Foreign Office, No. 1545, 15 June 1965, PREM 13/392, TNA.

[19] Sykes to Bottomley, 'Pakistan: The Rann of Kutch Dispute', 16 July 1965, PREM 13/393, TNA.

[20] Freeman to CRO, No. 1360, 26 April 1965, PREM 13/191, TNA.

advised the CRO. '[I]n the absence of any gesture by Pakistan, I guess that his fear is that at worst he might have either to launch some retaliation which he knows to be highly dangerous or else make way for someone else who will.'[21]

In Pakistan, coverage of the Rann fighting within the nation's tightly controlled media was muted. In contrast, India's free press took on an increasingly jingoistic tone as the Kutch crisis developed. With the Lok Sabha in session, some Indian parliamentarians played to the public gallery and engaged in 'hysterical' public denunciations of Pakistan. On 28 April, an uncharacteristically bellicose Shastri informed India's lower chamber of parliament that, 'If Pakistan continues to discard reason and persists in its aggressive activities, our Army will defend the country and it will decide its own strategy and employment of its manpower and equipment in a manner which it deems best.'[22] Chester Bowles was unimpressed by Shastri's tough rhetoric. The American ambassador lamented that the Indian premier's response to his first major external challenge had been 'weak, unsophisticated and needlessly fearful of his parliamentary opposition'.[23] The chances of preventing the clash in the Rann from expanding into a general Indo-Pakistani war looked unpromising, not least because a considerable divergence existed in the ceasefire demands issued by both sides. Pakistan insisted all military forces should leave the Rann under a ceasefire, thereby placing the onus upon India to relinquish its hold over the lion's share of the territory under dispute. India made it equally clear that it regarded Pakistan's unilateral withdrawal from Kanjarkot as a prerequisite to any cessation of hostilities, a precondition that Ayub Khan's government dismissed as unacceptable.[24] Yet, from a seemingly hopeless position, and after considerable diplomatic prodding by James and Freeman, on 30 April, the British managed to broker an informal ceasefire.

On the Indian side, the success of Britain's diplomatic initiative owed much to Shastri's desire to avoid all-out war with Pakistan. Shastri and his senior military commanders recognised that pressure from India's press, public and hawks within the Congress Party hierarchy to hit back at Pakistan outside Kutch would become irresistible if the fighting in

[21] Freeman to CRO, No. 1369, 27 April 1965, PREM 13/191, TNA.
[22] Sykes to Bottomley, 'Pakistan: The Rann of Kutch Dispute', 16 July 1965, PREM 13/393, TNA; Chakravorty, *Indo-Pak War*, p. 35.
[23] Bowles to Rusk, No. 3210, 10 May 1965, NSF Country File, India, Box 129 [1 of 2], Folder 2 India Cables [2 of 2], Vol. IV, 12-64 to 6-65, LBJL.
[24] CRO Circular, No. 118, 'The Dispute between India and Pakistan over the Rann of Kutch', 28 April 1965, PREM 13/391, TNA.

the Rann continued.[25] Ignoring protests from opposition groups, such as the Jan Sangh and Praya Socialist Party, and the misgivings of some malcontents within his own government, Shastri convinced a majority of the Congress Parliamentary Party to endorse a de facto ceasefire. Addressing the Rajya Sabha on 3 May, Shastri declared that

the Indian Government and the Indian people have no ill-will against the people of Pakistan. We wish them well and we would be happy to see them progress on the road to prosperity. We are aware that their prosperity as well as the prosperity of the people of India, of 600 million people who inhabit the subcontinent, depends upon the preservation of peace.[26]

The British discovered that Ayub Khan was equally willing to end the hostilities in Kutch, albeit for different reasons. Pakistan's armed forces had gained ground in the Rann and generally acquitted themselves well against their Indian adversaries. Consequently, Pakistan's government felt able to enter into negotiations with India from a position of strength. Pakistani officials, the British observed, had crowed at having 'seen the Indians off as effectively as the Chinese had done in 1962, except that the Chinese had needed a couple of divisions to do the job whereas the Pakistanis had only a couple of brigades'.[27] Occupying additional territory in Kutch would, in any event, become impossible after late May, when the onset of the monsoon ended the military campaigning season. Furthermore, Pakistan had come under increasing pressure from Washington to desist from using its US-supplied arms against India.[28] If nothing else, Ayub Khan's administration reasoned that India's agreement to convene talks on the Sind–Kutch border had validated its contention that the boundary was in dispute. The Rann crisis, Pakistan's president informed one Western official, had exposed Shastri as a week reed, a man as diminutive in character as he was in stature, and who 'seemed to be talking through his dhoti'.[29]

---

[25] Freeman to Bottomley, 'India: The Rann of Kutch Dispute', 30 July 1965, PREM 13/393, TNA.

[26] C. P. Srivastava, *Lal Bahadur Shastri: A Life of Truth in Politics* (New Delhi: Oxford University Press, 1995), pp. 199–200.

[27] Sykes to Bottomley, 'Pakistan: The Rann of Kutch Dispute', 16 July 1965, PREM 13/393, TNA.

[28] McConaughy to State Department, 30 April 1965, RG 59, Central Files 1964–6, POL 32-1 INDIA–PAK, National Archives and Records Administration, College Park, Maryland (hereafter NARA).

[29] Sykes to Bottomley, 'Pakistan: The Rann of Kutch Dispute', 16 July 1965, PREM 13/393, TNA. Morrice James noted that Ayub Khan, ever since his first meeting with Shastri in October 1964, 'in private conversation with Westerners ... has spoken of him [Shastri] in terms of the greatest disrespect'. James to Bottomley, 'Pakistan and Kashmir: A Tragic Misadventure', 25 October 1965, DO 196/388, TNA.

On 5 May, Shastri and Ayub Khan publicly confirmed that Indian and Pakistani forces had received orders to cease offensive operations. Behind the scenes, Freeman and James assumed the roles of honest brokers in the negotiations between Indian and Pakistani officials that followed.[30] In James and Freeman, the British were fortunate to have two experienced, respected and politically adroit individuals to represent their interests. Having previously served as Deputy High Commissioner in India between 1958 and 1961, James was on especially good terms with senior government figures in New Delhi and Rawalpindi.[31] The British mediators initially struggled to make any impression on their Indian and Pakistani colleagues, who engaged in a series of 'bitter and strenuously fought' bilateral exchanges. In particular, Pakistan's 'deeply negative and suspicious' Foreign Secretary, Aziz Ahmed, who one senior British official characterised as '65 per cent brains, 15 per cent real charm and 20 per cent mad', exasperated James by treating 'every drafting point as a life-and-death matter for Pakistan'.[32]

India's provocative decision to move 'very powerful' military forces close to its borders with East and West Pakistan while the Kutch talks were still ongoing, injected further unwelcome tension into the proceedings. As one British official put it, by deciding to redeploy the Indian Army and place the Pakistani city of Lahore 'under a greater threat than it had even been in 1947', Shastri was deemed by Ayub Khan to have committed an act of bad faith.[33] In turn, the Indian government resented Pakistan's attempts to broaden the scope of the ceasefire discussions to include other, unrelated issues. It was not until 12 May that an exhausted Morrice James was able to advise London that 'against the odds ... a substantial measure of agreement on essentials' had been reached between India and Pakistan.[34]

### A fragile peace

A month later, however, in mid-June, India and Pakistan were still haggling over the finer points of a Kutch agreement. On 14 June, Shastri instructed Indian's ambassador in Washington, B. K. Nehru, to inform

---

[30] Sykes to Bottomley, 'Pakistan: The Rann of Kutch Dispute', 16 July 1965, PREM 13/393, TNA.

[31] Morrice James, *Pakistan Chronicle* (London: Hurst, 1992), p. 124.

[32] Gore-Booth to Sir Saville Garner, 28 February 1965, MSS.Gore-Booth Eng.4535, Gore-Booth Papers, Bodleian Library, University of Oxford; James to CRO, 12 May 1965, PREM 13/391, TNA.

[33] Sykes to Bottomley, 'Pakistan: The Rann of Kutch Dispute', 16 July 1965, PREM 13/393, TNA.

[34] James to CRO, 12 May 1965, PREM 13/391, TNA.

Dean Rusk that New Delhi's patience with Pakistan was wearing thin. In the search for a diplomatic solution to the Kutch dispute, Nehru advised Rusk, India had conceded all that could be reasonably expected of it. Any further equivocation on the part of Ayub Khan's government might compel India to drive Pakistan out of the Rann by force of arms. India, Rusk was assured, had

taken full account of the military, political, economic, and social consequences of such action in the sub-continent, but had decided that there was no alternative if the Pakistanis would not vacate the Rann. India had been humiliated by her apparent defeat by the Chinese in 1962 and could not accept a similar humiliation at the hands of the Pakistanis now. If Shastri did not act he would be deposed and his successor would act in his stead.[35]

With the ceasefire under threat, the CRO, under the direction of Cyril Pickard, redoubled its efforts to push India and Pakistan into a formal settlement. Toward the end of the month, after some last-minute arm-twisting by Harold Wilson and his Secretary of State for Commonwealth Relations, Arthur Bottomley, at the Commonwealth Prime Ministers' Conference in London, Shastri and Ayub Khan agreed to settle the Rann of Kutch dispute through a process of binding international arbitration.[36]

Inevitably, the arbitration procedure proved more difficult, and took a good deal longer to conclude, than had been anticipated. In October, the UN Secretary General appointed Gunnar Lagergren, an eminent Swedish judge, to chair an award tribunal. Pakistan nominated Iran's former foreign minister, Nasrollah Entezam, to serve as the second member of the tribunal, while India selected a prominent Yugoslav jurist, Ales Bebler, as its nominee. The tribunal met for the first time in Geneva, on 19 February 1966. Its decision, which was announced two years later, in February 1968, largely upheld India's claim that the Sind–Kutch border ran along the Rann's northern edge, and not through its centre. Having laid claim to half the Rann, when the formal arbitration agreement was signed, in July 1965, Pakistan received only 320 square miles (828 square kilometres) of territory, although to Rawalpindi's satisfaction this included Kanjarkot and Chhad Bet.[37]

Having been instrumental in bringing the Kutch dispute to a peaceful conclusion, British officials congratulated themselves on a job

---

[35] Sir Patrick Dean to Foreign Office, No. 1545, 15 June 1965, PREM 13/392, TNA; James, *Pakistan Chronicle*, p. 126.
[36] Sykes to Bottomley, 'Pakistan: The Rann of Kutch Dispute', 16 July 1965, PREM 13/393, TNA; James, *Pakistan Chronicle*, p. 126.
[37] Chakravorty, *Indo-Pak War*, p. 35.

well done. In Pakistan, Ayub Khan's government privately acknowledged that it had probably gained more territory in the Rann through third-party mediation than it could have secured militarily. Moreover, the Rann negotiations rekindled international interest in the Kashmir issue, on which a considerable body of world opinion sympathised with Pakistan.[38] 'The British Government's efforts', the UK High Commission in Karachi exalted, 'have brought widespread and genuine gratitude from all sections of the [Pakistani] community.'[39] Whitehall considered Britain's diplomatic intervention in the subcontinent to have been particularly important, given other countries' apparent reluctance to become enmeshed in Indo-Pakistani affairs. The bitterness in India and Pakistan caused by Lyndon Johnson's decision earlier in the year to withdraw invitations for Shastri and Ayub Khan to visit the United States discouraged Washington from playing a prominent role in the Rann crisis. Alexei Kosygin, the Soviet premier, appeared equally reticent about offering India and Pakistan his services as a third-party mediator and, the British suspected, would have been rejected as an impartial intermediary by Pakistan in any case. Likewise, the Afro-Asian bloc's focus was centred upon its upcoming conference in Algiers, while the UN was preoccupied with its own internal problems. In John Freeman's view, had Britain not stepped in when it did to broker a ceasefire, the Indian subcontinent might have experienced 'the double shock of widespread military conflict and communal massacre on a vast scale'.[40]

Harold Wilson was particularly gratified by the plaudits his government received for helping to avert a disaster in South Asia. Dean Rusk emphasised to Johnson that Wilson and his officials had 'worked like Trojans, under the most complicated and frustrating circumstances' to bring peace to the subcontinent, an endorsement that prompted the president to send a personal note of thanks to 10 Downing Street.[41] Shastri was similarly appreciative of Wilson's efforts. In conversation with the editor of The Indian Express, Frank Moraes, Shastri praised his British counterpart's 'very helpful' intervention during the final

---

[38] James to Bottomley, 'Pakistan and Kashmir: A Tragic Misadventure', 25 October 1965, DO 196/388, TNA.

[39] James, Pakistan Chronicle, p. 126; E. L. Sykes to Bottomley, 'Pakistan: The Rann of Kutch Dispute', 16 July 1965, PREM 13/393, TNA.

[40] Freeman to Bottomley, 'India: The Rann of Kutch Dispute', 16 July 1965, PREM 13/393, TNA.

[41] Rusk to Johnson, 30 June 1965, NSF, Robert W. Komer Files, Box 53, Folder United Kingdom Jan 1964–Mar 1966 [2 of 2], LBJL.

stages of the Rann negotiations.[42] To some British officials, the Kutch incident confirmed that British 'credit' was 'still good in the subcontinent'.[43] Other senior figures in the British establishment were less sure. On a visit to New Delhi in May, Lord Mountbatten, Britain's Chief of Defence Staff, observed that during talks with Indian military commanders and civil officials:

he had sensed a feeling of restraint on the Indian side and it was clear to him that relations were very different from the last time he had visited India … he was sure that there was much [Indian] irritation about the British attitude in regard to the Rann of Kutch and particular disquiet that the British had not come out more strongly to support the Indian's cast-iron case in this dispute.[44]

Indeed, given his proclivity to court honours of any and every description, Mountbatten was dismayed to discover that India's Chief of Army Staff, General Joyanto Nath (J. N.) Chaudhuri, had abandoned plans to offer him the Colonelcy of a regular Indian Army regiment, due to the poor state of Anglo-Indian relations.[45] John Freeman cautioned Whitehall that it would be as well not to read too much into the Rann success, when the underlying issues perpetuating Indo-Pakistani enmity remained unresolved and continued to pose a threat to Britain's relations with both countries. In helping to avert a major clash between New Delhi and Rawalpindi over the Rann, Freeman counselled London, 'We have remedied a symptom, but the basic *malaise* still exists.'[46]

From the Johnson administration's perspective, the Rann episode acted as a further irritant in its faltering relationship with the subcontinent. The Indian government was angry that the United States had not done more to prevent Pakistan's use of US-supplied military equipment against its armed forces, despite past assurances from Washington that it would do so. Chester Bowles bemoaned that many Indian policymakers had become 'angry', 'unreasonable' and 'irrational' in the aftermath of the Kutch affair. After taking informal soundings from a number of moderate and generally pro-American Indians, including Chavan,

[42] Entry for 29 June 1965, PP MS 24, Box 2, Folder 14, 'Janta' Diary, Frank Moraes Papers, School of Oriental and African Studies, University of London (hereafter FMP).

[43] Freeman to Bottomley 'India: The Rann of Kutch Dispute', 16 July 1965, PREM 13/393, TNA.

[44] Record of a meeting held in Rashtrapati Bhavan, 7 May 1965, MB1/J507, Visit to India, May 1965, Lord Mountbatten Papers, Hartley Library, University of Southampton (hereafter MBP).

[45] Mountbatten to Chaudhuri, 7 May 1965, MB1/J507, Visit to India, May 1965, MBP.

[46] Freeman to Bottomley 'India: The Rann of Kutch Dispute', 16 July 1965, PREM 13/393, TNA.

Jha, Radhakrishnan and Morarji Desai, a worried Bowles found that each was 'concern[ed] about [the] future of US–India relations'. Urgent action was required, Bowles argued, 'if we are to prevent [the] rapid and disastrous erosion of [the] US position in South Asia which we have been laboriously building up for [the] last decade'.[47] Pakistan felt similarly aggrieved that American commitments to restrain Indian 'aggression' had proved to be hollow. On 14 July, as large anti-American rallies occurred across Pakistan, Ayub Khan attacked the United States at a public meeting of the Muslim League. Americans, Pakistan's president declared, were 'power drunk' and unable to understand, or work in partnership with, their allies.[48] At the beginning of August, an exasperated State Department asked the British to warn Ayub Khan and his ministers to tone down their anti-US diatribes. 'This is exactly why we look to the British to help us', an America official reasoned. '[N]ot because of their power and influence but because their present situation enables them to say some hard truths on our behalf that we would not want to say ourselves.'[49]

## Operation Gibraltar and the road to war

The most insidious threat to Western interests in the subcontinent, however, lay not in an upsurge of anti-American sentiment. Far more troubling was an emerging consensus amongst senior Pakistani politicians and military leaders that, having used military force as a lever to extract territorial concessions from India in the Rann, the same tactic could be repeated with similar results when applied to the Kashmir dispute. Pakistan's policymakers had taken heart from the outcome of the Kutch crisis. India, they believed, had shown itself to be an enfeebled and divided nation, yet to recover militarily, or psychologically, from its defeat at the hands of China in 1962. Mounting an operation to 'liberate' Kashmir before further British, American and Soviet military aid had strengthened India's armed forces, or New Delhi developed a nuclear capability, had, as the British later recognised, 'great

---

[47] Bowles to Secretary of State, No. 2349, 10 May 1965, NSF Country File, India, Box 129 [1 of 2], Folder 2 India Cables [2 of 2], Vol. IV, 12-64 to 6-65, LBJL; Green to Secretary of State, No. 3430, 25 May 1965, NSF Country File, India, Box 129 [1 of 2], Folder 2 India Cables [2 of 2], Vol. IV, 12-64 to 6-65, LBJL.
[48] Robert J. McMahon, *The Cold War on the Periphery: The United States, India and Pakistan* (New York: Columbia University Press, 1994), p. 325.
[49] State Department to Karachi, 8 August 1965, No. 255, NSF Country File, Pakistan, Box 151, Folder 6 Pakistan Cables [2 of 2], Vol. IV, 8-65 to 9-65, LBJL.

intrinsic attraction for Pakistanis and probably received early support from senior members of the army and Civil Service'.[50]

Foremost amongst those pushing Ayub Khan to exploit India's perceived weaknesses, and move against Kashmir, was a clique led by Pakistan's charismatic foreign minister Zulfikar Ali Bhutto, which also included Foreign Secretary Aziz Ahmed and Major-General Akhtar Hussain Malik, commander of Pakistan's forces in Azad Kashmir. Far more comfortable as a soldier than a diplomat, Ayub Khan leant heavily on Pakistan's foreign affairs experts for advice and guidance, and none more so than Bhutto. Harold Wilson worried that Pakistan's president was 'basically a simple and deeply patriotic soldier capable of being pushed around by unscrupulous politicians'.[51] In particular, British and American officials viewed Bhutto as the sort of 'reckless' and 'crooked' manipulator that could lead Pakistan, and its president, to the brink of disaster.[52] Moreover, to London and Washington's vexation, Bhutto's bellicose anti-Indian rhetoric and socialist pretensions earned him the support of a wide cross-section of Pakistan's underclass, many of whom felt politically alienated and economically overlooked by Ayub Khan's semi-authoritarian regime.[53]

At some point during the spring of 1965, Pakistan's foreign policy hawks persuaded Ayub Khan that a fresh bout of Indo-Pakistani fighting in Kashmir would act as a trigger for British and American diplomatic intervention in the dispute. Under international pressure, a weakened India would then, the president was assured, be squeezed into ceding territory to Pakistan.[54] Pakistani plans for a military operation in Kashmir were in place by May 1965, if not earlier, and well before the Kutch settlement with India had been signed.[55] At one stage in the Rann negotiations, Aziz Ahmed confirmed as much to a startled Morrice James. Pointing to the British High Commissioner in Ayub Khan's presence, Ahmed blurted out the words 'I think we've found our Kashmir negotiator.'[56]

---

[50] James to Bottomley, 'Pakistan and Kashmir: A Tragic Misadventure', 25 October 1965, DO 196/388, TNA; James, *Pakistan Chronicle*, p. 125.

[51] Wilson to Lyndon Johnson, 12 December 1965, PREM 13/396, TNA.

[52] C. C. W. Adams to Oliver Wright, 22 October 1965, DO 196/224, TNA.

[53] Record of meeting between James and Freeman in Karachi, 1 and 2 February 1966, FO 371/186952/F1041/30, TNA.

[54] Muhammad Musa, *My Version: India–Pakistan War 1965* (Lahore: Wajidalis, 1983), p. 54; James to Bottomley, 'Pakistan and Kashmir: A Tragic Misadventure', 25 October 1965, DO 196/388, TNA.

[55] James to Bottomley, 'Pakistan and Kashmir: A Tragic Misadventure', 25 October 1965, DO 196/388, TNA; Chakravorty, *Indo-Pak War*, p. 47.

[56] James, *Pakistan Chronicle*, p. 130.

By mid-summer, after months of training and preparation, irregular Pakistani forces were ready to launch 'Operation Gibraltar' and enter Indian-controlled Kashmir. Pakistan's plan was to foment disorder inside the state by cutting lines of communication, blowing up bridges and roads, and conducting hit-and-run raids on Indian military posts.[57] This, it was hoped, would spark a popular uprising against Indian rule, at which point regular Pakistani forces would enter Kashmir on the pretext of restoring law and order. Pakistan envisaged that external powers, led by Britain and the United States, would then step in, as they had during the Rann crisis, to arrange a ceasefire and broker a Kashmir settlement. Instead, as the British later lamented, 'By sending several thousand guerrillas across the Kashmir cease-fire line in early August, President Ayub's regime initiated a train of events which ... brought the Indo-Pakistan sub-continent to the edge of disaster.'[58]

'Operation Gibraltar' was set in motion on the night of 5–6 August, when over a thousand Pakistani insurgents dressed in civilian clothes crossed the 500 mile-long ceasefire line that had separated Indian and Pakistani forces in Kashmir since July 1949. The rugged mountain terrain surrounding the ceasefire line, and the frequency with which both sides had sent small patrols across it in the past, meant that it was some days before the Indian government recognised the seriousness of the situation.[59] On 8 August, Shastri hurriedly convened a meeting of the emergency committee of the Indian cabinet, and instructed General Chaudhuri to take immediate steps to stem the flow of Pakistani forces entering Kashmir.[60] That evening, the British and American governments were made aware for the first time of the crisis developing in the subcontinent. Having summoned John Freeman and Chester Bowles to his office in the Ministry of External Affairs, C. S. Jha informed the Western diplomats that large numbers of well-armed Pakistani soldiers

---

[57] 'Operation Gibraltar' took its name from the Arab general Abdur Rahman Tariq, who commanded an assault on Jablul Tariq (Gibraltar) in 711. Tariq ordered his men to burn their boats after sailing from North Africa to the Iberian Peninsula. When his men asked how they would return to their homeland, Tariq responded that their destiny lay in Spain and Gibraltar, and there was no question of turning back.

[58] James to Bottomley, 'Pakistan and Kashmir: A Tragic Misadventure', 25 October 1965, DO 196/388, TNA.

[59] The Australian Lieutenant General in charge of the UN Military Observer Group (UNMOGIP) in Kashmir, Robert Nimmo, informed Frank Moraes that in 1954 the UN had recorded 27 violations of the ceasefire line by Indian and Pakistani military forces and civilians. In 1964, as tensions rose between New Delhi and Rawalpindi, the number of UN recorded infringements rose dramatically to 2,200. Entry for 2 June 1965, PP MS 24, Box 2, Folder 14, 'Janta' Diary, FMP.

[60] Srivastava, *Lal Bahadur Shastri*, p. 212.

had crossed into Indian-controlled Kashmir, and had begun 'urging the local population to insurrection'. The following day, a full-length front-page headline in Pakistan's semi-official daily, *Dawn*, proclaimed, 'Revolutionary Council Held in Kashmir: Liberation War to be Waged'. In an accompanying article, *Dawn* praised 'the people of the occupied part of Kashmir' who had risen up to 'conduct an all-out war of liberation against Indian imperialism'. By now, following the arrival of thousands of reinforcements, Pakistani forces inside Kashmir had occupied strategic positions immediately to the west of the Kashmir Valley, one of which included a landing strip suitable for light aircraft. However, after some initial success, the momentum behind Pakistan's thrust into Kashmir slowed, and the state's inhabitants rejected exhortations from the Pakistani insurgents to join them in taking up arms against their Indian 'oppressors'.[61]

Pakistan's inability to muster support from the local Kashmiri population proved a disaster, both militarily and politically. On 13 August, a defiant Shastri assured his countrymen in a nationwide address broadcast on All India Radio that

There is no doubt that this is a thinly disguised armed attack on our country organised by Pakistan and it has to be met as such … There is no revolution in Kashmir nor is there any revolutionary council. The people in Jammu and Kashmir have, in fact, themselves given lie to Pakistan's propaganda … If Pakistan has any ideas of annexing any part of our territories by force, she should think afresh. I want to state categorically that force will be met with force and aggression against us will never be allowed to succeed.[62]

India's premier reiterated his determination to respond forcefully to Pakistan's provocation in a round of interviews with Western press correspondents. 'If this [infiltration in Kashmir] continues,' Shastri stated to the *New York Times*' New Delhi correspondent, Tony Lukas, 'we will have to carry the fight to the other side. It all depends on what Pakistan does now. It is up to them.'[63] Back in London, the possibility that the subcontinent might once again be plunged into 'chaos' unnerved Whitehall. On the face of things, India's superior military and industrial strength looked certain to prove decisive in a protracted Indo-Pakistani conflict. But, as Algernon Rumbold, Deputy Under Secretary of State at the CRO, reminded Arthur Bottomley, the associated economic,

[61] Freeman to Bottomley, 'India: India and Pakistan: The Three Weeks' War', 19 October 1965, DO 196/387, TNA.

[62] Srivastava, *Lal Bahadur Shastri*, pp. 214–15.

[63] *The New York Times*, 21 August 1965.

communal and psychological costs suggested that 'in this sort of war neither side can win'.[64]

On 28 August, with Pakistani forces edging further toward the heart of Kashmir, Shastri authorised India's army to go onto the offensive. Crossing the ceasefire line in the Uri sector, in the north-west of the state, Indian infantry engaged a large Pakistani force threatening the Kashmir Valley. By 30 August, the Indian Army had begun advancing into Azad Kashmir on three fronts, at Kargil, Tithwal and the Punch–Uri bulge.[65] On 1 September, Pakistan responded by initiating 'Operation Grand Slam', an armoured thrust with strong infantry support in the direction of Chhamb, at the southern end of the ceasefire line. Pakistan's leaders framed their decision to escalate the fighting in Kashmir as a necessary defensive reaction to India's assault on Pakistan's sovereignty, and more broadly, in terms of a moral obligation to support the Muslim 'sons of the soil of Kashmir' in their struggle 'against Indian tyranny'. In a letter to Wilson, Ayub Khan intimated that 'Gland Slam's' purpose was twofold: firstly, to preserve Pakistan's territorial integrity, and secondly, to challenge 'Indian repression of Kashmiris [which] has now assumed the proportions of genocide'.[66] Characteristically, Bhutto was even more outspoken in condemning India for forcing Pakistan's hand in Kashmir. On 3 September, Pakistan's foreign minister announced publicly that his government had taken a 'solemn pledge' to end India's 'barbaric policy of ... eliminating the Moslem majority [in the State] by Hitlerite extermination'.[67]

'Operation Grand Slam' threatened strategic disaster for Shastri's government. With India's forces around Chhamb thrown back onto the defensive by Pakistani armour, New Delhi's hold on Jammu was endangered. Sandwiched between the Vale of Kashmir to the north and the Daman Koh Plains to the south, Jammu contained the only road link between India and the Vale, and beyond that Ladakh. Without free passage through Jammu, Indian soldiers facing the Chinese on the country's northern border would be left isolated and exposed. On 2 September, Shastri met with the emergency committee of his cabinet to consider whether India should mount a diversionary attack on West Pakistan in order to relieve the pressure on Chhamb. Having considered the matter overnight, at a second emergency committee meeting held the following morning India's political leaders voted unanimously

---

[64] Rumbold to Bottomley, 'India/Pakistan' (draft), 10 September 1965, DO 196/384, TNA.
[65] Srivastava, *Lal Bahadur Shastri*, p. 220; James, *Pakistan Chronicle*, p. 131.
[66] Ayub Khan to Wilson, 1 September 1965, PREM 13/393, TNA.
[67] *The Economist*, 25 September 1965.

to launch a military operation against Pakistan in the Punjab.[68] Shastri's patience with Ayub Khan had been exhausted. Speaking at a meeting of India's National Development Council, the Indian premier explained:

We cannot allow this thing to continue. We do not want that there should be a continuous conflict forced on us by Pakistan, and that they should cross into our territory and then sue for peace, in the hope that we will agree to some kind of a ceasefire. This has become intolerable. We do not and cannot accept it. We have to bring this matter to an end.[69]

On 6 September, the Indian Army's I and XI corps crossed the Indo-Pakistani border in the Punjab, and headed for the cities of Sialkot and Lahore, Pakistan's cultural capital.[70] The Indian assault caught Pakistan by surprise. Some startled Pakistani soldiers rushed to the front line still wearing their pyjamas.[71] By threatening to cut the road and railway arteries running through the Punjab that linked Rawalpindi in the north with Karachi in the south, and effectively splitting West Pakistan in two, India regained the military initiative.[72]

On the streets of India's capital, confirmation that the nation's army had entered Western Punjab and was heading for Lahore 'probably caused more excitement ... than any other news since 1947'. The 'wild scenes of enthusiasm' in New Delhi reminded one British official of the public reaction to the outbreak of war in Europe in 1914. Residents who had left their ancestral homes in Lahore at the time of partition openly voiced the hope that India would reclaim the city of their birth. Across India, street hawkers gave away sweets to passers-by, newspaper offices distributed free updates on the fighting, workers called off strikes, trade unions withdrew pay claims and donations poured in to the National Defence Fund, a remnant of the Chinese invasion in 1962.[73] More troublingly, police patrols and self-appointed civil defence vigilantes roamed the capital's streets and rounded up suspected Pakistani agents, spies and saboteurs. 'To be a Muslim', an officer at the British High Commission noted, '(and Delhi has a considerable Muslim population) is now to be in some degree of danger.' Despite stern warnings from Shastri and his ministers that they would crack down severely on outbreaks of communal violence, a darker side to India's outpouring of patriotism came to the surface.[74] American policymakers were equally

---

[68] Srivastava, *Lal Bahadur Shastri*, p. 229.
[69] *The Hindustan Times*, 6 September 1965.
[70] Chakravorty, *Indo-Pak War*, p. 122.
[71] Ian Talbot, *Pakistan: A Modern History* (London: Hurst & Company, 2009), p. 177.
[72] James, *Pakistan Chronicle*, p. 136.
[73] Furness to Ewans, 'India Goes to War', 17 September 1965, DO 196/385, TNA.
[74] *Ibid.*

concerned by the prospect of an outbreak of communal disorder. On 9 September, Dean Rusk advised Lyndon Johnson that 'the prospect is grim'. Were Indo-Pakistani hostilities to spiral out of control, Rusk warned, 'the 50 million Moslems in India and upwards of 10 million Hindus in Pakistan [might be subsumed by] unbelievable blood baths … call[ing] into question the future of the subcontinent itself'.[75]

Back in the United Kingdom, the British government reacted with horror at India's decision to broaden the field of Indo-Pakistani hostilities beyond Kashmir. Harold Wilson confided to Westminster's lobby journalists that he regarded 'the war between India and Pakistan as one of the gravest international developments since the end of the war against Japan'.[76] Pakistan's assertion that India's attack across an internationally recognised border in the Punjab was of a different order of magnitude from the fighting that had hitherto occurred in Kashmir, garnered some sympathy in Whitehall. India's 'belligerent' policy, British ministers feared, would make it harder for Ayub Khan to overcome opposition from hardliners in his cabinet and move toward a settlement with Shastri. Moreover, any escalation in hostilities was certain to complicate an initiative by the United Nations to broker a ceasefire.[77] On 7 September, Wilson rounded on Pakistan's High Commissioner, Agha Hilaly, for his government's recklessness in infiltrating forces across the ceasefire line in Kashmir. 'Nonetheless,' Wilson added, 'Britain regarded yesterday's attack by India across the international boundary as different in kind and degree from attacks across the ceasefire line. We took a very grave view of attacks across the ceasefire line, but we took a still graver view of attacks across the international frontier.'[78] Well-established British friends of India questioned the wisdom of Shastri's action. Having watched television reports of the 'developing war' in South Asia, Harold Wilson's Postmaster General, Tony Benn, noted in his diary that 'All my instinct is pro-India but I think they may have made a grave mistake.'[79]

---

[75] Rusk to Johnson, 'India and Pakistan', 9 September 1965, NSF Country File, Pakistan, Box 151, Folder 7, Pakistan Memos, Vol. IV, 8-65 to 9-65, LBJL.

[76] *The Times*, 7 September 1965.

[77] 'Anglo-American Meeting on Indo-Pakistan Dispute', London, 8 September 1965, NSF, Robert W. Komer Files, Box 53, Folder United Kingdom Jan 1964–Mar 1966 [2 of 2], LBJL.

[78] Memorandum of conversation between Wilson and Hilaly, 7 September, PREM 13/393, TNA.

[79] Entry for 7 September 1965, Tony Benn, *Out of the Wilderness: Diaries 1963–67* (London: Hutchinson, 1987), p. 317.

## The 6 September furore and Anglo-Indian relations

On 3 September, Harold Wilson had despatched letters to Shastri and Ayub Khan urging both to exercise restraint. The following day, the United Nations Security Council passed a resolution calling for a cease-fire in the subcontinent. When both interventions went unheeded, and India's armoured forces struck out in the direction of Lahore, the CRO suggested to Wilson that he send further, 'rather stiff messages' to India and Pakistan. At the time, Arthur Bottomley had left London for a holiday in Scotland. Responsibility for drafting the texts of Wilson's letters to Shastri and Ayub Khan, and an accompanying public statement, therefore fell to Cledwyn Hughes, Minister of State for Commonwealth Relations, and senior officials at the CRO. The CRO's civil servants favoured taking a particularly strong line with India, given Shastri's decision to send Indian forces across an international border into West Pakistan. British military assistance to India, it was suggested, should be halted, and consideration given to suspending economic aid should the United States do likewise. It was important, Hughes advised Wilson, 'to try to shake [the] Indians' confidence in their rectitude'. 'The Americans might be reluctant today to agree to language [in the Security Council] which implies that India is guilty of aggression,' Hughes added, 'but we could go as far in that direction as the Americans prove willing to go.'[80] The CRO counselled against a British peace-making initiative akin to that undertaken during the Rann crisis and, instead, recommended leaving such matters to the UN, and its Secretary General, U Thant. A British mission would take time to put together, Wilson was cautioned, and the seriousness of the situation developing in the subcontinent called for immediate action. Moreover, previous British interventions in the Kashmir dispute had been resented, particularly by India. 'While we can properly urge them [India and Pakistan] both to a ceasefire, for us to get involved in the search for a settlement on the future of Kashmir', Hughes argued, 'would be likely to lead to us burning our fingers.'[81]

After first pausing to consult with his Foreign Secretary, Michael Stewart, late on 6 September Wilson sanctioned the delivery of messages to Shastri and Ayub Khan, which called on both, 'in the most urgent terms', to bring an immediate end to hostilities. At the same moment, 10 Downing Street issued a public statement expressing the British premier's deep concern at 'the increasingly serious fighting'

[80] Hughes to Wilson, 6 September 1965, PREM 13/393, TNA.
[81] Ibid.

taking place in South Asia, and 'especially at the news that Indian forces have today attacked Pakistan territory across the international frontier in the Punjab'. The latter, Wilson's statement underlined, constituted 'a distressing response to the resolution adopted by the Security Council on September 4, calling for a cease-fire'.[82] By singling out India for particular censure, the British expected to elicit a sharp retort from New Delhi. Oliver Wright, Wilson's private secretary, informed McGeorge Bundy in Washington that having 'issued a pretty tough (on India) statement from No. 10 Downing Street ... We fully expect India to react strongly to these actions.'[83]

The intensity of the cold fury that Wilson's statement provoked in India, however, took the British by surprise. Shastri deeply resented his government being cast as an aggressor by Wilson when Pakistan's earlier infringements of the ceasefire line in Kashmir had drawn only a muted British rebuke. To add insult to Indian injury, a second message from Wilson to Shastri asked the Indian leader to ensure that weapons Britain had sent to the subcontinent for use against the Chinese were not employed against Pakistan.[84] Indian policymakers apparently discounted the fact that Britain had issued a statement in the United Nations Security Council endorsing reports critical of Pakistan's violations of the ceasefire agreement in Kashmir. On 6 September, during a stormy interview with Wilson and Hughes, Dr Jivraj Narayan (J. N.) Mehta, India's High Commissioner in London, 'protested strongly that the British prime minister should have pilloried India without a mention of Pakistan's similar violations'. 'This [6 September] statement', the enraged High Commissioner warned, 'would be read by the world and the Indian Parliament would receive it in anger.'[85] Shastri's reaction to Wilson's intervention, although more measured in tone, was equally critical in substance. Writing to Wilson the same day, Shastri complained that it had been Ayub Khan's government that, back at the beginning of August, had attempted to seize control of Kashmir by force with insurgents 'trained and equipped in Pakistan'. Moreover, in early September, Pakistan had initiated a major military operation in the region of Chhamb, which had been supported by artillery, tanks and aircraft. It was not India's attack in the Punjab, Shastri insisted, that had 'altered the whole area of the conflict', but rather, 'massive attack by the regular forces of Pakistan ... not across the ceasefire line but

---

[82] *The Times*, 7 September 1965.
[83] Wright to McGeorge Bundy, 6 September 1965, PREM 13/393, TNA.
[84] CRO to New Delhi, No. 3050, 8 September 1965, PREM 13/393, TNA.
[85] Memorandum of conversation between Hughes and Mehta, 6 September 1965, PREM 13/393, TNA.

across the international boundary between the Indian state of Jammu and Kashmir and West Punjab in Pakistan'.[86] Shastri's broadside persuaded a chastened Wilson that henceforth the UN should be left to broker an Indo-Pakistan ceasefire. There were to be 'no new [British] initiatives' in the subcontinent, Wilson instructed his ministers on 7 September, and 'no new announcements'.[87]

Most officials in Whitehall remained adamant that Britain had been correct to administer India a 'severe crack' for crossing the international frontier in the Punjab. At the Foreign Office, the Permanent Under Secretary Paul Gore-Booth, who had been Freeman's immediate predecessor in New Delhi, defended Wilson's statement as 'quite proper' in the circumstances.[88] Likewise, Algernon Rumbold at the CRO maintained that it had been right to condemn an Indian attack on West Pakistan that had greatly increased the risk of Chinese and American intervention in the conflict 'and a full-scale nuclear war developing'. In Rumbold's opinion, such an appalling prospect justified Britain's decision to take 'some risks on 6th September in our relations with India', and probably helped to persuade India and Pakistan to reconsider 'the dangers in which they were involving themselves and others'. Besides which, Rumbold argued, India's politicians and press 'were bound to attack us, whatever we did. Whenever the Kashmir dispute is active, their position has always been that, unless we declare our unqualified acceptance of their case on Kashmir, we are hostile to them. All that has varied from time to time in the past is the shrillness of their criticism'.[89]

In contrast, once back in London, Arthur Bottomley, although supportive of Wilson's decision to issue a statement on 6 September, expressed misgivings that it 'had perhaps been a little hard on India'.[90] From his post in New Delhi, John Freeman voiced consternation at Downing Street's conduct. 'Britain's popularity in India', Freeman informed the CRO on 13 September, 'has taken a severe knock as a result of our open criticism of India's escalation of the conflict.'[91] Indians felt particularly bitter, Freeman informed Bottomley, that having been

[86] Shastri to Wilson, 6 September 1965, PREM 13/393, TNA.
[87] Memorandum of conversation between Wilson, Stewart and Bottomley, 'Kashmir', 7 September 1965, PREM 13/393, TNA.
[88] Gore-Booth, 'British Attitude to the Indo-Pakistani Dispute', 8 September 1965, DO 196/385, TNA.
[89] Rumbold to Freeman, 30 September 1965, PREM 13/395, TNA.
[90] Memorandum of conversation between Wilson, Stewart and Bottomley, 'Kashmir', 7 September 1965, PREM 13/393, TNA.
[91] 'Hostilities between India and Pakistan', India Fortnightly Summary, Part I, 31 August–13 September 1965, No. 13, 13 September 1965, DO 196/385, TNA.

provoked by Pakistan's attack around Chhamb, Wilson had 'jumped with indecent haste' to condemn India's counterstroke in the Punjab. 'Indians,' Freeman observed dolefully, 'wrongly perhaps but genuinely, had persuaded themselves that former Conservative Governments in Britain had consistently tended to show a pro-Pakistan bias, but that the Labour Government would be much more favourably disposed towards India.' Wilson's message to Shastri on 6 September, and its accompanying public statement, had, the British High Commissioner confirmed, 'shattered this feeling' in India.[92] In conversation with Chester Bowles, L. K. Jha affirmed that Wilson's actions had reinforced the suspicion amongst 'most Indians' that the British were 'pro-Pakistan, and had been long before independence'.[93] 'America and Russia', Shastri notified Freeman in mid-September, '... were [now] considered by his government to be more trustworthy friends than ourselves.'[94]

### Playing games with history: Harold Wilson and the CRO

The events of early September 1965 cast a long shadow over Britain's political and economic relationships with India. The damage that Wilson's statement wrought on Anglo-Indian relations lasted, in Gore-Booth's view, 'for years rather than months'.[95] Controversially, in the memoir of his first premiership, which was serialised in *The Sunday Times* in June 1971, and published in full later that year, Wilson blamed Whitehall officials for the 6 September debacle. In his book, Wilson stated that he had been badly served by mandarins in the CRO, who had 'inveigled' him to condemn India for an act of aggression. 'I had been taken for a ride by a pro-Pakistani faction in the CRO', Wilson bemoaned, 'it did not remain there for long.'[96] Former CRO officials were incensed at Wilson's accusation that they had somehow acted improperly, and openly challenged his version of events. In a letter sent to Wilson, on 17 June 1971, Joe Garner, the Permanent Under Secretary at the CRO in September 1965, castigated the Labour leader for unjustly besmirching the CRO's reputation. Having checked his recollection of events against

---

[92] Freeman to Bottomley, 'India: India and Pakistan: The Three Weeks' War', 19 October 1965, DO 196/387, TNA.

[93] Bowles to State Department, No. 503, 7 September 1965, NSF Country File, India, Box 129 [2 of 2], Folder 3 India Cables [3 of 3], Vol. V, 6-65 to 9-65, LBJL.

[94] Freeman to Bottomley, 16 September 1965, PREM 13/394, TNA.

[95] Paul Gore-Booth, *With Great Truth and Respect* (London: Constable, 1974), pp. 320–1.

[96] Harold Wilson, *Labour Government 1964–1970: A Personal Record* (London: Weidenfeld & Nicolson, 1971), pp. 133–4.

the relevant written record held in the Foreign and Commonwealth Office's archive, Garner informed Wilson that

It is clear that the initiative for an early statement [on 6 September] came from No. 10 and that the CRO were under pressure from your Office. A statement was drafted in the CRO and submitted to you with the specific warning that, if issued in this form, it would be likely to have serious repercussions on our relations with India.[97]

Moreover, Garner rubbished Wilson's claim that a pro-Pakistani faction inside the CRO had been sacked at the prime minister's behest as a direct consequence of the 6 September furore. '[T]his was not so,' Garner assured Wilson, 'no staff changes were made as a result of this matter and, according to my recollection, no complaints were made to me at the time.' In the circumstances, Garner insisted, Wilson ought to correct subsequent editions of his book in order that the historical record was 'kept straight'.[98]

Revealingly, the Cabinet Secretary, Sir Burke Trend, supported Garner's disquiet at Wilson's propensity to play fast and loose with historical facts. On 2 July 1971, Trend reassured Garner that in writing to Wilson he had been 'absolutely right to say what you did'.[99] In seeking to assuage Garner's anger over his 'unfair' treatment of the CRO, Wilson blundered into more trouble. In August, during an appearance on Britain's ITV television network to promote his memoir, Wilson accepted responsibility for the 6 September statement. However, later in the same interview, he added that he had been let down at the time by a senior figure in the CRO, clearly identifiable as Algernon Rumbold. Rumbold had retired from the CRO, in February 1966, upon reaching pensionable age, and not as a consequence of any association, real or imagined, with a 'pro-Pakistani' faction in Whitehall.[100] Furious at having his professional reputation called into question, Rumbold denounced Wilson's allegation as 'completely baseless'. On 5 August, in a letter published in *The Times*, Rumbold questioned Wilson's integrity, stating 'I am strongly of the view that civil servants should be silent. But when politicians defend changes in their own views by attacking the judgment of their officials, which at the time they accepted, the situation differs.'[101]

---

[97] Garner to Wilson, 17 June 1971, CAB 164/887, TNA.
[98] Garner to Wilson, 17 June 1971 and 15 July 1971, CAB 164/887, TNA.
[99] Trend to Garner, 2 July 1971, CAB 164/887, TNA.
[100] Joe Garner, *The Commonwealth Office, 1925–1968* (London: Heinemann, 1978), p. 404.
[101] *The Times*, 5 August 1971.

Wilson emerged with little credit from his unseemly spat with former CRO officials. In the wider context of Anglo-Indian relations, Wilson's attempt to bring about an Indo-Pakistani ceasefire in 1965 proved disastrous. Given the speed at which events were moving on the ground in the subcontinent, the confusion of having to interpret events through the 'fog of war' and the unfortunate absence from London of his Commonwealth Secretary, it is possible to excuse Wilson, at least partially, for making an error of judgement. Moreover, as Garner, Gore-Booth and James all subsequently acknowledged, the advice that Wilson received at the time from officials at best 'fell short of even-handedness' and, at worse, was simply 'faulty'.[102] Yet, British officials had clearly and explicitly warned the prime minister of the likely repercussions for Anglo-Indian relations of condemning Indian aggression. Ultimately, it was Wilson's decision to intervene in the Indo-Pakistani conflict and, having done so, risk dislocating Anglo-Indian relations by appearing to take sides in an intra-Commonwealth dispute. It reflects none too well on Wilson that, after Britain's relationship with India suffered as a consequence of political decisions taken in 10 Downing Street, in the autumn of 1965, he sought to shift responsibility for the 6 September statement away from himself, and onto the CRO. Such conduct, as one British official reflected, was 'neither appropriate nor convincing'.[103]

### India, Pakistan and Anglo-American military assistance

Wilson's public censure of Shastri's government was not the only British action to raise Indian hackles during the Indo-Pakistani War. To India's alarm, as fighting escalated in the subcontinent, Britain halted all forms of military assistance to New Delhi and Rawalpindi. Shipments of British arms to India and Pakistan were suspended, collaboration on the development of military ordnance facilities curtailed, and bilateral training and liaison activities stopped. Whereas Pakistan received the overwhelming majority of its military hardware from the United States, the British arms embargo hit India hard. Of the £32 million in military aid that Britain had promised India since 1962, some £10.7 million had yet to be delivered.[104] In London, J. N. Mehta emphasised to Wilson

---

[102] Garner to Wilson, 17 June 1971, CAB 164/887, TNA; Gore-Booth, *Truth and Respect*, pp. 320–1; James, *Pakistan Chronicle*, p. 139.

[103] Gore-Booth, *Truth and Respect*, pp. 320–1.

[104] 'Indo-Pakistan Conflict: Implications for the Ministry of Defence', Overseas Policy and Defence Committee (OPD) memorandum, 15 September 1965, DO 133/178, TNA; James, *Pakistan Chronicle*, p. 141.

that the Indian Army's preference for British military equipment had left it 'gravely handicapped' by the imposition of an arms embargo. The Pakistanis, Mehta complained bitterly, had circumvented the suspension of American arms shipments by taking delivery of US-manufactured arms from their Muslim neighbours, Turkey and Iran.[105] Shastri's government were especially incensed that, with Beijing making menacing noises in support of Pakistan, Britain had elected not 'to make any public statement indicating her willingness to resume arms aid in the event of a Chinese attack [on India]'.[106] Britain's decision to suspend arms shipments to India and Pakistan was entirely appropriate in the circumstances. Nevertheless, it added to Anglo-Indian tension by exacerbating New Delhi's sense of insecurity in relation to Pakistan and China. As India's Deputy High Commissioner in London, Parmeshwar Narayan Haksar, made clear to Paul Gore-Booth, his government resented the fact that 'at a moment of real national crisis like the war with Pakistan, vital military supplies could be cut off [by Britain] in a way over which India had no control'.[107]

As Pakistan's principal supplier of military aid, and following the Sino-Indian War of 1962, an important player alongside the British in efforts to modernise India's armed forces, the US government was placed in an awkward position by the outbreak of Indo-Pakistani hostilities. From the mid-1950s, the Eisenhower and Kennedy administrations had invested significant amounts of American political, economic and military capital in the subcontinent in a bid to turn India and Pakistan into bulwarks against communist expansion in Asia and the Middle East. Instead, it appeared that America's Cold War outlay in South Asia risked being squandered in a fratricidal regional squabble. In the US Congress, calls to halt the delivery of American arms to the subcontinent garnered strong bipartisan support. The Republican minority leader in the House of Representatives, Gerald Ford, and the senior Democratic Senator and member of the Senate Foreign Relations committee, Frank Church, were prominent amongst those advocating a suspension of arms shipments to India and Pakistan. Within the House of Representatives, sixty-two Democrats and eighty-one Republicans attempted to go further and derail the Johnson administration's foreign

[105] Memorandum of conversation between Wilson and Mehta, 15 September 1965, PREM 13/394, TNA.
[106] Freeman to Bottomley, 'India: India and Pakistan: The Three Weeks' War', 19 October 1965, DO 196/387, TNA.
[107] Memorandum of conversation between Gore-Booth and Haksar, 7 December 1965, FO371/180965/F1051/45, TNA.

assistance programme, by voting to curtail all American aid to South Asia, inclusive of economic and food assistance.[108]

On 6 September, Washington dismissed an attempt by Ayub Khan to invoke the US–Pakistan mutual defence agreement of 1959. In a cable sent to Walter McConaughy and Bowles, later that day, Dean Rusk confirmed that the United States would refuse all requests from India and Pakistan for military assistance while fighting continued in the sub-continent. '[W]e are being asked [by India and Pakistan] to come in on the crash landing,' Rusk observed, 'where we had no chance to be in on the take-off.'[109] Two days later, on 8 September, the US govern-ment suspended supplies of American military equipment to India and Pakistan.[110] Despite Indian protests to the contrary, policymakers on both sides of the Atlantic calculated that Pakistan would suffer dispro-portionately from the imposition of a Western arms embargo, giving Ayub Khan a powerful incentive to sue for peace. In conversation with Wilson, George Ball, US Under Secretary of State, noted that 'Pakistan had [military] supplies only for three weeks, while India was in a much better position: in appearing to treat both sides equally, they [Britain and the US] had in fact treated them unequally'.[111] Wilson did his utmost to impress upon Ayub Khan the precariousness of Pakistan's military situ-ation, and its likely impact upon Rawalpindi's wider political objectives. On 17 September, the British premier implored Pakistan's leader, 'most urgently as a friend to consider whether Pakistan would not be wise to stop the firing while the military situation is in reasonable balance in order to give pause for further negotiation'. 'To do so', Ayub Khan was reassured, 'would put you in a much stronger position to ask the world to tackle the Kashmir problem.'[112]

## China and the Indo-Pakistani War

In another sense, British and American policymakers were concerned to bring an end to the fighting on the subcontinent before the People's Republic of China was tempted to intervene on the side of its new best friend, Pakistan. In early September, Wilson warned Agha Hilaly that 'no one should be under any illusion but that the sole object of the

---

[108] McMahon, *Cold War on the Periphery*, pp. 328–9.
[109] Rusk to Bowles and McConaughy, No. 293 to Karachi and No. 364 to New Delhi, RG 59, Central Files 1964–6, POL 32-1 INDIA–PAK, NARA.
[110] McMahon, *Cold War on the Periphery*, pp. 328–9.
[111] Memorandum of conversation between Wilson and George Ball, 8 September 1965, PREM 13/393, TNA.
[112] Wilson to Ayub Khan, No. 2155, 17 September 1965, PREM 13/394, TNA.

Chinese was to fish in troubled waters and that it would be a thousand pities if the Kashmir problem became a happy hunting ground for other countries'.[113] The prospect that a nuclear-armed China might flex its regional muscle, and seek to humiliate India by securing a Kashmir settlement favourable to Pakistan, worried the British. Any extension of the Sino-Pakistan border promised to bring with it an unwelcome expansion of Beijing's sphere of influence in South Asia. Worse still, direct Chinese support for Pakistan appeared certain to be met by an American riposte, opening up the possibility of a global nuclear conflagration.[114] Since early 1964, information received by the CIA had indicated the existence of some form of 'secret Sino-Pakistan mutual defence agreement'. On 6 September, CIA analysts advised Washington policymakers that 'however loose and "uncommitted"' the understanding that China might have reached with Pakistan, it nonetheless gave 'Pakistan something which Rawalpindi can consider an "ace in the hole" in the present confrontation'.[115]

British and American fears that China would find 'the chance of embarrassing India was too good to miss' proved to be well founded. As the intensity of the fighting between India and Pakistan increased during September, China's state media began 'trumpeting loudly' the merits of Pakistan's claim on Kashmir and denouncing India as an imperialist aggressor. Frustrated British officials grumbled that the Indo-Pakistani War had presented China with 'a heaven-sent opportunity for a vicious campaign against her varied enemies – the Americans, the Indians, the Russians, the British (in a minor way) and the United Nations'.[116] On 8 September, China issued a formal protest to the Shastri government over alleged Indian violations of its northern border. In a note delivered to the Indian foreign ministry, Beijing warned:

China cannot but pay serious attention to the Indian Government's expansionist action against its neighbours ... The Chinese Government once again solemnly warns the Indian Government: India must ... withdraw its aggressive armed forces and stop all its acts of aggression and provocation against China

---

[113] Memorandum of conversation between Wilson and Hilaly, 7 September, PREM 13/393, TNA.
[114] Rumbold to Freeman, 30 September 1965, PREM 13/395; Rumbold to Wright, 6 October 1965, PREM 13/395, TNA.
[115] 'Possible Sino-Pakistani Military Arrangement', CIA Intelligence Memorandum, ICI No. 2316/65, 6 September 1965, NSF Country File, Pakistan, Box 151, Folder 7 Pakistan Memos, Vol. IV, 8-65 to 9-65, LBJL.
[116] D. C. Hopson to Michael Stewart 'China and the Indo-Pakistan Conflict', 29 September 1965, DO 196/387, TNA.

... Otherwise India must bear responsibility for all the consequences arising there from.[117]

China's bellicose rhetoric suggested to Dean Rusk that Beijing might be prepared to 'convert the Pakistan-Indian war into a Free World–Communist confrontation'. It was not only Kashmir's future at stake, the US Secretary of State believed, but also 'the whole Western power position in Asia'. If India were to buckle under Communist Chinese pressure, Rusk cautioned Lyndon Johnson, 'we would face a new situation in many ways as serious as the loss of China. And as India goes, so eventually will Pakistan.'[118]

In the State Department's estimation, the long-term risks to America's interests in Asia posed by a continuation of hostilities in the subcontinent warranted a renewed US effort at 'resolving outstanding Indo-Pak[istan] differences, including Kashmir'.[119] Lyndon Johnson thought otherwise, and ruled out a US-led mediation initiative on Kashmir that previous experience indicated was likely to prove unproductive and, quite possibly, detrimental to American regional interests. In common with Wilson, Johnson deemed it prudent to let the UN take the lead in brokering a peace agreement between India and Pakistan. Soundings taken by American officials in the subcontinent supported Johnson's circumspection. Although the United States' standing in New Delhi remained higher than that of the British, Pakistan's use of US military equipment against India had fostered a degree of anti-American sentiment in Indian political circles. In the circumstances, L. K. Jha advised Chester Bowles that 'he did not think that we [the US] could act effectively in the role of peacemaker'. It would be better, Jha indicated, for such matters to be left to U Thant, a fellow Asian deeply respected in India.[120]

Shastri's government were less concerned than Dean Rusk that the Chinese would launch a major attack on India, akin to that of 1962. Indian government officials reasoned that with no immediate and overriding stake of their own in the Indo-Pakistan dispute, China would baulk at instigating a conflict with the United States merely to advance Pakistan's interests. It seemed more likely that Chinese forces might mount a limited incursion across India's northern border, sufficient in size to bruise Indian egos, but small enough to avoid an American

[117] Chakravorty, *Indo-Pak War*, p. 307.
[118] Rusk to Johnson, 'India and Pakistan', 9 September 1965, NSF Country File, Pakistan, Box 151, Folder 7 Pakistan Memos, Vol. IV, 8-65 to 9-65, LBJL.
[119] Rusk to Johnson, 'India and Pakistan', 9 September 1965, NSF Country File, Pakistan, Box 151, Folder 7 Pakistan Memos, Vol. IV, 8-65 to9-65, LBJL.
[120] Bowles to State Department, No. 503, 7 September 1965, NSF Country File, India, Box 129 [2 of 2], Folder 3 India Cables [3 of 3], Vol. V, 6-65 to 9-65, LBJL.

military riposte.[121] India's comparatively benign assessment of Beijing's intentions was called into question on 16 September, when, with Indian and Pakistani forces still heavily engaged, the Chinese government sent New Delhi a second diplomatic note. On this occasion, China charged that India had sent patrols into Chinese territory, abducted two Chinese peasants and their livestock, and constructed military emplacements on the wrong side of the Tibet–Sikkim border. India had three days to dismantle the latter, the Chinese note stipulated, or face 'grave consequences'. The incredulous Indian chargé d'affaires in Beijing sought clarification from Chinese colleagues on whether the latest message from his government was an ultimatum of war. 'Yes, it is,' replied the Chinese official, 'and India should be prepared to face the consequences if she did not accept it.'[122] When India's press published news of Beijing's ultimatum, an Indian crowd herding a flock of sheep surrounded the Chinese Embassy in New Delhi, and waved placards proclaiming, 'Eat me, but save the world.'[123] In the Lok Sabha, Shastri sought to extract some of the sting from China's threat by indicating India's willingness to have joint inspection teams examine any contentious border posts, with a view to resolving any disputes amicably. 'We hope that China would not take advantage of the present situation and attack India', Shastri added defiantly. 'The House may rest assured that we are fully vigilant ... The might of China will not deter us from defending our territorial integrity.'[124]

Back in Whitehall, the prospect that China might intervene in the Indo-Pakistani War engendered considerable foreboding. Having witnessed his colleagues discuss the latest twist in the Kashmir saga around the cabinet table in 10 Downing Street, Richard Crossman, Wilson's minister for housing, confided to his diary:

Listening to this debate I began to wonder whether we weren't behaving like the Liberal Government in 1914 before Sarajevo. In 1914 Sarajevo was as far away from London as Nepal is today. If the Chinese actually go to war with the Indians, the Americans will come to the help of India and the war with China might then be extended to Vietnam; Britain might be committed as well and a world war might be in the offing.[125]

[121] Srivastava, *Lal Bahadur Shastri*, pp. 275–6.
[122] *The Hindustan Times*, 18 September 1965.
[123] *Time*, 1 October 1965.
[124] Srivastava, *Lal Bahadur Shastri*, p. 278.
[125] Diary entry for 16 September 1965, Richard Crossman, *The Diaries of a Cabinet Minister*, vol. 1: *Minister of Housing 1964–66* (London: Jonathan Cape, 1975), p. 328.

In Moscow, India's ambassador to the Soviet Union, Triloki Nath (T. N.) Kaul sought out the Soviet premier, Alexei Kosygin, and his foreign minister, Andrei Gromyko, to gauge Russia's reaction to China's sabre-rattling. Kaul was comforted to discover that Soviet support for India's claim on Kashmir remained unchanged, and that the USSR was committed to work within the UNSC for an immediate ceasefire between India and Pakistan.[126] The Soviet government was anxious to avoid China profiting from the conflagration in South Asia by extending its influence over Pakistan. On a more parochial level, Moscow was also concerned that Beijing's brinkmanship could transform a regional squabble close to the USSR's borders into a wider communal conflict with ramifications for the Soviet Union's adjacent, and predominately Muslim, southern republics.[127] On 18 September, Nikolai Fedorenko, the Soviet representative on the Security Council, reiterated his government's call for a UN-administered ceasefire in the subcontinent, and condemned Mao Zedong's regime for pursuing a 'criminal policy of driving the world's people to serve their own imperialist and expansionist aims'.[128]

The United States joined with the Soviet Union in warning China against adding to the subcontinent's troubles. Arthur Goldberg, America's ambassador to the United Nations, cautioned Beijing that dire consequences would follow were it 'to spread the [Indo-Pakistan] conflict and exploit what was already a tragedy'.[129] Outside the UN, US diplomats urged 'hard-liners' inside Ayub's government not to 'encourage, or even – by failing to agree to a ceasefire – create the situation which produces Chinese intervention'. 'President Johnson', Pakistani ministers were reminded, 'is not the sort of man who will ever give his approval to one thin dime for a country which supports or encourages the aggressive pressures of Red China.'[130] As a final precaution against China's entry into the Indo-Pakistani War, and in line with a request B. K. Nehru made on 17 September for direct US military assistance should China attack India, Lyndon Johnson ordered the Joint Chiefs of Staff to dust down contingency plans for American military intervention in South Asia.[131]

---

[126] *The Hindu*, 18 September 1965.
[127] Freeman to Bottomley, 'India: India and Pakistan: The Three Weeks' War', 19 October 1965, DO 196/387, TNA.
[128] *The Hindu*, 20 September 1965.
[129] *The Hindu*, 20 September 1965; *The New York Times*, 20 September 1965.
[130] Rusk to McConaughy, 18 September 1965, NSF Country File, Pakistan, Box 152, Folder 2 Pakistan Cables [2 of 2], Vol. V, 9-65 to 1-66, LBJL.
[131] Memorandum of conversation between Walt Rostow and B. K. Nehru, 18 September 1965, NSF Country File, India, Box 129 [2 of 2], Folder 5 India Memos & Misc. [2 of 3], Vol. V, 6-65 to 9-65, LBJL.

Shortly before China's ultimatum to India was due to expire, Beijing extended the deadline for New Delhi to comply with its demands by a further three days. The extra time enabled China to consider Pakistan's response to a UNSC meeting scheduled to take place on 20 September, which was expected to table a resolution calling upon India and Pakistan to declare an immediate ceasefire and withdraw their armed forces to lines of control that had existed in early August. Satisfied that it had secured a strategic and psychological victory over Pakistan by frustrating its attempt to seize Kashmir by force, when the UN resolution was passed, India accepted its terms. In Pakistan, Ayub Khan confided to Iran's ambassador that he feared being lynched by his fellow countrymen for accepting a UN resolution that made no mention of a plebiscite in Kashmir, much less guarantee one. But, with Pakistan's stocks of ammunition and other essential supplies all but exhausted, and with the military balance tipping steadily in India's favour, Ayub Khan's hands were tied.[132] On 22 September, Bhutto was sent to New York to address an emergency session of the Security Council. Criticising the UN's ceasefire proposal as 'unsatisfactory', Bhutto nonetheless confirmed that, in the name of peace, Pakistan would adhere to its terms.[133]

Once Pakistan had agreed to a ceasefire, China promptly confirmed that all Indian outposts on its territory had been removed, and that its latest border dispute with New Delhi was at an end.[134] The British suspected that China's decision to extricate itself from involvement in the Indo-Pakistani clash had, in part, been prompted by Rawalpindi's belated insistence that Beijing stay out of the conflict, at least in a military sense.[135] Although 'glad of China's vocal support', Pakistan's government appeared to recognise that accepting anything more from Beijing 'might tip the balance of world sympathy against her'.[136] Pakistani officials subsequently asserted that Ayub Khan and Bhutto had undertaken a clandestine visit to Beijing, on the night of 19–20 September, during which the Pakistani president had rejected an offer of Chinese military assistance.[137] Western diplomats felt that China's decision to pull back

---

[132] James to Bottomley, 'Pakistan and Kashmir: A Tragic Misadventure', 25 October 1965, DO 196/388, TNA.

[133] *The Hindu*, 23 September 1965.

[134] Chakravorty, *Indo-Pak War*, p. 310.

[135] 'China and the Indian-Pakistan Crisis', Foreign Office and CRO Circular, No. 389, 28 September 1965, DO 196/387, TNA.

[136] Hopson to Stewart, 'China and the Indo-Pakistan Conflict', 29 September 1965, DO 196/387, TNA; James, *Pakistan Chronicle*, p. 114.

[137] Notably, Altaf Gauhar, *Ayub Khan: Pakistan's First Military Ruler* (Lahore: Sang-e-Meel Publications, 1993), pp. 351–3. Other Pakistani sources have corroborated Gauhar's claim, although former British officials have questioned their credibility.

from the military precipice was indicative of Beijing's highly developed sense of political expediency. Mao Zedong's government had demonstrated its sensitivity to 'overstepping the mark in matters close to home thereby inviting United States retaliation' in the past, most notably during the Sino-Indian War of 1962. The principal watchwords of Chinese diplomacy, it seemed, were 'maximum noise' and 'minimum risk'. The British assumed that in supporting Pakistan, China had 'gone as far as they safely could without risk of retaliation' and having seen 'the red light glowing which suggested the possibility of effective United States support for India, they quietly backed down'.[138]

China reaped decidedly mixed dividends from its brief involvement in the Indo-Pakistani War. Pakistanis certainly appreciated the moral support that they had received from Beijing. In the streets of Karachi and Lahore, Pakistani crowds paraded portraits of Zhou Enlai, tore down US, British and United Nations flags, and smashed the windows of British and American diplomatic buildings, libraries and commercial premises.[139] Yet, as Morrice James observed, even the most ardent Sinophile in Rawalpindi had found it difficult to dispute that by raising the spectre of a nuclear war, China's ultimatum to India had rebounded to Pakistan's disadvantage. Ayub Khan's government had emerged diplomatically and militarily weakened from a conflict that, from Pakistan's perspective, represented a 'startling failure'.[140] Indeed, the British expressed hope that by appearing as a 'paper tiger' and issuing idle threats, China might have encouraged Pakistan's policymakers to undertake 'a fundamental re-examination of their relationship with ... China'.[141]

In a broader sense, international opinion found little to commend in China's latest demonstration of bellicosity and propensity to threaten war over trivial border disputes. While others had worked hard to bring about an Indo-Pakistan ceasefire, China's conduct created the impression that it was 'violently opposed to the efforts of the United States, the Soviet Union and the United Nations to bring an end to the fighting', and consequently was 'the odd man out in the eyes of the world'.[142]

---

See, for example, G. W. Choudhury, *India, Pakistan, Bangladesh and the Major Powers* (New York: Free Press, 1975), pp. 190–1; and James, *Pakistan Chronicle*, p. 146.

[138] Hopson to Stewart, 'China and the Indo-Pakistan Conflict', 29 September 1965, DO 196/387, TNA.

[139] *The Economist*, 25 September 1965; *The Times*, 22 September 1965.

[140] James to Bottomley, 'Pakistan and Kashmir: A Tragic Misadventure', 25 October 1965, DO 196/388, TNA.

[141] 'Future British Policy towards India and Pakistan', undated, FO 371/180965/F1051/37A, TNA.

[142] 'China and the Indian-Pakistan Crisis', Foreign Office and CRO Circular, No. 389, 28 September 1965, DO 196/387, TNA; Hopson to Stewart, 'China and the Indo-Pakistan Conflict', 29 September 1965, DO 196/387, TNA.

When set against the comparatively measured support that Moscow had offered India, Beijing's intercession on Pakistan's behalf appeared ill judged and reckless. 'On balance,' the British felt, 'it is likely to prove that China lost more than she gained by her aggressive intervention in this [Indo-Pakistan] crisis. In contrast, the moderation shown by the Soviet Union will generally rebound to their advantage.'[143] Much of the Western press delighted in chiding China for the ineptness of its Machiavellian diplomacy. In an article entitled 'Thanks for Muffing it', the London *Economist* mocked Mao Zedong's government for 'irresponsibly meddling' in Indo-Pakistani affairs and unwittingly giving 'America and Russia something to collaborate about'. 'Like Mephistopheles,' *The Economist* crowed, 'China is a power that desperately tries to do bad things but the result perversely turns out good.'[144]

Having confronted and overcome challenges from Pakistan and China, India's government, and more particularly Lal Bahadur Shastri, emerged from the Indo-Pakistani War brimming with confidence and domestic authority. On 26 September, Shastri joked with a vast audience gathered at the Ramlila Grounds, outside Delhi's historic Red Fort, that 'President Ayub had declared he would soon walk through to Delhi. He is a great person, high and mighty of stature. I thought he should not undergo the travail of such a long walk. We should ourselves march towards Lahore to greet him.'[145] Indian politicians, flushed with the nation's battlefield success, felt sufficiently emboldened to chastise Britain and the United States as fair-weather friends. On 4 October, Y. B. Chavan accused Wilson and Johnson of siding with 'Pakistani dictatorship' against 'Indian democracy'. 'Any country that extends aid to Pakistan', added Congress Party president Kumarasami Kamaraj, 'is an enemy of India.' The British and American governments' conduct during the war was vilified in equal measure in Pakistan. The Johnson administration, in particular, was transformed into a convenient 'whipping boy' by Ayub Khan's administration to explain away the failure of its ill-conceived Kashmir adventure. 'Our Pak[istan]/Indian affairs', Robert Komer informed McGeorge Bundy on 5 October, 'are in sad disarray. We are now beginning to get the worst of both worlds in both India and Pakistan with little light at the end of the tunnel.'[146]

---

[143] 'China and the Indian-Pakistan Crisis', Foreign Office and CRO Circular, No. 389, 28 September 1965, DO 196/387, TNA.
[144] *The Economist*, 25 September 1965.
[145] Srivastava, *Lal Bahadur Shastri*, p. 319.
[146] Komer to McGeorge Bundy, 5 October 1965, NSF, Robert W. Komer Files, Box 23, Folder 5 India 1965 [1 of 4], LBJL.

## Britain, the United States and the lessons of September 1965

Lyndon Johnson despaired at the apparent inability of India and Pakistan to break free from an enervating cycle of internecine conflict. The Indo-Pakistani War served, above all, to reinforce the American president's conviction that both Eisenhower and Kennedy had inflated South Asia's strategic importance in the wider Cold War. In consequence, the process of American disengagement from the Indian subcontinent, which had started in the first weeks of Johnson's presidency, gathered momentum in the autumn of 1965. Unlike South Vietnam, where he believed that pledges made by his predecessors precluded US withdrawal from a country in the grip of a communist-led insurgency, Johnson judged that America had little to lose politically, or strategically, from winding down its involvement in India and Pakistan.[147] In November, George Ball forewarned the British that the United States was taking a 'very hard look' at its future role in the subcontinent. The White House was increasingly doubtful, Ball made clear, 'whether it is prudent and wise to provide resources to two nations which are more obsessed with each other than with their own development'.[148]

Harold Wilson drew a rather different lesson from the Indo-Pakistani War. The British premier believed that the conflict had validated the premise that the 'struggle for the soul of Asia' was fundamentally a battle for ideological supremacy between a libertarian democratic model, embodied by India, and a repressive and militant brand of communism, championed by the People's Republic of China. It remained very much in the West's interest, Wilson concluded, to ensure that India prevailed in such a contest. Speaking on 15 November at London's Guildhall, Wilson reiterated the importance that his government attached to Britain's connection with South Asia. 'If I once said that Britain's frontier is on the Himalayas,' the British leader exclaimed, 'that frontier is perhaps not so much a military frontier, it is economic, indeed it is moral and philosophical.'[149] The Wilson government's ability to wield influence on its 'Himalayan frontier', however, had all but evaporated by the autumn of 1965. In New Delhi, John Freeman reported that Britain's 'public attitudes and actions over the Indo-Pakistani dispute

---

[147] McMahon, *Cold War on the Periphery*, pp. 334–5.

[148] Anglo-American meeting on India and Pakistan, Washington, DC, 16 November 1965, NSF, Robert W. Komer Files, Box 53, Folder United Kingdom Jan 1964–Mar 1966 [1 of 2], LBJL.

[149] Wilson Guildhall speech, 15 November 1965, FO 371/180965/F1051/43, TNA.

have been extremely badly received by both government and by normally pro-British elements in public life'. The Anglophile former Indian High Commissioner in London, Vijaya Lakshmi Pandit, concurred. On 26 November, Pandit stressed to Britain's solicitor general, Sir Dingle Foot, that 'It would be difficult to exaggerate Britain's unpopularity in India.'[150]

Britain and India had quarrelled and made up in the past over Suez, the Congo and Goa. On this occasion, however, fallout from the Indo-Pakistani War looked set to have a more lasting impact upon Anglo-Indian relations. John Freeman worried that Britain might have reached a tipping point in its relationship with India. 'At the moment we have virtually no influence at all on general political matters', Freeman informed the CRO. 'All will be well if a natural resumption of cordiality leads to a natural resumption of influence. Will it?' It seemed equally probable to the British High Commissioner that India might turn away from Britain, and seek to strengthen its links with the Soviet Union, the United States or possibly both.[151] Prior to the Indo-Pakistani War, Freeman had questioned the wisdom of Whitehall's established policy of impartiality with regard to India and Pakistan. In a letter to Mountbatten back in May, Freeman suggested that Britain's long-term interests might be better served by tilting toward India, the region's pre-eminent economic, military and political power. '[T]he time may well have come', Freeman argued, 'when we should take this assumption [of equality between India and Pakistan] out, dust it off and give it a really critical examination. What is undesirable, in other words, in my view, is that it should be accepted as a stereotype which is beyond challenge.'[152] Pakistan's failure to settle the Kashmir dispute by force strengthened Freeman's conviction that Britain would benefit from adopting a more pragmatic attitude to the future status of Kashmir, and Anglo-Indian relations in general.

In a series of cables that he sent from New Delhi to the CRO between mid-September and mid-October, Freeman made the case for adopting a new and 'iconoclastic' British regional policy. The Indo-Pakistani War, he contended, had placed India in a position to dictate the terms of a Kashmir settlement. The Indian government could not now, as the British had traditionally assumed, be cajoled into relinquishing its hold

---

[150] Freeman to Bottomley, 16 September 1965, PREM 13/394, TNA; Memorandum of Conversation between Dingle Foot and Pandit, 26 November 1965, PREM 13/2160, TNA.

[151] Freeman to Pickard, 1 October 1965, DO 196/224, TNA.

[152] Freeman to Mountbatten, 19 May 1965, MB1/J507, Visit to India, May 1965, MBP.

over portions of the Vale, Jammu or Ladakh. 'We must carefully and radically reassess our policies towards India and Pakistan', the High Commissioner reasoned. 'The result of such a reassessment could be a decision to accept and unobtrusively facilitate an Indian solution to the Kashmir problem.' By continuing to oppose a Kashmir agreement on terms favourable to India, Freeman insisted, Britain would most likely prolong conflict and instability in the subcontinent, impart further strain on Anglo-Indian relations and strengthen Soviet influence in South Asia. A British tilt toward India might occasion a rupture in Anglo-Pakistani relations and push Rawalpindi closer to China. The chances that this would happen, however, were offset, in part, Freeman considered, by Pakistan's dependency on American military and economic aid and the difficulties an Islamic country would face in allying itself too closely with a communist state. '[D]uring the past 18 years we and the Americans have, for reasons which were good at the time but may now be irrelevant, permitted a distortion of relations between the largest and most powerful nation of South Asia (India) and her much less powerful neighbour', Freeman argued. The time had arrived to correct this anomaly.[153]

From his vantage point in Karachi, Morrice James vigorously contested the validity of Freeman's analysis. In James' opinion, rushing to implement an 'Indian solution' to the Kashmir problem would needlessly undercut Britain's position in Pakistan. While Pakistani policies might in time compel Britain to shift to a more pro-Indian policy, especially if the more militant Bhutto replaced Ayub Khan as Pakistan's leader, James saw it as unnecessarily precipitate and counterproductive to force the pace of change. Were Britain to endorse a Kashmir settlement that denied Pakistan a substantial stake in the Vale, James made clear, 'I would expect our [British] influence here to be eclipsed very quickly and our material assets to be soon harried out of existence'. In such a scenario, neither the carrot of British developmental aid, nor Rawalpindi's military alliance with the United States, could reasonably be expected to mitigate the damage to Britain's substantial political and commercial interests in Pakistan. It appeared foolhardy, in James' view, for Britain to take sides in the subcontinent when, with American support, 'there is still some hope – as I believe there is – of reasserting Western influence [in Pakistan] and preventing a Chinese political take-over here'. It was surely better, James declared, to retain a foot

---

[153] Freeman to CRO, No. 3428, 23 September 1965, PREM 13/395, TNA; Freeman to Bottomley, 'India: India and Pakistan: The Three Weeks' War', 19 October 1965, DO 196/387, TNA.

in both the Indian and Pakistani camps by continuing to work with Washington in pursuit of a Kashmir solution acceptable to New Delhi and Rawalpindi.[154]

During October and November, senior Whitehall officials met with Freeman and James in London to review Britain's South Asia policy. Before reaching any firm conclusions, the British were careful to solicit input from their American allies. Over the course of several Anglo-American meetings, held in the late autumn of 1965, the State Department endorsed Freeman's position that India was of pre-eminent importance to Western interests in the subcontinent and wider Asia. In common with James, senior American policymakers were more concerned, however, 'that a policy of clearly siding with India could be self-defeating in view of Pakistan's destructive potential'.[155] On 16 November, Michael Stewart, Cyril Pickard and Sir Patrick Dean, Britain's ambassador to the United States, met with George Ball and Robert Komer, in Washington, to discuss the coordination of Anglo-American regional policy. A clear consensus emerged from the meeting in favour of a policy of continuity in South Asia. The United Kingdom, it was accepted, would continue to adopt an even-handed attitude in relation to India and Pakistan, 'since scope still remains for [the] exercise of UK influence toward resolving Indo-Pak[istan] differences'.[156]

On the question of whether Britain and the United States should resume military and economic aid to India and Pakistan, British and American policymakers found themselves at odds. The State Department opposed British plans to ease restrictions on the export of non-lethal military equipment to the subcontinent, and authorise the delivery of military items to India and Pakistan for which licences had been agreed before the war, which included twenty-six Hunter fighter jets ordered by New Delhi. Such a move, the Americans pointed out, 'would greatly favour India' and risk having 'a severe effect on Pakistan at a critical time when it is considering the orientation of its future foreign policy'. Furthermore, the US Congress was unwilling to sanction a similar resumption in United States military aid to New

---

[154] James to Bottomley, 'Pakistan and Kashmir: A Tragic Misadventure', 25 October 1965, DO 196/388, TNA.

[155] 'Future British Policy towards India and Pakistan', 25 October 1965, DO 196/225, TNA; Raymond A. Hare to Acting Secretary, 15 November 1965, RG 59, Records Relating to Indian Political Affairs 1964–6, Lot 69D52, Box 8, Pickard–Belcher Visit Nov. 1965 folder, NARA.

[156] Anglo-American meeting on India and Pakistan, Washington, DC, 16 November 1965, NSF, Robert W. Komer Files, Box 53, Folder United Kingdom Jan 1964–Mar 1966 [1 of 2], LBJL.

Delhi and Rawalpindi without firm evidence of a rapprochement in Indo-Pakistani relations, a reduction in military spending in the sub-continent, and a commitment on the part of Shastri and Ayub Khan to implement much-needed economic and agricultural reforms. A British decision to recommence military sales to India, US officials worried, would sour Anglo-Pakistani relations and might lead Pakistan to 'turn their anger against us unless there is some breakthrough on the US aid freeze'.[157] In defending Britain's position, Sir Patrick Dean emphasised to his American colleagues that the Indian government had reacted angrily to the suspension of commercial military shipments by Britain during the Indo-Pakistani War, which had threatened to immobilise its British-supplied Centurion tanks and Gnat and Hunter aircraft.[158] Maintaining an embargo on military sales to New Delhi now a cease-fire was in place would, the British felt, 'have a catastrophic effect' on their political and economic interests in India. Britain's special plead-ing failed to impress Johnson's administration. Having listened to their argument, George Ball urged the British to think very carefully before deciding to get out of step with the United States and begin shipping military equipment to South Asia.[159]

## The Noel-Baker affair

British concern over the negative impact that the Indo-Pakistani War had had on Anglo-Indian relations intensified the following month. On 1 December, having just returned from a visit to the subcontinent with parliamentary colleagues, the Labour MP Francis Noel-Baker wrote to Wilson to voice his concern at the 'constant reproaches' that he had received in India over the 'pro-Pakistan' attitude of Wilson, his govern-ment, the British press and the BBC. On 21 December, Wilson wrote back to Noel-Baker, noting in his letter that, amongst other things, the bad press that the Indian government had received in the UK was largely attributable to the ineptness of its public relations machinery; that the British public's reaction to India's decision to attack West Pakistan had made his 6 September statement unavoidable; and that some Indians had 'undoubtedly' exaggerated the statement's intention,

---

[157] Raymond A. Hare to Acting Secretary, 15 November 1965, RG 59, Records Relating to Indian Political Affairs 1964–6, Lot 69D52, Box 8, Pickard–Belcher Visit Nov. 1965 folder, NARA.

[158] *The Times*, 28 September 1965.

[159] Anglo-American meeting on India and Pakistan, Washington, DC, 16 November 1965, NSF, Robert W. Komer Files, Box 53, Folder United Kingdom Jan 1964–Mar 1966 [1 of 2], LBJL.

'read[ing] more into it than was ever intended'. To Whitehall's dismay, without allowing sufficient time 'for publication to be stopped', Noel-Baker informed 10 Downing Street of his intention to share his correspondence with Wilson with the British press.[160] The response in India to the publication of the Wilson/Noel-Baker letters was explosive. In the Lok Sabha, India's minister of external affairs, Swaran Singh, stated that the Indian government was 'naturally distressed and unhappy over the contents of the correspondence and the general attitude of the Government of the United Kingdom in relation to the recent India–Pakistan conflict'.[161] Under the headline, 'Mr. Wilson Opens Old Wounds in Delhi Controversy', the *Times'* correspondent in New Delhi reported that Indians appeared to have taken even 'more ground for offence' in Wilson's correspondence with Noel-Baker than in the prime minister's statement of 6 September.[162] Characteristically, rather than accept responsibility for Downing Street's latest diplomatic faux pas, Wilson again found the CRO, and Algernon Rumbold in particular, to be culpable. 'The fault is Rumbold's,' Wilson grumbled to his private secretary, 'both on Sept. 6th and for framing this draft [of Wilson's letter to Noel-Baker].'[163]

John Freeman despaired at Whitehall's failure to forestall the 'so unnecessary' Noel-Baker saga. The publication of extracts from Wilson's correspondence had, Freeman assured the CRO, 'gravely damaged our Prime Minister's personal prestige in India', 'caused the maximum embarrassment to this office' and 'undone careful work' that he had undertaken to rebuild Britain's position in India.[164] Worse still, release of Wilson's letter had occurred at a particularly delicate point in the immediate post-war period, as Indian and Pakistani leaders gathered for peace talks in the Soviet city of Tashkent. Indian rumour mills suggested that Wilson had deliberately engineered the Noel-Baker furore to disrupt the Tashkent meeting. The subcontinent's press printed a raft of conspiracy theories, the foremost of which alleged that Wilson's

---

[160] CRO to New Delhi, Nos. 58, 59 and 60, 5 January 1966, PREM 13/1051, TNA. CRO to New Delhi, No. 99, 7 January 1966, PREM 13/1051, TNA. Noel-Baker subsequently extracted an assurance from Wilson that 'I had his permission to publish his letter to me, and he told me that he had already made this plain to lobby correspondents which had asked him about it. He did add, however, that had he had time to re-read the letter he would, on reflection, have asked me to treat it as confidential. But he made it clear that, in his view, I had acted perfectly properly throughout.' Noel-Baker to Freeman, 10 March 1966, PREM 13/970, TNA.

[161] Freeman to CRO, No. 33, 1 March 1966, PREM 13/1051, TNA.

[162] *The Times*, 8 January 1966.

[163] Handwritten note from Wilson to Oliver Wright, 20 January 1966, PREM 13/1051, TNA.

[164] Freeman to Garner, 15 January 1966, PREM 13/1051, TNA.

'pro-Pakistani' letter was designed to encourage Pakistani intransigence on Kashmir and break up the talks, thereby denying 'the Russians a diplomatic success which Whitehall envies'.[165]

## Tashkent and the erosion of Anglo-American influence in South Asia

In truth, the British attitude ahead of the Tashkent talks, which took place between 4 and 10 January 1966, was somewhat conflicted. For much of the previous century the British had engaged Moscow in a 'Great Game', with a view to keeping Russian influence out of South Asia. Indian political commentators suspected that while the official British attitude had been 'perhaps genuinely appreciative of Soviet efforts' to host the Tashkent talks, behind the scenes in Whitehall, 'those who worked in, and remember the old Empire, see Tashkent as a portent of the waning influence of Britain in the Commonwealth'.[166] The London press deduced much the same. 'How strange and intolerable it would have seemed to [Lord] Curzon', *The Times* opined, 'that the affairs of the sub-continent he ruled should be taken to Tashkent to be discussed under the patronage of a Russian.'[167] Yet, during the Indo-Pakistani War, the Soviets had shown a willingness to work with Britain and the United States for peace and stability in the subcontinent, and to contain the spread of China's regional influence. From a British perspective, by bringing Shastri and Ayub Khan together in Tashkent, the Soviets had demonstrated that they could exercise 'the responsibilities of power in a way the West – indeed everybody except Mr Mao and his followers – can applaud'.[168]

Under the terms of the Tashkent declaration, India and Pakistan agreed to withdraw their armed forces to positions held prior to 5 August 1965; renounce the use of force to settle disputes, including Kashmir; and to seek to normalise bilateral economic, trade and cultural relations. The agreement, which required both sides to make significant concessions, was heavily criticised in India and Pakistan. Many Pakistanis were unhappy that in renouncing the use of force, their government appeared to have abandoned any hope of 'liberating' Kashmir. In Lahore, students from the Punjab University rioted, and leaders of opposition parties, including the Jamiat-i-Islami, Awami League and

---

[165] See *Patriot*, 7 January 1966; and *The Sunday Statesman*, 9 January 1966.
[166] *The Hindustan Times*, 6 January 1966.
[167] *The Times*, 3 January 1966.
[168] *The Economist*, 15 January 1966.

Shaukat Hayat (Council Muslim League), denounced Ayub Khan for his 'unpardonable weakness' in buying peace with India at the cost of Pakistan's national honour.[169] Large numbers of Indians were equally displeased with Shastri's agreement to withdraw Indian troops from the Uri–Punch bulge, a strategically important patch of territory that straddled the road from Kashmir to the Chinese border.[170]

The extent of the Soviets' success in cajoling India and Pakistan to come to terms at Tashkent appeared to unnerve the British. The Foreign Office acknowledged that for 'the Russians, the Tashkent meeting is a considerable diplomatic triumph … It may well give them a new and better entree into the affairs of the sub-continent.'[171] With its own 'stock in New Delhi … at rock-bottom', there was never any realistic question that the Wilson government could play a leading role brokering an Indo-Pakistan accord, as it had during the Kutch crisis.[172] Writing to Lyndon Johnson, in December 1965, Harold Wilson nonetheless continued to hold out the hope that some form of Anglo-American involvement in the peace process might eventually be required. 'I think that if Tashkent fails,' Wilson informed Johnson, 'which is likely since Kosygin will do no more than act as host, we may have to consider whether there should be a new initiative either by the United States with strong British support or possibly within the Commonwealth.'[173] In the event, members of Wilson's own cabinet felt that the Tashkent declaration represented a watershed in Britain's relationship with the Indian subcontinent. Denis Healey, Britain's Secretary of State for Defence, suggested retrospectively that Wilson's insistence that the United Kingdom's frontier stood on the Himalayas 'was exposed as an embarrassing farce' in January 1966.[174] At the time, Michael Stewart lamented that Britain's standing in South Asia had suffered a significant blow at the hands of the Soviets. George Brown, deputy leader of the Labour Party and First Secretary of State, went further, suggesting that, in exposing the weakness of the Commonwealth, Tashkent helped to convince Wilson that Britain's future was in Europe, rather than Africa or Asia.[175] John Freeman took an almost equally gloomy

---

[169] Talbot, *Pakistan*, p. 179.
[170] 'The Tashkent Meeting', undated, FO 371/186953/F1042/19, TNA.
[171] 'The Tashkent Meeting', E. Bolland, 13 January 1966, FO 371/186953, TNA.
[172] *The Economist*, 25 September 1965.
[173] Wilson to Johnson, 12 December 1965, NSF, Robert W. Komer Files, Box 53, Folder United Kingdom Jan 1964–Mar 1966 [1 of 2], LBJL.
[174] Denis Healey, *The Time of My Life* (London: Michael Joseph, 1989), p. 280.
[175] OPD (65) 40th, 22 September 1965, CAB 148/18, TNA; Entry for 20 January 1966, Cecil King, *The Cecil King Diary, 1967–1970* (London: Jonathan Cape, 1972), p. 56.

view of the Anglo-Indian relationship. In February 1966, with almost no British political sway to speak of in India, Freeman conceded that the United Kingdom had little option other than to 'lie low for the time being and leave it to the Russians to make the running, in the hope of gradually recovering our influence and eventually making a comeback later'.[176]

In the United States, senior policymakers in the Johnson administration recognised that the Soviets' success at Tashkent might circumscribe American influence in the subcontinent. But, although Moscow and Washington remained Cold War rivals, their strategic objectives in South Asia of building a strong and stable India and limiting Sino-Pakistani ties were much the same. With US and Soviet interests in the region running along broadly parallel lines, the US government saw little wrong in encouraging the Soviets in their bid to broker a peace agreement between India and Pakistan. In explaining America's position in relation to Tashkent, Dean Rusk confirmed that the Johnson administration had

encouraged the Russians to go ahead with the Tashkent idea, because we felt we had nothing to lose. If they succeeded in bringing about any detente at Tashkent, then there would be more peace on the subcontinent between India and Pakistan, and we would gain from that fact. If the Russians failed at Tashkent, at least the Russians would have the experience of some of the frustration that we had for twenty years in trying to sort out things between India and Pakistan.[177]

Indeed, the level of vexation that Lyndon Johnson and many of his senior officials harboured toward India and Pakistan by late 1965 suggested that, having worked to keep the Soviets out of South Asia over the previous decade, the United States was now more than content to usher Moscow in.

Yet, perhaps the most significant challenge to British and American authority in the subcontinent came not from the Tashkent meeting itself, but rather from the process of political transformation in India that occurred in its wake. Having committed India to the Tashkent declaration the previous day, in the early hours of 11 January, Lal Bahadur Shastri suffered a third, and on this occasion, fatal heart attack. Following Shastri's death, Jawaharlal Nehru's daughter, Indira Gandhi, assumed the reins of power in India. In Washington, Gandhi's elevation to the Indian premiership was greeted with a good deal of

---

[176] Memorandum of meeting between James and Freeman, Karachi, 1 and 2 February 1966, FO 371/186952/F1041/30, TNA.
[177] Dean Rusk, OH Interview, 2 January 1970, p. 36, LBJL.

apprehension. American diplomats viewed India's new leader as 'vain', 'emotional', 'authoritarian' and prone to 'irrational' fits of pique when events turned against her.[178] Moreover, as one US intelligence report subsequently noted, 'left-of-centre Indian officials, including Mrs. Gandhi, have long held a conspiratorial view of US activities in India which has been a smouldering source of resentment against the United States'.[179] Many of Gandhi's actions and utterances, in particular, appeared to Washington to be influenced by an anti-American and pro-Soviet tendency that the Indian premier was commonly perceived to have inherited from her father.[180]

Opinion in Britain was equally concerned by evidence that indicated Gandhi shared 'her father's preferences' for, amongst other things, the public sector over private enterprise. Moreover, the new Indian premier appeared worryingly predisposed to take a more charitable view of the Soviet Union's conduct than the West's indiscretions, real and imagined. In late January 1966, the *The Economist* noted that Gandhi appeared to have imbibed 'something of Nehru's love–hate attitude toward Britain in particular, though ... the love part has been notably absent, even in comparison with other Indian ministers, from hers'.[181] Inside the British High Commission in New Delhi, officials began to refer to the 'Gandhi factor' in Indo-British relations. Nehru had been at ease with his anglicised background, and looked back on his education at Harrow and Cambridge with a degree of pride and affection. In May 1960, the then Indian leader took time out from the Commonwealth Prime Ministers' Conference in London to visit Harrow. One Indian newspaper reported that Nehru had been 'visibly affected' by a special concert held in his honour, 'removing his glasses many times and wiping them vigorously' while joining in with the singing of the school song.[182] In contrast, Gandhi appeared to carry a considerable 'chip on the shoulder' when it came to her connections with Britain. Diplomats working for John Freeman speculated whether Britain would, in fact, pay 'a very heavy price in bilateral relations for Oxford University having ... chucked Mrs Gandhi out, or certainly made life difficult for her

---

[178] 'Mrs. Indira Gandhi', 15 January 1964, RG 59, Records Relating to Indian Political Affairs 1964–6, Lot 68D207, Box 5, Prime Minister Nehru Jan–May 1964, NARA.

[179] 'National Intelligence Survey: India September 1973', CIA-RDP01-00707000200070032-3, CIA Records Search Tool (CREST), NARA.

[180] Moynihan to Kissinger, No. 3458, 27 March 1973, Record Group 59, Central Foreign Policy Files, Electronic Telegrams, 1/1/1973–21/31/1973, NARA.

[181] *The Economist*, 22 January 1966.

[182] 'Harrow's Welcome To An "Old Boy"', *Amrita Bazar Patrika (Calcutta)*, 4 May 1960.

as a result of some academic failure, which was not forgotten'.[183] In April 1966, John Freeman cautioned London that shifts in India's political landscape meant that Britain could 'no longer depend on warm feelings from the past and we must look forward to a pragmatic relation of mutual benefit in the future'.[184] In fact, under the leadership of Indira Gandhi, as the British and American governments were to discover in the months and years ahead, Indian pragmatism resulted in the steady erosion of Western influence in the subcontinent. It was not until the conclusion of the Cold War in the early 1990s, and the process of economic and social liberalisation in India that followed on from it, that the standings of Britain and the United States in South Asia recovered to approach something like their pre-1965 levels.

[183] Peter Hall, DOHP 89, British Diplomatic Oral History Programme, Churchill College Cambridge.
[184] Freeman to Johnston, 13 April 1966, PREM 13/967, TNA.

# Conclusion: the erosion of Anglo-American influence in India and Pakistan

In April 1967, Chester Bowles entitled his regular column in the *American Reporter*, a mass circulation newspaper published by the US government in the subcontinent, 'Keep the Cold War Out of India'. In a thinly veiled attack on the Soviet Union, the US ambassador charged that sections of India's communist press were engaged in a 'carefully calculated, massively financed campaign', designed to 'create distrust and antagonism between the world's two largest democracies, the United States and India'. The delivery of subsidised American grain shipments to India and the educational, health and rural development programmes undertaken by US non-governmental organisations in the subcontinent, Bowles charged, were being maliciously misrepresented as part of a 'nefarious plot to undermine Indian self-reliance' and turn India over to 'Wall Street Imperialists', 'Neo-Colonialists' and 'Neo-Cultural Penetrationists'. Fulminating with righteous indignation, the US ambassador declared that in seeking to undermine American efforts to support India's development plans, the dissemination of 'devious' and 'false' communist propaganda risked imperilling the futures of all the subcontinent's citizens.[1] Bowles' exhortation to the Soviets to 'Keep the Cold War Out of India' while laudable, was woefully outmoded, and given America's record of intervention in South Asia over the preceding decade, smacked of hypocrisy. The ambassador's detractors were quick to charge that by entering into a military alliance with Pakistan back in 1954, Washington had, as Nehru bemoaned at the time, done more than anyone to bring the Cold War to the subcontinent.[2]

---

[1] Chester Bowles, 'Ambassador's Report: Keep the Cold War Out of India', *American Reporter*, 26 April 1967.

[2] In March 1954, Nehru had criticised the Eisenhower administration's decision to disturb the subcontinent's 'normality', and extend military aid to Pakistan. America's decision, the Indian leader complained bitterly, had upset the region's equilibrium, and was 'likely to create conditions which facilitate and encourage aggression'. *The New York Times*, 'Nehru Decries US Policy on Asia and the "Cold War"', 2 March 1954.

In the late 1940s, the newly independent states of India and Pakistan had barely registered on the Truman administration's geopolitical radar. In comparison with Western Europe, the considerable military-industrial resources of which appeared poised to fall into the Soviets' lap, US policymakers evidenced little interest in the Indian subcontinent, viewing the region as distant, impoverished, technologically regressive and strategically insignificant. A decade later, with Europe's ideological battle lines having solidified, the People's Republic of China flexing its regional muscle, war having broken out in Korea, an upsurge underway in Afro-Asian nationalism and Western colonialism in retreat, the Cold War had expanded to encompass the developing world. In the process, first the Eisenhower, and subsequently the Kennedy administration, came to view South Asia, and India in particular, as a strategic Cold War prize deserving of American patronage. The decision taken by the Eisenhower government to broker a formal alliance with Pakistan, and the notion that later gained currency amongst some senior Washington policymakers that India's democratic credentials, vast labour pool, latent economic power and political influence with the non-aligned movement could, and should, be harnessed to the West's advantage, was not rooted in a desire to control or exploit South Asia (and, in this sense, was not innately neo-imperialist). Rather, from the mid-1950s, American interventions in the Indian subcontinent invariably represented the responses of US officials to a series of (largely illusory) anxieties. Anxiety that the Soviet Union sought new satellite states in the Middle East and Persian Gulf; anxiety that Soviet commercial and economic links with India would erode Anglo-American influence in South Asia; anxiety over the strength of indigenous Indian communism; anxiety over Chinese Communist sway in South East Asia; anxiety that India would lose an economic 'race' with the PRC, debasing the Western model of democratic capitalist development; and anxiety that the 'loss' of South Asia to the forces of communism would weaken Western standing across the developing world.

The excessive weight attached by the Eisenhower and Kennedy administrations to the threats that the Soviet Union and PRC posed to Western authority in the subcontinent, and by extension, wider Asia, led the United States to embark upon a succession of ill-conceived forays into the internal affairs of India and Pakistan. Notably, between the late 1950s and the mid-1960s, Washington sank substantial amounts of political, economic and military capital into South Asia, in a bid to neutralise a largely hollow communist threat. The United States' return on its substantial investment in the region was, at best, negligible. A lavish, long-term American military assistance programme failed to transform Pakistan into anything like a credible deterrent to Soviet expansion into the Middle East. Likewise, having showered abundant economic assistance, political support and even some military aid on the Indian government, by the end of the 1960s Washington found that its relations with New Delhi were no better, and in many respects were much worse, than they had been a decade earlier. Moreover, South Asia's transformation from an international backwater into a major theatre in what, by now, had become a global Cold War, merely encouraged Soviet and Chinese interest and activity in the region. In short, American interventions in South Asia proved to be costly and, when judged against the objectives laid out by US policymakers, largely counterproductive.

By helping to usher the Cold War into South Asia, and inaugurate a fresh chapter in the 'Great Game', which over the course of the previous century had seen Britain, France, Russia and China jostle for pre-eminence in the Indian subcontinent, the United States also contributed to the erosion of residual British influence in the region (or at least helped to accelerate its decline). In the nineteenth century, at the zenith of its global power, Britain had vigorously defended its Indian Empire from external threats, real and imagined. Half a century later, following two debilitating global conflicts and the 'loss' of India, the British were ill equipped to play a major role in a new and modern variant of the 'Great Game'. The public reassurances offered by successive British post-war leaders, Labour and Conservative, that the United Kingdom remained an influential world power, belied the reality of a nation weighed down by an enervating combination of internal lassitude and extensive global commitments that it found increasingly difficult to meet. Between 1945 and 1965, Britain experienced a period of profound international adjustment, as its Empire contracted, its economic competitiveness slumped and its military capabilities diminished. The challenges Whitehall faced in managing such a transition were immense. Not least, a British exchequer plagued by recurrent balance of payments problems and monetary crises, severely restricted the United Kingdom's capacity for action on the world stage.

In South Asia, Britain remained a considerable commercial, cultural and diplomatic force well into the 1960s. At the same time, after August 1947, British influence in the subcontinent, as Whitehall privately acknowledged, yet Washington was surprisingly slow to accept, had come to represent a wasting asset. The broader socio-economic and political trends that made it progressively more difficult for British governments to maintain the pretence, much less the substance, of their former international power and authority were as evident in South Asia as elsewhere. In a sense, the death of India's prime minister Jawaharlal Nehru, in May 1964, marked a turning point in Britain's relationship with the subcontinent. The first generation of post-independence leaders in India and Pakistan were, for better or worse, products of the British colonial system. In later life the Harrow-, Trinity College, Cambridge-, and Inner Temple-educated Nehru, reflected mischievously that he would be the last Englishman to govern India, while the Pakistan leader, Ayub Khan, was marked out for his 'Sandhurst bearing' and 'clipped English accent'.[3] In Nehru's wake, a new generation of leaders emerged in India and Pakistan who evidenced far less interest in, and displayed little affinity for, things British. During the brief premiership of Lal Bahadur Shastri, it quickly became apparent that henceforth India would adopt a more pragmatic view of its relationship with London. In December 1965, Harold Wilson reminded Lyndon Johnson that India's next general elections, which were due in 1967, would be the first to 'be conducted without the presence of the father-figure of Nehru'. In Nehru's absence, Wilson cautioned the US president, 'Shastri was bound to be responsive to the almost intolerable pressures of visceral, irrational Indian politics, amongst which we must not underrate the importance of the anti-British and anti-American lobbies'.[4]

Under the leadership of Shastri's successor, and Nehru's daughter Indira Gandhi, India's once 'special' relationship with Britain proved to be anything but 'special'. To political commentators, Gandhi's appointment of Shanti Swaroop Dhavan as India's High Commissioner in London, in 1967, was indicative of Britain's reduced status in New Delhi. Reporting the news of Dhavan's appointment under the headline, 'London Slips Down the India League', *The Guardian* noted that although 'by all accounts, a talented, charming, somewhat elderly man … in total contrast to predecessors, he has little weight in Delhi'.[5] A year

---

[3] Viscount Hood to Lord Home, 'President Ayub's State Visit to the United States', 27 July 1961, DO 196/132, The United Kingdom National Archives, Kew, London (hereafter TNA); John Kenneth Galbraith, *Name-Dropping: From F.D.R. On* (New York: Houghton Mifflin, 1999), p. 132.

[4] Wilson to Johnson, 12 December 1965, National Security File (NSF), Robert W. Komer Files, Box 53, Folder United Kingdom Jan 1964–Mar 1966 [1 of 2], Lyndon Baines Johnson Library, Austin, Texas (hereafter LBJL).

[5] 'London Slips down the India League', *The Guardian*, 1 November 1967.

earlier, Dhavan had publicly announced that he 'foresaw no future for Indo-British friendship as Britain was not interested in seeing a strong India'.[6] Likewise, in early 1968, in Pakistan, Ayub Khan noted that a second devaluation of sterling, Britain's failure to secure entry into the Common Market, and its economic and military dependence on the United States, all suggested that 'if realism were to prevail, she [Britain] should become part of the USA and bargain to be counted not just as the 51st state but perhaps the fourth or fifth'.[7] Once a sick and increasingly marginalised Ayub Khan had been eased into retirement the following year, power in Pakistan passed to a succession of military leaders, such as Yahya Khan, and political opportunists, such as Zulfikar Ali Bhutto, whose attitude toward Britain was ambivalent at best. Bhutto, in particular, looked upon Britain as an imperial anachronism whose international role was distorted by burdensome historical ties to Asia and Africa. In applauding the decision taken by Harold Wilson's government to withdraw British armed forces from East of Suez, Bhutto maintained that

Britain's place is in Europe and the sooner Britain finds it the better it will be for Europe and for world peace. Britain began from Europe and to Europe she must now return. At present her tentacles are spread far beyond her capacity. She must adjust herself to the call of the times and reorientate her policies, primarily in respect of Europe.[8]

During the latter half of the 1960s, symbols of a second post-imperial British retreat from the subcontinent were abundant. In northern India, pressure to remove the status of English as an official language of the Indian Union manifested itself in an 'Out with English', or Angrezi Hatao, campaign. In February 1965, activists from the right-wing Bharatiya Jana Sangh party were to be found roaming the streets of New Delhi slopping tar over English-printed signboards and blacking out English street names.[9] At the same time, in an outbreak of imperial iconoclasm, effigies of prominent figures associated with British colonial power, such as Queen Victoria and Lord Curzon, were hauled

---

[6] Meeting between Minoo Masani and Marguerite Cooper (US Consulate General Bombay), 8 November 1967, RG 59, Bureau of Near Eastern and South Asian Affairs, Records Relating to India 1966–75, Lot file 71D385, Box 4, Folder Political Affairs & Relations India 1967, Swatantra Party, National Archives and Records Administration, College Park, Maryland (hereafter NARA).

[7] Diary entry for January–March 1968, in Craig Baxter (ed.), *Diaries of Field Marshal Mohammad Ayub Khan, 1966–1972* (Karachi: Oxford University Press, 2007), p. 209.

[8] Zulfikar Ali Bhutto, *The Myth of Independence* (London: Oxford University Press, 1969), p. 24.

[9] 'Tar-brush Tactics in the Language Crisis', *The Observer*, 21 February 1965.

down in public spaces across the subcontinent. In nominally secular India, where Islamic traditions governing idolatry were not enforced, symbols of Britain's former power were replaced with statues of Indian nationalist icons, such as Subas Chandra Bose and Bal Gangadhar Tilak.[10]

Yet, the decline in British power and influence in the subcontinent in the two decades following the formal transfer of power to India and Pakistan, and that reflected, in part, a diminution in the United Kingdom's global standing, was undoubtedly quickened by the extension of the Cold War to South Asia. In retrospect, it is possible to contend that the United States' strategic objectives in the Indian subcontinent would have been better served had the Eisenhower and Kennedy administrations resisted the temptation to intervene so often, and so directly, in its affairs. Adopting a regional policy of interested detachment and even-handedness in relation to India and Pakistan might well have served US interests better, and at a much reduced cost, by prolonging informal British authority in the subcontinent. In the mid-1950s, however, American policymakers had begun to question the utility of continuing to treat South Asia as predominantly a British responsibility. Not least, evidence of faltering British power and prestige in the Middle East and South East Asia suggested that the United States could no longer rely on the United Kingdom to uphold its vital national interests in the developing world. Notably, in Iran and Egypt, nationalist governments emerged, led by charismatic figures such Mohammad Mosaddegh and Gamal Abdel Nasser, the strident anti-imperialist agendas of which challenged established British hegemony in the Middle East. The impact of rising anti-British sentiment in the region was reflected in the Eden government's abortive attempt to cajole former regional allies into joining a scheme for collective Middle East defence. Likewise, Britain's apparent reluctance, or inability, to confront the political and economic problems that it had bequeathed India and Pakistan, or to fully comprehend the communist threat to the subcontinent posed by the Soviet Union and the PRC, frustrated the Eisenhower government. Moreover, Washington came to suspect that the Commonwealth Relations Office perceived the United States to be less of a benign and largely silent regional partner, and more of a looming competitive menace to Britain's valuable commercial and political stake in South Asia.

[10] A. K. Goldsmith (New Delhi) to D. M. Kerr (CRO), 30 April 1964, DO 174/54, TNA. See also ' Victory for the Iconoclasts', *The Times*, 11 May 1964.

Toward the end of the 1950s, an increasing emphasis in the United States on the importance of winning 'hearts and minds' in the developing world, and nowhere more so than in India, coupled with a growing realisation on the part of American officials of the limitations inherent in working alongside an instinctively circumspect British partner in South Asia, encouraged Washington to pursue a more assertive regional policy. Whenever possible, however, both the Eisenhower and Kennedy governments retained a strong preference for coordinating their regional policymaking with the British. Britain's long experience in the subcontinent and extensive network of political, economic and military connections within South Asia remained highly valued by the State Department. Besides which, pushing the British to assume a prominent role in joint Anglo-American initiatives was seen as advantageous in a number of respects. Not least, collaborating with the British in South Asia was expected to moderate criticism at an American 'tilt' toward India from Washington's Pakistani ally and a US legislature allergic to Nehru's policy of Cold War non-alignment. Moreover, using the British as a stalking horse in the subcontinent was expected to lessen the possibility of large-scale Soviet or Chinese intervention in the region; dampen the developing world's concern over America's purportedly neo-imperialist agenda; and go some way toward ensuring that the British made an appropriate contribution to the defence of the 'free world'.

In the event, Washington found it to be almost as frustrating and disappointing working with the British in South Asia in the early 1960s, as it was working without them in South Vietnam in the second half of the decade. In the United Kingdom, the Conservative governments of Harold Macmillan and Alec Douglas-Home, and their Labour successors led by Harold Wilson, welcomed the opportunity to consolidate Britain's status as the United States' foremost ally by supporting American efforts to enhance the security, stability and economic prosperity of India and Pakistan. At the same time, policymakers in London were acutely conscious of the need to safeguard valuable British diplomatic and financial interests in the subcontinent. More often than not, in seeking to balance the competing and invariably contradictory demands made upon them by the governments of the United States, India and Pakistan, the British found themselves caught on the horns of a dilemma. Above all, the British bridled at the imposition of pressure from Washington to act as an American surrogate in South Asia and operate as a conduit for the delivery of US support to India. Assuming such a role, Whitehall calculated, would prove financially prohibitive and politically toxic, not least when it came to Britain's relationship

with Pakistan. Furthermore, it threatened to overextend Britain's limited military resources and raised the alarming prospect of the United
Kingdom becoming embroiled in armed conflagration in South Asia.
The latter was of particular concern to British officials who worried
that America's bellicose attitude toward the PRC might land Britain
in a war with Beijing, with disastrous consequences for the country's
interests in places such as Hong Kong. After the brief Sino-Indian border war of late 1962, in marked contrast to his American colleagues,
Terence Garvey, Britain's chargé d'affaires in China, was to be found
reassuring Whitehall that

China's territorial and military intentions in the present dispute with India are
strictly limited ... If Mr. [Averell] Harriman supposes that the Chinese aim at
physical control of the South-East Asian 'rice-bowl', I think he is seeing the
wrong danger ... the danger to my mind is China's bid to make South-East
Asia not her province but her zone of influence ... The Chinese will pursue it
by economic and political means, by subversion and the threat of force, but I
would not expect them to do so by armed aggression beyond the 'traditional
frontiers.'[11]

Indeed, the growing disparity between post-war British and American
power, and the divergent perspectives from which London and
Washington approached their relationships with India, Pakistan, the
Soviet Union and Communist China, militated against the establishment of an effective Anglo-American modus operandi in the Indian
subcontinent.

While their strategic aspirations in South Asia were broadly similar, the existence of sharp tactical differences between British and
American policymakers over how best to meet regional 'threats', or
exploit regional 'opportunities', habitually resulted in tardy, muddled
and half-baked joint interventions in the affairs of India and Pakistan.
Whether attempting to broker a settlement to the Indo-Pakistan dispute over Kashmir, prevent India's purchase of Soviet fighter aircraft,
coax New Delhi into becoming a de facto member of the West's system of collective security or halt Indo-Pakistani hostilities in 1965,
Britain and the United States invariably succeeded only in antagonis-
ing New Delhi and Rawalpindi, and, more often than not, each other.
Moreover, the record of Anglo-American intervention in South Asia
after 1947 strongly suggests that senior policymakers in Washington
and Whitehall had a profoundly inadequate understanding of the degree
to which the region's previously intractable problems were susceptible
to external manipulation. Emotive issues such as Kashmir were too

[11]  Terence Garvey to Lord Home, 20 February 1963, DO 196/174, TNA.

bound up in the religious, communal and political fabric of India and Pakistan to yield easily, if at all, to outside pressures. The boundaries of Western power and influence in South Asia were not readily apparent to post-war American and British governments, who frequently ignored or contested constraints on external influence in the region, usually with disastrous results.

In retrospect, it is clear that the Indo-Pakistani War of 1965 represented a watershed in the West's association with the subcontinent. In the two centuries preceding the conflict, first Great Britain and latterly the United States had dominated South Asia's political and economic landscape, and worked assiduously to limit Russian and Chinese influence in the region. In 1965, the outbreak of Indo-Pakistani hostilities proved instrumental in bringing to a head simmering feelings of mutual disillusionment that had been building between India, Pakistan, the United Kingdom and the United States over much of the previous decade. The rancour that infused Britain's relations with India following the diplomatic rupture between London and New Delhi in September that year was captured vividly in the pages of the country's press. In *The Indian Express*, Frank Moraes decried Britain and the Commonwealth's 'hard white core' as 'embarrassing', 'irksome' and increasingly devoid of 'validity and relevance'. Observing pointedly that the world 'no longer revolves around London', the generally pro-Western Moraes called for India to cultivate closer relations with fellow Asian powers, including the Soviet Union, and to avoid repeating the 'mistake' of concentrating 'our political and economic eggs in too few baskets'. 'The era of the colonels and withered dowagers of Cheltenham is over,' Moraes proclaimed, 'even if some among this seemingly indestructible tribe continue to hug their illusions and think otherwise.'[12]

For all Harold Wilson's 'New Britain' rhetoric, the British leader's reluctance to confront the inevitability of his nation's diminished role on the world stage at times made him appear little more than a parody of Moraes' hidebound imperial relic. Following the Soviets' diplomatic triumph at the Tashkent peace talks, the British press dusted down 'Great Game' analogies and wrote in apocalyptic terms of the looming Russian shadow being cast across Britain's 'frontiers on the Himalayas'. In turn, Wilson continued to justify his government's enervating commitment to preserving a sizeable British military force 'East of Suez', in part, in terms of a moral obligation to defend the subcontinent and

---

[12] Frank Moraes, 'Indo-British Relations', *The Indian Express*, 20 September 1965.

the United Kingdom's interests in it from external threats.[13] The tendency amongst British officials was to draw a different lesson from Harold Wilson from the events of 1965. Britain's High Commissioner in New Delhi, John Freeman, maintained that Indo-British relations had shifted fundamentally as a result of the Indo-Pakistani War. In its wake, Freeman advised Whitehall that the United Kingdom 'could no longer depend on warm [Indian] feelings from the past and we must look forward to a pragmatic relation of mutual benefit in the future'.[14]

Within the CRO, where concern persisted over the propensity of 'too many Britishers' to 'express dislike of and contempt for India', senior officials went further and suggested that in certain areas British retrenchment from South Asia had not only become inevitable but was, in fact, desirable.[15] In a minute written in May 1966, one CRO official observed that after years of

exchanging views with the Americans and wringing our hands jointly and severally with them at our inability to dissuade the Indians from behaving wickedly and the Pakistanis from behaving stupidly ... the right policy for us should I think be one of unobtrusive disengagement. The harsh truth is that India and Pakistan will be more inclined to listen to the major power, Russia, than the middle power, Britain. All our experience ... is that when we take an active role [in South Asian affairs], we are far more likely to incur odium from one party or the other than appreciation for our efforts. Let us now quietly step back so that the Russians can fill the role we have tried to fill on and off for the last nineteen years.[16]

While instinctively recoiling from the 'very unheroic policy' advocated by his more junior colleagues, Sir Saville Garner, Permanent Under Secretary at the CRO, commended it as 'one no doubt adjusted to our [Britain's] changed status in the world'. The reality, Garner underlined, however unpalatable it might be to his political masters, was that in South Asia, 'the United States and the Soviet Union have more influence and means of persuasion than we do'. 'I do not think', the veteran Whitehall mandarin added wistfully, 'that we should have included this sentence 15 years ago.'[17]

In Wilson's cabinet, which had been infused with political modernisers such as Roy Jenkins, the focus of most ministers was on securing a

---

[13] Speech by Harold Wilson to the Parliamentary Labour Party, 15 June 1966, PLP Minutes 1964–6, Box of PLP Papers, Labour Party Archive (LPA), Manchester Museum of Labour History, Manchester, United Kingdom.

[14] John Freeman to Sir J. Johnston (CRO), 13 April 1966, PREM 13/967, TNA.

[15] Saville Garner to John Freeman, 28 September 1965, DO 196/224, TNA.

[16] Sir J. Johnston minute, 4 May 1966, DO 196/225, TNA.

[17] Saville Garner to Sir J. Johnston, Sir A. Snelling and Mr Duff, 30 December 1966, DO 196/225, TNA.

leading role for Britain in a new Europe, rather than seeking to perpetuate old and increasingly problematic imperial connections. Labour's 1964 general election manifesto, 'The New Britain', had underlined the importance of India, Pakistan and the wider Commonwealth. 'Though we shall seek to achieve closer links with our European neighbours,' Britain's electorate had been assured, 'the Labour Party is convinced that the first responsibility of a British Government is still to the Commonwealth.' Less than two years later, in March 1966, Labour's subsequent election manifesto, 'Time for Decision', barely referenced the Commonwealth and completely omitted any mention of India and Pakistan. That year, India severed an important economic connection with Britain when it left the sterling area. On a broader level, the Indian decision was reflective of a decline in the relative importance of British trade with the subcontinent and the wider Commonwealth, the latter having shrunk by over a quarter in the preceding eight years.[18] Having hosted three Commonwealth conferences between June 1965 and September 1966, during one of which Wilson had grumbled that Britain was being treated as 'if it were a bloody colony', the British premier waited until January 1969 before convening another.[19]

Elsewhere, in July 1967, with Britain's involvement in the Indonesia–Malaysia confrontation having ended the previous summer and the Treasury pressing for deep cuts in overseas spending in the face of sluggish domestic economic performance and incessant financial pressures, Wilson's government confirmed plans to withdraw British forces from bases East of Suez, qualifying the UK's status as a global military force. In November, the Arab-Israeli War and the Nigerian Civil War reduced Britain's oil supplies and contributed to the devaluation of sterling. A month later, in another blow to London's international pretensions, France rejected a second British application to join the European Economic Community. In January 1968, continued economic debility led the Wilson government to announce that it would bring forward plans to pull out from military bases in Asia, underlining Britain's status as primarily a European power with limited international reach. In the United States, the Johnson administration reacted with dismay at the British decision to sound an imperial retreat. With the Vietnam War consuming ever-greater amounts of American blood and treasure, the White House resented what it saw as Wilson's weakness in embracing a 'Little England' mentality and shirking Cold War responsibilities.

[18] 'Britain Reappraising the Commonwealth', *The New York Times*, 23 January 1966.
[19] Wilson cited in John W. Young, *The Labour Governments 1964–1970*, vol. 2: *International Policy* (Manchester University Press, 2003), p. 11.

In Washington, on 11 January 1968, in what he characterised subsequently as a 'bloody unpleasant' encounter, Britain's Foreign Secretary, George Brown, was urged by his American counterpart, Dean Rusk, to 'For God's sake be Britain.'[20]

In a sense, Britain's formal retreat from South East Asia and the Persian Gulf mirrored a decision taken by the Johnson administration earlier in the decade to disengage from South Asia. More sceptical of the subcontinent's centrality to US national security than his immediate predecessors in the White House, the outbreak of Indo-Pakistani hostilities in 1965 'raised grave doubts' in Lyndon Johnson's mind over the wisdom of continuing to furnish New Delhi and Rawalpindi with American military and economic aid. In what he described as 'one of the most difficult and lonely struggles of my Presidency', Johnson chose to ignore the advice of the South Asian experts that he had inherited from President Kennedy, and to implement a tough and uncompromising regional policy that proved deeply unpopular in India and Pakistan.[21] On 20 October 1965, in a blunt public statement delivered at the signing of his administration's foreign aid bill, the president made clear that henceforth Washington would evaluate its overseas assistance programmes not merely in terms of nations' needs, but also in respect of their economic policies and political attitudes. 'While our wealth is great,' Johnson emphasised, 'it is not unlimited.' 'It must be used not merely to apply Band-Aids to superficial wounds but to remove the cause of deeper and more dangerous disorders ... Our assistance must and will go to those nations that will most use it. Action, not promises, will be the standard of our assistance.'[22]

In a bid to induce the Indian government to divert resources away from industrial projects and into much-needed agricultural reforms, US food aid to the subcontinent was placed on a 'short tether' by Johnson and approved by the president on a month-by-month basis. With India then in the midst of a severe drought, which for the first time since the Second World War saw wheat, rice and sugar rationed in New Delhi, the 'short tether' approach infuriated Indian politicians. The following summer, India's ambassador to the United States,

---

[20] George Brown to the Foreign Office, 'Defence Cuts', 11 January 1968, PREM 13/1999; Memorandum of Conversation between George Brown and Dean Rusk, FCO 46/43, 11 January 1968, TNA. See also Memorandum to the President re Rusk meeting with Brown, Washington, DC, NSF, 11 January 1968, LBJL.

[21] Lyndon Baines Johnson, *The Vantage Point: Perspectives of the Presidency, 1963–1969* (New York: Holt, Rinehart and Winston, 1971), p. 225.

[22] Lyndon B. Johnson, 'Statement by the President Upon Signing the Foreign Assistance and Related Agencies Appropriation Act', 20 October 1965, The American Presidency Project, www.presidency.ucsb.edu.

B. K. Nehru, cautioned Walt Rostow, Johnson's National Security Advisor, that anti-American sentiment was gaining significant traction in the subcontinent. Rumours that the United States had pressed India to devalue its currency, and was considering resuming arms sales to Pakistan, served to exacerbate festering Indian resentment toward Johnson's food aid policy. More and more Indians, Rostow was advised by Nehru, were arguing that in order to 'recapture their sovereignty' it would be better to 'get rid of foreign aid whatever the consequences'.[23] Friction over Johnson's decision to escalate American military operations in support of South Vietnam added to the feelings of animosity between Washington and New Delhi. Visiting US diplomats, who had been feted by Indian ministers earlier in the decade, began to receive 'a conspicuously cold shoulder' when passing through the subcontinent.[24] British officials in India noted with concern the increasingly 'bitter' tone of Indo-US exchanges. In December 1966, with the Indian government still smarting over delays in the delivery of US wheat supplies, when Dean Rusk paid a brief visit to New Delhi, the Secretary of State was greeted by India's minister for external affairs, M. C. Chagla, with the words, 'What have you come here for if you have brought nothing with you?' During a terse and acrimonious exchange with Chagla, Rusk excoriated India for its failure to support the cause of 'freedom' in South Vietnam. 'Did India really wish the United States to withdraw from Vietnam?', Rusk challenged Chagla. 'Yes', the Indian minister replied bluntly.[25]

The United States' relationship with Pakistan proved to be equally testy in the second half of the 1960s. Under the guidance of Bhutto, whom British and American officials disparaged as 'neutralist', 'frequently spiteful' and 'bitterly anti-western', Ayub Khan's government adopted an increasingly independent and assertive course in the international arena. To Johnson's irritation, Pakistan cultivated ties with the PRC, set about building bridges with Moscow and re-established dialogue with the Afro-Asian non-aligned group, which Rawalpindi had left a decade earlier when it joined the Western alliance system.[26] In an

---

[23] Walt Rostow, memorandum of conversation, 12 August 1966, NSF Country File, India, Box 131 [1 of 2], Folder 1 India Memos & Misc. [1 of 3], Vol. VII, 1-66 to 8-66, LBJL.
[24] Inder Malhotra, 'US Given Indian Cold Shoulder', *The Guardian*, 1 November 1966.
[25] J. P. Waterfield to A. A. Duff (CRO), 'Indo-US Relations', 22 December 1966, DO 196/408, TNA.
[26] 'Pakistan's Foreign Policy Under Ayub and Bhutto', CIA Special Report, 16 April 1965, NSF Country File, Pakistan, Box 151, Folder 4 Pakistan Memos, Vol. III, 12-64 to 7-65, LBJL.

era when left-wing nationalism held sway in Egypt under Nasser, Ghana under Nkrumah and Indonesia under Sukarno, Bhutto's populist anti-Indian, anti-American and anti-capitalist rhetoric resonated with many of Pakistan's disenfranchised poor. Having hoped that Bhutto would be held publicly accountable for his country's disastrous showing in the Indo-Pakistani conflict of 1965 and suffer an 'abrupt eclipse', a dejected Morrice James informed the Commonwealth Relations Office in London that 'unfortunately the war has consolidated his [Bhutto's] following among the disaffected intelligentsia and student communities whose support it is essential for President Ayub to try to maintain'.[27] Bhutto would later coin the slogan *roti, kapra aur makan* (or bread, clothes and housing) and, at the head of his own Pakistan People's Party, preside over a disastrous experiment in socio-economic re-engineering in Pakistan in the early 1970s.[28] In June 1966, Ayub Khan attempted to stifle Bhutto's political ambition by expelling the unruly political firebrand from his cabinet. Rationalising a decision that enraged 'leftist elements' in Pakistan, the president recorded in his diary that Bhutto had

started using provocative language even on international platforms and started behaving in an objectionable manner. He was working fast in the direction of becoming another Krishna Menon or Subandiro. Demagogy became his stock in trade. Several warnings went unheeded. So, there was no alternative but to tell him to go ... His real trouble was that he started running a personal policy assisted by a few elements in the Foreign Office instead of the national policy; also he was distrusted and disliked in most capitals.[29]

Although delighted to see the back of Bhutto, moving forward British and American policymakers detected little, if any, change in what some international observers characterised as Pakistan's 'Red Shift'.[30]

The Johnson administration's determination to place its relationship with Pakistan on a new and more circumscribed basis following the events of 1965, encouraged Pakistan to hedge its Cold War bets and solicit greater amounts of economic and military aid from Beijing and Moscow. In April 1967, the State Department confirmed that the

---

[27]  Morrice James to Arthur Bottomley, 'Pakistan and Kashmir: A Tragic Misadventure', CRO Ref: 2SEA 65/164/1, 25 October 1965, DO 196/388, TNA.

[28]  Anatol Lieven, *Pakistan: A Hard Country* (London: Penguin, 2012), pp. 72–4.

[29]  Diary entry for Friday 2 September 1966, in Baxter (ed.), *Diaries of Field Marshal Mohammad Ayub Khan, 1966–1972*, p. 3.

[30]  Harold Wilson, who had problems managing his own outspoken and alcoholic Foreign Secretary, George Brown, confided in Ayub Khan shortly after Bhutto's dismissal, 'I'm glad you got rid of Bhutto. He was not trustworthy.' Diary entry for Friday 18 November 1966, in Baxter (ed.), *Diaries of Field Marshal Mohammad Ayub Khan, 1966–1972*, p. 29. See also 'A Medical Discharge', *Time*, 1 July 1966.

United States would not resume the military assistance programmes to Pakistan and India that had been suspended in September 1965. As America's 'most allied ally', Pakistan had roundly condemned the Soviet intervention in Hungary in 1956. In 1968, when Russian tanks rolled into Czechoslovakia to crush the 'Prague Spring', Pakistan's ambassador to the United Nations, Agha Shahi, adopted a position in New York that American diplomats decried as 'just short of alignment with the Soviets'.[31] The 'old special relationship' between the United States and Pakistan had, American and Pakistani policymakers agreed, been dealt a terminal blow by the Indo-Pakistani War. The 'low level of intensity' that had come to characterise Washington's interaction with Islamabad by the end of the 1960s was seen by American officials as, on the whole, a positive development more in keeping with the two countries' location, size and interests.[32] Likewise, many Pakistani politicians, while acknowledging the substantial economic and military assistance their country had received from Washington, came to echo Bhutto's assessment that the price of America's friendship had been exorbitantly high. Writing in 1969, Bhutto contended that in entering into an alliance with the United States

Pakistan had undertaken to stretch her defence commitments against the Communist powers without a categorical assurance with regard to her security against India. She had incurred the hostility of the Soviet Union, which openly supported Afghanistan and India against Pakistan. The policy of alignment also damaged Pakistan's image in the United Nations, strained her relations with neighbouring Islamic Arab states, and drove her towards isolation in the community of Asia and Africa.[33]

The decision taken by Ayub Khan's government around this time not to renew the lease on the American-run intelligence-gathering facility at Badaber, which was set to expire in 1969, drew a symbolic line under Pakistan's Cold War alliance with the United States. In dismissing American requests to reconsider shutting down the Badaber base, Ayub Khan underlined the heightened sense of vulnerability that Pakistan felt in the aftermath of the Indo-Pakistani War of 1965. The United States, Pakistan's president noted bitterly,

---

[31] State Department Intelligence Note 706, 6 September 1968, 'Pakistani Neutralism: The Czech Case', POL-27-1, Com Bloc-Czech, DSR, NARA.
[32] Thomas P. Thornton to James W. Spain and Granville S. Austin, 'Post-Peshawar Political Perspective, Prospects and Problems', 19 June 1968, RG 59, Bureau of Near Eastern and South Asian Affairs, Records Relating to India 1966–75, Lot file 72D5, Box 5, Folder Pakistan 1968, NARA.
[33] Bhutto, *The Myth of Independence*, p. 58.

forgets that our security hazards and political liabilities have increased to a dangerous level due to this installation. We knew this and yet we kept our part of the contract whilst the Americans betrayed us at every turn. They built up India against us, failed to come to our assistance in 1965, despite bilateral defence agreement, and finally stopped military aid ... Yet they expect us to expose ourselves to the enmity of India and China. They think that we exist for their convenience and that our freedom is negotiable.[34]

The Badaber announcement generated few ripples in Washington outside of the CIA's Langley headquarters. Once highly prized by US policymakers, with the advent of sophisticated satellite technology, the intelligence facility, much like the US-Pakistani relationship itself, appeared an historical anomaly that had largely outlived its usefulness.[35]

From the late 1950s, the United States had focused its efforts to contain the spread of communism in Asia on the Indian subcontinent. During the presidency of Lyndon Johnson, the locus of the US policy of containment in the Far East switched decisively to South Vietnam. 'It is an unhappy fact', lamented the NSC staffer Howard Wriggins, in July 1967, 'that our immediate effort to hold the Asian balance in Vietnam is so pressing that we cannot release more than 1/20th of what goes there to this huge [Indian] sub-continent which, in the long run, may contribute much more to this same policy objective.'[36] In New Delhi, Chester Bowles shared Wriggins' exasperation that the strategic importance of the subcontinent was being overlooked by an administration back in Washington that had become fixated with the war in Vietnam. Writing in May 1968 to Harrison Salisbury, the *New York Times'* assistant managing editor, Bowles suggested in vain that the influential US newspaper should consider publishing a series of articles highlighting South Asia's continued significance in the broader context of the Cold World. '[T]he US Government, diverted and confused by Vietnam and social tensions, seems to be pulling back from an effort which I believe is on the verge of success', Bowles informed Salisbury. 'In the meantime

---

[34] Diary entry for Monday 17 July 1968, in Baxter (ed.), *Diaries of Field Marshal Mohammad Ayub Khan, 1966–1972*, p. 242.

[35] Thomas P. Thornton to James W. Spain and Granville S. Austin, 'Post-Peshawar Political Perspective, Prospects and Problems', 19 June 1968, RG 59, Bureau of Near Eastern and South Asian Affairs, Records Relating to India 1966–75, Lot file 72D5, Box 5, Folder Pakistan 1968, NARA.

[36] Howard Wriggins to Walt Rostow, 'Thoughts on India/Pakistan', 24 July 1967, NSF Country File, Pakistan, Box 153, Folder 2 Pakistan Memos [1 of 2], Vol. VII, 10-66 to 7-67, LBJL.

the Soviets are successfully stepping up their efforts here with a great amount of skills and resources.'[37]

Indeed, under Indira Gandhi's leadership, Indo-Soviet relations grew increasingly close. After visiting Moscow in July 1966, Gandhi returned home with a Soviet pledge of increased economic and technical support for India's development plans. The following year, the Soviets went further and agreed to assist in the modernising of India's armed forces. In addition to ramping up its economic and military support for Gandhi's government, the Soviet Union also began to import substantial quantities of raw materials and manufactured goods from India. All of which, from Washington's perspective, appeared 'designed not only to undercut Western ties [to India] and strengthen the "socialist" sector of the [Indian] economy, but also to facilitate further strengthening of the military supply relationship' between Moscow and New Delhi'.[38] A marked deterioration in Sino-Soviet relations in 1969, which culminated in a border skirmish that briefly threatened to escalate into general war between the two Communist titans, acted as a further stimulus to Indo-Soviet friendship. At the beginning of the 1960s, India had looked to the United States to underwrite its security in relation to China. By the end of the decade, that responsibility had been transferred to a Soviet government that, in a throwback to the Kennedy administration, now favoured the establishment of a collective security system in Asia to contain the PRC. In August 1971, after a number of false starts, India and the Soviet Union cemented their strategic partnership by signing a 'Treaty of Peace, Friendship, and Cooperation'. At the end of that year, having supported New Delhi in the brief war with Pakistan that gave birth to the new state of Bangladesh, Moscow was feted as India's most loyal and trusted ally.[39]

While they regretted the heightened 'mutual irritation and suspicion' that came to cloud the United States' relations with India and Pakistan, senior policymakers in Washington wearied of dealing with the subcontinent and its seemingly intractable problems. In March 1970, one

---

[37] Chester Bowles to Harrison E. Salisbury, 2 May 1968, Box 1 Folder Chester Bowles, Harrison Salisbury Papers, Butler Library, Columbia University, New York.

[38] Carlton Coon to M. Heck, 'Indian Security Concerns and US Policy', 4 March 1968, RG 59, Bureau of Near Eastern and South Asian Affairs, Records Relating to India 1966–75, Lot file 72D5, Box 5, Folder India 1968, NARA.

[39] See 'International Images in India (based on Surveys by Indian Institute of Public Opinion, New Delhi)', April 1974, I-376 Folder India, Subject File Public Opinion 1974, Daniel Patrick Moynihan Papers, Manuscript Division, Library of Congress, Washington, DC.

State Department official noted that following South Asia's transition to a 'lower ranking in our [US] global priorities', the United States was content to limit its regional ambition to ensuring that India and Pakistan avoided implementing policies 'destructive of our efforts to build a stable and self-reliant system in Asia'.[40] Such pragmatism represented a far cry from the sweeping interventions in the affairs of India and Pakistan undertaken by the United States between the late 1950s and the early 1960s.

Over the past five decades, the importance attached to the subcontinent by British and American governments has fluctuated considerably. On occasions, South Asia has returned to the forefront of American strategic thinking. Notably, in 1971, the Nixon White House came to value Pakistan's close diplomatic relations with the PRC as it embarked upon a clandestine courtship of Communist China. Likewise, the controversial American decision to 'tilt' toward Pakistan during the Indo-Pakistani War that December, was informed by Richard Nixon's conviction that his government's credibility, in the eyes of its Chinese ally and Soviet adversary, hinged on making a strong show of support for Islamabad. Moreover, in 1979, the Soviet Union's ill-fated invasion of Afghanistan had a further transformative impact upon Pakistan's relationship with the United States. By serving as the principal conduit for the delivery of US supplies to resistance forces inside Soviet-occupied Afghanistan, Pakistan temporarily returned to the top of Washington's list of strategically important partners. Of late, in the aftermath of the attacks perpetrated in the United States in September 2001, and a further, American-led intervention in Afghanistan, India and Pakistan have assumed a prominent place in the West's strategy for combatting global terrorism.

Indeed, the history of the Cold War in South Asia between 1945 and 1965 offers up salutary lessons for contemporary international policymakers as they confront a new and amorphous global conflict, in which the subcontinent has bulked large. Specifically, the record of Anglo-American interventions in India and Pakistan is illustrative of how inflated fears of nebulous external threats can have a profound psychological impact upon a nation's sense of security. The British spent much of the nineteenth century preparing to defend India against a

---

[40] Carlton Coon to M. Heck 'Indian Security Concerns and US Policy', 4 March 1968, RG 59, Bureau of Near Eastern and South Asian Affairs, Records Relating to India 1966–75, Lot file 72D5, Box 5, India 1968; 'Indo-American Relations 1970', 2 March 1970, RG 59, Bureau of Near Eastern and South Asian Affairs, Records Relating to India 1966–75, Lot file 74D17, Box 14, India – Gen. Policy, NARA.

Russian invasion, the plans for which, if they ever existed, never progressed beyond a St Petersburg drawing board. Half a century later, excessive anxiety over the inroads that the Soviet Union and People's Republic of China were making in the developing world, and the danger that this posed to American national interests, prompted the United States to intervene in South Asia. Yet, in India and Pakistan, as elsewhere across the globe, the United States and its British partner found nascent post-colonial states to be frustratingly resistant to external pressures and outside direction. Raw Anglo-American power lost much of its potency when projected into Asia, Latin America or Africa. In the hands of Western leaders, the lure of economic aid, military assistance and collective security pacts, were blunt and ineffectual tools that proved incapable of regulating the international outlook or internal politics of India and Pakistan. By extending the Cold War into South Asia, however, the United States did succeed in disturbing the subcontinent's established politico-military equilibrium; undermining British influence in the region; embittering relations between India and Pakistan; and, ironically, facilitating the expansion of communist influence in the developing world. When viewed through the prism of the most recent Western intervention in South Asia, few, if any, lessons appear to have been absorbed from the past. In Afghanistan, where the United States and its allies have struggled for over a decade to fashion a stable, secure and pro-Western nation state, questions surrounding the arrogance and limitations of Western power remain as pertinent today as at any time during the Cold War period. Looking forward, it is to be hoped that future generations of British and American policymakers are able to engage with South Asia, and the wider developing world, on terms that are more informed, constructive and mutually beneficial than has hitherto been the case.

# Select bibliography

## MANUSCRIPT COLLECTIONS

UNITED KINGDOM

**Bodleian Library, University of Oxford**
Clement Attlee Papers
Harold Macmillan Papers
Harold Wilson Papers
Paul Gore-Booth Papers

**British Library, India Office Select Materials, London**
Alexander Symon Papers
Indian Civil Service (Retired) Association Papers
Olaf Caroe Papers
Sir John Gilbert Laithwaite Papers

**Churchill Archives Centre, Churchill College Cambridge**
Baron Gordon Walker Papers
Dingle Foot Papers
Duncan Sandys Papers
Earl of Swinton Papers
Leopold Amery Papers
Lord Hailsham Papers
Thomas Elmhirst Papers
William John Haley Papers

**Royal Commonwealth Society Library, University of Cambridge**
Cyril Pickard Papers

**Hartley Library, University of Southampton**
Lord Mountbatten Papers

**Houses of Parliament Archives, London**
John Tilney Papers
Reginald Sorenson Papers

**Palace Green Library, University Of Durham**
Malcolm MacDonald Papers

**School of Oriental and African Studies, University of London**
Frank Moraes Papers

**Unpublished UK Government Documents, National Archives, Kew, London**
Records of the Cabinet Office
Records of the Colonial Office
Records of the Commonwealth Relations Office
Records of the Foreign Office
Records of the Ministry of Defence
Records of the Prime Minister
Records of the Security Service
Records of the Treasury

UNITED STATES

**Library of Congress, Washington, DC**
Averell Harriman Papers
Daniel Patrick Moynihan Papers
Loy W. Henderson Papers

**Butler Library, Columbia University, New York**
Dorothy Norman Papers
Harrison Salisbury Papers

**Sterling Memorial Library, Yale University, Connecticut**
Chester Bowles Papers
Walter Lippmann Papers

**Harry S. Truman Library, Independence, Missouri**
Dean Acheson Papers
Harry S. Truman Papers

**Dwight D. Eisenhower Library, Abilene, Kansas**
Dwight D. Eisenhower Papers
John Foster Dulles Papers

**John F. Kennedy Library, Boston, Massachusetts**
Carl Kaysen Papers
George Ball Papers
John F. Kennedy Papers
John Kenneth Galbraith Papers
McGeorge Bundy Papers
Robert Komer Papers

Roger Hilsman Papers
Roswell Gilpatric Papers

**Lyndon Baines Johnson Library, Austin, Texas**
Bromley Smith Papers
Drew Pearson Papers
George Ball Papers
Lyndon B. Johnson Papers
Robert Komer Papers

**Unpublished US Government Documents, NARA, National Archives of the United States II, College Park, Maryland**
Record Group 59, General Records of the Department of State
Record Group 218, Records of the Joint Chiefs of Staff
Record Group 306, Records of the United States Information Agency
Record Group 273, Records of the National Security Council
Central Intelligence Agency Records Search Tool (CREST)

INDIA

**Nehru Memorial Museum and Library, New Delhi**
C. Rajagopalachari Papers
G. D. Birla Papers
K. P. S. Menon Papers
P. N. Haksar Papers
Subimal Dutt Papers
T. N. Kaul Papers
Vijaya Lakshmi Pandit Papers

**National Archives of India**
Records of the Ministry of External Affairs

PUBLISHED PRIMARY SOURCES

INDIA

Appadorai, A (ed.). *Select Documents on India's Foreign Policy and Relations, 1947–1972*, vol. 1. New Delhi: Oxford University Press, 1982.
    *Select Documents on India's Foreign Policy and Relations, 1947–1972*, vol. 2. New Delhi: Oxford University Press, 1985.
Chakravorty, B. C. *History of the Indo-Pak War, 1965*, ed. S. N. Prasad. New Delhi: History Division, Ministry of Defence, Government of India, 1992.
Choudhary, Valmiki (ed.). *Dr. Rajendra Prasad: Correspondence and Select Documents*, vol. 21, January 1960 to February 1963. New Delhi: Allied Publishers Limited, 1995.
Gandhi, Indira. *India: The Speeches and Reminiscences of Indira Gandhi, Prime Minister of India*. London: Hodder & Stoughton, 1975.

Gopal, Sarvepalli (ed.) *The Essential Writings of Jawaharlal Nehru*, vol. 2. Oxford University Press, 2003.

Hasan, Mushirul (ed.). *Selected Works of Jawaharlal Nehru*, Second Series, vol. 36, 1 December 1956–21 February 1957. New Delhi: Oxford University Press, 2005.

Hasan, Mushirul, Sharad Prasad, H. Y. and Damodaran, A. K. (eds.). *Selected Works of Jawaharlal Nehru*, Second Series, vol. 33, 1 May 1956–20 June 1956. New Delhi: Oxford University Press, 2004.

Kumar, Ravinder and Sharada Prasad, H. Y. (eds.). *Selected Works of Jawaharlal Nehru*, Second Series, vol. 27, 1 October 1954–31 January 1955. New Delhi: Oxford University Press, 2000.

*Selected Works of Jawaharlal Nehru*, vol. 28, 1 February–31 May 1955. New Delhi: Oxford University Press, 2001.

Parthasarathi, G. (ed.). *Jawaharlal Nehru: Letters to Chief Ministers, 1947–1964*, vol. 3: *1952–1954*. New Delhi: Oxford University Press, 1989.

*Jawaharlal Nehru: Letters to Chief Ministers, 1947–1964*, vol. 5: *1958–1964*. New Delhi: Oxford University Press, 1989.

Prasad, S. N. (ed.). *History of the Conflict With China, 1962*. New Delhi: History Division, Ministry of Defence, 1992.

*Prime Minister on Chinese Aggression*. New Delhi: Publications Division, Ministry of External Affairs, 1963.

*We Accept China's Challenge: Speeches in the Lok Sabha on India's Resolve to Drive out the Aggressor*. New Delhi: Government of India, Ministry of Information and Broadcasting Publications Division, 1962.

PAKISTAN

Ayub Khan, Mohammad. *Speeches and Statements by Field Marshal Mohammad Ayub Khan*, vol. 1, October 1958–June 1959. Karachi: Pakistan Government Publications, 1959.

*Speeches and Statements by Field Marshal Mohammad Ayub Khan*, vol. 4, July 1961–June 1962. Karachi: Pakistan Government Publications, 1962.

Baxter, Craig (ed.). *Diaries of Field Marshal Mohammad Ayub Khan, 1966–1972*. Karachi: Oxford University Press, 2007.

Ghani, Nadia (ed.). *Field Marshal Mohammad Ayub Khan: A Selection of Talks and Interviews, 1964–1967*. Karachi: Oxford University Press, 2010.

Jinnah, Mohammed Ali. *Speeches and Statements, 1947–1948*. Karachi: Oxford University Press, 1999.

SOVIET UNION

Bulganin, N. A. and Khrushchev, N. S. *Visit of Friendship to India, Burma and Afghanistan: Speeches and Official Documents, November–December 1955*. Moscow: Foreign Languages Publishing House, 1955.

UNITED STATES

Committee on Foreign Relations, United States Senate, Eighty-Third Congress, Second Session. Washington, DC: Government Printing Office, 1954.

*Foreign Relations of the United States, 1952–54*, vol. XI, Africa and South Asia, Part I. Washington, DC: Government Printing Office, 1983.

*Foreign Relations of the United States, 1952–54*, vol. XI, Africa and South Asia, Part II. Washington, DC: Government Printing Office, 1983.

*Foreign Relations of the United States, 1952–54*, vol. XII, East Asia and the Pacific. Washington, DC: Government Printing Office, 1984.

*Foreign Relations of the United States, 1952–54*, vol. XIII, Indochina. Washington, DC: Government Printing Office, 1982.

*Foreign Relations of the United States, 1955–57*, vol. VIII, South Asia. Washington, DC: Government Printing Office, 1987.

*Foreign Relations of the United States, 1958–60*, vol. XV, South and Southeast Asia. Washington, DC: Government Printing Office, 1992.

*Foreign Relations of the United States, 1961–63*, vol. XIX, South Asia. Washington, DC: Government Printing Office, 1996.

*Foreign Relations of the United States, 1964–68*, vol. XI, South Asia Crisis 1971. Washington, DC: Government Printing Office, 2005.

*Foreign Relations of the United States, 1964–68*, vol. XXV, South Asia. Washington, DC: Government Printing Office, 2000.

Galbraith, John Kenneth. *Letters to Kennedy*. London: Harvard University Press, 1998.

Kennedy, John F. *A Compilation of Statements and Speeches Made During His Service in the United States Senate and the House of Representatives*. Washington, DC: Government Printing Office, 1964.

Norman, Dorothy. *Indira Gandhi: Letters to an American Friend, 1950–1984*. New York: Harcourt Brace Jovanovich, 1985.


NEWSPAPERS AND PERIODICALS

*Amrita Bazar Patrika (Calcutta)*
*Business Week*
*The Daily Mail*
*The Daily Telegraph*
*Dawn (Karachi)*
*The Economist*
*The Guardian*
*The Hindu (Madras)*
*The Hindustan Times (New Delhi)*
*Indiagram*
*The Indian Express (Bombay)*
*National Herald (Lucknow)*
*New Republic*
*The New York Times*
*Patriot*
*The Statesman (Calcutta)*

*The Sunday Express*
*The Sunday Statesman (Calcutta)*
*Time*
*The Times*
*The Washington Post*


ONLINE PRIMARY SOURCES

The Cold War International History Project Digital Archive, Woodrow Wilson International Center for Scholars, Washington, DC, www.wilsoncenter. org/digital-archive

The Foreign Affairs Oral History Collection, Library of Congress, Washington, DC, http://memory.loc.gov/ammem/collections/diplomacy/

*Hansard, 1803–2005*, London, http://hansard.millbanksystems.com

Miller Center Presidential Recordings Program, University of Virginia, Virginia, http://millercenter.org/academic/presidentialrecordings

The National Security Archive, The George Washington University, Washington, DC, www.gwu.edu/~nsarchiv/

*Public Papers of the Presidents of the United States*, The American Presidency Project, www.presidency.ucsb.edu


SECONDARY SOURCES AND MEMOIRS

Abramson, Rudy. *Spanning the Century: The Life of W. Averell Harriman, 1891–1986*. New York: Morrow, 1992.

Acheson, Dean. *Present at the Creation: My Years at the State Department*. New York: Norton, 1969.

Aldous, Richard and Lee, Sabine (eds.). *Harold Macmillan: Aspects of a Political Life*. Basingstoke: Macmillan, 1988.

Aldrich, Richard. *The Hidden Hand: Britain, America and Cold War Secret Intelligence*. London: John Murray, 2001.

Ali, Chaudri Mohammed. *The Emergence of Pakistan*. New York: Columbia University Press, 1967.

Allen, Charles. *Plain Tales from the Raj: Images of India in the Twentieth Century*. London: Andre Deutsch, 1975.

Ambrose, Stephen E. *Eisenhower*, vol. 2: *The President*. New York: Simon and Schuster, 1984.

Andrew, Christopher. *The Defence of the Realm: The Authorized History of MI5*. London: Allen Lane, 2009.

Andrew, Christopher and Mitrokhin, Vasili. *The KGB and the World: The Mitrokhin Archive II*. London: Allen Lane, 2005.

Ashton, Nigel J. 'Harold Macmillan and the "Golden Days" of Anglo-American Relations Revisited, 1957–63', *Diplomatic History*, 29 (September 2005), 691–723.

   *Kennedy, Macmillan and the Cold War: The Irony of Interdependence*. Basingstoke: Palgrave Macmillan, 2002.

Ayub Khan, Mohammad. *Friends Not Masters: A Political Autobiography*. London: Oxford University Press, 1967.

'Pakistan Perspective', *Foreign Affairs* (July 1960), 547–56.

Ball, George. *The Past Has Another Pattern: Memoirs*. New York: W. W. Norton & Company, 1982.

Barnds, William J. *India, Pakistan and the Great Powers*. London: Pall Mall Press, 1972.

Barnett, Corelli. *The Verdict of Peace: Britain between Her Yesterday and the Future*. London: Macmillan, 2001.

Bartlett, C. J. *'The Special Relationship': A Political History of Anglo-American Relations since 1945*. London: Longman, 1992.

Benn, Tony. *Out of the Wilderness: Diaries 1963–67*. London: Hutchinson, 1987.

Bergan, Ronald. *Beyond the Fringe … and Beyond: A Critical Biography of Alan Bennett, Peter Cook, Jonathan Miller, Dudley Moore*. London: Virgin, 1989.

Beschloss. Michael R. *The Crisis Years: Kennedy and Khrushchev, 1960–1963*. New York: HarperCollins, 1991.

*Mayday: The U-2 Affair*. New York: Harper and Row, 1986.

Bhutto, Zulfikar Ali. *The Myth of Independence*. London: Oxford University Press, 1969.

Bowles, Chester. *Ambassador's Report*. New York: Harper, 1954.

'The "China Problem" Reconsidered', *Foreign Affairs*, 38 (April 1960), 476–86.

*Promises to Keep: My Years in Public Life, 1941–1969*. New York: Harper, 1971.

Brands, H. W. *Inside the Cold War: Loy Henderson and the Rise of the American Empire, 1918–1961*. New York: Oxford University Press, 1991.

*The Spectre of Neutralism: The United States and the Emergence of the Third World, 1947–1960*. New York: Columbia University Press, 1989.

Brass, Paul. *The Politics of India since Independence*. Cambridge University Press, 1990.

Brecher, Michael. *India and World Politics: Krishna Menon's View of the World*. London: Oxford University Press, 1968.

'Non-Alignment Under Stress: The West and the India–China Border War', *Pacific Affairs*, 52, 4 (1979–80), 612–30.

*The Struggle for Kashmir*. New York: Oxford University Press, 1953.

*Succession in India: A Study in Decision-Making*. London: Oxford University Press, 1966.

Brooker, Christopher. *The Neophiliacs: The Revolution in English Life in the Fifties and Sixties*. London: Pimlico, 1992.

Brown, Judith M. *Modern India: The Origins of an Asian Democracy*. Oxford University Press, 1985.

*Nehru: A Political Life*. New Haven: Yale University Press, 2003.

Bullock, Alan. *Ernest Bevin: Foreign Secretary, 1945–1954*. London: Heinemann, 1983.

Butler, Lord. *The Art of the Possible: The Memoirs of Lord Butler*. London: Hamish Hamilton, 1971.

Buzan, Barry and Gowher, Rizvi (eds.). *South Asian Insecurity and the Great Powers*. New York: St. Martin's Press, 1986.

Carpenter, Humphrey. *That Was Satire That Was: The Satire Boom of the 1960s*. London: Phoenix, 2002.

Castle, Barbara. *The Castle Diaries, 1964–1976*. London: Weidenfeld and Nicolson, 1980.

Choudhury, G. W. *India, Pakistan, Bangladesh and the Major Powers*. New York: Free Press, 1975.

Cohen, Stephen P. *The Pakistan Army*. Berkeley: University of California Press, 1984.

'US Weapons and South Asia: A Policy Analysis', *Pacific Affairs*, 49 (1976), 49–69.

Cohen, Warren I. *Dean Rusk*. Totowa, NJ: Cooper Square, 1982.

Crocker, Walter. *Nehru: A Contemporary's Estimate*. New York: Oxford University Press, 1966.

Crossman, Richard. *The Diaries of a Cabinet Minister*, vol. 1: *Minister of Housing 1964–66*. London: Jonathan Cape, 1975.

Dallek, Robert. *John F. Kennedy: An Unfinished Life, 1917–1963*. London: Allen Lane, 2003.

Dalton, Hugh. *High Tide and After: Memoirs 1945–1960*. London: Frederick Mueller, 1962.

Darwin, John. *Britain and Decolonisation: The Retreat from Empire in the Post-War World*. London: Macmillan, 1988.

Day, Anthony and Liem, Maya H. T. (eds.). *Cultures at War: The Cold War and Cultural Expression in Southeast Asia*. Ithaca, NY: Cornell University Press, 2010.

Desai, Morarji. *The Story of My Life*. New Delhi: S. Chand, 1978.

*The Story of My Life*, vol. 2. Oxford: Pergamon Press, 1979.

Desai, Tripta. *Indo-US Relations, 1947–1974*. Washington, DC: University Press of America, 1977.

Dickie, John. *'Special' No More: Anglo-American Relations: Rhetoric and Reality*. London: Weidenfeld and Nicolson, 1994.

Dimbleby, David and Reynolds, David. *An Ocean Apart: The Relationship between Britain and America in the Twentieth Century*. London: Hodder & Stoughton, 1988.

Dobson, Alan. *The Politics of the Anglo-American Economic Special Relationship, 1940–87*. Brighton: Wheatsheaf, 1988.

Dockrill, Michael and Young, John (eds.). *British Foreign Policy, 1945–56*. London: Macmillan, 1986.

Dockrill, Saki. *Britain's Retreat from East of Suez: The Choice between Empire and the World?* London: Palgrave Macmillan, 2002.

Dumbrell, John. *A Special Relationship: Anglo-American Relations in the Cold War and After*. Basingstoke: Palgrave Macmillan, 2000.

Duncan, Peter J. S. *The Soviet Union and India*. London: Routledge, 1989.

Dutt, Subimal. *With Nehru in the Foreign Office*. Calcutta: Minerva, 1977.

Eisenhower, Dwight D. *The White House Years: Mandate for Change, 1953–1956*. New York: Doubleday & Co., 1963.

*The White House Years: Waging Peace, 1956–1961*. New York: Doubleday & Co., 1965.

Evans, Harold. *Downing Street Diary: The Macmillan Years, 1957–1963*. London: Hodder & Stoughton, 1981.

Fair, John D. 'The Intellectual JFK: Lessons in Statesmanship from British History', *Diplomatic History*, 30 (January 2006), 119–42.

Frank, Katherine. *Indira: The Life of Indira Nehru Gandhi*. London: HarperCollins, 2002.

Galbraith, John Kenneth. *The Affluent Society*. London: Penguin Books, 1958.

*Ambassador's Journal: A Personal Account of the Kennedy Years*. Boston: Houghton Mifflin, 1969.

*The Liberal Hour*. London: Hamish Hamilton, 1960.

*A Life in Our Times*. London: Andre Deutsch, 1981.

*Name-Dropping: From F.D.R. On*. New York: Houghton Mifflin, 1999.

Ganguly, Sumit. *Conflict Unending: India–Pakistan Tensions since 1947*. New York: Columbia University Press, 2001.

Garner, Joe. *The Commonwealth Office, 1925–1968*. London: Heinemann, 1978.

Garver, John. *Protracted Contest: Sino-Indian Rivalry in the Twentieth Century*. Seattle: University of Washington Press, 2001.

Gauhar, Altaf. *Ayub Khan: Pakistan's First Military Ruler*. Lahore: Sang-e-Meel Publications, 1993.

Goldsworthy, David. *Colonial Issues in British Politics, 1945–1961: From 'Colonial Development' to 'Winds of Change'*. Oxford: Clarendon Press, 1971.

Gopal, Sarvepalli. *Jawaharlal Nehru: A Biography*, vol. 1: *1889–1947*. London: Jonathan Cape, 1975.

*Jawaharlal Nehru: A Biography*, vol. 2: *1947–1956*. London: Jonathan Cape, 1979.

*Jawaharlal Nehru: A Biography*, vol. 3: *1956–1964*. London: Jonathan Cape, 1984.

Gore-Booth, Paul. *With Great Truth and Respect*. London: Constable, 1974.

Goscha, Christopher E. and Ostermann, Christian F. (eds.). *Connecting Histories: Decolonization and the Cold War in Southeast Asia, 1945–1962*. Palo Alto: Stanford University Press, 2009.

Guha, Ramachandra. *India After Gandhi: The History of the World's Largest Democracy*. London: Macmillan, 2007.

Gundevia, Y. D. *Outside the Archives*. New Delhi: Sangam Books, 1984.

Gupta, Partha Sarathi. *Imperialism and the British Labour Movement, 1914–1964*. London: The Macmillan Press, 1975.

Halberstam, David. *The Best and the Brightest*. London: Barrie and Jenkins, 1972.

Hangen, Welles. *After Nehru, Who?* London: Rupert Hart-Davis, 1963.

Harris, Kenneth. *Attlee*. London: Weidenfeld and Nicolson, 1982.

Harrison, Selig S. *The Widening Gulf: Asian Nationalism and United States Policy*. New York: Free Press, 1978.

Harrison, Selig S. (ed.). *India and the United States*. New York: Macmillan, 1961.

Healey, Denis. *The Time of My Life*. London: Michael Joseph, 1989.

Hersh, Seymour. *The Dark Side of Camelot*. New York: Back Bay Books, 1998.

Hilsman, Roger. *To Move a Nation: The Politics of Foreign Policy in the Administration of John F. Kennedy*. New York: Delta, 1967.

Hoffmann, Steven. *India and the China Crisis*. Berkeley: University of California Press, 1990.

Hopkirk, Peter. *The Great Game: On Secret Service in High Asia*. London: John Murray, 1990.

Horn, Robert C. *Soviet-Indian Relations: Issues and Influence*. New York: Praeger, 1982.

Horne, Alistair. *Macmillan, 1894–1956*. London: Macmillan, 1988.

*Macmillan, 1957–1986*. London: Macmillan, 1989.

Hunt, Michael H. *Ideology and US Foreign Policy*. New Haven: Yale University Press, 1987.

Inder Singh, Anita. *The Limits of British Influence: South Asia and the Anglo-American Relationship, 1947–56*. London: Pinter, 1993.

Irial, Glynn. '"An Untouchable in the Presence of Brahmins": Lord Wavell's Disastrous Relationship with Whitehall During His Time as Viceroy, 1943–47', *Modern Asian Studies*, 41, 3 (2007), 639–63.

Issacs, Harold. *Scratches on Our Minds: American Views of China and India*. New York: John Day, 1958.

Jain, B. M. 'The Kennedy Administration's Policy towards Colonialism: A Case Study of Goa, 1961, in the Indian Context', *The Indian Journal of American Studies*, 14 (July 1984), 145–54.

Jalal, Ayesha. *The Sole Spokesman: Jinnah, the Muslim League and the Demand for Pakistan*. Cambridge University Press, 1985.

*The State of Martial Rule: The Origins of Pakistan's Political Economy of Defence*. Cambridge University Press, 1990.

James, Morrice. *Pakistan Chronicle*. London: Hurst, 1992.

Jeffrey, Robin. 'Jawaharlal Nehru and the Smoking Gun: Who Pulled the Trigger on Kerala's Communist Government in 1959?', *The Journal of Commonwealth and Comparative Politics*, 29 (1991), 72–85.

Jha, C. S. *From Bandung to Tashkent: Glimpses of India's Foreign Policy*. London: Sangam, 1983.

Jian, Chen. *Mao's China and the Cold War*. Chapel Hill: University of North Carolina Press, 2001.

Johnson, Alastair Iain and Ross, Robert S. (eds.). *New Directions in the Study of China's Foreign Policy*. Stanford University Press, 2008.

Johnson, Chalmers. *Blowback: The Costs and Consequences of American Empire*. London: Little Brown, 2000.

Johnson, Lyndon B. *The Vantage Point: Perspectives of the Presidency, 1963–1969*. New York: Holt, Rinehart and Winston, 1971.

Johnson, Robert. *Spying for Empire: The Great Game in Central and South-East Asia, 1757–1947*. London: Greenhill Books, 2006.

Jones, Matthew. *After Hiroshima: The United States, Race, and Nuclear Weapons in Asia, 1945–1965*. Cambridge University Press, 2010.

*Conflict and Confrontation in South East Asia, 1961–1965: Britain, the United States, and the Creation of Malaysia*. Cambridge University Press, 2002.

Jones, Matthew and Young, John. 'Polaris, East of Suez: British Plans for a Nuclear Force in the Indo-Pacific, 1964–1968', *Journal of Strategic Studies*, 33, 6 (2010), 1–24.

Kaul. T. N. *Diplomacy in Peace and War: Recollections and Reflections.* New Delhi: Vikas, 1979.

*Reminiscences: Discreet and Indiscreet.* New Delhi: Lancers, 1982.

Kennedy, John F. *The Strategy of Peace.* New York: Popular Library Publishers, 1961.

Kennedy, Paul. *The Realities Behind Diplomacy: Background Influences on British External Policy, 1865–1980.* London: Allen & Unwin, 1981.

*The Rise and Fall of the Great Powers: Economic Change and Military Confrontation 1500 to 2000.* London: Unwin Hyman, 1988.

Khrushchev, Nikita S. *Khrushchev Remembers: The Last Testament.* Boston: Little Brown, 1974.

*Memoirs: Time, People, Power,* vol. 3. Moscow: Moskovskie Novosti, 1999.

King, Cecil. *The Cecil King Diary, 1967–1970.* London: Jonathan Cape, 1972.

Kipling, Rudyard. *Kim.* London: Macmillan, 1901.

Kochavi, Noam. *A Conflict Perpetuated: China Policy during the Kennedy Years.* London: Praeger, 2002.

Kunz, Diane. '"Somewhat Mixed up Together": Anglo-American Defence and Financial Policy during the 1960s', *Journal of Imperial and Commonwealth History,* 27, 2 (1999), 213–32.

Kux, Dennis. *India and the United States: Estranged Democracies, 1941–1991.* Washington, DC: National Defense University Press, 1993.

*The United States and Pakistan, 1947–2000: Disenchanted Allies.* Baltimore: The Johns Hopkins University Press, 2001.

Lamb, Richard. *The Macmillan Years: The Emerging Truth.* London: John Murray, 1995.

Leffler, Melvyn P. *A Preponderance of Power: National Security, the Truman Administration and the Cold War.* Stanford University Press, 1992.

Lieven, Anatol. *Pakistan: A Hard Country.* London: Penguin, 2012.

Longford, Frank Pakenham. *Eleven at Number Ten: A Personal View of Prime Ministers, 1931–1984.* London: Harrap, 1984.

*The Grain of Wheat: An Autobiography.* London: Collins, 1974.

Louis, Wm. Roger and Bull, Hedley (eds.). *The Special Relationship: Anglo-American Relations Since 1945.* Oxford: Clarendon, 1986.

Lucas, Ivor. *A Road to Damascus: Mainly Diplomatic Memoirs from the Middle East.* London: The Radcliffe Press, 1997.

MacDonald, Malcolm. *Titans and Others.* London: Collins, 1972.

Macmillan, Harold. *At the End of the Day, 1961–1963.* London: Macmillan, 1973.

*Pointing the Way, 1959–1961.* London: Macmillan, 1972.

*Riding the Storm, 1956–1959.* London: Macmillan, 1971.

Mahmud Ali, S. *Cold War in the High Himalayas: The USA, China and South Asia in the 1950s.* New York: St. Martin's Press, 1999.

Malhotra, Inder. *Indira Gandhi: A Personal Memoir and Political Biography.* London: Hodder & Stoughton, 1989.

Manor, James (ed.). *Nehru to the Nineties: The Changing Office of the Prime Minister in India.* London: Hurst & Company, 1994.

Mastny, Vojtech. 'The Soviet Union's Partnership with India', *Journal of Cold War Studies,* 12, 3 (2010), 50–90.

Mathai, M. O. *Reminiscences of the Nehru Age*. New Delhi: Vikas, 1978.

Maxwell, Neville. *India's China War*. London: Cape, 1970.

McCullough, David G. *Truman*. New York: Simon & Schuster, 1992.

McGhee, George. *Envoy to the Middle World: Adventures in Diplomacy*. New York: Harper and Row, 1983.

McMahon, Robert J. *The Cold War on the Periphery: The United States, India and Pakistan*. New York: Columbia University Press, 1994.

*Dean Acheson and the Creation of an American World Order*. Dulles, VA: Potomac Books, 2008.

'US Policy toward South Asia and Tibet during the Early Cold War', *Journal of Cold War Studies*, 8, 3 (2006), 133–44.

Merrill, Dennis. *Bread and the Ballot: The United States and India's Economic Development, 1947–1963*. Chapel Hill: The University of North Carolina Press, 1990.

Milne, David. *America's Rasputin: Walt Rostow and the Vietnam War*. New York: Hill and Wang, 2008.

Moon, Pendrel (ed.). *Wavell: The Viceroy's Journal*. London: Oxford University Press, 1973.

Moore, R. J. *Escape from Empire: The Attlee Government and the Indian Problem*. Oxford: Clarendon Press, 1983.

Moraes, Frank. *Jawaharlal Nehru: A Biography*. New York: Macmillan, 1956.

Morgan, Kenneth O. *Labour in Power, 1945–1951*. Oxford: Clarendon Press, 1984.

Moynihan, Daniel Patrick. *A Dangerous Place*. Boston: Little Brown, 1978.

Mullik, B. N. *My Years with Nehru, 1948–1964*. New Delhi: Allied Publishers, 1972.

Musa, Muhammad. *My Version: India–Pakistan War 1965*. Lahore: Wajidalis, 1983.

Naipaul, V. S. *An Area of Darkness: A Discovery of India*. New York: Vintage Books, 2002.

Nanda, B. R. 'Nehru and the British', *Modern Asian Studies*, 30, 2 (1996), 469–79.

Nanda, B. R. (ed.). *Indian Foreign Policy: The Nehru Years*. New Delhi: Sangam Books, 1990.

Nehru, Jawaharlal. *Discovery of India*. New York: John Day, 1946.

*Soviet Russia: Some Random Sketches and Impressions*. Allahabad: Law Journal Press, 1928.

Nitze, Paul H. *From Hiroshima to Glasnost: At the Centre of Decision, A Memoir*. New York: Grove Weidenfeld, 1989.

Nixon, R. N. *RN: The Memoirs of Richard Nixon*. New York: Grosset and Dunlap, 1978.

Palit, D. K. *War in High Himalaya: The Indian Army in Crisis, 1962*. London: Hurst, 1991.

Palliser, Michael. 'Foreign Policy', in Michael Parsons (ed.), *Looking Back: The Wilson Years*. The University of Pau Press, 1999.

Pandit, Vijaya Lakshmi. *The Scope of Happiness: A Personal Memoir*. London: Weidenfeld & Nicolson, 1979.

Pannikar, K. M. *An Autobiography*. Madras: Oxford University Press, 1977.

*In Two Chinas: Memoirs of a Diplomat*. London: Allen and Unwin, 1955.

Parker, Richard. *John Kenneth Galbraith: His Life, His Politics, His Economics*. New York: Farrar, Straus and Giroux, 2005.

Pearce, Kimber Charles. *Rostow, Kennedy and the Rhetoric of Foreign Aid*. East Lansing: Michigan State University Press, 2001.

Pimlott, Ben. *Wilson*. London: HarperCollins, 1992.

Ponting, Clive. *Breach of Promise: Labour in Power 1964–1970*. London: Hamish Hamilton, 1989.

Prados, John. *Keepers of the Keys: A History of the National Security Council from Truman to Bush*. New York: Morrow, 1991.

Prozumenshchikov, Mikhail Y. 'The Sino-Indian Conflict, the Cuban Missile Crisis, and the Sino-Soviet Split, October 1962: New Evidence from the Russian Archives', *Cold War International History Project Bulletin*, no. 8–9 (1996–7), 251–7.

Qureshi, Ishtiaq Hussain. *The Pakistani Way of Life*. London: Heinemann, 1956.

Rahman, Habibur. 'India's Liberation of Goa and the Anglo-American Stand', *Journal of South Asian Studies*, 19, 1 (1996), 37–48.

Redding, Saunders. *An American in India: A Personal Report on the Indian Dilemma and the Nature of Her Conflicts*. New York: The Bobbs-Merrill Company, 1954.

Reid, Escott. *Envoy to Nehru*. New York: Oxford University Press, 1981.

Reynolds, David. *Britannia Overruled: British Policy and World Power in the 20th Century*. London: Longman, 1991.

'A "Special Relationship"? America, Britain and the International Order Since the Second World War', *International Affairs*, 62, 1 (1985–6), 1–20.

Ribeiro de Meneses, Filipe. *Salazar: A Political Biography*. London: Enigma, 2010.

Roosevelt, Eleanor. *India and the Awakening East*. London: Hutchinson, 1954.

Rostow, Walt W. *Diffusion of Power: An Essay in Recent History*. New York: Macmillan, 1972.

*Eisenhower, Kennedy and Foreign Aid*. Austin: University of Texas Press, 1985.

*The Stages of Economic Growth: A Non-Communist Manifesto*. Cambridge University Press, 1960.

Rotter, Andrew. *Comrades at Odds: The United States and India, 1947–1964*. London: Cornell University Press, 2000.

Rubinoff, Arthur. *India's Use of Force in Goa*. Bombay: Popular Prakashan, 1971.

Rusk, Dean. *As I Saw It*. New York: Norton, 1990.

Saggar, Shamit. *Race and Politics in Britain*. London: Philip Allan, 1991.

Salisbury, Harrison. *India: The Most Dangerous Decades*. Princeton University Press, 1960.

Sandbrook, Dominic. *Never Had it So Good: A History of Britain from Suez to the Beatles*. London: Little Brown, 2005.

*White Heat: A History of Britain in the Swinging Sixties*. London: Little Brown, 2006.

Sanger, Clyde. *Malcolm MacDonald: Bringing an End to Empire*. Liverpool University Press, 1995.

Schaffer, Howard B. *Chester Bowles: New Dealer in the Cold War*. Cambridge, MA: Harvard University Press, 1993.

*Ellsworth Bunker: Global Troubleshooter, Vietnam Hawk*. Chapel Hill: The University of South Carolina Press, 2003.

Schlesinger Jr, Arthur M. *A Thousand Days: John F. Kennedy in the White House*. Boston: Houghton Mifflin, 1965.

Schoenbaum, Thomas J. *Waging Peace and War: Dean Rusk in the Truman, Kennedy and Johnson Years*. New York: Simon and Schuster, 1988.

Singh, Jaswant. *Jinnah: India, Partition, Independence*. Oxford University Press, 2010.

Sorensen, Theodore. *Kennedy*. New York: Harper & Row, 1965.

Srivastava, C. P. *Lal Bahadur Shastri: A Life of Truth in Politics*. New Delhi: Oxford University Press, 1995.

Stein, Arthur. *India and the Soviet Union: The Nehru Era*. University of Chicago Press, 1972.

Stephens, Ian. *Pakistan: Old Country/New Nation*. London: Penguin Books, 1964.

Stiegler, Kurt. 'Communism and "Colonial Evolution": John Foster Dulles' Vision of India and Pakistan', *Journal of South Asian and Middle Eastern Studies*, 12 (Winter 1991), 68–89.

Strober, Gerald and Strober, Deborah (eds.). *'Let us Begin Anew': An Oral History of the Kennedy Presidency*. New York: HarperCollins, 1993.

Sulzberger, C. L. *Last of the Giants*. London: Weidenfeld & Nicolson, 1972.

Talbot, Ian. *Pakistan: A Modern History*. London: Hurst & Company, 2009.

Thakur, Ramesh and Thayer, Carlyle A. *Soviet Relations with India and Vietnam, 1945–1992*. New York: St. Martin's Press, 1992.

Turner, John. *Macmillan*. London: Longman, 1994.

Vertzberger, Yaccov. 'India's Border Conflict with China: A Perceptual Analysis', *Journal of Contemporary History*, 17, 4 (1982), 607–31.

Vu, Tuong and Wongsurawat, Wasana (eds.). *Dynamics of the Cold War in Asia: Ideology, Identity, and Culture*. New York: Palgrave Macmillan, 2009.

Westad, Odd Arne. *The Global Cold War: Third World Interventions and the Making of Our Times*. Cambridge University Press, 2007.

Whiting, Allen. *The Chinese Calculus of Deterrence*. Ann Arbor: University of Michigan Press, 1975.

Wilson, Harold. *Labour Government 1964–1970: A Personal Record*. London: Weidenfeld & Nicolson, 1971.

*The New Britain: Labour's Plan: Selected Speeches 1964*. London: Harmondsworth, 1964.

Wolpert, Stanley. *Jinnah of Pakistan*. Oxford University Press, 1984.

*Nehru: A Tryst with Destiny*. Oxford University Press, 1996.

Yangwen, Zheng, Liu, Hong and Szonyi, Michael (eds.). *The Cold War in Asia: The Battle for Hearts and Minds*. Leiden: Brill, 2010.

Young, John W. *The Labour Governments 1964–1970*, vol. 2: *International Policy*. Manchester University Press, 2003.

Zachariah, Benjamin. *Nehru*. London: Routledge, 2004.
Ziegler, Philip. *Mountbatten: The Official Biography*. London: Collins, 1985.
    *Wilson: The Authorised Life*. London: Weidenfeld and Nicolson, 1993.
Zubok, Vladislav. 'The Khrushchev–Mao Conversations, 31 July–3 August
    1958 and 2 October 1959', *Cold War International History Project Bulletin*,
    no. 12–13 (Fall/Winter 2001).

# Index

27928586R00223

Printed in Great Britain
by Amazon